W9-DGO-092

Stan Towerman

משכן הנפש
MISHKAN HANEFESH

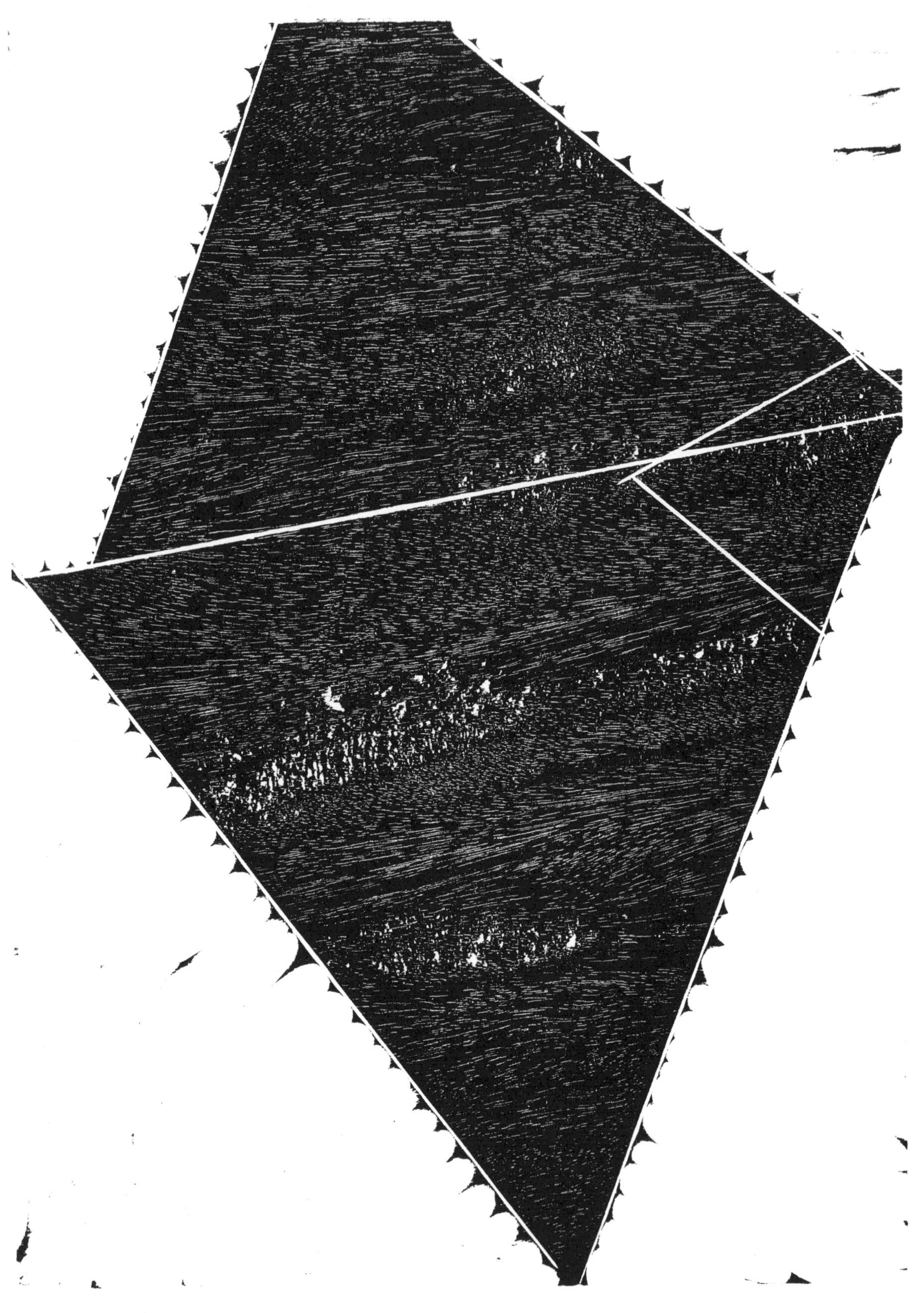

YOM KIPPUR

CCAR PRESS · NEW YORK · 2015/5776

For additional copyright information, see pp. 679–700, which constitute a continuation of this copyright page.

LIBRARY OF CONGRESS CATALOGING-IN-PUBLICATION DATA
Mishkan haNefesh = [Mahzor le-Yamim Nora'im] : Machzor for the Days of Awe / editors, Rabbi Edwin C. Goldberg, Rabbi Janet Ross Marder, Rabbi Sheldon Joseph Marder, Rabbi Leon Morris, Rabbi Hara E. Person ; woodcuts, Joel Shapiro ; translations, original compositions, and commentaries, Rabbi Janet Marder and Rabbi Sheldon Marder.
volumes cm
Text in both Hebrew and English.
Contents: Vol. 1: Rosh haShanah — Vol. 2: Yom Kippur.
Summary: "Prayer Book for the High Holy Days (Rosh HaShanah and Yom Kippur), includes 11 pieces of original art by Joel Shapiro"— Provided by publisher.
ISBN 978-0-88123-208-0 (set : alk. paper) — ISBN 978-0-88123-244-8 (v. 1: Rosh haShanah : alk. paper) — ISBN 978-0-88123-245-5 (v. 2: Yom Kippur : alk. paper) 1. Mahzorim—Texts. 2. Reform Judaism—Liturgy—Texts. 3. Mahzor (Reform, Central Conference of American Rabbis). High Holidays. I. Goldberg, Edwin C., editor. II. Marder, Janet Ross, 1954- editor translator author of added commentary. III. Marder, Sheldon Joseph, 1949- editor translator author of added commentary. IV. Shapiro, Joel, illustrator. V. Central Conference of American Rabbis, issuing body. VI. Mahzor (Reform, Central Conference of American Rabbis). High Holidays. Hebrew. VII. Mahzor (Reform, Central Conference of American Rabbis). High Holidays. English. VIII. Title: Machzor for the Days of Awe. IX. Title: Mahzor le-Yamim Nora'im.

BM675.H5Z667 2015
296.4'531—dc23

2015006277

Printed in the United States of America by Courier Corporation, Westford, MA.
Bound by Courier Corporation and Acme Bookbinding, Charlestown, MA.
Produced at The Philidor Company, Lexington, MA.

10 9 8 7 6 5 4 3 2 1

CCAR Press, 355 Lexington Avenue, New York, NY 10017
(212) 972-3636
ccarpress.org

In memory of my parents

CAROLINE AND JOSEPH GRUSS

whose philanthropy was directed

to the Jewish people and

their principles, as set

forth in the Torah.

EVELYN GRUSS LIPPER

EDITORS

Rabbi Edwin Goldberg · Rabbi Janet Marder · Rabbi Sheldon Marder · Rabbi Leon Morris

EDITORIAL TEAM ADVISORS

Rabbi Elaine Zecher · Cantor Evan Kent · Rabbi Peter Berg

WOODCUTS

Joel Shapiro

TRANSLATIONS, ORIGINAL COMPOSITIONS, AND COMMENTARIES

Rabbi Janet Marder and Rabbi Sheldon Marder

EXECUTIVE EDITOR AND PUBLISHER, CCAR PRESS

Rabbi Hara E. Person

CHIEF EXECUTIVE, CENTRAL CONFERENCE OF AMERICAN RABBIS

Rabbi Steven A. Fox

SPECIAL CONSULTANTS

Rabbi Lawrence A. Hoffman, PhD · Rabbi Tamara Eskenazi, PhD · Rabbi Dalia Marx, PhD
Rabbi Richard Sarason, PhD · Rabbi Margaret Moers Wenig

MACHZOR ADVISORY GROUP

Rabbi Elaine Zecher, *Chair*
Rabbi Steven A. Fox, *CCAR Chief Executive* · Rabbi Richard Block, *CCAR President* (2013–2015)
Rabbi Ellen Weinberg Dreyfus, *CCAR Past President* (2009–2011) · Rabbi Lance Sussman
Cantor Evan Kent, *ACC Representative* · Rabbi Peter Berg, *Membership Liaison*
Katherine Schwartz, *NATE Representative* · Marilynn Yentis, *URJ Representative*
Rabbi Lawrence A. Hoffman, PhD, *Academic Advisor* · Rabbi Rex Perlmeter, *Machzor Engagement*

PROJECT MANAGER AND ASSISTANT COMPOSITOR

Rabbi David E. S. Stein

PRODUCER, DESIGNER, AND TYPOGRAPHER

Scott-Martin Kosofsky at The Philidor Company

MANAGING EDITOR

Deborah Smilow

PILOT COORDINATION, MARKETING AND SALES

Ortal Bensky

יום כיפור
Yom Kippur

Acknowledgments

The CCAR, the Reform Movement, and the entire Jewish community are deeply indebted to Rabbi Edwin Goldberg, Rabbi Janet Marder, Rabbi Sheldon Marder, Rabbi Leon Morris, Rabbi Elaine Zecher, Rabbi Peter Berg, and Cantor Evan Kent—the editorial team of *Mishkan HaNefesh*—who gave fully of their souls, intellects, and talents to create this new *machzor*. Their tremendous dedication to this project and the gifts they each brought to the task were true offerings of the heart, which came together in a powerful vision of a new *machzor* for the next generation. We are uplifted by their beautiful work.

The editorial team, in turn, thanks the group that created the predecessor to this *machzor*, the *Mishkan T'filah* siddur. We are indebted to the inspirational work of Rabbi Elyse D. Frishman, editor, and the Siddur Publishing Team that worked with her: Rabbi Peter S. Knobel, Rabbi Lawrence A. Hoffman, PhD, Rabbi Bernard H. Mehlman, and Rabbi Elaine Zecher.

Rabbi Steven A. Fox and Rabbi Hara E. Person envisioned this *machzor* project, from the first Think Tank meeting in December 2008 through to publication. Together Rabbis Fox and Person selected the editors and the advisory board who shepherded this process. Rabbi Fox combined his rabbinic leadership and business acumen to ensure the success of the *machzor*, from strategic thinking to economic funding. Rabbi Person balanced patient guidance with clarity of focus to bring this project from dream to reality. With a steady, creative hand, she oversaw every step of the process, from planning to team building, from editorial to design, from production to marketing.

Rabbi David E. S. Stein and Scott-Martin Kosofsky were exemplary partners. Their professionalism, patience, unique skill sets, and good humor were much appreciated. We also thank proofreaders Michelle Kwitkin-Close and Ben Denckla.

In addition, we express our gratitude to those who have contributed their wisdom and guidance: Rabbi Ofer Sabath Beit-Halachmi; Nancy Berman; Rabbi Debra Reed Blank, PhD; Chana Bloch; Marc Brettler, PhD; Rabbi Carey Brown; Cantor Susan Caro; Cantor Ellen Dreskin; Larry Dressler; Rabbi Denise Eger; Rabbi Edward Feld; Howard and Mary Frank, PhD; Rabbi Don Goor; Jessica Greenbaum; Rabbi Alan Henkin; Joel Hoffman, PhD; Rabbi Yaron Kapitulnik; Rabbi Elliot Kukla; Henry Lefkowitz; Rabbi Carol Levithan; Catherine Madsen; Rabbi Dalia Marx, PhD; Rabbi Dan Medwin; Rabbi Heather Ellen Miller;

Mike Milov, Alan Morinis; Laurie Pinho; Rabbi Charles Rabinowitz; Rabbi Don Rossoff; Cantor Bruce Ruben; Cantor Benjie Ellen Schiller; Jeffrey Shandler, PhD; Ranen Omer-Sherman, PhD; Rabbi David Silber; Cantor Dan Singer; Rabbi Joseph Skloot; Rabbi Howard Stein; Bruce Turkel; Rabbi David A. Teutsch, PhD; Yaffa Weisman, PhD; and Rabbi Mary Zamore.

We are grateful to Joel Shapiro for his partnership and generosity with his inspirational art. We are also grateful to Leslie Miller of Greenfell Press for the beautiful prints. Many thanks to Jo Carole Lauder for introducing us to Joel Shapiro. A very special thanks to our generous funder, EGL Charitable Foundation, and to Rabbi Leon Morris for connecting us to both the funder and to Mrs. Lauder.

Thank you to the 2008–2015 CCAR Presidents, Rabbi Peter Knobel, Rabbi Ellen Weinberg Dreyfus, Rabbi Jonathan Stein, and Rabbi Richard Block, and the CCAR Board for their support. We are pleased to thank the congregations who graciously hosted meetings of the editorial team over the five years of the development of this *machzor*, including Congregation Beth Am, Los Altos Hills; Brooklyn Heights Synagogue, Brooklyn; Temple Judea, Coral Gables; Temple Israel, Boston; Temple Sholom, Chicago; Temple Adas Israel, Sag Harbor; and Temple Judea, Tarzana.

Deep thanks also to the many rabbis, cantors, presidents, board members, congregants, synagogues, Hillels, day schools, and youth groups—too many to name—who enthusiastically agreed to pilot early drafts, gave us helpful feedback, and supported the development of *Mishkan HaNefesh* from the start.

Many people made it possible for the editors to devote themselves to the work on *Mishkan HaNefesh*. We thank the following: the members of Temple Sholom of Chicago, the members of Temple Judea in Coral Gables, Florida, Rabbi Judith Siegal, Rabbi Shoshanah Conover, Daphne Parker, and Lori Curtis (EG); Sheba Solomon for her patience and careful attention to detail (JM); the members of Temple Adas Israel, Sag Harbor, New York, and the Shalom Hartman Institute (LM); the leaders and clergy of Temple Israel, Boston, Laurena Rosenberg, and Brigid Goggin (EZ); The Temple, Atlanta (PB); the Brooklyn Heights Synagogue, Rabbi Serge Lippe, and Congregation B'nai Olam, Fire Island Pines (HP).

The most supportive people of all were the members of our families, our spouses and children, who encouraged the tremendous undertaking of this endeavor and its related travel, and who understood why, when asked, we each said yes. We acknowledge all our loved ones, including Melanie Cole Goldberg (EG); daughters Betsy Marder Friedman and Rachel Marder (JM and SM); parents Irene and Alan Ross (JM); parents Frances and Jack Marder (ז״ל) (SM); Dasee Berkowitz (LM); Rabbi Donald Goor (EK); David Eisenberg and Jacob, Benjamin, and Naomi Eisenberg (EZ); Karen Kerness, Matan, Lior, and Noah Berg (PB); Yigal, Liya, and Yoni Rechtman, and Diane Person (HP).

MACHZOR TEAM MEMBERS, INITIAL DEVELOPMENTAL PHASE

ALTERNATIVE READINGS
Rabbi Leah Berkowitz, *team leader*
Rabbi Lewis Kamrass, *team leader*
Rabbi Neal Borovitz
Rabbi Michael Latz
Rabbi Tamar Malino
Rabbi Sarah Reines
Rabbi Jack Romberg
Rabbi Phyllis Sommer

SPIRITUAL COMMENTARY
Rabbi Rosie Haim, *team leader*
Rabbi Jill Cozen-Harel
Rabbi Jeffrey Goldwasser
Rabbi Scott Hausman-Weiss
Rabbi Steven Moss
Rabbi Beth Schwartz
Rabbi Stephen Wise

POETRY
Rabbi Scott Corngold ז״ל, *team leader*
Rabbi Alan Cook
Rabbi Lisa Edwards, PhD
Rabbi Yoel Kahn, PhD
Rabbi Karyn Kedar
Rabbi Yair Robinson
Rabbi Zachary Shapiro
Rabbi Andy Vogel

STUDY TEXTS
Rabbi Audrey Korotkin, *team leader*
Rabbi Judith Z. Abrams ז״ל
Rabbi Ruth Gais
Rabbi Greg Litcofsky
Rabbi Joel Mosbacher
Rabbi Suzanne Singer
Rabbi Mark Strauss-Cohn
Rabbi Irwin Zeplowitz

TRANSLATION
Rabbi Larry Englander · Rabbi Oren Hayon

MACHZOR THINK TANK PARTICIPANTS, 2008

Rabbi Elaine Zecher, *chair*
Rabbi Melanie Aron
Rabbi Richard Block
Rabbi Ellen Weinberg Dreyfus
Rabbi Larry Englander
Rabbi Karen Fox
Rabbi Steven Fox
Rabbi Edwin Goldberg
Rabbi Don Goor
Rabbi Lawrence A. Hoffman, PhD
Rabbi Rick Jacobs
Rabbi Serge Lippe
Rabbi Robert Loewy
Rabbi Sheldon Marder
Rabbi Michelle Missaghieh
Rabbi Joel Mosbacher
Rabbi Melinda Panken
Rabbi Steven Pearce, PhD
Rabbi Hara Person
Rabbi Richard Sarason, PhD
Rabbi Mark Dov Shapiro
Rabbi David Stern
Rabbi Jack Stern ז״ל
Rabbi Mark Strauss-Cohn
Rabbi Lance Sussman, PhD
Rabbi/Cantor Angela Warnick-Buchdahl
Rabbi Irwin Zeplowitz

RABBINIC INTERNS

Andrue Kahn

Rabbi Josh Beraha
Rabbi Yael Rooks-Rapport
Rabbi Sara Newman Rich
Rabbi Daniel Kirzane
Rabbi Adena Kemper Blum
Rabbi April Peters
Rabbi Jillian Cameron
Rabbi Liz Piper-Goldberg

Introduction

OPENING A PRAYER BOOK on the High Holy Days, what do we hope to find? This is not an easy question, since the *machzor* (if it succeeds) leads us on a path across rough terrain: honest soul-searching; reflection on our deeds, especially on how we have fallen short; introspection about our personal qualities and how they impact our closest relationships; examination of our beliefs about what it means to be human and Jewish in relation to the world and to God; feeling the loss of loved ones and thinking about our own mortality; asking forgiveness and bestowing it. The inner path that we travel on these days is not smooth; it is paved with remorse, grief, and guilt; but also with holiness, awe, gratitude, and hope. It tests our spiritual stamina; and we do well to make use of imagination and memory.

The concerns to which this *machzor* speaks are as wide and profound as the human condition itself. But the preeminent focus throughout *Mishkan HaNefesh* is on the two all-important themes of Rosh HaShanah and Yom Kippur: *t'shuvah* (return) and *cheshbon hanefesh* (accounting of the soul). These two themes form the Jewish purpose of the High Holy Days. And like the holy days themselves, these themes tower above all else.

The work of *t'shuvah* and *cheshbon hanefesh* — which Judaism deems so vital — requires unflinching honesty, concentration, dedicated space, and uninterrupted time. It is best undertaken in solitude, for it entails an inward-focused journey that is deeply personal. Yet this journey is enriched by a sense of shared endeavor and communal support. The Days of Awe provide the time for this inner work; the gathered community and its spiritual leaders provide inspiration; and the *machzor* provides both a script and springboard for our efforts.

Our hope is that this *machzor* will

- inspire participation in the multifaceted experience of the High Holy Days — from feelings of awe to moments of solace, from the solitude of contemplation to the solidarity of song and worship;
- guide worshipers, in accessible ways, through the journey of *t'shuvah* and *cheshbon hanefesh*;
- bridge the personal and the communal, the ritual and the ethical dimensions of the High Holy Days; and
- provide meaningful liturgy to those who pray regularly, and welcome those who are new to Jewish practice.

Mishkan HaNefesh draws from the deep wellsprings of Jewish liturgy, history, thought, music, interpretation and creativity. We embrace the rich liturgical voices of the Jewish past and the aspirations of our people today. Our hope is to offer metaphors and images of God that will speak to our time, as the prayers of the *Union Prayer Book* and *Gates of Repentance* spoke with depth and authenticity to theirs; our goal is a book whose tone and theological range are uplifting, inviting, and challenging.

Most important to our work are the people for whom this book is intended: the members of a dynamic, ever-changing, and diverse Reform Movement who gather in community to experience awe and forgiveness and hope, as well as all others who seek to find a spiritual home in this prayer book. Some call themselves classical Reform; some seek to recover and reinterpret the broader Jewish heritage. Some resonate with traditional views of God; others find it hard to believe in God at all.

We believe that the Reform nature of this *machzor* will be most evident in its respectful yet fresh approach to tradition; in its unwavering commitment to the equality of men and women; in its attention to concerns that are both immediate and timeless — the fears and hopes of the people who will pray from its pages; in its faithfulness to the ethical and justice-seeking dimension of Judaism; in its embrace of the universal and the particular; and perhaps, most of all, in its effort to deal with the tension between the historical theology of the High Holy Days (God's sovereignty and judgment) and more contemporary beliefs, such as the theology of human empowerment.

Mishkan T'filah has provided the paradigm and framework for this *machzor*. Its right-side/left-side format encourages diversity, choice, and the inclusion of many "voices." We have sought to create a dialogue — or confrontation — between the texts on facing pages; to enliven, question, challenge, and engage passionately with the tradition bequeathed to us by our ancestors.

Commentary is an integral part of this prayer book. Our hope and expectation is that High Holy Day worship will entail silent time for individual study. The commentary aims not only to explain the themes and vocabulary of the traditional liturgy, but also to encourage deep reflection in a manner both intellectually engaging and spiritually provocative.

Each service in *Mishkan HaNefesh* begins with a thematic phrase that is intended to highlight the essence of the service, as shown in the table on the facing page. There is in this sequence of services and themes a trajectory — a thematic arc — from the opening of the High Holy Days to their close. We navigate our way from "*Avinu Malkeinu,* renew us" to "You hold out Your hand." We begin with supplication; we end with an affirmation. We begin with a personal hope (Can we truly begin again? Can we start fresh?); we end by feeling the reality of a relationship with One beyond ourselves — the God whose hand is stretched out to meet us, whose transformative power is manifest within and around us. The gates of *N'ilah* close; the New Year begins, and we know ourselves called — individually and communally — to live with love, awe, integrity, and joy. Ten Days of Return. Ten services of Rosh HaShanah and Yom Kippur: each one a rung on the ladder that spans earth and heaven, elevating our thoughts and our lives to higher purpose.

Worship Service	Theme	Source
ROSH HASHANAH		
Evening	*Avinu Malkeinu*, renew us	Liturgy
Morning	Hear the call of the shofar	Liturgy
Afternoon	And we shall bless the Eternal, from this time and forever	Psalm 115:18
YOM KIPPUR		
Evening	I forgive, as you have asked	Numbers 14:20
Morning	You stand this day, all of you, in the presence of Adonai your God	Deuteronomy 29:9
Afternoon	You shall be holy	Leviticus 19:2
Avodah	May we ascend toward the holy	Liturgy
Eileh Ezk'rah	For these things I weep	Lamentations 1:16
Yizkor	These are the lights that guide us . . . These are the ways we remember	Hana Senesh
N'ilah	You hold out Your hand	Liturgy

What is the meaning of the name *Mishkan HaNefesh*? In the Book of Exodus, we read that artisans designed and built a *mishkan* — a dwelling-place or sanctuary — for Israel's communal worship of the God who wrought the miracle of freedom. The word *nefesh* usually means soul or person. One way to translate *Mishkan HaNefesh* is "Sanctuary of the Soul," which suggests that each person's spiritual quest happens within the holy space of the community. We hope that this *machzor* will be a "meeting place" for the inner life of each individual, the warm embrace of community, and the sacred traditions of the Jewish people. May this book be a source of healing and repair; and may it provide nourishment to meet the spiritual hunger of our times.

About *Mishkan HaNefesh*

A Note on Philosophy and Design

THE DESIGN OF *Mishkan HaNefesh* reflects the following philosophy of prayer:

1. Varied theological approaches that enable a diverse congregation to share religious experience and spiritual growth.
2. Universal access to the worship experience within a liberal Jewish setting.
3. An inclusive and egalitarian spirit.
4. An insistence on intellectual honesty and authenticity.
5. Integration of the communal nature of Jewish worship with opportunities for individual prayer and silent reflection.
6. Creative innovation to address contemporary Jewish concerns.
7. Commitment to Reform tradition, as well as the larger Jewish tradition.

This *machzor* has been structured to encourage individuals to participate at their own pace and in their own way. Some may wish to focus on a commentary or a challenging poem while the congregation sings a prayer.

Mishkan HaNefesh features three kinds of pages: WHITE pages with three basic elements: a traditional Hebrew prayer, a faithful translation, and a transliteration; GRAY-tinted pages for alternative translations, poems, counter-texts, and creative readings; and bordered, BLUE-tinted pages for study texts or silent meditations. All three have commentary of a spiritual, historical, or literary nature at the bottom of the page, as well as source citations. Thus this *machzor* encourages learning both during worship and in preparation for the High Holy Days.

The white pages may be called *keva* (fixed prayer); their corresponding gray pages may be called *kavanah* (focusing prayer); and the blue pages are intended for private devotion and study. But prayer-leaders and worshipers may choose to vary the use of these pages.

Much of this *machzor* follows the "two-page spread" format of *Mishkan T'filah*. However, the use of three distinctive page styles creates greater variety in the present volumes. Pages of the same type may occasionally occur in series. The three services for Yom Kippur afternoon — *Avodah*, *Eileh Ezk'rah*, and *Yizkor* — contain only white pages on which the *keva* prayers are integrated with creative prayers and poetry. (Yizkor begins with its own brief introduction regarding usage, on pages 528–29.)

There are very few instructions in *Mishkan HaNefesh*, in order to allow for *minhag hamakom* (local custom) and flexibility from congregation to congregation. Where they exist, the instructions are intended to provide clarity, not uniformity. Headings at the top of each page and vertical "navigations bars" (in Hebrew on the right side and in English on the left side) help worshipers to identify a prayer unit within the liturgical rubrics.

About the Translation

We have approached the work of translation as a sacred challenge: namely, to create a prayerful, meaningful experience in English that is equivalent to the experience of praying in Hebrew. Not identical, but equivalent. A literal or "word for word" translation cannot fully achieve such an experience because of the ways in which languages differ from one another: in sound, syntax, rhythm, and structure; and in the layered meanings of words and idioms that are unique to the culture in which a language grows.

The English versions of the prayers, Torah readings, and haftarah readings in *Mishkan HaNefesh* are original, faithful translations. This means that we render texts "idea for idea" or "feeling for feeling" instead of "word for word." And it means that we may use an English idiom that differs from the original idiom. Our goal is to convey the intention of the Hebrew prayer and its impact, though a given English word may not match a dictionary gloss of the corresponding Hebrew word. Fidelity in the translation of a prayer book requires faithfulness also to the overall experience of Jewish worship.

Traditional Hebrew prayer is intimate and direct; poetic and musical; allusive and highly charged with meaning. It is a powerful meeting-place of sound and sense. In our faithful translation we aim for these qualities in English. And we strive for language that conveys the values, hopes, and aspirations of the Jewish people in relationship with the Holy.

About the Transliteration

Our transliteration reflects spoken rather than written Hebrew. In general, it does not replicate (nearly) silent letters or doubled Hebrew consonants. Well-known Hebrew words are spelled conventionally, while the pronunciation of biblical Hebrew is treated with the greatest precision.

To encourage participation, we do not use unfamiliar and distracting signs and characters. Aside from the English alphabet, we use only the following symbols: an APOSTROPHE, to indicate a vocal *sh'va* (the half-vowel sound heard in the first syllable of the word "about"); a HYPHEN between certain words, to show the correct rhythm and syllable stress; and a RAISED DOT, to separate certain letters so that each one is pronounced distinctly — for example: *va·ed, yit·halal.*

The *Bayit* and the *K'neset*

RABBI DALIA MARX, PhD

THE WRITER and satirist Harry Golden once asked his atheist father why he went to shul so religiously. The reply: Garfinkel goes to talk to God. I go to talk to Garfinkel. This anecdote reveals an ancient truth: Jews come to the synagogue for many reasons, not all of which have to do with faith, though they are all legitimate and welcome reasons. Maybe this is why we call the synagogue a *Beit K'neset*, the House of Gathering, rather than the House of Prayer or the House of God. Scholars of ancient Judaism describe the early institution as closer to a modern-day Jewish Community Center than to a House of Prayer in the modern sense. But on a more profound level, a *Beit K'neset* is indeed a house of prayers. The synagogue houses the prayers of all Israel — much the way the Israeli parliament, the Knesset, is more than a gathering place for the country's politicians and lawmakers: it is meant to be the locus of Israelis' deepest concerns and aspirations.

As a child visiting monasteries in the Judean desert and seeing the monks spend their lives in solitude, meditation, and contemplation, I had mixed feelings of both appreciation and sadness that they could not share their religious experiences with others. Faith, however, is a personal matter; it is no one else's business to know what, how, or why we believe. Even the most extreme ultra-Orthodox groups, who control every aspect of their members' lives, focus on their behavior; they do not get involved with matters of faith and belief.

Yet prayer is different from faith. While one's beliefs are a private matter, our Jewish values, our struggles, and even our doubts are expressed primarily in a communal fashion. Of course, one can pray alone at home or on a beautiful mountaintop. Having a personal prayer life is considered praiseworthy. But Jewish tradition insists that the individual needs a minyan — a quorum of at least ten Jews with whom to pray. In the minyan, every individual counts. When you are not present, your voice is missed. The Midrash teaches that God's presence rests on a community gathered in prayer, citing this verse from Psalms: "God stands in the divine congregation" (Psalm 82:1).

Who counts in the minyan?

When referring to the various components of the incense offering used in the days of the Temple, the Sages stress that not only sweet-smelling frankincense, myrrh, and cinnamon are necessary, but also foul-smelling galbanum (as in Exodus 30:34). They teach that each of these components represents a different type of person, and that each is necessary for the preparation of the offering. According to the Talmud (*K'ritot* 6a), the inclusion of all the components is so crucial that if a person omits even one ingredient, that person is liable to the death penalty (not by a human court, but by the "heavenly court"). Thus, for the Sages, a congregation by definition must include diverse individuals with a range of ideas, feelings, and practices. Moreover, the richest experience comes when all of us bring our full selves into the community — not only our pious thoughts and positive feelings, but the full range of our our selves and our emotions, including questions, skepticism, and anger.

If this is true for the entire year, it is even more essential during the High Holy Days, arguably the most spiritually intense days of the Jewish year. Rabbi Shimon the Pious taught: "A fast that does not include the sinners of Israel is no fast; for behold, the odor of galbanum is unpleasant, and yet it was included in the spices for the incense" (Talmud *K'ritot* 6b). The ritual of Yom Kippur — confession, atonement, and forgiveness — cannot be complete without the inclusion of the wrongdoers. Similarly, Rabbi Meir of Rothenburg (13th-century Ashkenaz) ordained that the following words be said before reciting *Kol Nidrei*: "By the authority of the Heavenly Court and by authority of the earthly court, by the permission of God and by the permission of this congregation, we hold it lawful to pray with those who have transgressed." No one is excluded from the sacred space or from sharing in the Holy Day.

The confessions that we recite on Yom Kippur are expressed in the first-person plural: "*Ashamnu, bagadnu, gazalnu.* . . ." The meaning of this formulation is twofold: first, we proclaim our communal responsibility, because the wrongdoing of even one individual casts a shadow on the entire community. Second, we avoid shaming individuals and show solidarity with those who have gone astray. Thus we acknowledge that no one is perfect or blameless. The sound of our voices lifted in unison, as we confess our human sins and frailties, gives courage and comfort to each fallible individual in the congregation.

According to the last paragraph of the Mishnah tractate *Yoma*, which contains the early Rabbinic laws of Yom Kippur:

> For transgressions against God, the Day of Atonement atones; but for transgressions of one human being against another, the Day of Atonement does not atone until they have made peace with each other. (8:9)

Only by participating in the rituals of the holy day in a communal setting, joining our voice with others in the words of our tradition, do we absorb the central message: Yom Kippur is not only "about me" — my personal and spiritual life, my well-being and peace of mind.

An individual may spend the day in solitary prayer and reflection, yet not accomplish the purpose of Yom Kippur. The Day of Atonement is about reconnecting us with our highest aspirations, but also about bringing us closer to God and other human beings. This process can take place only when the community sets aside a time and a place for us to come together to engage in this crucial activity. Jewish tradition does not leave this up to the whim of the individual, but ordains a systematic, communal framework that engages each individual in the work of *t'shuvah*.

Our fellow worshipers go through their own repentance process while, at the same time, serving as witnesses to ours. Individual commitment is strengthened as we bear witness to one another's efforts. It is no coincidence that the Hebrew words *yachid* (individual) and *yachad* (together) come from the same etymological root.

The interplay of *yachid* and *yachad*

There is an inherent tension between the individual and the community, manifested in every generation and in every culture. Jewish tradition does not ask us to choose between the private and the public, the personal and the communal. Rather, it calls us to exist in both of these realms, actively living in the tension. No community is perfect, just as no individual is perfect. Yet, for all its frustrations, Jewish community remains a sacred vessel for our shared hopes, yearnings, struggles, and fears. The whole is greater than the sum of its parts; the community elevates and enhances each individual's experience.

Judaism insists, somewhat paradoxically, that we discover our uniqueness and become our best selves, not through solitary contemplation, but by having significant encounters with others and positive experiences as part of a collective. Our personal spiritual journey is enriched when we open ourselves to the journeys and struggles of others. By participating in communal life, an individual takes on responsibility, but paradoxically the burden is also lightened, for we see that there are others who join with us in prayer and *t'shuvah*. The task of soul searching required by the High Holy Days is demanding, even draining. When we are on our own, praying in solitude, the weight falls solely on our shoulders. Going through the demanding journey together may ease the burden and allow a certain sense of relief.

When I am in the community, I can be carried on the wings of other worshipers' prayers. If I am tired or distracted, I may doze off for a moment or drift into my own thoughts, but the community's worship will carry on. Then, when I am ready, I can come back and be fully present in the liturgy, carrying with me those worshipers who need my support.

The *Beit K'neset*, the synagogue where we pray, is not the "House of God," as some religions call their place of worship. God does not require a home; God cannot be "housed." At the dedication of the First Temple in Jerusalem, King Solomon made this clear, saying: "Behold, the highest heavens cannot contain You; how much less this House that I have built" (I Kings 8:27). What a bold statement! While dedicating this sacred place, Solomon acknowledges that the magnificent edifice of the Temple could not house God. The entire universe is God's "dwelling place"; the Temple was meant for the people. This physical structure, created by the community, served as a focal point to orient the people's prayers toward God.

In the same way, when we pray within its walls, the synagogue is *our* house — the place where we gather and, as a community, turn to God. In the *Beit K'neset* we need not feel like guests or visitors; this is our *bayit*, the home we share. So maybe Garfinkel and Golden had it wrong, with their bifurcated notions of why we go to synagogue. For the tradition asserts that, when we meet each other in a deep and authentic way, we may also meet the Divine.

Why Do We Need This Day of Atonement?

RABBI RICHARD S. SARASON, PhD

THE PACE of our lives today is very fast and only getting faster. We are often so preoccupied with the business of daily living that we don't pause to consider the bigger picture: What do we want our lives to *mean*? What do we want to leave behind as our legacy? Every year, as the season turns, the High Holy Days present us with the opportunity to take stock. In Hebrew, this is called *cheshbon hanefesh* — accounting for our souls, our selves. We are challenged to reevaluate our lives in the light of what really matters: our ultimate values, our relationships to others and to God (however we understand the Divine), and our own limitations of both time and ability. We must honestly confront those things that we most regret about ourselves: our mortality, our failures, the hurt that we have caused to others, and the harm we have done to the image of God — perhaps understood as violations against the natural world, the moral order, the sanctity of life, and our better selves. We must acknowledge our imperfections, all the while striving to transcend them. Rosh HaShanah, Yom Kippur, and the Ten Days of Repentance between them form a dramatic arc. We pass through it as we subject ourselves to this unflinching self-scrutiny — both as individuals and as a community. We attempt to learn from it how to correct our course on the journey of our personal and communal lives, to become better at the art and practice of sacred living.

While Rosh HaShanah inaugurates this passage with its themes of judgment and accountability, remembrance, and acknowledgment of a higher reality (*Malchuyot* — the proclamation of divine sovereignty), and the seven intermediate days focus on the processes of repentance and return, growth and change (*t'shuvah*), Yom Kippur is the climax of the entire movement. In Rabbinic literature it is often called *yoma*, "*The* Day": the most important day of the year. The dramatic movement of the day itself is from the depths to the heights, from anxiety to reassurance and reconciliation, wiping clean once again the tarnished slates of our lives as we enter upon a new year with renewed hope for the future. Its best-known activity is fasting, while its main themes and images — the stages through which we pass — are those of sin, confession, repentance, and finally forgiveness and atonement. We offer an interpretation of each of these in turn.

Fasting is an act of restraint and self-denial. For twenty-five hours, we refrain from the pleasures of eating and drinking — of nourishment and refreshment This is a way to help us focus on our spiritual rather than our physical needs. Alternatively, fasting underscores that we have physical needs, by intensifying them. On this day of annual self-scrutiny we need to be reminded that we are needy and not self-sufficient. The widespread custom of donating food on Yom Kippur to the hungry in our midst can enlarge our sense of social responsibility and larger purpose.

The traditional Jewish theological vocabulary can often be daunting, even off-putting, for many of us. The fact that these English words, and their synonyms in all other European languages, are inherently laden with Christian theological resonances frequently adds to the discomfort. A way out of this unease is to recognize that the language of our liturgy — indeed, all religious language — is not literal, but figurative, poetic, allusive. It remains an imperfect attempt to verbalize that which cannot be expressed fully, if at all, in words; it can merely point us toward something. Our experience of Yom Kippur, its worship and its work, needs to go beyond the words and images on the page; it needs to be felt deeply. (This is why musical expression is so important: it unlocks dimensions that words by themselves cannot utter.)

How then can the words themselves — the traditional vocabulary and images of Yom Kippur — help us to move beyond those words? If we can see through them to the basic, shared human experiences and dilemmas that lie at their core, we can better appreciate and identify with the internal, personal work that Yom Kippur challenges us to do. I find it helpful to view the dramatic ritualized movement through the day — and the work that it entails — as a cathartic process, aimed at healing the soul, the self, and the community.

We begin with our very real imperfections. "Sin" is a challenging word, since it carries for some the Christian theological connotations of an imperfect state of being that is beyond our ability to change. It provokes guilt, suggesting that we are somehow "bad" people. However, the Hebrew word for sin, *cheit*, literally means missing the mark, failing. It refers to our actions, not to who we are. "Transgression" (*aveirah*) might be a more understandable term. It means crossing a line or a boundary, violating a rule, invading someone else's space (human or divine) without permission. On Yom Kippur we must deal with the ways in which we have hurt both others and the world around us. We must wrestle with our failures, and with our *feelings* of failure and inadequacy, even of guilt and shame, however much those feelings may be concealed. In other words, we must come to terms with the fragile reality of our daily lives and be able to see ourselves — however painfully — as vulnerable. The purpose of this work on Yom Kippur, however, is to be able to move in a positive direction beyond these uncomfortable feelings and realities — to confront them in order to transcend them and to arrive at a better place.

The way we confront our failings is, first of all, by acknowledging them. That is why a verbal confession (*vidui*) — out loud, as an entire community — is a major part of the work of Yom Kippur. The embarrassment of doing this is eased somewhat by the fact that we do it all together, giving voice to the same words at the same time, in the first-person plural. Likely none of us have performed all of the misdeeds listed in the liturgy — but some of them may strike too close for comfort and some relate to what we have done or failed to do as a society. While the language of these confessions and of the *S'lichot* prayers for forgiveness sometimes might feel *too* self-abasing (how many times can we say, "I am nothing"?), a certain amount of this can be helpful to break through our resistance.

The process of *t'shuvah* — repentance, return, realignment — follows upon the acknowledgment of our failings and our recognition of what needs to change. What does *t'shuvah* mean in practical terms? Maimonides (*Mishneh Torah, Hilchot T'shuvah* 2.1) provided a brief definition that remains powerful today:

> What is perfect repentance? It is when an opportunity presents itself to repeat the same behavior, and, while being physically able to do so, you nonetheless refrain, because you have had a change of heart and resolved not to behave this way.

Although *t'shuvah* is a focus of the entire period between Rosh HaShanah and Yom Kippur, it is really an ongoing process, requiring attentiveness to our habitual behavior (since we are creatures of habit) and active intervention to change it. In Jewish ethical literature, this process is also referred to as *tikkun hamidot*, the repair or improvement of our character that is expressed through our personal behavior. That is why the Afternoon Service in this prayer book focuses on *tikkun midot* as "the heart of Yom Kippur."

At the very summit of Yom Kippur lies forgiveness, reconciliation, atonement. How is this to be achieved after the long, difficult work of the day? We can understand the insistence of our tradition that "for transgressions between one person and another, Yom Kippur does not effect atonement until that person reconciles with the other" (Mishnah *Yoma* 8:9). The responsibility for reconciling with someone whom we have offended rests squarely with ourselves. But how do we deal with the emotional residue and scars — some lack of trust, some lingering feelings of guilt or of shame — that so often remain even after we have reconciled? Emotionally speaking, can we truly be forgiven? Can we forgive ourselves?

Can we give ourselves permission to let go of these feelings? Here is where the ritualized passage and work of Yom Kippur becomes powerful and cathartic.

For the Sages of old believed in the power of this day to wipe the slate clean even when our own efforts at reconciliation with others and with God fall short. Jewish tradition asserts: the day itself — including the process that we experience between *Kol Nidrei* and *N'ilah* — effects atonement. In other words, within the rituals of Yom Kippur a transcendent power resides.

This power of the day is available to us, too. Can we give ourselves up to this process? Can we let ourselves go through its stages, its lows and its highs, so deeply and resonantly that the final shofar blast is a moment of catharsis? In the end, that is why we need this Day of Atonement: it has the potential to bring a sublime change in how we see ourselves, our community, and our world. It can inspire us to carry our insights beyond the confines of the synagogue, beyond the pages of a prayer book, and act upon them every day. For we do well to remember that the ultimate purpose of this day, and of the entire High Holy Day season, is to help us shape lives that are more thoughtful and compassionate, more ethical, and more reverent.

Changing Your Past: Reflection on Forgiveness

RABBI ELLEN LEWIS, NCPsyA

YOU CAN change your past. That is the emotional premise of forgiveness. No, you cannot change what happened. You can change only your emotional relationship to what happened. And it might very well be the hardest thing you ever try to do.

Choosing to forgive is exactly that — a choice. If a person feels coerced, it is no longer a choice. If the choice were an easy one, the *machzor* would not command, inspire, prod, praise, or cajole us toward forgiveness. To make the point, the sages of the Talmud boldly evoke a God who struggles with this very issue, offering as evidence God's own "personal prayer": "May it be My will that My mercy suppress my anger, and that it may prevail over My attributes of justice and judgment; and that I may deal with My children according to the attribute of compassion, and that I may not act toward them according to the strict line of justice" (*B'rachot* 7a). We identify with the God whom we encounter in this prayer; we too feel a tension between the urge to be compassionate and the wish to punish or exact revenge. The Sages validate, comfort, and challenge us with a message that our struggle is the mirror-image of God's.

Although the *machzor*'s urgency about forgiveness is felt just once a year, the wisdom of forgiveness is valued continually by our secular and religious cultures: in the research of psychologists, for example, who encourage us to forgive for our own good, if not for the good of others; in the religious writings of Maimonides, who not only says we must forgive but also tells how to feel during the act of forgiveness: "When the person who wronged [you] asks for forgiveness, [you] should forgive him with a complete heart and a willing spirit. Even if he aggravated and wronged [you] severely, [you] should not seek revenge or bear a grudge." (*Mishneh Torah, Hilchot T'shuvah* 2.10)

Compelling evidence offered both by modern psychology and by Jewish tradition would seem to make forgiveness an irresistible path to follow. And yet, the powerful chorus of voices exhorting us to forgive underlines the task's difficulty. For we are confronted by an inescapable human paradox: the more we are told to forgive, the more we resist. Think of how often a parent urges a child to say "I'm sorry," while parent and child both know that the words the child utters do not match her feelings. Behind this "civilizing process" lies the hope that someday the grudging apologies of childhood will lead the (now adult) child to genuine feelings of remorse.

Despite the best parental efforts, however, our long-ago child lives on in the unconscious mind of the adult we become. Old, unresolved feelings have gone underground and become inaccessible, but they are not gone. They lie in wait for a new wound to open, allowing old pain to come flooding back, and blending today's feelings with those of the child who felt in the right even when saying the obligatory "I'm sorry." The old feelings are ingrained, etched onto the psyche by years of practice and repetition. They make their appearance in our adult lives as a finely honed resistance to change of any kind.

Unearthing and working through the old feelings begins the process of forgiveness, setting us on the right path but offering no guarantees about how long it will take. Today's feelings are clues to the mysterious emotions of the past; and these clues can help us expose culprits of all kinds — shame, inadequacy, rejection, hatred, yearning, betrayal, anger, righteous indignation, hopelessness.

Only after allowing the painful, buried feelings to rise to the surface do we begin to understand why we hold on to those feelings and how we benefit from them. One might even say we hold on to them "for dear life," because the intensity of old feelings can feel like a life-and-death conflict. Children often experience not getting what they want as the end of the world, since they do not yet know that feelings can change in a heartbeat. Not unlike the forgotten children within us, adults often respond to emotional challenges by clinging to familiar responses that long ago outlived their usefulness. Old emotional protections lock into place out of habit, which inevitably locks us into pain and out of a happy life.

Why do people choose suffering over happiness, resentment over forgiveness? Almost always, the answer is embedded in old emotional wishes. For example, we hold on tight to the enduring hope that mother will rescue us from our torment, or that father will at long last acknowledge his culpability. We cling to the old fantasy that hearing the magic words will grant us freedom from pain and hurt, and offer us the love we crave. Though our personal motivations may vary, our unconscious wish for childhood vindication remains so powerful that it overrides our conscious desire to choose happiness. Who would not want to become the person whom Maimonides believes we can be? Who would not want to rise above the desire for revenge in order to forgive with a willing spirit? Yet, in its insistence that winning depends on being right, the unconscious part of the brain fights our desire to rise to a higher self. Being right trumps being happy. But, in the end, this kind of winning does not bring happiness. "Being right" does not release us from self-imposed emotional bondage; inevitably and ironically, it guarantees continued misery.

Forgiveness can come. But it comes only by understanding how we have constructed our own emotional history, and by reevaluating whether that version of our personal story still suits us. We may need to "try on" a new story for size. Like childhood clothing we outgrow and discard, we can also outgrow the old narrative. We can wait until a new feeling inspires a new effort, but we may find that, despite our best efforts, conjuring up the right feeling eludes us. Sometimes that old forced lesson (saying "sorry" when we do not mean it) is worth trying again — this time as an adult choice; this time with confidence that the act of forgiveness will allow us to develop a new feeling.

The *machzor* challenges us to forgive, leading many of us to berate ourselves for why we can't. If we think of *forgiving* as the right thing to do and *not forgiving* as wrong, we limit ourselves to the perspective of a struggling young child. Only if we reframe the question — not "What's the right thing to do?" and "Why can't I just forgive?"— but rather, "What stops me from forgiving?" — can we get unstuck from the old narrative and move toward more satisfying possibilities. Ask a question that opens up a sympathetic investigation rather than one that closes off possible new avenues of inquiry. Imagine what it would look like if we could forgive. And what will it look like if we can't?

Even if we create a different and more satisfying narrative, still we might not find forgiveness as a possibility in this moment. Despite all the benefits that forgiveness promises, it does not make sense in all situations. If we find ourselves caught up in a relentless cycle of being hurt and then forgiving, our haste to forgive might actually be appeasement masquerading as forgiveness. In this case, forgiveness is less an act of generosity than it is a seductive trap that merely allows for prolonged abusive behavior. When hate is the response to an offer of love, forgiveness is not the right path. Better to be kind to oneself than to offer premature forgiveness.

A person in this position is not helpless. We have choices: we can grieve the loss rather than punish ourselves for something that we cannot do. We can grieve the loss of the imperfect parent, sibling, child, partner, or friend. We can grieve the loss of our old self. We can move on and make progress in our life by engaging in the process of grief, which leads to an experience of freedom and gives us a new perspective on life. That new view may even open our heart to finding forgiveness in unexpected places — giving and receiving it not necessarily in the context of past conflict, but, more likely, in new situations where forgiveness, blessedly, is now an option. Just as we can change our past, so we can write a new story going forward.

God is slow to anger and quick to forgive, says the Psalmist. God wants to forgive us. A midrash teaches that during the Days of Awe, God is poised between the throne of judgment and the throne of mercy; in the end, God rejects the throne of judgment and, through the strength of our prayers, ascends the throne of mercy (*Leviticus Rabbah* 29.3–4). Seeking to emulate God's qualities, we aspire to the same: to reach for our higher, more compassionate selves, to ascend to mercy. But sometimes we lose sight of the crucial distinction between the desire to be compassionate (as God is compassionate) and the desire to be perfect (as God is perfect). Thinking of ourselves as "little lower than the angels" can blind us to that distinction; and so we forget that God does not require us to be perfect. Indeed, we forget that it is the very imperfection of our striving and the sincerity of our attempt that move God from one throne to the other.

Not perfect, but fully human: this is what God asks of us. And, in response, this may be the best we can do: forgive ourselves for our yearnings and failings, for being human and not God; and accept the imperfections, satisfactions, and challenges of being a person. Only having made that choice can we walk unburdened and openhearted into the new year.

Yizkor and Yom Kippur

RABBI MARGARET MOERS WENIG

MULTIPLE TIMES over the course of this most holy day, we recite, "Blessed are You, Eternal God, Sovereign of the Universe, who sanctifies . . . Yom HaKippurim." Some say that we call the Day of Atonement "Yom HaKippurim" — in the plural — because *both* the living and the dead are in need of *kapparah* (atonement), not infrequently from each other. *Yizkor* is not about the futility of human endeavors that evaporate with death. *Yizkor* is about what remains.

Maimonides is clear that the living may need absolution from the dead:

> If you sin against someone who dies before you have had a chance to make amends and ask forgiveness, you bring ten Israelites to the dead person's grave as witnesses and say before them: I have sinned in such and such a way against so-and-so. If the deceased has heirs, you pay your debt to the heirs. If the deceased has no heirs, you pay your debt to the *beit din* and confess. (*Hilchot T'shuvah* 2.9)

A Chasidic tale imagines the other side of the dynamic, in which a dead husband seeks forgiveness from his surviving spouse:

> In the night after the seven-day mourning for Reb Abraham the Angel, his wife had a dream. She saw a vast hall; and in it, thrones — set in a semicircle. On each throne sat one of the greats. A door opened, and . . . Abraham, her husband, entered. "Friends, my wife is angry with me because in my earthly life I lived apart from her. She is right and therefore I must obtain her forgiveness." His wife cried out: "With all my heart, I forgive you." And [she] awoke comforted. (Martin Buber, *Tales of the Hasidim*, vol. 1, p. 117)

An attempt to earn *kapparah* is built into the traditional Yizkor formula: "*Yizkor Elohim et nishmat ____, baavur she-ani nodeir/noderet tz'dakah baado/baadah* (May God remember the soul of ____, on whose behalf I pledge *tzedakah*). . . ."

Pledges and acts of *tzedakah* were believed to add merit to the soul of the deceased as he or she faced judgment. The pledge was omitted from many Reform *Yizkor* liturgies, out of discomfort with the underlying notion that a person may face judgment following death — and/or that the verdict could possibly be improved by deeds that the living perform on his or her behalf. *Mishkah HaNefesh* has retrieved this language from Jewish tradition and imbued it with new meaning and resonance for Reform and other liberal Jews: "For the sake of *tikkun olam*, I freely give *tzedakah* in his/her memory" (pages 570–71).

Yom Kippur is the cathartic climax to (though not the final end of) a long period of repentance, during which we examine our words, our thoughts, and our deeds and endeavor to change them for the better, if only incrementally. We work to improve our relationships with our peers, with those who depend on us — and with those upon whom we depend, including, I believe, the dead. For isn't it often difficult to separate our relationships with the living from our relationships with the dead?

During the *Yizkor* service, when we say *Yizkor Elohim et nishmat ____, baavur she·ani noderet tz'dakah baadah*, we might mean:

> May God take note of ____, for whom I pledge ____ so that her sins may be diminished and her merits magnified.
> or: . . . for whom I pledge ____ so that *my* sins may be diminished and *my* merits magnified.
> or: . . . for whom I pledge ____ as an expression of gratitude for all that she has taught me.
> or: . . . for whom I pledge ____ so that her death not be entirely in vain.
> or: . . . for whom I pledge ____ so that I may be worthy of the gift that she has bequeathed to me.

And if we are able, we might add:

> I hereby forgive ____ for the sin that he/she committed against me.
> I hereby ask ____ to forgive me for the sin that I committed against him/her.

Reciting *Yizkor* on Yom Kippur is less about mourning, mortality, or memory and more about connection, continuity, and change in our relationships with those whose lives impacted our own. And it is this change that we appeal to God to "remember."

WHEN WE recite *Yizkor Elohim et nishmat ____*, in what sense are we uttering a petition? "*May* God remember (or notice) the soul of ____"? Does the God whom we imagine ever *forget* what is written in *Sefer HaZichronot* (Book of Remembrance)? What is written by a person in *Sefer HaZichronot* is not written in ink that fades, or on paper that deteriorates with time. *Yizkor Elohim* cannot be a petition — *May* God remember, *May* God take note — *unless* we are asking God to take note of something that has not yet happened: namely, a *change* in our relationship with the deceased, a change in the deceased, a change in ourselves that we are about to attempt to bring about, such as:

- "By pledging and then doing this act of *tzedakah*, I hope to extend the reach of my mother's legacy."
- "By pledging and doing this act of *tzedakah*, I hope to open my grandmother's heart a little more in forgiveness."
- "By pledging and doing this act of *tzedakah*, I hope to add to my father's merit to tip the scales a bit from his bad deeds to his good deeds."
- "By pledging and doing this act of *tzedakah*, I hope to resurrect in my life a person from whom I have been estranged."
- "By pledging and doing this act of *tzedakah*, I hope, little by little, to externalize and thus internalize my lost one's love and, perhaps, feel her presence more and more, and grieve her absence less and less."

That is to say: "*Yizkor Elohim et nishmat* ____, *baavur she·ani noderet tz'dakah baadah*. . . . May God notice how the soul or the legacy *of the deceased* will change, if ever so slightly, through this act of *tzedakah*; and may God notice how *my* own soul, my inner life, and my outer life will change, if ever so slightly, through this act of *tzedakah*. For with this pledge and act of *tzedakah*, I open the files inscribed and stored in my brain and *edit* them before resaving them."

Yizkor on Yom Kippur is, I believe, not about human frailty or the futility of human endeavors. *Yizkor* on Yom Kippur is about the power of others to affect us, about our power to affect others, about the power of the dead and the living to continue to affect each other. *Yizkor* on Yom Kippur is, I believe, not simply about remembering the dead, but about attempting to effect *change* in our relationships with the dead and thus to effect change in ourselves and in our relationships with those who are still among the living.

עַרְבִית לְיוֹם כִּפּוּר
Yom Kippur Evening Service

I forgive, as you have asked.

—NUMBERS 14:20

בְּשַׁעֲרֵי יוֹם הַכִּפּוּרִים
B'Shaarei Yom HaKippurim
Entering into Yom Kippur

טַלִּית
Tallit

הַדְלָקַת נֵרוֹת
Hadlakat Nerot

תְּפִלָּה זַכָּה
T'filah Zakah

For those who wear the tallit:

My soul, bless Adonai.
Adonai, my God,
You are very great.
You are clothed in beauty and splendor,
wrapped in a robe of light.
You unfurl the heavens like the curtains of a tent.

from Psalm 104

בָּרוּךְ אַתָּה, יְיָ,
אֱלֹהֵינוּ מֶלֶךְ הָעוֹלָם,
אֲשֶׁר קִדְּשָׁנוּ בְּמִצְוֹתָיו,
וְצִוָּנוּ לְהִתְעַטֵּף בַּצִּיצִית.

Baruch atah, Adonai,
Eloheinu melech haolam,
asher kid'shanu b'mitzvotav,
v'tzivanu l'hitateif batzitzit.

Source of blessings — Eternal, our God, majestic in power:
Your mitzvot are paths of holiness;
You give us the mitzvah of wrapping ourselves in
the fringed tallit.

For those who do not wear the tallit:

Source of blessings — Eternal, our God, majestic in power:
Your splendor reveals the way to holiness;
Your light wraps us in the beauty of this sacred day.

FRINGED TALLIT צִיצִת. The 11th-century commentator Rashi notes that the numerical value of the word *tzitzit* (fringes), when fully spelled out, is 600 (צ *tzadi* = 90; י *yod* = 10; צ *tzadi* = 90; י *yod* = 10; ת *tav* = 400). The fringe is tied with 8 threads and 5 knots, totaling 613 — which, according to tradition, is the number of mitzvot in the Torah. Thus, in looking upon the fringes, we call to mind a life grounded in sacred commitment.

Commentary: Why Is the Tallit Worn This Night of Kol Nidrei?

"Look at it and recall all the mitzvot": these words of the Torah refer to the obligation to wear *tzitzit* (fringes) on the corners of one's garment. That is why we normally wear the fringed tallit only during the day—the hours when there is natural light to see the fringe and be reminded of our sacred obligations. Many Jews have worn the tallit both day night on Yom Kippur since the thirteenth century, when Rabbi Meir of Rothenburg taught the following link between the tallit and prayers of forgiveness (*s'lichot*).

When Moses ascended Mount Sinai with the second set of stone tablets, he asked God's forgiveness on behalf of the Israelites who had built and worshiped the Golden Calf. As God passed before him, Moses heard these words, known as God's Thirteen Attributes of Mercy: *Adonai, Adonai—God, compassionate, gracious, endlessly patient, loving, and true; showing mercy to the thousandth generation; forgiving evil, defiance, and wrongdoing; granting pardon*. According to the Talmud, this was the moment when the Divine Presence, wrapped in a tallit, taught Moses how to pray and ask forgiveness by uttering the Thirteen Attributes.

On this night of *Kol Nidrei*, when our prayers include songs of forgiveness, it is the custom of many Jews to wrap themselves in the tallit and feel its warm embrace while recalling God's compassion, patience, and love.

Open Closed Open

וּמַדּוּעַ הַטַּלִּית בְּפַסִּים וְלֹא בְּמִשְׁבְּצוֹת־שָׁחוֹר־לָבָן
כְּמוֹ לוּחַ שַׁחְמַט. כִּי הָרִבּוּעִים הֵם סוֹפִיִּים וּבְלִי תִּקְוָה,
הַפַּסִּים בָּאִים מֵאֵין־סוֹף וְיוֹצְאִים לְאֵין־סוֹף
כְּמוֹ מַסְלוּלֵי הַמְרָאָה בִּשְׂדֵה תְּעוּפָה
לִנְחִיתַת הַמַּלְאָכִים וּלְהַמְרָאָתָם.

And why is the tallis striped and not checkered black-and-white
like a chessboard? Because squares are finite and hopeless.
Stripes come from infinity and to infinity they go
like airport runways where angels land and take off.

—Yehuda Amichai (1924–2000), excerpted

---

look at it, Numbers 15:40.
adonai, adonai, Exodus 34:6–7.
this was the moment, Talmud *Rosh HaShanah* 17b.

Meditations

The most beautiful thing that one can do is to forgive a wrong.

—Rabbi Eleazar ben Judah of Worms (ca. 1165–1238)

It is the custom to visit one's friends on the eve of Yom Kippur to beseech their forgiveness, though there is generally no need to do so, for one has not sinned against one's friends, and even if one has sinned against them, it was unintentional, and love covers all sins; their enmity certainly must have left them already. Yet being an ancient custom, it is worthy of respect, for there is no knowing what feelings are stored up in the hearts of one's friends.

—Rabbi Joseph Yuspa Hahn of Frankfort-on-the-Main, 1723

For on this day *atonement shall be made for you to purify you from all your wrongs. And pure you shall be in the presence of Adonai* (Leviticus 16:30). Rabbi Eleazar ben Azariah has expounded this verse in the following way: Yom Kippur brings atonement for wrongs between people and God [which is why the Torah says *in the presence of Adonai*], but Yom Kippur can bring atonement for transgressions between one person and another only if the person offended has first been reconciled.

—Mishnah *Yoma* 8:9

Jewish thought pays little attention to inner tranquility and peace of mind. The feeling of "behold, I've arrived" could well undermine the capacity to continue, suggesting as it does that the Infinite can be reached in a finite number of steps. In fact, the very concept of the Divine as infinite implies an activity that is endless, of which one must never grow weary. At every rung of [the] ascent, the penitent, like any person who follows the way of God, perceives mainly the remoteness. Only in looking back can one obtain some idea of the distance already covered, of the degree of progress. Repentance does not bring a sense of serenity or of completion but stimulates a reaching out in further effort.

—Rabbi Adin Steinsaltz (b. 1937)

Humility is the root and beginning of repentance.

—Bachya ibn Pakuda (ca. 1255–1340), *Duties of the Heart* 2:125

On this journey our soul will awaken to itself. We will venture from innocence to sin and back to innocence again. This is a journey from denial to awareness, from self-deception to judgment. We will learn our Divine Name. We will move from self-hatred to self-forgiveness, from anger to healing, from hard-heartedness to brokenheartedness. This is the journey the soul takes to transform itself and to evolve, the journey from boredom and staleness—from deadness—to renewal. . . . It is the journey from little mind to big mind, from confinement in the ego to a sense of ourselves as a part of something larger. It is the journey from isolation to a sense of our intimate connection to all being. . . .

Every soul needs to express itself. Every heart needs to crack itself open. Every one of us needs to move from anger to healing, from denial to consciousness, from boredom to renewal. These needs did not arise yesterday. They are among the most ancient of human yearnings, and they are fully expressed in the pageantry and ritual of the Days of Awe, in the great journey we make between Rosh HaShanah and Yom Kippur.

—Rabbi Alan Lew (1944–2009)

Praying is more than merely reciting words; it's about encountering aspects of ourselves we rarely if ever see, shifting our perspective and seeing all things anew, awakening our spirits and sense of wonder. Prayer is about connection—with ourselves, with a community of other seekers, and with Someone or Something beyond ourselves. . . .

On the High Holy Days in particular, our prayer has some additional goals. We're trying to remove our protective armor—ego, self-deception, rationalization, external and internal "makeup," posturing—anything that keeps us from seeing ourselves as we really are. We're trying to experience both our vulnerability, and the true source of our strength. And perhaps most importantly, we're trying to get past our self-judgment and locate a place of gentleness and tenderness—that place where we feel deeply loved and valued, and where we feel most loving of others. Even if just for a moment.

—Rabbi Jan Uhrbach (b. 1963)

טַלִּית
Tallit

הַדְלָקַת נֵרוֹת
Hadlakat Nerot

תְּפִלָּה זַכָּה
T'filah Zakah

The impact of *erev Yom Kippur* was more powerful in my life than that of Yom Kippur itself. What really changed my life, and shaped my character, were the few hours before Yom Kippur. I am not going to give you a description. I can only say that they were moments in my life when I felt somehow more than human. These were difficult hours. It was a great challenge for us to discover whether it was still possible for us in our civilization to go through such great experiences. It was great fear and trembling, great *pachad*, great awareness that you are now to be confronted. There was no fear of punishment, not even a fear of death, but the expectation of standing in the presence of God. This was the decisive moment. Get ready, purify yourself. Terribly lacking in explicitness, but tremendously powerful. And behind it a full sense of one's own unworthiness and a sense of contrition.

—Rabbi Abraham Joshua Heschel (1907–1972), adapted

What an extraordinary gift it is—what a blessing, what a miracle
to have been raised by imperfect parents who did their very best;
to share our life with a partner no more flawed than we are;
to count as a friend one who understands and accepts us most of the time.
How brave, how hard it is to be "good enough" in our ties to one another:
to give, even when we're exhausted; to love faithfully;
to receive with grace the love imperfectly offered to us.

Can this night set us free from the tyranny of expectations?
Can this night release us from fantasies impossible to fulfill?

We resolve this night to embrace the practice of forgiveness:
to forgive others who fail to be all we hoped they would be;
to forgive ourselves when we fall short of what others hoped we would be.
We declare this night that we will cherish goodness wherever it is found,
and open ourselves to the gifts that are before us.

—Rabbi Lewis Kamrass (b. 1959), adapted

In the Bible, as in our own lives, personal experience led people to different ideas about God. Moses said: *The great, mighty, and awesome God* (Deuteronomy 10:17). But Jeremiah prayed, *O great and mighty God* (32:18). And Daniel prayed, *O great and awesome God* (9:4). How could Jeremiah and Daniel each omit a word uttered by Moses? Rabbi Eleazar said: Since they knew that the Holy One insists on truth, they were unable to say anything false about God. Sincere prayer demands complete honesty, because God can see through false piety—even if some people cannot.

—A teaching on Talmud *Yoma* 69b by Rabbi Amy Scheinerman (b. 1957), adapted

Yom Kippur is a scandalous day for those of us who live in the modern world. It conjures up the prospect of death, still a great taboo in our society. It enjoins healthy and vigorous people to step off their treadmills for a moment and listen to the fragile beating of their own hearts.

Many of us, regardless of denomination or stated belief, find the challenge and scandal of Yom Kippur too difficult to bear. As a consequence, inventive techniques are developed that help keep its subversive message at bay.

We busy ourselves with the business of fasting, or revel in the rebellion of eating as normal. We obsess on the seating arrangements, or the heating arrangements. Some have other, more subtle methods. They allow the nostalgia of tunes and prayers to mask the uncomfortable implications of the day.

When it comes to the Day of Atonement, there are no experts, and no masters. Each person is exposed as mortal; those of us who like to think of themselves as significant may be particularly offended by the very thought.

My own personal version of preparation for Yom Kippur always begins with a sense of how absurd and limited I am, and how grand I pretend to be. I try to bring to mind the inadequacies and the errors, the times when I was angry instead of smart, and when I was clever instead of genuine.

Whoever is too self-impressed to come to terms with these truths might just as well skip straight forward to Sukkot: Yom Kippur will pass them by.

However macabre it sounds, Yom Kippur is meant to be a near-death experience. Confronted with the scandal of my own inevitable demise, this year or next or in seventy years' time, I need to acknowledge my weaknesses and vulnerabilities.

—Rabbi Michael Marmur (b. 1962), adapted

I REMEMBER how the women would make candles for Yom Kippur many years ago, when I was a small girl. . . .

Sarah—who filled her days with good works for the sick, the poor, and the bereaved—appeared early in the morning on the eve of Yom Kippur, bearing a stack of the Yiddish prayer books for women known as *T'chines* (Supplications). She brought, as well, an enormous ball of wick-thread and a large piece of wax. The women prepared for their work of candle-making by praying in Yiddish from the *T'chines*, weeping intensely. And until the candle was finished, my mother ate nothing, so that her spirit would be softer and she would be more inclined to weep.

Sarah placed the ball of wick-thread inside her apron pocket; she and my mother stood facing one another, about three feet apart. While they passed the thread back and forth, my mother—in a voice filled with tears—spoke the names of family members who had died, recalling aloud their acts of kindness. A thread was added for each person she remembered, until the wick was good and thick. Then living members of the family were remembered for life—the dead and the living joined together in the Yom Kippur candle.

—Pauline Wengeroff (1833–1916), adapted

YOM KIPPUR SONNET, WITH A LINE FROM LAMENTATIONS

Can a person atone for pure bewilderment?
For hyperbole? for being wrong
In a thousand categorical opinions?
For never opening her mouth, except too soon?
For ignoring, all week long, the waning moon
Retreating from its haunt above the local canyons,
Signaling her season to repent,
Then deflecting her repentance with a song?
Because the rest is just too difficult to face—
What we are—I mean—in all its meagerness—
The way we stint on any modicum of kindness—
What we allow ourselves—what we don't learn—
How each lapsed, unchanging year resigns us—
Return us, Lord, to you, and we'll return.

—Jacqueline Osherow (b. 1956)

טַלִּית
Tallit

הַדְלָקַת נֵרוֹת
Hadlakat Nerot

תְּפִלָּה זַכָּה
T'filah Zakah

Tallit Blessing

Candlelighting

A Prayer for Purity and Worthiness

Candlelighting for Home and Synagogue

The first blessing is said when lighting a ner n'shamah (memorial candle).

בָּרוּךְ אַתָּה, יְיָ,
נוֹטֵעַ בְּתוֹכֵנוּ חַיֵּי עוֹלָם.

Baruch atah, Adonai,
notei·a b'tocheinu chayei olam.

You are blessed, Eternal One, who places within us life everlasting.

The human spirit is the lamp of God,
searching out what lies within us.
Guided by the flame of conscience,
on this sacred night we search for truth.
Shine Your light upon us as we strive to serve You;
may we find safety in Your faithful love.
We light the flame of healing and forgiveness;
on this Atonement night, we give thanks for love.

בָּרוּךְ אַתָּה, יְיָ,
אֱלֹהֵינוּ מֶלֶךְ הָעוֹלָם,
אֲשֶׁר קִדְּשָׁנוּ בְּמִצְוֹתָיו,
וְצִוָּנוּ לְהַדְלִיק נֵר
[שֶׁל שַׁבָּת וְ] שֶׁל יוֹם הַכִּפּוּרִים.

Baruch atah, Adonai,
Eloheinu melech haolam,
asher kid'shanu b'mitzvotav,
v'tzivanu l'hadlik ner
[*shel Shabbat v'*] *shel Yom HaKippurim.*

Source of blessing, Eternal our God,
You fill the universe with majestic might,
teaching us holiness through sacred obligations,
giving us the mitzvah of bringing light on [Shabbat and] Yom Kippur.

בָּרוּךְ אַתָּה, יְיָ,
אֱלֹהֵינוּ מֶלֶךְ הָעוֹלָם,
שֶׁהֶחֱיָנוּ וְקִיְּמָנוּ וְהִגִּיעָנוּ
לַזְּמַן הַזֶּה.

Baruch atah, Adonai,
Eloheinu melech haolam,
shehecheyanu v'kiy'manu v'higianu
laz'man hazeh.

Source of blessing, Eternal our God,
You fill the universe with majestic might—
giving us life, upholding the life within us, and bringing us to this time.

THE HUMAN SPIRIT, Proverbs 20:27.
SHINE YOUR LIGHT. Based on Psalm 31:17.

Three Meditations

טַלִּית
Tallit

הַדְלָקַת נֵרוֹת
Hadlakat Nerot

תְּפִלָּה זַכָּה
T'filah Zakah

1. *The Five Disciplines of Yom Kippur*

Can I learn from deprivation? Can I grow from self-restraint?
For this holy day, our Mishnah prescribes five disciplines:
Refrain from food and drink, from bathing, from cosmetics,
from wearing leather shoes, from sexual intimacy.

Withdrawing from physical nourishment,
may I nourish my soul instead.
Rejecting adornment, pampering, and vanity,
may I turn my focus inward now.
Stepping out of comfort and self-indulgence,
may I stand this day more simply, in humility.
Denied the body's pleasure and release,
may my desire be for insight, self-improvement,
and the courage to change.

2. *For Those Who Must Eat During Yom Kippur*

Rofei chol basar—Healer of all living creatures:
I thank You for the breath that is in me
for the community of Israel that lives
for the possibilities of today and tomorrow.

May my eating be as a fast;
May it be dedicated to You, to *t'shuvah*—
to the renewal and restoration of my relationship
to You, to others, and to myself.

OUR MISHNAH, *Yoma* 8:1.

T'FILAH ZAKAH — A PRAYER FOR PURITY AND WORTHINESS (*overleaf*). Moments before we are lifted by the first notes of *Kol Nidrei*, we find before us a prayer for silent contemplation on this holy day's themes: forgiveness and atonement, human weakness and moral strength. *T'filah Zakah* offers us the inspiration and the tools we need to enter Yom Kippur with a repentant mind, and a heart that is open to sincere accounting of the soul. *Kol Nidrei* itself, like the confessions that come later in the service, speaks in the communal language of "we." The intensity of *T'filah Zakah* is different; the pronoun "I" throughout the prayer encourages the introspection that *t'shuvah* requires.

3. *The Fasts of Yom Kippur*

The Sages of the Mishnah teach:

On the Day of Atonement, these are forbidden:
eating and drinking; washing for pleasure; perfuming the body;
sexual relations; and wearing leather shoes.

It shall be, says the Bible, a sabbath of sabbaths for you,
and you shall practice self-denial;
from evening to evening you shall observe this:
your sabbath.

Abstention, affliction, self-denial:
it is a sabbath — a full rest, a complete stop,
a cessation from everyday pleasure.
Some wish us an "easy fast" — thinking only of food;
it is more than that.

Eating and drinking; washing, perfuming, and sex . . .
but leather shoes — why this?
Of all these pleasant acts, wearing shoes is the most public,
the one most seen by others.
But perhaps it is because shoes are a symbol of the path our lives take,
the choices we make along the way, the roads not taken —
a symbol of our journey in the year to come.

A Blessing to Begin the Fast

Blessed are You, Soul of the universe,
Creator of many creatures and their varied needs.
For sustaining the lives of all beings,
Life of the universe —
we praise You.
Now we prepare to abstain from food and drink,
that we may dedicate ourselves to the spiritual tasks of this holy day.
Blessed is the Source of All: You open us to Your nourishment.
Be with us —
throughout this time of intentional fasting.

THE SAGES OF THE MISHNAH TEACH. Based on *Yoma* 8:1.
SAYS THE BIBLE. Based on Leviticus 23:32.

טַלִּית
Tallit

הַדְלָקַת נֵרוֹת
Hadlakat Nerot

תְּפִלָּה זַכָּה
T'filah Zakah

T'filah Zakah — A Prayer for Purity and Worthiness

God, my Creator and Guide,
as I seek purity of soul on this holiest of days,
I contemplate Your gifts of love and forgiveness.

I know that perfect righteousness is beyond human reach:
the earth overflows with pain caused by word and deed;
the wounds we inflict are physical and emotional;
the damage we do is spiritual and material.

This night we remember the teaching of our Sages:
"For transgressions against God, the Day of Atonement atones;
but for transgressions of one human being against another,
the Day of Atonement does not atone
until they have made peace with each other."

And so my heart aches within me. I am shaken to my bones —
for nothing, not even death, can take the place of true repentance.
Therefore, I offer this humble prayer:

May I be worthy of grace, kindness, and mercy
in Your eyes and in the eyes of all human beings.
I hereby forgive all who have broken faith
by harming me physically or materially,
or by using thoughtless, unethical, and malicious speech.
Let no one be punished because of me.
As I forgive those who have hurt me,
so let others view me with favor and forgiveness.

Let me always remember:
every aspect of creation is a sign of something greater than itself —

You created my heart and mind.
I am grateful for the blessings of thought, feeling, and understanding,
the gift of an inner will to act for the greater good.
But thoughtlessness, a lack of sympathy, and self-centeredness
have diminished my soul.

T'FILAH ZAKAH. Rabbi Abraham Danzig (1748–1820) is said to have copied this prayer from early sources, publishing it in his law code *Chayei Adam* (Vilna, 1812). It soon found its way into many High Holy Day prayer books.

FOR TRANSGRESSIONS AGAINST GOD, Mishnah *Yoma* 8:9.

Tallit Blessing

Candlelighting

A Prayer for Purity and Worthiness

You created my eyes and ears.
I am grateful for this blessing that allows me to read, hear,
study, and learn Torah,
and enables me to appreciate wisdom, beauty, and truth.
But I have closed my eyes and ears to suffering and injustice
and this has diminished my soul.

You created my mouth and tongue.
I am grateful for the blessings of language and speech,
by which I praise You and connect with all human beings.
But raising my voice in anger and saying things I regret
have diminished my soul.

You created my hands and legs.
I am grateful for the blessings of movement and activity,
the gift of work and the gift of engaging in *tikkun olam.*
But laziness, apathy, and hurriedness
have diminished my soul.

You created my body with sexuality.
I am grateful for the blessings of intimacy and pleasure,
the gift of love in all its fullness.
But I have neglected the spiritual essence of the physical act
and this has diminished my soul.

Every aspect of my creation — every organ of my body —
reminds me of my moral frailty and failures,
my need to repent, to change, to grow:

I withheld at a time for giving;
I spoke at a time for silence;
I was silent at a time of urgency.

God, my Creator and Guide,
on this Day of Atonement
let my fasting and other intentional acts of self-discipline
make me attentive to repentance and forgiveness,
to the potential of my soul,
and to the holy purpose of my life.

מָבוֹא
Mavo

כָּל נִדְרֵי
Kol Nidrei

וְנִסְלַח
V'nislach

סְלַח־נָא
S'lach Na

סֵדֶר כָּל נִדְרֵי

Seder Kol Nidrei · Release from Vows

Opening the Ark, Opening Ourselves

Yom Kippur: the Jewish people's Festival of the Soul
and *Kol Nidrei* its sacred portal — a night of deep emotions,
a night, as the Psalmist wrote, to "rejoice with trembling."

We rejoice at the sound of *Kol Nidrei* — rhythmic words of release
from vows, oaths, and promises to God we fail to keep.

We tremble at the melody. Music of spiritual amazement,
it fills us with awe as we stand before God and Torah.

We rejoice that we stand together, strengthened by community
in this hour of shared weakness and humility.

We tremble — for tonight we confess our flaws, admit our imperfection,
and acknowledge a Power far beyond our understanding.

We rejoice that we commit ourselves to great endeavors
because we feel so deeply and think so nobly.

We tremble — for we find that our ideals are far greater than our ability;
our promises surpass our might.

We rejoice in the freedom that is *Kol Nidrei*'s true gift:
the freedom to begin a new year without fear of failure,
to aspire to be God's image in the world.

We tremble because we are mortal;
we rejoice in our gratitude for life.

We rejoice with trembling, and enter *Kol Nidrei* to face our humanity.

REJOICE WITH TREMBLING, Psalm 2:11.

AS THE CONGREGATION RISES, the holy ark (*aron hakodesh*) is opened in preparation for removing the Torah scrolls and reciting *Kol Nidrei*. This act symbolically sets the stage for the *t'shuvah*-work that will occupy us for the next twenty-four hours. We have no access to Torah's wisdom and truth until the ark is opened. So also, a searching moral assessment depends on opening the self: stripping away disguises and self-deception, disclosing secrets, exploring shadowy corners of the psyche in the clear light of truth. Our success in this labor depends, as well, on opening ourselves sincerely to the words of prayer and teaching we will encounter throughout the holy day.

Introduction

Kol Nidrei

Forgiveness

Rabbi Leizer survived the death camps and returned to his hometown, Czenstochow, Poland. For years following the Shoah, he roamed the streets playing a hand organ. At regular intervals, amid the numerous tunes he played, he would intentionally play *Kol Nidrei*. As he did so, he would look into the eyes of the children who walked by, looking for a hint of recognition. In this way, he was able to bring many children back in contact with their people.

For us, too, *Kol Nidrei* is a moment of recognition—
a sound that brings us back to our people.

Kol nidrei: a chant that begins in a whisper and rises to a cry.
On this night of promises remembered,
each soul in solitude communes with the Soul of the universe.

God, from this Day of Atonement to the next—
may we reach it in peace—
all Israel makes these vows:
to turn from wrong, dishonesty, and greed,
to walk in the path of justice and right.

Yet we know our weakness—how prone we are to fail:
help us to keep our word;
help us to act with humility and integrity.
We seek pardon and forgiveness.
We seek Your radiance and light.

Or zarua latzadik;	אוֹר זָרֻעַ לַצַּדִּיק,
ulyishrei-lev simchah.	וּלְיִשְׁרֵי־לֵב שִׂמְחָה.

Light is sown for the righteous,
radiance and joy for the pure of heart.

Bishivah shel malah,	בִּישִׁיבָה שֶׁל מַעְלָה
uvishivah shel matah —	וּבִישִׁיבָה שֶׁל מַטָּה,
al daat hamakom	עַל דַּעַת הַמָּקוֹם
v'al daat hakahal:	וְעַל דַּעַת הַקָּהָל,
anu matirin l'hitpaleil	אָנוּ מַתִּירִין לְהִתְפַּלֵּל
im haavaryanim.	עִם הָעֲבַרְיָנִים.

With one voice, assembled Sages past and present declare:
all may pray as one on this night of repentance;
let none be excluded from our community of prayer.

With one voice, God and congregation proclaim:
all may pray as one on this day of return;
let all find a place in this sacred assembly.

LIGHT IS SOWN FOR THE RIGHTEOUS אוֹר זָרֻעַ לַצַּדִּיק. This verse (Psalm 97:11) offers the beautiful image of light sown like a seed in the dark earth, to burst forth only in the distant future. According to Rabbi Samson Raphael Hirsch (1808–1888), the verse promises "that evil cannot last forever in this world, that the future belongs to the righteous, and that with every human act of intervention against evil the sovereignty of God . . . is brought one step nearer." Even as we acknowledge the reality of human sin, we celebrate the inevitable blossoming of good.

WITH ONE VOICE בִּישִׁיבָה שֶׁל מַעְלָה. In our imaginations we stand before the Heavenly Court and the assembled Sages of Israel; while, in our synagogues, we also create the sense of a solemn legal proceeding, our leaders standing at attention, holding the scrolls of the Torah before the gathered community.

ALL MAY PRAY AS ONE אָנוּ מַתִּירִין לְהִתְפַּלֵּל. The traditional text grants permission to "pray with the *avaryanim* (transgressors)," for no true community excludes those who have stumbled and fallen. Rabbi Meir of Rothenburg, a 13th-century sage, inserted these lines in the liturgy, basing himself on the Talmudic statement (*K'ritot* 6b) that "a public fast that does not include the sinners of Israel is no fast." All of us are *avaryanim*; none of us is unworthy to join with others in prayer.

Reflections on Kol Nidrei

In its emphasis on humility, *Kol Nidrei* provides a corrective to the toxic certainties of polarized discourse. What if we approached each other with the humility to recognize that our most confident convictions will always be qualified by the limits of our own knowledge and understanding? In its haunting melody and strangely legalistic language, we begin to sense the twilight truth: our high horses too often stumble, and our soapboxes stand on shaky ground. *Kol Nidrei* grants us the gift of sacred uncertainty: the chance to begin this new year with a sense of what we do not know, rather than a narrow certainty about what we do. It's what Buddhists call "beginner's mind." What if every time I were ready to proclaim some self-evident truth, I allowed *Kol Nidrei* to whisper in my ear, "Says who?"

—Rabbi David Stern (b. 1961)

As a legal enactment (the annulling of vows), *Kol Nidrei* is recited in the presence of the Torah scrolls and of a *Beit Din*, a Jewish court, traditionally composed of three scholars. In many communities, congregational leaders hold the scrolls, flanking the person who chants *Kol Nidrei*. This symbolic gesture also recalls how Moses lifted his hands and offered prayers for the people, flanked by two loyal companions: "Aaron and Hur, one on each side, supported his hands; thus his hands remained steady until the sun set" (Exodus 17:12). In the same way, the synagogue's lay leaders uphold the Torah, offering strength and support to the rabbi and cantor as together they serve the congregation.

It is customary to clothe the Torah scrolls in white during the High Holy Days, and to clothe ourselves in white garments from *Erev Kol Nidrei* through the end of Yom Kippur. White refers not to purity and unblemished perfection but to forgiveness, as Scripture says: *Though your sins be as scarlet, they shall be white as snow* (Isaiah 1:18).

מָבוֹא
Mavo
כָּל נִדְרֵי
Kol Nidrei
וְנִסְלַח
V'nislach
סְלַח־נָא
S'lach Na

Kol Nidrei

Kol nidrei — ve·esarei, vacharamei,	כָּל נִדְרֵי וֶאֱסָרֵי וַחֲרָמֵי,
v'konamei, v'chinuyei,	וְקוֹנָמֵי וְכִנּוּיֵי,
v'kinusei, ushvuot —	וְקִנּוּסֵי וּשְׁבוּעוֹת,
dindarna ud·ishtabana,	דִּנְדַֽרְנָא וּדְאִשְׁתַּבַּֽעְנָא,
ud·acharimna,	וּדְאַחֲרִֽימְנָא,
v'daasarna al nafshatana,	וְדַאֲסַֽרְנָא עַל נַפְשָׁתָֽנָא,
miyom kipurim zeh	מִיּוֹם כִּפּוּרִים זֶה
ad yom kipurim haba, aleinu l'tovah:	עַד יוֹם כִּפּוּרִים הַבָּא עָלֵֽינוּ לְטוֹבָה:
kulhon icharatna v'hon;	כֻּלְּהוֹן אִחֲרַֽטְנָא בְהוֹן,
kulhon y'hon sharan,	כֻּלְּהוֹן יְהוֹן שָׁרָן,
sh'vikin, sh'vitin,	שְׁבִיקִין שְׁבִיתִין,
b'teilin, umvutalin —	בְּטֵלִין וּמְבֻטָּלִין,
la sh'ririn v'la kayamin.	לָא שְׁרִירִין וְלָא קַיָּמִין.
Nidrana la nidrei;	נִדְרָֽנָא לָא נִדְרֵי,
ve·esarana la esarei;	וֶאֱסָרָֽנָא לָא אֱסָרֵי,
ushvuatana — la sh'vuot.	וּשְׁבוּעָתָֽנָא לָא שְׁבוּעוֹת.

All vows —
resolves and commitments, vows of abstinence and terms of obligation,
sworn promises and oaths of dedication —
that we promise and swear to God, and take upon ourselves
from this Day of Atonement until next Day of Atonement, may it find us well:
we regret them and for all of them we repent.
Let all of them be discarded and forgiven, abolished and undone;
they are not valid and they are not binding.
Our vows shall not be vows; our resolves shall not be resolves;
and our oaths — they shall not be oaths.

THAT WE PROMISE AND SWEAR TO GOD, AND TAKE UPON OURSELVES. The medieval authority Rabbeinu Tam (Rashi's grandson, ca. 1100–1171) declared that *Kol Nidrei* applies only to personal vows made on one's own initiative — that is, obligations a person undertakes in relation to God. This principle is derived from the phrase *v'daasarna al nafshatana* (which we take upon ourselves). This annulment of vows has nothing to do with our obligations to other human beings.

Introduction

Kol Nidrei

Forgiveness

Let our speech be pure and our promises sincere.
Let our spoken words
—every vow and every oath—
be honest and well-intentioned.
Let our words cause no pain, bring no harm,
and never lead to shame, distrust, or fear.
And if, after honest effort,
we are unable to fulfill a promise, a vow, or an oath,
may we be released from its obligation
and forgiven for our failure.
Let our speech be pure and our promises sincere.

Give us the strength to keep our promises—
the sacred vows of partners in marriage,
the promises of love and care between parents and children,
the promises of duty between citizens and country,
the oaths of doctors, the sacred trust of teachers.
Give us the strength to keep our promises
to our friends and colleagues,
to those who live with us and depend on us,
to those who work for us and those for whom we work,
to those who pray with us and those for whom we pray,
to those we love and those we serve.
Give us the courage to keep our promises—
to ourselves, to one another,
and to future generations.

---

all vows כָּל נִדְרֵי (*facing page*). The custom of reciting *Kol Nidrei* three times, gradually increasing in volume, is first recorded in *Machzor Vitry* (France, 12th century): "The first time the prayer leader must utter it very softly, like one who hesitates to enter the Sovereign's palace to request a favor; the second time somewhat louder; and the third time more loudly still, as one who is accustomed to dwell in the palace and approach the Sovereign as a friend." Thus, with each repetition we express growing confidence in our relationship with the One who offers us the gift of renewal.

V'nislach l'chol-adat b'nei Yisrael,

v'lager hagar b'tocham —

ki l'chol-haam bishgagah.

וְנִסְלַח לְכָל־עֲדַת בְּנֵי יִשְׂרָאֵל,
וְלַגֵּר הַגָּר בְּתוֹכָם,
כִּי לְכָל־הָעָם בִּשְׁגָגָה.

מָבוֹא
Mavo

כָּל נִדְרֵי
Kol Nidrei

וְנִסְלַח
V'nislach

סְלַח־נָא
S'lach Na

All shall be forgiven —
the entire community of Israel,
and the stranger who lives in their midst —
for all have gone astray in error.

"S'lach na laavon haam hazeh

k'godel chasdecha,

v'chaasher nasata laam hazeh

miMitzrayim v'ad heinah."

סְלַח־נָא לַעֲוֹן הָעָם הַזֶּה
כְּגֹדֶל חַסְדֶּךָ,
וְכַאֲשֶׁר נָשָׂאתָה לָעָם הַזֶּה
מִמִּצְרַיִם וְעַד־הֵנָּה.

Moses prayed to God:
"As You have been faithful to this people ever since Egypt,
please forgive their failings now,
in keeping with Your boundless love."

V'sham ne·emar:

Vayomer Adonai: "Salachti, kidvarecha."

וְשָׁם נֶאֱמַר:
וַיֹּאמֶר יְיָ: סָלַחְתִּי כִּדְבָרֶךָ.

And God responded: "I forgive, as you have asked."

BORACHU NEXT

ALL SHALL BE FORGIVEN וְנִסְלַח, Numbers 15:26.
AS YOU HAVE BEEN FAITHFUL סְלַח נָא, Numbers 14:19.
AND GOD RESPONDED וַיֹּאמֶר יְיָ, Numbers 14:20.

Kol Nidrei

My neighbor's roses are blooming, blooming;
their perfume spills past me and into the street.
The world gives us so much
without being asked.

But again and again
we break our promises to it:
we breathe, eat, sleep away
the glittering nights, spend
the tapestried days.

These broken promises,
let them be forgotten.
Our sworn oaths, unswear.
They drop noiseless on the earth,
become the earth.

Prayer from the Heart

I bow.
I face the ground.
I fall before the Most High.
Farther than heaven's heaven are You,
nearer to me than the flesh on my bones. . . .
What have I to offer You but my spirit?

How shall I lift my eyes to You?
How can my tongue give praise?

The signs of Your love are countless,
as are my sins: more numerous than the sands of the sea.
So guide me toward the right path,
my teacher, my keeper of faith—source of all that I know.

When my heart speaks I hear the words myself.
And You—may You hear me, too.

KOL NIDREI. By Nan Cohen (b. 1968).
PRAYER FROM THE HEART. By Rabbi Abraham Ibn Ezra (1089–1164), adapted.

שְׁמַע וּבִרְכוֹתֶיהָ
Sh'ma Uvirchoteha · Sh'ma and Its Blessings

בָּרְכוּ
Bar'chu

מַעֲרִיב עֲרָבִים
Maariv Aravim

אַהֲבַת עוֹלָם
Ahavat Olam

קְרִיאַת שְׁמַע
K'riat Sh'ma

אֱמֶת וֶאֱמוּנָה
Emet ve·Emunah

מִי־כָמֹכָה
Mi Chamocha

הַשְׁכִּיבֵנוּ
Hashkiveinu

וְשָׁמְרוּ
V'sham'ru

כִּי־בַיּוֹם הַזֶּה
Ki-vayom Hazeh

חֲצִי קַדִּישׁ
Chatzi Kaddish

Chant your supplications to God
in a melody that makes the heart weep,
and your praises of God
in one that will make it sing.
Thus you will be filled with love and joy
for the One who sees the heart.

—RABBI JUDAH BEN SAMUEL

Shine praises upon God, all nations;
let all the world approach with worship.

For Your love has won us over;
Your loyalty exists for all time — praise God.

—PSALM 117, adapted

Bar'chu et Adonai hamvorach.	בָּרְכוּ אֶת יְיָ הַמְבֹרָךְ.
Baruch Adonai hamvorach l'olam va·ed.	בָּרוּךְ יְיָ הַמְבֹרָךְ לְעוֹלָם וָעֶד.

Bless the Eternal, the Blessed One.
Blessed is the Eternal, the Blessed One, now and forever.

CHANT YOUR SUPPLICATIONS. Rabbi Judah ben Samuel of Regensburg (1150–1217) was known as Judah the Pious. As the melody of *Kol Nidrei* makes the heart weep, the call to worship joyously summons us to prayer.

Call to Prayer
Twilight Prayer
Revelation of Torah
Sh'ma and Its Sections
Redemption
Peace in the Night
Keep Shabbat
On This Day
Reader's Kaddish

בָּרְכוּ אֶת עֵין הַחַיִּים.

Bar'chu et ein hachayim.

Let us bless the source of life.

נְבָרֵךְ אֶת עֵין הַחַיִּים
וְכֹה נִתְבָּרֵךְ.

N'vareich et ein hachayim
v'choh nitbareich.

As we bless the source of life
so we are blessed.

נְבָרֵךְ אֶת עֵין הַחַיִּים
וְכֹה נִתְבָּרֵךְ.

N'vareich et ein hachayim
v'choh nitbareich.

As we bless the source of life
so may we be blessed.

Steal into the prayerbook
Like a stowaway.
Fasting, without a bite,
Travel for days,
Till you reach the shore.
Lie folded up in your hideout.
Do not stir through the whole journey.
And if, with a right word, you get
Into the proper place
And light up the little prayerbook
With Jewish joy,
That will be it.
The little prayerbook will have to
Carry you through all eternities,
And they will *doven* you too,
Will say you.

LET US BLESS. By Marcia Falk (b. 1946).
STEAL INTO THE PRAYERBOOK. By Jacob Glatshteyn (1896–1971).
DOVEN. The Yiddish word that means "pray." It refers to the rhythmic chanting of the Hebrew liturgy. Also pronounced: *davven*.

בָּרְכוּ
Bar'chu
מַעֲרִיב עֲרָבִים
Maariv Aravim
אַהֲבַת עוֹלָם
Ahavat Olam
קְרִיאַת שְׁמַע
K'riat Sh'ma
אֱמֶת וֶאֱמוּנָה
Emet ve-Emunah
מִי־כָמֹכָה
Mi Chamocha
הַשְׁכִּיבֵנוּ
Hashkiveinu
וְשָׁמְרוּ
V'sham'ru
כִּי־בַיּוֹם הַזֶּה
Ki-vayom Hazeh
חֲצִי קַדִּישׁ
Chatzi Kaddish

בָּרוּךְ אַתָּה, יְיָ,	*Baruch atah, Adonai,*
אֱלֹהֵינוּ מֶלֶךְ הָעוֹלָם,	*Eloheinu melech haolam,*
אֲשֶׁר בִּדְבָרוֹ מַעֲרִיב עֲרָבִים,	*asher bidvaro maariv aravim;*
בְּחָכְמָה פּוֹתֵחַ שְׁעָרִים,	*b'chochmah potei·ach sh'arim,*
וּבִתְבוּנָה מְשַׁנֶּה עִתִּים,	*uvitvunah m'shaneh itim,*
וּמַחֲלִיף אֶת הַזְּמַנִּים,	*umachalif et haz'manim,*
וּמְסַדֵּר אֶת הַכּוֹכָבִים	*umsadeir et hakochavim*
בְּמִשְׁמְרוֹתֵיהֶם בָּרָקִיעַ כִּרְצוֹנוֹ.	*b'mishm'roteihem barakia kirtzono.*
בּוֹרֵא יוֹם וָלָיְלָה,	*Borei yom valailah —*
גּוֹלֵל אוֹר מִפְּנֵי חֹשֶׁךְ,	*goleil or mip'nei choshech,*
וְחֹשֶׁךְ מִפְּנֵי אוֹר.	*v'choshech mip'nei or.*
וּמַעֲבִיר יוֹם וּמֵבִיא לָיְלָה,	*Umaavir yom umeivi lailah;*
וּמַבְדִּיל בֵּין יוֹם וּבֵין לָיְלָה,	*umavdil bein yom uvein lailah —*
יְיָ צְבָאוֹת שְׁמוֹ.	*Adonai Tz'vaot sh'mo.*
אֵל חַי וְקַיָּם,	*El chai v'kayam,*
תָּמִיד יִמְלֹךְ עָלֵינוּ לְעוֹלָם וָעֶד.	*tamid yimloch aleinu l'olam va·ed.*

Blessed are You, Adonai.
Your great name fills the universe with majestic might.
Your word creates twilight and dusk,
as Your wisdom opens the gates of night.
Your discernment separates the changing seasons
and causes the passage of time.
The stars, arrayed across the sky, reveal Your design.
You roll out the cycle of darkness and light, shaping day and night.
You sweep away day and carry the world into nightfall,
setting day apart from nighttime.
You are God of all we can perceive,
and all that is beyond our perception.

Living, Eternal God: be our sovereign to the end of time.

בָּרוּךְ אַתָּה, יְיָ, הַמַּעֲרִיב עֲרָבִים.
Baruch atah, Adonai, hamaariv aravim.
Blessed are You, Adonai, Creator of twilight and dusk.

DAY AND NIGHT are Yours, Creative Spirit of the universe—
the muted colors of twilight, the radiance of dawn.
Yours are the spreading wings of light,
the deepening shadows of darkness, an ever-changing drama.

In the human heart, too, the struggle between darkness and light unfolds.
From sunlit heights of generosity,
the human heart sinks to the gloomy depths of selfishness.
Although we fall, You give us the strength to rise again.
You call on those who hurt through word or deed
to break free from wrongdoing and return to You.
All who hear Your call to goodness are embraced;
all who reject emptiness and evil find acceptance from You.

We come into Your presence, this night of *Kol Nidrei*,
aware that our shortcomings and weaknesses are many.
Yet, encouraged by Your promise of forgiveness,
we choose freely the path of repentance,
restoring wholeness to our lives and holiness to the world.

בָּרוּךְ אַתָּה, יְיָ, הַמַּעֲרִיב עֲרָבִים.

Baruch atah, Adonai, hamaariv aravim.

Blessed are You, Adonai, Creator of twilight and dusk.

DAY AND NIGHT. Linking the natural phenomena of darkness and light to themes of repentance and human nature, this prayer brings a Yom Kippur dimension to words that are recited in every evening service. Inspired by a creative interpretation in Rabbi David Einhorn's 19th-century prayer book *Olat Tamid* (A Regular Offering), these words prepare us for the confessions and songs of forgiveness that are the focal point of this holy day.

בָּרְכוּ
Bar'chu

מַעֲרִיב עֲרָבִים
Maariv Aravim

אַהֲבַת עוֹלָם
Ahavat Olam

קְרִיאַת שְׁמַע
K'riat Sh'ma

אֱמֶת וֶאֱמוּנָה
Emet ve·Emunah

מִי־כָמֹכָה
Mi Chamocha

הַשְׁכִּיבֵנוּ
Hashkiveinu

וְשָׁמְרוּ
V'sham'ru

כִּי־בַיּוֹם הַזֶּה
Ki-vayom Hazeh

חֲצִי קַדִּישׁ
Chatzi Kaddish

אַהֲבַת עוֹלָם בֵּית יִשְׂרָאֵל עַמְּךָ אָהָבְתָּ,
תּוֹרָה וּמִצְוֹת, חֻקִּים וּמִשְׁפָּטִים
אוֹתָנוּ לִמַּדְתָּ.
עַל כֵּן, יְיָ אֱלֹהֵינוּ, בְּשָׁכְבֵנוּ
וּבְקוּמֵנוּ נָשִׂיחַ בְּחֻקֶּיךָ,
וְנִשְׂמַח בְּדִבְרֵי תוֹרָתֶךָ
וּבְמִצְוֹתֶיךָ לְעוֹלָם וָעֶד.
כִּי הֵם חַיֵּינוּ וְאֹרֶךְ יָמֵינוּ,
וּבָהֶם נֶהְגֶּה יוֹמָם וָלָיְלָה.
וְאַהֲבָתְךָ אַל תָּסִיר מִמֶּנּוּ לְעוֹלָמִים.

Ahavat olam beit Yisrael am'cha ahavta;
Torah umitzvot, chukim umishpatim
otanu limadta.
Al kein, Adonai Eloheinu, b'shochbeinu
uvkumeinu nasiach b'chukecha;
v'nismach b'divrei Toratecha
uvmitzvotecha l'olam va·ed.
Ki heim chayeinu v'orech yameinu;
uvahem negeh yomam valailah.
V'ahavat'cha al tasir mimenu l'olamim.

Love beyond all space and time —
Your love enfolds Your people, *Yisrael.*
We receive it in Your teaching:
Your gift of Torah, sacred obligations, discipline, and law.
So let us speak these teachings when we lie down and rise up
and find joy forever in Your Torah and mitzvot.
They are the very essence of our life —
ours to ponder and study all our days.
May we never lose or be unworthy of Your love . . .

בָּרוּךְ אַתָּה, יְיָ, אוֹהֵב עַמּוֹ יִשְׂרָאֵל.
Baruch atah, Adonai, oheiv amo Yisrael.
. . . for You are blessed: the One who loves Your people, *Yisrael.*

LOVE BEYOND ALL SPACE AND TIME אַהֲבַת עוֹלָם.In the evening service, four blessings surround the *Sh'ma*, two before and two after. The first one (*Maariv Aravim*) is universal in its focus, and it celebrates divine wisdom as manifest in the cycles of nature. The second blessing (*Ahavat Olam*) celebrates God's love, manifest in the gift of Torah to the Jewish people. The last two (after the *Sh'ma*) are *Emet ve·Emunah* and *Hashkiveinu* — the first centering on God's power to redeem, and the second on God's power to protect. This sequence of four blessings suggests a progression in human character: we should learn and strive for wisdom so that we may act with love, using our power to rescue and protect the vulnerable.

WHO LOVES YOUR PEOPLE, YISRAEL אוֹהֵב עַמּוֹ יִשְׂרָאֵל. The words of *Sh'ma Yisrael*, proclaiming God's unity, are bracketed by liturgical expressions of love: this prayer (*Ahavat Olam*), which speaks of God's love for us, and *V'ahavta*, which speaks of our love for God. Love is the meeting point where human beings touch the Divine; unity will be realized when our perceptions and actions are guided by love.

We pause in reverence before the gift of self:
The vessel shatters, the divine spark shines through,
And our solitary self becomes a link in Israel's golden chain.
For what we are, we are by sharing. And as we share
We move toward the light.

We pause in reverence before the mystery of a presence:
The near and far reality of God.
Not union, but communion is our aim.
And we approach the mystery
With deeds. Words lead us to the edge of action.
But it is deeds that bring us closer to the God of light.

We pause in terror before the human deed:
The cloud of annihilation, the concentrations for death,
The cruelly casual way of each to each.
But in the stillness of this hour
We find our way from darkness into light.

May we find our life so precious
That we cannot but share it with the other,
That light may shine brighter than a thousand suns,
With the presence among us of the God of light.

---

we pause. By Rabbi Albert Friedlander (1927–2004).

You are My witnesses, says Adonai.
God is the first, God is the last,
there is no God but Adonai.

Testify for Me, says Adonai;
in your love for Me teach your children,
embracing Torah now and forever.

We accept God's sovereignty in reverence,
treating others with love, studying Torah.
May this be our will as we witness. . . .

שמע ישראל יהוה
בָּרוּךְ שֵׁם כְּבוֹד

Sh'ma, Yisrael: Adonai Eloheinu, Adonai echad!
Listen, Israel: Adonai is our God, Adonai is One!

Baruch shem k'vod malchuto l'olam va·ed.
Blessed is God's glorious majesty forever and ever.

SH'MA, YISRAEL שְׁמַע יִשְׂרָאֵל, Deuteronomy 6:4.
BLESSED IS GOD'S GLORIOUS בָּרוּךְ שֵׁם כְּבוֹד, Mishnah *Yoma* 3:8, inspired by Nehemiah 9:5.

אלהינו יהוה אחד

מַלְכוּתוֹ לְעוֹלָם וָעֶד.

ONCE WE AFFIRM that God is one and infinite and also that God's image is inscribed in all people (and all creation, for that matter), we find ourselves in deep waters. Within the world's vast diversity, primal unity inheres. Infinite depths dwell within every finite crumb of matter. (Rabbi Jeremy Kalmanofsky, b. 1966)

Sh'ma: How Do We Respond to God's Oneness?

By Loving God and Devoting Ourselves to Torah

וְאָהַבְתָּ אֵת יְיָ אֱלֹהֶיךָ	*V'ahavta et Adonai Elohecha —*
בְּכׇל־לְבָבְךָ	*b'chol-l'vav'cha,*
וּבְכׇל־נַפְשְׁךָ	*uvchol-nafsh'cha,*
וּבְכׇל־מְאֹדֶךָ׃	*uvchol-m'odecha.*
וְהָיוּ הַדְּבָרִים הָאֵלֶּה	*V'hayu had'varim ha·eileh*
אֲשֶׁר אָנֹכִי מְצַוְּךָ הַיּוֹם	*asher anochi m'tzav'cha hayom*
עַל־לְבָבֶךָ׃	*al-l'vavecha.*
וְשִׁנַּנְתָּם לְבָנֶיךָ וְדִבַּרְתָּ בָּם	*V'shinantam l'vanecha v'dibarta bam*
בְּשִׁבְתְּךָ בְּבֵיתֶךָ	*b'shivt'cha b'veitecha,*
וּבְלֶכְתְּךָ בַדֶּרֶךְ	*uvlecht'cha vaderech,*
וּבְשׇׁכְבְּךָ וּבְקוּמֶךָ׃	*uvshochb'cha, uvkumecha.*
וּקְשַׁרְתָּם לְאוֹת עַל־יָדֶךָ	*Ukshartam l'ot al-yadecha;*
וְהָיוּ לְטֹטָפֹת בֵּין עֵינֶיךָ׃	*v'hayu l'totafot bein einecha;*
וּכְתַבְתָּם עַל־מְזֻזוֹת בֵּיתֶךָ	*uchtavtam al-m'zuzot beitecha*
וּבִשְׁעָרֶיךָ׃	*uvisharecha.*

You shall love Adonai your God with all your mind,
with all your soul, and with all your strength.
Set these words, which I command you this day, upon your heart.
Teach them faithfully to your children.
Speak of them in your home and on your way,
when you lie down and when you rise up.
Bind them as a sign upon your hand;
let them be a symbol before your eyes;
inscribe them on the doorposts of your house, and on your gates.

Some congregations continue with V'hayah Im Shamoa (Section 2 of the Sh'ma) on page 34.

בָּרְכוּ
Bar'chu
מַעֲרִיב עֲרָבִים
Maariv Aravim
אַהֲבַת עוֹלָם
Ahavat Olam
קְרִיאַת שְׁמַע
K'riat Sh'ma
אֱמֶת וֶאֱמוּנָה
Emet ve·Emunah
מִי־כָמֹכָה
Mi Chamocha
הַשְׁכִּיבֵנוּ
Hashkiveinu
וְשָׁמְרוּ
V'sham'ru
כִּי־בַיּוֹם הַזֶּה
Ki-vayom Hazeh
חֲצִי קַדִּישׁ
Chatzi Kaddish

V'AHAVTA וְאָהַבְתָּ. Section 1 of the *Sh'ma*, Deuteronomy 6:5–9.

"WITH ALL YOUR STRENGTH . . ."

Our Sages teach:
Love God with all your strength.

This means:
"Show love with your wealth;
put your resources toward good purposes;
serve the Most High with everything you possess."

Those who reject all material possessions;
who spurn comfort and wealth; who deny the body—
they lose their ability to appreciate life's value.

Poverty and suffering do not cultivate the love of God.
Rather: learn to love life; live fully; cherish the world and enjoy its treasures.
Then you will gain a full measure of love.
Then will your heart expand with gratitude.
And only then will you give with a joyful heart.

LISTEN, all you who wrestle with your fate: the intimate and the infinite are one. Trust that unity with your whole heart, doubt and all; with your whole soul, and with all the powers at your command. Remember it; repeat it everywhere, working or resting, sitting or walking, night and morning, alone and to all you love. See it written on your hand, on your brow, in every common place and in every face.

SHOW LOVE WITH YOUR WEALTH. Mishnah *B'rachot* 9:5 interprets the Hebrew phrase *b'chol m'odecha* (normally translated "with all your strength") as *b'chol mamoncha* ("with all your wealth"); the Aramaic *Targum Onkelos* renders it, "with all your possessions."

THOSE WHO REJECT ALL MATERIAL POSSESSIONS. Adapted from the teachings of Rabbi Abraham Isaac Kook (1865–1935).

LISTEN. By Catherine Madsen (b. 1952).

לְמַעַן תִּזְכְּרוּ וַעֲשִׂיתֶם
אֶת־כָּל־מִצְוֺתָי
וִהְיִיתֶם קְדֹשִׁים לֵאלֹהֵיכֶם:
אֲנִי יְיָ אֱלֹהֵיכֶם
אֲשֶׁר הוֹצֵאתִי אֶתְכֶם מֵאֶרֶץ
מִצְרַיִם לִהְיוֹת לָכֶם לֵאלֹהִים
אֲנִי יְיָ אֱלֹהֵיכֶם:

L'maan tizk'ru vaasitem
et-kol-mitzvotai,
viyitem k'doshim l'Eloheichem.
Ani, Adonai, Eloheichem,
asher hotzeiti et·chem mei·eretz
Mitzrayim liyot lachem l'Elohim —
ani Adonai Eloheichem.

Be mindful of all My mitzvot,
and do them;
thus you will become holy to your God.
I, Adonai, am your God,
who brought you out of Egypt to be your God —
I, Adonai your God.

יְיָ אֱלֹהֵיכֶם אֱמֶת.
Adonai Eloheichem emet.
Adonai your God is true.

Continue on page 38. 39

L'MAAN TIZK'RU לְמַעַן תִּזְכְּרוּ. The last part of Section 3 of the *Sh'ma*, Numbers 15:40–41.
BE HOLY TO YOUR GOD וִהְיִיתֶם קְדֹשִׁים לֵאלֹהֵיכֶם. The third section of the *Sh'ma* sets forth an aspirational view of Jewish identity. The Israelites are not told that they are a holy people — a description that would lead to complacency and disengagement from the world's problems. Instead, they are offered mitzvot as a path *toward* holiness; and they are commanded to build communities that embody sacred values. Moses teaches the former slaves that they were liberated in order to direct their energies toward divine service, bringing *k'dushah* (holiness) into every aspect of their lives.

Throughout the year, our actions condemn us;
throughout the year our deeds are open to blame.
But on this day we rise above our human failings.
Fasting, praying, wrapped in white *tallitot*,
we stand like angels, reaching for the Divine.
On this one day, we catch a glimpse of what we could be—
we celebrate the better angels of our nature.

At the beginning of creation God spoke;
and primordial light infused all existence, contained in radiant vessels.

An intention arose in the mind of God: to create a being capable of choice,
able to distinguish good from bad, holy from profane.

God breathed in—*tzimtzum*—and for the smallest moment was absent,
to make space for human beings to develop their godly essence,
as expressed in the divine intention:
"Let us make the human being according to our image."

Utter darkness reigned, the forces of chaos tore at the cosmos;
the vessels were broken. All creation threatened to fall asunder.

At that instant, when darkness was complete and creation was in peril,
the human being came into existence.

And God breathed out again, filling the universe once more with splendor.

But what of the rays of light that escaped from the broken vessels—
were they lost forever?

Now the fusion of divine intention and human potential became clear.
For human beings are able and thus commanded to retrieve the wandering rays of light—those entangled in darkness, lost in unlikely corners of the universe.

Each act of kindness, each effort to be human in inhuman circumstances,
returns a spark of light to its Source.

The rays of light are everywhere. And when all have been retrieved and uplifted,
the messianic time of peace will be upon us.

THROUGHOUT THE YEAR . . . WE STAND LIKE ANGELS. Based on *Midrash T'hilim* 27:4.

THE BETTER ANGELS OF OUR NATURE. From Abraham Lincoln's First Inaugural Address, March 4, 1861.

AT THE BEGINNING. This parable, central to the Jewish mystical tradition, originated with the 16th-century kabbalist Rabbi Isaac Luria. It is adapted from a version recounted by Rabbi Awraham Soetendorp (b. 1943).

בָּרְכוּ
Bar'chu
מַעֲרִיב עֲרָבִים
Maariv Aravim
אַהֲבַת עוֹלָם
Ahavat Olam
קְרִיאַת שְׁמַע
K'riat Sh'ma
אֱמֶת וֶאֱמוּנָה
Emet ve·Emunah
מִי־כָמֹכָה
Mi Chamocha
הַשְׁכִּיבֵנוּ
Hashkiveinu
וְשָׁמְרוּ
V'sham'ru
כִּי־בַיּוֹם הַזֶּה
Ki-vayom Hazeh
חֲצִי קַדִּישׁ
Chatzi Kaddish

Responding to God's Oneness by Performing Mitzvot

וְהָיָה אִם־שָׁמֹעַ תִּשְׁמְעוּ אֶל־מִצְוֺתַי	*V'hayah im-shamoa tishm'u el-mitzvotai*
אֲשֶׁר אָנֹכִי מְצַוֶּה אֶתְכֶם הַיּוֹם	*asher anochi m'tzaveh et·chem hayom —*
לְאַהֲבָה אֶת־יְיָ אֱלֹהֵיכֶם	*l'ahavah et-Adonai Eloheichem,*
וּלְעָבְדוֹ בְּכָל־לְבַבְכֶם	*ulovdo b'chol-l'vavchem*
וּבְכָל־נַפְשְׁכֶם׃	*uvchol nafsh'chem —*
וְנָתַתִּי מְטַר־אַרְצְכֶם בְּעִתּוֹ	*v'natati m'tar-artz'chem b'ito,*
יוֹרֶה וּמַלְקוֹשׁ	*yoreh umalkosh.*
וְאָסַפְתָּ דְגָנֶךָ	*V'asafta d'ganecha*
וְתִירֹשְׁךָ וְיִצְהָרֶךָ׃	*v'tirosh'cha v'yitz·harecha;*
וְנָתַתִּי עֵשֶׂב בְּשָׂדְךָ לִבְהֶמְתֶּךָ	*v'natati eisev b'sad'cha livhemtecha.*
וְאָכַלְתָּ וְשָׂבָעְתָּ׃	*V'achalta v'savata.*
הִשָּׁמְרוּ לָכֶם פֶּן יִפְתֶּה לְבַבְכֶם	*Hisham'ru lachem, pen yifteh l'vavchem,*
וְסַרְתֶּם וַעֲבַדְתֶּם אֱלֹהִים אֲחֵרִים	*v'sartem vaavadtem elohim acheirim*
וְהִשְׁתַּחֲוִיתֶם לָהֶם׃	*v'hishtachavitem lahem.*
וְחָרָה אַף־יְיָ בָּכֶם	*V'charah af Adonai bachem —*
וְעָצַר אֶת־הַשָּׁמַיִם	*v'atzar et-hashamayim,*
וְלֹא־יִהְיֶה מָטָר	*v'lo yiyeh matar,*
וְהָאֲדָמָה לֹא תִתֵּן אֶת־יְבוּלָהּ	*v'haadamah lo titein et-y'vulah;*
וַאֲבַדְתֶּם מְהֵרָה	*v'avadtem m'heirah*
מֵעַל הָאָרֶץ הַטֹּבָה	*mei·al haaretz hatovah*
אֲשֶׁר יְיָ נֹתֵן לָכֶם׃	*asher Adonai notein lachem.*

If, indeed, you obey My commandments, which I instruct you this day — loving Adonai your God and serving God with all your heart and soul — I will grant rain for your land in season, the early rain and the late. And you will gather in your new grain and wine and oil; and I will provide grassland for your cattle. Thus you will eat and be satisfied. Be careful not to be lured away to serve other gods, bowing down to them. For then the anger of Adonai will flare up against you, and God will hold back the skies so that there will be no rain and the ground will not yield its crops; and you will soon perish from the good land that Adonai is giving you.

V'HAYAH IM SHAMOA וְהָיָה אִם שָׁמֹעַ. Section 2 of the *Sh'ma*, Deuteronomy 11:13–21.

וְשַׂמְתֶּם֙ אֶת־דְּבָרַ֣י אֵ֔לֶּה עַל־
לְבַבְכֶ֖ם וְעַל־נַפְשְׁכֶ֑ם
וּקְשַׁרְתֶּ֨ם אֹתָ֤ם לְאוֹת֙ עַל־יֶדְכֶ֔ם
וְהָי֥וּ לְטוֹטָפֹ֖ת בֵּ֥ין עֵינֵיכֶֽם׃
וְלִמַּדְתֶּ֥ם אֹתָ֛ם אֶת־בְּנֵיכֶ֖ם
לְדַבֵּ֣ר בָּ֑ם
בְּשִׁבְתְּךָ֤ בְּבֵיתֶ֨ךָ֙
וּבְלֶכְתְּךָ֣ בַדֶּ֔רֶךְ
וּֽבְשָׁכְבְּךָ֖ וּבְקוּמֶֽךָ׃
וּכְתַבְתָּ֛ם עַל־מְזוּז֥וֹת בֵּיתֶ֖ךָ
וּבִשְׁעָרֶֽיךָ׃
לְמַ֨עַן יִרְבּ֤וּ יְמֵיכֶם֙ וִימֵ֣י בְנֵיכֶ֔ם
עַ֚ל הָֽאֲדָמָ֔ה אֲשֶׁ֨ר נִשְׁבַּ֧ע יְיָ
לַאֲבֹתֵיכֶ֖ם לָתֵ֣ת לָהֶ֑ם
כִּימֵ֥י הַשָּׁמַ֖יִם עַל־הָאָֽרֶץ׃

V'samtem et-d'varai eileh al-
l'vavchem v'al-nafsh'chem.
Ukshartem otam l'ot al-yedchem;
v'hayu l'totafot bein eineichem.
V'limadtem otam et-b'neichem
l'dabeir bam —
b'shivt'cha b'veitecha,
uvlecht'cha vaderech,
uvshochb'cha uvkumecha.
Uchtavtam al-m'zuzot beitecha
uvisharecha,
l'maan yirbu y'meichem vimei v'neichem
al haadamah asher nishba Adonai
laavoteichem lateit lahem,
kimei hashamayim al-haaretz.

Therefore place these, My words, upon your heart and upon your very being. Bind them as a sign upon your hand; let them be a symbol before your eyes. Teach them to your children; speak of them in your home and on your way, when you lie down and when you rise up. Inscribe them on the doorposts of your house and on your gates, so that your days and the days of your children may increase upon the land that Adonai swore to give to your ancestors, for as long as the heavens are over the earth.

בָּרְכוּ
Bar'chu
מַעֲרִיב עֲרָבִים
Maariv Aravim
אַהֲבַת עוֹלָם
Ahavat Olam
קְרִיאַת שְׁמַע
K'riat Sh'ma
אֱמֶת וֶאֱמוּנָה
Emet ve-Emunah
מִי־כָמֹכָה
Mi Chamocha
הַשְׁכִּיבֵנוּ
Hashkiveinu
וְשָׁמְרוּ
V'sham'ru
כִּי־בַיּוֹם הַזֶּה
Ki-vayom Hazeh
חֲצִי קַדִּישׁ
Chatzi Kaddish

Responding to God's Oneness by Wearing Tzitzit

Vayomer Adonai el-Mosheh leimor:	וַיֹּ֥אמֶר יְיָ֖ אֶל־מֹשֶׁ֥ה לֵּאמֹֽר׃
Dabeir el-b'nei Yisrael v'amarta aleihem —	דַּבֵּ֞ר אֶל־בְּנֵ֤י יִשְׂרָאֵל֙ וְאָמַרְתָּ֣ אֲלֵהֶ֔ם
v'asu lahem tzitzit al-kanfei vigdeihem l'dorotam;	וְעָשׂ֨וּ לָהֶ֥ם צִיצִ֛ת עַל־כַּנְפֵ֥י בִגְדֵיהֶ֖ם לְדֹרֹתָ֑ם
v'nat'nu al-tzitzit hakanaf p'til t'cheilet.	וְנָֽתְנ֛וּ עַל־צִיצִ֥ת הַכָּנָ֖ף פְּתִ֥יל תְּכֵֽלֶת׃
V'hayah lachem l'tzitzit, uritem oto,	וְהָיָ֣ה לָכֶם֮ לְצִיצִת֒ וּרְאִיתֶ֣ם אֹת֗וֹ
uzchartem et-kol-mitzvot Adonai.	וּזְכַרְתֶּם֙ אֶת־כָּל־מִצְוֺ֣ת יְיָ֔
Vaasitem otam;	וַעֲשִׂיתֶ֖ם אֹתָ֑ם
v'lo-taturu acharei l'vavchem v'acharei eineichem	וְלֹֽא־תָת֜וּרוּ אַחֲרֵ֤י לְבַבְכֶם֙ וְאַחֲרֵ֣י עֵֽינֵיכֶ֔ם
asher-atem zonim achareihem.	אֲשֶׁר־אַתֶּ֥ם זֹנִ֖ים אַחֲרֵיהֶֽם׃
L'maan tizk'ru vaasitem et-kol-mitzvotai,	לְמַ֣עַן תִּזְכְּר֔וּ וַעֲשִׂיתֶ֖ם אֶת־כָּל־מִצְוֺתָ֑י
viyitem k'doshim l'Eloheichem.	וִהְיִיתֶ֥ם קְדֹשִׁ֖ים לֵאלֹהֵיכֶֽם׃
Ani Adonai Eloheichem —	אֲנִ֞י יְיָ אֱלֹהֵיכֶ֗ם
asher hotzeiti et·chem mei·eretz Mitzrayim	אֲשֶׁ֨ר הוֹצֵ֤אתִי אֶתְכֶם֙ מֵאֶ֣רֶץ מִצְרַ֔יִם
liyot lachem l'Elohim:	לִהְי֥וֹת לָכֶ֖ם לֵאלֹהִ֑ים
ani Adonai Eloheichem.	אֲנִ֖י יְיָ אֱלֹהֵיכֶֽם׃

Adonai said to Moses: Speak to the people of Israel, and tell them to make for themselves *tzitzit* — fringes — on the corners of their clothing, throughout their generations; and let them place upon the corner-fringe a thread of violet-blue. The fringes will be yours to see and remember all the mitzvot — the sacred obligations — of Adonai. Do them; and do not be misled by the lustful urges of your heart and your eyes. Be mindful of all My mitzvot, and do them; thus you will become holy to your God. I, Adonai, am your God, who brought you out of Egypt to be your God — I, Adonai your God.

יְיָ אֱלֹהֵיכֶם אֱמֶת.

Adonai Eloheichem emet.

Adonai your God is true.

VAYOMER וַיֹּאמֶר. Section 3 of the *Sh'ma*, Numbers 15:37–41.

Lest We Serve Other Gods . . .

Something will have gone out of us as a people if we ever let the remaining wilderness be destroyed; if we permit the last virgin forests to be turned into comic books and plastic cigarette cases; if we drive the few remaining members of the wild species into zoos or to extinction; if we pollute the last clear air and dirty the last clean streams and push our paved roads through the last of the silence, so that never again will Americans be free in their own country from the noise, the exhausts, the stinks of human and automotive waste. And so that never again can we have the chance to see ourselves single, separate, vertical and individual in the world, part of the environment of trees and rocks and soil, brother to the other animals, part of the natural world and competent to belong in it. Without any remaining wilderness we are committed wholly, without chance for even momentary reflection and rest, to a headlong drive into our technological termite-life, the Brave New World of a completely man-controlled environment.

We need wilderness preserved—as much of it as is still left, and as many kinds—because it was the challenge against which our character as a people was formed. The reminder and the reassurance that it is still there is good for our spiritual health even if we never once in ten years set foot in it. It is good for us when we are young, because of the incomparable sanity it can bring briefly, as vacation and rest, into our insane lives. It is important to us when we are old simply because it is there—important, that is, simply as an idea.

And you *shall make fringes on the corners of your garments.*
And you shall leave the corners of your fields for the poor.
Behold, I clothe myself tonight in this four-cornered tallit
whose fringes recall my sacred obligations.
Let me open my field of vision to recognize the poor.
Let me open the clenched fist of my selfishness
and extend my hand to the hungry.
Let me open the darkest corners of my heart
to the light of truth.

---

lest we serve other gods. This excerpt from the famous 1960 "Wilderness Letter" by Wallace Stegner (1909–1993) is an eloquent plea that restates in a modern context *V'hayah Im Shamoa*, the second section of the *Sh'ma*. The classic passage from Deuteronomy warns the Israelites that if they adopt false gods, they risk impoverishing themselves—for the land will not tolerate their abuses. Similarly, if we give ourselves over to the worship of progress and technology with no thought of ultimate ideals, warns Stegner, we may well bring physical and spiritual destruction upon ourselves.

אֱמֶת וֶאֱמוּנָה כָּל זֹאת, וְקַיָּם עָלֵינוּ,
כִּי הוּא יְיָ אֱלֹהֵינוּ וְאֵין זוּלָתוֹ,
וַאֲנַחְנוּ יִשְׂרָאֵל עַמּוֹ.
הַפּוֹדֵנוּ מִיַּד מְלָכִים,
מַלְכֵּנוּ הַגּוֹאֲלֵנוּ מִכַּף כָּל הֶעָרִיצִים.
הָעוֹשֶׂה גְדוֹלוֹת עַד אֵין חֵקֶר,
וְנִפְלָאוֹת עַד אֵין מִסְפָּר,
הַשָּׂם נַפְשֵׁנוּ בַּחַיִּים,
וְלֹא נָתַן לַמּוֹט רַגְלֵנוּ.
הָעוֹשֶׂה לָּנוּ נִסִּים בְּפַרְעֹה,
אוֹתוֹת וּמוֹפְתִים בְּאַדְמַת בְּנֵי חָם.
וַיּוֹצֵא אֶת עַמּוֹ יִשְׂרָאֵל מִתּוֹכָם
לְחֵרוּת עוֹלָם.

Emet ve·emunah kol zot, v'kayam aleinu,
ki hu Adonai Eloheinu — v'ein zulato;
vaanachnu Yisrael amo.
Hapodeinu miyad m'lachim;
malkeinu hago·aleinu mikaf kol haaritzim.
Ha·oseh g'dolot ad ein cheiker,
v'niflaot ad ein mispar;
hasam nafsheinu bachayim,
v'lo natan lamot ragleinu.
Ha·oseh-lanu nisim b'Pharoh;
otot umoftim b'admat b'nei cham.
Vayotzei et amo Yisrael mitocham
l'cheirut olam.

Truth and faith —

these are fundamental to our existence.
God alone is their source,
and we are Israel, a people of God.

Our Sovereign saves us from tyranny,
redeems us from its violence through countless wonders,
from its brutality through great feats beyond measure.

We are Israel, a people of God —
the Giver of life, who would not let our feet give way;
the Maker of miracles for us against Pharaoh,
of signs and portents in the land of Egypt —
the One who brought our people Israel from its midst
to enduring freedom.

TRUTH AND FAITH אֱמֶת וֶאֱמוּנָה. This blessing is called *Emet ve·Emunah.* Like its counterpart in the morning service (*Emet v'Yatziv*, "True and Steadfast"), it expresses trust in God's redemptive power. Remarkably, our Sages insist that this power, revealed in the liberation of the Israelite slaves, is still with us today. But after the Holocaust — in a world rife with violence, hatred, and suffering — how can we say "our Sovereign saves us from tyranny"? Perhaps our continued survival and our enduring Jewish commitment testify to the existence of a redemptive force beyond ourselves. God "saves" us by implanting in us the will to live, the desire to resist oppression, and the determination to liberate all who are enslaved.

Call to Prayer
Twilight Prayer
Revelation of Torah
Sh'ma and Its Sections
Redemption
Peace in the Night
Keep Shabbat
On This Day
Reader's Kaddish

Emet ve·Emunah: Truth and Faithfulness in the Night

Our Sages taught:
It is proper to mention the Exodus from Egypt in our morning prayers
and also at night.

We celebrate the going-out from Egypt in the morning light,
full of confidence and vigor as we enter the new day.

But in the evening, weary from the day's exertions,
cast down and fearful at the coming of the night—
what can the Exodus teach us then?

Our nighttime prayer brings hope and trust in the future.
As God did not abandon our people long ago—through the long,
dark night of exile—
so the Holy One will be with us in time to come.
To stand by the one you love: that is the true essence of faithfulness,
the meaning of *emunah*.

So it is written in the Psalms:
"To proclaim Your kindness in the morning, and Your faithfulness in the nights."

Sing with joy in the mornings of your life,
when light surrounds you and the world seems beautiful and good.
And in the evenings of your life,
when you dwell in sorrow and the world seems dark,
do not despair.

OUR SAGES TAUGHT. Based on Talmud *B'rachot* 12a and the 12th-century sage Maimonides, who taught: "We are commanded to mention the Exodus both during the day and at night" (a mitzvah fulfilled by reciting the prayer *Emet v'Yatziv* during the morning service, and *Emet ve·Emunah* during the evening service). This mitzvah is derived from Deuteronomy 16:3: "in order that you shall remember your leaving the land of Egypt all the days of your life." It would have been sufficient for the Torah to say "the days of your life." The extra "all" implies that a full solar day is meant—including the night as well.

HOPE AND TRUST IN THE FUTURE. Based on the teachings of the medieval commentators Rashi and *Tosafot* on the differing emphases of *Emet v'Yatziv* (the morning version of this prayer) and *Emet ve·Emunah* (the evening version).

TO PROCLAIM YOUR KINDNESS, Psalm 92:3.

בָּרְכוּ *Bar'chu*
מַעֲרִיב עֲרָבִים *Maariv Aravim*
אַהֲבַת עוֹלָם *Ahavat Olam*
קְרִיאַת שְׁמַע *K'riat Sh'ma*
אֱמֶת וֶאֱמוּנָה ***Emet ve·Emunah***
מִי־כָמֹכָה ***Mi Chamocha***
הַשְׁכִּיבֵנוּ *Hashkiveinu*
וְשָׁמְרוּ *V'sham'ru*
כִּי־בַיּוֹם הַזֶּה *Ki-vayom Hazeh*
חֲצִי קַדִּישׁ *Chatzi Kaddish*

וְרָאוּ בָנָיו גְּבוּרָתוֹ, — *V'ra·u vanav g'vurato,*
שִׁבְּחוּ וְהוֹדוּ לִשְׁמוֹ. — *shib'chu v'hodu lishmo.*
וּמַלְכוּתוֹ בְּרָצוֹן קִבְּלוּ עֲלֵיהֶם. — *Umalchuto b'ratzon kib'lu aleihem.*
מֹשֶׁה וּמִרְיָם וּבְנֵי יִשְׂרָאֵל לְךָ עָנוּ — *Mosheh uMiryam uvnei Yisrael l'cha anu*
שִׁירָה בְּשִׂמְחָה רַבָּה, וְאָמְרוּ כֻלָּם: — *shirah b'simchah rabah; v'am'ru chulam:*

Witnesses to this heroic might,
the people thanked and praised God by name,
freely accepting the reign of heaven.

Then Moses and Miriam and all Israel sang to You this song of utter joy:

מִי־כָמֹכָה בָּאֵלִם, יְיָ, — *"Mi-chamocha ba·eilim, Adonai?*
מִי כָּמֹכָה נֶאְדָּר בַּקֹּדֶשׁ, — *Mi kamocha — nedar bakodesh,*
נוֹרָא תְהִלֹּת, עֹשֵׂה פֶלֶא. — *nora t'hilot, oseih-fele?"*
מַלְכוּתְךָ רָאוּ בָנֶיךָ, — *Malchut'cha ra·u vanecha —*
בּוֹקֵעַ יָם לִפְנֵי מֹשֶׁה וּמִרְיָם, — *bokei·a yam lifnei Mosheh uMiryam —*
זֶה אֵלִי עָנוּ. — *"Zeh Eili!" anu.*
וְאָמְרוּ: יְיָ יִמְלֹךְ לְעֹלָם וָעֶד. — *V'am'ru: "Adonai yimloch l'olam va·ed."*
וְנֶאֱמַר: כִּי פָדָה יְיָ אֶת־יַעֲקֹב, — *V'ne·emar: "Ki fadah Adonai et-Yaakov;*
וּגְאָלוֹ מִיַּד חָזָק מִמֶּנּוּ. — *ug·alo miyad chazak mimenu."*

"Of all that is worshiped, is there another like You?
Maker of wonders, who is like You —
in holiness sublime, evoking awe and praise?"

When Your children saw Your sovereign might —
the splitting of the sea before Moses and Miriam —
they responded, "This is my God!"
And they said, "The Eternal will reign till the end of time."

As it is written: "Adonai will save Jacob,
and redeem him from one stronger than himself."

בָּרוּךְ אַתָּה, יְיָ, גָּאַל יִשְׂרָאֵל.
Baruch atah, Adonai, gaal Yisrael.

Blessed are You in our lives, Eternal One, who redeemed Israel.

IS THERE ANOTHER LIKE YOU מִי־כָמֹכָה, Exodus 15:11.
THE ETERNAL WILL REIGN יְיָ יִמְלֹךְ, Exodus 15:18.
ADONAI WILL SAVE כִּי פָדָה יְיָ, Jeremiah 31:11.

For every exile who walked out
of Egypt between walls of water,
for everyone who remembered
the feel of sea bottom underfoot,
the sibilant roar of water rearing
on the right, on the left, someone
forgot. Someone scanning

the dry horizon for a well,
or already mourning the musky
smell of autumn in her father's
fig trees, forgot the hosannahs,
and, by the bitter waves of Marah,
forgot the flash of dancing feet,
the shimmer of timbrels.

For every proselyte at Sinai,
someone never heard of horns
at all. Someone turned back from
the mountain to bank the fire,
feed the baby, steal a secret
moment with another.

Revelation begins in attention:
while the elders trembled before
the word of God flowing down
the scorched north flank of Sinai,
someone, rising from a last long
embrace, gazed into the rapt face
of the beloved and saw
that it was good.

בָּרוּךְ אַתָּה, יְיָ, גָּאַל יִשְׂרָאֵל.

Baruch atah, Adonai, gaal Yisrael.

Blessed are You in our lives, Eternal One who redeemed Israel.

FOR EVERY EXILE. By Jacqueline Kudler (b. 1935). The poem evokes our propensity to "forget" the miracles in our lives—due to preoccupation with the past, or worries about the future. Yet it also points to a different kind of miraculous "revelation": God's love and power as experienced in loving relationships with others.

Hashkiveinu, Adonai Eloheinu, l'shalom;

v'haamideinu, Malkeinu, l'chayim.

Ufros aleinu sukat sh'lomecha,

v'tak'neinu b'eitzah tovah mil'fanecha.

V'hoshi·einu l'maan sh'mecha —

v'hagein baadeinu;

v'haseir mei·aleinu oyeiv:

dever, v'cherev, v'raav, v'yagon;

v'harcheik mimenu avon vafesha.

Uvtzeil k'nafecha tastireinu —

ki El shomreinu umatzileinu atah;

ki El melech chanun v'rachum atah.

Ushmor tzeiteinu uvo·einu,

l'chayim ulshalom — mei·atah v'ad olam.

Ufros aleinu sukat sh'lomecha.

הַשְׁכִּיבֵנוּ, יְיָ אֱלֹהֵינוּ, לְשָׁלוֹם,

וְהַעֲמִידֵנוּ, מַלְכֵּנוּ, לְחַיִּים.

וּפְרוֹשׂ עָלֵינוּ סֻכַּת שְׁלוֹמֶךָ,

וְתַקְּנֵנוּ בְּעֵצָה טוֹבָה מִלְּפָנֶיךָ.

וְהוֹשִׁיעֵנוּ לְמַעַן שְׁמֶךָ:

וְהָגֵן בַּעֲדֵנוּ,

וְהָסֵר מֵעָלֵינוּ אוֹיֵב –

דֶּבֶר, וְחֶרֶב, וְרָעָב, וְיָגוֹן –

וְהַרְחֵק מִמֶּנּוּ עָוֹן וָפֶשַׁע.

וּבְצֵל כְּנָפֶיךָ תַּסְתִּירֵנוּ –

כִּי אֵל שׁוֹמְרֵנוּ וּמַצִּילֵנוּ אָתָּה,

כִּי אֵל מֶלֶךְ חַנּוּן וְרַחוּם אָתָּה.

וּשְׁמוֹר צֵאתֵנוּ וּבוֹאֵנוּ,

לְחַיִּים וּלְשָׁלוֹם, מֵעַתָּה וְעַד עוֹלָם.

וּפְרֹשׂ עָלֵינוּ סֻכַּת שְׁלוֹמֶךָ.

בָּרְכוּ
Bar'chu

מַעֲרִיב עֲרָבִים
Maariv Aravim

אַהֲבַת עוֹלָם
Ahavat Olam

קְרִיאַת שְׁמַע
K'riat Sh'ma

אֱמֶת וֶאֱמוּנָה
Emet ve·Emunah

מִי־כָמֹכָה
Mi Chamocha

הַשְׁכִּיבֵנוּ
Hashkiveinu

וְשָׁמְרוּ
V'sham'ru

כִּי־בַיּוֹם הַזֶּה
Ki-vayom Hazeh

חֲצִי קַדִּישׁ
Chatzi Kaddish

Bless our sleep with peace, Adonai, and awaken us to life when we rise.
With power sublime, spread over us Your shelter of shalom;
and through Your wisdom restore us — make us whole.
Let Your name proclaim Your presence in our lives —
be our shield; make us stronger than the enemies we face:
illness and war, famine and sorrow;
and stronger than the enemies in our hearts: wickedness and sin.
Carry us to safety as on wings —
for You are the Monarch of grace, the Sovereign of compassion;
You are the One who cares for us and sets us free.
Watch over us, we who go forth to life; watch over us,
that we may come home in peace — now, and till the end of time.

SERMON

בָּרוּךְ אַתָּה, יְיָ, הַפּוֹרֵשׂ סֻכַּת שָׁלוֹם עָלֵינוּ,
וְעַל כָּל עַמּוֹ יִשְׂרָאֵל, וְעַל יְרוּשָׁלָיִם.

*Baruch atah, Adonai, haporeis sukat shalom aleinu,
v'al kol amo Yisrael, v'al Y'rushalayim.*

Blessed One, You spread over us a canopy of peace —
a shelter of shalom over all Israel, Your people, and over Jerusalem.

*Go to
46*

On weekdays, continue on page 45.

When fears multiply
and danger threatens;
when sickness comes,
when death confronts us—
it is God's blessing of shalom
that sustains us
and upholds us.

Lightening our burden,
dispelling our worry,
restoring our strength,
renewing our hope—
reviving us.

The Peace of Wild Things

When despair for the world grows in me
and I wake in the night at the least sound
in fear of what my life and my children's lives may be,
I go and lie down where the wood drake
rests in his beauty on the water, and the great heron feeds.
I come into the peace of wild things
who do not tax their lives with forethought
of grief. I come into the presence of still water.
And I feel above me the day-blind stars
waiting with their light. For a time
I rest in the grace of the world, and am free

בָּרוּךְ אַתָּה, יְיָ, הַפּוֹרֵשׂ סֻכַּת שָׁלוֹם עָלֵינוּ,
וְעַל כָּל עַמּוֹ יִשְׂרָאֵל, וְעַל יְרוּשָׁלָיִם.

Baruch atah, Adonai, haporeis sukat shalom aleinu,
v'al kol amo Yisrael, v'al Y'rushalayim.

Blessed One, You spread over us a canopy of peace—
a shelter of shalom over all Israel, Your people, and over Jerusalem.

WHEN FEARS MULTIPLY. By Rabbi Hershel Matt (1922–1987).
THE PEACE OF WILD THINGS. By Wendell Berry (b. 1934).

On Shabbat:

וְשָׁמְרוּ בְנֵי יִשְׂרָאֵל אֶת־הַשַּׁבָּת,	*V'sham'ru v'nei Yisrael et-haShabbat,*
לַעֲשׂוֹת אֶת־הַשַּׁבָּת לְדֹרֹתָם	*laasot et-haShabbat l'dorotam*
בְּרִית עוֹלָם.	*b'rit olam.*
בֵּינִי וּבֵין בְּנֵי יִשְׂרָאֵל	*Beini uvein b'nei Yisrael*
אוֹת הִיא לְעֹלָם,	*ot hi l'olam,*
כִּי־שֵׁשֶׁת יָמִים עָשָׂה יְיָ	*ki-sheishet yamim asah Adonai*
אֶת־הַשָּׁמַיִם וְאֶת־הָאָרֶץ,	*et-hashamayim v'et-haaretz,*
וּבַיּוֹם הַשְּׁבִיעִי שָׁבַת וַיִּנָּפַשׁ.	*uvayom hash'vi·i shavat vayinafash.*

Let all Israel keep Shabbat
and celebrate Shabbat for all generations
as an everlasting covenant.
It is a sign forever —
a bond between Me and Israel —
that in six days the Eternal One made the heavens and the earth;
but on the seventh day God stopped,
and breathed a new soul into the world.

V'SHAM'RU וְשָׁמְרוּ, Exodus 31:16–17.

IT IS A SIGN FOREVER. Why is Shabbat an eternal sign of Israel's relationship with God? Among the days, Shabbat is unique: a monument to God's withdrawal from creative activity, the moment in cosmic time when God "took a breath." When we celebrate this unique day, we emulate our Maker — and therein, perhaps, experience the breathing space that comes after six days of making and doing. Shabbat is a sign that we, in our own human way, are following in God's footsteps. By keeping Shabbat, we bear witness that the covenant endures.

כִּי־בַיּוֹם הַזֶּה יְכַפֵּר עֲלֵיכֶם
לְטַהֵר אֶתְכֶם,
מִכֹּל חַטֹּאתֵיכֶם לִפְנֵי יְיָ תִּטְהָרוּ.

Ki-vayom hazeh y'chapeir aleichem
l'taheir et·chem;
mikol chatoteichem lifnei Adonai tit·haru.

For on this day atonement shall be made for you
to purify you from all your wrongs.
And pure you shall be in the presence of Adonai.

יִתְגַּדַּל וְיִתְקַדַּשׁ שְׁמֵהּ רַבָּא,
בְּעָלְמָא דִּי בְרָא כִרְעוּתֵהּ.
וְיַמְלִיךְ מַלְכוּתֵהּ בְּחַיֵּיכוֹן
וּבְיוֹמֵיכוֹן,
וּבְחַיֵּי דְכָל בֵּית יִשְׂרָאֵל,
בַּעֲגָלָא וּבִזְמַן קָרִיב.
וְאִמְרוּ: אָמֵן.
יְהֵא שְׁמֵהּ רַבָּא מְבָרַךְ
לְעָלַם וּלְעָלְמֵי עָלְמַיָּא.
יִתְבָּרַךְ וְיִשְׁתַּבַּח וְיִתְפָּאַר וְיִתְרוֹמַם
וְיִתְנַשֵּׂא וְיִתְהַדָּר וְיִתְעַלֶּה וְיִתְהַלָּל
שְׁמֵהּ דְּקֻדְשָׁא, בְּרִיךְ הוּא,
לְעֵלָּא **וּלְעֵלָּא מִכָּל** בִּרְכָתָא וְשִׁירָתָא,
תֻּשְׁבְּחָתָא וְנֶחֱמָתָא דַּאֲמִירָן בְּעָלְמָא.
וְאִמְרוּ: אָמֵן.

Yitgadal v'yitkadash sh'meih raba,
b'alma di v'ra chiruteih.
V'yamlich malchuteih b'chayeichon
uvyomeichon,
uvchayei d'chol beit Yisrael —
baagala uvizman kariv;
v'imru: Amen.
Y'hei sh'meih raba m'varach
l'alam ul·almei almaya.
Yitbarach v'yishtabach v'yitpaar v'yitromam
v'yitnasei v'yit·hadar v'yitaleh v'yit·halal
sh'meih d'kudsha — b'rich hu —
l'eila ***ul·eila mikol*** *birchata v'shirata,*
tushb'chata v'nechemata daamiran b'alma;
v'imru: Amen.

May God's great name come to be magnified and sanctified in the world God brought into being. May God's majestic reign prevail soon in your lives, in your days, and in the life of the whole House of Israel; and let us say: *Amen.*

May God's great name be blessed to the end of time.

May God's holy name come to be blessed, acclaimed, and glorified; revered, raised, and beautified; honored and praised. Blessed is the One who is **entirely** beyond all the blessings and hymns, all the praises and words of comfort that we speak in the world; and let us say: *Amen.*

FOR ON THIS DAY כִּי־בַיּוֹם הַזֶּה, Leviticus 16:30.

הַתְּפִלָּה
HaT'filah · Standing before God

Have mercy upon me, O God,
as befits Your faithfulness;
in keeping with Your abundant compassion,
blot out my transgressions.
Wash me thoroughly of my iniquity,
and purify me of my sin;
for I recognize my transgressions,
and am ever conscious of my sin.

—PSALM 51:3–5

Adonai, s'fatai tiftach,	אֲדֹנָי, שְׂפָתַי תִּפְתָּח,
ufi yagid t'hilatecha.	וּפִי יַגִּיד תְּהִלָּתֶךָ.

Adonai, open my lips,
that my mouth may declare Your praise.

כַּוָּנָה
Kavanah

אָבוֹת וְאִמָּהוֹת
Avot v'Imahot

גְּבוּרוֹת
G'vurot

קְדֻשַּׁת הַשֵּׁם
K'dushat HaShem

קְדֻשַּׁת הַיּוֹם
K'dushat HaYom

עֲבוֹדָה
Avodah

הוֹדָאָה
Hodaah

שָׁלוֹם
Shalom

תְּפִלַּת הַלֵּב
T'filat HaLev

SING FROM FLOOR

HAVE MERCY. These verses from Psalm 51 offer us a concise model as we stand before God on the Day of Atonement — a day of confessions, long and short, public and private. The speaker (King David, according to ancient Jewish tradition) affirms three truths about God: divine faithfulness; divine compassion; and divine ability to purify from sin. Most important, though, is what comes next: "I recognize my transgressions. I am ever conscious of my sin." When we confess, what matters most are self-knowledge, ceaseless self-awareness, and acknowledgment of our responsibility.

ADONAI . . . MY LIPS אֲדֹנָי, שְׂפָתַי, Psalm 51:17.

The High Holy Day T'filah: An Introductory Note

Today—and throughout the High Holy Days—the *Amidah* includes four special insertions:

Remember us for life, sovereign God who treasures life.
Inscribe us in the Book of Life, for Your sake, God of life.
(in the blessing "God of All Generations")

Who compares with You, merciful God?
With tenderness and compassion You remember the living for life.
(in the blessing "God's Powers")

Inscribe Your covenant partners for a life of goodness.
(in the blessing "Thanksgiving")

Let us and the whole family of Israel be remembered and inscribed in the Book of Life.
May it be a life of goodness, blessing, and prosperity!
May it be a life of peace!
(in the blessing "Peace")

Perhaps what strikes us most about these four prayers is the recurring language; but taking a closer look at the repetition of words we notice something more subtle—an artful symmetry that unites them into a single structure:

Remember and Inscribe . . . Book of Life
Remember . . . Life
Inscribe . . . Life
Remember and Inscribe . . . Book of Life

This poetic symmetry gives the High Holy Day *Amidah* a profound coherence and unity; it fills us, the worshipers, with clarity of purpose and a sense of this moment's urgency. At the same time we notice a gradual expansion of what it means to pray for life. It is as if we discover, as we move through the *Amidah*, that it is not enough to pray for life itself. What we fervently desire is a life of goodness; and not just a life of goodness, but, ultimately a life of goodness, blessing, prosperity, and peace. The unique character of the High Holy Day *Amidah* flows from this sense of increasing intensity, and from the dramatic image of the Book of Life.

בָּרוּךְ אַתָּה, יְיָ,
אֱלֹהֵינוּ וֵאלֹהֵי אֲבוֹתֵינוּ וְאִמּוֹתֵינוּ:
אֱלֹהֵי אַבְרָהָם, אֱלֹהֵי יִצְחָק,
וֵאלֹהֵי יַעֲקֹב,
אֱלֹהֵי שָׂרָה, אֱלֹהֵי רִבְקָה,
אֱלֹהֵי רָחֵל, וֵאלֹהֵי לֵאָה,
הָאֵל הַגָּדוֹל הַגִּבּוֹר וְהַנּוֹרָא,
אֵל עֶלְיוֹן,
גּוֹמֵל חֲסָדִים טוֹבִים, וְקוֹנֵה הַכֹּל –
וְזוֹכֵר חַסְדֵי אָבוֹת וְאִמָּהוֹת,
וּמֵבִיא גְאֻלָּה לִבְנֵי בְנֵיהֶם,
לְמַעַן שְׁמוֹ בְּאַהֲבָה.

זָכְרֵנוּ לְחַיִּים,
מֶלֶךְ חָפֵץ בַּחַיִּים.
וְכָתְבֵנוּ בְּסֵפֶר הַחַיִּים,
לְמַעַנְךָ אֱלֹהִים חַיִּים.

מֶלֶךְ עוֹזֵר וּמוֹשִׁיעַ וּמָגֵן –

Baruch atah, Adonai,
Eloheinu v'Elohei avoteinu v'imoteinu:
Elohei Avraham, Elohei Yitzchak,
v'Elohei Yaakov;
Elohei Sarah, Elohei Rivkah,
Elohei Rachel, v'Elohei Leah;
haEl hagadol hagibor v'hanora,
El elyon,
gomeil chasadim tovim, v'koneih hakol —
v'zocheir chasdei avot v'imahot,
umeivi g'ulah livnei v'neihem,
l'maan sh'mo b'ahavah.

Zochreinu l'chayim,
Melech chafeitz bachayim.
V'chotveinu b'sefer hachayim,
l'maancha, Elohim chayim.

Melech ozeir umoshia umagein —

You are the Source of blessing, Adonai, our God
and God of our fathers and mothers:
God of Abraham, God of Isaac, and God of Jacob;
God of Sarah, God of Rebecca, God of Rachel, and God of Leah;
exalted God, dynamic in power, inspiring awe,
God sublime, Creator of all —
yet You offer us kindness,
recall the loving deeds of our fathers and mothers,
and bring redemption to their children's children,
acting in love for the sake of Your name.

Remember us for life, sovereign God who treasures life.
Inscribe us in the Book of Life, for Your sake, God of life.

Sovereign of salvation, Pillar of protection —

בָּרוּךְ אַתָּה, יְיָ, מָגֵן אַבְרָהָם וְעֶזְרַת שָׂרָה.

Baruch atah, Adonai, magein Avraham v'ezrat Sarah.

Blessed are You in our lives, Adonai, Shield of Abraham, Sustainer of Sarah.

From T'filah to Vidui to S'lichot

T'filah is a journey
from the God of the ancients
to my Rock
and my Redeemer. . . .

On most nights
you stand on the holy summit of *T'filah*
and see before you
a land that calls out
for redemption,
for healing,
for peace—
a world that needs you

Kol Nidrei is different

T'filah tonight
is an inward journey
that takes you
deep within yourself,
pierces you to the core. . . .
You stand on the holy summit
of this *T'filah*
and see before you the land within:
a weary soul
yearning to be forgiven,
longing to be loved

בָּרוּךְ אַתָּה, יְיָ, מָגֵן אַבְרָהָם וְעֶזְרַת שָׂרָה.

Baruch atah, Adonai, magein Avraham v'ezrat Sarah.

Blessed are You in our lives, Adonai, Shield of Abraham, Sustainer of Sarah.

FROM T'FILAH TO VIDUI TO S'LICHOT. *T'filah* (literally "prayer") refers to the series of blessings called, in these pages, *HaT'filah*: "The Prayer" or "Standing before God." *Vidui* and *S'lichot* refer to later sections of the Yom Kippur service: Confession, and Songs of Forgiveness.

In Hebrew, choose either hakol *or* meitim.

כַּוָּנָה
Kavanah
אָבוֹת וְאִמָּהוֹת
Avot v'Imahot
גְּבוּרוֹת
G'vurot
קְדֻשַּׁת הַשֵּׁם
K'dushat HaShem
קְדֻשַּׁת הַיּוֹם
K'dushat HaYom
עֲבוֹדָה
Avodah
הוֹדָאָה
Hodaah
שָׁלוֹם
Shalom
תְּפִלַּת הַלֵּב
T'filat HaLev

אַתָּה גִּבּוֹר לְעוֹלָם, אֲדֹנָי –	*Atah gibor l'olam, Adonai —*
מְחַיֵּה הַכֹּל\מֵתִים אַתָּה,	*m'chayeih hakol/meitim atah,*
רַב לְהוֹשִׁיעַ.	*rav l'hoshia.*
מוֹרִיד הַטָּל.	*Morid hatal.*
מְכַלְכֵּל חַיִּים בְּחֶסֶד,	*M'chalkeil chayim b'chesed,*
מְחַיֵּה הַכֹּל\מֵתִים	*m'chayeih hakol/meitim*
בְּרַחֲמִים רַבִּים –	*b'rachamim rabim —*
סוֹמֵךְ נוֹפְלִים,	*someich noflim,*
וְרוֹפֵא חוֹלִים וּמַתִּיר אֲסוּרִים,	*v'rofei cholim umatir asurim;*
וּמְקַיֵּם אֱמוּנָתוֹ לִישֵׁנֵי עָפָר.	*umkayeim emunato lisheinei afar.*
מִי כָמוֹךָ, בַּעַל גְּבוּרוֹת,	*Mi chamocha, baal g'vurot;*
וּמִי דּוֹמֶה לָּךְ,	*umi domeh-lach? —*
מֶלֶךְ מֵמִית וּמְחַיֶּה	*melech meimit umchayeh*
וּמַצְמִיחַ יְשׁוּעָה.	*umatzmiach y'shuah.*
מִי כָמוֹךְ, אֵל הָרַחֲמִים,	*Mi chamocha, El harachamim? —*
זוֹכֵר יְצוּרָיו לְחַיִּים בְּרַחֲמִים.	*zocheir y'tzurav l'chayim b'rachamim.*
וְנֶאֱמָן אַתָּה לְהַחֲיוֹת הַכֹּל\מֵתִים.	*V'ne·eman atah l'hachayot hakol/meitim.*

GO BACK DOWN

Your life-giving power is forever, Adonai — with us in life and in death.
You liberate and save, cause dew to descend;
and with mercy abundant, lovingly nurture all life.
From life to death, You are the force that flows without end —
You support the falling, heal the sick, free the imprisoned and confined;
You are faithful, even to those who rest in the dust.

Power-beyond-Power, from whom salvation springs,
Sovereign over life and death — who is like You?
Merciful God, who compares with You?
With tender compassion You remember all creatures for life.
Faithful and true, worthy of our trust —
You sustain our immortal yearnings; in You we place our undying hopes.

בָּרוּךְ אַתָּה, יְיָ, מְחַיֵּה הַכֹּל\הַמֵּתִים.

Baruch atah, Adonai, m'chayeih hakol/hameitim.

Wellspring of blessing, Power eternal, You are the One who gives and renews all life.

FALL, FALLING, FALLEN. That's the way the season
Changes its tense in the long-haired maples
That dot the road; the veiny hand-shaped leaves
Redden on their branches (in a fiery competition
With the final remaining cardinals) and then
Begin to sidle and float through the air, at last
Settling into colorful layers carpeting the ground.
At twilight the light, too, is layered in the trees
In a season of odd, dusky congruences—a scarlet tanager
And the odor of burning leaves, a golden retriever
Loping down the center of a wide street and the sun
Setting behind smoke-filled trees in the distance,
A gap opening up in the treetops and a bruised cloud
Blamelessly filling the space with purples. Everything
Changes and moves in the split second between summer's
Sprawling past and winter's hard revision, one moment
Pulling out of the station according to schedule,
Another moment arriving on the next platform. It
Happens almost like clockwork: the leaves drift away
From their branches and gather slowly at our feet,
Sliding over our ankles, and the season begins moving
Around us even as its colorful weather moves us,
Even as it pulls us into its dusty, twilit pockets.
And every year there is a brief, startling moment
When we pause in the middle of a long walk home and
Suddenly feel something invisible and weightless
Touching our shoulders, sweeping down from the air:
It is the autumn wind pressing against our bodies;
It is the changing light of fall falling on us.

בָּרוּךְ אַתָּה, יְיָ, מְחַיֵּה הַכֹּל\הַמֵּתִים.

Baruch atah, Adonai, m'chayeih hakol/hameitim.

We praise You, eternal Power, the One who gives and renews all life.

HEAL THE SICK, FREE THE IMPRISONED וְרוֹפֵא חוֹלִים, וּמַתִּיר אֲסוּרִים (*facing page*). And what if the sick can no longer be healed? Perhaps it is then that God frees the captive soul and allows it to return to the Source of being.

FALL, FALLING, FALLEN. By Edward Hirsch (b. 1950).

קְדֻשַּׁת הַשֵּׁם
K'dushat HaShem
God's Holiness: Awe, Honor, and Righteousness

What is the purpose of our prayers? Connection with the past; the expression of hopes for the future; a moment of personal transcendence and clarity; a strong bond with a community that shares our values and sings the melodies we cherish: these are all worthy reasons to pray. But during this sacred season our liturgy also gives us an extended opportunity to ponder the holiness of God.

During the Days of Awe, three short prayers are added to the third blessing of *HaT'filah*—the blessing that is known as the *K'dushah* (short for *K'dushat HaShem*, the Sanctification of God's Name). These passages, each beginning with the Hebrew word *uvchein* ("and so"), explore the implications of a world suffused with God's holiness. What would that look like?

In the first passage, all creation is united by a sense of AWE and REVERENCE for the Divine; in the second, the Jews—a people historically vulnerable and often despised—receive *kavod* (HONOR and RESPECT); and in the third, evil has been vanquished by RIGHTEOUSNESS. Together, these three prayers set forth a vision of a world in which God's presence is felt and experienced every day. We sanctify God not only verbally, by reciting these words, but also by realizing that vision through our actions: showing REVERENCE for all creation, giving *kavod* to all people—especially those who are vulnerable and needy—and embodying RIGHTEOUSNESS in all that we do.

The message of these three passages is reinforced by the compelling climax of the evening *K'dushah*: "The Source of all might is exalted through justice, the God of holiness made holy through righteousness" (Isaiah 5:16; see page 58). Why, during this season, do we take time to understand the meaning of God's holiness? Because God's holiness is dependent on human beings, who extend the reach of the Divine into dark corners of the world by embracing AWE, showing HONOR, and acting with RIGHTEOUSNESS.

אַתָּה קָדוֹשׁ, וְשִׁמְךָ קָדוֹשׁ,
Atah kadosh, v'shimcha kadosh,

וּקְדוֹשִׁים בְּכָל יוֹם יְהַלְלְוּךָ סֶּלָה.
ukdoshim b'chol yom y'hal'lucha selah.

You are holy. Your name is holy.
Seekers of holiness praise You day by day. *Selah.*

How Do We Sense God's Holiness?

Through Awe

וּבְכֵן תֵּן פַּחְדְּךָ, יְיָ אֱלֹהֵינוּ,
Uvchein tein pachd'cha, Adonai Eloheinu,

עַל כָּל מַעֲשֶׂיךָ,
al kol maasecha;

וְאֵימָתְךָ עַל כָּל מַה שֶּׁבָּרָאתָ.
v'eimat'cha al kol mah shebarata.

וְיִירָאְוּךָ כָּל הַמַּעֲשִׂים,
V'yira·ucha kol hamaasim;

וְיִשְׁתַּחֲווּ לְפָנֶיךָ כָּל הַבְּרוּאִים.
v'yishtachavu l'fanecha kol hab'ruim.

וְיֵעָשׂוּ כֻלָּם אֲגֻדָּה אֶחָת,
V'yei·asu chulam agudah echat,

לַעֲשׂוֹת רְצוֹנְךָ בְּלֵבָב שָׁלֵם,
laasot r'tzoncha b'leivav shaleim —

כְּמוֹ שֶׁיָּדַֽעְנוּ, יְיָ אֱלֹהֵינוּ,
k'mo sheyadanu, Adonai Eloheinu,

שֶׁהַשָּׁלְטָן לְפָנֶיךָ,
shehasholtan l'fanecha,

עֹז בְּיָדְךָ, וּגְבוּרָה בִּימִינֶךָ,
oz b'yad'cha, ugvurah biminecha,

וְשִׁמְךָ נוֹרָא עַל כָּל מַה שֶּׁבָּרָאתָ.
v'shimcha nora al kol mah shebarata.

And so, in Your holiness,
give all creation the gift of awe.
Turn our fear to reverence;
let us be witnesses of wonder —
perceiving all nature as a prayer come alive.
We bow to the sovereignty of Your strength,
the primacy of Your power.
We yearn for connection with all that lives,
doing Your will with wholeness of heart.
Awe-inspiring is Your creation,
all-encompassing Your transcendent name.

SELAH סֶלָה. Most likely *selah* is a musical reference that signaled a pause or break to the psalm singers and instrumentalists of ancient Temple worship. We too might understand *selah* in that way, and see it as a message woven into our prayer: "Slow down. Let go of words. Take a moment for stillness, for silence and for meditation."

כּוָּנָה
Kavanah

אָבוֹת וְאִמָּהוֹת
Avot v'Imahot

גְּבוּרוֹת
G'vurot

קְדֻשַּׁת הַשֵּׁם
K'dushat HaShem

קְדֻשַּׁת הַיּוֹם
K'dushat HaYom

עֲבוֹדָה
Avodah

הוֹדָאָה
Hodaah

שָׁלוֹם
Shalom

תְּפִלַּת הַלֵּב
T'filat HaLev

How Do We Sense God's Holiness?
Through Honor

Uvchein tein kavod, Adonai, l'amecha;	וּבְכֵן תֵּן כָּבוֹד, יְיָ, לְעַמֶּךָ,
t'hilah lirei·echa;	תְּהִלָּה לִירֵאֶיךָ
v'tikvah tovah l'dorshecha;	וְתִקְוָה טוֹבָה לְדוֹרְשֶׁיךָ,
ufit·chon peh lamyachalim lach,	וּפִתְחוֹן פֶּה לַמְיַחֲלִים לָךְ,
simchah l'artzecha,	שִׂמְחָה לְאַרְצֶךָ
v'sason l'irecha;	וְשָׂשׂוֹן לְעִירֶךָ,
utzmichat keren l'David avdecha;	וּצְמִיחַת קֶרֶן לְדָוִד עַבְדֶּךָ,
vaarichat ner l'ven Yishai m'shichecha,	וַעֲרִיכַת נֵר לְבֶן יִשַׁי מְשִׁיחֶךָ,
bimheirah v'yameinu.	בִּמְהֵרָה בְיָמֵינוּ.

And so, in Your holiness,
give Your people the gift of honor.
Bless with praise those who praise You.
Bless with hope those who seek You.
Give Your believers a basis for faith:
true happiness for the Land of Israel,
true joy in Jerusalem.
May the sparks of David, Your servant,
soon grow bright enough for us to see
a beam of light in the darkness,
a promise of perfection.

KADOSH קָדוֹשׁ. The enlarged Hebrew word for "holy" beside the headings of the three sections of *K'dushat HaShem* echoes the threefold declaration of God's holiness in Isaiah 6:3: "Holy, Holy, Holy is the God of heaven's hosts. The fullness of the whole earth is God's glory."

THE GIFT OF HONOR כָּבוֹד. The first prayer in this three-part series conveys a yearning for all creation to experience "the gift of awe" — a universal theme (page 53). This second prayer focuses on the Jewish people, speaking of "the gift of honor" for those often marginalized and despised, seeking hope for those who have loyally held fast to the faith of Israel. The prayer culminates in a messianic vision in which the Jewish homeland, too, will experience honor and joy. King David, traditionally viewed as the ancestor of the Messiah, is here evoked as an emblematic figure who shines through Jewish history as a symbol of hope.

"GIVE YOUR BELIEVERS A BASIS FOR FAITH . . ."

אַתָּה יוֹדֵעַ לִבְרֹא לֵב
אֶבֶן שֶׁאַתָּה יָכוֹל גַּם לְהָרִים

אַתָּה יוֹדֵעַ לִבְרֹא לֵב
שֶׁיֵּדַע גַּם לָצֵאת מִבּוֹרוֹת,
שֶׁהִפִּיל עַצְמוֹ, שֶׁנִּמְכַּר

אַתָּה יוֹדֵעַ לְהָחֵם בְּכַף יָדְךָ לֵב
קָפוּא מֵרֹב

אַתָּה יוֹדֵעַ

You know how to create a heart
of stone that You can lift

You know how to create a heart
that will know how to get out of pits,
that cast itself, that was sold

You know how to warm with Your hand a heart
frozen from too much

You know

YOU KNOW. Poet Elhanan Nir (b. 1980) borrows the philosopher's conundrum of whether the omnipotent God can create a stone too heavy for God to lift. But, as a poet of faith, Nir is more interested in God's participation in our lives: God's ability to lift up even the heaviest of human hearts—"a heart of stone." And he is interested in how God creates within us the capacity (the heart) to "get out of" the dire circumstances we create for ourselves—that is, the "pits" into which we cast ourselves. And last, says commentator David C. Jacobson (b. 1947), the poem's speaker "celebrates God's power to revive people who have become spiritually frozen" and relieve the heart's pain.

HOW TO GET OUT OF PITS. In Genesis 37, Joseph's brothers cast him into a pit and sell him into slavery. Later, Potiphar has Joseph imprisoned in a dungeon that is also described as a "pit."

קדוש

How Do We Sense God's Holiness?
Through Righteousness

וּבְכֵן צַדִּיקִים יִרְאוּ וְיִשְׂמָחוּ,
וִישָׁרִים יַעֲלֹזוּ,
וַחֲסִידִים בְּרִנָּה יָגִילוּ,
וְעוֹלָתָה תִּקְפָּץ־פִּיהָ,
וְכָל הָרִשְׁעָה כֻּלָּהּ כְּעָשָׁן תִּכְלֶה,
כִּי תַעֲבִיר מֶמְשֶׁלֶת זָדוֹן מִן הָאָרֶץ.

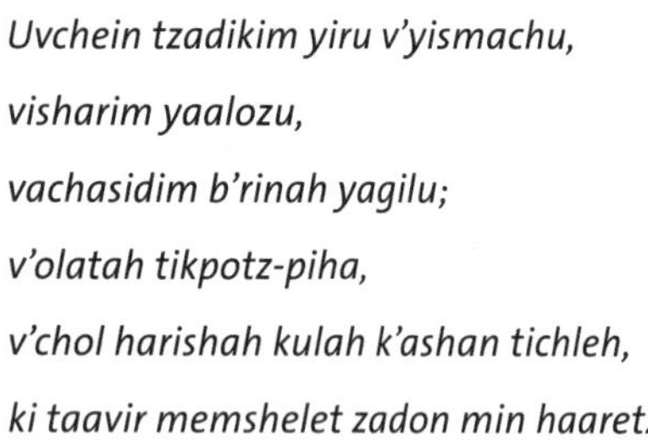

Uvchein tzadikim yiru v'yismachu,
visharim yaalozu,
vachasidim b'rinah yagilu;
v'olatah tikpotz-piha,
v'chol harishah kulah k'ashan tichleh,
ki taavir memshelet zadon min haaretz.

And so, in Your holiness,
give the righteous the gift of a vision bright with joy:
a world where evil has no voice
and the rule of malevolence fades like wisps of smoke.
Good people everywhere will celebrate
the stunning sight of arrogance gone from the earth.

כַּוָּנָה *Kavanah*
אָבוֹת וְאִמָּהוֹת *Avot v'Imahot*
גְּבוּרוֹת *G'vurot*
קְדֻשַּׁת הַשֵּׁם *K'dushat HaShem*
קְדֻשַּׁת הַיּוֹם *K'dushat HaYom*
עֲבוֹדָה *Avodah*
הוֹדָאָה *Hodaah*
שָׁלוֹם *Shalom*
תְּפִלַּת הַלֵּב *T'filat HaLev*

THE RULE OF MALEVOLENCE וְכָל הָרִשְׁעָה כֻּלָּהּ. This prayer, last in a three-part series, each beginning with the word *Uvchein* (And so), looks toward a time when the righteous will rejoice and wickedness will be permanently vanquished. But does it make sense to yearn for such a day? The political philosopher John Gray (b. 1948), a critic of utopian thinking, rejects this view, citing "the human proclivity to hatred and destruction." He writes: "The point is that destructive behavior of this kind flows from inherent human flaws. Crucially, these defects are not only or even mainly intellectual. No advance in human knowledge can stop humans attacking and persecuting others."

Jewish tradition acknowledges that aggression and hostility are inborn human tendencies, and that we are prone to behavior that is both self-destructive and harmful to others. Yet it insists that human beings also possess *yetzer hatov* — a moral instinct that controls and channels our harmful drives, gives rise to generous and cooperative acts, and inspires us to work for a better world. And Judaism rests on a belief that evil will not forever dominate the world — not because human beings will be miraculously transformed and aggression will be eradicated, but because we can establish just and equitable social institutions and non-violent ways of resolving conflict. Thus, Isaiah (ch. 2) and Micah (ch. 4) envision a messianic age in which Jerusalem becomes a spiritual center with a kind of World Court for the peaceful adjudication of disputes: "And they shall beat their swords into plowshares and their spears into pruning hooks."

Who is righteous?
One who gives to others and sustains them.
So it is written: "Noah was a righteous man."
Why? Because he fed the animals in the ark.
Joseph, too, is called righteous, for he sustained those around him
for seven years of famine in Egypt.
Nourishing God's creatures made them like their Creator.
Thus Scripture says: "Adonai is righteous; God loves righteous deeds;
the upright shall behold God's face."

So a river gives life to the land with its waters;
so the wise are like candles, kindling light in their students;
so the generous bring comfort with compassionate gifts.
All are righteous, for goodness and blessing flow from their deeds.
As Scripture says: "They give freely to those in need;
their righteousness endures forever."

The Merit of Righteous Women

Rabbi Akiva taught: Through the merit of the righteous women of that generation, Israel was redeemed from Egypt. . . . What did they do? When they would go and draw water, God would bring small fish to their pails and they would draw pails half full of water and half full of fish. The women would go to their husbands and pour them two bowls—one of warm water and one of fish—and they would feed them and wash them and anoint them and give them drink and have relations with them . . . and when they conceived, they would return home.

NOAH WAS A RIGHTEOUS MAN, Genesis 6:9.

BECAUSE HE FED THE ANIMALS. Based on Midrash *Tanchuma* (Buber), *Noach* 2.

JOSEPH . . . IS CALLED RIGHTEOUS. The Rabbinic sages called him *Yosef HaTzadik* (Joseph the Righteous). He is the only character in the *Tanach* whom the Rabbis described in this way.

FOR HE SUSTAINED THOSE AROUND HIM. Midrash *Tanchuma* (Buber), *Noach* 2.

SEVEN YEARS OF FAMINE, Genesis 41:53–57.

ADONAI IS RIGHTEOUS, Psalm 11:7.

THE WISE ARE LIKE CANDLES. Medieval mystics likened Rabbi Shimon to a candle—a source of enlightenment for his students (*Zohar* 2:86b).

THEY GIVE FREELY. Adapted from Psalm 112:9.

MERIT OF RIGHTEOUS WOMEN. From Talmud *Sotah* 11b; Midrash *Exodus Rabbah* 1.12. The midrash celebrates the initiative of righteous Israelite women, who did not give up hope and persuaded their husbands to engage in the mitzvah of procreation, thereby saving the nation and ensuring Jewish survival.

וְתִמְלֹךְ, אַתָּה, יְיָ, לְבַדֶּךָ עַל כָּל מַעֲשֶׂיךָ,
בְּהַר צִיּוֹן מִשְׁכַּן כְּבוֹדֶךָ,
וּבִירוּשָׁלַיִם עִיר קָדְשֶׁךָ,
כַּכָּתוּב בְּדִבְרֵי קָדְשֶׁךָ:
יִמְלֹךְ יְיָ לְעוֹלָם,
אֱלֹהַיִךְ, צִיּוֹן, לְדֹר וָדֹר, הַלְלוּ־יָהּ.

V'timloch — atah, Adonai — l'vadecha al kol maasecha,
b'Har Tziyon, mishkan k'vodecha,
uviYrushalayim, ir kodshecha —
kakatuv b'divrei kodshecha:
"Yimloch Adonai l'olam;
Elohayich, Tziyon, l'dor vador — hal'lu-Yah!"

You, and You alone, Adonai, will reign over Creation,
upon Mount Zion, home of Your Presence,
and in Jerusalem, a city set apart by You —
as the Psalmist believed: "Adonai will reign eternally;
your God, Zion, for all generations. Halleluyah!"

קָדוֹשׁ אַתָּה, וְנוֹרָא שְׁמֶךָ,
וְאֵין אֱלוֹהַּ מִבַּלְעָדֶיךָ, כַּכָּתוּב:
וַיִּגְבַּהּ יְיָ צְבָאוֹת בַּמִּשְׁפָּט,
וְהָאֵל הַקָּדוֹשׁ נִקְדַּשׁ בִּצְדָקָה.

Kadosh atah, v'nora sh'mecha;
v'ein elo·ah mibaladecha, kakatuv:
"Vayigbah Adonai tz'vaot bamishpat;
v'haEl hakadosh nikdash bitzdakah."

You are holy.
Your name is Awe.
There is nothing divine beyond You —
as the prophet Isaiah taught:
"The Source of all might is exalted through justice,
the God of holiness made holy through righteousness."

בָּרוּךְ אַתָּה, יְיָ, הַמֶּלֶךְ הַקָּדוֹשׁ.

*Baruch atah, Adonai, **haMelech** hakadosh.*

Blessed are You, Adonai, holy Sovereign.

כַּוָּנָה
Kavanah
אָבוֹת וְאִמָּהוֹת
Avot v'Imahot
גְּבוּרוֹת
G'vurot
קְדֻשַּׁת הַשֵּׁם
K'dushat HaShem
קְדֻשַּׁת הַיּוֹם
K'dushat HaYom
עֲבוֹדָה
Avodah
הוֹדָאָה
Hodaah
שָׁלוֹם
Shalom
תְּפִלַּת הַלֵּב
T'filat HaLev

ADONAI WILL REIGN ETERNALLY יִמְלֹךְ יְיָ לְעוֹלָם, Psalm 146:10.
THE SOURCE OF ALL MIGHT IS EXALTED וַיִּגְבַּהּ יְיָ צְבָאוֹת, Isaiah 5:16.

Traveling to Jerusalem on a Moon Night

הַחַלּוֹן נוֹסֵעַ הָעֲנָנִים נוֹסְעִים אֲנִי
נוֹסַעַת הַכְּבִישׁ נוֹסֵעַ הַיָּרֵחַ נוֹסֵעַ הָעֵצִים נוֹסְעִים הַזְּגוּגִית
נוֹסַעַת הַיָּרֵחַ נוֹסֵעַ הַנּוֹסְעִים נוֹסְעִים
הָאָרֶץ נוֹסַעַת הֶהָרִים נוֹסְעִים הַפְּלָנֶטָה נוֹסַעַת הַמַּחֲשָׁבוֹת נוֹסְעוֹת
הַזְּמַן נוֹסֵעַ
הָאוֹר נוֹסֵעַ הַזְּכוּכִית נוֹסַעַת הָאֲבָנִים נוֹסְעוֹת הַגָּלַקְסְיָה
נוֹסַעַת הַקּוֹסְמוֹס נוֹסֵעַ הַגָּלַקְסְיָה נוֹסַעַת הַיָּרֵחַ נוֹסֵעַ
וֵאלֹהִים
לְעוֹלָם
עוֹמֵד

The window travels the clouds travel I
travel the road travels the moon travels the trees travel the pane
travels the moon travels the passengers travel
the earth travels the mountains travel the planet travels the thoughts travel
the time travels
the light travels the glass travels the stones travel the galaxy
travels the cosmos travels the galaxy travels the moon travels
and God
eternally
stands

בָּרוּךְ אַתָּה, יְיָ, הַמֶּלֶךְ הַקָּדוֹשׁ.

Baruch atah, Adonai, haMelech hakadosh.

Blessed are You, Adonai, holy Sovereign.

TRAVELING TO JERUSALEM ON A MOON NIGHT. By Rachel Chalfi (b. ca. 1945).

כַּוָּנָה
Kavanah
אָבוֹת וְאִמָּהוֹת
Avot v'Imahot
גְּבוּרוֹת
G'vurot
קְדֻשַּׁת הַשֵּׁם
K'dushat HaShem
קְדֻשַּׁת הַיּוֹם
K'dushat HaYom
עֲבוֹדָה
Avodah
הוֹדָאָה
Hodaah
שָׁלוֹם
Shalom
תְּפִלַּת הַלֵּב
T'filat HaLev

אַתָּה בְחַרְתָּנוּ מִכָּל הָעַמִּים,
אָהַבְתָּ אוֹתָנוּ וְרָצִיתָ בָּנוּ.
וְרוֹמַמְתָּנוּ מִכָּל הַלְּשׁוֹנוֹת,
וְקִדַּשְׁתָּנוּ בְּמִצְוֹתֶיךָ.
וְקֵרַבְתָּנוּ, מַלְכֵּנוּ, לַעֲבוֹדָתֶךָ,
וְשִׁמְךָ הַגָּדוֹל וְהַקָּדוֹשׁ
עָלֵינוּ קָרָאתָ.

Atah v'chartanu mikol haamim;
ahavta otanu, v'ratzita banu.
V'romamtanu mikol hal'shonot,
v'kidashtanu b'mitzvotecha.
V'keiravtanu, Malkeinu, laavodatecha;
v'shimcha hagadol v'hakadosh
aleinu karata.

You chose us, with love, to be messengers of mitzvot;
and through us You made known Your aspirations.

Among all the many peoples,
You gave us a pathway to holiness.
Among all the great nations,
You uplifted us and made Yourself our Sovereign —
and so we seek You and serve You
and celebrate our nearness to Your presence.

Your great and sacred name has become our calling.

YOU CHOSE US, WITH LOVE אַתָּה בְחַרְתָּנוּ. This prayer has nothing to do with superiority, even if Jews and non-Jews have at times so construed it. The sins of chauvinism and racism were not fathered by the Jew. Chosenness does not imply limited access to God; there are many ways to serve God. Nor is Israel by definition a limited people. It is so by dint of history and circumstance. Israel's unique way of serving God is open to all who would join in. (Rabbi W. Gunther Plaut, 1912–2012; adapted)

AMONG ALL THE MANY PEOPLES מִכָּל הָעַמִּים. The Talmud (*Sanhedrin* 37a) teaches that one reason the human race descended from a single set of parents is so that no person can claim ancestral superiority over others. All human beings constitute one family, and all are equal in God's sight. Said the prophet Malachi (2:10): "Have we not all one Parent? Did not one God create us?"

TO ME, O ISRAELITES, you are just like the Ethiopians—declares Adonai.
True, I brought Israel up from the land of Egypt,
But also the Philistines from Caphtor and the Arameans from Kir.

The idea that Jews are a chosen people does not imply biological or racial superiority. Jews belong to all races, and welcome as converts people of all races, ethnic groups, and nations. Neither does it imply moral superiority; the Hebrew Bible, a profoundly self-critical document, contains sharp prophetic rebukes of Israelite morality.

Commenting on *parashat K'doshim*, which contains the call "You shall be holy, for I, Adonai your God, am holy," Martin Buber noted that the biblical God does not withdraw from the world. Hence: "In imitating God by being a holy nation, Israel must not withdraw from the world of the nations, but rather radiate a positive influence on them through every aspect of Jewish living." Chosenness does not connote superiority, but it does confer special responsibility to strive for moral excellence.

TODAY THE JEWISH MISSION is not diminished. In a world that still cries out for healing, where suffering and narrowness are endemic, to be chosen means to have a special calling to teach that all human beings are children of God created in God's image and must be treated as sacred.

That Judaism is a small nation is no bar to this task. Many of the nations that have changed the world have been small: the Athens of Socrates and Plato, the England of Queen Elizabeth and Shakespeare, the America of Washington and Jefferson. No nation, great or small, has touched humanity more deeply than the tiny nation of Isaiah and Jeremiah.

Chosenness is not a privilege to boast of but a task to be undertaken. It is to keep constantly in mind the words of the prophet Micah: "It has been told you, O mortal, what is good, and what the Eternal requires of you—Only this: to do justly, and love mercy, and walk humbly with your God."

TO ME, O ISRAELITES, Amos 9:7. Rabbi Abraham Joshua Heschel (1907–1972) points out that both the Philistines and the Arameans were enemies of the people of Israel; the Ethiopians, commonly sold as slaves, had low social status. Thus the prophet Amos' argument is particularly forceful: Israel enjoys no special status in God's eyes. All peoples are equally beloved, and equally subject to divine judgment. Even Israel's foundational story of the Exodus is not unique; other peoples have their own stories of the journey to redemption.

YOU SHALL BE HOLY, Leviticus 19:2.

MARTIN BUBER. 1878–1965.

TODAY THE JEWISH MISSION. By Rabbi David J. Wolpe (b. 1958).

IT HAS BEEN TOLD YOU, Micah 6:8.

כַּוָּנָה *Kavanah*
אָבוֹת וְאִמָּהוֹת *Avot v'Imahot*
גְּבוּרוֹת *G'vurot*
קְדֻשַּׁת הַשֵּׁם *K'dushat HaShem*
קְדֻשַּׁת הַיּוֹם *K'dushat HaYom*
עֲבוֹדָה *Avodah*
הוֹדָאָה *Hodaah*
שָׁלוֹם *Shalom*
תְּפִלַּת הַלֵּב *T'filat HaLev*

וַתִּתֶּן־לָנוּ, יְיָ אֱלֹהֵינוּ, בְּאַהֲבָה אֶת
[יוֹם הַשַּׁבָּת הַזֶּה
לִקְדֻשָּׁה וְלִמְנוּחָה, וְאֶת]
יוֹם הַכִּפּוּרִים הַזֶּה,
לִמְחִילָה וְלִסְלִיחָה וּלְכַפָּרָה,
וְלִמְחָל־בּוֹ אֶת כָּל עֲוֹנוֹתֵינוּ [בְּאַהֲבָה],
מִקְרָא קֹדֶשׁ, זֵכֶר לִיצִיאַת מִצְרָיִם.

Vatiten-lanu, Adonai Eloheinu, b'ahavah et
[Yom haShabbat hazeh
likdushah v'limnuchah, v'et]
Yom HaKippurim hazeh —
limchilah v'lislichah ulchaparah —
v'limchol-bo et kol avonoteinu [b'ahavah],
mikra-kodesh, zeicher litziat Mitzrayim.

In Your love, Eternal our God, You have given us this
[Shabbat — for holiness and rest — and this] Yom Kippur:
a day on which our wrongs are forgiven with love;
a day of sacred assembly;
a day to be mindful of our people's going-out from Egypt.

אֱלֹהֵינוּ וֵאלֹהֵי אֲבוֹתֵינוּ וְאִמּוֹתֵינוּ,
יַעֲלֶה וְיָבֹא וְיַגִּיעַ, וְיֵרָאֶה וְיֵרָצֶה
וְיִשָּׁמַע וְיִפָּקֵד וְיִזָּכֵר
זִכְרוֹנֵנוּ וּפִקְדוֹנֵנוּ,
וְזִכְרוֹן אֲבוֹתֵינוּ וְאִמּוֹתֵינוּ,
וְזִכְרוֹן יְרוּשָׁלַיִם עִיר קָדְשֶׁךָ,
וְזִכְרוֹן כָּל עַמְּךָ בֵּית יִשְׂרָאֵל,
לְפָנֶיךָ לִפְלֵיטָה לְטוֹבָה,
לְחֵן וּלְחֶסֶד וּלְרַחֲמִים,
לְחַיִּים וּלְשָׁלוֹם,
בְּיוֹם הַכִּפּוּרִים הַזֶּה.

Eloheinu v'Elohei avoteinu v'imoteinu,
yaaleh v'yavo v'yagia, v'yeira·eh v'yeiratzeh
v'yishama, v'yipakeid, v'yizacheir
zichroneinu ufikdoneinu —
v'zichron avoteinu v'imoteinu,
v'zichron Y'rushalayim ir kodshecha,
v'zichron kol am'cha beit Yisrael
l'fanecha — lifleitah l'tovah,
l'chein ulchesed ulrachamim,
l'chayim ulshalom,
b'Yom HaKippurim hazeh.

Our God, and God of the generations before us —
may a memory of us ascend and come before You.
May it be heard and seen by You,
winning Your favor and reaching Your awareness —
together with the memory of our ancestors,
the memory of Your sacred city, Jerusalem,
and the memory of Your people, the family of Israel.
May we be remembered —
for safety, well-being, and favor,
for love and compassion,
for life, and for peace —
on this Day of Atonement.

LIKE SMOKE above the altar
may a memory of us ascend and come before You.

As Israel once came to You with offerings from the flock,
so we bring to You the offerings of our mouth—
not lip service but heartfelt prayer.

So the prophet taught:
"Return, O Israel, to Adonai your God,
for you have fallen because of your sin.
Take words with you
and return to Adonai."

Accept the words we set before You,
awkward and imperfect as they are:
our hesitant questions, our corrosive doubts.
Accept, too, our silences:
our thoughts that rise in the stillness,
our faith that coheres for a fragile instant—
then dissipates
like smoke above the altar.

MAY A MEMORY OF US ASCEND (*facing page*). The traditional version of this prayer includes five mentions of Israel's remembrance (*zichron*). Some commentators link this to a verse in the Torah (Numbers 8:19) in which God mentions the Israelites five times. Such repetition, they said, is a sign of love, for all of us take pleasure in mentioning the name of a person we love. For our Sages, the repeated mention of the Israelites was a reassuring sign that God indeed lovingly remembers our people and will soon redeem them.

RETURN, O ISRAEL, Hosea 14:2.

זָכְרֵנוּ, יְיָ אֱלֹהֵינוּ, בּוֹ לְטוֹבָה. אָמֵן.
וּפָקְדֵנוּ בוֹ לִבְרָכָה. אָמֵן.
וְהוֹשִׁיעֵנוּ בוֹ לְחַיִּים. אָמֵן.

Zochreinu, Adonai Eloheinu, bo l'tovah. Amen.
Ufokdeinu vo livrachah. Amen.
V'hoshi·einu vo l'chayim. Amen.

Eternal our God,
remember us, *Amen*
be mindful of us, *Amen*
and redeem us
for a life of goodness and blessing. *Amen*

וּבִדְבַר יְשׁוּעָה וְרַחֲמִים חוּס וְחָנֵּנוּ,
וְרַחֵם עָלֵינוּ וְהוֹשִׁיעֵנוּ,
כִּי אֵלֶיךָ עֵינֵינוּ,
כִּי אֵל מֶלֶךְ חַנּוּן וְרַחוּם אָתָּה.

Uvidvar y'shuah v'rachamim chus v'choneinu;
v'racheim aleinu v'hoshi·einu —
ki eilecha eineinu;
ki El melech chanun v'rachum atah.

Favor us with words of deliverance and mercy.
Show us the depth of Your care.
God, we await Your redemption,
for You reign with grace and compassion.

YOU REIGN WITH GRACE AND COMPASSION אֵל מֶלֶךְ חַנּוּן וְרַחוּם אָתָּה. The Hebrew description of God as *melech chanun v'rachum* (literally "gracious and compassionate ruler") conveys an unusual combination of power and restraint. The image is of one who uses power gently, sensitively, and generously, or who employs power in the service of kindness and mercy. The Torah devotes much attention to instructing those who enjoy social power or privilege — the wealthy, employers, those in the prime of life, those who are blessed with extended kinship networks and intact families — in how to care for the vulnerable: the poor, day laborers, the frail elderly, widows, orphans, and strangers. Thus, the idea of a God who unites infinite power with infinite compassion provides inspiration for human beings and societies that seek to avoid the abuse of power.

They Said Redemption Would Come

הֵם אָמְרוּ שֶׁתָּבוֹא הַגְּאֻלָּה רַק כְּשֶׁאִישׁ
כְּבָר לֹא יְצַפֶּה לָהּ,
וְלַיְלָה תָּמִים יָשְׁבוּ עֵרִים בְּפִתְחֵי חֲנֻיּוֹת וּבָתִּים
וְלֹא צִפּוּ לִגְאֻלָּה
וּכְשֶׁעָלָה הַשַּׁחַר הָיוּ דְּמָעוֹת מִתְגַּלְגְּלוֹת מִכָּל הַגַּגּוֹת.

They said redemption would come only when no one's
expecting it anymore,
and one night they sat silent and awake at the thresholds
of their stores and homes and didn't expect redemption
and when dawn rose there were tears rolling down from
all the rooftops

In the Time of Redemption

The Sages and the prophets did not yearn for the messianic time in order to have dominion over the entire world, to rule over the gentiles, to be exalted by the nations, or to eat, drink, and celebrate. Rather, they desired to be free from oppression or disturbance, so that they might immerse themselves in Torah and wisdom and thus merit the world-to-come. . . . In that era, there will be neither famine nor war, envy nor competition—for goodness will flow in abundance, and all delights will be freely available as dust of the earth. The entire world will be occupied solely in seeking to know God . . . as Scripture says, *The earth shall be full of the knowledge of God as water covers the sea.*

Let this be my prayer for personal redemption:
uninterrupted time to breathe and think;
time to ask myself the purpose of all my frantic striving;
time to bask in the radiance of what is.

THEY SAID REDEMPTION WOULD COME. By Rivka Miriam (b. 1952).

THE SAGES AND THE PROPHETS . . . AS WATER COVERS THE SEA. By Rabbi Moses Maimonides (1135–1204). A rationalist, Maimonides taught that the messianic age would not require supernatural miracles that violate the natural order. For him, the essence of the messianic time was the absence of political oppression and economic need, allowing for uninterrupted Torah study. Thus human consciousness would rise to a higher level: the intellectual apprehension of God, which he considered the highest good.

THE EARTH SHALL BE FULL, Isaiah 11:9.

כַּוָּנָה
Kavanah
אָבוֹת וְאִמָּהוֹת
Avot v'Imahot
גְּבוּרוֹת
G'vurot
קְדֻשַּׁת הַשֵּׁם
K'dushat HaShem
קְדֻשַּׁת הַיּוֹם
K'dushat HaYom
עֲבוֹדָה
Avodah
הוֹדָאָה
Hodaah
שָׁלוֹם
Shalom
תְּפִלַּת הַלֵּב
T'filat HaLev

אֱלֹהֵינוּ וֵאלֹהֵי אֲבוֹתֵינוּ וְאִמּוֹתֵינוּ,
מְחַל
לַעֲוֹנוֹתֵינוּ בְּיוֹם
[הַשַּׁבָּת הַזֶּה וּבְיוֹם]
הַכִּפּוּרִים הַזֶּה.
מְחֵה וְהַעֲבֵר פְּשָׁעֵינוּ וְחַטֹּאתֵינוּ
מִנֶּגֶד עֵינֶיךָ, כָּאָמוּר:
אָנֹכִי אָנֹכִי הוּא מֹחֶה פְשָׁעֶיךָ
לְמַעֲנִי,
וְחַטֹּאתֶיךָ לֹא אֶזְכֹּר.
וְנֶאֱמַר: מָחִיתִי כָעָב פְּשָׁעֶיךָ,
וְכֶעָנָן חַטֹּאתֶיךָ,
שׁוּבָה אֵלַי כִּי גְאַלְתִּיךָ.
וְנֶאֱמַר: כִּי־בַיּוֹם הַזֶּה יְכַפֵּר
עֲלֵיכֶם לְטַהֵר אֶתְכֶם,
מִכֹּל חַטֹּאתֵיכֶם לִפְנֵי יְיָ תִּטְהָרוּ.

Eloheinu v'Elohei avoteinu v'imoteinu,
m'chal
laavonoteinu b'Yom
[haShabbat hazeh uvYom]
HaKippurim hazeh.
M'cheih v'haaveir p'sha·einu v'chatoteinu
mineged einecha, kaamur:
"Anochi, anochi hu mocheh f'sha·echa
l'maani;
v'chatotecha lo ezkor."
V'ne·emar: "Machiti kaav p'sha·echa,
v'che·anan chatotecha —
shuvah eilai, ki g'alticha."
V'ne·emar: "Ki-vayom hazeh y'chapeir
aleichem l'taheir et·chem;
mikol chatoteichem lifnei Adonai tit·haru."

Our God and God of our forebears,
pardon
our failings on [this day of Shabbat, and] this Day of Atonement;
erase our misdeeds; see beyond our defiance.

For Isaiah said in Your name: "It is I, I alone
who wipe away your defiant acts — this is My essence.
I shall pay no heed to your errors."

And the prophet said: "As a cloud fades away, as mist dissolves into air,
so your wrongs and mistakes shall be gone; I will wipe them away —
come back to Me, that I may redeem you."

As You said to Moses: "For on this day atonement shall be made for you
to purify you from all your wrongs.
And pure you shall be in the presence of Adonai."

IT IS I אָנֹכִי אָנֹכִי, Isaiah 43:25.
AS A CLOUD FADES AWAY מָחִיתִי כָעָב, Isaiah 44:22.
FOR ON THIS DAY כִּי־בַיּוֹם הַזֶּה, Leviticus 16:30.

The Promise of Your Forgiveness

Adonai, all-merciful and gracious, on this night of *Kol Nidrei* we are filled with confidence and faith as we awaken to the promise of Your forgiveness. Like a generous father, You accept our weakness; like a kind and caring mother, You see beyond our faults—for Your desire to pardon the penitent is true and enduring. And yet, how can we come close to You, near enough to know Your living fountain of love? You are near when we banish hatred from our hearts. You are near when we cast out cruelty and spite. You are the Source of Life—Mother and Father of all that lives. But we cannot call You our parent unless we first treat all people as our brothers and sisters—asking forgiveness from those we have hurt, bringing healing to the places where we have done harm.

God, we thank You for signs of Your grace and love. We thank You for courage and inspiration in the work of *tikkun midot*—the task of shaping our lives for the better. You have shown us that repentance requires not ceremony but return to the path of duty, sincerity, and truth; not offerings at the altar but a mending of ways; not strength beyond human powers but a belief in the ability to change. We do not trust in miracles to rid the world of madness and evil, but in a Supreme Wisdom that guides our lives and deeds toward goodness. May our prayers be pleasing in Your sight. May our actions be acceptable before You. May our journey of atonement be a source of joy and gladness.

Out of the depths I call You—
hear me in this darkness
as I cry for mercy.
I long for Your word; I wait for Your forgiveness.
You offer love; You free me from my sins.
I yearn for Your light, more eager than watchers for the morning.
Help me to know Your peace.

THE PROMISE OF YOUR FORGIVENESS. Inspired by Fanny Neuda (1819–1894), who published her book of prayers and meditations for Jewish women, *Stunden der Andacht* (Hours of Devotion), in 1855. It was, for many years, a best seller in the original German, as well as in Yiddish and English translations. In the book's preface, Neuda explains her motivation: "I have frequently felt powerful, inescapable urges to enter into dialogue with the sublime Spirit of the Universe." The prayer on this page is a contemporary adaptation of the 1866 translation by Rabbi Moritz Mayer (1821–1867).

OUT OF THE DEPTHS. Based on Psalm 130, traditionally recited on Yom Kippur.

אֱלֹהֵינוּ וֵאלֹהֵי אֲבוֹתֵינוּ וְאִמּוֹתֵינוּ,
[רְצֵה בִמְנוּחָתֵנוּ,]
קַדְּשֵׁנוּ בְּמִצְוֹתֶיךָ
וְתֵן חֶלְקֵנוּ בְּתוֹרָתֶךָ.
שַׂבְּעֵנוּ מִטּוּבֶךָ
וְשַׂמְּחֵנוּ בִּישׁוּעָתֶךָ.
[וְהַנְחִילֵנוּ, יְיָ אֱלֹהֵינוּ,
בְּאַהֲבָה וּבְרָצוֹן שַׁבַּת קָדְשֶׁךָ,
וְיָנוּחוּ בָהּ יִשְׂרָאֵל,
מְקַדְּשֵׁי שְׁמֶךָ.]

Eloheinu v'Elohei avoteinu v'imoteinu,
[r'tzeih vimnuchateinu,]
kad'sheinu b'mitzvotecha;
v'tein chelkeinu b'Toratecha.
Sab'einu mituvecha;
v'sam'cheinu bishuatecha.
[V'hanchileinu, Adonai Eloheinu,
b'ahavah uvratzon Shabbat kodshecha;
v'yanuchu vah Yisrael,
m'kad'shei sh'mecha.]

God who is ours
and God of our fathers and mothers:
[may our rest on this Shabbat bring You pleasure;]
lead us to holiness through Your mitzvot;
and may each of us find a portion of Torah that is ours.
You bestow such goodness — teach us to be satisfied,
and to know the joy of Your salvation.
[Let Your holy Shabbat be our heritage,
embraced freely and with love;
and may all our people bring holiness to Your name
by resting on this day.]

כַּוָּנָה *Kavanah*
אָבוֹת וְאִמָּהוֹת *Avot v'Imahot*
גְּבוּרוֹת *G'vurot*
קְדֻשַּׁת הַשֵּׁם *K'dushat HaShem*
קְדֻשַּׁת הַיּוֹם *K'dushat HaYom*
עֲבוֹדָה *Avodah*
הוֹדָאָה *Hodaah*
שָׁלוֹם *Shalom*
תְּפִלַּת הַלֵּב *T'filat HaLev*

GOD WHO IS OURS אֱלֹהֵינוּ. This prayer, known as *K'dushat HaYom* (The Day's Holiness), is added to *HaT'filah* for Shabbat and festivals, replacing the prayers of petition recited at this point on weekdays. On holy days, we focus not on our needs and desires but on spiritual growth, celebration, and appreciation.

EMBRACED FREELY AND WITH LOVE בְּאַהֲבָה וּבְרָצוֹן. The traditional prayer says that God gave Shabbat to the Jewish people as an inheritance "with love and favor" (*b'ahavah uvratzon*). The translation above emphasizes the human dimension: our heritage offers us Shabbat, an extraordinary gift to be "embraced freely and with love." The phrase *b'ahavah* (with love) often accompanies mention of Shabbat in the liturgy, suggesting that the Sabbath signifies the bond of love between God and Israel. The day of rest is a gift bestowed in love; this prayer awakens us to the prospect of embracing this weekly gift "freely and with love" — and sharing it with future generations.

A BUTTERFLY comes and stays on a leaf—a leaf much warmed by the sun—and shuts his wings. In a minute he opens them, shuts them again, half wheels round, and by-and-by—just when he chooses, and not before—floats away. The flowers open, and remain open for hours, to the sun. Hastelessness is the only word one can make up to describe it; there is much rest, but no haste. Each moment, as with the greenfinches, is so full of life that it seems so long and so sufficient in itself. Not only the days, but life itself lengthens in summer. I would spread abroad my arms and gather more of it to me, could I do so.

WHATEVER IS FORESEEN in joy
Must be lived out from day to day.
Vision held open in the dark
By our ten thousand days of work.
Harvest will fill the barn; for that
The hand must ache, the face must sweat.

And yet no leaf or grain is filled
By work of ours; the field is tilled
And left to grace. That we may reap,
Great work is done while we're asleep.
When we work well, a Sabbath mood
Rests on our day, and finds it good.

WAKING in the morning
Time smiles in my hand.
This dawn
Lasts all day.

A BUTTERFLY COMES. By Richard Jefferies (1848–1887).
WHATEVER IS FORESEEN. By Wendell Berry (b. 1934).
WAKING IN THE MORNING. By Deena Metzger (b. 1936).

וְטַהֵר לִבֵּנוּ לְעָבְדְּךָ בֶּאֱמֶת,	*V'taheir libeinu l'ovd'cha be·emet —*
כִּי אַתָּה סָלְחָן לְיִשְׂרָאֵל,	*ki atah solchan l'Yisrael,*
וּמָחֳלָן לְשִׁבְטֵי יְשֻׁרוּן	*umocholan l'shivtei Y'shurun*
בְּכָל דּוֹר וָדוֹר,	*b'chol dor vador;*
וּמִבַּלְעָדֶיךָ אֵין לָנוּ מֶלֶךְ מוֹחֵל	*umibaladecha ein lanu melech mocheil*
וְסוֹלֵחַ אֶלָּא אָתָּה.	*v'solei·ach ela atah.*

Help us to serve you truly, with purity of heart —
for You are the Forgiver of Israel,
in every generation granting pardon to the tribes of Yeshurun.
We have no God of forgiveness and pardon but You, You alone.

בָּרוּךְ אַתָּה, יְיָ,	*Baruch atah, Adonai —*
מֶלֶךְ מוֹחֵל וְסוֹלֵחַ לַעֲוֹנוֹתֵינוּ	*melech mocheil v'solei·ach laavonoteinu*
וְלַעֲוֹנוֹת עַמּוֹ בֵּית יִשְׂרָאֵל,	*v'laavonot amo beit Yisrael,*
וּמַעֲבִיר אַשְׁמוֹתֵינוּ בְּכָל שָׁנָה	*umaavir ashmoteinu b'chol shanah*
וְשָׁנָה,	*v'shanah —*
מֶלֶךְ עַל כָּל הָאָרֶץ,	*melech al kol haaretz,*
מְקַדֵּשׁ [הַשַּׁבָּת וְ] יִשְׂרָאֵל	*m'kadeish [haShabbat v'] Yisrael*
וְיוֹם הַכִּפּוּרִים.	*v'Yom HaKippurim.*

You are blessed, Adonai, Sovereign who forgives our failings
and pardons the failings of Your people, the House of Israel.
You banish our guilt, from year to year,
You reign in majesty over all the earth;
You sanctify [Shabbat,] the people Israel and the Day of Atonement.

כַּוָּנָה *Kavanah*
אָבוֹת וְאִמָּהוֹת *Avot v'Imahot*
גְּבוּרוֹת *G'vurot*
קְדֻשַּׁת הַשֵּׁם *K'dushat HaShem*
קְדֻשַּׁת הַיּוֹם *K'dushat HaYom*
עֲבוֹדָה *Avodah*
הוֹדָאָה *Hodaah*
שָׁלוֹם *Shalom*
תְּפִלַּת הַלֵּב *T'filat HaLev*

THE TRIBES OF YESHURUN שִׁבְטֵי יְשֻׁרוּן. Yeshurun (Hebrew: *Y'shurun*) is a name for the Jewish people, derived from *yashar*, meaning "upright; straight and true." While the name *Yisrael* ("one who struggles with God") focuses on the theological wrestling and questioning that are inherent in Jewish identity, the name *Y'shurun* emphasizes the ethical obligations that are central to being a Jew. In Isaiah 44:2, *Y'shurun* appears in parallel with the name *Yaakov* (Jacob). The parallelism implies a kind of spiritual evolution in which *Yaakov* ("the supplanter"), a deceitful and self-interested person, may grow into *Y'shurun*, a principled, morally upright individual.

Pure heart
Clear mind
Generous vision
Gentle words
The courage to say yes
The strength to say no
Steadiness in Your work
Purpose every day

I set You before me always;
Mindful of You, may I never be shaken.

On this night of Atonement, grant us, God,
A sense of Your presence, as we call upon Your name.

Speak Your hopeful message to each yearning heart;
And answer the worthy petitions of each searching soul.

Purify and strengthen our noble strivings;
And cleanse us of all our unworthy desires.

Join us together in fellowship and in love;
And grant us the joy which comes from enriching other lives.

Help us to be loyal to the heritage we share;
Draw us near to Torah in wisdom and in faith.

Strengthen our devotion to our people everywhere;
Keep alive our faith in righteousness and truth.

Bless us with hopes to uplift our daily lives;
And keep steadfast our courage and our resolve at all times.

On this night of Atonement, help us, God,
To be worthy of Your presence, as we call upon Your name.

I set You, Psalm 16:8.
On this night. By Rabbi Sidney Greenberg (1917–2003) and Rabbi Jonathan D. Levine (b. 1944).

כַּוָּנָה
Kavanah
אָבוֹת וְאִמָּהוֹת
Avot v'Imahot
גְּבוּרוֹת
G'vurot
קְדֻשַּׁת הַשֵּׁם
K'dushat HaShem
קְדֻשַּׁת הַיּוֹם
K'dushat HaYom
עֲבוֹדָה
Avodah
הוֹדָאָה
Hodaah
שָׁלוֹם
Shalom
תְּפִלַּת הַלֵּב
T'filat HaLev

רְצֵה, יְיָ אֱלֹהֵינוּ, בְּעַמְּךָ יִשְׂרָאֵל.
וּתְפִלָּתָם בְּאַהֲבָה תְקַבֵּל בְּרָצוֹן,
וּתְהִי לְרָצוֹן תָּמִיד עֲבוֹדַת
יִשְׂרָאֵל עַמֶּךָ.
אֵל קָרוֹב לְכָל קֹרְאָיו,
פְּנֵה אֶל עֲבָדֶיךָ וְחָנֵּנוּ.
שְׁפֹךְ רוּחֲךָ עָלֵינוּ,
וְתֶחֱזֶינָה עֵינֵינוּ בְּשׁוּבְךָ לְצִיּוֹן
בְּרַחֲמִים.

R'tzeih, Adonai Eloheinu, b'am'cha Yisrael.
Utfilatam b'ahavah t'kabeil b'ratzon,
ut·hi l'ratzon tamid avodat
Yisrael amecha.
El karov l'chol korav,
p'neih el avadecha v'choneinu.
Sh'foch ruchacha aleinu,
v'techezenah eineinu b'shuvcha l'Tziyon
b'rachamim.

Eternal, our God, Your people Israel yearns for Your favor.
Receive their prayer with loving acceptance,
and may You always desire Your people's worship.
Divine One, close to all who call upon You,
bring Your grace and presence near to those who serve You.
Pour forth Your spirit on us,
and may our eyes see Your merciful return to Zion.

בָּרוּךְ אַתָּה, יְיָ, הַמַּחֲזִיר שְׁכִינָתוֹ לְצִיּוֹן.
Baruch atah, Adonai, hamachazir Sh'chinato l'Tziyon.
Blessed are You whose Divine Presence is felt again in Zion.

RECEIVE THEIR PRAYER וּבִתְפִלָּתָם ... תְקַבֵּל. Known as the *Avodah* (literally "worship; service") blessing, this prayer sets forth the hope that God will lovingly accept both the Jewish people and our offering of worship, today and always. The traditional form of this blessing calls for the restoration of sacrificial offerings in the Jerusalem Temple; Reform prayer books speak instead of prayer — called by our Sages "the service of the heart." Both versions of the blessing conclude by calling to mind Zion, site of the ancient Temple and center of Jewish spiritual life. But what would it mean for God to "accept" our worship? Perhaps these words can help us be mindful of offering worthy prayers — heartfelt rather than superficial, inclusive rather than selfish in their concerns, appreciative and grateful as well as need-focused.

PRAYER is for the soul what food is for the body.

The strength we get from one meal lasts until the next;
so too, the blessings of a prayer last until we pray again.

The longer the pause between one prayer and the next,
the more we're mired in worldly pursuits,
in words that dim the purity of the soul, in speech that dulls its brightness.

When we pray we wash away all that clouds our vision
and satisfy our spirit's hunger for a higher calling.

Prayer gives the soul what food gives the body.

EVERY DAY I want to speak with you. And every day something more important
calls for my attention—the drugstore, the beauty products, the luggage

I need to buy for the trip.
Even now I can hardly sit here

among the falling piles of paper and clothing, the garbage trucks outside
already screeching and banging.

The mystics say you are as close as my own breath.
Why do I flee from you?

My days and nights pour through me like complaints
and become a story I forgot to tell.

Help me. Even as I write these words I am planning
to rise from the chair as soon as I finish this sentence.

PRAYER IS FOR THE SOUL. Based on a passage in the *Kuzari*, written ca. 1140 by the Spanish poet, philosopher, and physician Yehudah Halevi. The *Kuzari* is one of his most famous works, setting forth his defense of Rabbinic Judaism against attacks from philosophers, Christian and Muslim theologians, and Karaites. In this passage, Halevi explains that Jewish tradition prescribes three daily times for prayer: *Shacharit* (morning worship), *Minchah* (afternoon worship), and *Arvit* (evening worship). He draws from this an analogy between physical and spiritual sustenance; as a person needs three meals daily, so the human soul yearns for the nourishment of prayer in equal measure.

EVERY DAY. By Marie Howe (b. 1950).

כַּוָּנָה *Kavanah*
אָבוֹת וְאִמָּהוֹת *Avot v'Imahot*
גְּבוּרוֹת *G'vurot*
קְדֻשַּׁת הַשֵּׁם *K'dushat HaShem*
קְדֻשַּׁת הַיּוֹם *K'dushat HaYom*
עֲבוֹדָה *Avodah*
הוֹדָאָה *Hodaah*
שָׁלוֹם *Shalom*
תְּפִלַּת הַלֵּב *T'filat HaLev*

מוֹדִים אֲנַחְנוּ לָךְ,
שָׁאַתָּה הוּא יְיָ אֱלֹהֵינוּ וֵאלֹהֵי
אֲבוֹתֵינוּ וְאִמּוֹתֵינוּ לְעוֹלָם וָעֶד.
צוּר חַיֵּינוּ, מָגֵן יִשְׁעֵנוּ,
אַתָּה הוּא לְדוֹר וָדוֹר.
נוֹדֶה לְּךָ וּנְסַפֵּר תְּהִלָּתֶךָ:
עַל חַיֵּינוּ הַמְּסוּרִים בְּיָדֶךָ,
וְעַל נִשְׁמוֹתֵינוּ הַפְּקוּדוֹת לָךְ,
וְעַל נִסֶּיךָ שֶׁבְּכָל יוֹם עִמָּנוּ,
וְעַל נִפְלְאוֹתֶיךָ וְטוֹבוֹתֶיךָ שֶׁבְּכָל עֵת,
עֶרֶב וָבֹקֶר וְצָהֳרָיִם.
הַטּוֹב, כִּי לֹא כָלוּ רַחֲמֶיךָ,
וְהַמְרַחֵם, כִּי לֹא תַמּוּ חֲסָדֶיךָ,
מֵעוֹלָם קִוִּינוּ לָךְ.

Modim anachnu lach,
shaatah hu Adonai Eloheinu v'Elohei
avoteinu v'imoteinu l'olam va·ed.
Tzur chayeinu, magein yisheinu,
atah hu l'dor vador.
Nodeh l'cha unsapeir t'hilatecha:
al chayeinu ham'surim b'yadecha,
v'al nishmoteinu hap'kudot lach,
v'al nisecha sheb'chol yom imanu,
v'al nifl'otecha v'tovotecha sheb'chol eit,
erev vavoker v'tzohorayim.
Hatov — ki lo chalu rachamecha;
v'hamracheim — ki lo tamu chasadecha:
mei·olam kivinu lach.

God who is ours,
God of all generations,
to You we are grateful forever.

Rock and Protector of our lives,
Your saving power endures from age to age.

We thank You and tell the tale of Your praise:
Your power in our lives,
Your caring for our souls,
the constant miracle of Your kindness.

Morning, noon, and night
we call You Goodness — for Your compassion never ends;
we call You Mercy — for Your love has no limit;
we call You Hope, now and for all time.

WE ARE GRATEFUL FOREVER מוֹדִים אֲנַחְנוּ לָךְ . . . לְעוֹלָם וָעֶד. One of the concluding prayers of *HaT'filah*, the *Hodaah* (Thanksgiving) blessing calls us to awareness of the "constant miracles" that are with us every day. What is ever-present soon becomes commonplace, and its wonders are too often ignored. The Thanksgiving blessing reminds us that miracles need not be supernatural or extraordinary events. If we pay attention, the smallest details of our surroundings and the very regularity of nature's laws can evoke awe.

MORNING, NOON, AND NIGHT עֶרֶב וָבֹקֶר וְצָהֳרָיִם. These might also symbolize the seasons of human life, each of which has its own opportunities for gratitude.

It doesn't have to be
the blue iris, it could be
weeds in a vacant lot, or a few
small stones; just
pay attention, then patch

a few words together and don't try
to make them elaborate, this isn't
a contest but the doorway

into thanks, and a silence in which
another voice may speak.

Is it not by his high superfluousness we know
Our God? For to be equal a need
Is natural, animal, mineral: but to fling
Rainbows over the rain
And beauty above the moon, and secret rainbows
On the domes of deep sea-shells,
And make the necessary embrace of breeding
Beautiful also as fire,
Not even the weeds to multiply without blossom
Nor the birds without music:
There is the great humaneness at the heart of things,
The extravagant kindness, the fountain
Humanity can understand, and would flow likewise
If power and desire were perch-mates.

---

it doesn't. By Mary Oliver (b. 1935).

is it not. By Robinson Jeffers (1887–1962). Here the poet finds evidence of the Divine in what he calls "high superfluousness"—the fact that we experience the most mundane phenomena of this world as saturated with beauty far beyond what we might expect. Traces of this beauty, from the pearly iridescence of seashells to birdsong, flowering weeds, and the exquisite "fire" of human sexuality, testify to a "fountain" of "extravagant kindness" from which we drink every day. We, too, might emulate such free-flowing kindness, Jeffers notes poignantly, could we only unite "power and desire."

וְעַל כֻּלָּם יִתְבָּרַךְ וְיִתְרוֹמַם שִׁמְךָ,
מַלְכֵּנוּ, תָּמִיד לְעוֹלָם וָעֶד.

V'al kulam yitbarach v'yitromam shimcha,
Malkeinu, tamid l'olam va·ed.

וּכְתֹב לְחַיִּים טוֹבִים
כָּל בְּנֵי בְרִיתֶךָ.

Uchtov l'chayim tovim
kol b'nei v'ritecha.

וְכֹל הַחַיִּים יוֹדוּךָ סֶּלָה,
וִיהַלְלוּ אֶת שִׁמְךָ בֶּאֱמֶת,
הָאֵל יְשׁוּעָתֵנוּ וְעֶזְרָתֵנוּ סֶלָה.

V'chol hachayim yoducha selah,
vihal'lu et shimcha be·emet —
haEl y'shuateinu v'ezrateinu selah.

And for all these gifts, God of majesty,
may Your name come to be blessed and praised —
our gratitude a daily offering until the end of time.

Inscribe Your covenant partners
for a life of goodness.

And may all life resound with gratitude and faith
in praise of Your name.
God, You free us and strengthen us.

בָּרוּךְ אַתָּה, יְיָ, הַטּוֹב שִׁמְךָ, וּלְךָ נָאֶה לְהוֹדוֹת.

Baruch atah, Adonai, hatov shimcha, ulcha na·eh l'hodot.

Blessed are You, Adonai, whose goodness
deserves thanks and praise.

כַּוָּנָה *Kavanah*
אָבוֹת וְאִמָּהוֹת *Avot v'Imahot*
גְּבוּרוֹת *G'vurot*
קְדֻשַּׁת הַשֵּׁם *K'dushat HaShem*
קְדֻשַּׁת הַיּוֹם *K'dushat HaYom*
עֲבוֹדָה *Avodah*
הוֹדָאָה *Hodaah*
שָׁלוֹם *Shalom*
תְּפִלַּת הַלֵּב *T'filat HaLev*

WHOSE GOODNESS DESERVES THANKS AND PRAISE הַטּוֹב שִׁמְךָ, וּלְךָ נָאֶה לְהוֹדוֹת. Both the Bible and the liturgy speak frequently of God's nearness. For example, in the *Avodah* prayer (page 72), we say "Divine One, close to all who call upon You"; likewise, Psalm 34:19 says "God is close to those who have a broken heart." These two verses suggest that those who are fearful, worried, or sad may sense God's presence in the act of reaching out for strength and comfort from a Power beyond themselves. But the *Hodaah* (Thanksgiving) prayer suggests a different view: by recognizing the endless, undeserved flow of goodness that we receive from the Source of life, we come closer to experiencing the Divine.

Focusing Prayer
God of All Generations
God's Powers
God's Holiness
The Day's Holiness
Our Offering
Thanksgiving
Peace
Prayer of the Heart

Permission

אֶת הַמִּלִּים שֶׁאָמַרְתִּי הַיּוֹם
לֹא בִּקַּשְׁתִּי מִלְּפָנֶיךָ
וְרָאִיתִי נוֹפִים לֹא שְׁאוּלִים מֵעִמְּךָ
וְהָאוֹטוֹבּוּס צָפוֹנָה הָלַךְ וְהִתְרַחֵק מִירוּשָׁלַיִם
וְעִם זֹאת הָיִיתִי בַּחֲצַר קָדְשְׁךָ
וְנִרְדַּמְתִּי עַל סַפְסַל־הַגַּן
וְכָל הַדְּבָרִים שֶׁאָמַרְתִּי הָיוּ שִׁמְךָ
וְכָל הַנּוֹפִים שֶׁרָאִיתִי – פֵּרוּשׁוֹ.

The words I said today
I did not request of You
I saw landscapes not borrowed from You
the bus to the north went more and more distant from Jerusalem
and even so I was in the courtyard of Your holiness
and I dozed on the garden bench
and all the words that I said were Your name
and all the landscapes I saw—its interpretation.

בָּרוּךְ אַתָּה, יְיָ, הַטּוֹב שִׁמְךָ, וּלְךָ נָאֶה לְהוֹדוֹת.

Baruch atah, Adonai, hatov shimcha, ulcha na·eh l'hodot.

Blessed are You, Adonai, whose goodness
deserves thanks and praise.

PERMISSION. Israeli poet Sivan Har-Shefi (b. 1978) describes a moment of religious revelation. A secular speaker declares that neither her own words nor the landscapes she has seen are of divine origin. Traveling far from the Holy City, she feels herself growing more distant from God. And then a sudden realization: throughout her journey, she has always been in God's presence. Even far from Jerusalem, she dwells, as it were, in the Temple "courtyard." She sees now that every word she has said expresses God's name (in which, according to tradition, God's essence is contained); and every view of the landscape is an "interpretation" of God's name. (David C. Jacobson, b. 1947; adapted)

The poem thus records an inner journey, from skepticism and religious alienation, to a mystic consciousness that the Divine pervades all things—as *Tikkunei Zohar* puts it, "No place is empty of God" (*leit atar panui minei*). This instant of ecstatic realization conveys something of the gratitude the author of the *Modim* prayer (*facing page*) might have felt: "May all life resound with gratitude and faith in praise of Your name."

כַּוָּנָה
Kavanah
אָבוֹת וְאִמָּהוֹת
Avot v'Imahot
גְבוּרוֹת
G'vurot
קְדֻשַּׁת הַשֵּׁם
K'dushat HaShem
קְדֻשַּׁת הַיּוֹם
K'dushat HaYom
עֲבוֹדָה
Avodah
הוֹדָאָה
Hodaah
שָׁלוֹם
Shalom
תְּפִלַּת הַלֵּב
T'filat HaLev

שָׁלוֹם רָב עַל יִשְׂרָאֵל עַמְּךָ תָּשִׂים
לְעוֹלָם,
כִּי אַתָּה הוּא מֶלֶךְ אָדוֹן לְכָל הַשָּׁלוֹם,
וְטוֹב בְּעֵינֶיךָ לְבָרֵךְ אֶת עַמְּךָ
יִשְׂרָאֵל,
בְּכָל עֵת וּבְכָל שָׁעָה, בִּשְׁלוֹמֶךָ.

Shalom rav al Yisrael am'cha tasim
l'olam —
ki atah hu melech adon l'chol hashalom;
v'tov b'einecha l'vareich et am'cha
Yisrael,
b'chol eit uvchol shaah, bishlomecha.

בְּסֵפֶר חַיִּים, בְּרָכָה, וְשָׁלוֹם,
וּפַרְנָסָה טוֹבָה,
נִזָּכֵר וְנִכָּתֵב לְפָנֶיךָ,
אֲנַחְנוּ וְכָל עַמְּךָ בֵּית יִשְׂרָאֵל,
לְחַיִּים טוֹבִים וּלְשָׁלוֹם.

B'sefer chayim, b'rachah, v'shalom,
ufarnasah tovah,
nizacheir v'nikateiv l'fanecha,
anachnu, v'chol am'cha beit Yisrael,
l'chayim tovim ulshalom!

Peace — profound and lasting, all-embracing.
Peace — let this be Your gift to Israel, Your people.
In Your goodness, Author of peace, bless us and all people —
every season, every hour —
with the peace that is Yours to give.

Let us, and the whole family of Israel,
be remembered and inscribed in the Book of Life.
May it be a life of goodness, blessing, and prosperity!
May it be a life of peace!

בָּרוּךְ אַתָּה, יְיָ, עוֹשֵׂה הַשָּׁלוֹם.
Baruch atah, Adonai, oseih hashalom.
You are the Blessed One, the Eternal One, Source of shalom.

PEACE — PROFOUND AND LASTING שָׁלוֹם רָב. *Shalom Rav*, the prayer for peace, is the last of the seven blessings in *HaT'filah*. This placement suggests that peace is the culmination of all our prayers, the ultimate goal for which we strive. Rabbi Sheldon Lewis (b. 1941) writes that within Jewish tradition "there are more expressions lauding the virtues of peace than of any other single value." While some biblical images of God suggest a militant deity, the Rabbinic sages rejected such notions. Lewis explains, "Nowhere does one find militant, angry, warlike, or violent images of God held up as worthy of emulation. The sages carefully filtered divine actions on their way to a more compassionate understanding of God, and that evolving belief shaped what they asked of the Jewish people. The softer, gracious image of God became the model to which to aspire."

GRANT US PEACE, Your most precious gift,
O Eternal Source of peace,
and give us the will to proclaim its message
to all the peoples of the earth.

Bless our country,
that it may always be a stronghold of peace,
and its advocate among the nations.
May contentment reign within its borders,
health and happiness within its homes.
Strengthen the bonds of friendship
among the inhabitants of all lands,
and may the love of Your name
hallow every home and every heart.

Inscribe us in the book of life, blessing, and peace.
We praise You, O God, the Source of peace.

ETERNAL Source and Soul of peace—
send Your peace into the midst of *Am Yisrael*, Your people.
Let it heal our rifts and soothe the bitterness of intolerance.
Let it overcome distrust, isolation, and rivalry.
May Your peace flow in every stream of Judaism; and may it inspire solidarity,
uniting us as one people.

Let peace grow and increase, and let it shape the lives of all human beings.
Let there be nothing but peace! No hatred or jealousy,
no victories that bring suffering and loss to people and nations—
only love and peace: strong, profound, and true.

We yearn for love that knits us together; we yearn for the wisdom of community:
shared knowledge, empathy, and trust.
May the words that we speak and the meditations of our hearts
open pathways of truth and understanding.

ETERNAL SOURCE. Inspired by a prayer of Rabbi Nachman of Breslov (1772–1810).

אֱלֹהַי,	*Elohai:*
נְצֹר לְשׁוֹנִי מֵרָע,	*N'tzor l'shoni meira;*
וּשְׂפָתַי מִדַּבֵּר מִרְמָה.	*usfatai midabeir mirmah.*
וְלִמְקַלְלַי נַפְשִׁי תִדֹּם,	*V'limkal'lai nafshi tidom;*
וְנַפְשִׁי כֶּעָפָר לַכֹּל תִּהְיֶה.	*v'nafshi ke·afar lakol tiyeh.*
פְּתַח לִבִּי בְּתוֹרָתֶךָ,	*P'tach libi b'Toratecha;*
וּבְמִצְוֹתֶיךָ תִּרְדֹּף נַפְשִׁי.	*uvmitzvotecha tirdof nafshi.*
וְכָל הַחוֹשְׁבִים עָלַי רָעָה,	*V'chol hachoshvim alai raah —*
מְהֵרָה הָפֵר עֲצָתָם,	*m'heirah hafeir atzatam,*
וְקַלְקֵל מַחֲשַׁבְתָּם.	*v'kalkeil machashavtam.*
עֲשֵׂה לְמַעַן שְׁמֶךָ.	*Aseih l'maan sh'mecha.*
עֲשֵׂה לְמַעַן יְמִינֶךָ.	*Aseih l'maan y'minecha.*
עֲשֵׂה לְמַעַן קְדֻשָּׁתֶךָ.	*Aseih l'maan k'dushatecha.*
עֲשֵׂה לְמַעַן תּוֹרָתֶךָ.	*Aseih l'maan Toratecha.*
לְמַעַן יֵחָלְצוּן יְדִידֶיךָ,	*L'maan yeichal'tzun y'didecha,*
הוֹשִׁיעָה יְמִינְךָ וַעֲנֵנִי.	*hoshiah y'mincha vaaneini.*

My God:
Keep my tongue from doing harm, and my lips from lies and deceit.
Before those who wrong me with words, may silence be my practice.
Before all human beings, let humility be my stance.
Open my heart to Your Torah, that I may follow its sacred path of duty.
Shatter, at once, the malicious plans of those who would do me harm.
Act, for the sake of Your name.
Act, for the sake of Your shielding hand.
Act, for the sake of Your holiness.
Act, for the sake of Your Torah.
For the sake of those who love You — their rescue and safety —
let Your shielding hand be the answer to my prayer.

כַּוָּנָה *Kavanah*
אָבוֹת וְאִמָּהוֹת *Avot v'Imahot*
גְּבוּרוֹת *G'vurot*
קְדֻשַּׁת הַשֵּׁם *K'dushat HaShem*
קְדֻשַּׁת הַיּוֹם *K'dushat HaYom*
עֲבוֹדָה *Avodah*
הוֹדָאָה *Hodaah*
שָׁלוֹם *Shalom*
תְּפִלַּת הַלֵּב *T'filat HaLev*

MY GOD — KEEP אֱלֹהַי, נְצֹר, based on Psalm 34:14.

KEEP MY TONGUE FROM DOING HARM נְצֹר לְשׁוֹנִי מֵרָע. The Talmud (*B'rachot* 17a) records several personal prayers of the sages, which they recited after concluding *HaT'filah*. One such prayer, uttered by a 4th-century rabbi, Mar son of Ravina, has entered the liturgy, in somewhat modified form. In its concern for *lashon hara* (harmful speech), emphasis on honesty, self-discipline, humility, and openness to learning, the prayer is especially appropriate for the High Holy Day work of character improvement.

FOR THE SAKE OF . . . THEIR RESCUE לְמַעַן יֵחָלְצוּן, Psalm 60:7.

Focusing Prayer
God of All Generations
God's Powers
God's Holiness
The Day's Holiness
Our Offering
Thanksgiving
Peace
Prayer of the Heart

Yiyu l'ratzon imrei-fi	יִהְיוּ לְרָצוֹן אִמְרֵי־פִי
v'hegyon libi l'fanecha,	וְהֶגְיוֹן לִבִּי לְפָנֶיךָ,
Adonai, tzuri v'go·ali.	יְיָ, צוּרִי וְגֹאֲלִי.

May the words of my mouth
and the meditation of my heart
be acceptable to You, Soul of Eternity,
my Rock and my Redeemer.

Oseh shalom bimromav,	עֹשֶׂה שָׁלוֹם בִּמְרוֹמָיו,
hu yaaseh shalom aleinu,	הוּא יַעֲשֶׂה שָׁלוֹם עָלֵינוּ,
v'al kol Yisrael	וְעַל כָּל יִשְׂרָאֵל
v'al kol yoshvei teiveil.	וְעַל כָּל יוֹשְׁבֵי תֵבֵל.
V'imru: Amen.	וְאִמְרוּ: אָמֵן.

May the Maker of peace above make peace for us,
all Israel, and all who dwell on earth. *Amen.*

Prayers for healing are on pages 271–73 and 340.

MAY THE WORDS OF MY MOUTH יִהְיוּ לְרָצוֹן, Psalm 19:15. After the concluding meditation of Mar son of Ravina (*facing page*), it is appropriate for individuals to offer silent personal prayers.

MAY THE MAKER OF PEACE ABOVE. The Talmud (*Yoma* 53b) offers instructions on concluding *HaT'filah* in a reverent manner: "Rabbi Alexandri said in the name of Rabbi Joshua ben Levi: After praying one should take three steps backward and say *shalom* (peace, farewell)" — a reference to the words "May the Maker of peace above make peace for us (*Oseh shalom bimromav, hu yaaseh shalom aleinu*)." To conclude the time of "standing before God" in a respectful manner, some have the custom of bowing when saying these words — first to the left, then to the right, and finally toward the center. If we believe that we are always in God's presence, we might understand these physical movements as reminders to be aware of the Presence everywhere and at all times.

ALL WHO DWELL ON EARTH, Psalm 33:8. Although God's covenant with the people of Israel is central to the Bible, a universalistic message is also pervasive throughout: God is the Creator of all life (Genesis 1–2); therefore, God's love and care extend to all who dwell on earth. *Shalom* means "wholeness" — a prayer for peace is necessarily a prayer for the whole human family.

וִדּוּי זוּטָא
Vidui Zuta

וִדּוּי רַבָּה
Vidui Rabbah

וִדּוּי

Vidui · Confession

Vidui Zuta — The Short Confession

אֱלֹהֵינוּ וֵאלֹהֵי אֲבוֹתֵינוּ וְאִמּוֹתֵינוּ,	*Eloheinu v'Elohei avoteinu v'imoteinu,*
תָּבֹא לְפָנֶיךָ תְּפִלָּתֵנוּ,	*tavo l'fanecha t'filateinu;*
וְאַל תִּתְעַלַּם מִתְּחִנָּתֵנוּ.	*v'al titalam mit'chinateinu.*
אֲנַחְנוּ עַזֵּי פָנִים וּקְשֵׁי עֹרֶף	*Anachnu azei fanim ukshei oref*
לוֹמַר לְפָנֶיךָ,	*lomar l'fanecha,*
יְיָ אֱלֹהֵינוּ וֵאלֹהֵי אֲבוֹתֵינוּ	*Adonai Eloheinu v'Elohei avoteinu*
וְאִמּוֹתֵינוּ:	*v'imoteinu:*
צַדִּיקִים אֲנַחְנוּ וְלֹא חָטָאנוּ.	*Tzadikim anachnu, v'lo chatanu.*
אֲבָל אֲנַחְנוּ חָטָאנוּ.	*Aval anachnu chatanu.*

Our God and God of all generations, may our prayers reach Your presence.
And when we turn to You, do not be indifferent.
Adonai, we are arrogant and stubborn, claiming to be blameless and free of sin.
In truth, we have stumbled and strayed. We have done wrong.

אָשַׁמְנוּ, בָּגַדְנוּ, גָּזַלְנוּ, דִּבַּרְנוּ דֹפִי.	*Ashamnu, bagadnu, gazalnu, dibarnu dofi.*
הֶעֱוִינוּ, וְהִרְשַׁעְנוּ, זַדְנוּ, חָמַסְנוּ,	*He·evinu, v'hirshanu, zadnu, chamasnu,*
טָפַלְנוּ שֶׁקֶר. יָעַצְנוּ רָע, כִּזַּבְנוּ,	*tafalnu sheker. Yaatznu ra, kizavnu,*
לַצְנוּ, מָרַדְנוּ, נִאַצְנוּ, סָרַרְנוּ, עָוִינוּ,	*latznu, maradnu, niatznu, sararnu, avinu,*
פָּשַׁעְנוּ, צָרַרְנוּ, קִשִּׁינוּ עֹרֶף. רָשַׁעְנוּ,	*pashanu, tzararnu, kishinu oref. Rashanu,*
שִׁחַתְנוּ, תִּעַבְנוּ, תָּעִינוּ, תִּעְתָּעְנוּ.	*shichatnu, tiavnu, ta·inu, titanu.*

Of these wrongs we are guilty:
We betray. We steal. We scorn. We act perversely.
We are cruel. We scheme. We are violent. We slander.
We devise evil. We lie. We ridicule. We disobey.
We abuse. We defy. We corrupt. We commit crimes.
We are hostile. We are stubborn. We are immoral. We kill.
We spoil. We go astray. We lead others astray.

Short Confession

Long Confession

Ashamnu

When I was young
And learned the alphabet,
Life was open to me
"A" was full of aspiration
"B" was for beauty; "C" for confidence
And "D" for dreams
And so on through the list—no fewer than twenty-six
opportunities, twenty-six possibilities.
And yet I fear that with the passage of time,
I've squandered them, creating instead
"A"s of apathy, "B"s of brusqueness, and "C"s of coarseness.
Help me, then, to return to that innocence.
Let the letters be letters once again,
And let them rise to the heavens
And form into the words
That You know I wish to say.

OF THESE WRONGS WE ARE GUILTY (*facing page*). Why do we confess to wrongs we have not personally committed? The 16th-century mystic Rabbi Isaac Luria teaches that the people of Israel may be likened to a body of which every Jew is a living part. The vitality of the whole depends upon the health of every organ and limb. That is how deeply we are connected to one another. Therefore, each individual sin inflicts damage on the whole organism, and all of us share responsibility for healing the body of Israel.

ASHAMNU. By Rabbi Alan Cook (b. 1970).

AND LEARNED THE ALPHABET. The confessions that are structured as alphabetical acrostics are intended to express, through their A to Z completeness, the totality of the congregation's sins. They do not replace our own personal confessions; rather, they remind us to expand upon them, as we aim for a complete recollection of our wrongful acts—an effort that Rabbi Moses Maimonides (1135–1204) calls praiseworthy (*Hilchot T'shuvah* 1.1).

וִדּוּי זוּטָא
Vidui Zuta

וִדּוּי רַבָּה
Vidui Rabbah

סַרְנוּ מִמִּצְוֹתֶֽיךָ וּמִמִּשְׁפָּטֶֽיךָ
הַטּוֹבִים, וְלֹא שָֽׁוָה לָֽנוּ.
וְאַתָּה צַדִּיק עַל כָּל הַבָּא עָלֵֽינוּ,
כִּי אֱמֶת עָשִֽׂיתָ, וַאֲנַֽחְנוּ הִרְשָֽׁעְנוּ.
מַה נֹּאמַר לְפָנֶֽיךָ, יוֹשֵׁב מָרוֹם,
וּמַה נְּסַפֵּר לְפָנֶֽיךָ, שׁוֹכֵן שְׁחָקִים.
הֲלֹא כָּל הַנִּסְתָּרוֹת וְהַנִּגְלוֹת
אַתָּה יוֹדֵֽעַ.

Sarnu mimitzvotecha umimishpatecha
hatovim, v'lo shavah-lanu.
V'atah tzadik al kol haba aleinu,
ki emet asita, vaanachnu hirshanu.
Mah nomar l'fanecha, yosheiv marom?
Umah n'sapeir l'fanecha, shochein sh'chakim?
Halo kol hanistarot v'haniglot
atah yodei·a.

Our turning away from Your mitzvot and laws of goodness is a hollow pursuit.
You are just, concerning all that happens in our lives.
Your way is the way of truth, while ours leads to error.
What can we say to You whose existence is beyond time and space?
What words of ours can reach Your realm
beyond the clouds, beyond heaven itself?
Every hidden mystery, every revelation — surely, You know them all.

אַתָּה יוֹדֵֽעַ רָזֵי עוֹלָם,
וְתַֽעֲלוּמוֹת סִתְרֵי כָּל חָי.
אַתָּה חוֹפֵשׂ כָּל־חַדְרֵי־בָֽטֶן,
וּבוֹחֵן כְּלָיוֹת וָלֵב.
אֵין דָּבָר נֶֽעְלָם מִמֶּֽךָּ,
וְאֵין נִסְתָּר מִנֶּֽגֶד עֵינֶֽיךָ.
וּבְכֵן יְהִי רָצוֹן מִלְּפָנֶֽיךָ,
יְיָ אֱלֹהֵֽינוּ וֵאלֹהֵי אֲבוֹתֵֽינוּ
וְאִמּוֹתֵֽינוּ:
שֶׁתִּסְלַח לָֽנוּ עַל כָּל חַטֹּאתֵֽינוּ,
וְתִמְחַל לָֽנוּ עַל כָּל עֲוֹנוֹתֵֽינוּ,
וּתְכַפֵּר לָֽנוּ עַל כָּל פְּשָׁעֵֽינוּ.

Atah yodei·a razei olam;
v'taalumot sitrei kol chai.
Atah chofeis kol-chadrei-vaten;
uvochein k'layot valev.
Ein davar ne·elam mimeka;
v'ein nistar mineged einecha.
Uvchein y'hi ratzon mil'fanecha,
Adonai Eloheinu v'Elohei avoteinu
v'imoteinu:
shetislach lanu al kol chatoteinu,
v'timchal lanu al kol avonoteinu,
ut·chapeir lanu al kol p'sha·einu.

You know the secrets of the universe and the secrets of the human heart.
You know and understand us, for You examine our inner lives.
Nothing is concealed from You, nothing hidden from Your sight.
Eternal One, our God and God of our ancestors,
we pray that this be Your will: forgive all our wrongs,
pardon us for every act of injustice, help us atone for all our moral failures.

Study Text on T'shuvah

Resh Lakish said: "Great is repentance, for it transforms one's deliberate sins into merits" (Talmud, *Yoma* 86b). In general, we think of repentance as a way of achieving expiation for the wrongs we have done. But Resh Lakish's teaching points us in a new and surprising direction.... The focus is not on changing the past, but on defining a new direction for the future. For *t'shuvah*, after all, is ultimately about changing ourselves, not only clearing our record of past deeds that we are now ashamed of. Through the process of *t'shuvah* we evolve morally, becoming the sort of people who can no longer conceive of falling back into the old patterns of misconduct that characterized our past. But how did this transformation occur if not through the examination of that very misconduct? Transgressions can become the springboard for tremendous moral growth, if only we do the hard work of *t'shuvah* that enables us to learn from our mistakes.

In this way, repentance enables us to turn our moral liabilities into assets. Rabbi Soloveitchik captures the spiritual dynamic of this process:

> The years of sin are transformed into powerful impulsive forces which propel the sinner toward God. Sin is not to be forgotten, blotted out or cast into the depths of the sea. On the contrary, sin has to be remembered. It is the memory of sin that releases the power within the inner depths of the soul of the penitent to do greater things than ever before. The energy of sin can be used to bring one to new heights.

It would be preposterous if an accountant suggested that a debit was really a credit. But what is impossible on a financial balance sheet is eminently doable in the context of soul reckoning. Indeed the very goal of *t'shuvah* is to transform the sins of the past into the roots of a new life. In a profound sense, repentance does turn our vices into virtues.

—Louis Newman (b. 1956)

RESH LAKISH SAID. This Talmudic teaching, as interpreted by Rabbi Joseph Soloveitchik (1903–1993), shows us the possibility of elevating past misconduct into the inspiration for a new and better life. The process of *t'shuvah* helps us understand the roots of our wrongdoing, perceive the damage we have done, and address the character flaws that led us to sin, thus freeing us to pursue goodness with renewed vigor. Soloveitchik argues, in effect, that those who have genuinely engaged in *t'shuvah* will live with more integrity and moral strength than they did before the sin.

וִדּוּי זוּטָא
Vidui Zuta

וִדּוּי רַבָּה
Vidui Rabbah

Vidui Rabbah — The Long Confession

For these sins, our God, we ask forgiveness:

Al cheit shechatanu l'fanecha	עַל חֵטְא שֶׁחָטָאנוּ לְפָנֶיךָ
b'zadon uvishgagah;	בְּזָדוֹן וּבִשְׁגָגָה,
v'al cheit shechatanu l'fanecha	וְעַל חֵטְא שֶׁחָטָאנוּ לְפָנֶיךָ
b'dibur peh.	בְּדִבּוּר פֶּה.

The ways we have wronged You deliberately and by mistake;
and harm we have caused in Your world through the words of our mouths.

Al cheit shechatanu l'fanecha	עַל חֵטְא שֶׁחָטָאנוּ לְפָנֶיךָ
b'imutz halev;	בְּאִמּוּץ הַלֵּב,
v'al cheit shechatanu l'fanecha	וְעַל חֵטְא שֶׁחָטָאנוּ לְפָנֶיךָ
b'tifshut peh.	בְּטִפְשׁוּת פֶּה.

The ways we have wronged You by hardening our hearts;
and harm we have caused in Your world through careless speech.

Al cheit shechatanu l'fanecha	עַל חֵטְא שֶׁחָטָאנוּ לְפָנֶיךָ
b'chachash uvchazav;	בְּכַחַשׁ וּבְכָזָב,
v'al cheit shechatanu l'fanecha	וְעַל חֵטְא שֶׁחָטָאנוּ לְפָנֶיךָ
birchilut.	בִּרְכִילוּת.

The ways we have wronged You through lies and deceit;
and harm we have caused in Your world through gossip and rumor.

FOR THESE SINS. As each harmful act is mentioned, both here and in the Short Confession (*Ashamnu*, page 82), some worshipers gently strike their hearts with the right hand. The Midrash identifies this not as an act of self-punishment but as a way of identifying the heart (that is, desire and impulse) as the source of sin, taking personal responsibility, and showing remorse (*Ecclesiastes Rabbah* 7.9). Rabbi Israel Meir Kagan (1838–1933), known as the Chofetz Chayim, taught: "God does not forgive us when we strike our hearts; rather, we are forgiven when our heart strikes us — that is, when we feel the pangs of conscience for our wrongdoing."

Short Confession

Long Confession

עַל חֵטְא שֶׁחָטָאנוּ לְפָנֶיךָ
בִּפְלִילוּת,
וְעַל חֵטְא שֶׁחָטָאנוּ לְפָנֶיךָ
בְּזִלְזוּל הוֹרִים וּמוֹרִים.

Al cheit shechatanu l'fanecha
biflilut;
v'al cheit shechatanu l'fanecha
b'zilzul horim umorim.

The ways we have wronged You by judging others unfairly;
and harm we have caused in Your world through disrespect to parents and teachers.

עַל חֵטְא שֶׁחָטָאנוּ לְפָנֶיךָ
בְּוִדּוּי פֶּה,
וְעַל חֵטְא שֶׁחָטָאנוּ לְפָנֶיךָ
בְּהוֹנָאַת רֵעַ.

Al cheit shechatanu l'fanecha
b'vidui peh;
v'al cheit shechatanu l'fanecha
b'honaat rei·a.

The ways we have wronged You through insincere apologies;
and harm we have caused in Your world by mistreating a friend or neighbor.

עַל חֵטְא שֶׁחָטָאנוּ לְפָנֶיךָ
בְּחֹזֶק יָד,
וְעַל חֵטְא שֶׁחָטָאנוּ לְפָנֶיךָ
בְּמַשָּׂא וּבְמַתָּן.

Al cheit shechatanu l'fanecha
b'chozek yad,
v'al cheit shechatanu l'fanecha
b'masa uvmatan.

The ways we have wronged You through violence and abuse;
and harm we have caused in Your world through dishonesty in business.

וְעַל כֻּלָּם, אֱלוֹהַּ סְלִיחוֹת,
סְלַח לָנוּ, מְחַל לָנוּ, כַּפֶּר־לָנוּ.

V'al kulam, Elo·ah s'lichot,
s'lach lanu, m'chal lanu, kaper-lanu.

For all these failures of judgment and will, God of forgiveness —
forgive us, pardon us, lead us to atonement.

THROUGH VIOLENCE AND ABUSE בְּחֹזֶק יָד. Such acts need not involve bodily harm. "Force may also be used in the market and with regard to people's money or property. Withholding by force that which belongs to another or withholding wages due, misusing trust funds or clients' investment monies, abusing charitable funds — all these are considered to be forms of violence." (Meir Tamari, b. 1927; adapted)

וִדּוּי זוּטָא
Vidui Zuta

וִדּוּי רַבָּה
Vidui Rabbah

עַל חֵטְא שֶׁחָטָאנוּ לְפָנֶיךָ
בַּגָּלוּי וּבַסָּתֶר,
וְעַל חֵטְא שֶׁחָטָאנוּ לְפָנֶיךָ
בִּפְרִיקַת עֹל.

Al cheit shechatanu l'fanecha
bagalui uvasater;
v'al cheit shechatanu l'fanecha
bifrikat ol.

The ways we have wronged You openly and secretly;
and harm we have caused in Your world by losing self-control.

עַל חֵטְא שֶׁחָטָאנוּ לְפָנֶיךָ
בְּגִלּוּי עֲרָיוֹת,
וְעַל חֵטְא שֶׁחָטָאנוּ לְפָנֶיךָ
בְּמַאֲכָל וּבְמִשְׁתֶּה.

Al cheit shechatanu l'fanecha
b'gilui arayot;
v'al cheit shechatanu l'fanecha
b'maachal uvmishteh.

The ways we have wronged You through sexual immorality;
and harm we have caused in Your world through consumption of food and drink.

עַל חֵטְא שֶׁחָטָאנוּ לְפָנֶיךָ
בְּיֵצֶר הָרָע,
וְעַל חֵטְא שֶׁחָטָאנוּ לְפָנֶיךָ
בְּנֶשֶׁךְ וּבְמַרְבִּית.

Al cheit shechatanu l'fanecha
b'yeitzer hara;
v'al cheit shechatanu l'fanecha
b'neshech uvmarbit.

The ways we have wronged You by giving in to our hostile impulses;
and harm we have caused in Your world through greed and exploitation.

עַל חֵטְא שֶׁחָטָאנוּ לְפָנֶיךָ
בְּלָצוֹן,
וְעַל חֵטְא שֶׁחָטָאנוּ לְפָנֶיךָ
בִּנְטִיַּת גָּרוֹן.

Al cheit shechatanu l'fanecha
b'latzon;
v'al cheit shechatanu l'fanecha
bintiyat garon.

The ways we have wronged You through cynicism and scorn;
and harm we have caused in Your world through arrogant behavior.

OPENLY AND SECRETLY בַּגָּלוּי וּבַסָּתֶר. Said the Rebbe of Kotzk (1787–1859): "Most people behave well in public, and act badly only in secret." But he taught the opposite: "Keep your good deeds private; do wrong only in public—since fear of exposure will reduce your misdeeds." We might ask: what would be the impact on us if all our deeds were widely known?

Short Confession

Long Confession

Failures of Integrity

We wrong You when we wrong ourselves.
For our failures of integrity, Adonai, we seek forgiveness.

For passing judgment without knowledge of the facts,
and for distorting facts to suit our purposes.

For succumbing in silence to social pressure,
and for acquiescing in beliefs we find offensive.

For using others' bad behavior to excuse our own,
and for blaming others for our mistakes and poor decisions.

For pretending to emotions we do not feel,
and for appearing to be other than what we are.

For condemning in our children the faults we tolerate in ourselves,
and for tolerating in ourselves the faults we condemn in our parents.

Failures of Justice

We dishonor You when we dishonor our society.
For our failures of justice, Adonai, we seek forgiveness.

For being indifferent to deprivation and hunger,
while accepting a culture of self-indulgence and greed.

For abuse of power in board rooms, court rooms, and classrooms,
and for accepting the neglect of children and elders, the ill and the weak.

For permitting social inequalities to prevail,
and for lacking the vision to transcend our selfishness.

For glorifying violence and turning hastily to war,
and for allowing history to repeat itself.

For behaviors that risk the future of our planet,
and for wreaking havoc on our only true inheritance—God's Creation.

וִדּוּי זוּטָא
Vidui Zuta

וִדּוּי רַבָּה
Vidui Rabbah

Al cheit shechatanu l'fanecha	עַל חֵטְא שֶׁחָטָאנוּ לְפָנֶיךָ
b'sinat chinam;	בְּשִׂנְאַת חִנָּם,
v'al cheit shechatanu l'fanecha	וְעַל חֵטְא שֶׁחָטָאנוּ לְפָנֶיךָ
b'tumat s'fatayim.	בְּטֻמְאַת שְׂפָתָיִם.

The ways we have wronged You by hating without cause;
and harm we have caused in Your world through offensive speech.

SIT
V'AL KULOM

Al cheit shechatanu l'fanecha	עַל חֵטְא שֶׁחָטָאנוּ לְפָנֶיךָ
bilshon hara;	בִּלְשׁוֹן הָרָע,
v'al cheit shechatanu l'fanecha	וְעַל חֵטְא שֶׁחָטָאנוּ לְפָנֶיךָ
b'tzarut-ayin.	בְּצָרוּת עָיִן.

The ways we have wronged You with a slanderous tongue;
and harm we have caused in Your world through a selfish or petty spirit.

V'al kulam, Elo·ah s'lichot,	וְעַל כֻּלָּם, אֱלוֹהַּ סְלִיחוֹת,
s'lach lanu, m'chal lanu, kaper-lanu.	סְלַח לָנוּ, מְחַל לָנוּ, כַּפֶּר־לָנוּ.

For all these failures of judgment and will, God of forgiveness—
forgive us, pardon us, lead us to atonement.

THROUGH OFFENSIVE SPEECH בְּטֻמְאַת שְׂפָתָיִם. Many of the wrongful and harmful acts in the litanies of confession refer to unethical speech: gossip, slander, and rumor-mongering; lies, large and small; careless and hurtful remarks. The "problem" of human speech is introduced at the beginning of the service, in *T'filah Zakah* (A Prayer for Purity and Worthiness, pp. 12–13); it is underscored by *Kol Nidrei*, as we acknowledge the vows and promises to God that we have failed to keep; and the confessions devote much attention to it. Seeing them as more than outpourings of remorse and guilt, the *machzor* frames the confessions as "teachable moments" in which we are instructed on the thoughtful, sensitive, and honorable use of language.

FOR ALL THESE FAILURES וְעַל כֻּלָּם. Both the Long Confession (*Al Cheit*) and the Short Confession (*Ashamnu*) provide a wide-ranging list of human sins and misdeeds, but our Sages recognized that no liturgical text could include the wrongful acts of every individual. The formal confessions are meant to stir the memory and prompt our private confession. We are part of a community that joins with us in the work of *t'shuvah*: introspection; acknowledgment of weaknesses and strengths; and, at the end of the day, a return to the right path.

Short Confession

Long Confession

Failures of Love

We sin against You when we hurt one another.
For our failures of love, Adonai, we seek forgiveness.

For exploiting another for our own pleasure,
and for the wounds we cause through betrayal and deception.

For withholding affection from those we claim to love,
and for using love to control our spouses and partners, our children and parents.

For abandoning friends and siblings whose love has sustained us,
and for neglecting those who love us when they need us most.

For harboring in our relationships mistrust, boredom and disloyalty,
and for rejecting our partner's efforts at repair and renewal.

For possessiveness, jealousy, and avarice,
and for lashing out in anger at those who are closest to us.

Who among us is blameless? Who shall say: "I have not erred;
I have not wronged or sinned"?

We **a**buse, we **b**rutalize, we **c**ovet, we **d**eceive, we **e**nslave, we **f**eud,
we **g**ossip, we **h**umiliate, we **i**njure, we **j**udge unfairly, we **k**ill, we **l**ie,
we **m**anipulate, we **n**eglect, we **o**stracize, we **p**lagiarize, we **q**uarrel,
we **r**age, we **s**hame, we **t**urn away, we **u**ndermine, we **v**ilify, we **w**aste,
we e**x**ploit the earth, we **y**earn too much for yesterday—and too easily forget **Z**ion.

Our sins are an alphabet of woe.

Help us, Holy One, to follow Your ways of integrity, justice, and love.
Teach us to seek forgiveness with humility and an open heart.

וְעַל כֻּלָּם, אֱלוֹהַּ סְלִיחוֹת,
סְלַח לָנוּ, מְחַל לָנוּ, כַּפֶּר־לָנוּ.

V'al kulam, Elo·ah s'lichot,
s'lach lanu, m'chal lanu, kaper-lanu.

For all these wrongs, God of forgiveness,
forgive us, pardon us, lead us to atonement.

וְדוּי זוּטָא
Vidui Zuta

וְדוּי רַבָּה
Vidui Rabbah

Confession: A Prayer for Repair of the Tablets

אֵל אֱלֹהֵי הָעֵדוּת.
יוֹדֵעַ לֵב וּבוֹרֵא עוֹלָם,
הַבֵּט מֵהַר חוֹרֵב,
וּסְלַח
וּשְׁלַח בְּחַסְדְּךָ
מָזוֹר וְתַקָּנָה
אֶל הַסְּדָקִים שֶׁנִּפְעֲרוּ בִּי
מֵהֶבֶל עֲבוֹדָה זָרָה.

סְלַח עַל הַשְּׁבָרִים שֶׁהוֹתַרְתִּי
בִּדְרָכַי,
שִׁבְרֵי הַנֶּפֶשׁ אוֹ שִׁבְרֵי הַגּוּף
כִּי בְּשׁוֹגֵג הָיוּ כָּל אֵלֶּה
וּמֵחוּלְשַׁת אֱנוֹשׁ.

סְלַח
וּשְׁלַח, בְּחַסְדְּךָ הַנֶּעֱלָם
תִּקּוּן שֶׁל קַבָּלָה וָאוֹר,
אֶל רְסִיסֵי לוּחוֹת.
וּשְׁלַח הַכֹּחַ לַעֲמֹד,
אֶל מוּל פָּנֶיךָ
אֵל.

God of the Covenant—
intimate of the heart, creator of the world:

Gaze from Horeb,
and forgive.
Through Your love,
send healing,
and mend
the cracks within me
caused by the senselessness of serving idols.

Forgive the shards
I left scattered
on my path—
broken bits of body, pieces of soul—
for it all happened by mistake,
the result of human frailty.

Forgive
and, through Your hidden love,
send to the shattered tablets
a mystical repair
of acceptance and light.
And send me strength,
my God,
to stand
before You.

A PRAYER FOR REPAIR OF THE TABLETS. By Rabbi Ofer Sabath Beit-Halachmi (b. 1965). According to Exodus 32:19, Moses, enraged by the Israelites' worship of the Golden Calf, shattered the tablets he had just brought down from Mount Sinai. Exodus 34 describes a second set of tablets, given by God to replace the first. For the Talmudic Sages, this gift of Torah, in the aftermath of the people's idolatry and Moses' anger, was the ultimate sign of God's forgiveness. Thus, the Sages believed that the second tablets were given to the Jewish people on Yom Kippur—the day we devote to deep reflection on wrongdoing and forgiveness (Midrash *Tanchuma, Ki Tisa* 31; Rashi on Exodus 33:11). This day, then, is the anniversary of God's boundless compassion and forgiveness—a day to proclaim: that which is broken can be made whole again.

Short Confession

Long Confession

For Acts of Healing and Repair

God our Creator and Guide,
Let us speak now of the healing acts by which we bring You into the world,
the acts of repair that make You a living presence in our lives:

Al hatikkun shetikanu l'fanecha . . . עַל הַתִּקּוּן שֶׁתִּקַּנּוּ לְפָנֶיךָ . . .

For the act of healing we have done openly or anonymously
and for the act of repair we have done without personal gain

Al hatikkun shetikanu l'fanecha . . . עַל הַתִּקּוּן שֶׁתִּקַּנּוּ לְפָנֶיךָ . . .

For the act of healing we have done by seeking forgiveness
and for the act of repair we have done by forgiving others

Al hatikkun shetikanu l'fanecha . . . עַל הַתִּקּוּן שֶׁתִּקַּנּוּ לְפָנֶיךָ . . .

For the act of healing we have done through righteous giving
and for the act of repair we have done by opening our hearts

Al hatikkun shetikanu l'fanecha . . . עַל הַתִּקּוּן שֶׁתִּקַּנּוּ לְפָנֶיךָ . . .

For the act of healing we have done by comforting the mourner and visiting the sick; and for the act of repair we have done by pursuing justice and human rights, fairness and civility

Al hatikkun shetikanu l'fanecha . . . עַל הַתִּקּוּן שֶׁתִּקַּנּוּ לְפָנֶיךָ . . .

For the act of healing we have done by making peace between one person and another; and for the act of repair we have done by protecting nature and all its creatures

Al hatikkun shetikanu l'fanecha . . . עַל הַתִּקּוּן שֶׁתִּקַּנּוּ לְפָנֶיךָ . . .

For the act of healing we have done by teaching our children the ways of peace; and for the act of repair we have done by teaching our children the ways of Torah

Al hatikkun shetikanu l'fanecha . . . עַל הַתִּקּוּן שֶׁתִּקַּנּוּ לְפָנֶיךָ . . .

For the act of healing we have done by honoring elders and loving the stranger; and for the act of repair we have done in response to Your commandment: choose life and blessing

V'al kulam . . . וְעַל כֻּלָּם . . .

And all these bring nearer the day when You shall be One and Your name shall be One.

וִדּוּי זוּטָא
Vidui Zuta

וִדּוּי רַבָּה
Vidui Rabbah

The Essence of Atonement

Facing Confession, Seeking Forgiveness: From Vidui to S'lichot

Our sins are like veils upon our faces,
Hiding us from our Maker!
—MOSES IBN EZRA

The medieval poet Moses ibn Ezra gives us a striking image for the Ten Days of Repentance that culminate in Yom Kippur: our sins are like a veil covering the face, separating us from God, from the people in our life and from our true self. The process of *t'shuvah* (repentance, literally "return") is meant to return us to our core, the person we really are—the good and worthy human being masked behind the veil. *T'shuvah* represents an optimistic outlook on life: change is always possible; wrongdoing does not stain us forever; a veil can be removed.

Vidui, the act of confession, represents our movement toward God; self-disclosure precedes the seeking of forgiveness. We can picture it as a ritualized "dance": first we take small steps (the short confession, called *Ashamnu*); then, feeling more confident, we immerse ourselves in a powerful piece of worship (the long confession, *Al Cheit*). During these confessions, some worshipers strike their chest in rhythm to the chant, so that, like a dance, the prayer is felt physically as well as emotionally.

Vidui leads to a series of pleas for reconciliation with God: the prayers called *S'lichot* (Songs of Forgiveness). They are grounded in two verses of Torah, known as the Thirteen Attributes of God: "Adonai, Adonai—God, compassionate, gracious, endlessly patient, loving, and true; showing mercy to the thousandth generation; forgiving evil, defiance, and wrongdoing; granting pardon" (Exodus 34:6–7).

In an astonishing midrash, the Talmudic Sage Rabbi Yochanan imagined God, majestically robed in a tallit, teaching Moses the order of the prayers, saying to him, "Whenever Israel 'misses the mark,' let them read the Thirteen Attributes in My presence, and I will forgive them." This portrait of an intimate relationship with God conveys the spiritual promise of the Songs of Forgiveness. For this is the moment when the veil is lifted from our faces and we no longer hide from our Maker. This is the precious moment when we reveal our true selves—and renew our relationship with the One who makes us whole.

ASTONISHING MIDRASH. Talmud *Rosh HaShanah* 17b.

Short Confession

Long Confession

Possible Answers to Prayer

Your petitions—though they continue to bear
just the one signature—have been duly recorded.
Your anxieties—despite their constant,

relatively narrow scope and inadvertent
entertainment value—nonetheless serve
to bring your person vividly to mind.

Your repentance—all but obscured beneath
a burgeoning, yellow fog of frankly more
conspicuous resentment—is sufficient.

Your intermittent concern for the sick,
the suffering, the needy poor is sometimes
recognizable to me, if not to them.

Your angers, your zeal, your lipsmackingly
righteous indignation toward the many
whose habits and sympathies offend you—

these must burn away before you'll apprehend
how near I am, with what fervor I adore
precisely these, the several who rouse your passions.

POSSIBLE ANSWERS TO PRAYER. By Scott Cairns (b. 1954). The poet adopts the dry, legalistic tone of an imagined bureaucratic deity who receives and critiques our prayers—a device designed to provoke our own self-critique. As we approach *S'lichot*, the Songs of Forgiveness, we assess the sincerity, scope, and generosity of the prayers we offer, and ask ourselves whether resentment and disdain for others hamper our ability to perceive a loving, accepting God.

סְלִיחוֹת
S'lichot · Songs of Forgiveness

יַעֲלֶה תַּחֲנוּנֵנוּ מֵעֶרֶב,	*Yaaleh tachanuneinu mei·erev,*
וְיָבֹא שַׁוְעָתֵנוּ מִבֹּקֶר,	*v'yavo shavateinu miboker,*
וְיֵרָאֶה רִנּוּנֵנוּ עַד עָרֶב.	*v'yeira·eh rinuneinu ad arev.*
יַעֲלֶה קוֹלֵנוּ מֵעֶרֶב,	*Yaaleh koleinu mei·erev,*
וְיָבֹא צִדְקָתֵנוּ מִבֹּקֶר,	*v'yavo tzidkateinu miboker,*
וְיֵרָאֶה פִּדְיוֹנֵנוּ עַד עָרֶב.	*v'yeira·eh pidyoneinu ad arev.*
יַעֲלֶה עִנּוּיֵנוּ מֵעֶרֶב,	*Yaaleh inuyeinu mei·erev,*
וְיָבֹא סְלִיחָתֵנוּ מִבֹּקֶר,	*v'yavo s'lichateinu miboker,*
וְיֵרָאֶה נַאֲקָתֵנוּ עַד עָרֶב.	*v'yeira·eh naakateinu ad arev.*
יַעֲלֶה מְנוּסֵנוּ מֵעֶרֶב,	*Yaaleh m'nuseinu mei·erev,*
וְיָבֹא לְמַעֲנוֹ מִבֹּקֶר,	*v'yavo l'maano miboker,*
וְיֵרָאֶה כִּפּוּרֵנוּ עַד עָרֶב.	*v'yeira·eh kipureinu ad arev.*

Let our needs rise up with the darkness,
our cries with the rays of the sun.
All day our praise is before You — songs of joy and bliss
till evening comes.

May our voices soar at nightfall,
our just deeds shine forth with the light.
All day we await deliverance — fervent our hope for redemption
till evening comes.

Let our suffering ascend at twilight,
our forgiveness with the break of dawn.
All day we sigh from oppression — cry out for right and justice
till evening comes.

May there be refuge when night surrounds us,
at sunrise — safe haven, for Your sake.
All day our words rise from a sea of sorrow — and they break
in waves of atonement
till evening comes.

Yaaleh yisheinu mei·erev,	יַעֲלֶה יִשְׁעֵנוּ מֵעֶרֶב,
v'yavo tohoreinu miboker,	וְיָבֹא טָהֳרֵנוּ מִבֹּקֶר,
v'yeira·eh chinuneinu ad arev.	וְיֵרָאֶה חִנּוּנֵנוּ עַד עָרֶב.
Yaaleh zichroneinu mei·erev,	יַעֲלֶה זִכְרוֹנֵנוּ מֵעֶרֶב,
v'yavo viudeinu miboker,	וְיָבֹא וִעוּדֵנוּ מִבֹּקֶר,
v'yeira·eh hadrateinu ad arev.	וְיֵרָאֶה הַדְרָתֵנוּ עַד עָרֶב.
Yaaleh dofkeinu mei·erev,	יַעֲלֶה דָּפְקֵנוּ מֵעֶרֶב,
v'yavo gileinu miboker,	וְיָבֹא גִּילֵנוּ מִבֹּקֶר,
v'yeira·eh bakashateinu ad arev.	וְיֵרָאֶה בַּקָּשָׁתֵנוּ עַד עָרֶב.
Yaaleh enkateinu mei·erev,	יַעֲלֶה אֶנְקָתֵנוּ מֵעֶרֶב,
v'yavo eilecha miboker,	וְיָבֹא אֵלֶיךָ מִבֹּקֶר,
v'yeira·eh eileinu ad arev.	וְיֵרָאֶה אֵלֵינוּ עַד עָרֶב.

Let evening bring salvation.
Let morning make all hearts pure.
This day our prayers spell healing — peace, peace, to all, far and near —
till evening comes.

May mindfulness of us rise with the evening star,
our worthy deeds revealed in the radiance of dawn.
All day we meditate on life's beauty — the precious jewels of creation —
till evening comes.

Let our pounding on the gates of mercy thunder on high, as darkness falls.
And with dawn, let the joy of renewal arrive.
The day holds the urgency of our prayers — confessions of the heart,
lamentations of the soul —
till evening comes.

May our yearnings rise above the shadows of dusk.
May the searching of our souls reach You in the morning.
All day our praise is before You — may it be acceptable, may it be received —
till evening comes.

LET OUR NEEDS RISE UP יַעֲלֶה. This prayer traces the spiritual arc of Yom Kippur from dusk to dawn and then, again, to twilight. Its acrostic flows from the end of the alphabet to the beginning — like a river of light flowing toward its origin, *Alef*: the One who unifies all of creation.

PEACE, PEACE. Isaiah 57:19, from the haftarah reading on Yom Kippur morning.

שְׁמַע קוֹלֵנוּ, יְיָ אֱלֹהֵינוּ.	*Sh'ma koleinu, Adonai Eloheinu.*
חוּס וְרַחֵם עָלֵינוּ.	*Chus v'racheim aleinu.*
וְקַבֵּל בְּרַחֲמִים וּבְרָצוֹן אֶת תְּפִלָּתֵנוּ.	*V'kabeil b'rachamim uvratzon et t'filateinu.*
הֲשִׁיבֵנוּ, יְיָ, אֵלֶיךָ וְנָשׁוּבָה,	*Hashiveinu, Adonai, eilecha — v'nashuvah;*
חַדֵּשׁ יָמֵינוּ כְּקֶדֶם.	*chadeish yameinu k'kedem.*
אֲמָרֵינוּ הַאֲזִינָה, יְיָ,	*Amareinu haazinah, Adonai,*
בִּינָה הֲגִיגֵנוּ.	*binah hagigeinu.*
יִהְיוּ לְרָצוֹן אִמְרֵי־פִינוּ וְהֶגְיוֹן לִבֵּנוּ לְפָנֶיךָ,	*Yiyu l'ratzon imrei-finu v'hegyon libeinu l'fanecha,*
יְיָ, צוּרֵנוּ וְגוֹאֲלֵנוּ.	*Adonai — tzureinu v'goaleinu.*
אַל־תַּשְׁלִיכֵנוּ מִלְּפָנֶיךָ,	*Al-tashlicheinu mil'fanecha;*
וְרוּחַ קָדְשְׁךָ אַל־תִּקַּח מִמֶּנּוּ.	*v'ruach kodsh'cha al-tikach mimenu.*
אַל־תַּשְׁלִיכֵנוּ לְעֵת זִקְנָה,	*Al-tashlicheinu l'eit ziknah;*
כִּכְלוֹת כֹּחֵנוּ אַל־תַּעַזְבֵנוּ.	*kichlot kocheinu, al-taazveinu.*
אַל־תַּעַזְבֵנוּ, יְיָ אֱלֹהֵינוּ,	*Al-taazveinu, Adonai Eloheinu;*
אַל־תִּרְחַק מִמֶּנּוּ.	*al-tirchak mimenu.*
כִּי־לְךָ, יְיָ, הוֹחָלְנוּ,	*Ki-l'cha, Adonai, hochalnu;*
אַתָּה תַעֲנֶה, אֲדֹנָי אֱלֹהֵינוּ.	*atah taaneh, Adonai Eloheinu.*

Hear our call, Adonai our God. Show us compassion.
Accept our prayer with love and goodwill.

Take us back, Adonai; let us come back to You;
renew our days as in the past.
Hear our words, Adonai; understand our unspoken thoughts.
May the speech of our mouth and our heart's quiet prayer
be acceptable to You, Adonai, our Rock and our Redeemer.

Do not cast us away from Your presence, or cut us off
from Your holy spirit.
Do not cast us away when we are old; as our strength diminishes,
do not forsake us.
Do not forsake us, Adonai; be not far from us, our God.

With hope, Adonai, we await You;
surely, You, Adonai our God — You will answer.

HEAR OUR CALL שְׁמַע קוֹלֵנוּ, based on Lamentations 5:21; Psalms 5:2, 19:15, 51:13, 71:9, 38:22, 38:16.

Will You Hear My Voice

הֲתִשְׁמַע קוֹלִי רְחוֹקִי שֶׁלִּי.
הֲתִשְׁמַע קוֹלִי בַּאֲשֶׁר הִנְּךָ –
קוֹל קוֹרֵא בְּעֹז קוֹל בּוֹכֶה בִּדְמִי
וּמֵעַל לַזְּמַן מְצַוֶּה בְּרָכָה.

תֵּבֵל זוֹ רַבָּה וּדְרָכִים בָּהּ רָב.
נִפְגָּשׁוֹת לְדַק נִפְרָדוֹת לָעַד –
מְבַקֵּשׁ אָדָם אַךְ כּוֹשְׁלוֹת רַגְלָיו
לֹא יוּכַל לִמְצֹא אֵת אֲשֶׁר אָבַד.

אַחֲרוֹן יָמַי כְּבָר קָרוֹב אוּלַי.
כְּבָר קָרוֹב הַיּוֹם שֶׁל דִּמְעוֹת פְּרֵידָה.
אֲחַכֶּה לְךָ עַד יִכְבּוּ חַיַּי
כְּחַכּוֹת רָחֵל לְדוֹדָהּ.

Will you hear my voice, you who are far from me?
Will you hear my voice, wherever you are;
a voice calling aloud, a voice silently weeping,
endlessly demanding a blessing.

This busy world is vast, its ways are many;
paths meet for a moment, then part forever;
we go on searching, but our feet stumble,
we cannot find that which we have lost.

Perhaps my last day is already drawing near,
drawing close are the tears of parting.
I will wait for you till my days flicker out,
like Rachel waiting for her beloved.

DO NOT CAST US AWAY WHEN WE ARE OLD (*facing page*). The power of *Sh'ma Koleinu* deepens for us as we age. Those aware of their aging often question the value and significance of their lives, seeking spiritual connection in questions such as "Did my life mean anything?" and "Of what use am I, now that I am old?" In *Sh'ma Koleinu* we hear a voice—perhaps our own—calling out from the winter of the heart, an inner landscape of loss and uncertainty about the future. We learn from this prayer that a person who feels this way needs, above all, to be heard. Relatedness and the warmth of spirituality begin with the first word of this prayer: *Sh'ma* (Hear).

WILL YOU HEAR MY VOICE. By Rachel Bluwstein, known as Rachel (1890–1931).

God of forgiveness, we come before You in need of compassion.

At Sinai You spoke words that guide our lives to this day,
but our ancestors lost faith in You, lost hope in their Redeemer.

With one voice, they had promised: "We will do and obey";
and yet, stiff-necked, they broke their word, adoring an idol of gold.

How wondrous Your compassion in the face of their rebellion,
Your forgiveness in that moment of human weakness and doubt!

We, too, have broken promises to You.
We, too, worship the work of our own hands.
We, too, make of gold a god.
And we, too, forsake Your word.

At Sinai You revealed thirteen attributes of mercy;
these aspects of Your nature — Your very essence — we now recall:

Adonai, Adonai — El rachum v'chanun;   יְיָ יְיָ, אֵל רַחוּם וְחַנּוּן,

erech apayim, v'rav-chesed ve·emet;   אֶרֶךְ אַפַּֽיִם, וְרַב־חֶֽסֶד וֶאֱמֶת.

notzeir chesed laalafim;   נֹצֵר חֶֽסֶד לָאֲלָפִים,

nosei avon vafesha v'chataah; v'nakeih.   נֹשֵׂא עָוֺן וָפֶֽשַׁע וְחַטָּאָה, וְנַקֵּה.

Adonai, Adonai —
God, compassionate, gracious, endlessly patient, loving, and true;
showing mercy to the thousandth generation;
forgiving evil, defiance, and wrongdoing; granting pardon.

יַעֲלֶה
Yaaleh

שְׁמַע קוֹלֵֽנוּ
Sh'ma Koleinu

שְׁלֹשׁ עֶשְׂרֵה מִדּוֹת
13 Middot

כְּרַחֵם אָב
K'Racheim Av

כִּי הִנֵּה כַּחֹֽמֶר
Ki Hineih KaChomer

אַל תַּעַזְבֵֽנוּ
Al Taazveinu

שְׁלֹשׁ עֶשְׂרֵה מִדּוֹת
13 Middot

כִּי אָֽנוּ עַמֶּֽךָ
Ki Anu Amecha

אָֽנוּ עַזֵּי פָנִים
Anu Azei Fanim

שְׁלֹשׁ עֶשְׂרֵה מִדּוֹת
13 Middot

מִי שֶׁעָנָה
Mi She·anah

אל רחום. This emblem ("God, compassionate") sets apart the Thirteen Attributes of Mercy
(Exodus 34:6–7) when they appear in the Songs of Forgiveness throughout Yom Kippur.
Rav Yehudah (Talmud *Rosh HaShanah* 17b) claims special status for the Thirteen Attri-
butes: "God said to Moses, 'Whenever the people of Israel sin, let them perform this
service before Me and I will forgive them.'" Some Sages took this to mean that saying the
words ensures divine mercy; but others note that it says "perform," not merely "recite."
Focusing on God's compassionate qualities is meant to prompt our own actions in kind.
ADONAI, ADONAI יְיָ יְיָ, Exodus 34:6–7.

כְּרַחֵם אָב עַל־בָּנִים,	*K'racheim av al-banim,*
רַחֵם יְיָ עַל־יְרֵאָיו.	*richam Adonai al-y'rei·av.*
כִּי כִגְבֹהַּ שָׁמַיִם עַל־הָאָרֶץ,	*Ki chigvo·ah shamayim al-haaretz,*
גָּבַר חַסְדּוֹ עַל־יְרֵאָיו.	*gavar chasdo al-y'rei·av.*
לַייָ הַיְשׁוּעָה,	*L'Adonai haishuah,*
עַל־עַמְּךָ בִרְכָתֶךָ סֶּלָה.	*al-am'cha virchatecha selah.*
יְיָ צְבָאוֹת עִמָּנוּ,	*Adonai Tz'vaot imanu;*
מִשְׂגָּב־לָנוּ אֱלֹהֵי יַעֲקֹב, סֶלָה.	*misgav-lanu Elohei Yaakov, selah.*
יְיָ צְבָאוֹת,	*Adonai Tz'vaot,*
אַשְׁרֵי אָדָם בֹּטֵחַ בָּךְ.	*ashrei adam botei·ach bach.*
יְיָ הוֹשִׁיעָה,	*Adonai, hoshiah!*
הַמֶּלֶךְ יַעֲנֵנוּ בְיוֹם־קָרְאֵנוּ.	*HaMelech yaaneinu v'yom-koreinu.*
סְלַח־נָא לַעֲוֹן הָעָם הַזֶּה	*"S'lach na laavon haam hazeh*
כְּגֹדֶל חַסְדֶּךָ,	*k'godel chasdecha,*
וְכַאֲשֶׁר נָשָׂאתָה לָעָם הַזֶּה	*v'chaasher nasata laam hazeh*
מִמִּצְרַיִם וְעַד־הֵנָּה.	*miMitzrayim v'ad heinah."*
וְשָׁם נֶאֱמַר:	*V'sham ne·emar:*
וַיֹּאמֶר יְיָ:	*Vayomer Adonai:*
סָלַחְתִּי כִּדְבָרֶךָ.	*"Salachti, kidvarecha."*

As parents show tenderness to their children,
may You show mercy to those who worship You.
Like the heavens that tower above the earth,
Your love is powerful for those who revere You.
Liberation is a gift from God — a blessing upon Your people.
You are the God of all we can perceive, our haven, the God of *Yaakov*.
And You are the God of all that is beyond our perception;
the one who has faith in You is fortunate.
Sovereign God, show us the way to freedom!
Answer us on this day of our calling out to You.

Moses prayed to God:
"As You have been faithful to this people ever since Egypt,
please forgive their failings now, in keeping with Your boundless love."
And God responded: "I forgive, as you have asked."

MOSES PRAYED סְלַח־נָא, Numbers 14:19–20.

כִּי הִנֵּה כַּחֹמֶר בְּיַד הַיּוֹצֵר
בִּרְצוֹתוֹ מַרְחִיב וּבִרְצוֹתוֹ מְקַצֵּר
כֵּן אֲנַחְנוּ בְיָדְךָ, חֶסֶד נוֹצֵר,
לַבְּרִית הַבֵּט וְאַל תֵּפֶן לַיֵּצֶר.

Ki hineih kachomer b'yad hayotzeir —
birtzoto marchiv uvirtzoto m'katzeir —
kein anachnu v'yad'cha, chesed notzeir.
Lab'rit habeit; v'al teifen layeitzer!

כִּי הִנֵּה כָּאֶבֶן בְּיַד הַמְסַתֵּת
בִּרְצוֹתוֹ אוֹחֵז וּבִרְצוֹתוֹ מְכַתֵּת
כֵּן אֲנַחְנוּ בְיָדְךָ, מְחַיֶּה וּמְמוֹתֵת,
לַבְּרִית הַבֵּט וְאַל תֵּפֶן לַיֵּצֶר.

Ki hineih ka·even b'yad hamsateit —
birtzoto ocheiz uvirtzoto m'chateit —
kein anachnu v'yad'cha, m'chayeh um'moteit.
Lab'rit habeit; v'al teifen layeitzer!

כִּי הִנֵּה כַּגַּרְזֶן בְּיַד הֶחָרָשׁ
בִּרְצוֹתוֹ דִּבֵּק לָאוּר וּבִרְצוֹתוֹ פֵּרַשׁ
כֵּן אֲנַחְנוּ בְיָדְךָ, תּוֹמֵךְ עָנִי וָרָשׁ,
לַבְּרִית הַבֵּט וְאַל תֵּפֶן לַיֵּצֶר.

Ki hineih kagarzen b'yad hecharash —
birtzoto dibeik la·ur uvirtzoto peirash —
kein anachnu v'yad'cha, tomeich ani varash.
Lab'rit habeit; v'al teifen layeitzer!

כִּי הִנֵּה כַּהֶגֶה בְּיַד הַמַּלָּח
בִּרְצוֹתוֹ אוֹחֵז וּבִרְצוֹתוֹ שִׁלַּח
כֵּן אֲנַחְנוּ בְיָדְךָ, אֵל טוֹב וְסַלָּח,
לַבְּרִית הַבֵּט וְאַל תֵּפֶן לַיֵּצֶר.

Ki hineih kahegeh b'yad hamalach —
birtzoto ocheiz uvirtzoto shilach —
kein anachnu v'yad'cha, El tov v'salach.
Lab'rit habeit; v'al teifen layeitzer!

כִּי הִנֵּה כִּזְכוּכִית בְּיַד הַמְזַגֵּג
בִּרְצוֹתוֹ חוֹגֵג וּבִרְצוֹתוֹ מְמוֹגֵג
כֵּן אֲנַחְנוּ בְיָדְךָ, מַעֲבִיר זָדוֹן וְשֶׁגֶג,
לַבְּרִית הַבֵּט וְאַל תֵּפֶן לַיֵּצֶר.

Ki hineih kiz·chuchit b'yad hamzageig —
birtzoto chogeig uvirtzoto m'mogeig —
kein anachnu v'yad'cha, maavir zadon v'shegeg.
Lab'rit habeit; v'al teifen layeitzer!

יַעֲלֶה *Yaaleh*
שְׁמַע קוֹלֵנוּ *Sh'ma Koleinu*
שְׁלֹשׁ עֶשְׂרֵה מִדּוֹת *13 Middot*
כְּרַחֵם אָב *K'Racheim Av*
כִּי הִנֵּה כַּחֹמֶר *Ki Hineih KaChomer*
אַל תַּעַזְבֵנוּ *Al Taazveinu*
שְׁלֹשׁ עֶשְׂרֵה מִדּוֹת *13 Middot*
כִּי אָנוּ עַמֶּךָ *Ki Anu Amecha*
אָנוּ עַזֵּי פָנִים *Anu Azei Fanim*
שְׁלֹשׁ עֶשְׂרֵה מִדּוֹת *13 Middot*
מִי שֶׁעָנָה *Mi She·anah*

CONSIDER THE CLAY כִּי הִנֵּה כַּחֹמֶר. This spiritual poem (*piyut*) from the 12th century is based on a vivid array of metaphors drawn from everyday life. Potters, masons, glass-blowers, and silversmiths work with the raw material at hand — repairing what is damaged, refining what is clumsy, continually reshaping their work into new and more beautiful forms. Inspired by the artisan's dedication to constant improvement, this prayer expresses confidence that God can help us to change the shape and direction of our lives for the better. The poet asks God to regard us with the loving vision of the artist — to see us not as flawed and damaged creatures, but as the people we could be: more perfect vessels of the divine spirit. This *piyut* was inspired by Jeremiah 18:3–6 and Isaiah 64:7: "We are the clay and You are the Potter; we are all the work of Your hands."

Consider the clay in the potter's hand, stretched and rolled
as the artist desires;
so are we in Your hand, our loving Protector.
Look to the covenant, not our imperfection.

Consider the stone in the mason's hand, broken or kept whole
as the stonecutter sees fit;
so are we in Your hand, Creator of life and death.
Look to the covenant, not our imperfection.

Consider the iron in the welder's hand, held to the flame
or removed at will;
so are we in Your hand, Provider for the poor and afflicted.
Look to the covenant, not our imperfection.

Consider the helm in the seafarer's hand, steering or drifting
as the sailor wills it;
so are we in Your hand, our God of goodness and forgiveness.
Look to the covenant, not our imperfection.

Consider the glass in the glazier's hand, rounded and melted
as the artist desires;
so are we in Your hand, the one who pardons our errors
and our wrongdoing.
Look to the covenant, not our imperfection.

LOOK TO THE COVENANT לַבְּרִית הַבֵּט. The poet asks God to consider our people in the light of the long and mutually loving relationship we share, rather than judging us strictly on our individual merits. Covenant (*b'rit*) also has a deeper meaning, specific to the High Holy Day season. According to the Talmud (*Rosh HaShanah* 17b), God established a covenant with the Jewish people by means of the Thirteen Attributes of Mercy (Exodus 34:6–7, pp. 100, 105, 107), the recitation of which assures divine forgiveness. Thus, this prayer of forgiveness urges God to "look to the covenant" — to see us through the lens of God's own qualities of compassion, patience, mercy, and grace. Though we inhabit an imperfect reality — a world rife with suffering, blemished by the human propensity for evil — this prayer sees human beings as a work in progress, and our covenantal partnership with the divine Artist as the basis for shaping something better.

אֱלֹהֵינוּ וֵאלֹהֵי אֲבוֹתֵינוּ וְאִמּוֹתֵינוּ,
אַל תַּעַזְבֵנוּ וְאַל תִּטְּשֵׁנוּ;
וְאַל תַּכְלִימֵנוּ וְאַל תָּפֵר בְּרִיתְךָ
אִתָּנוּ.
קָרְבֵנוּ לְתוֹרָתֶךָ,
לַמְּדֵנוּ מִצְוֹתֶיךָ,
הוֹרֵנוּ דְּרָכֶיךָ,
הַט לִבֵּנוּ לְיִרְאָה אֶת שְׁמֶךָ,
וּמוֹל אֶת לְבָבֵנוּ לְאַהֲבָתֶךָ,
וְנָשׁוּב אֵלֶיךָ בֶּאֱמֶת וּבְלֵב שָׁלֵם.
וּלְמַעַן שִׁמְךָ הַגָּדוֹל תִּמְחַל
וְתִסְלַח לַעֲוֹנֵינוּ,
כַּכָּתוּב בְּדִבְרֵי קָדְשֶׁךָ:
לְמַעַן־שִׁמְךָ, יְיָ,
וְסָלַחְתָּ לַעֲוֹנִי,
כִּי רַב־הוּא.

Eloheinu v'Elohei avoteinu v'imoteinu,
al taazveinu v'al tit'sheinu;
v'al tachlimeinu v'al tafeir brit'cha
    itanu!
Kar'veinu l'Toratecha,
lam'deinu mitzvotecha,
horeinu d'rachecha,
hat libeinu l'yirah et sh'mecha,
umol et l'vaveinu l'ahavatecha —
v'nashuv eilecha be·emet, uvlev shaleim.
Ulmaan shimcha hagadol timchal
    v'tislach laavoneinu,
kakatuv b'divrei kodshecha:
"L'maan-shimcha, Adonai,
v'salachta laavoni —
ki rav hu."

יַעֲלֶה
Yaaleh

שְׁמַע קוֹלֵנוּ
Sh'ma Koleinu

שְׁלֹשׁ עֶשְׂרֵה מִדּוֹת
13 Middot

כְּרַחֵם אָב
K'Racheim Av

כִּי הִנֵּה כַּחֹמֶר
Ki Hineih KaChomer

אַל תַּעַזְבֵנוּ
Al Taazveinu

שְׁלֹשׁ עֶשְׂרֵה מִדּוֹת
13 Middot

כִּי אָנוּ עַמֶּךָ
Ki Anu Amecha

אָנוּ עַזֵּי פָנִים
Anu Azei Fanim

שְׁלֹשׁ עֶשְׂרֵה מִדּוֹת
13 Middot

מִי שֶׁעָנָה
Mi She·anah

Our God and God of our fathers, God of our mothers —
Do not abandon us, leaving us in shame.
Do not dissolve the covenant You made with us.

Rather, draw us near to Your Teaching.
Show us Your ways and teach us how to live.
Let us be open to Your love, ready to revere Your very being.
Cut away the hardness of our hearts,
so that we may turn to You with all our heart's devotion —
truly repentant.

For the sake of Your great name,
pardon our failures, forgive our moral weakness,
as in the holy words of Your Psalmist:
"Adonai, as befits Your name,
forgive my sin, no matter how great."

ADONAI, AS BEFITS YOUR NAME לְמַעַן־שִׁמְךָ, יְיָ, Psalm 25:11.

אל רחום

In all your ways, be aware of God.
For there is no sovereign without a people —
ein melech b'lo am. אֵין מֶלֶךְ בְּלֹא עָם.

We are the chariot on which God's glory rides.
For there is no sovereign without a people.

Let the love of God be spread through our deeds.
For there is no sovereign without a people.

You are My servant, Israel; I will be glorified through you.
For there is no sovereign without a people.

Where is God? Anywhere we let God in.
For there is no sovereign without a people —
ein melech b'lo am. אֵין מֶלֶךְ בְּלֹא עָם.

Eternal God, You revealed to Moses Your thirteen attributes of mercy:
they exist in the world through our awareness;
they transform the world through our actions.
We speak them now as prayer and aspiration.

Adonai, Adonai — El rachum v'chanun;	יְיָ יְיָ, אֵל רַחוּם וְחַנּוּן,
erech apayim, v'rav-chesed ve·emet;	אֶרֶךְ אַפַּיִם, וְרַב־חֶסֶד וֶאֱמֶת.
notzeir chesed laalafim;	נֹצֵר חֶסֶד לָאֲלָפִים,
nosei avon vafesha v'chataah; v'nakeih.	נֹשֵׂא עָוֹן וָפֶשַׁע וְחַטָּאָה, וְנַקֵּה.

Adonai, Adonai —
God, compassionate, gracious, endlessly patient, loving, and true;
showing mercy to the thousandth generation;
forgiving evil, defiance, and wrongdoing; granting pardon.

IN ALL YOUR WAYS, Talmud *B'rachot* 63a.
FOR THERE IS NO SOVEREIGN WITHOUT A PEOPLE. A principle cited by Rabbeinu Bachya ben Asher (1255–1390), in his comment on Genesis 38:30. (See also Midrash *Pirkei d'Rabbi Eliezer*, chapter 3.)
LET THE LOVE OF GOD, Talmud *Yoma* 86a, adapted.
YOU ARE MY SERVANT, Isaiah 49:3, as understood in Talmud *Yoma* 86a.
WHERE IS GOD? Adapted from Rabbi Menachem Mendel of Kotzk ("the Kotzker Rebbe"; 1787–1859).
ADONAI, ADONAI יְיָ, יְיָ, Exodus 34:6–7.

Ki anu amecha, v'atah Eloheinu;	כִּי אָֽנוּ עַמֶּֽךָ, וְאַתָּה אֱלֹהֵֽינוּ,
anu vanecha, v'atah avinu.	אָֽנוּ בָנֶֽיךָ, וְאַתָּה אָבִֽינוּ.
Anu avadecha, v'atah adoneinu;	אָֽנוּ עֲבָדֶֽיךָ, וְאַתָּה אֲדוֹנֵֽנוּ,
anu k'halecha, v'atah chelkeinu.	אָֽנוּ קְהָלֶֽךָ, וְאַתָּה חֶלְקֵֽנוּ.
Anu nachalatecha, v'atah goraleinu;	אָֽנוּ נַחֲלָתֶֽךָ, וְאַתָּה גוֹרָלֵֽנוּ,
anu tzonecha, v'atah ro·einu.	אָֽנוּ צֹאנֶֽךָ, וְאַתָּה רוֹעֵֽנוּ.
Anu charmecha, v'atah notreinu;	אָֽנוּ כַרְמֶֽךָ, וְאַתָּה נוֹטְרֵֽנוּ,
anu f'ulatecha, v'atah yotzreinu.	אָֽנוּ פְעֻלָּתֶֽךָ, וְאַתָּה יוֹצְרֵֽנוּ.
Anu rayatecha, v'atah dodeinu;	אָֽנוּ רַעְיָתֶֽךָ, וְאַתָּה דוֹדֵֽנוּ,
anu s'gulatecha, v'atah k'roveinu.	אָֽנוּ סְגֻלָּתֶֽךָ, וְאַתָּה קְרוֹבֵֽנוּ.
Anu amecha, v'atah malkeinu;	אָֽנוּ עַמֶּֽךָ, וְאַתָּה מַלְכֵּֽנוּ,
anu maamirecha, v'atah maamireinu.	אָֽנוּ מַאֲמִירֶֽךָ, וְאַתָּה מַאֲמִירֵֽנוּ.

Our God and God of our ancestors —

We are Your people; and You are our God.
We are Your children; and You are our father, our mother.
We are the people who serve You; and You call us to serve.
We are Your community; and You are our portion.
We are Your legacy; and You are our purpose.
We are Your flock; and You are our shepherd.
We are Your vineyard; and You watch over us.
We are Your work; and You are our maker.
We are Your beloved; and You are our lover.
We are Your treasure; and You are the one we cherish.
We are Your people; and You reign over us.
We offer You our words; and You offer us Yours.

So forgive us, pardon us, lead us to atonement.

KI ANU AMECHA כִּי אָֽנוּ עַמֶּֽךָ. Father, mother, shepherd, creator, companion, sovereign — these evocative words encourage and enable us to contemplate aspects of our relationship with God. Israeli philosopher Rabbi Moshe Halbertal (b. 1958) points out that language, unlike painting or sculpture, is an appropriate Jewish medium for representing God because language gives us only a partial description. Art is too fixed, too definite, and too concrete for this task; it tells us too much — and because of that, it is apt to be wrong. But language leaves "open spaces" in which we can use our imaginations to confront the complexity of the Sublime.

אֵל רַחוּם

אָֽנוּ עַזֵּי פָנִים, וְאַתָּה רַחוּם וְחַנּוּן.
אָֽנוּ קְשֵׁי עֹֽרֶף, וְאַתָּה אֶֽרֶךְ אַפַּֽיִם.
אָֽנוּ מְלֵאֵי עָוֹן, וְאַתָּה מָלֵא רַחֲמִים.
אָֽנוּ יָמֵֽינוּ כְּצֵל עוֹבֵר,
וְאַתָּה הוּא וּשְׁנוֹתֶֽיךָ לֹא יִתָּֽמּוּ.

Anu azei fanim, v'atah rachum v'chanun.
Anu k'shei oref, v'atah erech apayim.
Anu m'lei·ei avon, v'atah malei rachamim.
Anu yameinu k'tzeil oveir,
v'atah — hu ushnotecha lo yitamu.

We are insolent —
but You are compassionate and gracious.

We are stubborn and stiff-necked —
but You are slow to anger.

We persist in doing wrong —
but You are the essence of mercy.

Our days are a shadow passing by, but You —
You are existence itself,
Your years never ending.

יְיָ יְיָ, אֵל רַחוּם וְחַנּוּן,
אֶֽרֶךְ אַפַּֽיִם, וְרַב־חֶֽסֶד וֶאֱמֶת.
נֹצֵר חֶֽסֶד לָאֲלָפִים,
נֹשֵׂא עָוֹן וָפֶֽשַׁע וְחַטָּאָה, וְנַקֵּה.

Adonai, Adonai — El rachum v'chanun;
erech apayim, v'rav-chesed ve·emet;
notzeir chesed laalafim;
nosei avon vafesha v'chataah; v'nakeih.

Adonai, Adonai —
God, compassionate, gracious, endlessly patient, loving, and true;
showing mercy to the thousandth generation;
forgiving evil, defiance, and wrongdoing; granting pardon.

ADONAI, ADONAI יְיָ, יְיָ, Exodus 34:6–7.

יַעֲלֶה
Yaaleh

שְׁמַע קוֹלֵנוּ
Sh'ma Koleinu

שָׁלֹשׁ עֶשְׂרֵה מִדּוֹת
13 Middot

כְּרַחֵם אָב
K'Racheim Av

כִּי הִנֵּה כַּחֹמֶר
Ki Hineih KaChomer

אַל תַּעַזְבֵנוּ
Al Taazveinu

שָׁלֹשׁ עֶשְׂרֵה מִדּוֹת
13 Middot

כִּי אָנוּ עַמֶּךָ
Ki Anu Amecha

אָנוּ עַזֵּי פָנִים
Anu Azei Fanim

שָׁלֹשׁ עֶשְׂרֵה מִדּוֹת
13 Middot

מִי שֶׁעָנָה
Mi She·anah

אֵל רַחוּם

לוּ אֶחֱזֶה פָנָיו בְּלִבִּי בָיְתָה . . .

If I could see God's face within my heart . . .

I'd see the face of a Gardener —
compassionate to weed and flower alike, patiently pruning,
graciously planting,
loving the endless hours of tending and nurturing the earth —
seeds, roots, all that grows;
and true to the essence of the gardener's work:
forgiving the fallen branches, the withered petals, the cracked stones,
the broken stems

לוּ אֶחֱזֶה פָנָיו בְּלִבִּי בָיְתָה . . .

If I could see God's face within my heart . . .

I'd see the human face in a thousand acts of mercy —
the one who gives bread to the hungry and shelters the lost,
who hears the voice of grief
and makes room for the stranger;
who brings relief to the blind, the bent, the unjustly imprisoned;
and is true to the essence of holy work:
defying evil, healing brokenness, easing pain;
and, in the end, forgiving ourselves as God forgives us.

IF I COULD SEE GOD'S FACE. This line is from "Vision of God," a religious poem (*piyut*) by Yehudah Halevi (ca. 1075–1141). The Hebrew may also be translated: "Would that I might see God's face within my heart."

"We Are Your People" (*Ki Anu Amecha*, p. 106) depicts the people Israel as God's vineyard and God as the one who cares for the vineyard. The meditation on this page encourages reflection on what it might mean to see ourselves as a garden tended by the Holy One. The image implies mutuality of purpose and action: as the garden grows and changes, the Gardener labors with love to bring out its potential beauty. Like the garden, we are always a work in progress. Our blossoming results both from our own striving and from God's compassionate, untiring efforts on our behalf. That compassion is central to the Thirteen Attributes of God, which appears as a recurring motif throughout the Songs of Forgiveness (pp. 100, 105, and 107).

When men were children, they thought of God as a father;
When men were slaves, they thought of God as a master;
When men were subjects, they thought of God as a king.
But I am a woman, not a slave, not a subject,
not a child who longs for God as father or mother.

I might imagine God as teacher or friend, but those images,
like king, master, father or mother, are too small for me now.

God is the force of motion and light in the universe;
God is the strength of life on our planet;
God is the power moving us to do good;
God is the source of love springing up in us.
God is far beyond what we can comprehend.

The Bronx, 1942

When I told him to shut up,
my father slammed on the brakes and left
me like a parcel in the car
on a strange street, to punish me
he said for lack of respect, though
what he always feared was lack of love.
I know now just how long

forgiveness can take
and that it can be harder than respect,
or even love. My father stayed angry
for a week. But I still remember
the gritty color of the sky through
that windshield and how, like a parcel,
I started to come apart.

---

when men were children. By Ruth Brin (1921–2009).
the bronx, 1942. By Linda Pastan (b. 1932).

יַעֲלֶה
Yaaleh

שְׁמַע קוֹלֵנוּ
Sh'ma Koleinu

שְׁלֹשׁ עֶשְׂרֵה מִדּוֹת
13 Middot

כְּרַחֵם אָב
K'Racheim Av

כִּי הִנֵּה כַּחֹמֶר
Ki Hineih KaChomer

אַל תַּעַזְבֵנוּ
Al Taazveinu

שְׁלֹשׁ עֶשְׂרֵה מִדּוֹת
13 Middot

כִּי אָנוּ עַמֶּךָ
Ki Anu Amecha

אָנוּ עַזֵּי פָנִים
Anu Azei Fanim

שְׁלֹשׁ עֶשְׂרֵה מִדּוֹת
13 Middot

מִי שֶׁעָנָה
Mi She·anah

מִי שֶׁעָנָה לְשָׂרָה אִמֵּנוּ בְּזִקְנָתָהּ,
הוּא יַעֲנֵנוּ.

Mi she·anah l'Sarah imeinu b'ziknatah,
hu yaaneinu!

מִי שֶׁעָנָה לְאַבְרָהָם אָבִינוּ
בְּהַר הַמּוֹרִיָּה, הוּא יַעֲנֵנוּ.

Mi she·anah l'Avraham avinu
b'Har HaMoriyah, hu yaaneinu!

מִי שֶׁעָנָה לְיִצְחָק בְּנָם כְּשֶׁנֶּעֱקַד
עַל גַּבֵּי הַמִּזְבֵּחַ, הוּא יַעֲנֵנוּ.

Mi she·anah l'Yitzchak b'nam k'shene·ekad
al gabei hamizbei·ach, hu yaaneinu!

מִי שֶׁעָנָה לְרִבְקָה בְּהֶרְיוֹנָהּ,
הוּא יַעֲנֵנוּ.

Mi she·anah l'Rivkah b'heryonah,
hu yaaneinu!

מִי שֶׁעָנָה לְיַעֲקֹב בְּבֵית אֵל,
הוּא יַעֲנֵנוּ.

Mi she·anah l'Yaakov b'Veit El,
hu yaaneinu!

מִי שֶׁעָנָה לְלֵאָה בְּעׇנְיָהּ,
הוּא יַעֲנֵנוּ.

Mi she·anah l'Leah b'onyah,
hu yaaneinu!

מִי שֶׁעָנָה לְרָחֵל בְּעִצְּבוֹנָהּ,
הוּא יַעֲנֵנוּ.

Mi she·anah l'Rachel b'itz'vonah,
hu yaaneinu!

מִי שֶׁעָנָה לְיוֹסֵף בְּבֵית
הָאֲסוּרִים, הוּא יַעֲנֵנוּ.

Mi she·anah l'Yosef b'veit
haasurim, hu yaaneinu!

מִי שֶׁעָנָה לַמְיַלְּדוֹת הָעִבְרִיּוֹת
עַל הָאׇבְנָיִם, הוּא יַעֲנֵנוּ.

Mi she·anah lamyal'dot ha·ivriyot
al haovnayim, hu yaaneinu!

מִי שֶׁעָנָה לְיוֹכֶבֶד עַל שְׂפַת
הַיְאֹר, הוּא יַעֲנֵנוּ.

Mi she·anah l'Yocheved al s'fat
hai·or, hu yaaneinu!

מִי שֶׁעָנָה לַאֲבוֹתֵינוּ וּלְאִמּוֹתֵינוּ
עַל יַם סוּף, הוּא יַעֲנֵנוּ.

Mi she·anah laavoteinu ul·imoteinu
al yam suf, hu yaaneinu!

מִי שֶׁעָנָה לְמֹשֶׁה בְּחוֹרֵב,
הוּא יַעֲנֵנוּ.

Mi she·anah l'Mosheh b'Choreiv,
hu yaaneinu!

מִי שֶׁעָנָה לִבְנוֹת צְלׇפְחָד בְּעׇמְדָן
פֶּתַח אֹהֶל מוֹעֵד, הוּא יַעֲנֵנוּ.

Mi she·anah livnot Tz'lofchad b'omdan
petach ohel mo·eid, hu yaaneinu!

מִי שֶׁעָנָה לְאֵלִיָּהוּ בְּקוֹל דְּמָמָה
דַקָּה בַּמִּדְבָּר, הוּא יַעֲנֵנוּ.

Mi she·anah l'Eliyahu b'kol d'mamah
dakah bamidbar, hu yaaneinu!

Answer us,
You who answered our mother Sarah in her old age
You who answered our father Abraham on Mount Moriah
You who answered their son Isaac, when bound upon the altar
You who answered Rebecca when she cried, "Why do I exist?"
You who answered Jacob at Beth El, "Israel shall be your name"
You who answered Leah in her sadness
You who answered Rachel in her pain
You who answered Joseph in the prison-house
You who answered the midwives — Shiphrah and Puah —
at the birthing stones
You who answered Yocheved's courage on the bank of the Nile
You who answered our fathers and our mothers at the Sea of Reeds
You who answered Moses at Sinai: "I bore you on eagles' wings"
You who answered the daughters of Zelophehad,
who stood up for their rights before Moses and God
You who answered Elijah with a "still, small voice" in the wilderness
You who answered the righteous ones before us,
men and women of integrity and compassion —
Answer us.

YOU WHO ANSWERED מִי שֶׁעָנָה. This is a contemporary version of a prayer that originates in the Mishnah, as part of a public fast during drought (*Taanit* 2:4). In keeping with the deeply relational nature of the Songs of Forgiveness, "You Who Answered" inspires relationship with biblical ancestors as well as God. For each stanza, the allusion is to the following biblical passage: Genesis 21:7 (Sarah); Genesis 22:12 (Abraham); Genesis 22:12 (Isaac); Genesis 25:23 (Rebecca); Genesis 35:10 (Jacob); Genesis 29:31 (Leah); Genesis 30:22 (Rachel); Genesis 39:21 (Joseph); Exodus 1:20 (Shiphrah and Puah); Exodus 2:3 (Yocheved); Exodus 14:19–30 (at the Sea of Reeds); Exodus 19:4 (Moses); Numbers 27:7 (the daughters of Zelophehad); I Kings 19:11–12 (Elijah).

אָבִינוּ מַלְכֵּנוּ
Avinu Malkeinu

אָבִינוּ מַלְכֵּנוּ
Avinu Malkeinu · Almighty and Merciful

אָבִינוּ מַלְכֵּנוּ,
הָאֵר לָנוּ אֶת דֶּרֶךְ חַיֵּינוּ.

Avinu Malkeinu,
ha·eir lanu et derech chayeinu.

Avinu Malkeinu — Illumine for us the path of our life.

Avinu Malkeinu — How shall we find the strength to take the road less traveled by?

Avinu Malkeinu — How shall we come to know the purpose of our existence?

Avinu Malkeinu — How shall we learn not to live life in vain?

Avinu Malkeinu — How shall we get out of our indifference?

Avinu Malkeinu — How shall we distinguish between truth and falsehood?

Avinu Malkeinu — How shall we find the answers to our questions?

Avinu Malkeinu — How shall we gird ourselves with strength to seek answers?

אָבִינוּ מַלְכֵּנוּ,
חָנֵּנוּ וַעֲנֵנוּ, חַזְּקֵנוּ וְאַמְּצֵנוּ,
כִּי בְךָ וְעִמְּךָ הַתְּשׁוּבוֹת.

Avinu Malkeinu,
choneinu vaaneinu, chaz'keinu v'am'tzeinu,
ki v'cha v'im'cha hat'shuvot.

Avinu Malkeinu — Be gracious to us, answer us,
empower us, and give us courage,
for the answers are both in You and with You.

AVINU MALKEINU אָבִינוּ מַלְכֵּנוּ. Based on a Hebrew prayer by Rabbi Mordechai Rotem (b. 1947).
HOW SHALL WE. Instead of the traditional petitions (pp. 114–15), this contemporary *Avinu Malkeinu* presents a series of questions acknowledging our responsibility for our lives. The prayer is an invitation to add other questions that may "illumine for us the path of our life."
LESS TRAVELED BY. From "The Road Not Taken" by Robert Frost (1874–1963).

Avinu Malkeinu

Avinu Malkeinu: A Prayer of Protest

Avinu Malkeinu—
Hear our voice:
Some of us have cancer.
Some have lost strength of body; some have lost memory and speech.
Some of us are in pain.
Some can't find work.
Some of us bear the marks of human cruelty—inside, where the scars don't show.
Some live with depression; some battle addiction; many feel alone.
Some have known shattered marriages, trust betrayed, hopes destroyed.
Some of us have lost the ones we love, far too soon.
And some have lost a child.
All of us have seen suffering in our midst.
All of us know the ravages of war—for which there are no words.

Avinu Malkeinu, why?
Avinu Malkeinu, are you there? Do you care?
Avinu Malkeinu, hear our pain.
Hear our anger. Hear our grief.
Avinu Malkeinu, here is our prayer:
Give us the strength to go on.
Give us reasons to get up each day; give us purpose and persistence.
Help us to fend off fear and to hold on to hope.
Help us to be kind.
Don't make us bow or grovel for your favor. Give us dignity and give us courage.

Avinu Malkeinu—
Show us the way to a year of goodness.
Renew our belief that the world can be better.
Restore our faith in life. Restore our faith in you.

אָבִֽינוּ מַלְכֵּֽנוּ
Avinu Malkeinu

אָבִֽינוּ מַלְכֵּֽנוּ, שְׁמַע קוֹלֵֽנוּ.
Avinu Malkeinu, sh'ma koleinu.
Avinu Malkeinu — Almighty and Merciful — hear our voice.

אָבִֽינוּ מַלְכֵּֽנוּ, חָטָֽאנוּ לְפָנֶֽיךָ.
Avinu Malkeinu, chatanu l'fanecha.
Avinu Malkeinu, we have strayed and sinned before You.

אָבִֽינוּ מַלְכֵּֽנוּ, חֲמֹל עָלֵֽינוּ, וְעַל עוֹלָלֵֽנוּ וְטַפֵּֽנוּ.
Avinu Malkeinu, chamol aleinu, v'al olaleinu v'tapeinu.
Avinu Malkeinu, have compassion on us and on our families.

אָבִֽינוּ מַלְכֵּֽנוּ, כַּלֵּה דֶּֽבֶר וְחֶֽרֶב וְרָעָב מֵעָלֵֽינוּ.
Avinu Malkeinu, kaleih dever v'cherev v'raav mei·aleinu.
Avinu Malkeinu, halt the onslaught of sickness, violence, and hunger.

אָבִֽינוּ מַלְכֵּֽנוּ, כַּלֵּה כָּל צַר וּמַשְׂטִין מֵעָלֵֽינוּ.
Avinu Malkeinu, kaleih kol tzar umastin mei·aleinu.
Avinu Malkeinu, halt the reign of those who cause pain and terror.

אָבִֽינוּ מַלְכֵּֽנוּ, כָּתְבֵֽנוּ בְּסֵֽפֶר חַיִּים טוֹבִים.
Avinu Malkeinu, kotveinu b'sefer chayim tovim.
Avinu Malkeinu, enter our names in the Book of Lives Well Lived.

אָבִֽינוּ מַלְכֵּֽנוּ, חַדֵּשׁ עָלֵֽינוּ שָׁנָה טוֹבָה.
Avinu Malkeinu, chadeish aleinu shanah tovah.
Avinu Malkeinu, renew for us a year of goodness.

אָבִֽינוּ מַלְכֵּֽנוּ, מַלֵּא יָדֵֽינוּ מִבִּרְכוֹתֶֽיךָ.
Avinu Malkeinu, malei yadeinu mibirchotecha.
Avinu Malkeinu, let our hands overflow with Your blessings.

אָבִֽינוּ מַלְכֵּֽנוּ, הָרֵם קֶֽרֶן מְשִׁיחֶֽךָ.
Avinu Malkeinu, hareim keren m'shichecha.
Avinu Malkeinu, let our eyes behold the dawn of redemption.

Avinu Malkeinu

אָבִֽינוּ מַלְכֵּֽנוּ, נָא אַל תְּשִׁיבֵֽנוּ רֵיקָם
מִלְּפָנֶֽיךָ.

Avinu Malkeinu, na al t'shiveinu reikam mil'fanecha.

Avinu Malkeinu, we pray: do not turn us away from You with nothing.

אָבִֽינוּ מַלְכֵּֽנוּ, קַבֵּל בְּרַחֲמִים
וּבְרָצוֹן אֶת תְּפִלָּתֵֽנוּ.

Avinu Malkeinu, kabeil b'rachamim uvratzon et t'filateinu.

Avinu Malkeinu, welcome our prayer with love; accept and embrace it.

אָבִֽינוּ מַלְכֵּֽנוּ, עֲשֵׂה עִמָּֽנוּ
לְמַֽעַן שְׁמֶֽךָ.

Avinu Malkeinu, aseih imanu l'maan sh'mecha.

Avinu Malkeinu, act toward us as befits Your name.

אָבִֽינוּ מַלְכֵּֽנוּ, עֲשֵׂה לְמַעַנְךָ אִם לֹא
לְמַעֲנֵֽנוּ.

Avinu Malkeinu, aseih l'maancha im lo l'maaneinu.

Avinu Malkeinu, act for Your sake, if not for ours.

אָבִֽינוּ מַלְכֵּֽנוּ, אֵין לָֽנוּ מֶֽלֶךְ אֶלָּא אָֽתָּה.

Avinu Malkeinu, ein lanu melech ela atah.

Avinu Malkeinu, You alone are our Sovereign.

אָבִֽינוּ מַלְכֵּֽנוּ, פְּתַח שַׁעֲרֵי שָׁמַֽיִם
לִתְפִלָּתֵֽנוּ.

Avinu Malkeinu, p'tach shaarei shamayim litfilateinu.

Avinu Malkeinu, let the gates of heaven be open to our prayer.

אָבִֽינוּ מַלְכֵּֽנוּ, שְׁמַע קוֹלֵֽנוּ, חוּס
וְרַחֵם עָלֵֽינוּ.

Avinu Malkeinu, sh'ma koleinu; chus v'racheim aleinu.

Avinu Malkeinu, hear our voice; treat us with tender compassion.

אָבִֽינוּ מַלְכֵּֽנוּ, חָנֵּֽנוּ וַעֲנֵֽנוּ,
כִּי אֵין בָּֽנוּ מַעֲשִׂים.
עֲשֵׂה עִמָּֽנוּ צְדָקָה וָחֶֽסֶד, וְהוֹשִׁיעֵֽנוּ.

Avinu Malkeinu, choneinu vaaneinu;
ki ein banu maasim.
Aseih imanu tz'dakah vachesed, v'hoshi·einu.

Avinu Malkeinu — Almighty and Merciful —
answer us with grace, for our deeds are wanting.
Save us through acts of justice and love.

סִיּוּם הָעַרְבִית
Siyum HaArvit · Concluding Prayers

עָלֵינוּ
Aleinu

קַדִּישׁ יָתוֹם
Kaddish Yatom

מִזְמוֹר כ״ז
Mizmor l'David

אֲדוֹן עוֹלָם
Adon Olam

Aleinu l'shabei·ach laadon hakol,	עָלֵינוּ לְשַׁבֵּחַ לַאֲדוֹן הַכֹּל,
lateit g'dulah l'yotzeir b'reishit —	לָתֵת גְּדֻלָּה לְיוֹצֵר בְּרֵאשִׁית,
shelo asanu k'goyei haaratzot,	שֶׁלֹּא עָשָׂנוּ כְּגוֹיֵי הָאֲרָצוֹת,
v'lo samanu k'mishp'chot haadamah;	וְלֹא שָׂמָנוּ כְּמִשְׁפְּחוֹת הָאֲדָמָה,
shelo sam chelkeinu kahem,	שֶׁלֹּא שָׂם חֶלְקֵנוּ כָּהֶם,
v'goraleinu k'chol hamonam.	וְגֹרָלֵנוּ כְּכָל הֲמוֹנָם.
Vaanachnu korim,	וַאֲנַחְנוּ כּוֹרְעִים
umishtachavim, umodim	וּמִשְׁתַּחֲוִים וּמוֹדִים
lifnei melech malchei ham'lachim:	לִפְנֵי מֶלֶךְ מַלְכֵי הַמְּלָכִים,
HaKadosh, baruch hu,	הַקָּדוֹשׁ בָּרוּךְ הוּא.

Ours is the duty to praise the All-Sovereign, to honor the Artist of Creation, who made us unique in the human family, with a destiny all our own. For this we bend our knees and bow with gratitude before the Sovereign Almighty — Monarch of All — the Wellspring of holiness and blessing,

shehu noteh shamayim v'yoseid aretz,	שֶׁהוּא נוֹטֶה שָׁמַיִם וְיוֹסֵד אָרֶץ,
umoshav y'karo bashamayim mimaal,	וּמוֹשַׁב יְקָרוֹ בַּשָּׁמַיִם מִמַּעַל,
ush·chinat uzo b'govhei m'romim.	וּשְׁכִינַת עֻזּוֹ בְּגָבְהֵי מְרוֹמִים.
Hu Eloheinu; ein od.	הוּא אֱלֹהֵינוּ, אֵין עוֹד.
Emet Malkeinu, efes zulato —	אֱמֶת מַלְכֵּנוּ אֶפֶס זוּלָתוֹ,
kakatuv b'Torato:	כַּכָּתוּב בְּתוֹרָתוֹ:
"V'yadata hayom v'hasheivota el-l'vavecha,	וְיָדַעְתָּ הַיּוֹם וַהֲשֵׁבֹתָ אֶל־לְבָבֶךָ,
ki Adonai hu haElohim	כִּי יְיָ הוּא הָאֱלֹהִים
bashamayim mimaal	בַּשָּׁמַיִם מִמַּעַל
v'al-haaretz mitachat — ein od."	וְעַל־הָאָרֶץ מִתָּחַת, אֵין עוֹד.

who spread out the sky and fashioned the land, who dwells in beauty far beyond sight, whose powerful presence is the loftiest height. You are our God; there is none else. We take as true Your sovereignty; there is no other — as Torah teaches: "Embrace and carry in your heart this day: In heaven above, on earth below, the Eternal is God. There is no other."

EMBRACE וְיָדַעְתָּ, Deuteronomy 4:39.

Our Destiny
Mourner's Kaddish
Psalm 27
Eternal God

עָלֵינוּ לְשַׁבֵּחַ לַאֲדוֹן הַכֹּל,	*Aleinu l'shabei·ach laadon hakol,*
לָתֵת גְּדֻלָּה לְיוֹצֵר בְּרֵאשִׁית,	*lateit g'dulah l'yotzeir b'reishit —*
שֶׁהוּא נוֹטֶה שָׁמַיִם וְיוֹסֵד אָרֶץ,	*shehu noteh shamayim v'yoseid aretz,*
וּמוֹשַׁב יְקָרוֹ בַּשָּׁמַיִם מִמַּעַל,	*umoshav y'karo bashamayim mimaal;*
וּשְׁכִינַת עֻזּוֹ בְּגָבְהֵי מְרוֹמִים,	*ush·chinat uzo b'govhei m'romim,*
הוּא אֱלֹהֵינוּ אֵין עוֹד.	*hu Eloheinu — ein od.*
וַאֲנַחְנוּ כּוֹרְעִים	*Vaanachnu korim,*
וּמִשְׁתַּחֲוִים וּמוֹדִים	*umishtachavim, umodim*
לִפְנֵי מֶלֶךְ מַלְכֵי הַמְּלָכִים,	*lifnei melech malchei ham'lachim:*
הַקָּדוֹשׁ בָּרוּךְ הוּא.	*HaKadosh, baruch hu.*

Let us now praise the Sovereign of the universe, and proclaim the greatness of the Creator—who spread out the heavens and established the earth, whose glory is revealed in the heavens above and whose greatness is manifest throughout the world. You are our God; there is none else. Therefore we bow in awe and thanksgiving before the One who is sovereign over all, the Holy and Blessed One.

• • • • •

עָלֵינוּ לְשַׁבֵּחַ לַאֲדוֹן הַכֹּל,	*Aleinu l'shabei·ach laadon hakol,*
לָתֵת גְּדֻלָּה לְיוֹצֵר בְּרֵאשִׁית,	*lateit g'dulah l'yotzeir b'reishit —*
שֶׁהוּא עָשָׂנוּ לְשׁוֹמְרֵי הָאֲדָמָה,	*shehu asanu l'shomrei haadamah,*
וְהוּא שָׂמָנוּ לִשְׁלִיחֵי הַתּוֹרָה,	*v'hu samanu lishlichei haTorah;*
שֶׁהוּא שָׂם חַיֵּינוּ אִתָּם,	*shehu sam chayeinu itam,*
וְגוֹרָלֵנוּ עִם כָּל הָעוֹלָם.	*v'goraleinu im kol haolam.*
וַאֲנַחְנוּ כּוֹרְעִים	*Vaanachnu korim,*
וּמִשְׁתַּחֲוִים וּמוֹדִים	*umishtachavim, umodim*
לִפְנֵי מֶלֶךְ מַלְכֵי הַמְּלָכִים,	*lifnei melech malchei ham'lachim:*
הַקָּדוֹשׁ בָּרוּךְ הוּא.	*HaKadosh, baruch hu.*

Our calling is to praise the Living Source. Our duty is to make known the greatness of the One Creator, who trusts us to be guardians of the earth and messengers of Torah; who gives us a destiny shared with all human beings, and who binds our lives to theirs. And so we bend, bow, and give thanks before the Blessed One whose realm is unfathomable, whose sovereignty over all makes all life holy and precious.

עָלֵינוּ
Aleinu

קַדִּישׁ יָתוֹם
Kaddish Yatom

מִזְמוֹר כ"ז
Mizmor l'David

אֲדוֹן עוֹלָם
Adon Olam

Al kein n'kaveh l'cha, Adonai Eloheinu,

lirot m'heirah b'tiferet uzecha,

l'haavir gilulim min haaretz;

v'ha·elilim karot yikareitun.

L'takein olam b'malchut Shaddai,

v'chol b'nei vasar yikr'u vishmecha;

l'hafnot eilecha kol rishei aretz.

עַל כֵּן נְקַוֶּה לְּךָ, יְיָ אֱלֹהֵינוּ,

לִרְאוֹת מְהֵרָה בְּתִפְאֶרֶת עֻזֶּךָ,

לְהַעֲבִיר גִּלּוּלִים מִן הָאָרֶץ,

וְהָאֱלִילִים כָּרוֹת יִכָּרֵתוּן.

לְתַקֵּן עוֹלָם בְּמַלְכוּת שַׁדַּי,

וְכָל בְּנֵי בָשָׂר יִקְרְאוּ בִשְׁמֶךָ,

לְהַפְנוֹת אֵלֶיךָ כָּל רִשְׁעֵי אָרֶץ.

And so, Adonai our God, we look to You,
hoping soon to behold the splendor of Your power revealed:
a world free of idolatry and false gods;
a world growing more perfect through divine governance;
a world in which all human beings make known Your name,
while those who do evil turn toward You.

V'ne·emar:

"V'hayah Adonai l'melech al-kol-haaretz,

bayom hahu yiyeh Adonai echad,

ushmo echad."

וְנֶאֱמַר:

וְהָיָה יְיָ לְמֶלֶךְ עַל־כָּל־הָאָרֶץ,

בַּיּוֹם הַהוּא יִהְיֶה יְיָ אֶחָד,

וּשְׁמוֹ אֶחָד.

As the prophet announced,
"The Eternal shall be sovereign over all the earth.
On that day the Eternal shall be one, and God's name shall be one."

THOSE WHO DO EVIL. The Jews, who throughout their history have suffered anguish and oppression at the hands of evil-doers, are, nevertheless, as concerned for the fate of their tormentors as they are for their own. So we stand, in solemn prayer, petitioning the Almighty to grant enlightenment to our enemies so that they may recognize God's sovereignty and share in the reward that is treasured up for the faithful. (Rabbi Jeffrey M. Cohen, b. 1950; adapted)

THE ETERNAL SHALL BE וְהָיָה יְיָ. This prophetic verse (Zechariah 14:9) points to a future in which all humanity will come to recognize one God — a fulfillment of the vision set forth in the *Sh'ma* (Deuteronomy 6:4), which proclaims God's unity, and in the first section of *Aleinu* (page 116), which calls God "Monarch of All."

May the time not be distant, our God,
when all shall turn to You in love,
when corruption and evil shall give way to integrity and goodness,
when lies and bigotry shall no longer enslave the mind,
nor idolatry blind the eye.
So may all, created in Your image,
become one in spirit and one in friendship,
forever united in Your service.
Then shall Your dominion be established on earth,
and the word of Your prophet fulfilled:
"Adonai will reign forever and ever."

וְנֶאֱמַר:
וְהָיָה יְיָ לְמֶלֶךְ עַל־כָּל־הָאָרֶץ.
בַּיּוֹם הַהוּא יִהְיֶה יְיָ אֶחָד,
וּשְׁמוֹ אֶחָד.

V'ne·emar:
"V'hayah Adonai l'melech al-kol-haaretz.
Bayom hahu yiyeh Adonai echad,
ushmo echad."

And it has been said: "Adonai shall reign over all the earth.
On that day Adonai shall be one, and God's name shall be one."

May we gain wisdom in our lives,
overflowing like a river with understanding.
Loved, each of us, for the peace we bring to others.
May our deeds exceed our speech,
and may we never lift up our hand
but to conquer fear and doubt and despair.
Rise up like the sun, O God, over all humanity.
Cause light to go forth over all the lands between the seas.
And light up the universe with the joy
of wholeness, of freedom, and of peace.

וְנֶאֱמַר:
וְהָיָה יְיָ לְמֶלֶךְ עַל־כָּל־הָאָרֶץ.
בַּיּוֹם הַהוּא יִהְיֶה יְיָ אֶחָד,
וּשְׁמוֹ אֶחָד.

V'ne·emar:
"V'hayah Adonai l'melech al-kol-haaretz.
Bayom hahu yiyeh Adonai echad,
ushmo echad."

Thus it has been said: "Adonai will be sovereign over all the earth.
On that day, Adonai will be one, and God's name will be one."

***How shall** the heart be reconciled*
to its feast of losses?
—Stanley Kunitz

יִתְגַּדַּל וְיִתְקַדַּשׁ שְׁמֵהּ רַבָּא
Yitgadal v'yitkadash sh'meih raba

This is the praise of the living,
praise for the gift of life.

Praise for loved ones and friends,
for listening hearts,
laughter and forgiveness.

Praise for their searching and striving,
for perseverance and vision,
minds that aspired to know and understand.

Praise for their courage and faith,
for souls that brought light to dark corners,
for hands that were gentle and strong.

Praise for those who walked before us
in valleys of darkest shadow,
who endured their grief, and brought forth new life.

יִתְגַּדַּל וְיִתְקַדַּשׁ שְׁמֵהּ רַבָּא
Yitgadal v'yitkadash sh'meih raba

Praise for the One who is always with us:
the Source of growth, the Promise of goodness.

Praise for the gift of life and memory.
Praise for the blessing of hope.

We stand as one on this night of remembrance.
United in grief, united in loss,
united in the power of a promise:
God has made us; God will sustain us.
We give praise to this life
and rise up together to renew our strength.

Our Destiny

Mourner's Kaddish

Psalm 27

Eternal God

Preparing for the Prayer of Memory

This holy night concludes with memory;
our last thoughts, always, are of those we have lost.

We miss them especially tonight,
yearning for their presence at our side.

The service we have shared once was theirs:
they spoke and sang the ancient words;
they prayed, repented, and yearned for better lives—as we have done.

Flawed in their deeds, imperfect in their faith,
they still drew strength from their tradition, as we seek fortitude in ours.

What was good and beautiful in their lives
once gave us joy and now inspires us to reach higher.

The knowledge that they loved us deeply brings comfort to our hearts.
So we light candles of remembrance and gratitude,
and we speak this timeless truth:

Zichronam livrachah — זִכְרוֹנָם לִבְרָכָה

Their memory is a blessing, now and forever.
We pray that their goodness will live on in our lives,
planting seeds of kindness and hope for generations to come.

Our thoughts turn to loved ones
whom death has taken from us in recent days,
and those who died at this season in years past.
Our hearts open, as well, to the wider circles of loss
in our community and wherever grief touches
the human family. . . .
Zichronam livrachah — זִכְרוֹנָם לִבְרָכָה
May their memories be a blessing in this new year—and always.

עָלֵינוּ
Aleinu
קַדִּישׁ יָתוֹם
Kaddish Yatom
מִזְמוֹר כ״ז
Mizmor l'David
אֲדוֹן עוֹלָם
Adon Olam

Mourner's Kaddish

Yitgadal v'yitkadash sh'meih raba,	יִתְגַּדַּל וְיִתְקַדַּשׁ שְׁמֵהּ רַבָּא,
b'alma di v'ra chiruteih.	בְּעָלְמָא דִּי בְרָא כִרְעוּתֵהּ.
V'yamlich malchuteih b'chayeichon uvyomeichon,	וְיַמְלִיךְ מַלְכוּתֵהּ בְּחַיֵּיכוֹן וּבְיוֹמֵיכוֹן,
uvchayei d'chol beit Yisrael —	וּבְחַיֵּי דְכָל בֵּית יִשְׂרָאֵל,
baagala uvizman kariv;	בַּעֲגָלָא וּבִזְמַן קָרִיב.
v'imru: Amen.	וְאִמְרוּ: אָמֵן.
Y'hei sh'meih raba m'varach	יְהֵא שְׁמֵהּ רַבָּא מְבָרַךְ
l'alam ul·almei almaya.	לְעָלַם וּלְעָלְמֵי עָלְמַיָּא.
Yitbarach v'yishtabach v'yitpaar v'yitromam v'yitnasei v'yit·hadar v'yitaleh v'yit·halal sh'meih d'kudsha — b'rich hu —	יִתְבָּרַךְ וְיִשְׁתַּבַּח וְיִתְפָּאַר וְיִתְרוֹמַם וְיִתְנַשֵּׂא וְיִתְהַדַּר וְיִתְעַלֶּה וְיִתְהַלַּל שְׁמֵהּ דְּקֻדְשָׁא, בְּרִיךְ הוּא,
l'eila ul·eila mikol birchata v'shirata,	לְעֵלָּא וּלְעֵלָּא מִכָּל בִּרְכָתָא וְשִׁירָתָא,
tushb'chata v'nechemata daamiran b'alma;	תֻּשְׁבְּחָתָא וְנֶחֱמָתָא דַּאֲמִירָן בְּעָלְמָא.
v'imru: Amen.	וְאִמְרוּ: אָמֵן.
Y'hei sh'lama raba min sh'maya,	יְהֵא שְׁלָמָא רַבָּא מִן שְׁמַיָּא,
v'chayim aleinu v'al kol Yisrael;	וְחַיִּים עָלֵינוּ וְעַל כָּל יִשְׂרָאֵל.
v'imru: Amen.	וְאִמְרוּ: אָמֵן.
Oseh shalom bimromav,	עֹשֶׂה שָׁלוֹם בִּמְרוֹמָיו
hu yaaseh shalom aleinu,	הוּא יַעֲשֶׂה שָׁלוֹם עָלֵינוּ
v'al kol Yisrael	וְעַל כָּל יִשְׂרָאֵל
v'al kol yoshvei teiveil;	וְעַל כָּל יוֹשְׁבֵי תֵבֵל.
v'imru: Amen.	וְאִמְרוּ: אָמֵן.

GO TO BEMA ADON OLOM AS RABBI BENEDICTION

May the Source of peace bestow peace on all who mourn,
and may we be a source of comfort to all who are bereaved.
Amen.

May God's great name come to be magnified and sanctified
in the world God brought into being.
May God's majestic reign prevail soon in your lives, in your days,
and in the life of the whole House of Israel;
and let us say: *Amen.*

May God's great name be blessed to the end of time.

May God's holy name come to be blessed, acclaimed, and glorified;
revered, raised, and beautified; honored and praised.
Blessed is the One who is entirely beyond
all the blessings and hymns,
all the praises and words of comfort
that we speak in the world;
and let us say: *Amen.*

Let perfect peace abound;
let there be abundant life for us and for all Israel.
May the One who makes peace in the high heavens
make peace for us,
all Israel,
and all who dwell on earth;
and let us say: *Amen.*

Sow In Tears

Those who sow, who sow in tears will reap in joy, will reap in joy.
Those who sow, who sow in tears will reap, will reap in joy.
It's the song of the dreamer, from a dark place it grows.
Like a flower in the desert, the oasis of our souls.
Come back, come back where we belong, You who hear our longing cries.
Our mouths, our lips are filled with song.
You can see our tear-filled eyes.

SOW IN TEARS. Lyrics by Debbie Friedman (1951–2011), based on Psalm 126:5. Part of a "Song of Ascents," these words once offered promise to sorrowing Israelites driven from the Land of Israel to exile in Babylonia. On this holiest of nights, we pray that these words will lift us up, as well, and help us to ascend — from regret to true repentance; from stubborn anger to forgiveness; from cynicism to principled ideals; from sorrow to hope renewed.

From Psalm 27

עָלֵינוּ
Aleinu

קַדִּיש יָתוֹם
Kaddish Yatom

מִזְמוֹר כ״ז
Mizmor l'David

אֲדוֹן עוֹלָם
Adon Olam

Adonai ori v'yishi — mimi ira?

Adonai maoz-chayai — mimi efchad?

יְיָ אוֹרִי וְיִשְׁעִי, מִמִּי אִירָא,
יְיָ מָעוֹז־חַיַּי, מִמִּי אֶפְחָד.

God is my light and my refuge secure —
whom shall I fear?
God is the stronghold of my life —
of whom should I be afraid?

Achat shaalti mei·eit-Adonai;

otah avakeish:

shivti b'veit-Adonai kol-y'mei chayai,

lachazot b'no·am-Adonai,

ulvakeir b'heichalo.

אַחַת שָׁאַלְתִּי מֵאֵת־יְיָ,
אוֹתָהּ אֲבַקֵּשׁ:
שִׁבְתִּי בְּבֵית־יְיָ כָּל־יְמֵי חַיַּי,
לַחֲזוֹת בְּנֹעַם־יְיָ,
וּלְבַקֵּר בְּהֵיכָלוֹ.

Just one thing I have asked of God;
only this do I seek:
to dwell in God's House all the days of my life,
to behold divine sweetness and beauty,
and to gaze in delight at God's Temple.

ADONAI IS MY LIGHT יְיָ אוֹרִי. Psalm 27 offers a statement of serenity and confidence appropriate to the mood of the Holy Days. Its words can help us summon the courage we need to confront our moral failings, which may be as challenging as any enemies we face.

A TEACHING of our Sages:

Adonai is my light and my help—
for so it is written:
Your word is a lamp to my feet, a light for my path.
There are some who stumble in darkness, like wanderers lost in the night.
But those who love and study Your words—
they carry a torch in the darkness:
they see the dangers, and they do not fall.

Adonai is my light—
This refers to Rosh HaShanah,
called *Yom HaDin*—day of judgment, time of truth,
for so it is written:
God will let your righteousness shine forth like the light;
the justice of your cause like the noonday sun.

Adonai is my help—
This refers to Yom Kippur,
the holy day when God helps us to atone and forgives our sins.

On this Atonement night, I pray:
Let the goodness within me shine forth.
As I struggle to overcome my flaws,
let me find forgiveness and peace.
So may I journey from darkness and confusion
to clarity and light.
And so may I learn not to fear.

A TEACHING OF OUR SAGES. Based on *Midrash T'hilim* 27:2 and 27:4. Probably because of this midrashic link between Psalm 27 and the Days of Awe, it became customary to recite this psalm each day from the beginning of the month of Elul through Hoshana Rabbah, the conclusion of the High Holy Day season.

ADONAI IS MY LIGHT AND MY HELP, Psalm 27:1.

YOUR WORD IS A LAMP TO MY FEET, Psalm 119:105.

GOD WILL LET YOUR RIGHTEOUSNESS SHINE FORTH, Psalm 37:6.

עָלֵינוּ
Aleinu

קַדִּישׁ יָתוֹם
Kaddish Yatom

מִזְמוֹר כ״ז
Mizmor l'David

אֲדוֹן עוֹלָם
Adon Olam

Adon Olam

אֲדוֹן עוֹלָם אֲשֶׁר מָלַךְ,
Adon olam asher malach,
בְּטֶרֶם כָּל יְצִיר נִבְרָא.
b'terem kol y'tzir nivra.
לְעֵת נַעֲשָׂה בְחֶפְצוֹ כֹּל,
L'eit naasah v'cheftzo kol,
אֲזַי מֶלֶךְ שְׁמוֹ נִקְרָא.
azai Melech sh'mo nikra.
וְאַחֲרֵי כִּכְלוֹת הַכֹּל,
V'acharei kichlot hakol,
לְבַדּוֹ יִמְלֹךְ נוֹרָא.
l'vado yimloch nora.
וְהוּא הָיָה, וְהוּא הֹוֶה,
V'hu hayah, v'hu hoveh,
וְהוּא יִהְיֶה, בְּתִפְאָרָה.
v'hu yiyeh, b'tifarah.
וְהוּא אֶחָד וְאֵין שֵׁנִי,
V'hu echad v'ein sheini,
לְהַמְשִׁיל לוֹ לְהַחְבִּירָה.
l'hamshil lo l'hachbirah.
בְּלִי רֵאשִׁית בְּלִי תַכְלִית,
B'li reishit b'li tachlit,
וְלוֹ הָעֹז וְהַמִּשְׂרָה.
v'lo haoz v'hamisrah.
וְהוּא אֵלִי וְחַי גֹּאֲלִי,
V'hu Eli v'chai go·ali,
וְצוּר חֶבְלִי בְּעֵת צָרָה.
v'tzur chevli b'eit tzarah.
וְהוּא נִסִּי וּמָנוֹס לִי,
V'hu nisi umanos-li,
מְנָת כּוֹסִי בְּיוֹם אֶקְרָא.
m'nat kosi b'yom ekra.
בְּיָדוֹ אַפְקִיד רוּחִי,
B'yado afkid ruchi,
בְּעֵת אִישַׁן וְאָעִירָה.
b'eit ishan v'a·irah.
וְעִם רוּחִי גְּוִיָּתִי,
V'im ruchi g'viyati,
יְיָ לִי וְלֹא אִירָא.
Adonai li v'lo ira.

Eternal God, who reigned before the earth was formed and life appeared,
when all came forth as You desired, You ruled supreme, Your name revered.

And after all shall fade away, alone our God of Awe remains;
You were, You are, shall always be; Your presence shines; Your glory reigns.

Our God is One, beyond compare; through You we glimpse pure unity.
Unbound by words like "first" and "last," our Moment of eternity.

My living God, my Rock, my Help, in times of grief I seek Your face;
my sign of hope, my cup of life — my prayer reveals Your sheltering place.

My soul entrusted to Your care, both when I sleep and when I rise.
My body, too, will rest in You. I have no fear — for God is mine.

Our Destiny
Mourner's Kaddish
Psalm 27
Eternal God

Hashiveinu / Return Again

הֲשִׁיבֵנוּ, יְיָ, אֵלֶיךָ
וְנָשׁוּבָה,
חַדֵּשׁ יָמֵינוּ כְּקֶדֶם.

Hashiveinu, Adonai, eilecha
v'nashuvah;
chadeish yameinu k'kedem.

Return again, return again,
return to the land of your soul.
Return to what you are, return to who you are,
return to where you are
Born and reborn again.

Renew Us

יְהִי רָצוֹן מִלְּפָנֶיךָ,
יְיָ אֱלֹהֵינוּ וֵאלֹהֵי אֲבוֹתֵינוּ
וְאִמּוֹתֵינוּ,
שֶׁתְּחַדֵּשׁ עָלֵינוּ שָׁנָה טוֹבָה
וּמְתוּקָה.

Y'hi ratzon mil'fanecha,
Adonai Eloheinu v'Elohei avoteinu
v'imoteinu,
shet'chadeish aleinu shanah tovah
umtukah.

Our God and God of our ancestors,
Eternal God of all generations:
May Your presence in our lives this New Year
renew our spirits and renew our strength.
May it be a good year.
May it be a sweet year.

לְשָׁנָה טוֹבָה תִּכָּתֵבוּ – וְתֵחָתֵמוּ!

L'shanah tovah tikateivu — v'teichateimu!

May you be inscribed — and sealed — for a good year!

HASHIVEINU הֲשִׁיבֵנוּ, Lamentations 5:21.
RETURN AGAIN. Lyrics by Rabbi Shlomo Carlebach (1924–1994).

שחרית ליום כיפור
Yom Kippur Morning Service

You stand this day, all of you,
in the presence of Adonai your God.

—DEUTERONOMY 29:9

בִּרְכוֹת הַשַּׁחַר
Birchot HaShachar · Morning Blessings

Tallit

בָּרְכִי, נַפְשִׁי, אֶת־יְיָ,
יְיָ אֱלֹהַי, גָּדַלְתָּ מְּאֹד,
הוֹד וְהָדָר לָבָשְׁתָּ,
עֹטֶה־אוֹר כַּשַּׂלְמָה,
נוֹטֶה שָׁמַיִם כַּיְרִיעָה.

Bar'chi, nafshi, et-Adonai!
Adonai Elohai, gadalta m'od:
hod v'hadar lavashta;
oteh-or kasalmah;
noteh shamayim kairiah.

Unnamable God, I summon all my strength to praise:
You are fathomless, yet close to me.
Clothed in splendor, wrapped in light like a cloak,
You stretch out the sky, celestial tent.

בָּרוּךְ אַתָּה, יְיָ,
אֱלֹהֵינוּ מֶלֶךְ הָעוֹלָם,
אֲשֶׁר קִדְּשָׁנוּ בְּמִצְוֹתָיו,
וְצִוָּנוּ לְהִתְעַטֵּף בַּצִּיצִת.

Baruch atah, Adonai,
Eloheinu melech haolam,
asher kid'shanu b'mitzvotav,
v'tzivanu l'hitateif batzitzit.

Source of blessings — Eternal, our God, majestic in power:
Your mitzvot are paths of holiness;
You give us the mitzvah of wrapping ourselves in
the fringed tallit.

For those who do not wear the tallit:

Source of blessings — Eternal, our God, majestic in power:
Your splendor reveals the way to holiness;
Your light wraps us in the beauty of this sacred day.

UNNAMABLE GOD בָּרְכִי, נַפְשִׁי, Psalm 104:1–2.

WRAP OURSELVES. It is written in the Book of Job: "I clothed myself in righteousness and it robed me; justice was my cloak and turban" (29:14). This biblical metaphor suggests a life lived with integrity, in which one's actions are "all of a piece," governed by an overarching principle. By wrapping ourselves in a garment whose fringes recall our Jewish obligations, we, too, try to "clothe ourselves in righteousness."

Tallit Blessing
Gratitude
Readiness
In God's Holy Place
Psalm 121
Psalm 27
Torah Blessings
Torah Study
Our Bodies
Our Souls
Everyday Miracles

Mah-yakar chasd'cha, Elohim!	מַה־יָּקָר חַסְדְּךָ, אֱלֹהִים,
Uvnei adam b'tzeil k'nafecha yechesayun.	וּבְנֵי אָדָם בְּצֵל כְּנָפֶיךָ יֶחֱסָיוּן.
Yirv'yun mideshen beitecha;	יִרְוְיֻן מִדֶּשֶׁן בֵּיתֶךָ,
v'nachal adanecha tashkeim.	וְנַחַל עֲדָנֶיךָ תַשְׁקֵם.
Ki im'cha m'kor chayim;	כִּי עִמְּךָ מְקוֹר חַיִּים,
b'orcha nireh-or.	בְּאוֹרְךָ נִרְאֶה־אוֹר.
M'shoch chasd'cha l'yodecha,	מְשֹׁךְ חַסְדְּךָ לְיֹדְעֶיךָ,
v'tzidkat'cha l'yishrei-lev.	וְצִדְקָתְךָ לְיִשְׁרֵי־לֵב.

Your faithful love—
a most precious gift
Your wings—
our shade and shelter
Your house—
a place of abundance
Your streams—
delightful to drink
With You there is life.
With You there is light, vision, and understanding.

Bestow kindness on all who would know You,
goodness on those who spread justice.

WALKERS WITH THE DAWN

Being walkers with the dawn and morning,
Walkers with the sun and morning,
We are not afraid of night,
Nor days of gloom,
Nor darkness—
Being walkers with the sun and morning.

YOUR FAITHFUL LOVE מַה־יָּקָר חַסְדְּךָ, Psalm 36:8–11.
WALKERS WITH THE DAWN. By Langston Hughes (1902–1967).

מוֹדֶה\מוֹדָה אֲנִי לְפָנֶיךָ,
מֶלֶךְ חַי וְקַיָּם,
שֶׁהֶחֱזַרְתָּ בִּי נִשְׁמָתִי בְּחֶמְלָה.
רַבָּה אֱמוּנָתֶךָ.

Modeh/Modah ani l'fanecha,
Melech chai v'kayam,
shehechezarta bi nishmati b'chemlah.
Rabah emunatecha.

I thank You, living and eternal Power,
for returning my soul to me with compassion.
Great is Your faithfulness.

הֲרֵינִי מְקַבֵּל\מְקַבֶּלֶת עָלַי
מִצְוַת הַבּוֹרֵא:
וְאָהַבְתָּ לְרֵעֲךָ כָּמוֹךָ.

Hareini m'kabeil/m'kabelet alai
mitzvat haborei:
"V'ahavta l'rei·acha kamocha."

I am ready to take upon myself
the sacred charge of my Creator:
"Love your neighbor as yourself."

I THANK YOU מוֹדֶה\מוֹדָה אֲנִי. Because consciousness is absent during sleep and our bodily functions are slowed, the Talmud (*B'rachot* 57b) calls sleep a kind of "mini-death" (literally, one-sixtieth of death). The *Modeh Ani* prayer expresses grateful delight in the return of consciousness in the morning. We thank God for granting us this day — a sign of divine compassion and also of God's faith in us, for we have been entrusted with another opportunity to bring goodness into the world.

I AM READY הֲרֵינִי. This *kavanah* (focusing meditation) before the morning service was introduced by the kabbalist Rabbi Isaac Luria of Safed (1534–1572). It reminds us that the ultimate purpose of our prayers is to create a strong and loving community.

LOVE YOUR NEIGHBOR AS YOURSELF וְאָהַבְתָּ לְרֵעֲךָ כָּמוֹךָ, Leviticus 19:18. The 18th-century rabbi Alexander Susskind of Grodno taught: "The positive mitzvah *You shall love your neighbor as yourself* can be fulfilled at any time, both through our deeds and through our thoughts. How? If we perform a kind act for another, we fulfill the mitzvah through our deeds. And if we see or hear something good concerning another person, and are happy and rejoice wholeheartedly, as if that good had actually come to ourselves, then we have fulfilled the mitzvah through our thoughts."

WE BREATHE YOUR NAME (*facing page*). Rabbi Lawrence Kushner (b. 1943) teaches that the Hebrew letters of God's name (*yod, hei, vav, hei*) cannot be pronounced as a word. He writes: "The holiest Name in the world, the Name of the Creator, is the sound of your own breathing."

Entering the Day

1.

We stand this day, all of us, in the presence of our God.
Youth and elders, women and men,
those close to tradition and those who have been estranged —
all are welcome in this community of prayer.
Around the world, all Israel greets this holy day.
We stand with them, a people united by our history and fate —
linked in mind and heart to generations past,
who stood before God to be cleansed of their sins
in Russia, Poland, Germany, and Spain;
in Morocco, Egypt, Brazil, and India.
Our great-grandparents are here with us today,
and our great-great-grandchildren, as well —
all are present in memory and hope.
We stand this sacred morning, all of us,
as one.

2.

We thank You, living and eternal One,
for morning light,
for the breath within us,
for strength and life renewed.
Now it opens before us:
this Sabbath of Sabbaths,
gift of spacious contemplation,
mirror for the soul.
May we see our lives reflected in this still, clear pool —
a day apart,
unhurried time,
and undivided mind.
Give us joy in this day that Israel shares;
give us presence and attention,
clear vision, a listening heart.
We wake to the morning.
We open our eyes.
We breathe Your name.

THE FAST WE CHOOSE

For animals, eating is a matter of appetite and instinct. As a human being, I give thanks for my ability to master my appetites and restrict my consumption for the sake of ethical and spiritual goals. As a Jew, I affirm the fast of Yom Kippur mandated by tradition: "Mark, the tenth day of this seventh month is the Day of Atonement. It shall be a sacred occasion for you; you shall practice self-denial" (Leviticus 23:26–27).

Having withdrawn from physical nourishment, may I fast consciously and with focused intention, attentive to the work of repentance and atonement.

Mindful of the words of the prophet Isaiah, I pray for a fast of moral significance: "*This* is the fast I desire: . . . to share your bread with the hungry" (58:7). Going without food on this day may bring me discomfort. Help me to feel the pain of those who lack food every day, and to remember that feeling when Yom Kippur has ended. May this act of self-denial inspire me to greater generosity toward those who have much less than I.

And may our congregation grow in spirit from this shared experience of deprivation. May we who constantly face the temptation to over-consume learn the virtues of moderation and self-control. May we spend less on ourselves and our families, and give more to charity and education.

God whose name is *Shaddai*—meaning "it is enough"—help us to curb our acquisitive hunger and find satisfaction in what is ours. As our Sages have taught: "Who is rich? One who is content with his or her portion" (Mishnah *Avot* 4:4).

בָּרוּךְ אַתָּה, יְיָ, שֶׁדְּרָכָיו דַּרְכֵי קְדֻשָּׁה,
מִצְוַת צוֹם נָתַתָּ לָנוּ בַּיּוֹם הַקָּדוֹשׁ הַזֶּה.

Baruch atah, Adonai, shed'rachav darchei k'dushah;
mitzvat tzom natata lanu bayom hakadosh hazeh.

We praise You, Adonai, whose mitzvot are paths of holiness;
You give us the mitzvah of fasting on this holy day.

MAY WE WHO CONSTANTLY FACE THE TEMPTATION . . . MORE TO CHARITY AND EDUCATION. From Rabbi Allen Maller (b. 1938), adapted.

SHADDAI. A midrash interprets this as a divine name implying limitation and restriction: "God, who said to the world '*Dai* (enough)!'" (*Genesis Rabbah* 46.3; Talmud *Chagigah* 12a).

טַלִּית / *Tallit*

מוֹדָה\מוֹדֶה אֲנִי / *Modeh/Modah Ani*

הֲרֵינִי / *Hareini*

מַה־טֹּבוּ / *Mah Tovu*

שִׁיר לַמַּעֲלוֹת / *Shir Lamaalot*

מִזְמוֹר כ"ז / *Mizmor l'David*

בִּרְכוֹת הַתּוֹרָה / *Birchot HaTorah*

תַּלְמוּד תּוֹרָה / *Talmud Torah*

אֲשֶׁר יָצַר / *Asher Yatzar*

אֱלֹהַי, נְשָׁמָה / *Elohai, N'shamah*

נִסִּים שֶׁבְּכָל יוֹם / *Nisim Sheb'chol Yom*

FOR THOSE UNABLE TO FAST

As I ENTER the holy day of Yom Kippur, I am mindful of the Torah's teaching for this day: "It shall be a sacred occasion for you; you shall practice self-denial" (Leviticus 23:27). The decision to fast is an expression of human freedom, our capacity to control our appetites rather than be enslaved to them. Our Sages have taught that we do not eat and drink so as to remove ourselves from normal concerns and focus our minds on the spiritual tasks of repentance and atonement.

But for those unable for reasons of health to participate in the fast, it is a commandment to eat and drink on Yom Kippur. For Torah is not a source of punishment, but an instrument of compassion and loving-kindness, intended to enrich and improve our lives. I honor the divine gift of my life and the sacred imperative to preserve life. Therefore, I am prepared to fulfill the mitzvah of eating and drinking on this day, in keeping with what is written in the Torah (Leviticus 18:5): "You shall keep My laws and My rules, by the pursuit of which you shall live; I am Adonai."

May I experience the spiritual intensity of this day with a whole heart, and may I go forward this year to fulfill many mitzvot, in life and health, in sincerity and dedication.

Amen.

AUTHOR OF LIFE—
Your care for us teaches us to care for ourselves.
Embraced by You,
I embrace Your mitzvah "Choose life"
on this holy Day of Atonement.
Let my spirit, as well as my body, be nourished
by the food and drink that will sustain me through the day.
Blessed with strength and well-being,
may I pursue a life of *t'shuvah*, *t'filah*, and *tzedakah*:
return to the right path, prayer, and righteous giving.

OUR SAGES HAVE TAUGHT. Rabbi Moses Maimonides (1135–1204), in his *Guide of the Perplexed* (3:43), teaches that refraining from work, food, drink, and other bodily concerns frees us from distraction and allows us to concentrate on the work of *t'shuvah*.

TORAH IS NOT A SOURCE OF PUNISHMENT. Based on Maimonides, *Mishneh Torah* (Laws of Shabbat 2.3), which permits one to perform otherwise forbidden labor on Shabbat in order to save life.

טַלִּית
Tallit

מוֹדֶה\מוֹדָה אֲנִי
Modeh/Modah Ani

הֲרֵינִי
Hareini

מַה־טֹּבוּ
Mah Tovu

שִׁיר לַמַּעֲלוֹת
Shir Lamaalot

מִזְמוֹר כ״ז
Mizmor l'David

בִּרְכוֹת הַתּוֹרָה
Birchot HaTorah

תַּלְמוּד תּוֹרָה
Talmud Torah

אֲשֶׁר יָצַר
Asher Yatzar

אֱלֹהַי, נְשָׁמָה
Elohai, N'shamah

נִסִּים שֶׁבְּכָל יוֹם
Nisim Sheb'chol Yom

מַה־טֹּבוּ אֹהָלֶיךָ, יַעֲקֹב,	*Mah-tovu ohalecha, Yaakov;*
מִשְׁכְּנֹתֶיךָ, יִשְׂרָאֵל.	*mishk'notecha, Yisrael!*
וַאֲנִי בְּרֹב חַסְדְּךָ אָבוֹא בֵיתֶךָ,	*Vaani b'rov chasd'cha avo veitecha;*
אֶשְׁתַּחֲוֶה אֶל־הֵיכַל־קָדְשְׁךָ	*eshtachaveh el-heichal-kodsh'cha*
בְּיִרְאָתֶךָ.	*b'yiratecha.*
יְיָ, אָהַבְתִּי מְעוֹן בֵּיתֶךָ,	*Adonai, ahavti m'on beitecha;*
וּמְקוֹם מִשְׁכַּן כְּבוֹדֶךָ.	*umkom mishkan k'vodecha.*
וַאֲנִי אֶשְׁתַּחֲוֶה וְאֶכְרָעָה,	*Vaani eshtachaveh v'echraah;*
אֶבְרְכָה לִפְנֵי־יְיָ עֹשִׂי.	*evr'chah lifnei-Adonai osi.*
וַאֲנִי תְפִלָּתִי־לְךָ, יְיָ, עֵת רָצוֹן.	*Vaani t'filati-l'cha, Adonai, eit ratzon.*
אֱלֹהִים בְּרָב־חַסְדֶּךָ,	*Elohim, b'rov-chasdecha,*
עֲנֵנִי בֶּאֱמֶת יִשְׁעֶךָ.	*aneini be·emet yishecha.*

How beautiful are your tents, Yaakov,
your dwelling places, Yisrael!
In Your great love, let me enter Your house,
to pray — awestruck — in Your holy place.
Your kindness has led me to Your house;
here I will honor You.
I pray to You, God,
that this may be a good time for our meeting.
Out of Your great love, let me perceive Your truth,
and find Your help.

HOW BEAUTIFUL מַה־טֹּבוּ, Numbers 24:5.

IN YOUR GREAT LOVE וַאֲנִי בְּרֹב חַסְדְּךָ, Psalm 5:8. These words describe a moment of intense spirituality and awareness of the abundance of God's *chesed* — a word that in the Bible conveys the essence of the covenant between God and Israel: the qualities of steadfast love, kindness, loyalty, responsibility, and care.

YOUR KINDNESS יְיָ, אָהַבְתִּי, Psalm 26:8.

HERE I WILL HONOR וַאֲנִי אֶשְׁתַּחֲוֶה, based on Psalm 95:6.

I PRAY TO YOU וַאֲנִי תְפִלָּתִי־לְךָ, Psalm 69:14. Reflecting on a midrashic reading of these words — "I am my prayer to You" (*va·ani t'filati l'cha*) — Rabbi Yoel Kahn (b. 1958) writes: "I yearn for the I–Thou of prayer in which I lose my self-consciousness and self-criticism, and can allow the prayers to flow through me. And I pray to internalize my prayers so that when I leave the sanctuary, I can fully embody them in the way I live."

אַנְעִים זְמִירוֹת, וְשִׁירִים אֶאֱרוֹג,
כִּי אֵלֶיךָ נַפְשִׁי תַעֲרוֹג.
נַפְשִׁי חָמְדָה בְּצֵל יָדֶךָ,
לָדַעַת כָּל רָז סוֹדֶךָ.
מִדֵּי דַבְּרִי בִּכְבוֹדֶךָ,
הוֹמֶה לִבִּי אֶל דּוֹדֶיךָ.
עַל כֵּן אֲדַבֵּר בְּךָ נִכְבָּדוֹת,
וְשִׁמְךָ אֲכַבֵּד בְּשִׁירֵי יְדִידוֹת.

Anim z'mirot, v'shirim e·erog —
ki eilecha nafshi taarog.
Nafshi cham'dah b'tzeil yadecha,
ladaat kol raz sodecha.
Midei dab'ri bichvodecha,
homeh libi el dodecha.
Al kein adabeir b'cha nichbadot,
v'shimcha achabeid b'shirei y'didot.

I would sing You the sweetest of songs, weave You tapestries of rhyme—
for You my soul is yearning. . . .

To know Your sheltering hand, to grasp Your deepest mysteries—
in these my soul delights.

The moment I speak of Your glory,
Your love overpowers my heart.

Through speech I honor Your praiseworthy deeds,
but I honor You best in love songs.

DEEPEST GOOD

When I sort through the layered texture
Of what clutters and claims my spirit,
I find you, Deepest Good, in residence.
You shine like a piece of gold inside of me.
In that tranquil, secluded district of soul
I discover my true, unblemished nature.
Teach me that there is much more to "me"
Than just my struggle and my failure.
Absorb me in the jewel of your love
Until I am fully one with your goodness.

ANIM Z'MIROT. This religious poem (*piyut*), in praise of God's glory, is ascribed to Rabbi Yehudah the Pious of Regensburg (d. 1217). It is customary to say the prayer while standing before the open ark.

DEEPEST GOOD. By Joyce Rupp (b. 1943).

From Psalm 121

Esa einai el-heharim:	אֶשָּׂא עֵינַי אֶל־הֶהָרִים
mei·ayin yavo ezri?	מֵאַיִן יָבֹא עֶזְרִי.
Ezri mei·im Adonai,	עֶזְרִי מֵעִם יְיָ
oseih shamayim vaaretz.	עֹשֵׂה שָׁמַיִם וָאָרֶץ.

I lift my eyes to the mountains:
From where will my help come?
My help comes from the Eternal,
Maker of heaven and earth.

From Psalm 27

Adonai ori v'yishi — mimi ira?	יְיָ אוֹרִי וְיִשְׁעִי, מִמִּי אִירָא,
Adonai maoz-chayai — mimi efchad?	יְיָ מָעוֹז־חַיַּי, מִמִּי אֶפְחָד.
Achat shaalti mei·eit-Adonai;	אַחַת שָׁאַלְתִּי מֵאֵת־יְיָ,
otah avakeish:	אוֹתָהּ אֲבַקֵּשׁ:
shivti b'veit-Adonai kol-y'mei chayai,	שִׁבְתִּי בְּבֵית־יְיָ כָּל־יְמֵי חַיַּי,
lachazot b'no·am-Adonai,	לַחֲזוֹת בְּנֹעַם־יְיָ,
ulvakeir b'heichalo.	וּלְבַקֵּר בְּהֵיכָלוֹ.

God is my light and my refuge secure —
whom shall I fear?
God is the stronghold of my life —
of whom should I be afraid?

Just one thing I have asked of God;
only this do I seek:
to dwell in God's House all the days of my life,
to behold divine sweetness and beauty,
and to gaze in delight at God's Temple.

טַלִּית
Tallit
מוֹדֶה\מוֹדָה אֲנִי
Modeh/Modah Ani
הֲרֵינִי
Hareini
מַה־טֹּבוּ
Mah Tovu
שִׁיר לַמַּעֲלוֹת
Shir Lamaalot
מִזְמוֹר כ״ז
Mizmor l'David
בִּרְכוֹת הַתּוֹרָה
Birchot HaTorah
תַּלְמוּד תּוֹרָה
Talmud Torah
אֲשֶׁר יָצַר
Asher Yatzar
אֱלֹהַי, נְשָׁמָה
Elohai, N'shamah
נִסִּים שֶׁבְּכָל יוֹם
Nisim Sheb'chol Yom

GOD IS MY LIGHT. Psalm 27 is an outpouring of deep faith that theologian Walter Brueggemann (b. 1933) calls a "Song of Confidence." On this holy day of contrition and confession, the spiritual confidence of Psalm 27 may give us the strength for "return to the right path" (*t'shuvah*).

A MORNING OFFERING

I bless the night that nourished my heart
To set the ghosts of longing free
Into the flow and figure of dream
That went to harvest from the dark
Bread for the hunger no one sees.

All that is eternal in me
Welcomes the wonder of this day,
The field of brightness it creates
Offering time for each thing
To arise and illuminate.

I place on the altar of dawn:
The quiet loyalty of breath,
The tent of thought where I shelter,
Waves of desire I am shore to
And all beauty drawn to the eye.

May my mind come alive today
To the invisible geography
That invites me to new frontiers,
To break the dead shell of yesterdays,
To risk being disturbed and changed.

May I have the courage today
To live the life that I would love,
To postpone my dream no longer
But do at last what I came here for
And waste my heart on fear no more.

USES OF SORROW

Someone I loved once gave me
a box full of darkness.

It took me years to understand
that this, too, was a gift.

A MORNING OFFERING. By John O'Donohue (1956–2008).
USES OF SORROW. By Mary Oliver (b. 1935), who notes: "In my sleep I dreamed this poem."

For Those Who Study Torah

His brothers took Joseph and cast him into the pit.
The pit was empty; there was no water in it.

Why does the verse tell us that there was no water?
If the pit was empty, is that not obvious?
It means that there was no water,
but there were snakes and scorpions within.

Our Sages teach:
water represents Torah, source of our life and sustenance.
When the mind is empty of Torah, snakes and scorpions will enter.

Fill your mind with wisdom, with moral values and teachings.
You will have no room for what is vulgar, trivial, or unworthy.

And so it is written: "Those who love Your Torah find peace;
guided by Your words, they will not stumble."

Blessings for Study

Baruch atah, Adonai,

Eloheinu melech haolam,

asher kid'shanu b'mitzvotav,

v'tzivanu laasok b'divrei Torah.

בָּרוּךְ אַתָּה, יְיָ,
אֱלֹהֵינוּ מֶלֶךְ הָעוֹלָם,
אֲשֶׁר קִדְּשָׁנוּ בְּמִצְוֹתָיו,
וְצִוָּנוּ לַעֲסֹק בְּדִבְרֵי תוֹרָה.

Blessed are You, Adonai our God,
supreme Power of the universe;
You sanctify our lives with mitzvot,
and give us the sacred obligation of learning and living Torah.

טַלִּית
Tallit

מוֹדֶה\מוֹדָה אֲנִי
Modeh/Modah Ani

הֲרֵינִי
Hareini

מַה־טֹּבוּ
Mah Tovu

שִׁיר לַמַּעֲלוֹת
Shir Lamaalot

מִזְמוֹר כ״ז
Mizmor l'David

בִּרְכוֹת הַתּוֹרָה
Birchot HaTorah

תַּלְמוּד תּוֹרָה
Talmud Torah

אֲשֶׁר יָצַר
Asher Yatzar

אֱלֹהַי, נְשָׁמָה
Elohai, N'shamah

נִסִּים שֶׁבְּכָל יוֹם
Nisim Sheb'chol Yom

HIS BROTHERS TOOK JOSEPH, Genesis 37:24.

THERE WERE SNAKES AND SCORPIONS. See Talmud *Shabbat* 22a.

WATER REPRESENTS TORAH. See Talmud *Bava Kamma* 82a.

WHEN THE MIND IS EMPTY. Based on the teaching of the Vilna Gaon (Rabbi Elijah ben Solomon of Vilna; 1720–1797) on this verse.

THOSE WHO LOVE YOUR TORAH. Adapted from Psalm 119:165.

Tallit Blessing
Gratitude
Readiness
In God's Holy Place
Psalm 121
Psalm 27
Torah Blessings
Torah Study
Our Bodies
Our Souls
Everyday Miracles

וְהַעֲרֶב־נָא, יְיָ אֱלֹהֵינוּ,
אֶת דִּבְרֵי תוֹרָתְךָ בְּפִינוּ,
וּבְפִי עַמְּךָ בֵּית יִשְׂרָאֵל,
וְנִהְיֶה אֲנַחְנוּ וְצֶאֱצָאֵינוּ,
וְצֶאֱצָאֵי עַמְּךָ בֵּית יִשְׂרָאֵל,
כֻּלָּנוּ יוֹדְעֵי שְׁמֶךָ,
וְלוֹמְדֵי תוֹרָתְךָ לִשְׁמָהּ.

V'haarev-na, Adonai Eloheinu,
et divrei Torat'cha b'finu,
uvfi am'cha beit Yisrael —
v'niyeh anachnu v'tze·etza·einu,
v'tze·etza·ei am'cha beit Yisrael,
kulanu yodei sh'mecha,
v'lomdei Toratecha lishmah.

Our God, Eternal,
let us taste the sweetness of Your Torah's words;
and let them give pleasure to Your people, the House of Israel —
so that we, our children and all generations of Israel to come
shall know Your name and study Your Torah for its own sake.

בָּרוּךְ אַתָּה, יְיָ, הַמְלַמֵּד תּוֹרָה לְעַמּוֹ יִשְׂרָאֵל.

Baruch atah, Adonai, hamlameid Torah l'amo Yisrael.

Blessed are You, Adonai, who instructs
our people Israel in the ways of Torah.

בָּרוּךְ אַתָּה, יְיָ,
אֱלֹהֵינוּ מֶלֶךְ הָעוֹלָם,
אֲשֶׁר בָּחַר־בָּנוּ מִכָּל הָעַמִּים,
וְנָתַן־לָנוּ אֶת תּוֹרָתוֹ.
בָּרוּךְ אַתָּה, יְיָ, נוֹתֵן הַתּוֹרָה.

Baruch atah, Adonai,
Eloheinu melech haolam,
asher bachar-banu mikol haamim,
v'natan-lanu et Torato.
Baruch atah, Adonai, notein haTorah.

Blessed are You, Adonai our God —
in Your sovereignty, You chose us
to bring the gift of Torah into the world.

בָּרוּךְ אַתָּה, יְיָ, נוֹתֵן הַתּוֹרָה.

Baruch atah, Adonai, notein haTorah.

Blessed are You, Adonai, Giver of Torah.

GIVER OF TORAH נוֹתֵן הַתּוֹרָה. The Torah is like a kaleidoscope — dazzlingly beautiful, infinitely complex, and differently configured each time we look at it anew. (Rabbi Eric Yoffie, b. 1947)

Study: Bible

וְהָיְתָה לָכֶם לְחֻקַּת עוֹלָם בַּחֹדֶשׁ הַשְּׁבִיעִי בֶּעָשׂוֹר
לַחֹדֶשׁ תְּעַנּוּ אֶת־נַפְשֹׁתֵיכֶם וְכָל־מְלָאכָה לֹא תַעֲשׂוּ
הָאֶזְרָח וְהַגֵּר הַגָּר בְּתוֹכְכֶם: כִּי־בַיּוֹם הַזֶּה יְכַפֵּר
עֲלֵיכֶם לְטַהֵר אֶתְכֶם מִכֹּל חַטֹּאתֵיכֶם לִפְנֵי יְיָ תִּטְהָרוּ:

And this shall be an eternal law for you:
In the seventh month, on the tenth day of the month,
you shall practice self-denial; and you shall not do any work—
the citizen and the foreigner who resides among you.
For on this day atonement shall be made for you to purify you
from all your wrongs.
And pure you shall be in the presence of Adonai.

—Leviticus 16:29–30

וַיְדַבֵּר יְיָ אֶל־מֹשֶׁה לֵּאמֹר: דַּבֵּר אֶל־בְּנֵי יִשְׂרָאֵל אִישׁ
אוֹ־אִשָּׁה כִּי יַעֲשׂוּ מִכָּל־חַטֹּאת הָאָדָם לִמְעֹל מַעַל בַּיְיָ
וְאָשְׁמָה הַנֶּפֶשׁ הַהִוא: וְהִתְוַדּוּ אֶת־חַטָּאתָם אֲשֶׁר עָשׂוּ
וְהֵשִׁיב אֶת־אֲשָׁמוֹ בְּרֹאשׁוֹ וַחֲמִישִׁתוֹ יֹסֵף עָלָיו וְנָתַן
לַאֲשֶׁר אָשַׁם לוֹ:

Adonai spoke to Moses, saying —
Speak to the people of Israel:
Those who break faith with Adonai—man or woman—
through wrongs against a person, and realize their guilt:
they shall confess the wrong they have done.
And, further, they shall make restitution for their wrong with
   its principal,
add one-fifth of it to the sum, and give it to the one who
   was wronged.

—Numbers 5:5–7

YOU SHALL PRACTICE SELF-DENIAL. Interpreted in the Mishnah (*Yoma* 8:1) as a prohibition of eating, drinking, washing oneself, anointing one's body with oil, wearing leather shoes, and sexual intercourse.

MAN OR WOMAN. This passage establishes the principle that confession and restitution are essential for wrongs committed against another person.

טלית
Tallit

מוֹדֶה\מוֹדָה אֲנִי
Modeh/Modah Ani

הֲרֵינִי
Hareini

מַה־טֹּבוּ
Mah Tovu

שִׁיר לַמַּעֲלוֹת
Shir Lamaalot

מִזְמוֹר כ"ז
Mizmor l'David

בִּרְכוֹת הַתּוֹרָה
Birchot HaTorah

תַּלְמוּד תּוֹרָה
Talmud Torah

אֲשֶׁר יָצַר
Asher Yatzar

אֱלֹהַי, נְשָׁמָה
Elohai, N'shamah

נִסִּים שֶׁבְּכָל יוֹם
Nisim Sheb'chol Yom

וַיֹּאמֶר מֹשֶׁה אֶל־יְיָ . . . וְעַתָּה יִגְדַּל־נָא כֹּחַ אֲדֹנָי כַּאֲשֶׁר
דִּבַּרְתָּ לֵאמֹר: יְיָ אֶרֶךְ אַפַּיִם וְרַב־חֶסֶד נֹשֵׂא עָוֹן וָפָשַׁע
וְנַקֵּה לֹא יְנַקֶּה פֹּקֵד עֲוֹן אָבוֹת עַל־בָּנִים עַל־שִׁלֵּשִׁים
וְעַל־רִבֵּעִים: סְלַח־נָא לַעֲוֹן הָעָם הַזֶּה כְּגֹדֶל חַסְדֶּךָ
וְכַאֲשֶׁר נָשָׂאתָה לָעָם הַזֶּה מִמִּצְרַיִם וְעַד־הֵנָּה: וַיֹּאמֶר יְיָ
סָלַחְתִּי כִּדְבָרֶךָ:

Moses said to Adonai . . . "And now, I pray, let God's forbearance be great, as You have declared, saying: 'Adonai is slow to anger and abounding in kindness, forgiving crime and offense; though not making one innocent—visiting the crime of parents upon children, upon the third and fourth generations.' As you have been faithful to this people ever since Egypt, please forgive their failings now, in keeping with Your boundless love." And Adonai responded: "I forgive, as you have asked."

—Numbers 14:13, 17–20

לְכוּ־נָא וְנִוָּכְחָה יֹאמַר יְיָ
אִם־יִהְיוּ חֲטָאֵיכֶם כַּשָּׁנִים
כַּשֶּׁלֶג יַלְבִּינוּ
אִם־יַאְדִּימוּ כַתּוֹלָע
כַּצֶּמֶר יִהְיוּ:

"Come, let us find common ground,"
—says Adonai.
"Be your sins like crimson,
they can turn white as snow;
be they red as dyed wool,
they can turn pure as fleece."

—Isaiah 1:18

VISITING THE CRIME פֹּקֵד עֲוֹן. The Talmud (*Yoma* 36b) defines the Hebrew word *avon* as intentional wrongdoing. Such acts committed by parents and grandparents may indeed have serious repercussions for their descendants—and may result in the suffering of innocents.

PLEASE FORGIVE THEIR FAILINGS סְלַח־נָא לַעֲוֹן הָעָם הַזֶּה. In these verses, Moses addresses God after the episode of the scouts, in which the Israelites resolved to return to Egypt and refused to enter the Promised Land. Here Moses intervenes on their behalf and secures for them God's forgiveness. The last part of this passage is recited early in the service on Yom Kippur evening, a sign of our confidence in God's forgiveness, even before we have confessed our wrongs.

Study: Mishnah

הָאוֹמֵר: אֶחֱטָא וְאָשׁוּב, אֶחֱטָא וְאָשׁוּב – אֵין מַסְפִּיקִין בְּיָדוֹ לַעֲשׂוֹת תְּשׁוּבָה. אֶחֱטָא וְיוֹם הַכִּפּוּרִים מְכַפֵּר – אֵין יוֹם הַכִּפּוּרִים מְכַפֵּר. עֲבֵרוֹת שֶׁבֵּין אָדָם לַמָּקוֹם – יוֹם הַכִּפּוּרִים מְכַפֵּר. עֲבֵרוֹת שֶׁבֵּין אָדָם לַחֲבֵרוֹ – אֵין יוֹם הַכִּפּוּרִים מְכַפֵּר, עַד שֶׁיְּרַצֶּה אֶת חֲבֵרוֹ. אֶת זוֹ דָּרַשׁ רַבִּי אֶלְעָזָר בֶּן עֲזַרְיָה, מִכֹּל חַטֹּאתֵיכֶם לִפְנֵי יְיָ תִּטְהָרוּ: עֲבֵרוֹת שֶׁבֵּין אָדָם לַמָּקוֹם, יוֹם הַכִּפּוּרִים מְכַפֵּר. עֲבֵרוֹת שֶׁבֵּין אָדָם לַחֲבֵרוֹ, אֵין יוֹם הַכִּפּוּרִים מְכַפֵּר, עַד שֶׁיְּרַצֶּה אֶת חֲבֵרוֹ.

One who says: "I will do wrong, and repent. . . . I will do wrong, and repent"—that person will not be given an opportunity to repent. One who says: "I will do wrong and the Day of Atonement will atone"—for that person the Day of Atonement does not atone. For wrongs between a person and the All-encompassing One, the Day of Atonement atones. For wrongs between one person and another, the Day of Atonement does not atone until the offender has put matters right with the one who was wronged.

Here is how Rabbi Eleazar ben Azariah interpreted the verse "From all your wrongs you shall be made pure in the presence of Adonai" (Leviticus 16:30): for wrongs between a person and the All-encompassing One, the Day of Atonement atones; for wrongs between one person and another, the Day of Atonement does not atone until the offender has put matters right with the one who was wronged.

—*Yoma* 8:9

ALL-ENCOMPASSING ONE הַמָּקוֹם. A common Rabbinic name for God, *HaMakom* (literally, "the Place") expresses the idea of God's pervasiveness. "The ancient charge against Judaism was that its God was transcendent and remote and therefore inaccessible. . . . To counter this, the Rabbis avowed that their God was both far and near, awesome and intimate. As the soul fills the body, God's presence pervades the universe. God as *HaMakom*, the Spacious One, was meant to convey as well that one could pray in one's heart without uttering a sound and still be heard by God. God was never out of reach. We were in fact immersed in God's ubiquitous presence." (Rabbi Ismar Schorsch, b. 1935)

RABBI ELAZAR BEN AZARIAH רַבִּי אֶלְעָזָר בֶּן עֲזַרְיָה. This interpretation rests on the phrase "in the presence of Adonai." Rabbi Elazar understands the biblical verse to mean that atonement on Yom Kippur applies specifically to sins "in the presence of Adonai"—that is, wrongs between a person and God, such as infractions of ritual law.

Tallit Blessing
Gratitude
Readiness
In God's Holy Place
Psalm 121
Psalm 27
Torah Blessings
Torah Study
Our Bodies
Our Souls
Everyday Miracles

סֵדֶר תַּעֲנִיּוֹת, כֵּיצַד? מוֹצִיאִין אֶת הַתֵּבָה לִרְחוֹבָהּ שֶׁל עִיר וְנוֹתְנִין אֵפֶר מַקְלֶה עַל גַּבֵּי הַתֵּבָה וּבְרֹאשׁ הַנָּשִׂיא וּבְרֹאשׁ אַב בֵּית דִּין, וְכָל אֶחָד וְאֶחָד נוֹתֵן בְּרֹאשׁוֹ. הַזָּקֵן שֶׁבָּהֶן אוֹמֵר לִפְנֵיהֶן דִּבְרֵי כִבּוּשִׁין: אַחֵינוּ, לֹא נֶאֱמַר בְּאַנְשֵׁי נִינְוֵה, וַיַּרְא הָאֱלֹהִים אֶת שַׂקָּם וְאֶת תַּעֲנִיתָם, אֶלָּא, וַיַּרְא הָאֱלֹהִים אֶת מַעֲשֵׂיהֶם, כִּי שָׁבוּ מִדַּרְכָּם הָרָעָה. וּבַקַּבָּלָה הוּא אוֹמֵר, וְקִרְעוּ לְבַבְכֶם וְאַל בִּגְדֵיכֶם.

What was the procedure for public fast days? They would bring the ark to the city square and place wood ash upon the ark and upon the heads of the chief rabbi and the chief justice; and all the people placed ash upon their own heads. Then a respected member of the community would address the people with words of admonition: "Friends, it is not said of the people of Nineveh that God saw their sackcloth and their fasting; but rather that 'God saw their deeds, how they were turning back from their evil ways' (Jonah 3:10). And in the Prophets it says: 'Rend your hearts, not your clothing' (Joel 2:13)."

—*Taanit* 2:1

אֵלּוּ דְבָרִים שֶׁאֵין לָהֶם שִׁעוּר:
הַפֵּאָה וְהַבִּכּוּרִים וְהָרֵאָיוֹן וּגְמִילוּת חֲסָדִים וְתַלְמוּד תּוֹרָה.

There is no limit to the fulfillment of these mitzvot: leaving the corners of your fields for the needy; giving to God the first fruits of your harvest; gathering with the community for festivals; acting with kindness and loyalty. And striving for knowledge of Torah.

—*Pei·ah* 1:1

PUBLIC FAST DAYS תַּעֲנִיּוֹת. In ancient Israel, drought was experienced as divine punishment, and the Sages would decree a series of public fasts to demonstrate to God that the people had repented. This mishnah records how the leaders of the community, in a striking ritual act, would humble themselves by placing ashes on their head and upon the holy ark. Even as they performed the ritual, they would remind the people that *t'shuvah* is accomplished through sincere remorse and behavioral change, not through rituals alone. The mishnah gives us an early example of rabbinic preaching, showing how the Sages drew an important lesson from the Book of Jonah, which is read on Yom Kippur afternoon.

Study: Talmud and Midrash

תְּנַן הָתָם, רַבִּי אֱלִיעֶזֶר אוֹמֵר: שׁוּב יוֹם אֶחָד לִפְנֵי מִיתָתָךְ.
שָׁאֲלוּ תַלְמִידָיו אֶת רַבִּי אֱלִיעֶזֶר: וְכִי אָדָם יוֹדֵעַ אֵיזֶהוּ יוֹם יָמוּת?
אָמַר לָהֶן: וְכָל שֶׁכֵּן יָשׁוּב הַיּוֹם, שֶׁמָּא יָמוּת לְמָחָר, וְנִמְצָא כָּל
יָמָיו בִּתְשׁוּבָה.

We learned (*Pirkei Avot* 2:15): Rabbi Eliezer said, "Repent one day before your death."

His students asked him, "But do people know on what day they will die?" He replied: "All the more reason to repent today, lest one die tomorrow; and thus one's whole life will be spent in *t'shuvah*."

—Talmud *Shabbat* 153a

COMMENTARY

Rabbi Eliezer's words reside at the heart of what it means to live a religious life. That is to say, the hardest time to embark on a sudden search for God is when a life-shaking crisis hits. It's nearly impossible to hand over the reins to God then, if we have spent our entire lives trying to wrest them away for ourselves. A peaceful co-existence with God is earned through a lifetime of humility and gratitude, wonderment instead of entitlement. There are surely many good reasons to pursue *t'shuvah* on a daily basis, but even the most doubtful among us would acknowledge that the kind of religious discipline prescribed by Rabbi Eliezer can provide extraordinary solace when we need it most.

The famed twentieth-century theologian Paul Tillich taught that there is no such thing as an atheist: we always make something or someone our God. By demanding that we repent one day before we die, Rabbi Eliezer essentially asks each one of us daily: Who is *your* God? Will your God be a source of comfort and strength when you're staring into the abyss—as we all will someday?

COMMENTARY. By Rabbi Kenneth Chasen (b. 1965).

טַלִּית
Tallit

מוֹדֶה\מוֹדָה אֲנִי
Modeh/Modah Ani

הֲרֵינִי
Hareini

מַה־טֹּבוּ
Mah Tovu

שִׁיר לַמַּעֲלוֹת
Shir Lamaalot

מִזְמוֹר כ"ז
Mizmor l'David

בִּרְכוֹת הַתּוֹרָה
Birchot HaTorah

תַּלְמוּד תּוֹרָה
Talmud Torah

אֲשֶׁר יָצַר
Asher Yatzar

אֱלֹהַי, נְשָׁמָה
Elohai, N'shamah

נִסִּים שֶׁבְּכָל יוֹם
Nisim Sheb'chol Yom

AND ADONAI PASSED before him and proclaimed: "Adonai, Adonai – God, compassionate, gracious, endlessly patient, loving, and true . . ."

—Exodus 34:6

When the Holy One, blessed be God, had passed by, God removed the hollow of the divine hand from Moses; and he saw the traces of the Divine Presence, as Scripture says: *And I will take away My hand, and you shall see My back* (Exodus 33:23). Moses began to cry with a loud voice, and he said: "Adonai, Adonai—God, compassionate, gracious . . ."

—Midrash *Pirkei d'Rabbi Eliezer* 47

COMMENTARY

An alternative reading of the biblical text is offered by the midrash in chapter 47 of *Pirkei d'Rabbi Eliezer*, and it is breathtaking in its boldness. It was not God who revealed these attributes to Moses, but rather Moses who revealed them to God. At first, this notion seems incredible: how is it possible that a mortal might reveal to God an aspect of God's own being? And yet, throughout the tale, it is Moses who is the voice of temperance and kindness, standing in stark contrast to God's volatile anger and retributive intent.

RABBI ISHMAEL BEN ELISHA SAID: "I once entered into the innermost part of the sanctuary to offer incense and saw Adonai seated upon a high and exalted throne. God said to me, 'Ishmael My son, bless Me.' I replied: May it be Your will that Your mercy may conquer Your anger, and Your mercy may prevail over Your other attributes—so that You may deal with Your children according to the attribute of mercy. . . .'"

—Talmud *B'rachot* 7a

COMMENTARY

The idea that God would desire the blessing of a mortal is almost too extreme to comprehend. And yet, it will not escape the reader's attention that Rabbi Ishmael's blessing is precisely what Moses had proclaimed to God generations earlier—that mercy is the essence of God's being. All else that we proclaim about God, that God is mighty, omnipotent, awe-inspiring, vast, grand, and so on, is self-evident. Seemingly, though, even God is grateful for our intercession on behalf of Divine mercies. Contrary to the Bard's saying, the quality of mercy is indeed strained. It is so hard to come by that even God prays for it.

COMMENTARY. Both commentaries by Bryna Jocheved Levy.

THE QUALITY OF MERCY. An allusion to *The Merchant of Venice* by William Shakespeare.

אֵלּוּ דְבָרִים שֶׁאָדָם אוֹכֵל פֵּרוֹתֵיהֶם בָּעוֹלָם הַזֶּה,
וְהַקֶּרֶן קַיֶּמֶת לוֹ לָעוֹלָם הַבָּא.
וְאֵלּוּ הֵן:
כִּבּוּד אָב וָאֵם,
וּגְמִילוּת חֲסָדִים,
וְהַשְׁכָּמַת בֵּית הַמִּדְרָשׁ שַׁחֲרִית וְעַרְבִית,
וְהַכְנָסַת אוֹרְחִים,
וּבִקּוּר חוֹלִים,
וְהַכְנָסַת כַּלָּה,
וּלְוָיַת הַמֵּת,
וְעִיּוּן תְּפִלָּה,
וַהֲבָאַת שָׁלוֹם בֵּין אָדָם לַחֲבֵרוֹ.
וְתַלְמוּד תּוֹרָה כְּנֶגֶד כֻּלָּם.

Some mitzvot sustain us not only in this world, but also in the world-to-come. They are: honoring our parents; acting with kindness and loyalty; eagerly pursuing Jewish learning at all times; welcoming guests; visiting the sick; rejoicing with couples under the chuppah; caring for the dead and mourners; delving deeply into prayer; making peace among human beings. And the study of Torah—this is the cornerstone.

— Based on Talmud *Shabbat* 127a

SOME MITZVOT SUSTAIN US שֶׁאָדָם אוֹכֵל פֵּרוֹתֵיהֶם. The Sages use an economic metaphor to describe the benefit of these crucial mitzvot: they generate "interest" (literally "a person eats their fruit") in this life, but the principal does not decrease "in the world-to-come." That is, these sacred acts yield immediate reward and continue to enrich us in time to come. All connect us more deeply to something beyond ourselves; in performing these mitzvot we strengthen our relationship to other human beings, to God, and to the wisdom of Jewish tradition.

EAGERLY PURSUING JEWISH LEARNING. Literally: "arriving early at the House of Study morning and evening." Such behavior suggests a sustained enthusiasm for Jewish study, and a commitment to such study, even for busy working people. We might understand this phrase metaphorically, as well: pursue Jewish learning in your youth and also in your later years, as it will enrich all seasons of life. Since Torah study inspires virtuous deeds, it is the foundation of a meaningful life.

There were some ruffians in the neighborhood of Rabbi Meir who caused him a great deal of trouble. So Rabbi Meir prayed that they would die. His wife, Beruriah, asked him, "What is your view [of the scriptural basis for this prayer]? Is it because of the verse 'may *chata·im* disappear'? Does the verse say *chot'im* (sinners)? No, it says *chata·im* (sins)! Moreover, look at the end of the verse, where it says 'and the wicked be no more.' This means: because their sins will cease, they will be wicked people no more. Rather, pray for them that they should repent and be wicked no more." Rabbi Meir did pray for them, and they repented.

—Talmud *B'rachot* 10a

COMMENTARY

In this celebrated story Beruriah, the learned wife of Rabbi Meir, teaches the great sage a lesson in patience and compassion. When he prays for the death of the enemies who persecute him, she offers a creative reinterpretation of a biblical verse (Psalm 104:35). The verse actually says: "May sinners disappear from the earth, and the wicked be no more." But Beruriah, in the tradition of the Rabbinic sages, suggests a slight change in the vocalization of the word *chata·im*, reading it as "sins," rather than "sinners."

She offers a similar creative reading of the end of the verse. In its original biblical context, the end of the verse simply offers a parallel to the beginning: "May sinners disappear . . . and the wicked be no more." Beruriah interprets it, instead, to mean "they will be wicked no more" (since they no longer engage in sinful behavior). She thus transforms a vengeful biblical verse yearning for the obliteration of sinners into a hopeful prayer for their rehabilitation through *t'shuvah* (return, repentance).

Beruriah encourages Rabbi Meir to view people who annoy and anger him through a more positive lens, seeing them as human beings like himself, capable of change and with goodness at their core. Such a perspective affirms that all people, including criminals, may return to a better path, especially if they receive support from those around them. Beruriah's teaching may also inspire us to relate more compassionately to the "ruffians" in our own life.

Study: Middle Ages

1. Who has attained complete *t'shuvah*? Those who confront the same situation in which they acted offensively, [but,] when they have the potential to do it again, nevertheless abstain from it because of their *t'shuvah* alone, and not because of fear [of getting caught] or lack of strength. For example, a man engaged in illicit sexual relations with a woman. Afterward, he found himself alone with her, in the same country and with continued love for her and unabated physical power. Nevertheless, he refrained and did no wrong—he has attained true *t'shuvah*.

2. What constitutes *t'shuvah*? It occurs when one abandons one's wrongdoing and removes it from one's thoughts, resolving in one's heart never to do it again, as Isaiah 55:7 states: "Let the wicked give up their ways, and those who do evil their thoughts; let them turn back to Adonai." . . . One must verbally confess and state these resolutions that were made in the heart.

3. One who confesses verbally but has not resolved to stop sinning is like a person who immerses [in a *mikveh*] while grasping an impure reptile. Unless you cast it away, the immersion will be useless. . . . One who confesses must specify the sin, as evidenced by [Moses' confession in Exodus 32:31]: "This people is guilty of a great offense in making for themselves a god of gold."

—Maimonides, *Mishneh Torah*, Laws of Repentance 2.1–3

COMPLETE T'SHUVAH. The *t'shuvah* process is complete only when one can demonstrate a change in character and behavior. Rabbi Moses Maimonides (1135–1204) draws on a statement in the Talmud: "How can one prove that one is truly penitent? Rabbi Judah said: If an opportunity to commit the same sin presents itself on two occasions and one does not yield to it" (*Yoma* 86b).

ONE WHO CONFESSES VERBALLY. Based on Talmud *Taanit* 16a. Although verbal confession is obligatory, Maimonides emphasizes that words are not enough to constitute *t'shuvah*; confession must be accompanied by renouncing the sin. Asks Rabbi Debra Orenstein (b. 1962): Is there any aspect of a sin, habit, or grudge that you want to let go, to which some part of you is still clinging? Are you ready to let that "snake" go completely?

THIS PEOPLE IS GUILTY. Moses' words to God after the Golden Calf episode. Maimonides, quoting Talmud *Yoma* 86b, cites the verse as an example of a confession that is specific in describing the sin.

טַלִּית
Tallit

מוֹדֶה\מוֹדָה אֲנִי
Modeh/Modah Ani

הֲרֵינִי
Hareini

מַה־טֹּבוּ
Mah Tovu

שִׁיר לַמַּעֲלוֹת
Shir Lamaalot

מִזְמוֹר כ״ז
Mizmor l'David

בִּרְכוֹת הַתּוֹרָה
Birchot HaTorah

תַּלְמוּד תּוֹרָה
Talmud Torah

אֲשֶׁר יָצַר
Asher Yatzar

אֱלֹהַי, נְשָׁמָה
Elohai, N'shamah

נִסִּים שֶׁבְּכָל יוֹם
Nisim Sheb'chol Yom

FREE WILL is granted to all people. If we desire to turn to the path of good and be righteous, the choice is ours. Should we desire to turn to the path of evil and be wicked, the choice is ours. . . . There is no one who compels us, sentences us, or leads us toward either of these two paths. Rather, all persons, at their own initiative and decision, turn to the path they desire.

—Maimonides, *Mishneh Torah*, Laws of Repentance 5.1, 3

BAALEI T'SHUVAH [those who repent] should not consider themselves distant from the level of the righteous because of their wrongdoing. . . . Such people are as beloved and precious to the Creator as if they had never done wrong. Furthermore, those who repent have a great reward, for they have tasted sin and yet have separated themselves from it—conquering their [evil] inclination. Our Sages declared: "In the place where *baalei t'shuvah* stand, even the wholly righteous cannot stand." The level of *baalei t'shuvah* transcends the level of those who never did wrong at all, for they had to make a greater effort to overcome their [evil] inclination.

—Maimonides, *Mishneh Torah*, Laws of Repentance 7.4

THE PUNISHMENT OF SINNERS who put off *t'shuvah* grows heavier day by day, for such people . . . know that there is a sanctuary to which they can flee, the sanctuary of *t'shuvah*, and yet they persist in their rebellion and continue in their wrongdoing.

—Rabbi Jonah of Gerona, *Gates of Repentance*; adapted

COMMENTARY

Rabbi Jonah of Gerona (d. 1263) called repentance a sanctuary, a place to escape the intensity of sin. It is also the place to embrace the strength needed to fight our hardest inner battles and our stubborn resistance to change. By calling repentance a sanctuary, Rabbi Jonah transformed an act into a space we can step into and know that we are home, and we are safe. We have returned to our essential selves, the people we like best. We are at one with forces that usually rage within us, pulling us between good and evil, generosity and self-absorption, selflessness and narcissism.

IN THE PLACE WHERE BAALEI T'SHUVAH STAND, Talmud *B'rachot* 34b.
COMMENTARY. By Erica Brown (b. 1966).

Study: Modern Era

Sin, in the context of relationship, is not a transgression of an abstract norm, but an injury toward an Other rendered vulnerable by his/her trust. *T'shuvah* is turning again to face the Other, not to annul what has occurred, but to sew up the wounds and determine how to go on. Relationships bear scars because they have memory. As memories accumulate, they carry consequences that bind us. They retell how we have come to be related in the way we are, but they also point us toward what we must become, what we must recreate, what we must repay. Without memory, there can be no covenants.

In a theology of relationship where there are flexible boundaries between God and others, both unity with and separation from God are possible. Imagine God as continually pregnant with, delivering, rearing, and separating from the world, like a tree at once bearing blossoms, unripe fruit, ripe fruit, and the stems and scars from fruit that has fallen from the tree. The world is inside God, outside God, part of God as in halachah the unborn infant is "part of its mother's body," and separate from God, as the emancipated child is separate from a parent who still watches its story unfold, sometimes with pride, sometimes with pain.

—Rabbi Rachel Adler (b. 1943)

If even some events in the future are fixed and immutable, then it is only reasonable to resign ourselves to the inevitable. To struggle against fate may be heroic, but it is ultimately futile. Indeed, much of the pathos of Greek tragedy derives from the ways in which the protagonists are unwittingly caught in a web of fate from which they cannot escape. Oedipus has been fated to kill his father and marry his mother, and no choices he makes can alter this horrible conclusion to the tale.

This tragic outlook on life is precisely antithetical to the view that gives rise to the idea of repentance. For if repentance means anything, it points to a radical human freedom, especially to the possibility of freeing ourselves from the effects of our own past transgressions. The past does not determine the future; our destiny is not fixed and beyond our power to change. No matter what we have done, we can make a decision to "turn" in a different direction tomorrow. In the most profound sense, no choice we made in the past is final or irredeemable, and even our most awful misdeeds can propel us in a radically new direction.

—Louis E. Newman (b. 1956)

טַלִּית
Tallit
מוֹדֶה\מוֹדָה אֲנִי
Modeh/Modah Ani
הֲרֵינִי
Hareini
מַה־טֹּבוּ
Mah Tovu
שִׁיר לַמַּעֲלוֹת
Shir Lamaalot
מִזְמוֹר כ״ז
Mizmor l'David
בִּרְכוֹת הַתּוֹרָה
Birchot HaTorah
תַּלְמוּד תּוֹרָה
Talmud Torah
אֲשֶׁר יָצַר
Asher Yatzar
אֱלֹהַי, נְשָׁמָה
Elohai, N'shamah
נִסִּים שֶׁבְּכָל יוֹם
Nisim Sheb'chol Yom

Yom kippur teaches that human beings inevitably fail or sin. But when people turn, they come out stronger. In a relationship between two people, love based on the assumption of perfection on both sides is vulnerable to the almost inevitable crack in the mirror. Once flaws are acknowledged and accepted, love becomes genuinely unconditional.

Rabbinic tradition claims that Moses broke the tablets of the Ten Commandments on the tenth of Tishrei, that is, on Yom Kippur. The original tablets were fashioned by the Divine, untouched by human flaws, but when the people sinned and created a Golden Calf, God despaired and wanted to get rid of them. Moses was so distressed that he smashed the tablets. It was almost as if the tablets were too pure to be left in human hands.

Then came forty days of working through the heartbreak. Reconciliation and catharsis were followed by forty days of Moses' labor fashioning new tablets. This set of tablets—the product of hard-won repentance based on realism, forgiveness, and acceptance of others' limitations—would guide the Israelites for centuries to come. Such tablets express the spirit of Yom Kippur, when out of our brokenness we become stronger than when we claimed to be whole.

—Rabbi Irving Greenberg (b. 1933), adapted

The divine voice speaks to Moses from the burning bush: "*Ehyeh asher Ehyeh* (I am who I am)." This is the name and self-description of the One in whose image we are made. Our God-likeness is at the essence of our humanness, and this story teaches that we are endowed with dignity and deserving of self-acceptance and respect by virtue of our being human.

On Yom Kippur, when we are inclined to self-doubt and perhaps harsh self-criticism, we can be uplifted and regain our lost dignity in the sure knowledge that however we have failed ourselves or others, or failed before God, "*Ehyeh asher Ehyeh*, I am as I am." I have come to appreciate how many of us, despite our accomplishments, our advanced degrees and our worldliness, can also be so fragile, anxious about our place in our families and the world, haunted by internal voices of rebuke and disappointment. God answers us in love: *Ehyeh asher Ehyeh*. Just as you are, however broken in spirit, however far you have wandered from your imagined path, however burdened or disappointed you may be—you and I each stand here as a reflection and image of the Holy One.

—Rabbi Yoel Kahn (b. 1958)

בָּרוּךְ אַתָּה, יְיָ,
אֱלֹהֵינוּ מֶלֶךְ הָעוֹלָם,
אֲשֶׁר יָצַר אֶת הָאָדָם בְּחָכְמָה,
וּבָרָא בוֹ נְקָבִים נְקָבִים,
חֲלוּלִים חֲלוּלִים.
גָּלוּי וְיָדוּעַ לִפְנֵי כִסֵּא כְבוֹדֶךָ
שֶׁאִם יִפָּתֵחַ אֶחָד מֵהֶם,
אוֹ יִסָּתֵם אֶחָד מֵהֶם,
אִי אֶפְשַׁר לְהִתְקַיֵּם
וְלַעֲמֹד לְפָנֶיךָ.

Baruch atah, Adonai,
Eloheinu melech haolam,
asher yatzar et haadam b'chochmah,
uvara-vo n'kavim n'kavim,
chalulim chalulim.
Galui v'yadua lifnei chisei ch'vodecha
she·im yipatei·ach echad meihem,
o yisateim echad meihem,
i efshar l'hitkayeim
v'laamod l'fanecha.

Blessed are You, Holy One, who has formed the human body with wisdom — an intricate network of channels, vessels, and openings. This wondrous structure, and the flow of life within us, allows us to stand before You and give thanks. Let us cherish this gift of flesh and blood, honor it as God's creation.

בָּרוּךְ אַתָּה, יְיָ, רוֹפֵא כָל בָּשָׂר, וּמַפְלִיא לַעֲשׂוֹת.
Baruch atah, Adonai, rofei chol basar, umafli laasot.
We praise You, Holy One,
for wondrous acts of creation and healing.

WHO HAS FORMED THE HUMAN BODY. The prayer *Asher Yatzar* views the human body with wonder, appreciation, and gratitude. The poem by May Sarton (*facing page*) sets forth a view of the body that is marked by tenderness, compassion, and forgiveness. Each work, in its own way, presents a countercultural perspective that challenges the message we receive from the secular world — that beauty resides only in the youthful and "perfect" body.

FOR WONDROUS ACTS OF CREATION AND HEALING. Based on Exodus 15:26; Judges 13:19; Talmud *B'rachot* 60b.

I CAN LOOK

At my body
As an old friend
Who needs my help,
Or an enemy
Who frustrates me
In every way
With its frailty
And inability to cope.
Old friend,
I shall try
To be of comfort to you
To the end.

THE GIFT OF HONOR

Ben Azzai used to say:

Treat no one with scorn;
regard nothing as useless,
for all people have their moment,
and all things have their place.

Diamonds, when found in the ground,
may look like worthless pieces of glass.
It takes an expert to see the precious gem that is hidden within.

Become an expert in human beings.
Learn to see each one as a diamond in the rough.

בָּרוּךְ אַתָּה, יְיָ, רוֹפֵא כָל בָּשָׂר, וּמַפְלִיא לַעֲשׂוֹת.

Baruch atah, Adonai, rofei chol basar, umafli laasot.

Blessed are You, God, who performs the miracles
of creation and healing.

I CAN LOOK. By May Sarton (1912–1995).
TREAT NO ONE WITH SCORN. *Pirkei Avot* 4:3.
DIAMONDS. Based on a teaching of Rabbi Abraham Twerski (b. 1930).

טַלִּית
Tallit
מוֹדֶה\מוֹדָה אֲנִי
Modeh/Modah Ani
הֲרֵינִי
Hareini
מַה־טֹּבוּ
Mah Tovu
שִׁיר לַמַּעֲלוֹת
Shir Lamaalot
מִזְמוֹר כ״ז
Mizmor l'David
בִּרְכוֹת הַתּוֹרָה
Birchot HaTorah
תַּלְמוּד תּוֹרָה
Talmud Torah
אֲשֶׁר יָצַר
Asher Yatzar
אֱלֹהַי, נְשָׁמָה
Elohai, N'shamah
נִסִּים שֶׁבְּכָל יוֹם
Nisim Sheb'chol Yom

אֱלֹהַי, נְשָׁמָה שֶׁנָּתַתָּ בִּי
טְהוֹרָה הִיא.
אַתָּה בְרָאתָהּ,
אַתָּה יְצַרְתָּהּ,
אַתָּה נְפַחְתָּהּ בִּי,
וְאַתָּה מְשַׁמְּרָהּ בְּקִרְבִּי.
וְאַתָּה עָתִיד לִטְּלָהּ מִמֶּנִּי,
וּלְהַחֲזִירָהּ בִּי לֶעָתִיד לָבוֹא.
כָּל זְמַן שֶׁהַנְּשָׁמָה בְקִרְבִּי,
מוֹדֶה\מוֹדָה אֲנִי לְפָנֶיךָ,
יְיָ אֱלֹהַי וֵאלֹהֵי אֲבוֹתַי וְאִמּוֹתַי,
רִבּוֹן כָּל הַמַּעֲשִׂים,
אֲדוֹן כָּל הַנְּשָׁמוֹת.

Elohai, n'shamah shenatata bi —
t'horah hi.
Atah v'ratah,
atah y'tzartah,
atah n'fachtah bi,
v'atah m'sham'rah b'kirbi.
V'atah atid lit'lah mimeni,
ulhachazirah bi le·atid lavo.
Kol z'man shehan'shamah v'kirbi,
modeh/modah ani l'fanecha,
Adonai Elohai v'Elohei avotai v'imotai,
Ribon kol hamaasim,
Adon kol han'shamot.

Pure, my God, is the soul You have given me.
You formed it. You shaped it. You breathed it into me.
You keep it safe within me.
Someday, when this soul returns to You,
I will find a place in eternity.
But as long as spirit breathes within me,
I place before You my thanks,
Eternal my God and God of my ancestors,
Creator of all creation, Sovereign of all souls.

בָּרוּךְ אַתָּה, יְיָ, אֲשֶׁר בְּיָדוֹ נֶפֶשׁ כָּל חָי, וְרוּחַ כָּל בְּשַׂר אִישׁ.

Baruch atah, Adonai, asher b'yado nefesh kol chai, v'ruach kol b'sar ish.

We give You praise, Adonai: all life is in Your hand;
and in Your care, the soul of every human being.

THE SOUL YOU HAVE GIVEN ME. Rabbi Shabtai Sheftel Horowitz (1565–1619) taught that the human soul is a part of God. He wrote that the only essential difference is that "the Creator is the totality of existence, the all-embracing Infinite Light, and the soul is a tiny particle of that great light."

AFTER A LONG INSOMNIAC NIGHT

I walked down to the sea in the early morning
after a long insomniac night.

I climbed over the giant gull-colored rocks
and moved past the trees,
tall dancers stretching their limbs
and warming up in the blue light.

I entered the salty water, a penitent
whose body was stained,
and swam toward a red star rising
in the east—regal, purple-robed.

One shore disappeared behind me
and another beckoned.
I confess
that I forgot the person I had been
as easily as the clouds drifting overhead.

My hands parted the water.
The wind pressed at my back, wings
and my soul floated over the whitecapped waves.

AS A BLADE of Your grass in a distant, wild field
Loses a seed in the lap of the earth
And dies away
Sow in me Your living breath
As You sow a seed in the earth.

בָּרוּךְ אַתָּה, יְיָ, אֲשֶׁר בְּיָדוֹ נֶפֶשׁ כָּל חָי, וְרוּחַ כָּל בְּשַׂר אִישׁ.

Baruch atah, Adonai, asher b'yado nefesh kol chai, v'ruach kol b'sar ish.

We give You praise, Adonai: all life is in Your hand;
and in Your care, the soul of every human being.

AFTER A LONG INSOMNIAC NIGHT. By Edward Hirsch (b. 1950).
AS A BLADE. By Kadya Molodowsky (1894–1975).

Baruch atah, Adonai,

Eloheinu melech haolam,

asher natan lasechvi vinah

l'havchin bein yom uvein lailah.

בָּרוּךְ אַתָּה, יְיָ,
אֱלֹהֵינוּ מֶלֶךְ הָעוֹלָם,
אֲשֶׁר נָתַן לַשֶּׂכְוִי בִינָה,
לְהַבְחִין בֵּין יוֹם וּבֵין לָיְלָה.

You are the Source of blessings, Adonai;
Your great power gave the mind discernment to distinguish
light from darkness.

Baruch atah, Adonai,

Eloheinu melech haolam,

pokei·ach ivrim.

בָּרוּךְ אַתָּה, יְיָ,
אֱלֹהֵינוּ מֶלֶךְ הָעוֹלָם,
פּוֹקֵחַ עִוְרִים.

You are the Source of blessings, Adonai;
Your great power opens eyes that cannot see.

Baruch atah, Adonai,

Eloheinu melech haolam,

matir asurim.

בָּרוּךְ אַתָּה, יְיָ,
אֱלֹהֵינוּ מֶלֶךְ הָעוֹלָם,
מַתִּיר אֲסוּרִים.

You are the Source of blessings, Adonai;
Your great power brings freedom to the captive.

Baruch atah, Adonai,

Eloheinu melech haolam,

zokeif k'fufim.

בָּרוּךְ אַתָּה, יְיָ,
אֱלֹהֵינוּ מֶלֶךְ הָעוֹלָם,
זוֹקֵף כְּפוּפִים.

You are the Source of blessings, Adonai;
Your great power lifts up the fallen.

Baruch atah, Adonai,

Eloheinu melech haolam,

roka haaretz al hamayim.

בָּרוּךְ אַתָּה, יְיָ,
אֱלֹהֵינוּ מֶלֶךְ הָעוֹלָם,
רוֹקַע הָאָרֶץ עַל הַמָּיִם.

You are the Source of blessings, Adonai;
Your great power spreads the land upon the waters.

טַלִּית
Tallit

מוֹדֶה\מוֹדָה אֲנִי
Modeh/Modah Ani

הֲרֵינִי
Hareini

מַה־טֹּבוּ
Mah Tovu

שִׁיר לַמַּעֲלוֹת
Shir Lamaalot

מִזְמוֹר כ"ז
Mizmor l'David

בִּרְכוֹת הַתּוֹרָה
Birchot HaTorah

תַּלְמוּד תּוֹרָה
Talmud Torah

אֲשֶׁר יָצַר
Asher Yatzar

אֱלֹהַי, נְשָׁמָה
Elohai, N'shamah

נִסִּים שֶׁבְּכָל יוֹם
Nisim Sheb'chol Yom

GAVE THE MIND DISCERNMENT נָתַן לַשֶּׂכְוִי בִינָה. Talmud *B'rachot* 60b teaches that this blessing should be said upon hearing the rooster crow in the morning. Thus, Rashi construes *sechvi* as "rooster." Others construe it as "heart" or "mind," based on Job 38:36.

LIGHT FROM DARKNESS בֵּין יוֹם וּבֵין לָיְלָה. Literally, "between day and night." This phrase may be understood metaphorically. Thus we offer thanks for the capacity to make moral, as well as perceptual, distinctions.

Tallit Blessing
Gratitude
Readiness
In God's Holy Place
Psalm 121
Psalm 27
Torah Blessings
Torah Study
Our Bodies
Our Souls
Everyday Miracles

בָּרוּךְ אַתָּה, יְיָ,
אֱלֹהֵינוּ מֶלֶךְ הָעוֹלָם,
שֶׁעָשָׂה לִי כָּל צָרְכִּי.

Baruch atah, Adonai,
Eloheinu melech haolam,
she·asah-li kol tzorki.

You are the Source of blessings, Adonai;
Your great power has made all I need.

בָּרוּךְ אַתָּה, יְיָ,
אֱלֹהֵינוּ מֶלֶךְ הָעוֹלָם,
הַמֵּכִין מִצְעֲדֵי־גָבֶר.

Baruch atah, Adonai,
Eloheinu melech haolam,
hameichin mitzadei-gaver.

You are the Source of blessings, Adonai;
Your great power gives firmness to our steps.

בָּרוּךְ אַתָּה, יְיָ,
אֱלֹהֵינוּ מֶלֶךְ הָעוֹלָם,
מַלְבִּישׁ עֲרֻמִּים.

Baruch atah, Adonai,
Eloheinu melech haolam,
malbish arumim.

You are the Source of blessings, Adonai;
Your great power clothes the naked.

בָּרוּךְ אַתָּה, יְיָ,
אֱלֹהֵינוּ מֶלֶךְ הָעוֹלָם,
הַנּוֹתֵן לַיָּעֵף כֹּחַ.

Baruch atah, Adonai,
Eloheinu melech haolam,
hanotein laya·eif ko·ach.

You are the Source of blessings, Adonai;
Your great power gives strength to the weary.

בָּרוּךְ אַתָּה, יְיָ,
אֱלֹהֵינוּ מֶלֶךְ הָעוֹלָם,
הַמַּעֲבִיר שֵׁנָה מֵעֵינַי,
וּתְנוּמָה מֵעַפְעַפָּי.

Baruch atah, Adonai,
Eloheinu melech haolam,
hamaavir sheinah mei·einai,
utnumah mei·afapai.

You are the Source of blessings, Adonai;
Your great power removes sleep from my eyes,
slumber from my eyelids.

EVERYDAY MIRACLES נִסִּים שֶׁבְּכָל יוֹם. In uttering these blessings, we express profound appreciation for the gifts of life and creation. We say, in effect, "Pay attention! Something awe-inspiring and praiseworthy is happening all around us." And so we come to realize, with each blessing we say, that our everyday world is filled with wonder and mystery. That is why Reform Jews call the morning blessings *Nisim Sheb'chol Yom* (Everyday Miracles). (Rabbi Micah Greenstein, b. 1963; adapted)

בָּרוּךְ אַתָּה, יְיָ,
אֱלֹהֵֽינוּ מֶֽלֶךְ הָעוֹלָם,
שֶׁעָשַֽׂנִי בְּצֶֽלֶם אֱלֹהִים.

Baruch atah, Adonai,
Eloheinu melech haolam,
she-asani b'tzelem Elohim.

You are the Source of blessings, Adonai;
Your great power made me in the image of God.

בָּרוּךְ אַתָּה, יְיָ,
אֱלֹהֵֽינוּ מֶֽלֶךְ הָעוֹלָם,
שֶׁעָשַֽׂנִי בֶּן\בַּת חוֹרִין.

Baruch atah, Adonai,
Eloheinu melech haolam,
she-asani ben/bat chorin.

You are the Source of blessings, Adonai;
Your great power endowed me with human freedom.

בָּרוּךְ אַתָּה, יְיָ,
אֱלֹהֵֽינוּ מֶֽלֶךְ הָעוֹלָם,
שֶׁעָשַֽׂנִי יִשְׂרָאֵל.

Baruch atah, Adonai,
Eloheinu melech haolam,
she-asani Yisrael.

You are the Source of blessings, Adonai;
Your great power has made me Yisrael.

בָּרוּךְ אַתָּה, יְיָ,
אֱלֹהֵֽינוּ מֶֽלֶךְ הָעוֹלָם,
אוֹזֵר יִשְׂרָאֵל בִּגְבוּרָה.

Baruch atah, Adonai,
Eloheinu melech haolam,
ozeir Yisrael bigvurah.

You are the Source of blessings, Adonai;
Your great power gives strength to Yisrael.

בָּרוּךְ אַתָּה, יְיָ,
אֱלֹהֵֽינוּ מֶֽלֶךְ הָעוֹלָם,
עוֹטֵר יִשְׂרָאֵל בְּתִפְאָרָה.

Baruch atah, Adonai,
Eloheinu melech haolam,
oteir Yisrael b'tifarah.

You are the Source of blessings, Adonai;
Your great power crowns Yisrael with glory.

טַלִּית
Tallit

מוֹדֶה\מוֹדָה אֲנִי
Modeh/Modah Ani

הֲרֵינִי
Hareini

מַה־טֹּֽבוּ
Mah Tovu

שִׁיר לַמַּעֲלוֹת
Shir Lamaalot

מִזְמוֹר כ״ז
Mizmor l'David

בִּרְכוֹת הַתּוֹרָה
Birchot HaTorah

תַּלְמוּד תּוֹרָה
Talmud Torah

אֲשֶׁר יָצַר
Asher Yatzar

אֱלֹהַי, נְשָׁמָה
Elohai, N'shamah

נִסִּים שֶׁבְּכָל יוֹם
Nisim Sheb'chol Yom

WHO HAS MADE ME YISRAEL שֶׁעָשַֽׂנִי יִשְׂרָאֵל. When Jacob (*Yaakov*) emerged from an encounter with God, and received a new name — Israel (*Yisrael*) — he was told its significance: "For you have striven with beings divine and human, and have prevailed" (Genesis 32:29). An equally faithful translation of this blessing could be: "Your great power has made me a Jew." But retaining the name *Yisrael* in this personal blessing returns each of us to the most ancient roots of our identity. To call ourselves *Yisrael* is to identify not only with Jacob but with all of his spiritual descendants who have wrestled with adversity and have grown from the experience.

SAID THE ROMAN PROCURATOR Turnus Rufus to Rabbi Akiva: "Whose acts are greater, those of human beings or those of God?"

Rabbi Akiva answered: "The deeds of human beings are greater."

Surprised, Turnus Rufus asked, "But can you create the heavens and the earth?"

Akiva replied, "Do not speak to me of what is beyond the reach of humankind. Speak of what is available to human beings."

Akiva then brought to Turnus Rufus wheat stalks and cakes, raw flax and fine linen. "The wheat and the flax are the work of God," said Akiva, "but the cakes and the linen were made by human beings. Are they not superior?"

So our Sages taught: "All created things require refining and improvement. The mustard seed needs to be sweetened; the lupine needs to be soaked; the wheat needs to be ground, and the human being needs to be repaired."

The world that is given into our hands is still incomplete. Go forth, then, and work to make it better.

—Based on Midrash *Tanchuma, Tazria* 5 and Midrash *Genesis Rabbah* 11.6

COMMENTARY

"The deeds of human beings are greater." Rabbi Harold Schulweis sees this statement as affirming the partnership of God and humanity, and reflecting two dimensions of the Divine: *Elohim*, Giver of the natural world, and *Adonai*, the godliness implanted within us. He writes:

"How do I understand Akiva's response? Is it a denigration of God? By no means. Akiva is here rejecting the split thinking of either/or. Either God or man. Either above or below. Either *Elohim* or *Adonai*.

"What Akiva insists is that both are involved in the benediction of creation. God and humanity. In the *motzi* benediction (*Baruch atah, Adonai, Eloheinu melech haolam, hamotzi lechem min haaretz*), *Elohim* is revealed in sun, seed, water, and soil—the raw material that none of us has created. Still the raw sheaf of wheat is inedible. One needs to have God-given human intelligence, human competence, and purpose to till the soil, to pull the weeds, to water the ground, to grind the wheat, to bake the bread. The *motzi* blessing expresses appreciation of the transaction between God and person that transforms sheaves into bread."

TURNUS RUFUS. A Roman governor in Judea during the 2nd century CE. Rabbinic literature presents debates between him and Rabbi Akiva. In some cases, these dialogues reflect our Sages' wrestling with issues that troubled them; questions placed in the mouth of a Roman leader allow the Rabbis a safe way to articulate their own doubts and struggles. Here, the discussion centers on whether it is proper for human beings to interfere with the order of creation—for example, by circumcising a child. Akiva's answer affirms that humanity is empowered and, indeed, enjoined to engage actively and creatively with the world.

RABBI HAROLD SCHULWEIS, 1925–2014.

בָּרוּךְ שֶׁאָמַר
Baruch she·Amar

שִׁירִים לְיוֹם הַשַּׁבָּת
Shirim l'Yom HaShabbat

אַשְׁרֵי
Ashrei

כֹּל הַנְּשָׁמָה
Kol HaN'shamah

אִלּוּ פִינוּ
Ilu Finu

הַמֶּלֶךְ
HaMelech

יִשְׁתַּבַּח
Yishtabach

חֲצִי קַדִּישׁ
Chatzi Kaddish

פְּסוּקֵי דְזִמְרָא
P'sukei d'Zimra · Songs of Praise

Baruch she·amar v'hayah haolam.	בָּרוּךְ שֶׁאָמַר וְהָיָה הָעוֹלָם,
Baruch hu.	בָּרוּךְ הוּא.
Baruch oseh v'reishit,	בָּרוּךְ עוֹשֶׂה בְרֵאשִׁית,
baruch omeir v'oseh;	בָּרוּךְ אוֹמֵר וְעוֹשֶׂה,
baruch gozeir umkayeim,	בָּרוּךְ גּוֹזֵר וּמְקַיֵּם,
baruch m'rachem al haaretz;	בָּרוּךְ מְרַחֵם עַל הָאָרֶץ,
baruch m'rachem al hab'riyot,	בָּרוּךְ מְרַחֵם עַל הַבְּרִיּוֹת,
baruch m'shaleim sachar tov lirei·av.	בָּרוּךְ מְשַׁלֵּם שָׂכָר טוֹב לִירֵאָיו.
Baruch chai laad, v'kayam lanetzach.	בָּרוּךְ חַי לָעַד, וְקַיָּם לָנֶצַח.
Baruch podeh umatzil. Baruch sh'mo.	בָּרוּךְ פּוֹדֶה וּמַצִּיל, בָּרוּךְ שְׁמוֹ.
Bishvachot uvizmirot,	בִּשְׁבָחוֹת וּבִזְמִירוֹת,
n'gadelcha unshabeichacha unfa·ercha;	נְגַדֶּלְךָ וּנְשַׁבֵּחֲךָ וּנְפָאֶרְךָ,
v'nazkir shimcha v'namlich'cha,	וְנַזְכִּיר שִׁמְךָ וְנַמְלִיכְךָ,
Malkeinu Eloheinu.	מַלְכֵּנוּ אֱלֹהֵינוּ.
Yachid, chei haolamim,	יָחִיד, חֵי הָעוֹלָמִים,
melech m'shubach umfo·ar —	מֶלֶךְ מְשֻׁבָּח וּמְפֹאָר,
adei ad sh'mo hagadol.	עֲדֵי עַד שְׁמוֹ הַגָּדוֹל.

Blessed is the One who spoke the world into being. Praised is God.
  Praised — the One who is ever creating.
Praised — the One who creates with a word.
  Praised — the One whose vision is made real.
Praised — the One who loves the earth.
  Praised — the One who loves earth's creatures.
Praised — the One whose worshipers know goodness.
  Praised — the One whose life and being last forever.
Praised — the One who rescues and sets free. Blessed is Your name.
  Our Sovereign, we praise You with songs of celebration.
  Your Oneness is the life of the cosmos.

בָּרוּךְ אַתָּה, יְיָ, מֶלֶךְ מְהֻלָּל בַּתִּשְׁבָּחוֹת.

Baruch atah, Adonai, Melech m'hulal batishbachot.

Blessed are You, Adonai. Your majesty is celebrated in songs of praise.

Blessed Is the One
Psalms 92 and 93
Psalm 145
Psalm 150
Our Words of Thanks
Majesty
Delighting in Song
Reader's Kaddish

Hal'li nafshi et Adonai!	הַלְלִי נַפְשִׁי אֶת־יְיָ.
Ahal'lah Adonai b'chayai,	אֲהַלְלָה יְיָ בְּחַיָּי,
azam'rah l'Elohai b'odi.	אֲזַמְּרָה לֵאלֹהַי בְּעוֹדִי.

I call my soul to give You praise!
Eternal, I will celebrate You as long as I live,
and sing to my God while I have breath.

Hall'lu Yah —	הַלְלוּ יָהּ
hal'lu et-Adonai min-hashamayim;	הַלְלוּ אֶת־יְיָ מִן־הַשָּׁמַיִם,
hal'luhu bam'romim.	הַלְלְוּהוּ בַּמְּרוֹמִים.
Hal'luhu kol-malachav;	הַלְלְוּהוּ כָל־מַלְאָכָיו,
hal'luhu kol-tz'vaav.	הַלְלְוּהוּ כָּל־צְבָאָיו.
Hal'luhu shemesh v'yarei·ach;	הַלְלְוּהוּ שֶׁמֶשׁ וְיָרֵחַ,
hal'luhu kol-koch'vei or.	הַלְלְוּהוּ כָּל־כּוֹכְבֵי אוֹר.
Hal'luhu sh'mei hashamayim,	הַלְלְוּהוּ שְׁמֵי הַשָּׁמָיִם,
v'hamayim asher mei·al hashamayim.	וְהַמַּיִם אֲשֶׁר מֵעַל הַשָּׁמָיִם.
Y'hal'lu et-shem Adonai,	יְהַלְלוּ אֶת־שֵׁם יְיָ,
ki hu tzivah v'nivra·u.	כִּי הוּא צִוָּה וְנִבְרָאוּ.
Vayaamideim laad l'olam;	וַיַּעֲמִידֵם לָעַד לְעוֹלָם,
chok-natan v'lo yaavor.	חָק־נָתַן וְלֹא יַעֲבוֹר.

Praise the Eternal, in the dome of heaven;
  from the skies above, give praise to God.
Praise the Eternal, all you messengers;
  let celestial beings give praise to God.
Praise the Eternal, sun and moon;
  let all bright stars give praise to God.
Praise the Eternal, vault of heaven;
  let the waters above give praise to God.
For the Infinite called them into being,
  founded them, and fixed their bounds.

I CALL MY SOUL הַלְלִי נַפְשִׁי, Psalm 146:1–2.
PRAISE THE ETERNAL הַלְלוּ יָהּ, Psalm 148:1–6.

ON SHABBAT:

Psalm Selections for Shabbat

Psalm 16–92:13

Tzadik katamar yifrach;	צַדִּיק כַּתָּמָר יִפְרָח,
k'erez baL'vanon yisgeh.	כְּאֶרֶז בַּלְּבָנוֹן יִשְׂגֶּה.
Sh'tulim b'veit Adonai;	שְׁתוּלִים בְּבֵית יְיָ,
b'chatzrot Eloheinu yafrichu.	בְּחַצְרוֹת אֱלֹהֵינוּ יַפְרִיחוּ.
Od y'nuvun b'seivah;	עוֹד יְנוּבוּן בְּשֵׂיבָה,
d'sheinim v'raananim yiyu.	דְּשֵׁנִים וְרַעֲנַנִּים יִהְיוּ.
L'hagid ki-yashar Adonai —	לְהַגִּיד כִּי־יָשָׁר יְיָ,
tzuri, v'lo-avlatah bo.	צוּרִי וְלֹא־עַוְלָתָה בּוֹ.

The righteous shall blossom like date-palms
and thrive like cedars of Lebanon.
Planted in the house of Adonai,
they shall flourish in the courts of our God —
full of sap and richness,
still bearing fruit in old age:
proof that Adonai is upright —
my Rock, in whom there is no wrong.

Psalm 93

God acts within every moment
and creates the world with each breath.
He speaks from the center of the universe,
in the silence beyond all thought.
Mightier than the crash of a thunderstorm,
mightier than the roar of the sea,
is God's voice silently speaking
in the depths of the listening heart.

PSALM 93. Adaptation by Stephen Mitchell (b. 1943).

בָּרוּךְ שֶׁאָמַר
Baruch she·Amar

שִׁירִים לְיוֹם הַשַׁבָּת
Shirim l'Yom HaShabbat

אַשְׁרֵי
Ashrei

כֹּל הַנְּשָׁמָה
Kol HaN'shamah

אֵלוּ פִינוּ
Ilu Finu

הַמֶּלֶךְ
HaMelech

יִשְׁתַּבַּח
Yishtabach

חֲצִי קַדִּישׁ
Chatzi Kaddish

Ashrei — David's Song of Praise

Adonai my sovereign God, I praise Your name,
Boundless is Your glory.

Compassionate and full of grace,
Deeply patient, gentle and just—

Each generation sings of You,
Forever tells Your story.

Goodness and mercy extend to all,
Hands opened wide to nourish life—

I celebrate Your faithful love;
Joyful forever we sing to You.

A Song to Lift Up the Name of God

I will hold you highest in my heart
Will pronounce with blessing Your unsayable name
Everywhere and always

Each of my days will be a blessing for you . . .
I will stop
and consider
Your burning beauty
Your wondrous deeds
I will stop and speak
Of your awesome acts
I will stop and remember
Your greatness

GOODNESS AND MERCY EXTEND TO ALL. The *S'fat Emet* (Rabbi Yehudah Aryeh Leib Alter; 1847–1905) taught that human beings cannot truly understand animals or feel as much compassion for them as they do for human beings. If they did, they would not consume animals for food, exploit, or torment them. In contrast, God's compassion is infinite, and it extends to all living things.

A SONG TO LIFT UP. From an adaptation by Norman Fischer (b. 1946) of Psalm 145.

Ashrei — Happy Are Those

אַשְׁרֵי יוֹשְׁבֵי בֵיתֶךָ, — *Ashrei yosh'vei veitecha,*
עוֹד יְהַלְלוּךָ, סֶּלָה. — *od y'hal'lucha, selah.*
אַשְׁרֵי הָעָם שֶׁכָּכָה לּוֹ, — *Ashrei haam shekacha lo,*
אַשְׁרֵי הָעָם שֶׁיְיָ אֱלֹהָיו. — *ashrei haam she·Adonai elohav.*

Happy are those who dwell in Your house;
they shall sing Your praises forever *Selah.*
Happy the people for whom it is so;
happy the people whose God is Adonai.

תְּהִלָּה לְדָוִד. — *T'hilah l'David.*
אֲרוֹמִמְךָ, אֱלוֹהַי הַמֶּלֶךְ, — *Aromimcha, Elohai HaMelech;*
וַאֲבָרְכָה שִׁמְךָ לְעוֹלָם וָעֶד. — *vaavar'cha shimcha l'olam va·ed.*
בְּכָל־יוֹם אֲבָרְכֶךָּ, — *B'chol-yom avar'cheka;*
וַאֲהַלְלָה שִׁמְךָ לְעוֹלָם וָעֶד. — *vaahal'lah shimcha l'olam va·ed.*
גָּדוֹל יְיָ וּמְהֻלָּל מְאֹד, — *Gadol Adonai umhulal m'od;*
וְלִגְדֻלָּתוֹ אֵין חֵקֶר. — *v'ligdulato ein cheiker.*
דּוֹר לְדוֹר יְשַׁבַּח מַעֲשֶׂיךָ, — *Dor l'dor y'shabach maasecha;*
וּגְבוּרֹתֶיךָ יַגִּידוּ. — *ugvurotecha yagidu.*
הֲדַר כְּבוֹד הוֹדֶךָ, — *Hadar k'vod hodecha;*
וְדִבְרֵי נִפְלְאֹתֶיךָ אָשִׂיחָה. — *v'divrei nifl'otecha asichah.*
וֶעֱזוּז נוֹרְאוֹתֶיךָ יֹאמֵרוּ — *Ve·ezuz nor'otecha yomeiru;*
וּגְדוּלָּתְךָ אֲסַפְּרֶנָּה. — *ugdulat'cha asap'renah.*
זֵכֶר רַב־טוּבְךָ יַבִּיעוּ, — *Zeicher rav-tuv'cha yabiu;*
וְצִדְקָתְךָ יְרַנֵּנוּ. — *v'tzidkat'cha y'raneinu.*
חַנּוּן וְרַחוּם יְיָ, — *Chanun v'rachum Adonai;*
אֶרֶךְ אַפַּיִם וּגְדָל־חָסֶד. — *erech apayim ugdol-chased.*

HAPPY ARE THOSE אַשְׁרֵי, Psalm 84:5 and 144:15.

T'HILAH L'DAVID תְּהִלָּה לְדָוִד, Psalm 145. This poem is an incomplete alphabetical acrostic — for unknown reasons, the verse beginning with the Hebrew letter *nun* is missing. The Talmud (*B'rachot* 4b) says that it is omitted because it hints at the word *n'filah* (falling); thus it might refer to the downfall of Israel, as Scripture says: "Fallen, not to rise again, is Maiden Israel" (Amos 5:2). But, the Talmud continues, the following verse (which begins with the letter *samech*) offers reassurance that even in times of destruction, our people knows God's sustenance: "Adonai supports all who fall."

טוֹב־יְיָ לַכֹּל,	*Tov Adonai lakol;*
וְרַחֲמָיו עַל־כׇּל־מַעֲשָׂיו.	*v'rachamav al-kol-maasav.*
יוֹדְוּךָ יְיָ כׇּל־מַעֲשֶׂיךָ,	*Yoducha Adonai kol-maasecha;*
וַחֲסִידֶיךָ יְבָרְכְוּכָה.	*vachasidecha y'var'chucha.*
כְּבוֹד מַלְכוּתְךָ יֹאמֵרוּ,	*K'vod malchut'cha yomeiru;*
וּגְבוּרָתְךָ יְדַבֵּרוּ.	*ugvurat'cha y'dabeiru.*
לְהוֹדִיעַ לִבְנֵי הָאָדָם גְּבוּרֹתָיו,	*L'hodia livnei haadam g'vurotav,*
וּכְבוֹד הֲדַר מַלְכוּתוֹ.	*uchvod hadar malchuto.*
מַלְכוּתְךָ מַלְכוּת כׇּל־עֹלָמִים,	*Malchut'cha malchut kol-olamim,*
וּמֶמְשַׁלְתְּךָ בְּכׇל־דּוֹר וָדֹר.	*umemshalt'cha b'chol-dor vador.*
סוֹמֵךְ יְיָ לְכׇל־הַנֹּפְלִים,	*Someich Adonai l'chol-hanof'lim,*
וְזוֹקֵף לְכׇל־הַכְּפוּפִים.	*v'zokeif l'chol-hak'fufim.*
עֵינֵי־כֹל אֵלֶיךָ יְשַׂבֵּרוּ,	*Einei-chol eilecha y'sabeiru;*
וְאַתָּה נוֹתֵן לָהֶם אֶת־אׇכְלָם בְּעִתּוֹ.	*v'atah notein lahem et-ochlam b'ito.*
פּוֹתֵחַ אֶת־יָדֶךָ,	*Potei·ach et-yadecha;*
וּמַשְׂבִּיעַ לְכׇל־חַי רָצוֹן.	*umasbia l'chol-chai ratzon.*
צַדִּיק יְיָ בְּכׇל־דְּרָכָיו,	*Tzadik Adonai b'chol-d'rachav,*
וְחָסִיד בְּכׇל־מַעֲשָׂיו.	*v'chasid b'chol-maasav.*
קָרוֹב יְיָ לְכׇל־קֹרְאָיו,	*Karov Adonai l'chol-kor'av —*
לְכֹל אֲשֶׁר יִקְרָאֻהוּ בֶאֱמֶת.	*l'chol asher yikra·uhu ve·emet.*
רְצוֹן־יְרֵאָיו יַעֲשֶׂה,	*R'tzon-y'rei·av yaaseh;*
וְאֶת־שַׁוְעָתָם יִשְׁמַע וְיוֹשִׁיעֵם.	*v'et-shavatam yishma v'yoshi·eim.*
שׁוֹמֵר יְיָ אֶת־כׇּל־אֹהֲבָיו,	*Shomeir Adonai et-kol-ohavav;*
וְאֵת כׇּל־הָרְשָׁעִים יַשְׁמִיד.	*v'et kol-har'sha·im yashmid.*
תְּהִלַּת יְיָ יְדַבֶּר־פִּי,	*T'hilat Adonai y'daber-pi;*
וִיבָרֵךְ כׇּל־בָּשָׂר שֵׁם קׇדְשׁוֹ	*vivareich kol-basar shem kodsho*
לְעוֹלָם וָעֶד.	*l'olam va·ed.*
וַאֲנַחְנוּ נְבָרֵךְ יָהּ	*Vaanachnu n'vareich Yah*
מֵעַתָּה וְעַד־עוֹלָם, הַלְלוּ־יָהּ.	*mei·atah v'ad-olam, hal'lu-Yah!*

VAANACHNU וַאֲנַחְנוּ, Psalm 115:18.

Psalm 150

הַלְלוּ יָהּ,
Hal'lu Yah!

הַלְלוּ־אֵל בְּקָדְשׁוֹ,
Hal'lu-El b'kodsho;

הַלְלְוּהוּ בִּרְקִיעַ עֻזּוֹ.
hal'luhu birkia uzo.

הַלְלְוּהוּ בִגְבוּרֹתָיו,
Hal'luhu bigvurotav;

הַלְלְוּהוּ כְּרֹב גֻּדְלוֹ.
hal'luhu k'rov gudlo.

הַלְלְוּהוּ בְּתֵקַע שׁוֹפָר,
Hal'luhu b'teika-shofar;

הַלְלְוּהוּ בְּנֵבֶל וְכִנּוֹר.
hal'luhu b'neivel v'chinor.

הַלְלְוּהוּ בְּתֹף וּמָחוֹל,
Hal'luhu b'tof umachol;

הַלְלְוּהוּ בְּמִנִּים וְעֻגָב.
hal'luhu b'minim v'ugav.

הַלְלְוּהוּ בְצִלְצְלֵי־שָׁמַע,
Hal'luhu v'tziltz'lei-shama;

הַלְלְוּהוּ בְּצִלְצְלֵי תְרוּעָה.
hal'luhu b'tziltz'lei t'ruah!

כֹּל הַנְּשָׁמָה תְּהַלֵּל יָהּ,
Kol han'shamah t'haleil Yah:

הַלְלוּ־יָהּ.
Hal'lu-Yah!

Halleluyah!
Praise God in our holy Temple;
give praise in the heavens, God's fortress.
Praise God for deeds of great power;
give praise for the depths of God's grandeur.
Praise God with the blast of the shofar;
give praise with the harp and the lyre.
Praise God with drumbeat and dancing;
give praise with the strings and the flute.
Praise God with the crash of cymbals,
and praise with the clash of resounding cymbals!
With every quiet breath, let everything that breathes
praise God — Halleluyah!

בָּרוּךְ שֶׁאָמַר
Baruch she-Amar
שִׁירִים לְיוֹם הַשַּׁבָּת
Shirim l'Yom HaShabbat
אַשְׁרֵי
Ashrei
כֹּל הַנְּשָׁמָה
Kol HaN'shamah
אִלּוּ פִינוּ
Ilu Finu
הַמֶּלֶךְ
HaMelech
יִשְׁתַּבַּח
Yishtabach
חֲצִי קַדִּישׁ
Chatzi Kaddish

PSALM 150 concludes the Book of Psalms on a note of ecstatic praise: a vision of God's greatness proclaimed in the high heavens (the celestial Temple), just as human beings join in songs of praise on earth. The final words of the psalm celebrate the sheer wonder and joy of being alive — a joy we feel most intensely, perhaps, on this day when we are especially conscious of our mortality.

אִלּוּ פִינוּ מָלֵא שִׁירָה כַּיָּם,
וּלְשׁוֹנֵנוּ רִנָּה כַּהֲמוֹן גַּלָּיו,
וְשִׂפְתוֹתֵינוּ שֶׁבַח כְּמֶרְחֲבֵי רָקִיעַ,
וְעֵינֵינוּ מְאִירוֹת כַּשֶּׁמֶשׁ וְכַיָּרֵחַ,
וְיָדֵינוּ פְרוּשׂוֹת כְּנִשְׁרֵי שָׁמָיִם,
וְרַגְלֵינוּ קַלּוֹת כָּאַיָּלוֹת,
אֵין אֲנַחְנוּ מַסְפִּיקִים לְהוֹדוֹת לְךָ,
יְיָ אֱלֹהֵינוּ וֵאלֹהֵי אֲבוֹתֵינוּ
וְאִמּוֹתֵינוּ,
וּלְבָרֵךְ אֶת שְׁמֶךָ עַל אַחַת מֵאֶלֶף
אַלְפֵי אֲלָפִים וְרִבֵּי רְבָבוֹת
פְּעָמִים הַטּוֹבוֹת
שֶׁעָשִׂיתָ עִם אֲבוֹתֵינוּ וְאִמּוֹתֵינוּ
וְעִמָּנוּ.

Ilu finu malei shirah kayam,
ulshoneinu rinah kahamon galav,
v'siftoteinu shevach k'meirchavei rakia,
v'eineinu m'irot kashemesh v'chayarei·ach,
v'yadeinu f'rusot k'nishrei shamayim,
v'ragleinu kalot kaayalot:
ein anachnu maspikim l'hodot l'cha,
Adonai Eloheinu v'Elohei avoteinu
v'imoteinu,
ulvareich et sh'mecha al achat mei·elef
alfei alafim v'ribei r'vavot
p'amim hatovot
she·asita im avoteinu v'imoteinu
v'imanu.

If our mouths were filled with song as the sea,
our tongues with music like the crash of ocean waves,
our lips with praise endless as sky above,
our eyes aglow like sun and moon,
our arms reaching toward heaven like eagle's wings,
our legs as graceful as the gazelle in flight—
still our words of thanks to You would not suffice,
Adonai our God and God of all ages,
nor could we bless Your name enough
for Your infinite acts of kindness to our ancestors and to us.

ONE GOES TO an earthly sovereign with arms full of gifts and returns empty-handed. To God, one goes with empty hands and returns full. (Midrash *P'sikta Rabbati* 44, *Shuvah* 185a)

A TEACHING of Rabbi Nachman of Breslov (1772–1810): A person should get into the habit of singing, for a holy melody is a great and wondrous thing. It can awaken the heart from sleep and bring it back to the divine Source of all.

מִמִּצְרַֽיִם גְּאַלְתָּֽנוּ, יְיָ אֱלֹהֵֽינוּ,
וּמִבֵּית עֲבָדִים פְּדִיתָֽנוּ.
בְּרָעָב זַנְתָּֽנוּ,
וּבְשָׂבָע כִּלְכַּלְתָּֽנוּ,
מֵחֶֽרֶב הִצַּלְתָּֽנוּ,
וּמִדֶּֽבֶר מִלַּטְתָּֽנוּ,
וּמֵחֳלָיִם רָעִים וְנֶאֱמָנִים דִּלִּיתָֽנוּ.
עַד הֵֽנָּה עֲזָרֽוּנוּ רַחֲמֶֽיךָ.
וְלֹא עֲזָבֽוּנוּ חֲסָדֶֽיךָ,
וְאַל תִּטְּשֵֽׁנוּ, יְיָ אֱלֹהֵֽינוּ, לָנֶֽצַח.

MiMitzrayim g'altanu, Adonai Eloheinu,
umibeit avadim p'ditanu.
B'raav zantanu
uvsava kilkaltanu;
meicherev hitzaltanu
umidever milattanu;
umeicholayim ra·im v'ne·emanim dilitanu.
Ad heinah azarunu rachamecha.
V'lo azavunu chasadecha;
v'al tit'sheinu, Adonai Eloheinu, lanetzach.

From Egypt You redeemed us, Adonai our God,
and from a world of slavery You saved us.
In times of hunger You fed us.
In times of plenty You nourished us.
You turned our blight to blessing,
spared us from suffering,
and rescued us from the sword.
Your mercy supports us
and Your love abides — now as in the past.
Never forsake us, Adonai our God; never turn away.

הָאֵל בְּתַעֲצוּמוֹת עֻזֶּךָ,
הַגָּדוֹל בִּכְבוֹד שְׁמֶךָ,
הַגִּבּוֹר לָנֶֽצַח,
וְהַנּוֹרָא בְּנוֹרְאוֹתֶֽיךָ,

HaEl b'taatzumot uzecha,
hagadol bichvod sh'mecha,
hagibor lanetzach,
v'hanora b'norotecha —

Holy One, infinite Your power,
radiant Your glory,
unbounded Your might,
awe-inspiring Your works —

FROM EGYPT YOU REDEEMED US. A provocative midrash suggests that the Israelite slaves at first did not welcome Moses' offer of freedom because they were attached to idolatry (*M'chilta d'Rabbi Yishmael, Pischa* 5). Jeffrey Spitzer (b. 1965) asks: "Do people deserve liberation or support because they are oppressed? Must people take some action on their own in order to effect redemption? How much time is needed to reject dysfunctional habits before requiring someone to move on to something better?"

HaMelech

yosheiv al kisei ram v'nisa, יוֹשֵׁב עַל כִּסֵּא רָם וְנִשָּׂא,

MAJESTIC GOD, today enthroned beyond time and space —

Shochein ad, marom v'kadosh sh'mo. שׁוֹכֵן עַד, מָרוֹם וְקָדוֹשׁ שְׁמוֹ.

V'chatuv: "Ran'nu tzadikim b'Adonai! וְכָתוּב: רַנְּנוּ צַדִּיקִים בַּייָ.

Laisharim navah t'hilah." לַיְשָׁרִים נָאוָה תְהִלָּה.

Eternally present,
Your name is hallowed on high.
And the Psalmist sang:
"Rejoice in Adonai, you righteous!
Let the upright adorn You with praise."

HAMELECH הַמֶּלֶךְ. This word ("Majestic God"), present in the liturgy for Shabbat and the festivals, is typically enlarged in the *machzor* for Rosh HaShanah and Yom Kippur, emphasizing the dramatic proclamation of God as sovereign of the world — a central theme of the Days of Awe.

REJOICE IN ADONAI רַנְּנוּ . . . בַּייָ, Psalm 33:1. The Psalmist expresses the joy of knowing and trusting in God's ultimate dominion over all creation. Despite the presence of evil around us and our own propensity for wrongdoing, joy is at the heart of these holy days. A better life is always possible — if we mobilize the good forces within ourselves and align ourselves with the Divine.

B'fi y'sharim titromam;

uvdivrei tzadikim titbarach;

uvilshon chasidim titkadash;

uvkerev k'doshim tit·halal.

Uvmak·halot riv'vot am'cha,

beit Yisrael,

b'rinah yitpaar shimcha, Malkeinu,

b'chol dor vador.

בְּפִי יְשָׁרִים תִּתְרוֹמָם,

וּבְדִבְרֵי צַדִּיקִים תִּתְבָּרַךְ,

וּבִלְשׁוֹן חֲסִידִים תִּתְקַדָּשׁ,

וּבְקֶרֶב קְדוֹשִׁים תִּתְהַלָּל.

וּבְמַקְהֲלוֹת רִבְבוֹת עַמְּךָ,

בֵּית יִשְׂרָאֵל,

בְּרִנָּה יִתְפָּאַר שִׁמְךָ, מַלְכֵּנוּ,

בְּכָל דּוֹר וָדוֹר.

בָּרוּךְ שֶׁאָמַר
Baruch she·Amar

שִׁירִים לְיוֹם הַשַּׁבָּת
Shirim l'Yom HaShabbat

אַשְׁרֵי
Ashrei

כֹּל הַנְּשָׁמָה
Kol HaN'shamah

אִלּוּ פִינוּ
Ilu Finu

הַמֶּלֶךְ
HaMelech

יִשְׁתַּבַּח
Yishtabach

חֲצִי קַדִּישׁ
Chatzi Kaddish

By the mouths of the upright You are raised up;
in the words of the righteous You are blessed;
on the tongues of the pious You are sanctified;
in the midst of the holy You are praised.
Your people by the thousands sing to glorify Your name.
In all generations we give voice to Your sovereignty.

BY THE MOUTHS OF THE UPRIGHT בְּפִי יְשָׁרִים. The liturgy imagines a chorus of good people everywhere singing praise of God. Four categories are mentioned: the upright, the righteous, the pious, and the holy. By joining in these words, we become part of the chorus. But how can we, flawed as we are, identify with the righteous and holy?

Rabbi Israel Friedman of Rizhyn (1796–1850) taught that each day God restores us to life anew. This realization should not only fill us with gratitude and joy, but give us the courage to pray. "For often when we try to raise ourselves in worship, our *yeitzer*, our self-destructive side, our own personal internal enemy, seeks to undermine our resolve by asking, 'Who are we to pray? How dare such a sinner open his or her mouth!' We must realize, says the Rizhyner, that each and every moment we are new creatures. Just this instant, again, we have been born anew. And therefore we are without sin!" (Rabbi Lawrence Kushner, b. 1943; and Rabbi Nehemia Polen, b. 1946)

יִשְׁתַּבַּח שִׁמְךָ לָעַד, מַלְכֵּנוּ,
הָאֵל הַמֶּלֶךְ הַגָּדוֹל וְהַקָּדוֹשׁ
בַּשָּׁמַיִם וּבָאָרֶץ.
כִּי לְךָ נָאֶה, יְיָ אֱלֹהֵינוּ וֵאלֹהֵי
אֲבוֹתֵינוּ וְאִמּוֹתֵינוּ,
שִׁיר וּשְׁבָחָה, הַלֵּל וְזִמְרָה,
עֹז וּמֶמְשָׁלָה, נֶצַח,
גְּדֻלָּה וּגְבוּרָה, תְּהִלָּה וְתִפְאֶרֶת,
קְדֻשָּׁה וּמַלְכוּת, בְּרָכוֹת וְהוֹדָאוֹת,
מֵעַתָּה וְעַד עוֹלָם.

Yishtabach shimcha laad, Malkeinu,
HaEl haMelech hagadol v'hakadosh
bashamayim uvaaretz.
Ki l'cha na·eh, Adonai Eloheinu v'Elohei
avoteinu v'imoteinu,
shir ushvachah, haleil v'zimrah,
oz umemshalah, netzach,
g'dulah ugvurah, t'hilah v'tiferet,
k'dushah umalchut, b'rachot v'hodaot —
mei·atah v'ad olam.

Our sovereign God, Source of holiness and greatness —
may Your name be praised forever in this world and beyond.
Eternal One, God of our mothers and our fathers,
Your strength, sanctity, glory, and dominion
are deserving of song, praise, poetry, hymn, sacred chant,
and blessings of thankfulness
for all time and eternity.

בָּרוּךְ אַתָּה, יְיָ, אֵל מֶלֶךְ גָּדוֹל בַּתִּשְׁבָּחוֹת, אֵל הַהוֹדָאוֹת,
אֲדוֹן הַנִּפְלָאוֹת, הַבּוֹחֵר בְּשִׁירֵי זִמְרָה, מֶלֶךְ, אֵל, חֵי הָעוֹלָמִים.

Baruch atah, Adonai, El melech gadol batishbachot, El hahodaot,
adon haniflaot, habocheir b'shirei zimrah, Melech, El, chei haolamim.

Blessed are You, Adonai, Sovereign of praise, Source of the impulse
to give thanks, Crown of wonders — who desires a world
filled with song and a universe of life.

DESERVING OF SONG, PRAISE, POETRY לְךָ נָאֶה . . . שִׁיר וּשְׁבָחָה, הַלֵּל. The liturgical rubric called "Songs of Praise" began with the words "Blessed is the One who spoke the world into being" (page 164). Here it reaches its climax with an exuberant catalogue of human speech acts to praise the Creator. In *Yishtabach* we reach, with an urgent joy, for the right words to express the depth of our gratitude; and though we know that our words cannot suffice, we express our aspiration.

יִתְגַּדַּל וְיִתְקַדַּשׁ שְׁמֵהּ רַבָּא,	*Yitgadal v'yitkadash sh'meih raba,*
בְּעָלְמָא דִּי בְרָא כִרְעוּתֵהּ.	*b'alma di v'ra chiruteih.*
וְיַמְלִיךְ מַלְכוּתֵהּ בְּחַיֵּיכוֹן	*V'yamlich malchuteih b'chayeichon*
וּבְיוֹמֵיכוֹן,	*uvyomeichon,*
וּבְחַיֵּי דְכָל בֵּית יִשְׂרָאֵל,	*uvchayei d'chol beit Yisrael —*
בַּעֲגָלָא וּבִזְמַן קָרִיב.	*baagala uvizman kariv;*
וְאִמְרוּ: אָמֵן.	*v'imru: Amen.*
יְהֵא שְׁמֵהּ רַבָּא מְבָרַךְ	*Y'hei sh'meih raba m'varach*
לְעָלַם וּלְעָלְמֵי עָלְמַיָּא.	*l'alam ul·almei almaya.*
יִתְבָּרַךְ וְיִשְׁתַּבַּח וְיִתְפָּאַר	*Yitbarach v'yishtabach v'yitpaar*
וְיִתְרוֹמַם וְיִתְנַשֵּׂא וְיִתְהַדָּר	*v'yitromam v'yitnasei v'yit·hadar*
וְיִתְעַלֶּה וְיִתְהַלָּל שְׁמֵהּ	*v'yitaleh v'yit·halal sh'meih*
דְּקֻדְשָׁא, בְּרִיךְ הוּא,	*d'kudsha — b'rich hu —*
לְעֵלָּא וּלְעֵלָּא מִכָּל בִּרְכָתָא וְשִׁירָתָא,	*l'eila ul·eila mikol birchata v'shirata,*
תֻּשְׁבְּחָתָא וְנֶחֱמָתָא	*tushb'chata v'nechemata*
דַּאֲמִירָן בְּעָלְמָא.	*daamiran b'alma;*
וְאִמְרוּ: אָמֵן.	*v'imru: Amen.*

May God's great name come to be magnified and sanctified in the world God brought into being. May God's majestic reign prevail soon in your lives, in your days, and in the life of the whole House of Israel; and let us say: *Amen.*

May God's great name be blessed to the end of time.

May God's holy name come to be blessed, acclaimed, and glorified; revered, raised, and beautified; honored and praised. Blessed is the One who is **entirely** beyond all the blessings and hymns, all the praises and words of comfort that we speak in the world; and let us say: *Amen.*

בָּרוּךְ שֶׁאָמַר *Baruch she·Amar*
שִׁירִים לְיוֹם הַשַּׁבָּת *Shirim l'Yom HaShabbat*
אַשְׁרֵי *Ashrei*
כֹּל הַנְּשָׁמָה *Kol HaN'shamah*
אִלּוּ פִינוּ *Ilu Finu*
הַמֶּלֶךְ *HaMelech*
יִשְׁתַּבַּח *Yishtabach*
חֲצִי קַדִּישׁ ***Chatzi Kaddish***

MAY GOD'S GREAT NAME יִתְגַּדַּל. Called the Reader's *Kaddish* (*Chatzi Kaddish*, literally "half-*Kaddish*"), this shorter form of the *Kaddish* has no connection with mourning; it serves instead as liturgical punctuation, to divide sections of the service. Despite its profusion of words in praise of God, the *Kaddish* asserts that Divinity is "entirely beyond" the power of human language. Nevertheless, the repetitive sound-pattern and rhythmic cadence of the Aramaic text demonstrate the power of prayer to shift our consciousness and transport us beyond ordinary language.

What Color Is Grass?

What color is grass?

The hurried eye said, green.
But following the sheen
of spring woods, there stretched
meadows marbled in such hues
of yellow green, red green, and blues
merging—below, between, above.

What color is grass?
The thoughtful eye said, Love.

What color is love?

The harried heart said, flame.
But following the changing years
there poured prisms of delight
and spectrum flowed out of the name
paling moon, stars, and sun.

What color is Love?
The knowing heart said, One.

Hey, Clockmaker—
I was looking for You.
Builder of the machine,
You lost interest, I guess, and walked away—
but I was looking for signs of You.
I saw accidents,
mutations,
disasters unpredicted and unexplained;
pretty sloppy work, if You ask me.
Hey, Clockmaker—
praised be Your name
and the names of Your mechanics.

---

what color is grass. By Ruth Finer Mintz (1919–1997).

שְׁמַע וּבִרְכוֹתֶיהָ
Sh'ma Uvirchoteha · Sh'ma and Its Blessings

בָּרְכוּ
Bar'chu

יוֹצֵר אוֹר
Yotzeir Or

אַהֲבָה רַבָּה
Ahavah Rabbah

קְרִיאַת שְׁמַע
K'riat Sh'ma

אֱמֶת וְיַצִּיב
Emet v'Yatziv

מִי־כָמֹכָה
Mi Chamocha

בָּרְכוּ אֶת יְיָ הַמְבֹרָךְ.
בָּרוּךְ יְיָ הַמְבֹרָךְ לְעוֹלָם וָעֶד.

Bar'chu et Adonai hamvorach.
Baruch Adonai hamvorach l'olam va·ed.

Bless the Eternal, the Blessed One.
Blessed is the Eternal, the Blessed One, now and forever.

בָּרוּךְ אַתָּה, יְיָ,
אֱלֹהֵינוּ מֶלֶךְ הָעוֹלָם,
הַפּוֹתֵחַ לָנוּ שַׁעֲרֵי רַחֲמִים,
וּמֵאִיר עֵינֵי הַמְחַכִּים לִסְלִיחָתוֹ,
יוֹצֵר אוֹר, וּבוֹרֵא חֹשֶׁךְ,
עֹשֶׂה שָׁלוֹם וּבוֹרֵא אֶת הַכֹּל.

Baruch atah, Adonai,
Eloheinu melech haolam,
hapotei-ach lanu shaarei rachamim,
umei-ir einei hamchakim lislichato;
yotzeir or, uvorei choshech —
oseh shalom uvorei et hakol.

אוֹר עוֹלָם בְּאוֹצַר חַיִּים,
אוֹרוֹת מֵאֹפֶל אָמַר: וַיֶּהִי.

Or olam b'otzar chayim.
Orot mei-ofel amar: Vayehi.

Praise to You, Adonai our God, whose power fills the cosmos —
who opens for us the gates of compassion
and lights up the eyes of those who await forgiveness —
Shaper of light, Source of the darkness,
Maker of peace, Creator of all.

Infinite light is preserved in life's treasure-house;
"Lights from the darkness!" said God — it was so.

WHO OPENS FOR US THE GATES OF COMPASSION הַפּוֹתֵחַ לָנוּ שַׁעֲרֵי רַחֲמִים. This two-line insertion for Yom Kippur morning links the renewal of light at dawn with the sense of renewed hope felt by those who await God's forgiveness. The phrase "opens for us the gates of compassion" points to the "closing of the gates"— the *N'ilah* prayers at the end of Yom Kippur, thus lending a sense of urgency to our prayers.

LIGHTS FROM THE DARKNESS אוֹרוֹת מֵאֹפֶל. Inserted on Rosh HaShanah and Yom Kippur, this sentence alludes to the first words spoken by God in the Bible: "Let there be light" (Genesis 1:3). We might read these words metaphorically, referring not only to the divine capacity to defeat darkness, but also to our own power to push back the darkness of our times.

In this circle of community, in this hour of striving for faith,
I believe in Your majesty, Your guiding presence within me.
To You I turn on this day of the spirit—seeking atonement,
longing to hear Your words: "I forgive."

בָּרוּךְ שֵׁם כְּבוֹד מַלְכוּתוֹ.

Blessed is God's glorious majesty. *Baruch shem k'vod malchuto.*

Holy One of Might—Your towering strength reaches from heaven's heights to the human heart.
Holy One of Mercy—Your forgiveness is profound; it embraces all who turn to You.
Holy One of Torah—the secrets You impart are radiant; they reach Your people, Your cherished ones.

Blessed is God's glorious majesty.

Holy One of the Heart—You forgive us in our weakness; You pardon us in our fear.
Holy One of Strength—we praise Your powers, the wonders of creation and redemption.
Holy One of Remembrance—You remember us with love, taking delight when we search our souls.

Blessed is God's glorious majesty.

Holy One of the Spirit—You accept our fast of repentance, and breathe into us purity and goodness.
Holy One of Conscience—You remove our wrongs, and reveal the way of righteousness.
Holy One of Existence—Your light is the glory of creation; Your mercy endures forever.

Blessed is God's glorious majesty. *Baruch shem k'vod malchuto.*

In this circle of community, in this hour of striving for faith,
I believe in Your majesty, Your guiding presence within me.
To You I turn on this day of the spirit—seeking atonement,
longing to hear Your words: "I forgive."

HOLY ONE OF MIGHT. Based on the liturgical poem *Kadosh Adir BaAliyato*, which is attributed to Rabbi Kalonymus ben Mosheh (10th century). In the traditional version of the *piyut* (which is said while standing), the refrain "Blessed is God's glorious majesty" is a congregational response.

בָּרְכוּ
Bar'chu

יוֹצֵר אוֹר
Yotzeir Or

אַהֲבָה רַבָּה
Ahavah Rabbah

קְרִיאַת שְׁמַע
K'riat Sh'ma

אֱמֶת וְיַצִּיב
Emet v'Yatziv

מִי־כָמֹכָה
Mi Chamocha

Hamei·ir laaretz v'ladarim aleha
  b'rachamim;
uvtuvo m'chadeish b'chol yom tamid
  maaseih v'reishit.
Mah rabu maasecha, Adonai —
kulam b'chochmah asita;
mal·ah haaretz kinyanecha!
Titbarach, Adonai Eloheinu,
al shevach maaseih yadecha;
v'al m'orei or she·asita —
y'faarucha selah.

הַמֵּאִיר לָאָרֶץ וְלַדָּרִים עָלֶיהָ
  בְּרַחֲמִים,
וּבְטוּבוֹ מְחַדֵּשׁ בְּכָל יוֹם תָּמִיד
  מַעֲשֵׂה בְרֵאשִׁית.
מָה רַבּוּ מַעֲשֶׂיךָ, יְיָ —
כֻּלָּם בְּחָכְמָה עָשִׂיתָ,
מָלְאָה הָאָרֶץ קִנְיָנֶךָ.
תִּתְבָּרַךְ, יְיָ אֱלֹהֵינוּ,
עַל שֶׁבַח מַעֲשֵׂה יָדֶיךָ,
וְעַל מְאוֹרֵי אוֹר שֶׁעָשִׂיתָ
יְפָאֲרוּךָ סֶּלָה.

In love You bring light to the earth and its creatures;
Your goodness renews the Creation each day.
Infinite, varied, and rich are Your works, Divine Artist —
all of them wrought with wisdom;
the whole earth is teeming with life!
Awe-struck by the universe, work of Your hands,
let all life bless You, praise You,
and celebrate the beauty of Your lights.

Or chadash al Tziyon ta·ir,
v'nizkeh chulanu m'heirah l'oro.

אוֹר חָדָשׁ עַל צִיּוֹן תָּאִיר
וְנִזְכֶּה כֻלָּנוּ מְהֵרָה לְאוֹרוֹ.

May You shine a new light on Zion;
and may we soon be privileged to share in that light.

בָּרוּךְ אַתָּה, יְיָ, יוֹצֵר הַמְּאוֹרוֹת.
Baruch atah, Adonai, yotzeir ham'orot.
Our praise to You, Adonai, Creator of the cosmic lights.

SHINE A NEW LIGHT ON ZION אוֹר חָדָשׁ עַל צִיּוֹן תָּאִיר. Saadia Gaon, a 10th-century leader
of Babylonian Jews, objected to this addition to the *Yotzeir Or* (Shaper of Light) prayer,
asserting that there is no place for the figurative light of Zion in a prayer that praises God
for the creation of "real" physical light. Poetry, however, prevailed — a testament to the
importance of metaphor in Jewish prayer; and a testament to the significance of the Land
of Israel in the constellation of Jewish faith.

THOSE WHO DWELL, as scientists or laymen, among the beauties and mysteries of the earth, are never alone or weary of life. Whatever the vexations or concerns of their personal lives, their thoughts can find paths that lead to inner contentment and to renewed excitement in living. Those who contemplate the beauty of the earth find reserves of strength that will endure as long as life lasts. There is symbolic as well as actual beauty in the migration of the birds, the ebb and flow of the tides, the folded bud ready for the spring. There is something infinitely healing in the repeated refrains of nature—the assurance that dawn comes after night, and spring after the winter.

LIKE AN unbroken current
energy streams from the Source.
Bathing the planet in light,
calling forth life,
movement, mind unfolding from matter,
the power to love.
And we offer it back to You—
our own creative energy,
ever-dreaming, building,
shaping patterns out of chaos,
searching out light in the darkness.
Creation never ceases, not for an instant:
All life is aglow with Your light;
All things draw sustenance from the Source.

בָּרוּךְ אַתָּה, יְיָ, יוֹצֵר הַמְּאוֹרוֹת.

Baruch atah, Adonai, yotzeir ham'orot.

Our praise to You, Adonai, Creator of the lights of heaven.

THOSE WHO DWELL. By Rachel Carson (1907–1964).

LIKE AN UNBROKEN CURRENT. Based on the teachings of Rabbi Levi Yitzchak of Berditchev (1740–1809) in his Chasidic commentary on the Torah and other sacred books, entitled *K'dushat Levi* (Holiness of Levi). There he declares that the *Yotzeir Or* prayer is formulated in the present tense (God shapes light and creates darkness) because the universe is animated by a continuous flow of divine creative energy: "For at every moment God creates; at every moment God bestows vitality on all living creatures, and all is from God."

בָּרְכוּ
Bar'chu
יוֹצֵר אוֹר
Yotzeir Or
אַהֲבָה רַבָּה
Ahavah Rabbah
קְרִיאַת שְׁמַע
K'riat Sh'ma
אֱמֶת וְיַצִּיב
Emet v'Yatziv
מִי־כָמֹכָה
Mi Chamocha

אַהֲבָה רַבָּה אֲהַבְתָּנוּ, יְיָ אֱלֹהֵינוּ,
חֶמְלָה גְדוֹלָה וִיתֵרָה חָמַלְתָּ עָלֵינוּ.
בַּעֲבוּר אֲבוֹתֵינוּ וְאִמּוֹתֵינוּ
שֶׁבָּטְחוּ בְךָ,
וַתְּלַמְּדֵם חֻקֵּי חַיִּים,
כֵּן תְּחָנֵּנוּ וּתְלַמְּדֵנוּ.
אָבִינוּ, הָאָב הָרַחֲמָן:
הַמְרַחֵם, רַחֵם עָלֵינוּ,
וְתֵן בְּלִבֵּנוּ לְהָבִין וּלְהַשְׂכִּיל,
לִשְׁמֹעַ, לִלְמֹד וּלְלַמֵּד,
לִשְׁמֹר וְלַעֲשׂוֹת וּלְקַיֵּם אֶת כָּל דִּבְרֵי
תַלְמוּד תּוֹרָתֶךָ בְּאַהֲבָה.
וְהָאֵר עֵינֵינוּ בְּתוֹרָתֶךָ,
וְדַבֵּק לִבֵּנוּ בְּמִצְוֹתֶיךָ.

Ahavah rabbah ahavtanu, Adonai Eloheinu,
chemlah g'dolah viteirah chamalta aleinu.
Baavur avoteinu v'imoteinu
shebat'chu v'cha
vat'lam'deim chukei chayim,
kein t'choneinu utlam'deinu.
Avinu, haAv harachaman:
hamracheim, racheim aleinu;
v'tein b'libeinu l'havin ulhaskil,
lishmoa, lilmod ul'lameid,
lishmor v'laasot ulkayeim et kol divrei
talmud Toratecha b'ahavah.
V'ha·eir eineinu b'Toratecha;
v'dabeik libeinu b'mitzvotecha.

Love abundant, love unstinting —
our God, You have enfolded us in love.
Tender compassion beyond all bounds —
Your precious gift.
Our fathers and mothers gave You their trust
and You gave them Torah, laws by which to live.
For their sake, teach us, as well; grace us with Your guidance.
Loving Father, Merciful Mother of us all:
Grant us clear understanding
that we may listen, learn, and teach,
preserve, practice, and fulfill with love
every lesson of Your Torah.
May learning Your Torah light up our eyes;
may our hearts embrace Your mitzvot.

MAY LEARNING YOUR TORAH LIGHT UP OUR EYES וְהָאֵר עֵינֵינוּ בְּתוֹרָתֶךָ. Attachment to Torah — divine teachings transmitted from generation to generation — has made the Jews an eternal people. As the Midrash says: When Israel stood at Sinai and received the Torah, the Holy Blessed One said to the Angel of Death, "You have power over all . . . but not over this people, for they are My portion" (*Leviticus Rabbah* 18.3).

You love us by helping us grow;
You give us Torah, a ladder for the soul.
Words that draw us upward;
Every mitzvah—an invitation to climb.
Forge and kiln and crucible
To purify our hearts—
You give us Torah;
You love us by helping us grow.

All who are thirsty, come here for water.
Drink deep of Torah, a fathomless well.

Seas spread out to distant horizons;
Torah encompasses all of the earth.

Water revives and refreshes the body;
Torah is potent, restoring the soul.

Soil and pollution swept away in pure waters;
immersing in Torah, the spirit is cleansed.

Earth's precious water, free and untrammeled—
Torah is open and belongs to all people.

Mighty waters pour down like thunder;
Torah is shared in a rainbow of voices.

Waters flow from the heights to the valleys;
Torah will dwell in the humble of heart.

Raindrops swell into powerful rivers;
begin in your learning and wisdom will grow.

Fountain of gardens, wellspring of fresh water;
words of Torah bring life to the world.

Our praise to You, Adonai:
with love You offer Israel the gift of Torah.

YOU LOVE US. Based on a midrash: "The mitzvot were given to Israel in order to refine and purify us. For what does the Holy One care whether a person kills an animal by the throat or the nape of the neck? Hence the purpose of the mitzvot is to refine our characters" (*Genesis Rabbah* 44.1; *Leviticus Rabbah* 13.3).

ALL WHO ARE THIRSTY, COME HERE FOR WATER. Adapted from Isaiah 55:1.

SEAS SPREAD OUT . . . LIFE TO THE WORLD. Based on Midrash *Song of Songs Rabbah* 1:19. "Fountain of gardens, wellspring of fresh water" is from Song of Songs 4:15.

בָּרְכוּ
Bar'chu
יוֹצֵר אוֹר
Yotzeir Or
אַהֲבָה רַבָּה
Ahavah Rabbah
קְרִיאַת שְׁמַע
K'riat Sh'ma
אֱמֶת וְיַצִּיב
Emet v'Yatziv
מִי־כָמֹכָה
Mi Chamocha

וְיַחֵד לְבָבֵנוּ לְאַהֲבָה וּלְיִרְאָה
אֶת שְׁמֶךָ.
וְלֹא נֵבוֹשׁ וְלֹא נִכָּלֵם,
וְלֹא נִכָּשֵׁל לְעוֹלָם וָעֶד.
כִּי בְשֵׁם קָדְשְׁךָ הַגָּדוֹל וְהַנּוֹרָא
בָּטָחְנוּ,
נָגִילָה וְנִשְׂמְחָה בִּישׁוּעָתֶךָ.

V'yacheid l'vaveinu l'ahavah ulyirah
et sh'mecha.
V'lo neivosh v'lo nikaleim;
v'lo nikasheil l'olam va·ed.
Ki v'shem kodsh'cha hagadol v'hanora
batachnu;
nagilah v'nism'chah bishuatecha.

Unite us in love and reverence for You,
that we may never feel ashamed of our deeds.
We have trusted in Your great and holy name;
now let us celebrate at last the joy of Your salvation.

וַהֲבִיאֵנוּ לְשָׁלוֹם
מֵאַרְבַּע כַּנְפוֹת הָאָרֶץ,
וְתוֹלִיכֵנוּ קוֹמְמִיּוּת לְאַרְצֵנוּ.
כִּי אֵל פּוֹעֵל יְשׁוּעוֹת אָתָּה,
וּבָנוּ בָחַרְתָּ מִכָּל עַם וְלָשׁוֹן.
וְקֵרַבְתָּנוּ לְשִׁמְךָ הַגָּדוֹל
סֶלָה בֶּאֱמֶת,
לְהוֹדוֹת לְךָ, וּלְיַחֶדְךָ בְּאַהֲבָה.

Vahavi·einu l'shalom
mei·arba kanfot haaretz;
v'tolicheinu kom'miyut l'artzeinu.
Ki El po·eil y'shuot atah —
uvanu vacharta mikol am v'lashon.
V'keiravtanu l'shimcha hagadol
selah be·emet,
l'hodot l'cha, ulyachedcha b'ahavah.

Bring us in peace from the four corners of the earth;
lead us with upright pride to the land that is ours.
For You are a God of miracles and wonders —
from all the peoples of the earth You sought us out
and brought us near to Your great, enduring truth.
So with love we acknowledge and proclaim that You are One.

בָּרוּךְ אַתָּה, יְיָ, הַבּוֹחֵר בְּעַמּוֹ יִשְׂרָאֵל בְּאַהֲבָה.

Baruch atah, Adonai, habocheir b'amo Yisrael b'ahavah.

Our praise to You, Adonai:
You have singled out Your people Israel with love.

MEDITATION BEFORE THE SH'MA

Hineini—
behold, I stand ready to listen and learn
to embrace in thought and deed
to proclaim with a whole heart
the sacred Unity of all being.

ADONAI ECHAD: WE PROCLAIM YOU ONE

You are the One who unites all things,
who links life to life in a sacred chain.

The forests anchored in the soil
breathe air into our lungs.

Our faces are reflected in the creatures of earth;
we carry the sea within us.

Our fate is connected to rivers and deserts,
our family a many-branched Tree of Life.

All beings intertwine in You;
all are encompassed in "*Adonai echad*."

Thus no man is an island;
no soul exists apart.

To say *echad* is to know this truth:
to see the world whole, humankind undivided.

Precious and holy are these words we speak:
Adonai echad—We proclaim You One.

בָּרוּךְ אַתָּה, יְיָ, הַבּוֹחֵר בְּעַמּוֹ יִשְׂרָאֵל בְּאַהֲבָה.

Baruch atah, Adonai, habocheir b'amo Yisrael b'ahavah.

Our praise to You, Adonai:
You have singled out Your people Israel with love.

NO MAN IS AN ISLAND. From John Donne, *Devotions upon Emergent Occasions*, Meditation XVII (1624).

Long ago, in the courtyard of the Temple, on the holy day of Yom Kippur,
the High Priest proclaimed aloud the sacred name of God.
And all the people fell to the ground, prostrated themselves and called:
"Blessed is God's glorious majesty forever and ever!"
Millennia have passed, but still we speak these words aloud,
witnesses forever to the truth of God's dominion.

בָּרְכוּ
Bar'chu

יוֹצֵר אוֹר
Yotzeir Or

אַהֲבָה רַבָּה
Ahavah Rabbah

קְרִיאַת שְׁמַע
K'riat Sh'ma

אֱמֶת וְיַצִּיב
Emet v'Yatziv

מִי־כָמֹכָה
Mi Chamocha

שְׁמַע יִשְׂרָאֵל יהוה

בָּרוּךְ שֵׁם כְּבוֹד

Sh'ma, Yisrael: Adonai Eloheinu, Adonai Echad!
Baruch shem k'vod malchuto l'olam va·ed.

Listen, Israel: Adonai is our God, Adonai is One!
Blessed is God's glorious majesty forever and ever.

LONG AGO. The Talmud (*Yoma* 66a) records that just once a year, on Yom Kippur, the High Priest would say aloud the four-letter Divine Name (*yod-hei-vav-hei*), which was otherwise never pronounced. The people's response (*Baruch shem k'vod malchuto l'olam va·ed*) is to this day recited aloud on Yom Kippur, though during the rest of the year, those words are traditionally spoken in a whisper.

Call to Prayer

Creation

Revelation

Sh'ma and Its Sections

Redemption

אלהינו יהוה אחד
מַלְכוּתוֹ לְעוֹלָם וָעֶד.

BLESSED IS GOD'S GLORIOUS MAJESTY בָּרוּךְ שֵׁם כְּבוֹד מַלְכוּתוֹ. When Israel Baal Shem Tov, the 18th-century founder of Chasidism, was five years old, his father, Eliezer, grew very ill. On the last day of his life, he called to the boy and said, "My child, always remember that God is with you. Never let this thought out of your mind. Go deeper and deeper into it every hour and every minute, and in every place." The Baal Shem Tov said: "My father's words are still fixed in my heart and engraved in my mind. After his death, I always went off alone in seclusion, in forests and fields, to strengthen this holy thought in my mind: the glory of the Holy One, blessed be God, fills the earth; and God is actually with me."

How Do We Respond to God's Oneness?

By Loving God and Devoting Ourselves to Torah

<table>
<tr>
<td>

V'ahavta et Adonai Elohecha —

b'chol-l'vav'cha,

uvchol-nafsh'cha,

uvchol-m'odecha.

V'hayu had'varim ha·eileh

asher anochi m'tzav'cha hayom

al l'vavecha.

V'shinantam l'vanecha v'dibarta bam

b'shivt'cha b'veitecha,

uvlecht'cha vaderech,

uvshochb'cha, uvkumecha.

Ukshartam l'ot al yadecha;

v'hayu l'totafot bein einecha;

uchtavtam al m'zuzot beitecha

  uvisharecha.

</td>
<td>

וְאָהַבְתָּ אֵת יְיָ אֱלֹהֶיךָ

בְּכָל־לְבָבְךָ

וּבְכָל־נַפְשְׁךָ

וּבְכָל־מְאֹדֶךָ:

וְהָיוּ הַדְּבָרִים הָאֵלֶּה

אֲשֶׁר אָנֹכִי מְצַוְּךָ הַיּוֹם

עַל־לְבָבֶךָ:

וְשִׁנַּנְתָּם לְבָנֶיךָ וְדִבַּרְתָּ בָּם

בְּשִׁבְתְּךָ בְּבֵיתֶךָ

וּבְלֶכְתְּךָ בַדֶּרֶךְ

וּבְשָׁכְבְּךָ וּבְקוּמֶךָ:

וּקְשַׁרְתָּם לְאוֹת עַל־יָדֶךָ

וְהָיוּ לְטֹטָפֹת בֵּין עֵינֶיךָ:

וּכְתַבְתָּם עַל־מְזֻזוֹת בֵּיתֶךָ

וּבִשְׁעָרֶיךָ:

</td>
</tr>
</table>

בָּרְכוּ
Bar'chu

יוֹצֵר אוֹר
Yotzeir Or

אַהֲבָה רַבָּה
Ahavah Rabbah

קְרִיאַת שְׁמַע
K'riat Sh'ma

אֱמֶת וְיַצִּיב
Emet v'Yatziv

מִי־כָמֹכָה
Mi Chamocha

You shall love Adonai your God with all your mind,
  with all your soul, and with all your strength.
Set these words, which I command you this day, upon your heart.
Teach them faithfully to your children.
Speak of them in your home and on your way,
  when you lie down and when you rise up.
Bind them as a sign upon your hand;
  let them be a symbol before your eyes;
inscribe them on the doorposts of your house, and on your gates.

V'AHAVTA וְאָהַבְתָּ, Deuteronomy 6:5–9.

YOU SHALL LOVE ADONAI. How in the world can one love God who is not a person, who has no arms, no legs, no lips? One of the familiar commentaries says: "Do not read it *v'ahavta* (you shall love). But read it *v'ihavta* (make God beloved). Act in such a way that, when people observe how you behave, they will believe in Godliness, in goodness, in hope, in compassion, in love." (Rabbi Harold M. Schulweis, 1925–2014)

V'AHAVTA — WHEN YOU LOVE

When you love *Adonai Elohecha* body and soul
these things I ask of you will be possible:

To answer your children's questions about Me
and believe your answers yourselves
To connect religion to your everyday
comings and goings . . .
for example,
when you hug them in bed at night
with tender words—*Sh'ma Yisrael*
or when you think to say *Modeh Ani*
in the rush of getting them up and out
in the morning
To be alert enough
to open doors for your children
in every waking moment
and when they dream.

And finally, to remember just why
all these things matter:

They matter because I, *Adonai Elohecha*,
brought you and your children out of Egypt
to be God for you.
I am your God.
And when you do these things
I will be your children's God.

I WILL BE YOUR CHILDREN'S GOD. How do we teach children about God? Rabbi Harold Schulweis (1925–2014) coined the term "predicate theology." When we encounter statements such as "God is love," "God is truth," "God is forgiving," we should focus not on the subject, God, but on the predicate—love, truth, forgiveness. Those are not statements about God. They are statements about the kind of qualities and experiences we consider godly. They don't so much teach us about God as they teach us to recognize when God comes into our lives. (Rabbi Harold Kushner, b. 1935; adapted)

Some congregations continue on the facing page.

בָּרְכוּ
Bar'chu

יוֹצֵר אוֹר
Yotzeir Or

אַהֲבָה רַבָּה
Ahavah Rabbah

קְרִיאַת שְׁמַע
K'riat Sh'ma

אֱמֶת וְיַצִּיב
Emet v'Yatziv

מִי־כָמֹכָה
Mi Chamocha

How Do We Respond to God's Oneness?

By Choosing to Do Mitzvot

If, indeed, you obey My commandments, which I instruct you this day — loving Adonai your God and serving God with all your heart and soul — I will grant rain for your land in season, the early rain and the late. And you will gather in your new grain and wine and oil; and I will provide grassland for your cattle. Thus you will eat and be satisfied. Be careful not to be lured away to serve other gods, bowing down to them. For then the anger of Adonai will flare up against you, and God will hold back the skies so that there will be no rain and the ground will not yield its crops; and you will soon perish from the good land that Adonai is giving you.

Therefore place these, My words, upon your heart and upon your very being. Bind them as a sign upon your hand; let them be a symbol before your eyes. Teach them to your children; speak of them in your home and on your way, when you lie down and when you rise up. Inscribe them on the doorposts of your house and on your gates, so that your days and the days of your children may increase upon the land that Adonai swore to give to your ancestors, for as long as the heavens are over the earth.

By Wearing Tzitzit as a Reminder of Sacred Obligation

Adonai said to Moses: Speak to the people of Israel, and tell them to make for themselves *tzitzit* — fringes — on the corners of their clothing, throughout their generations; and let them place upon the corner-fringe a thread of violet-blue. The fringes will be yours to see and remember all the *mitzvot* — the sacred obligations — of Adonai. Do them; and do not be misled by the lustful urges of your heart and your eyes.

IF, INDEED, YOU OBEY, Deuteronomy 11:13–21, the second section of the *Sh'ma*. One need not read these words as a literal statement about divine reward and punishment. In a world whose survival depends partly on our capacity to value creation and care for it wisely, it is possible to interpret the passage more naturalistically, as a dire prediction of the consequences of human arrogance. If we develop an ecological consciousness, if we treat the earth with respect, if we see ourselves embedded in a great web of life of which God is the ultimate source and sustainer, then the earth will bear fruit for us and the rain will come in its season. But if we forget the sacredness of all things, exploit the earth for short-term profit, and make idols of human comfort and convenience, "the ground will not yield its produce," and both we and our world may perish.

THE ETERNAL ONE SAID, Numbers 15:37–39, the start of the third section of the *Sh'ma*.

Call to Prayer
Creation
Revelation
Sh'ma and Its Sections
Redemption

לְמַעַן תִּזְכְּרוּ וַעֲשִׂיתֶם
אֶת־כׇּל־מִצְוֺתָי
וִהְיִיתֶם קְדֹשִׁים לֵאלֹהֵיכֶם:
אֲנִי יְיָ אֱלֹהֵיכֶם
אֲשֶׁר הוֹצֵאתִי אֶתְכֶם מֵאֶרֶץ מִצְרַיִם
לִהְיוֹת לָכֶם לֵאלֹהִים
אֲנִי יְיָ אֱלֹהֵיכֶם:

L'maan tizk'ru vaasitem
et-kol-mitzvotai,
viyitem k'doshim l'Eloheichem.
Ani Adonai Eloheichem —
asher hotzeiti et·chem mei·eretz Mitzrayim
liyot lachem l'Elohim:
ani Adonai Eloheichem.

Be mindful of all My mitzvot,
and do them;
thus you will become holy to your God.
I, Adonai, am your God,
who brought you out of Egypt to be your God —
I, Adonai your God.

יְיָ אֱלֹהֵיכֶם אֱמֶת.
Adonai Eloheichem emet.
Adonai your God is true.

L'MAAN TIZK'RU לְמַעַן תִּזְכְּרוּ, Numbers 15:40–41, the conclusion of the third section of the *Sh'ma*.

BE MINDFUL . . . AND DO THEM לְמַעַן תִּזְכְּרוּ וַעֲשִׂיתֶם. The proclamation of God's unity is followed by a call to love the Eternal, internalize words of Torah, and teach them to the next generation. The final section of the *Sh'ma* focuses on the ultimate purpose of our study and teaching: to inspire actions that will bring divine goodness into the world. The *tzitzit* (fringes) act as visual reminders of our sacred obligations; we wrap ourselves in a fringed garment as a sign that the mitzvot are all-encompassing — enriching and enhancing all of life.

TO BE YOUR GOD לִהְיוֹת לָכֶם לֵאלֹהִים. Numbers 15:40–41 asserts that God liberated the Israelite slaves from Egypt in order to create a relationship with them. Throughout the Torah, God is portrayed as seeking out connection with human beings — bringing them into being, summoning Abraham and his descendants, inviting them into a covenant that is then extended to an entire people at Sinai. Far from the impassive Unmoved Mover of Aristotle (4th century BCE) and Maimonides (1135–1204), the Torah's God is impassioned, fiercely loving, and deeply invested in the human enterprise and the fate of the earth.

בָּרְכוּ
Bar'chu
יוֹצֵר אוֹר
Yotzeir Or
אַהֲבָה רַבָּה
Ahavah Rabbah
קְרִיאַת שְׁמַע
K'riat Sh'ma
אֱמֶת וְיַצִּיב
Emet v'Yatziv
מִי־כָמֹכָה
Mi Chamocha

אֱמֶת וְיַצִּיב וְאָהוּב וְחָבִיב
וְנוֹרָא וְאַדִּיר וְטוֹב וְיָפֶה
הַדָּבָר הַזֶּה עָלֵינוּ לְעוֹלָם וָעֶד.
אֱמֶת אֱלֹהֵי עוֹלָם מַלְכֵּנוּ,
צוּר יַעֲקֹב, מָגֵן יִשְׁעֵנוּ.
לְדֹר וָדֹר הוּא קַיָּם,
וּשְׁמוֹ קַיָּם,
וְכִסְאוֹ נָכוֹן,
וּמַלְכוּתוֹ וֶאֱמוּנָתוֹ לָעַד קַיָּמֶת.
וּדְבָרָיו חָיִים וְקַיָּמִים,
נֶאֱמָנִים וְנֶחֱמָדִים לָעַד
וּלְעוֹלְמֵי עוֹלָמִים.

Emet v'yatziv v'ahuv v'chaviv
v'nora v'adir v'tov v'yafeh
hadavar hazeh aleinu l'olam va·ed.
Emet: Elohei olam malkeinu,
tzur Yaakov, magein yisheinu.
L'dor vador hu kayam,
ushmo kayam;
v'chiso nachon,
umalchuto ve·emunato laad kayamet.
Udvarav chayim v'kayamim;
ne·emanim v'nechemadim laad
ul·olmei olamim.

True and steadfast is this teaching:
beloved and treasured, a source of wonder, a fount of goodness,
a thing of beauty — and ours for all time.
And true it is: the eternal God is our sovereign,
the Rock of Jacob, our protecting shield.
Through all generations, God's name lives on,
God's throne stands firm, God's dominion prevails.
God's grandeur and faithfulness endure through eternity;
God's words are precious; they will live forever.

THIS TEACHING IS TRUE אֱמֶת ... הַדָּבָר הַזֶּה. The three letters that make up the word אמת *emet* (true) are far apart in the Hebrew alphabet; they are respectively the first, middle, and last letter. On the other hand, the letters of the word for falsehood, שקר *sheker*, are clustered together toward the end of the alphabet. Our Sages derived from this the lesson that truth is hard to find in this world, but lies are common and easy to find (Talmud *Shabbat* 104a). In addition: lies reflect a narrow outlook, but truth is all-encompassing. Another lesson comes from the letters' shape: א, מ, and ת all stand firm on two "legs" (like a capital "A"), while each letter in *sheker* stands on a single "leg" (like a capital "P"). Thus we learn that lies are precarious, destined to collapse in the end, but truth endures because it rests on a solid foundation. As the Talmud says, "God's signature is truth" (*Shabbat* 55a).

אֱמֶת וְיַצִּיב *Emet v'yatziv*

True and enduring
All else is fluid, impermanent, fleeting.

Unsteady, we falter; in chaos we cry.
In quest for some certainty, an anchor for trust.

צוּר חַיֵּינוּ, מָגֵן יִשְׁעֵנוּ *Tzur chayeinu, magein yisheinu*

Rock of our lives, our Shield and Protector,
You are the constant, abiding through time.

The Rock, whose works speak of wholeness and justice;
You: the still center, fixed point where we stand.

From the ends of the earth, from the depths of despair,
We call, with the Psalmist, to our Fortress and Refuge:
"Lead me to the rock that is higher than I."

Our Rock and Salvation,
Our shelter and strength;
Grounded in You, we shall never be shaken.

The towers of cities will crumble with age
And iron corrodes and decays into rust;

But the words and teachings that echo from Sinai
are true and enduring; forever they stand.

TZUR CHAYEINU, MAGEIN YISHEINU. From the *Modim* (Gratitude) prayer in the Amidah.

THE ROCK, WHOSE WORKS. From Deuteronomy 32:4, often included as part of the funeral service: "The Rock!—whose deeds are perfect, / Yea, all God's ways are just; / A faithful God, never false, / True and upright indeed."

FROM THE ENDS OF THE EARTH. Adapted from Psalm 61:3–4.

OUR ROCK AND SALVATION. Adapted from Psalm 62:7–8.

THE TOWERS OF CITIES. Inspired by the words of Rabbi Abraham Joshua Heschel (1907–1972): "We are impressed by the towering buildings of New York City. Yet not the rock of Manhattan nor the steel of Pittsburgh but the law that came from Sinai is their ultimate foundation. The true foundation upon which our cities stand is a handful of spiritual ideas."

בָּרְכוּ
Bar'chu
יוֹצֵר אוֹר
Yotzeir Or
אַהֲבָה רַבָּה
Ahavah Rabbah
קְרִיאַת שְׁמַע
K'riat Sh'ma
אֱמֶת וְיַצִּיב
Emet v'Yatziv
מִי־כָמֹֽכָה
Mi Chamocha

MiMitzrayim g'altanu, Adonai Eloheinu;	מִמִּצְרַֽיִם גְּאַלְתָּֽנוּ, יְיָ אֱלֹהֵֽינוּ,
umibeit avadim p'ditanu.	וּמִבֵּית עֲבָדִים פְּדִיתָֽנוּ.
Al zot shib'chu ahuvim	עַל זֹאת שִׁבְּחוּ אֲהוּבִים
v'rom'mu El;	וְרוֹמְמוּ אֵל,
v'nat'nu y'didim z'mirot,	וְנָתְנוּ יְדִידִים זְמִירוֹת,
shirot v'tishbachot,	שִׁירוֹת וְתִשְׁבָּחוֹת,
b'rachot v'hodaot	בְּרָכוֹת וְהוֹדָאוֹת
l'melech El chai v'kayam —	לְמֶֽלֶךְ אֵל חַי וְקַיָּם.
ram v'nisa, gadol v'nora,	רָם וְנִשָּׂא, גָּדוֹל וְנוֹרָא,
mashpil gei·im, umagbiah sh'falim,	מַשְׁפִּיל גֵּאִים, וּמַגְבִּֽיהַּ שְׁפָלִים,
motzi asirim, ufodeh anavim,	מוֹצִיא אֲסִירִים, וּפוֹדֶה עֲנָוִים,
v'ozeir dalim.	וְעוֹזֵר דַּלִּים,
V'oneh l'amo b'eit shav'am eilav.	וְעוֹנֶה לְעַמּוֹ בְּעֵת שַׁוְּעָם אֵלָיו.
T'hilot l'El elyon —	תְּהִלּוֹת לְאֵל עֶלְיוֹן,
baruch hu umvorach.	בָּרוּךְ הוּא וּמְבֹרָךְ.
Mosheh uMiryam uvnei Yisrael	מֹשֶׁה וּמִרְיָם וּבְנֵי יִשְׂרָאֵל
l'cha anu shirah b'simchah rabah,	לְךָ עָנוּ שִׁירָה בְּשִׂמְחָה רַבָּה,
v'am'ru chulam. . . .	וְאָמְרוּ כֻלָּם:

From Egypt You redeemed us, Adonai our God;
and from the slave-house You set us free.
For this the people who felt Your love exalted You;
and the ones You found precious sang hymns of praise,
blessing, and thanks
to the living God who reigns forever —
high and exalted, inspiring wonder,
who humbles the proud and raises the lowly,
who frees the captive, redeems the oppressed,
and sustains the poor.
God responds to the cry of our people — their prayer in time of need.
Sing praise to God Most High, most blessed source of blessing,
as Moses, Miriam, and all Israel sang this joyous song to You. . . .

ME CHA MOICA
196

"**AND THEY SHALL KNOW** that I, Adonai, am their God,
who brought them out of the land of Egypt,
that I might abide among them—
I, Adonai their God."

You took us out of the darkness
so that Your light might dwell among us.

You showed us Your power
to bring down the powerful,
uplift the enslaved,
transform the social order.

You showed us Your strength
so that we might remember our own.

We carry the Exodus vision wherever we go:
Lest we forget our sense of liberation—
Lest we lose the joy of breathing free—
Lest we grow indifferent and blind to others' pain.

So long as we work to make You present
we walk the path of freedom.
But if we forget to bring You into this world
then we return to the darkness.

AND THEY SHALL KNOW, Exodus 29:46. The 11th-century commentator Rashi reads this verse in conditional form: "On the condition that I abide among [the people], I have brought them out of Egypt."

YOU TOOK US . . . RETURN TO THE DARKNESS. Inspired by these words of Rabbi Jill Jacobs (b. 1975): "As long as the people allow the divine presence to dwell among them, they will remain free from Mitzrayim (Egypt). But the moment the people stop actively trying to make the divine presence manifest, they will metaphorically return to the constricted space of Mitzrayim. By giving *tzedakah*, by working for policies that will create opportunity for everyone, and by helping to create a more just society, we too can make the divine presence manifest among us, even—or especially—in difficult times, and will lift ourselves collectively out of the narrowness of Mitzrayim."

מִי־כָמְכָה בָּאֵלִם, יְיָ,
מִי כָּמְכָה נֶאְדָּר בַּקֹּדֶשׁ,
נוֹרָא תְהִלֹּת, עֹשֵׂה פֶֽלֶא.
שִׁירָה חֲדָשָׁה שִׁבְּחוּ גְאוּלִים
לְשִׁמְךָ עַל שְׂפַת הַיָּם,
יַֽחַד כֻּלָּם הוֹדוּ וְהִמְלִֽיכוּ, וְאָמְרוּ:
יְיָ יִמְלֹךְ לְעֹלָם וָעֶד.

"Mi-chamocha ba·eilim, Adonai?
Mi kamocha — nedar bakodesh,
nora t'hilot, oseih-fele?"
Shirah chadashah shib'chu g'ulim
l'shimcha al s'fat hayam.
Yachad kulam hodu v'himlichu, v'am'ru:
"Adonai yimloch l'olam va·ed."

צוּר יִשְׂרָאֵל, קֽוּמָה בְּעֶזְרַת יִשְׂרָאֵל,
וּפְדֵה כִנְאֻמֶךָ יְהוּדָה וְיִשְׂרָאֵל.
גֹּאֲלֵֽנוּ, יְיָ צְבָאוֹת שְׁמוֹ,
קְדוֹשׁ יִשְׂרָאֵל.

Tzur Yisrael, kumah b'ezrat Yisrael.
Ufdeih chinumecha Y'hudah v'Yisrael.
Go·aleinu, Adonai Tz'vaot sh'mo,
k'dosh Yisrael.

"Of all that is worshiped, is there another like You?
Maker of wonders, who is like You —
in holiness sublime, evoking awe and praise?"

At the sea — with a new song on their lips —
the redeemed praised Your name.
Overflowing with gratitude, they proclaimed Your sovereignty
and spoke as one, declaring:
"The Eternal will reign till the end of time."

Rock of Israel, arise and come to the help of Your people Israel.
Keep Your word by redeeming Judah and Israel.
The Eternal and Infinite One is our redeemer,
our source of holiness.

בָּרוּךְ אַתָּה, יְיָ, גָּאַל יִשְׂרָאֵל.
Baruch atah, Adonai, gaal Yisrael.
Blessed are You in our lives, Eternal One, who redeemed Israel.

IS THERE ANOTHER LIKE YOU מִי־כָמְכָה, Exodus 15:11.
THE ETERNAL WILL REIGN יְיָ יִמְלֹךְ, Exodus 15:18.

Who is like You
among the silent?
Mute and inscrutable
You witness our pain.

Once upon a time, the sea was split,
and Israel marveled at Your outstretched arm.
How many have cried out since then?
How many have sunk beneath the waves?

Centuries of innocent blood—
lives lost to hunger, war, to cruelty or indifference;
and those who died with Your name on their lips.
And still they perish in distant lands,
and still they languish on our chilly streets.

Your creatures are drowning even now,
so why should we sing?

Ever-silent, hiding out in history,
You have Your reasons—or so they say.
You left us on our own, so let us give You leave:
withdraw into Yourself,
withhold Your saving power.

And we will live on memories of joy;
and stubborn and stiff-necked, we'll cling to hope;
and gather strength to fight the Pharaohs when we must.
And hold fast to freedom, and celebrate in song—
and vow that we will never be
among the silent.

WHO IS LIKE YOU / AMONG THE SILENT? The question that opens this contemporary poem comes from an ancient midrash (*M'chilta, Shirata* 8; Talmud *Gittin* 56b). It is a question that haunted Jews in the Middle Ages and followed us into the modern world. With the addition of a single letter to the verse Exodus 15:11, "Who is like You, Adonai, among the celestials (*eilim*)?" the authors of this midrash turn praise to condemnation: "Who is like You, Adonai, among the silent ones (*il'mim*)? Who is like You—seeing the shame suffered by Your children and keeping silent!" For this midrash, God's stunning "silence" when the Temple was destroyed is a source of pain and bewilderment. The 12th-century poet Isaac bar Shalom, who quoted the midrash in a religious poem (*piyut*), grieved over God's silence during the persecution of French and German Jewry at the time of the Second Crusade (circa 1145–1149). And the question of God's silence persists "after Auschwitz" as Jews continue to wrestle with a history defined by hope and despair.

הַתְּפִלָּה
HaT'filah · Standing before God

כַּוָּנָה
Kavanah

אָבוֹת וְאִמָּהוֹת
Avot v'Imahot

גְּבוּרוֹת
G'vurot

וּנְתַנֶּה תְּקֶף
Untaneh Tokef

קְדֻשַּׁת הַשֵּׁם
K'dushat HaShem

קְדֻשַּׁת הַיּוֹם
K'dushat HaYom

עֲבוֹדָה
Avodah

הוֹדָאָה
Hodaah

שָׁלוֹם
Shalom

תְּפִלַּת הַלֵּב
T'filat HaLev

In the depths of night, by the edge of the river,
Jacob was left alone.

In heartfelt longing, in the temple of God,
Channah uttered her prayer alone.

In the barren wilderness, in doubt and despair,
Elijah found God alone.

On the holiest day, in the Holy of Holies,
the High Priest entered alone.

We are bound to one another in myriad ways,
but each soul needs time to itself.

In solitude we meet the solitary One;
silence makes space for the still small voice.

For the Psalmist says: "Deep calls unto deep."
From the depths of our soul, we seek what is most profound.

Adonai, s'fatai tiftach,

ufi yagid t'hilatecha.

אֲדֹנָי, שְׂפָתַי תִּפְתָּח,
וּפִי יַגִּיד תְּהִלָּתֶךָ.

A DO NOI.

Adonai, open my lips,
that my mouth may declare Your praise.

IN THE DEPTHS OF NIGHT. Genesis 32:25 recounts the story of Jacob's wrestling
with a mysterious figure by night.
CHANNAH UTTERED HER PRAYER, I Samuel 1:10.
IN THE BARREN WILDERNESS. I Kings 19:12 recounts Elijah's encounter with
God in the form of a "still small voice."
ON THE HOLIEST DAY, Leviticus 16:17.
DEEP CALLS UNTO DEEP. Psalm 42:8, where *t'hom* (deep) is the same word
used to describe the primordial depths over which God's spirit hovered in the
Creation story (Genesis 1:2).
ADONAI . . . MY LIPS, אֲדֹנָי שְׂפָתַי, Psalm 51:17.

מִסּוֹד חֲכָמִים וּנְבוֹנִים,
וּמִלֶּמֶד דַּעַת מְבִינִים,
אֶפְתְּחָה פִי בִּתְפִלָּה וּבְתַחֲנוּנִים,
לְחַלּוֹת וּלְחַנֵּן פְּנֵי מֶלֶךְ מָלֵא
רַחֲמִים,
מוֹחֵל וְסוֹלֵחַ לַעֲוֹנִים.

Misod chachamim unvonim,
umilemed daat m'vinim,
eft'chah fi bitfilah uvtachanunim —
l'chalot ulchanen p'nei melech malei rachamim,
mocheil v'solei·ach laavonim.

Guided by the wisdom of our tradition
and the spiritual insights of our Sages,
I open myself through prayer to the Sovereign of Compassion;
I open my lips to seek the Soul of Forgiveness.

FROM "TFILES (PRAYERS)"

I still don't know whom,
I still don't know why I ask.
A prayer lies bound in me,
And implores a god,
And implores a name.

I pray
In the field,
In the noise of the street,
Together with the wind, when it runs before my lips,
A prayer lies bound in me,
And implores a god,
And implores a name.

To the west, when the sun sets,
To the east, when it rises there,
To each spark
That it show me the light
And make my eyes bright,
To each worm that glows in the darkness at night,
Then it shall bring its wonder before my heart
And redeem the darkness that is enclosed in me.

GUIDED BY THE WISDOM מִסּוֹד חֲכָמִים. With these words, we add focused intention to the hope that prayer will have a profound impact on us—that it will stir us spiritually and open us to God's forgiveness.

TFILES (PRAYERS). From the Yiddish, by Kadya Molodowsky (1894–1975).

Baruch atah, Adonai,	בָּרוּךְ אַתָּה, יְיָ,
Eloheinu v'Elohei avoteinu v'imoteinu:	אֱלֹהֵינוּ וֵאלֹהֵי אֲבוֹתֵינוּ וְאִמּוֹתֵינוּ:
Elohei Avraham, Elohei Yitzchak,	אֱלֹהֵי אַבְרָהָם, אֱלֹהֵי יִצְחָק,
v'Elohei Yaakov;	וֵאלֹהֵי יַעֲקֹב,
Elohei Sarah, Elohei Rivkah,	אֱלֹהֵי שָׂרָה, אֱלֹהֵי רִבְקָה,
Elohei Rachel, v'Elohei Leah;	אֱלֹהֵי רָחֵל, וֵאלֹהֵי לֵאָה,
haEl hagadol hagibor v'hanora,	הָאֵל הַגָּדוֹל הַגִּבּוֹר וְהַנּוֹרָא,
El elyon,	אֵל עֶלְיוֹן,
gomeil chasadim tovim, v'koneih hakol —	גּוֹמֵל חֲסָדִים טוֹבִים, וְקוֹנֵה הַכֹּל –
v'zocheir chasdei avot v'imahot,	וְזוֹכֵר חַסְדֵי אָבוֹת וְאִמָּהוֹת,
umeivi g'ulah livnei v'neihem,	וּמֵבִיא גְאֻלָּה לִבְנֵי בְנֵיהֶם,
l'maan sh'mo b'ahavah.	לְמַעַן שְׁמוֹ בְּאַהֲבָה.

You are the Source of blessing, Adonai, our God
and God of our fathers and mothers:
God of Abraham, God of Isaac, and God of Jacob;
God of Sarah, God of Rebecca, God of Rachel, and God of Leah;
exalted God, dynamic in power, inspiring awe,
God sublime, Creator of all —
yet You offer us kindness,
recall the loving deeds of our fathers and mothers,
and bring redemption to their children's children,
acting in love for the sake of Your name.

כַּוָּנָה *Kavanah*
אָבוֹת וְאִמָּהוֹת *Avot v'Imahot*
גְּבוּרוֹת *G'vurot*
וּנְתַנֶּה תֹּקֶף *Untaneh Tokef*
קְדֻשַּׁת הַשֵּׁם *K'dushat HaShem*
קְדֻשַּׁת הַיּוֹם *K'dushat HaYom*
עֲבוֹדָה *Avodah*
הוֹדָאָה *Hodaah*
שָׁלוֹם *Shalom*
תְּפִלַּת הַלֵּב *T'filat HaLev*

GOD OF OUR FATHERS AND MOTHERS אֱלֹהֵינוּ וֵאלֹהֵי אֲבוֹתֵינוּ וְאִמּוֹתֵינוּ. We begin *HaT'filah* by summoning the memory of those who went before us, linking our own "standing before God" to the spiritual lives of our parents, grandparents, and great-grandparents, in a long line stretching back to Abraham and Sarah.

Rabbi Angela Buchdahl (b. 1972) reminds us that the High Holy Day liturgy likens our relationship with God to our relationship with elders who both love us and challenge us to do better, as when we call God *Avinu Malkeinu*, both caring parent and demanding sovereign: "We see God as a parent-figure, who throughout our *machzor* asks us to take responsibility for ourselves as the new year turns, to look hard at our errors and make them right in the time that's left. We may decide to ignore God's message — to treat God as the aging parent, who has outlived his usefulness. But it is precisely in these moments of our self-sufficiency and even arrogance that the Fifth Commandment comes to remind us that we must honor the source of our life — that honoring our parents or God is not contingent on what they can do for us. It is a test of who we are and what we hope to be."

I WENT to my grandfather's to say good-bye:
I was going away to a school out West.
As I came in,
my grandfather turned from the window at which he sat
(sick, skin yellow, eyes bleary—
but his hair still dark,
for my grandfather had hardly any grey hair in his beard or on his head—
he would sit at the window, reading a Hebrew book).
He rose with difficulty—
he had been expecting me, it seemed—
stretched out his hands and blessed me in a loud voice:
in Hebrew, of course,
and I did not know what he was saying.
When he had blessed me,
my grandfather turned aside and burst into tears.
"It is only for a little while, Grandpa," I said
in my broken Yiddish. "I'll be back in June."
(By June my grandfather was dead.)
He did not answer.
Perhaps my grandfather was in tears for other reasons:
perhaps, because, in spite of all the learning I had acquired in high school,
I knew not a word of the sacred text of the Torah
and was going out into the world
with none of the accumulated wisdom of my people to guide me,
with no prayers with which to talk to the God of my people,
a soul—
for it is not easy to be a Jew or, perhaps, a man—
doomed by his ignorance to stumble and blunder.

WITHOUT PROFOUND REVERENCE for father and mother, our ability to observe the other commandments is dangerously impaired. The problem we face, the problem I as a father face, is why my child should revere me. Unless my child will sense in my personal existence acts and attitudes that evoke reverence—the ability to delay satisfactions, to overcome prejudices, to sense the holy, to strive for the noble—why should she revere me?

I WENT TO MY GRANDFATHER'S. By Charles Reznikoff (1894–1976).
WITHOUT PROFOUND REVERENCE. By Rabbi Abraham Joshua Heschel (1907–1972).

Zochreinu l'chayim,

Melech chafeitz bachayim.

V'chotveinu b'sefer hachayim,

l'maancha Elohim chayim.

Melech ozeir umoshia umagein —

זָכְרֵנוּ לְחַיִּים,

מֶלֶךְ חָפֵץ בַּחַיִּים.

וְכָתְבֵנוּ בְּסֵפֶר הַחַיִּים,

לְמַעַנְךָ אֱלֹהִים חַיִּים.

מֶלֶךְ עוֹזֵר וּמוֹשִׁיעַ וּמָגֵן –

כַּוָּנָה
Kavanah

אָבוֹת וְאִמָּהוֹת
Avot v'Imahot

גְּבוּרוֹת
G'vurot

וּנְתַנֶּה תֹּקֶף
Untaneh Tokef

קְדֻשַּׁת הַשֵּׁם
K'dushat HaShem

קְדֻשַּׁת הַיּוֹם
K'dushat HaYom

עֲבוֹדָה
Avodah

הוֹדָאָה
Hodaah

שָׁלוֹם
Shalom

תְּפִלַּת הַלֵּב
T'filat HaLev

Remember us for life, sovereign God who treasures life.
Inscribe us in the Book of Life, for Your sake, God of life.

Sovereign of salvation, Pillar of protection —

בָּרוּךְ אַתָּה, יְיָ, מָגֵן אַבְרָהָם וְעֶזְרַת שָׂרָה.

Baruch atah, Adonai, magein Avraham v'ezrat Sarah.

Blessed are You in our lives, Adonai,
Shield of Abraham, Sustainer of Sarah.

REMEMBER US FOR LIFE . . . GOD OF LIFE. This passage is the first of four
special insertions in the *Amidah* for the Days of Awe. They are found in the *Avot
v'Imahot*, *G'vurot*, *Hodaah*, and *Shalom* blessings. Usually we do not include
bakashot (petitionary prayers) in the *Amidah* on Shabbat or festivals, focusing
instead on gratitude and praise. Yet three of these special High Holy Day insertions
are petitionary prayers: "Remember us for life"; "Inscribe Your covenant partners for
a life of goodness"; and "Let us, and the whole family of Israel, be remembered and
inscribed in the Book of Life."

Commentators have justified their inclusion by pointing out that they are not
individual petitions but communal requests ("remember us"). Furthermore, we ask
to be remembered and inscribed not for our personal benefit but "for Your sake, God
of life."

These words thus convey more than our self-interested desire for added years
of life. We ask to go on living for God's sake — so that we might use our additional
years to do God's work and make God's presence manifest in the world.

Focusing Prayer
God of All Generations
God's Powers
The Power of This Day
God's Holiness
The Day's Holiness
Our Offering
Thanksgiving
Peace
Prayer of the Heart

בּוֹדֵק אֶת עַצְמוֹ. הוֹפֵךְ וְהוֹפֵךְ
כָּל צַד
בְּקֶר וְעֶרֶב
עִתִּים בְּאֶמְצַע הַלַּיְלָה
כְּרוֹאֶה חֶשְׁבּוֹן מֻטְרָד
אֲבָל אֵינֶנּוּ חָזָק בָּזֶה.
לֹא בְּחֶשְׁבּוֹן־
הַנֶּפֶשׁ וְלֹא בְּחֶשְׁבּוֹן
כְּלָל. מִשְׁתַּדֵּל אֵפוֹא
לְהַבְדִּיל בֵּין זְכוּת
לְחוֹבָה
צַד
צַד
אֲבָל כִּכְלוֹת־הַכֹּל,
מַה זֶּה חָשׁוּב!
הַחַיִּים – אִלּוּ יָכוֹל הָיָה
הָיָה זֶה רְצוֹנוֹ לוֹמַר לָךְ:
הַחַיִּים עִם כָּל הַשְּׁאֵרִית
קָשֶׁה לְוַתֵּר עֲלֵיהֶם
קָשֶׁה
גַּם עַכְשָׁו.

LIKE AN ACCOUNTANT

Self-examination. Turning the pages
over and over
morning and evening
sometimes in the middle of the night
like an anxious accountant
but not very strong,
neither at spiritual
accounting nor any other
kind. He tries to distinguish
between credit
and debit
page
by page
but in the last analysis,
what does it matter!
Life—if he could,
what he would like to tell you is this:
life what is left of it
is hard to give up
hard
even now.

THE SHATTERED vessel
awaits mending
once again.
When we exalt
God's creation
will the Maker
find the blueprint
in time
to remember us
unto life?

LIKE AN ACCOUNTANT. By Abba Kovner (1918–1987).
THE SHATTERED VESSEL. By Rabbi Israel Zoberman (b. 1945).

In Hebrew, choose either hakol *or* meitim.

אַתָּה גִּבּוֹר לְעוֹלָם, אֲדֹנָי –
מְחַיֵּה הַכֹּל\מֵתִים אַתָּה,
רַב לְהוֹשִׁיעַ.

מוֹרִיד הַטָּל.

מְכַלְכֵּל חַיִּים בְּחֶסֶד,
מְחַיֵּה הַכֹּל\מֵתִים
בְּרַחֲמִים רַבִּים –
סוֹמֵךְ נוֹפְלִים,
וְרוֹפֵא חוֹלִים וּמַתִּיר אֲסוּרִים,
וּמְקַיֵּם אֱמוּנָתוֹ לִישֵׁנֵי עָפָר.
מִי כָמוֹךָ, בַּעַל גְּבוּרוֹת,
וּמִי דּוֹמֶה לָּךְ,
מֶלֶךְ מֵמִית וּמְחַיֶּה
וּמַצְמִיחַ יְשׁוּעָה.

מִי כָמוֹךָ, אֵל הָרַחֲמִים,
זוֹכֵר יְצוּרָיו לְחַיִּים בְּרַחֲמִים.

וְנֶאֱמָן אַתָּה לְהַחֲיוֹת הַכֹּל\מֵתִים.

Atah gibor l'olam, Adonai —
m'chayeih hakol/meitim atah,
rav l'hoshia.

Morid hatal.

M'chalkeil chayim b'chesed,
m'chayeih hakol/meitim
b'rachamim rabim —
someich noflim,
v'rofei cholim umatir asurim;
umkayeim emunato lisheinei afar.
Mi chamocha, baal g'vurot;
umi domeh-lach? —
melech meimit umchayeh
umatzmiach y'shuah.

Mi chamocha, El harachamim? —
zocheir y'tzurav l'chayim b'rachamim.

V'ne·eman atah l'hachayot hakol/meitim.

Your life-giving power is forever, Adonai — with us in life and in death.
You liberate and save, cause dew to descend;
and with mercy abundant, lovingly nurture all life.
From life to death, You are the force that flows without end —
You support the falling, heal the sick, free the imprisoned and confined;
You are faithful, even to those who rest in the dust.

GO BACK TO SEATS

Power-beyond-Power, from whom salvation springs,
Sovereign over life and death — who is like You?
Merciful God, who compares with You?
With tender compassion You remember all creatures for life.
Faithful and true, worthy of our trust —
You sustain our immortal yearnings; in You we place our undying hopes.

בָּרוּךְ אַתָּה, יְיָ, מְחַיֵּה הַכֹּל\הַמֵּתִים.

Baruch atah, Adonai, m'chayeih hakol/hameitim.

Wellspring of blessing, Power eternal, You are the One who gives and renews all life.

ONCE WE STOP acting like God, we might allow God's presence to be more active in our lives. Belief in God is difficult for many of us, but it is impossible if we consider ourselves the Highest Power in the universe. Being humble enough to consider that there may be something greater than we are is a first step toward faith. And if we believe that there could be a power greater than we are, we might turn to that power for strength, comfort, guidance, and love when we are facing moments of our own helplessness. As the Psalmist says, "God is our refuge and stronghold, a help in trouble, very near. Therefore we are not afraid, though the earth reels, though mountains topple into the sea" (46:2–4). Or, more famously, "Yea, though I walk through the valley of the shadow of death, I will fear no evil, for Thou art with me; Thy rod and Thy staff, they comfort me" (23:4). Not being God allows us to experience what a relationship with the real God might be like.

"YOU . . . FREE THE IMPRISONED AND CONFINED"

The phrase conjures up instances of redeeming captives and prisoners, and it certainly denotes that. The same words, though, are used in the early morning blessings, where, according to the Talmud (*B'rachot* 60b), they denote the ability just to sit up in bed on the way to getting up in the morning. Anyone who has ever been bedridden or seen someone else in that state will recognize the poignancy of the blessing in that context: we who can get up bless God for freeing us from being chained to our beds. The phrase can also be interpreted metaphorically to refer to releasing someone from intellectual or psychological bonds—superstitious beliefs, for example, or prejudice toward others. All of these instances of liberating the bound require both power and goodness—two of God's chief characteristics—and therefore, these too are godly acts.

ONCE WE STOP. By Rabbi Sarah Weissman (b. 1981).
THE PHRASE CONJURES UP. By Rabbi Elliot N. Dorff (b. 1943).

Study Texts for Untaneh Tokef (Part I)

1

On Rosh HaShanah this is written;
on the Fast of Yom Kippur this is sealed . . .
who will live and who will die;
who will reach the ripeness of age,
who will be taken before their time;
who by fire and who by water . . .
who by earthquake and who by plague . . .
who will rest and who will wander;
who will be tranquil and who will be troubled. . . .

I sat in shul for years reading these words before I realized the answer. The answer to each of these questions is "me." Who will live and who will die? I will. Who at their end and who not at their end? Me. Like every human being, when I die it will be at the right time, and it will also be too soon. Fire, water, earthquake, plague? In my lifetime, I've been scorched and drowned, shaken and burdened, wandering and at rest, tranquil and troubled. That has been my life's journey.

Of course, I prefer to deflect this truth. I would much prefer to let the prayers talk about someone else, perhaps the fellow in the next row. It has taken a lifetime to reveal that defense as a lie. The prayer is not about someone else. It's about me. It is a frightfully succinct summary of my existence. So now I read it again, but in the first person, and it makes me shiver.

I will live and I will die, at the right time, and before my time,
I will wander but I might yet find rest.
I will be troubled but I may achieve tranquility.

This is the central truth of the High Holy Days. This is what makes them *Yamim Nora'im*, days of terror. We are vulnerable.

—Rabbi Edward Feinstein (b. 1954)

2

In truth,
You are judge. . . .
As a shepherd considers the flock. . . .

Judge and shepherd play different roles. The shepherd who "has his sheep pass under his staff" is the same shepherd who "makes me lie down in green pastures, who restores my soul" (Psalm 23). The shepherd's job is to protect his sheep from predators and accidents, thirst and starvation, and to find and rescue them if they wander off and become lost.

How can one be both judge and shepherd? Parents who impose expectations upon us may also care for us. A teacher who grades us may also encourage us. An employer who could fire us may stop us from doing something foolish, steer us back on course, and never tell a soul.

—Rabbi Margaret Moers Wenig (b. 1957)

3

Who by fire? Who by water? Who in the sunshine? Who in the night time? Who by high ordeal? Who by common trial? Who in your merry, merry month of May? Who by very slow decay? *And who shall I say is calling?*

Who in her lonely slip? Who by barbiturate? Who in these realms of love? Who by something blunt? Who by avalanche? Who by powder? Who for his greed? Who for his hunger? *And who shall I say is calling?*

Who by brave ascent? Who by accident? Who in solitude? Who in this mirror? Who by his lady's command? Who by his own hand? Who in mortal chains? Who in power? *And who shall I say is calling?*

—Leonard Cohen (b. 1934)

וּבְכֵן וּלְךָ תַעֲלֶה קְדֻשָּׁה,
כִּי אַתָּה אֱלֹהֵינוּ מֶלֶךְ מוֹחֵל
וְסוֹלֵחַ.

Uvchein ulcha taaleh k'dushah,
ki atah Eloheinu melech mocheil
v'solei·ach.

Our Sovereign,
God of pardon and forgiveness,
let these words of sanctity ascend to You.

וּנְתַנֶּה תֹּקֶף קְדֻשַּׁת הַיּוֹם –
כִּי הוּא נוֹרָא וְאָיֹם.
וּבוֹ תִנָּשֵׂא מַלְכוּתֶךָ,
וְיִכּוֹן בְּחֶסֶד כִּסְאֶךָ,
וְתֵשֵׁב עָלָיו בֶּאֱמֶת.

Untaneh-tokef k'dushat hayom —
ki hu nora v'ayom.
Uvo tinasei malchutecha,
v'yikon b'chesed kisecha;
v'teisheiv alav be·emet.

Let us proclaim the power of this day —
a day whose holiness awakens deepest awe
and inspires highest praise for Your dominion,
for Your throne is a throne of love;
Your reign is a reign of truth.

אֱמֶת כִּי אַתָּה הוּא דַיָּן,
וּמוֹכִיחַ וְיוֹדֵעַ וָעֵד,
וְכוֹתֵב וְחוֹתֵם, וְסוֹפֵר וּמוֹנֶה,
וְתִזְכֹּר כָּל הַנִּשְׁכָּחוֹת.
וְתִפְתַּח אֶת סֵפֶר הַזִּכְרוֹנוֹת,
וּמֵאֵלָיו יִקָּרֵא –
וְחוֹתָם יַד כָּל אָדָם בּוֹ.

Emet ki atah hu dayan,
umochiach v'yodei·a va·eid,
v'choteiv v'choteim, v'sofeir umoneh,
v'tizkor kol hanishkachot.
V'tiftach et sefer hazichronot,
umei·eilav yikarei —
v'chotam yad kol adam bo.

In truth,
You are judge and plaintiff, counselor and witness.
You inscribe and seal. You record and recount.
You remember all that we have forgotten.
And when You open the Book of Memories,
it speaks for itself —
for every human hand leaves its mark,
an imprint like no other.

UNTANEH TOKEF

Today we call it by its rightful name:
A Day of Dread—*nora v'ayom*.
Unwelcome visitor, for we want to live
in a sunny world where God is love
and all endings are happy.

But the drumbeat sounds
and the words tumble down
and even the angels tremble with fear.
For all things are judged
and all things will pass
and life ends in a heartbeat,
and death knows our name.

At the start of the year,
in the season of truth,
comes the Day of Remembrance
for all we forget
and all we deny;
and we fall on our knees
in the depths of our hearts
for we know that the bell tolls
for us.

The words are old and the language was theirs,
but the call is real and the message is ours:
Take hold of your life
while you still have the chance;
for your story will end
and it might be this year
in a way you don't know.
Take hold of your life:
make things right while you can;
and don't miss the call of the Day of Dread.

Uvshofar gadol yitaka.

V'kol d'mamah dakah yishama.

Umalachim yeichafeizun,

v'chil uradah yocheizun,

v'yomru: "Hineih yom hadin" —

lifkod al tz'va marom badin;

ki lo yizku v'einecha badin.

V'chol ba·ei olam yaavrun l'fanecha
    kivnei maron.

K'vakarat ro·ei edro,

maavir tzono tachat shivto,

kein taavir v'tispor v'timneh,

v'tifkod nefesh kol chai.

V'tachtoch kitzbah l'chol b'riyah;

v'tichtov et g'zar dinam.

וּבְשׁוֹפָר גָּדוֹל יִתָּקַע.

וְקוֹל דְּמָמָה דַקָּה יִשָּׁמַע.

וּמַלְאָכִים יֵחָפֵזוּן,

וְחִיל וּרְעָדָה יֹאחֵזוּן,

וְיֹאמְרוּ: הִנֵּה יוֹם הַדִּין —

לִפְקֹד עַל צְבָא מָרוֹם בַּדִּין,

כִּי לֹא יִזְכּוּ בְעֵינֶיךָ בַּדִּין.

וְכָל בָּאֵי עוֹלָם יַעַבְרוּן לְפָנֶיךָ
    כִּבְנֵי מָרוֹן.

כְּבַקָּרַת רוֹעֶה עֶדְרוֹ,

מַעֲבִיר צֹאנוֹ תַּחַת שִׁבְטוֹ,

כֵּן תַּעֲבִיר וְתִסְפֹּר וְתִמְנֶה,

וְתִפְקֹד נֶפֶשׁ כָּל חָי.

וְתַחְתֹּךְ קִצְבָּה לְכָל בְּרִיָּה,

וְתִכְתֹּב אֶת גְּזַר דִּינָם.

כַּוָּנָה
Kavanah

אָבוֹת וְאִמָּהוֹת
Avot v'Imahot

גְּבוּרוֹת
G'vurot

וּנְתַנֶּה תֹּקֶף
Untaneh Tokef

קְדֻשַּׁת הַשֵּׁם
K'dushat HaShem

קְדֻשַּׁת הַיּוֹם
K'dushat HaYom

עֲבוֹדָה
Avodah

הוֹדָאָה
Hodaah

שָׁלוֹם
Shalom

תְּפִלַּת הַלֵּב
T'filat HaLev

And so a great shofar will cry — t'kiah.
A still small voice will be heard.
Angels, in a whirl of fear and trembling, will say:
"Behold the day of judgment" —
  for they too are judged;
  in Your eyes even they are not blameless.

All who come into the world pass before You
    like sheep before their shepherd.
As a shepherd considers the flock,
when it passes beneath the staff,
You count and consider every life.
You set bounds; You decide destiny;
You inscribe judgments.

A GREAT SHOFAR WILL CRY. The scene now switches to heaven, as the poet imagines a cosmic drama in which even the angels are summoned to divine judgment. Two sounds — a shofar blast and a "still small voice" (1 Kings 19:12) — evoke two dimensions of the Divine: God's majesty, before whom all beings stand accountable; and the gentle, insistent voice of conscience, God's presence within us.

Study Texts for Untaneh Tokef (Part II)

4

Untaneh Tokef, the prayer that imagines God inscribing in the heavenly book who shall live and who shall die in the year to come, has become for many a riveting and troubling image of the High Holy Days. I remember one year that the *Untaneh Tokef* prayer found me painfully aware that a friend, a beloved member of our community, who had known much tragedy in her life, was now in the final stages of a long and valiant cancer journey. We were quite sure that our friend would not live to see another Rosh HaShanah, and *Untaneh Tokef* took us deep into our grief. And I remember the year that I listened to the *Untaneh Tokef* on Rosh HaShanah, having been told that I might have ovarian cancer. I was lucky—by Yom Kippur I had good news. But the words shook me to my core. . . .

In a sense, *Untaneh Tokef* invites the whole community into the truth with which sick and grieving people live every day. Rosh HaShanah assaults the denial of the healthy, so that on this day, the ill—beset with clear awareness of mortality—are at one with the whole community, all of us knowing the fundamental uncertainty of life. *We are made of dust*, as the *Untaneh Tokef* concludes, *and to dust we return; like clay vessels, we can break, like flowers we fade, and like shadows we pass, and like a dream we will someday pass from sight*. This is the truth, and there can be comfort in standing in the sacred circle of community affirming it, at the same time committing to savor the fragile gift of life we are given.

So, too, on Yom Kippur we enact a 25-hour period of practice for the experience of dying. Deprived of food, drink, and sexual pleasure, dressed in the white of the shroud, constantly reminded that the gates will soon close, we come face-to-face with our own mortality.

This confrontation with mortality can lead to a sense of dread, despair, and overwhelming grief. At the same time, this recognition can motivate us to embrace the beauty of our lives, and to make changes so that we can live truly, righteously, and generously with the time that remains to us. . . . The goal of the High Holidays, perhaps like the journey of life itself, is to emerge on the other end as a more righteous and godly person, more conscious of life's fragility and beauty, and more grateful for the blessings of life.

—Rabbi Amy Eilberg (b. 1954)

בְּרֹאשׁ הַשָּׁנָה יִכָּתֵבוּן,
וּבְיוֹם צוֹם כִּפּוּר יֵחָתֵמוּן:

כַּמָּה יַעַבְרוּן,
וְכַמָּה יִבָּרֵאוּן.
מִי יִחְיֶה, וּמִי יָמוּת.
מִי בְקִצּוֹ, וּמִי לֹא בְקִצּוֹ.
מִי בָאֵשׁ, וּמִי בַמַּיִם.
מִי בַחֶרֶב, וּמִי בַחַיָּה.
מִי בָרָעָב, וּמִי בַצָּמָא.
מִי בָרַעַשׁ, וּמִי בַמַּגֵּפָה.
מִי בַחֲנִיקָה, וּמִי בַסְּקִילָה.
מִי יָנוּחַ, וּמִי יָנוּעַ.
מִי יַשְׁקִיט, וּמִי יְטֹּרַף.
מִי יִשָּׁלֵו, וּמִי יִתְיַסֵּר.
מִי יֵעָנִי, וּמִי יַעֲשִׁיר.
מִי יֻשְׁפַּל, וּמִי יָרוּם —

B'Rosh HaShanah yikateivun;
uvYom Tzom Kippur yeichateimun:

kamah yaavorun,
v'chamah yibarei·un;
mi yichyeh, umi yamut;
mi v'kitzo, umi lo v'kitzo;
mi va·eish, umi vamayim;
mi vacherev, umi vachayah;
mi varaav, umi vatzama;
mi varaash, umi vamageifah;
mi vachanikah, umi vas'kilah;
mi yanuach, umi yanua;
mi yashkit, umi y'toraf;
mi yishaleiv, umi yityaseir;
mi yaani, umi yaashir;
mi yushpal, umi yarum —

On Rosh HaShanah this is written;
on the Fast of Yom Kippur this is sealed:

How many will pass away from this world,
how many will be born into it;
who will live and who will die;
who will reach the ripeness of age,
who will be taken before their time;
who by fire and who by water;
who by war and who by beast;
who by famine and who by drought;
who by earthquake and who by plague;
who by strangling and who by stoning;
who will rest and who will wander;
who will be tranquil and who will be troubled;
who will be calm and who tormented;
who will live in poverty and who in prosperity;
who will be humbled and who exalted —

THE POWER OF THIS DAY

An empty page
An open book
A day of ultimate questions

Will I still be here next year at this time
with the ones I love beside me?

What is in store for my family?
And what will become of my friends?

Who will have reason to celebrate?
Who will contend with grief?

New love, new babies, marriages deepening or breaking apart,
prosperity, struggle, reversals of fortune, illness, and health await us.

Who will be missing when we gather next?
Who will stand apart? Who will be estranged?
And who will have joined us, enriching our community?

On the edge of the unknown we tremble:
What lies ahead for us all?

An empty page
An open book
Nothing is written and nothing is sealed.

Flesh and blood, frail creatures,
our lives are fleeting and subject to chance.

Yet this we possess: the strength to persist,
to prevail, to comfort one another in the dark.

Prayer, right action, a turning toward the good—
These give us hope and help us bear the pain of life.

WHAT IS AT THE CORE of our life? What will live on after we are wind and space? What will be worthy of that endless, infinitely powerful silence? And what are we clinging to that isn't important, that won't endure, that isn't worthy? (Rabbi Alan Lew, 1944–2009)

Utshuvah, utfilah, utzdakah
maavirin et roa hag'zeirah.

וּתְשׁוּבָה, וּתְפִלָּה, וּצְדָקָה
מַעֲבִירִין אֶת רֹעַ הַגְּזֵרָה.

But through return to the right path,
through prayer and righteous giving,
we can transcend the harshness of the decree.

Ki k'shimcha kein t'hilatecha:
kasheh lichos v'no·ach lirtzot.
Ki lo tachpotz b'mot hameit,
ki im b'shuvo midarko v'chayah.
V'ad yom moto t'chakeh lo;
im yashuv, miyad t'kab'lo.
Emet ki atah hu yotzram,
v'yodei·a yitzram;
ki heim basar vadam.

כִּי כְּשִׁמְךָ כֵּן תְּהִלָּתֶךָ:
קָשֶׁה לִכְעֹס וְנוֹחַ לִרְצוֹת.
כִּי לֹא תַחְפֹּץ בְּמוֹת הַמֵּת,
כִּי אִם בְּשׁוּבוֹ מִדַּרְכּוֹ וְחָיָה.
וְעַד יוֹם מוֹתוֹ תְּחַכֶּה לּוֹ,
אִם יָשׁוּב, מִיָּד תְּקַבְּלוֹ.
אֱמֶת כִּי אַתָּה הוּא יוֹצְרָם,
וְיוֹדֵעַ יִצְרָם,
כִּי הֵם בָּשָׂר וָדָם.

You are everything that we praise You for:
slow to anger, quick to forgive.
You do not wish the death of sinners,
but urge them to return from their ways and live.
Until the day of death, You wait for them;
You accept them at once if they return.
Since You created us, You know our impulses;
we are but flesh and blood.

כַּוָּנָה *Kavanah*
אָבוֹת וְאִמָּהוֹת *Avot v'Imahot*
גְּבוּרוֹת *G'vurot*
וּנְתַנֶּה תֹּקֶף *Untaneh Tokef*
קְדֻשַּׁת הַשֵּׁם *K'dushat HaShem*
קְדֻשַּׁת הַיּוֹם *K'dushat HaYom*
עֲבוֹדָה *Avodah*
הוֹדָאָה *Hodaah*
שָׁלוֹם *Shalom*
תְּפִלַּת הַלֵּב *T'filat HaLev*

WE WHO LIVED in concentration camps can remember the ones who walked through the huts comforting others, giving away their last piece of bread. They may have been few in number, but they offer sufficient proof that everything can be taken from a person but one thing: the last of the human freedoms — to choose one's attitude in any given set of circumstances, to choose one's own way. (Viktor E. Frankl, 1905–1997)

AND LET US GIVE OURSELVES OVER to the power of this day. . . .
And let us give ourselves over to holiness and awe
And let us calm the voice of dread and fear
And let us submit to the Power beyond and within
And let us take the path of sincere return
And let us give ourselves over to prayer of the heart
And let us feel the pull of righteousness
And let us give ourselves over to the still small voice
And let us awaken to the wholeness of body and soul
And let us awaken to the wholeness of thought and deed
And let us see in the darkness a doorway of hope
And let us give ourselves over to the power of this day.

WHEN WE WALK through a valley of darkness,
but find courage to live in the shadow of pain . . .

we transcend the harshness of the decree.

When we speak about fear with honesty,
and share what is hardest to say . . .

we transcend the harshness of the decree.

When day becomes night,
but we let ourselves hope . . .

we transcend the harshness of the decree.

When we feel far from caring and friendship,
but let go of pride to ask for help . . .

we transcend the harshness of the decree.

When, in grief, we are crushed by the absence of love,
but open ourselves to Your presence . . .

we transcend the harshness of the decree.

AND LET US GIVE. The phrase that opens and closes this prayer—"And let us give ourselves over to the power of this day"—is from a translation by Rabbi Elyse D. Frishman (b. 1954) of the Hebrew words *Untaneh-tokef k'dushat hayom*.

WALK THROUGH A VALLEY OF DARKNESS. See Psalm 23:4.

FAR FROM CARING AND FRIENDSHIP. See Psalm 88:19—"You have put friend and neighbor far from me, and my companions into darkness."

Adam — y'sodo mei·afar, v'sofo le·afar.

אָדָם יְסוֹדוֹ מֵעָפָר, וְסוֹפוֹ לֶעָפָר.

B'nafsho yavi lachmo —

בְּנַפְשׁוֹ יָבִיא לַחְמוֹ —

mashul kacheres hanishbar,

מָשׁוּל כַּחֶֽרֶס הַנִּשְׁבָּר,

k'chatzir yaveish, uchtzitz noveil,

כְּחָצִיר יָבֵשׁ, וּכְצִיץ נוֹבֵל,

k'tzeil oveir, uch·anan kaleh,

כְּצֵל עוֹבֵר, וּכְעָנָן כָּלָה,

uchruach noshavet, uchavak porei·ach,

וּכְרֽוּחַ נוֹשָֽׁבֶת, וּכְאָבָק פּוֹרֵֽחַ,

v'chachalom ya·uf.

וְכַחֲלוֹם יָעוּף.

> We who are mortal — our origin is dust, and so is our end.
> We wear out our lives to get our bread —
> like broken vessels, like withered grass,
> like a flower that must fade,
> a shadow moving on, a cloud passing by,
> mere dust on the wind, a dream that flies away.

V'atah hu melech,

וְאַתָּה הוּא מֶֽלֶךְ,

El chai v'kayam.

אֵל חַי וְקַיָּם.

Ein kitzbah lishnotecha,

אֵין קִצְבָּה לִשְׁנוֹתֶֽיךָ,

v'ein keitz l'orech yamecha,

וְאֵין קֵץ לְאֹֽרֶךְ יָמֶֽיךָ,

v'ein l'sha·eir mark'vot k'vodecha —

וְאֵין לְשַׁעֵר מַרְכְּבוֹת כְּבוֹדֶֽךָ —

v'ein l'fareish eilom sh'mecha.

וְאֵין לְפָרֵשׁ עֵילוֹם שְׁמֶֽךָ.

Shimcha na·eh l'cha,

שִׁמְךָ נָאֶה לְךָ,

v'atah na·eh lishmecha.

וְאַתָּה נָאֶה לִשְׁמֶֽךָ,

Ushmeinu karata vishmecha.

וּשְׁמֵֽנוּ קָרֵֽאתָ בִּשְׁמֶֽךָ.

> But for You, ever-living Sovereign, time has no limits.
> Your presence, unbounded by days and years, is everywhere —
> a glorious mystery none can decipher.
> Your name is worthy of You, and You are worthy of Your name.
> And our name You have linked with Yours.

כַּוָּנָה
Kavanah

אָבוֹת וְאִמָּהוֹת
Avot v'Imahot

גְּבוּרוֹת
G'vurot

וּנְתַנֶּה תֹּֽקֶף
Untaneh Tokef

קְדֻשַּׁת הַשֵּׁם
K'dushat HaShem

קְדֻשַּׁת הַיּוֹם
K'dushat HaYom

עֲבוֹדָה
Avodah

הוֹדָאָה
Hodaah

שָׁלוֹם
Shalom

תְּפִלַּת הַלֵּב
T'filat HaLev

AND OUR NAME YOU HAVE LINKED WITH YOURS וּשְׁמֵֽנוּ קָרֵֽאתָ בִּשְׁמֶֽךָ. Our mortality gains significance because it exists under the aspect of God's eternity. Our acts of compassion matter because they transpire in the context of God's goodness. God is, in the words of Rabbi Samuel Karff, a "Conserver of value." The faith of *Untaneh Tokef* is that the acts of mortal beings have timeless significance even in a world that sometimes breaks our hearts. (Rabbi David Stern, b. 1961)

Focusing Prayer

God of All Generations

God's Powers

The Power of This Day

God's Holiness

The Day's Holiness

Our Offering

Thanksgiving

Peace

Prayer of the Heart

THE HOLY WAY:
A Kavanah before K'dushat HaShem

The spirit is not holy;
nor ideals, intention or will.

To love God in the heart, to carry a spiritual thought—
this is not the holy way.

Holiness resides in deeds alone;
only these are our task in this world.

But to act without thought is empty,
a mechanical rite without soul.

Consciousness and action,
matter and spirit—all unite in a mitzvah mindfully performed.

We change the world not through our dreams,
but through the way we consume, do our work,
make Shabbat, give to one another.

Were we angels, pure disembodied souls,
we would not need the discipline of deeds.
Were we animals, pure instinct and drive,
we could not rise to touch the sacred.

To join body and mind,
to live our ideals,
to serve in the fullness of our humanity:
this is the challenge of holy living.

THE HOLY WAY. Based on the writings of Rabbi Eliezer Berkovits (1908–1992).
KAVANAH. A focusing meditation.

N'kadeish et shimcha baolam,	נְקַדֵּשׁ אֶת שִׁמְךָ בָּעוֹלָם,	כַּוָּנָה Kavanah
k'shem shemakdishim oto	כְּשֵׁם שֶׁמַּקְדִּישִׁים אוֹתוֹ	
bishmei marom;	בִּשְׁמֵי מָרוֹם,	אָבוֹת וְאִמָּהוֹת Avot v'Imahot
kakatuv al yad n'vi·echa:	כַּכָּתוּב עַל יַד נְבִיאֶךָ:	
V'kara zeh el-zeh v'amar:	וְקָרָא זֶה אֶל־זֶה וְאָמַר:	גְּבוּרוֹת G'vurot
"Kadosh, kadosh, kadosh Adonai tz'vaot,	קָדוֹשׁ, קָדוֹשׁ, קָדוֹשׁ יְיָ צְבָאוֹת,	וּנְתַנֶּה תֹּקֶף Untaneh Tokef
m'lo chol-haaretz k'vodo."	מְלֹא כָל־הָאָרֶץ כְּבוֹדוֹ.	
Adir adireinu, Adonai adoneinu —	אַדִּיר אַדִּירֵנוּ, יְיָ אֲדֹנֵינוּ —	קְדֻשַּׁת הַשֵּׁם K'dushat HaShem
mah-adir shimcha b'chol haaretz.	מָה־אַדִּיר שִׁמְךָ בְּכָל־הָאָרֶץ.	קְדֻשַּׁת הַיּוֹם K'dushat HaYom
"Baruch k'vod-Adonai mim'komo."	בָּרוּךְ כְּבוֹד־יְיָ מִמְּקוֹמוֹ.	עֲבוֹדָה Avodah
Echad hu eloheinu, hu avinu,	אֶחָד הוּא אֱלֹהֵינוּ, הוּא אָבִינוּ,	הוֹדָאָה Hodaah
hu malkeinu, hu moshi·einu —	הוּא מַלְכֵּנוּ, הוּא מוֹשִׁיעֵנוּ —	
v'hu yashmi·einu b'rachamav	וְהוּא יַשְׁמִיעֵנוּ בְּרַחֲמָיו	שָׁלוֹם Shalom
l'einei kol chai:	לְעֵינֵי כָּל חָי:	תְּפִלַּת הַלֵּב T'filat HaLev
"Ani Adonai Eloheichem."	אֲנִי יְיָ אֱלֹהֵיכֶם.	

We sanctify Your name in the world,
as celestial song sanctifies You in realms beyond our world,
in the words of Your prophet:

Holy   Holy   Holy   is the God of heaven's hosts.
The fullness of the whole earth is God's glory.

God of Strength who gives us strength,
God of Might who gives us might —
how magnificent the signs of Your Being throughout the earth.

Blessed is the splendor that shines forth from the Eternal.

Our God is one —
Avinu and *Malkeinu*, sovereign Source of life and liberation —
revealing with mercy to all who live: "I am Adonai your God."

HOLY קָדוֹשׁ, Isaiah 6:3.
GOD OF MIGHT יְיָ אֲדֹנֵינוּ, Psalm 8:2, 10.
BLESSED בָּרוּךְ, Ezekiel 3:12.
I AM אֲנִי, Numbers 15:41.

PURITY

Far away from our humble world,
far above its dampness, its air of decay,
you flourish, heavenly bush—
young fire-tree
planted in the coldness of empty space.

Your buds—galaxies of stars,
modest in their glory—gleam and glisten through eternity:
down channels of gold
a radiance flows, pure and primal,
toward the pitch-black watches of our nights.

Our ears have grown weary from the clamor of the day—
Where is the stone that hasn't sharpened a knife?
Where is the tongue that hasn't sharpened a lie?
Bless us, burning bush—
by your light, by your truth, by your peace!

הַרְחֵק מֵעוֹלָמֵנוּ הַשָּׁפָל,
רָם מִנֶּשֶׁם טַחַב סַגְרִירָיו
תְּלַבְלֵב, הַסְּנֶה הַשְּׁמֵימִי,
נֶטַע דִּי־נוּר
שָׁתוּל בַּבְּלִימָה הַצּוֹנֶנֶת.

מְנַצְנְצִים בַּנֶּצַח צְנוּעֵי זִיו
נִצָּנֶיךָ – כּוֹכָבִים וּמַזָּלוֹת,
זַךְ נוֹזֵל בְּצִנּוֹרוֹת זָהָב
זִיו הִיּוּלִי
אֶל שְׁחוֹר אַשְׁמוּרוֹת לֵילוֹתֵינוּ.

עָיְפָה אָזְנֵנוּ מִשְּׁאוֹנוֹ שֶׁל יוֹם –
אֶבֶן אֵי בָּהּ לֹא מֹרְטָה סַכִּין?
שֶׁקֶר אֵי בוֹ לֹא לֻטְּשָׁה לָשׁוֹן?
בָּרְכֵנוּ, הַסְּנֶה,
בְּאוֹרְךָ, בַּאֲמִתְּךָ, בִּשְׁלוֹמֶךָ!

I KNOW NOT YOUR WAYS

I know not your ways—
A sunset is for me
a Godset.
Where are you going,
God?
Take me along,
if, in the along,
it is light,
God.

I am afraid of the dark

PURITY. By Haim Lensky (1905–ca. 1941).
I KNOW NOT YOUR WAYS. By Malka Heifetz Tussman (1893–1987); transl. Marcia Falk.

"Yimloch Adonai l'olam;

Elohayich, Tziyon, l'dor vador —

hal'lu-Yah!"

L'dor vador nagid godlecha.

Ulneitzach n'tzachim k'dushat'cha nakdish.

V'shivchacha, Eloheinu, mipinu lo yamush

l'olam va·ed,

ki El melech gadol v'kadosh atah.

יִמְלֹךְ יְיָ לְעוֹלָם,
אֱלֹהַיִךְ, צִיּוֹן, לְדֹר וָדֹר,
הַלְלוּ־יָהּ.

לְדוֹר וָדוֹר נַגִּיד גָּדְלֶךָ.
וּלְנֵצַח נְצָחִים קְדֻשָּׁתְךָ נַקְדִּישׁ.
וְשִׁבְחֲךָ, אֱלֹהֵינוּ, מִפִּינוּ לֹא יָמוּשׁ
לְעוֹלָם וָעֶד,
כִּי אֵל מֶלֶךְ גָּדוֹל וְקָדוֹשׁ אָתָּה.

כַּוָּנָה
Kavanah

אָבוֹת וְאִמָּהוֹת
Avot v'Imahot

גְּבוּרוֹת
G'vurot

וּנְתַנֶּה תְּקֶף
Untaneh Tokef

קְדֻשַּׁת הַשֵּׁם
K'dushat HaShem

קְדֻשַּׁת הַיּוֹם
K'dushat HaYom

עֲבוֹדָה
Avodah

הוֹדָאָה
Hodaah

שָׁלוֹם
Shalom

תְּפִלַּת הַלֵּב
T'filat HaLev

"The Eternal shall reign for all time,
  your God for all generations, Zion — Halleluyah!"

We will teach Your greatness
  l'dor vador — from generation to generation.
And to the end of time
  we will affirm Your holiness.
Our God, Your praise shall ever be on our lips,
  for Your power is boundless — sovereign and holy.

THE ETERNAL SHALL REIGN יִמְלֹךְ יְיָ, Psalm 146:10.
FOR ALL TIME לְעוֹלָם. In I Kings 1:31, Bathsheba offers the traditional greeting to a monarch:
  "May my lord King David live forever!"—a sentiment expressed in many Western nations as
  "Long live the king!" Here the wish is extended to the divine sovereign, conveying both the
  joyous certainty of God's eternal reign and a prayer that God's rule be extended throughout all
  space and time. In a personal sense, we might see these words as expressing a desire to place
  ourselves in alignment with divine rule — to live in service to the Holy One and to further
  God's work through our own acts.
WE WILL TEACH YOUR GREATNESS L'DOR VADOR לְדוֹר וָדוֹר נַגִּיד גָּדְלֶךָ. How can we
  imbue the next generation with a sense of God's greatness? Perhaps by showing the young
  people in our care that we discern God's presence in the world — in the wonders of creation; in
  the order and elegance of nature's laws; in just and compassionate acts; in the persistent human
  striving to make a better world.

LETTER TO A HUMANIST

Men and women are the messengers of God;
There are neither angels nor emanations;
Only people like you, in whom God has planted
A striving for justice and freedom and peace.

Inspiration and dedication and every inward joy
Are the gifts of God, who makes us equal with equal love
And appoints us, every one, God's messengers and workers
To bring another springtime to the world.

Listen to your own inner conversation:
You will learn that
When you work for justice,
You are bringing redemption;
When you work for freedom and peace,
You are praying for salvation;
When you accept and love another person,
The Messiah draws near.

AND THIS IS YOUR PRAISE

אֱלֹהִים שׁוֹכֵב עַל גַּבּוֹ מִתַּֽחַת לַתֵּבֵל,
תָּמִיד עָסוּק בְּתִקּוּן, תָּמִיד מַֽשֶּׁהוּ מִתְקַלְקֵל.
רָצִֽיתִי לִרְאוֹתוֹ כֻּלּוֹ, אַךְ אֲנִי רוֹאֶה
רַק אֶת סֻלְיוֹת נְעָלָיו וַאֲנִי בּוֹכֶה.
וְהִיא תְּהִלָּתוֹ.

God lies on his back under the world,
always busy with repairs, always something
going wrong.
I wanted to see all of him, but all I can see
are the soles of his shoes—hence my tears.
And this is his praise.

LETTER TO A HUMANIST. By Ruth Brin (1921–2009).

AND THIS IS YOUR PRAISE. A phrase from a medieval *piyut* (religious poem) for the Days of Awe.

GOD LIES ON HIS BACK. By Yehuda Amichai (1924–2000); excerpt. Playing with conventional imagery of God dwelling above, the poet imagines God as a mechanic stretched out under a car, forever tinkering with the works—an image both humble and celebratory, since this God is continually trying to set things right. The mechanic's operations are mysterious, however, since (as Exodus 33:20 says) human beings may not see God's face and live.

כַּוָּנָה
Kavanah
אָבוֹת וְאִמָּהוֹת
Avot v'Imahot
גְּבוּרוֹת
G'vurot
וּנְתַנֶּה תֹּקֶף
Untaneh Tokef
קְדֻשַּׁת הַשֵּׁם
K'dushat HaShem
קְדֻשַּׁת הַיּוֹם
K'dushat HaYom
עֲבוֹדָה
Avodah
הוֹדָאָה
Hodaah
שָׁלוֹם
Shalom
תְּפִלַּת הַלֵּב
T'filat HaLev

How Do We Sense God's Holiness?
Through Awe

וּבְכֵן תֵּן פַּחְדְּךָ, יְיָ אֱלֹהֵינוּ,
עַל כָּל מַעֲשֶׂיךָ,
וְאֵימָתְךָ עַל כָּל מַה שֶּׁבָּרָאתָ.
וְיִירָאוּךָ כָּל הַמַּעֲשִׂים,
וְיִשְׁתַּחֲווּ לְפָנֶיךָ כָּל הַבְּרוּאִים.
וְיֵעָשׂוּ כֻלָּם אֲגֻדָּה אֶחָת,
לַעֲשׂוֹת רְצוֹנְךָ בְּלֵבָב שָׁלֵם,
כְּמוֹ שֶׁיָּדַעְנוּ, יְיָ אֱלֹהֵינוּ,
שֶׁהַשִּׁלְטָן לְפָנֶיךָ,
עֹז בְּיָדְךָ, וּגְבוּרָה בִּימִינֶךָ,
וְשִׁמְךָ נוֹרָא עַל כָּל מַה שֶּׁבָּרָאתָ.

Uvchein tein pachd'cha, Adonai Eloheinu,
al kol maasecha;
v'eimat'cha al kol mah shebarata.
V'yira·ucha kol hamaasim;
v'yishtachavu l'fanecha kol hab'ruim.
V'yei·asu chulam agudah echat,
laasot r'tzoncha b'leivav shaleim —
k'mo sheyadanu, Adonai Eloheinu,
shehasholtan l'fanecha,
oz b'yad'cha, ugvurah biminecha,
v'shimcha nora al kol mah shebarata.

And so, in Your holiness,
give all creation the gift of awe.
Turn our fear to reverence;
let us be witnesses of wonder —
perceiving all nature as a prayer come alive.
We bow to the sovereignty of Your strength,
the primacy of Your power.
We yearn for connection with all that lives,
doing Your will with wholeness of heart.
Awe-inspiring is Your creation,
all-encompassing Your transcendent name.

AND SO וּבְכֵן. This prayer is the first of a trio added to the High Holy Day liturgy, all of which begin with the phrase "And so" (*Uvchein*). Tradition relates this word to its occurrence in the Bible, when, after preparing herself by prayer and fasting, Esther says "And so (*Uvchein*), I will go to the king" (Esther 4:16). In the same manner, we approach the divine sovereign after spiritual preparation.

IN YOUR HOLINESS. This prayer offers a powerful, universalistic vision of the future, in which all beings will unite in reverence for God and pursue goodness with "wholeness of heart" (*leivav shaleim*). The phrase suggests both unity and single-minded dedication to what is right — without the distraction, moral confusion, ambivalence, and hostile impulses that mar our world.

I STAND AT THE SEASHORE, alone, and start to think. There are the rushing waves . . . mountains of molecules, each stupidly minding its own business . . . trillions apart, yet forming white surf in unison.

Ages on ages . . . before any eyes could see . . . year after year . . . thunderously pounding the shore as now. For whom, for what? . . . on a dead planet, with no life to entertain.

Never at rest . . . tortured by energy . . . wasted prodigiously by the sun . . . poured into space. A mite makes the sea roar.

Deep in the sea, all molecules repeat the patterns of one another till complex new ones are formed. They make others like themselves, and a new dance starts.

Growing in size and complexity . . . living things, masses of atoms, DNA, protein . . . dancing a pattern ever more intricate.

Out of the cradle onto the dry land . . . here it is standing . . . atoms with consciousness . . . matter with curiosity.

Stands at the sea . . . wonders at wondering . . . I . . . a universe of atoms . . .
an atom in the universe.

TO BE AWAKE is to be alive.

Only that day dawns to which we are awake.

One cannot help but be in awe when one contemplates the mysteries of eternity, of life, of the marvelous structure of reality.

It is enough if one tries merely to comprehend a little of this mystery every day. Never lose a holy curiosity.

Wisdom begins with awe of the Eternal.

I STAND AT THE SEASHORE. By Richard P. Feynman (1918–1988).
TO BE AWAKE . . . WE ARE AWAKE. By Henry D. Thoreau (1817–1862).
ONE CANNOT HELP . . . HOLY CURIOSITY. By Albert Einstein (1879–1955).
WISDOM BEGINS, Psalm 111:10.

How Do We Sense God's Holiness?

Through Honor

וּבְכֵן תֵּן כָּבוֹד, יְיָ, לְעַמֶּךָ,
תְּהִלָּה לִירֵאֶיךָ
וְתִקְוָה טוֹבָה לְדוֹרְשֶׁיךָ,
וּפִתְחוֹן פֶּה לַמְיַחֲלִים לָךְ,
שִׂמְחָה לְאַרְצֶךָ
וְשָׂשׂוֹן לְעִירֶךָ,
וּצְמִיחַת קֶרֶן לְדָוִד עַבְדֶּךָ,
וַעֲרִיכַת נֵר לְבֶן יִשַׁי מְשִׁיחֶךָ,
בִּמְהֵרָה בְיָמֵינוּ.

Uvchein tein kavod, Adonai, l'amecha;
t'hilah lirei·echa;
v'tikvah tovah l'dorshecha;
ufit·chon peh lamyachalim lach,
simchah l'artzecha,
v'sason l'irecha;
utzmichat keren l'David avdecha;
vaarichat ner l'ven Yishai m'shichecha,
bimheirah v'yameinu.

And so, in Your holiness,
give Your people the gift of honor.
Bless with praise those who praise You.
Bless with hope those who seek You.
Give Your believers a basis for faith:
true happiness for the Land of Israel,
true joy in Jerusalem.
May the sparks of David, Your servant,
soon grow bright enough for us to see—
a beam of light in the darkness,
a promise of perfection.

כַּוָּנָה *Kavanah*
אָבוֹת וְאִמָּהוֹת *Avot v'Imahot*
גְּבוּרוֹת *G'vurot*
וּנְתַנֶּה תֹּקֶף *Untaneh Tokef*
קְדֻשַּׁת הַשֵּׁם **K'dushat HaShem**
קְדֻשַּׁת הַיּוֹם *K'dushat HaYom*
עֲבוֹדָה *Avodah*
הוֹדָאָה *Hodaah*
שָׁלוֹם *Shalom*
תְּפִלַּת הַלֵּב *T'filat HaLev*

THE GIFT OF HONOR תֵּן כָּבוֹד. The particular *kavod* (honor) that Israel has sought is not some vague token feelings of admiration for having been history's spiritual pioneers, but rather the very real, tangible, and practical demonstrations of *kavod*, by ensuring that we can enjoy "true happiness for the Land of Israel, true joy in Jerusalem." Indeed, *kavod* in the Bible has the regular meaning of "material possessions," "abundance," in addition to its usual sense of "honor" and "glory." (Rabbi Jeffrey M. Cohen, b. 1950; adapted).

SPARKS OF DAVID קֶרֶן לְדָוִד. The prayer expresses the messianic hope that the radiance of David will someday "sprout forth" (*tz'michat keren l'David*)—a metaphor that links the image of light with the image of a growing plant. We find a similar linking of light and organic growth in a verse from Psalms chanted on Yom Kippur eve: "Light is sown for the righteous" (97:11). Both phrases convey the idea that light will dawn gradually—in a slow, evolutionary process in which the darkness of ignorance and cruelty is transformed into the radiant glow of enlightenment and goodness.

A MIDRASH: FAITHFUL TO THE COVENANT

The king was absent for many years;
his beloved wife was left alone.
Her neighbors taunted her:
"Your husband has abandoned you—marry someone else!"
But she would withdraw into her bridal chamber
and read her *ketubah*, with its promises of love and support,
and in this she found comfort.
When at last the king returned, he said to her:
"I am amazed that you waited for me all these years!"
And she replied:
"Were it not for the *ketubah* you gave me so many years ago,
I would have been lost."

So it is with the people Israel.
We go into our synagogues and study houses,
and in words of Torah we find comfort.
When at last redemption comes,
and God says to us:
"How were you able to wait so long?
How did you survive among the nations?"
We will answer:
"If not for the memory of Your love
we would have been lost."

And thus Scripture says:
"But this do I call to mind—therefore I have hope."

A MIDRASH. This rabbinic parable is based on a verse in Lamentations: "But this do I call to mind—therefore I have hope" (3:21). The Sages imagined the relationship between God and the Jewish people as one of enduring love and commitment, despite centuries of persecution in which God's presence was difficult to discern. The Torah, a record of God's promises and care for Israel, has provided grounds for hope that allowed the Jewish people to resist the pressure to assimilate and disappear from history.

How Do We Sense God's Holiness?
Through Righteousness

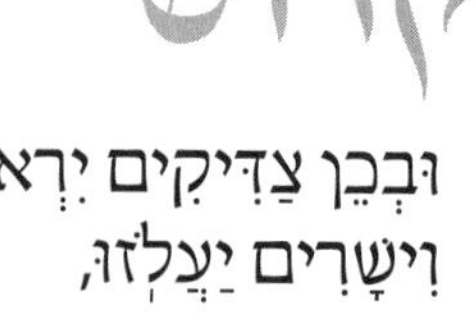

וּבְכֵן צַדִּיקִים יִרְאוּ וְיִשְׂמָחוּ,
וִישָׁרִים יַעֲלֹזוּ,
וַחֲסִידִים בְּרִנָּה יָגִילוּ,
וְעוֹלָתָה תִּקְפָּץ־פִּיהָ,
וְכָל הָרִשְׁעָה כֻּלָּהּ כְּעָשָׁן תִּכְלֶה,
כִּי תַעֲבִיר מֶמְשֶׁלֶת זָדוֹן מִן הָאָרֶץ.

Uvchein tzadikim yiru v'yismachu,
visharim yaalozu,
vachasidim b'rinah yagilu;
v'olatah tikpotz-piha,
v'chol harishah kulah k'ashan tichleh,
ki taavir memshelet zadon min haaretz.

And so, in Your holiness,
give the righteous the gift of a vision bright with joy:
a world where evil has no voice
and the rule of malevolence fades like wisps of smoke.
Good people everywhere will celebrate
the stunning sight of arrogance gone from the earth.

GIVE THE RIGHTEOUS THE GIFT OF A VISION צַדִּיקִים יִרְאוּ. The Yom Kippur prayers emphasize honest self-scrutiny and unflinching acknowledgment of how we have harmed ourselves, those around us, and the larger world. Yet, at the same time, the Day of Atonement is rich in the liturgy of hope. Here, in the conclusion of a three-part sequence that explores divine holiness, the poet imagines a world in which evil has been vanquished and good people celebrate the fulfillment of their dreams. Confrontation with dispiriting realities must be balanced by a beautiful vision that inspires us to persist in the work of *tikkun* (healing and repair).

THE RIGHTEOUS, they say, are invisible to all.
Hidden and unknown, they live in quiet decency,
hurting no one but suffering the pain of the world.
Were it not for these thirty-six, the Sages say,
the universe could not exist.

If you think you might be one of the thirty-six,
chances are you're wrong.
They labor in obscurity,
bombarded every minute of every day
by unbearable sounds from everywhere:
the weeping of sick and hungry children,
abused women; sad and wounded men,
tormented souls who feel they're all alone.

The thirty-six shudder; they cover their ears.
They can't bear the anguish, the assault of tears—
and their hearts break, over and over
and over again, and the bleeding never stops.
But they are the righteous;
they have to endure it
every minute of every day
so that the world can go on,
and the rest of us can live
in peace.

FOR RIGHTEOUS GENTILES

Our Sages teach: The righteous of all nations have a place in the world-to-come.
And Scripture says: My House shall be called a house of prayer for all peoples.
So let them be blessed:
all those who pursue justice and act with compassion;
those who give strength to the Jewish people and help to build our future;
cherished family and friends; allies and supporters.
With gratitude and love, we give them praise.

INVISIBLE TO ALL. Based on the legend of the *Lamed-Vavniks*, thirty-six hidden righteous individuals for whose sake the world endures. (In *gimatriyah*, the numerical value of the letters *lamed* and *vav* is thirty-six.) The legend comes from a Talmudic statement: "There are no less than thirty-six righteous persons in the world who receive the Divine Presence" (*Sanhedrin* 97b; *Sukkah* 45b).

THE RIGHTEOUS OF ALL NATIONS, *Tosefta Sanhedrin* 13:2; Maimonides, Laws of *T'shuvah* 3.5.

MY HOUSE SHALL BE CALLED, Isaiah 56:7.

וְתִמְלֹךְ, אַתָּה, יְיָ, לְבַדֶּךָ
עַל כָּל מַעֲשֶׂיךָ,
בְּהַר צִיּוֹן מִשְׁכַּן כְּבוֹדֶךָ,
וּבִירוּשָׁלַיִם עִיר קָדְשֶׁךָ,
כַּכָּתוּב בְּדִבְרֵי קָדְשֶׁךָ:
יִמְלֹךְ יְיָ לְעוֹלָם,
אֱלֹהַיִךְ, צִיּוֹן, לְדֹר וָדֹר,
הַלְלוּ־יָהּ.

V'timloch — atah, Adonai — l'vadecha
al kol maasecha,
b'Har Tziyon, mishkan k'vodecha,
uviYrushalayim, ir kodshecha —
kakatuv b'divrei kodshecha:
"Yimloch Adonai l'olam;
Elohayich, Tziyon, l'dor vador —
hal'lu-Yah!"

You, and You alone, Adonai, will reign over creation,
upon Mount Zion, home of Your Presence,
and in Jerusalem, a city set apart by You —
as the Psalmist believed:
"The Eternal shall reign for all time,
your God for all generations, Zion — Halleluyah!"

קָדוֹשׁ אַתָּה, וְנוֹרָא שְׁמֶךָ,
וְאֵין אֱלוֹהַּ מִבַּלְעָדֶיךָ, כַּכָּתוּב:
וַיִּגְבַּהּ יְיָ צְבָאוֹת בַּמִּשְׁפָּט,
וְהָאֵל הַקָּדוֹשׁ נִקְדַּשׁ בִּצְדָקָה.

Kadosh atah, v'nora sh'mecha;
v'ein elo·ah mibaladecha, kakatuv:
"Vayigbah Adonai tz'vaot bamishpat;
v'haEl hakadosh nikdash bitzdakah."

You are holy.
Your name is Awe.
There is nothing divine beyond You —
as the prophet Isaiah taught:
"The Source of all might is exalted through justice,
the God of holiness made holy through righteousness."

בָּרוּךְ אַתָּה, יְיָ, הַמֶּלֶךְ הַקָּדוֹשׁ.

*Baruch atah, Adonai, **haMelech** hakadosh.*

Blessed are You, Adonai, holy Sovereign.

THE ETERNAL SHALL REIGN יִמְלֹךְ יְיָ, Psalm 146:10.

THE SOURCE OF ALL MIGHT IS EXALTED וַיִּגְבַּהּ יְיָ צְבָאוֹת, Isaiah 5:16.

Focusing Prayer
God of All Generations
God's Powers
The Power of This Day
God's Holiness
The Day's Holiness
Our Offering
Thanksgiving
Peace
Prayer of the Heart

FROM MOUNT SCOPUS

רָאִיתִי אֶת יְרוּשָׁלַיִם מֵעַל
הַר־הַצּוֹפִים
וְהִיא שְׁלֵמָה וּכְלוּלָה,
קְטַנָּה, אַךְ אֵין לָהּ סוֹפִים,
וּמִתְכַּנֶּסֶת וְאֵינָהּ מִתְכַּנֶּסֶת בִּגְבוּלָהּ.

I gazed on Jerusalem from
Har HaTzofim—
she was perfect, and she was whole;
so small, and yet endless;
contained, but not confined by
her borders.

מִזְרָחָה, עֲטוּפִים כְּחוֹל,
לָבָן וּתְכֵלֶת,
מְכַהֲנִים הָרֵי יְהוּדָה, וּדְמוּמֵי קוֹל
מְהַרְהֲרִים בְּרָכָה וּמַקְטִירִים סַמְמָנֵי
הַשְּׁחֵלֶת.

To the east,
the hills of Judah are hushed priests
wrapped in azure, blue and white—
their incense a sharp and spicy
offering, their blessing softly said.

מַעֲרָבָה מִשְׂתָּרֵעַ מִדְבַּר הַשְּׁמָמָה,
וְהוּא חַדְגּוֹנִי וְגַם מִתְהַפֵּךְ בִּגְוָנָיו.
וְהַדְּמָמָה, זֹאת הַדְּמָמָה,
שֶׁל עוֹלָם גָּלוּם עִם אִיָּיו וַאֲבָנָיו.

To the west,
harsh wilderness unfolds—
a sameness of color, but not without
its subtleties.
And the silence is the silent world of
islands and stones.

וְעַל הַגְּבָעוֹת וְהַגְּמָמוֹת
עוֹד לוֹחֲשׁוֹת גֶּחָלִים,
וּכְאִלּוּ הַמֻּגְמָר מִתְגַּמֵּר שָׁם בֵּין
הַשְּׁמָמוֹת
מֵהִבְהוּב גַּחֲלֵי שֶׁמֶשׁ עַל מַחְתּוֹת
הַצְּלָלִים.

And on the hills and in the hollows
of rock
warm embers whisper still—
and there, amid the harshness,
perfumed spices rise up,
roasted by the sun's coals on fire-pans
of shadow—or so it seems.

וַתְּהִי לִי כָּל יְרוּשָׁלַיִם
כְּגַחֶלֶת אַחַת, הַנִּשְׁמֶרֶת
עַל הַמִּזְבֵּחַ, וּבָאוּ וְהֵיטִיבוּהָ בְּמֶלְקָחַיִם,
וְלָקְחוּ מִמֶּנָּה רִצְפָּה כָּל לְאֹם וְכָל
מִשְׁמֶרֶת.

For me, all of Jerusalem
was like a solitary coal, guarded on
the altar,
so that every people and protector
would arrive—fire tongs in hand—
to add to her radiance, to take from
her a spark.

FROM MOUNT SCOPUS. By Yehuda Karni (1884–1949).
MOUNT SCOPUS. In Hebrew: *Har HaTzofim* (Mount Lookout). Located in northeast Jerusalem.

אַתָּה בְחַרְתָּנוּ מִכָּל הָעַמִּים,	*Atah v'chartanu mikol haamim;*
אָהַבְתָּ אוֹתָנוּ וְרָצִיתָ בָּנוּ.	*ahavta otanu, v'ratzita banu.*
וְרוֹמַמְתָּנוּ מִכָּל הַלְּשׁוֹנוֹת,	*V'romamtanu mikol hal'shonot,*
וְקִדַּשְׁתָּנוּ בְּמִצְוֹתֶיךָ.	*v'kidashtanu b'mitzvotecha.*
וְקֵרַבְתָּנוּ, מַלְכֵּנוּ, לַעֲבוֹדָתֶךָ,	*V'keiravtanu, Malkeinu, laavodatecha;*
וְשִׁמְךָ הַגָּדוֹל וְהַקָּדוֹשׁ עָלֵינוּ קָרָאתָ.	*v'shimcha hagadol v'hakadosh aleinu karata.*

You chose us, with love, to be messengers of mitzvot;
and through us You made known Your aspirations.

Among all the many peoples,
You gave us a pathway to holiness.
Among all the great nations,
You uplifted us and made Yourself our Sovereign —
and so we seek You and serve You
and celebrate our nearness to Your presence.

Your great and sacred name has become our calling.

וַתִּתֶּן־לָנוּ, יְיָ אֱלֹהֵינוּ, בְּאַהֲבָה אֶת	*Vatiten-lanu, Adonai Eloheinu, b'ahavah et*
[יוֹם הַשַּׁבָּת הַזֶּה	*[Yom haShabbat hazeh*
לִקְדֻשָּׁה וְלִמְנוּחָה, וְאֶת]	*likdushah v'limnuchah, v'et]*
יוֹם הַכִּפּוּרִים הַזֶּה,	*Yom HaKippurim hazeh —*
לִמְחִילָה וְלִסְלִיחָה וּלְכַפָּרָה,	*limchilah v'lislichah ulchaparah —*
וְלִמְחָל־בּוֹ אֶת כָּל עֲוֹנוֹתֵינוּ [בְּאַהֲבָה],	*v'limchol-bo et kol avonoteinu [b'ahavah],*
מִקְרָא קֹדֶשׁ,	*mikra-kodesh,*
זֵכֶר לִיצִיאַת מִצְרָיִם.	*zeicher litziat Mitzrayim.*

In Your love, Eternal our God,
You have given us this [Shabbat — for holiness and rest —
and this] Yom Kippur:
a day on which our wrongs are forgiven [with love];
a day of sacred assembly;
a day to be mindful of our people's going-out from Egypt.

YOU HAVE GIVEN US THIS YOM KIPPUR וַתִּתֶּן־לָנוּ . . . אֶת יוֹם הַכִּפּוּרִים הַזֶּה. This blessing in the festival and High Holy Day *T'filah* celebrates the gift of the festival calendar as a mark of God's love for the Jewish people. On each holiday, this prayer mentions the distinctive theme of the occasion. Thus, on Yom Kippur we give thanks for a day on which we can ask and receive forgiveness.

"YOU CHOSE US, WITH LOVE . . ."

More than any event since the destruction of the Second Temple in Jerusalem, the Holocaust put the notion of chosenness to the test. If the Jews are God's chosen people, why have we repeatedly been the target of the worst excesses of human depravity? . . .

Some Jews, both religious and secular, have tried to make the point that the continuing survival of the Jewish people, even after the Holocaust, is proof of Jewish chosenness. For the Zionists, the miracle is the rebirth of the Jewish state after almost two thousand years of exile; for the ultra-Orthodox, it is the recreation of the shtetl way of life in various places in the new world; and for the semi-assimilated, it is the continuing importance of the Jew in Western culture.

I dissent from all these "explanations." The chosenness of the Jews is a mystery. Only God knows the purpose of setting apart an obscure tribe to suffer and to achieve more than could be expected from so small a band on so stormy a journey. All that we Jews can know about ourselves is that after every tragedy we have always made new beginnings. . . .

There is no quiet life for Jews anywhere, at least not for long. The only question is whether one lives among the tempests with purpose and dignity. We Jews know why we suffer. Society resents anyone who challenges its fundamental beliefs, behavior, and prejudices. The ruling class does not like to be told that morality overrules power. The claim to chosenness guarantees that Jews will live unquiet lives. I say it is far better to be the chosen people, the goad and the irritant to much of humanity, than to live timidly and fearfully. Jews exist to be bold. We cannot hide from the task of making the world more just and decent. In a society without law, where brute power prevails, no one is safe, and most often the Jew is the least safe of all. Jews, therefore, must stand up for a society that is bound by human morality—and speak truth to power.

MORE THAN ANY EVENT. By Rabbi Arthur Hertzberg (1921–2006).

אֱלֹהֵינוּ וֵאלֹהֵי אֲבוֹתֵינוּ וְאִמּוֹתֵינוּ,
יַעֲלֶה וְיָבֹא וְיַגִּיעַ, וְיֵרָאֶה וְיֵרָצֶה
וְיִשָּׁמַע וְיִפָּקֵד וְיִזָּכֵר
זִכְרוֹנֵנוּ וּפִקְדוֹנֵנוּ,
וְזִכְרוֹן אֲבוֹתֵינוּ וְאִמּוֹתֵינוּ,
וְזִכְרוֹן יְרוּשָׁלַיִם עִיר קָדְשֶׁךָ,
וְזִכְרוֹן כָּל עַמְּךָ בֵּית יִשְׂרָאֵל, לְפָנֶיךָ
לִפְלֵיטָה לְטוֹבָה,
לְחֵן וּלְחֶסֶד וּלְרַחֲמִים,
לְחַיִּים וּלְשָׁלוֹם,
בְּיוֹם הַכִּפּוּרִים הַזֶּה.

Eloheinu v'Elohei avoteinu v'imoteinu,
yaaleh v'yavo v'yagia, v'yeira·eh v'yeiratzeh
v'yishama, v'yipakeid, v'yizacheir
zichroneinu ufikdoneinu —
v'zichron avoteinu v'imoteinu,
v'zichron Y'rushalayim ir kodshecha,
v'zichron kol am'cha beit Yisrael l'fanecha —
lifleitah l'tovah,
l'chein ulchesed ulrachamim,
l'chayim ulshalom,
b'Yom HaKippurim hazeh.

Our God, and God of the generations before us,
may a memory of us ascend and come before You.
May it be heard and seen by You,
winning Your favor and reaching Your awareness —
together with the memory of our ancestors,
the memory of Your sacred city, Jerusalem,
and the memory of Your people, the family of Israel.
May we be remembered —
for safety, well-being, and favor,
for love and compassion,
for life,
and for peace —
on this Day of Atonement.

DAY OF ATONEMENT יוֹם הַכִּפּוּרִים. In the Torah, the festival is actually called *Yom Kippurim* or *Yom HaKippurim* — literally, "the Day of Atonements." Why the plural? Perhaps because on this day we seek expiation not only for our individual misdeeds but also for wrongs committed by our community. Others argue that the plural term *kippurim* is appropriate, because the true focus of Yom Kippur is interpersonal behavior — sins committed by one person against another.

Rabbi Marc Angel (b. 1945) suggests that the plural term refers to the diversity of individuals present in the congregation. He writes: "The plural form reminds us that there are many roads to atonement. Each person is different and is on a unique spiritual level; each comes with different insights, experiences, memories. The roads to atonement are plural, because no two of us have identical needs."

זָכְרֵנוּ, יְיָ אֱלֹהֵינוּ, בּוֹ לְטוֹבָה. אָמֵן.
וּפָקְדֵנוּ בוֹ לִבְרָכָה. אָמֵן.
וְהוֹשִׁיעֵנוּ בוֹ לְחַיִּים. אָמֵן.

Zochreinu, Adonai Eloheinu, bo l'tovah. Amen.
Ufokdeinu vo livrachah. Amen.
V'hoshi·einu vo l'chayim. Amen.

Eternal our God,
remember us, *Amen*
be mindful of us, *Amen*
and redeem us
for a life of goodness and blessing. *Amen*

וּבִדְבַר יְשׁוּעָה וְרַחֲמִים חוּס וְחָנֵּנוּ,
וְרַחֵם עָלֵינוּ וְהוֹשִׁיעֵנוּ,
כִּי אֵלֶיךָ עֵינֵינוּ,
כִּי אֵל מֶלֶךְ חַנּוּן וְרַחוּם אָתָּה.

Uvidvar y'shuah v'rachamim chus v'choneinu;
v'racheim aleinu v'hoshi·einu —
ki eilecha eineinu;
ki El melech chanun v'rachum atah.

Favor us with words of deliverance and mercy.
Show us the depth of Your care.
God, we await Your redemption,
for You reign with grace and compassion.

OUR GOD, REMEMBER US זָכְרֵנוּ, יְיָ אֱלֹהֵינוּ, בּוֹ לְטוֹבָה. The phrase "*zochreinu, Adonai Eloheinu, bo l'tovah*" recalls the prayer of Nehemiah, governor of Judah, following the return from Babylonian exile (Nehemiah 5:19): "My God, remember to my credit . . ." (*Zochrah-li, Elohai, l'tovah*). Nehemiah utters several prayers of this kind, in each case seeking to be remembered favorably for his meritorious deeds, which he enumerates and describes. Strikingly, when this phrase is incorporated into the liturgy — as a communal prayer for God's favor — no meritorious deeds are specified. We come before the Holy One more modestly, without claiming that our virtue entitles us to God's attentive response. We rely, instead, on divine love and mercy. The prayer might provoke us to ask whether others always need to earn our forgiveness by proving themselves worthy, or whether we have the capacity to bestow forgiveness as a gift of love and compassion.

כַּוָּנָה
Kavanah
אָבוֹת וְאִמָּהוֹת
Avot v'Imahot
גְּבוּרוֹת
G'vurot
וּנְתַנֶּה תֹּקֶף
Untaneh Tokef
קְדֻשַּׁת הַשֵּׁם
K'dushat HaShem
קְדֻשַּׁת הַיּוֹם
K'dushat HaYom
עֲבוֹדָה
Avodah
הוֹדָאָה
Hodaah
שָׁלוֹם
Shalom
תְּפִלַּת הַלֵּב
T'filat HaLev

אֱלֹהֵינוּ וֵאלֹהֵי אֲבוֹתֵינוּ וְאִמּוֹתֵינוּ,
מְחַל
לַעֲוֹנוֹתֵינוּ בְּיוֹם
[הַשַּׁבָּת הַזֶּה וּבְיוֹם]
הַכִּפּוּרִים הַזֶּה.
מְחֵה וְהַעֲבֵר פְּשָׁעֵינוּ וְחַטֹּאתֵינוּ
מִנֶּגֶד עֵינֶיךָ, כָּאָמוּר:
אָנֹכִי אָנֹכִי הוּא מֹחֶה פְשָׁעֶיךָ
לְמַעֲנִי,
וְחַטֹּאתֶיךָ לֹא אֶזְכֹּר.
וְנֶאֱמַר: מָחִיתִי כָעָב פְּשָׁעֶיךָ,
וְכֶעָנָן חַטֹּאתֶיךָ,
שׁוּבָה אֵלַי כִּי גְאַלְתִּיךָ.
וְנֶאֱמַר: כִּי־בַיּוֹם הַזֶּה יְכַפֵּר
עֲלֵיכֶם לְטַהֵר אֶתְכֶם,
מִכֹּל חַטֹּאתֵיכֶם לִפְנֵי יְיָ תִּטְהָרוּ.

Eloheinu v'Elohei avoteinu v'imoteinu,
m'chal
laavonoteinu b'Yom
[haShabbat hazeh uvyom]
HaKippurim hazeh.
M'cheih v'haaveir p'sha·einu v'chatoteinu
mineged einecha, kaamur:
"Anochi, anochi hu mocheh f'sha·echa
l'maani;
v'chatotecha lo ezkor."
V'ne·emar: "Machiti kaav p'sha·echa,
v'che·anan chatotecha —
shuvah elai, ki g'alticha."
V'ne·emar: "Ki-vayom hazeh y'chapeir
aleichem l'taheir et·chem;
mikol chatoteichem lifnei Adonai tit·haru."

Our God and God of our forebears,
pardon
our failings on [this day of Shabbat, and] this Day of Atonement;
erase our misdeeds; see beyond our defiance.

For Isaiah said in Your name: "It is I, I alone
who wipe away your defiant acts — this is My essence.
I shall pay no heed to your errors."

And the prophet said: "As a cloud fades away, as mist dissolves into air,
so your wrongs and mistakes shall be gone; I will wipe them away —
come back to Me, that I may redeem you."

As You said to Moses: "For on this day atonement shall be made for you
to purify you from all your wrongs.
And pure you shall be in the presence of Adonai."

IT IS I אָנֹכִי אָנֹכִי, Isaiah 43:25.
AS A CLOUD FADES AWAY מָחִיתִי כָעָב, Isaiah 44:22.
FOR ON THIS DAY כִּי־בַיּוֹם הַזֶּה, Leviticus 16:30.

IT IS NOT EASY to forgive God. It takes huge effort. It is painful, contradictory, and maddening. The human suffering that surrounds us feels utterly unforgivable. But I will forgive God because I do not want to write off the relationship. Because I feel there is too much to be lost by simply walking away. Because I want my children to develop their own relationships and come to their own conclusions. Because, despite the pain, sorrow, and suffering, I want my universe full of miracles, not void of them. Because I do not want to be one more angry, old cynic in the world. I want to believe a voice still calls out from Sinai, from heaven. That is why I will forgive God.

I want to engage in the eternal conversations with the ancestors and sages. Despite it all, I want to live my life in praise and awe—in wonder and hope. Even if I am wrong. Even if at the end there is nothing but darkness.

A TEACHING of the Baal Shem Tov:
Your fellow human being is a mirror for you.
If there is love and compassion in your soul,
you will see the goodness in others.
If you see a blemish in another,
it is your own imperfection you encounter.
Take careful note of the flaws you perceive in others.
This is a lesson for you:
they are your own flaws set before you,
a reminder of your own spiritual work.

IT IS FORBIDDEN for a person to be cruel and refuse to be appeased. Rather, one should be easily pacified and difficult to anger. When someone who has wronged you asks for forgiveness, you should forgive that person with a whole heart and a willing spirit—even if the person aggravated and sinned against you greatly. Let the offender come three times and ask sincerely for forgiveness. If the offended person continues to be stubborn and refuses to forgive, one is not required to beg forgiveness any longer; the one who refuses to forgive is now the sinner.

IT IS NOT EASY. By Rabbi Will Berkovitz (b. 1968).
BAAL SHEM TOV. "Master of the Good Name"; a popular appellation for Rabbi Israel ben Eliezer, the founder of Chasidism (1698–1760).
IT IS FORBIDDEN. Based on Maimonides (1135–1204), *Laws of T'shuvah* 2.9–10.

אֱלֹהֵינוּ וֵאלֹהֵי אֲבוֹתֵינוּ וְאִמּוֹתֵינוּ,	*Eloheinu v'Elohei avoteinu v'imoteinu,*
[רְצֵה בִמְנוּחָתֵנוּ,]	*[r'tzeih vimnuchateinu,]*
קַדְּשֵׁנוּ בְּמִצְוֹתֶיךָ,	*kad'sheinu b'mitzvotecha;*
וְתֵן חֶלְקֵנוּ בְּתוֹרָתֶךָ.	*v'tein chelkeinu b'Toratecha.*
שַׂבְּעֵנוּ מִטּוּבֶךָ,	*Sab'einu mituvecha;*
וְשַׂמְּחֵנוּ בִּישׁוּעָתֶךָ.	*v'sam'cheinu bishuatecha.*
[וְהַנְחִילֵנוּ, יְיָ אֱלֹהֵינוּ,	*[V'hanchileinu, Adonai Eloheinu,*
בְּאַהֲבָה וּבְרָצוֹן שַׁבַּת קָדְשֶׁךָ,	*b'ahavah uvratzon Shabbat kodshecha;*
וְיָנוּחוּ בָהּ יִשְׂרָאֵל,	*v'yanuchu vah Yisrael,*
מְקַדְּשֵׁי שְׁמֶךָ.]	*m'kad'shei sh'mecha.]*

God who is ours
and God of our fathers and mothers:
[may our rest on this Shabbat bring You pleasure;]
lead us to holiness through Your mitzvot;
and may each of us find a portion of Torah that is ours.
You bestow such goodness — teach us to be satisfied,
and to know the joy of Your salvation.
[Let Your holy Shabbat be our heritage,
embraced freely and with love;
and may all our people bring holiness to Your name
by resting on this day.]

כַּוָּנָה *Kavanah*
אָבוֹת וְאִמָּהוֹת *Avot v'Imahot*
גְּבוּרוֹת *G'vurot*
וּנְתַנֶּה תֹּקֶף *Untaneh Tokef*
קְדֻשַּׁת הַשֵּׁם *K'dushat HaShem*
קְדֻשַּׁת הַיּוֹם *K'dushat HaYom*
עֲבוֹדָה *Avodah*
הוֹדָאָה *Hodaah*
שָׁלוֹם *Shalom*
תְּפִלַּת הַלֵּב *T'filat HaLev*

MAY EACH OF US FIND A PORTION OF TORAH וְתֵן חֶלְקֵנוּ בְּתוֹרָתֶךָ. This phrase is found in the Mishnah (*Avot* 5:24). It may also be translated "Grant us our share in Your Torah." The *Zohar* teaches that there are 600,000 letters in the Torah — each representing one of the 600,000 souls present at Sinai. In fact, the name *Yisrael* may be read as an acronym for *yeish shishim ribo otiyot laTorah* (there are 600,000 letters in the Torah). While not a numerically accurate count, this mystical teaching conveys the sense that each of us can have a personal connection to the foundational Jewish text — and contribute unique insights and interpretations.

Focusing Prayer
God of All Generations
God's Powers
The Power of This Day
God's Holiness
The Day's Holiness
Our Offering
Thanksgiving
Peace
Prayer of the Heart

V'taheir libeinu l'ovd'cha be·emet —	וְטַהֵר לִבֵּנוּ לְעָבְדְּךָ בֶּאֱמֶת,
ki atah solchan l'Yisrael,	כִּי אַתָּה סָלְחָן לְיִשְׂרָאֵל,
umocholan l'shivtei Y'shurun	וּמָחֳלָן לְשִׁבְטֵי יְשֻׁרוּן
b'chol dor vador;	בְּכָל דּוֹר וָדוֹר,
umibaladecha ein lanu melech mocheil	וּמִבַּלְעָדֶיךָ אֵין לָנוּ מֶלֶךְ מוֹחֵל
v'solei·ach ela atah.	וְסוֹלֵחַ אֶלָּא אָתָּה.

Help us to serve you truly, with purity of heart —
for You are the Forgiver of Israel,
in every generation granting pardon to the tribes of Yeshurun.
We have no God of forgiveness and pardon but You, You alone.

Baruch atah, Adonai —	בָּרוּךְ אַתָּה, יְיָ,
melech mocheil v'solei·ach laavonoteinu	מֶלֶךְ מוֹחֵל וְסוֹלֵחַ לַעֲוֹנוֹתֵינוּ
v'laavonot amo beit Yisrael,	וְלַעֲוֹנוֹת עַמּוֹ בֵּית יִשְׂרָאֵל,
umaavir ashmoteinu b'chol shanah	וּמַעֲבִיר אַשְׁמוֹתֵינוּ בְּכָל שָׁנָה
v'shanah —	וְשָׁנָה,
melech al kol haaretz,	מֶלֶךְ עַל כָּל הָאָרֶץ,
m'kadeish [haShabbat v'] Yisrael	מְקַדֵּשׁ [הַשַּׁבָּת וְ] יִשְׂרָאֵל
v'Yom HaKippurim.	וְיוֹם הַכִּפּוּרִים.

You are blessed, Adonai, Sovereign who forgives our failings
and pardons the failings of Your people, the House of Israel.
You banish our guilt, from year to year,
You reign in majesty over all the earth;
You sanctify [Shabbat,] the people Israel and the Day of Atonement.

IN EVERY GENERATION . . . TRIBES OF YESHURUN יְשֻׁרוּן בְּכָל דּוֹר וָדוֹר. Rabbi Meir Simcha of Dvinsk (1843–1926) teaches that, on Yom Kippur, God offers forgiveness not only for our present wrongs, but also for the wrongdoing of "the tribes of Yeshurun" — a reference to the crime committed against Joseph by his brothers (Genesis 37), who seized him and sold him into slavery (an act that, according to a midrash, occurred on Yom Kippur). Family conflict and resentment among siblings remain common; hence these wrongs persist "in every generation."

YESHURUN יְשֻׁרוּן. A poetic name for the Jewish people, apparently related to the Hebrew word *yashar* (straight, honorable, morally upright). Deuteronomy 32:15, where the name first appears, suggests that material wealth has a corrupting affect on the Israelites' moral vocation.

רְצֵה, יְיָ אֱלֹהֵינוּ, בְּעַמְּךָ יִשְׂרָאֵל.
וּתְפִלָּתָם בְּאַהֲבָה תְקַבֵּל בְּרָצוֹן,
וּתְהִי לְרָצוֹן תָּמִיד עֲבוֹדַת
יִשְׂרָאֵל עַמֶּךָ.
אֵל קָרוֹב לְכָל קֹרְאָיו,
פְּנֵה אֶל עֲבָדֶיךָ וְחָנֵּנוּ.
שְׁפֹךְ רוּחֲךָ עָלֵינוּ,
וְתֶחֱזֶינָה עֵינֵינוּ בְּשׁוּבְךָ לְצִיּוֹן
בְּרַחֲמִים.

R'tzeih, Adonai Eloheinu, b'am'cha Yisrael.
Utfilatam b'ahavah t'kabeil b'ratzon,
ut·hi l'ratzon tamid avodat
Yisrael amecha.
El karov l'chol korav,
p'neih el avadecha v'choneinu.
Sh'foch ruchacha aleinu,
v'techezenah eineinu b'shuvcha l'Tziyon
b'rachamim.

Eternal, our God, Your people Israel yearns for Your favor.
Receive their prayer with loving acceptance,
and may You always desire Your people's worship.
Divine One, close to all who call upon You,
bring Your grace and presence near to those who serve You.
Pour forth Your spirit on us,
and may our eyes see Your merciful return to Zion.

בָּרוּךְ אַתָּה, יְיָ, הַמַּחֲזִיר שְׁכִינָתוֹ לְצִיּוֹן.
Baruch atah, Adonai, hamachazir Sh'chinato l'Tziyon.
Blessed are You whose Divine Presence is felt again in Zion.

RECEIVE THEIR PRAYER וּבִתְפִלָּתָם . . . תְּקַבֵּל. The function of prayer (as I understand it) is not intellectual but affective. Does it ease pain and nurture hope to stand as a member of a historic community in a ritual recitation? One is not required to perceive the world through a jeweler's glass, rigorously scrutinizing each event and each word for its compatibility with logic. Descartes was very wrong with his "I think, therefore I am." What distinguishes the human being, what constitutes our "is-ness" and dignifies us beyond the Cartesian model, is precisely the connection between thinking and feeling. No apology whatever is required for affect, nor need we feel that we are, somehow, "indulging" our weakness when we repair to it. (Leonard Fein, 1934–2014)

Focusing Prayer
God of All Generations
God's Powers
The Power of This Day
God's Holiness
The Day's Holiness
Our Offering
Thanksgiving
Peace
Prayer of the Heart

FROM "THE BLUE CANDLE"

A blue candle is my Zion.
Its pure light

blesses the silence
of this sleeping house.

I do not wish
to leave—soon enough

something
will take my hand

and quietly lead me away.

I CALLED GOD

I called God but there's no
God. But there was
God because I called
God. And if there wasn't
God what
Did I call? And I called, I called
God. And there was, for a split
Second, and there will be. Won't
Die. As long as
I keep calling
God.

קָרָאתִי אֱלֹהִים וְאֵין
אֱלֹהִים. אֲבָל הָיָה
אֱלֹהִים כִּי קָרָאתִי
אֱלֹהִים. וְאִלְמָלֵא
הָיָה אֱלֹהִים מָה
קָרָאתִי? וְקָרָאתִי. קָרָאתִי
אֱלֹהִים. וְהָיָה, וְלוּ
לְרֶגַע, וְיִהְיֶה. לֹא
יָמוּת. כָּל עוֹד
אֲנִי שָׁב וְקוֹרֵא
אֱלֹהִים.

בָּרוּךְ אַתָּה, יְיָ, הַמַּחֲזִיר שְׁכִינָתוֹ לְצִיּוֹן.

Baruch atah, Adonai, hamachazir Sh'chinato l'Tziyon.

Blessed are You whose Divine Presence is felt again in Zion.

A BLUE CANDLE IS MY ZION. By William Pillin (1910–1985). In this poem of old age, Zion is the symbol of a personal piety and reverence, rather than a point on the map. The pure light of the candle suggests the waning of life and the preciousness of home.

I CALLED GOD. By Adi Assis (b. 1967). While the *Avodah* prayer (*facing page*) addresses God directly and confidently as "Divine One, close to all who call upon You," this contemporary poem instead places its faith in the continuing quest for God.

Modim anachnu lach,

shaatah hu Adonai Eloheinu v'Elohei

    avoteinu v'imoteinu l'olam va·ed.

Tzur chayeinu, magein yisheinu,

atah hu l'dor vador.

Nodeh l'cha unsapeir t'hilatecha:

al chayeinu ham'surim b'yadecha,

v'al nishmoteinu hap'kudot lach,

v'al nisecha sheb'chol yom imanu,

v'al nifl'otecha v'tovotecha sheb'chol eit,

erev vavoker v'tzohorayim.

Hatov — ki lo chalu rachamecha;

v'hamracheim — ki lo tamu chasadecha:

mei·olam kivinu lach.

מוֹדִים אֲנַחְנוּ לָךְ,

שָׁאַתָּה הוּא יְיָ אֱלֹהֵינוּ וֵאלֹהֵי

אֲבוֹתֵינוּ וְאִמּוֹתֵינוּ לְעוֹלָם וָעֶד.

צוּר חַיֵּינוּ, מָגֵן יִשְׁעֵנוּ,

אַתָּה הוּא לְדוֹר וָדוֹר.

נוֹדֶה לְּךָ וּנְסַפֵּר תְּהִלָּתֶךָ:

עַל חַיֵּינוּ הַמְּסוּרִים בְּיָדֶךָ,

וְעַל נִשְׁמוֹתֵינוּ הַפְּקוּדוֹת לָךְ,

וְעַל נִסֶּיךָ שֶׁבְּכָל יוֹם עִמָּנוּ,

וְעַל נִפְלְאוֹתֶיךָ וְטוֹבוֹתֶיךָ שֶׁבְּכָל עֵת,

עֶרֶב וָבֹקֶר וְצָהֳרָיִם.

הַטּוֹב, כִּי לֹא כָלוּ רַחֲמֶיךָ,

וְהַמְרַחֵם, כִּי לֹא תַמּוּ חֲסָדֶיךָ,

מֵעוֹלָם קִוִּינוּ לָךְ.

כַּוָּנָה
Kavanah

אָבוֹת וְאִמָּהוֹת
Avot v'Imahot

גְּבוּרוֹת
G'vurot

וּנְתַנֶּה תְּקֶף
Untaneh Tokef

קְדֻשַּׁת הַשֵּׁם
K'dushat HaShem

קְדֻשַּׁת הַיּוֹם
K'dushat HaYom

עֲבוֹדָה
Avodah

הוֹדָאָה
Hodaah

שָׁלוֹם
Shalom

תְּפִלַּת הַלֵּב
T'filat HaLev

God who is ours,
God of all generations,
to You we are grateful forever.

Rock and Protector of our lives,
Your saving power endures from age to age.

We thank You and tell the tale of Your praise:
Your power in our lives,
Your caring for our souls,
the constant miracle of Your kindness.

Morning, noon, and night
we call You Goodness — for Your compassion never ends;
we call You Mercy — for Your love has no limit;
we call You Hope, now and for all time.

HODAAH הוֹדָאָה. When offering this prayer of thanksgiving it is traditional to bow twice: at the beginning, when reciting the word מוֹדִים *modim* (we are grateful); and at the end (page 242), at the word בָּרוּךְ *baruch* (blessed). The gesture of bowing conveys humility — it is a mark of deference to another, or making room for the other. In a culture unaccustomed to bowing, this act has particular force, teaching that we express gratitude for the inexplicable gift of life by living with awareness of that which is beyond the self. Reverent attention to the "constant miracles" that surround us — and to the needs of other people who inhabit this world — is a way of carrying this posture of bowing into our everyday life.

AN AWE so quiet
I don't know when it began.

A gratitude
had begun
to sing in me.

Was there some moment
dividing
song from no song?

When does dewfall begin?

When does night
fold its arms over our hearts
to cherish them?

When is daybreak?

THE PATIENCE OF ORDINARY THINGS

It is a kind of love, is it not?
How the cup holds the tea,
How the chair stands sturdy and foursquare,
How the floor receives the bottoms of shoes
Or toes. How soles of feet know
Where they're supposed to be.
I've been thinking about the patience
Of ordinary things, how clothes
Wait respectfully in closets
And soap dries quietly in the dish,
And towels drink the wet
From the skin of the back.
And the lovely repetition of stairs.
And what is more generous than a window?

AN AWE. By Denise Levertov (1923–1997).
THE PATIENCE OF ORDINARY THINGS. By Pat Schneider (b. 1934).

V'al kulam yitbarach v'yitromam shimcha,	וְעַל כֻּלָּם יִתְבָּרַךְ וְיִתְרוֹמַם שִׁמְךָ,
Malkeinu, tamid l'olam va·ed.	מַלְכֵּנוּ, תָּמִיד לְעוֹלָם וָעֶד.
Uchtov l'chayim tovim	וּכְתֹב לְחַיִּים טוֹבִים
kol b'nei v'ritecha.	כָּל בְּנֵי בְרִיתֶךָ.
V'chol hachayim yoducha selah,	וְכֹל הַחַיִּים יוֹדוּךָ סֶּלָה,
vihal'lu et shimcha be·emet —	וִיהַלְלוּ אֶת שִׁמְךָ בֶּאֱמֶת,
haEl y'shuateinu v'ezrateinu selah.	הָאֵל יְשׁוּעָתֵנוּ וְעֶזְרָתֵנוּ סֶלָה.

And for all these gifts, God of majesty,
may Your name come to be blessed and praised —
our gratitude a daily offering until the end of time.

Inscribe Your covenant partners
for a life of goodness.

And may all life resound with gratitude and faith
in praise of Your name.
God, You free us and strengthen us.

בָּרוּךְ אַתָּה, יְיָ, הַטּוֹב שִׁמְךָ, וּלְךָ נָאֶה לְהוֹדוֹת.
Baruch atah, Adonai, hatov shimcha, ulcha na·eh l'hodot.
Blessed are You, Adonai, whose goodness
deserves thanks and praise.

כַּוָּנָה *Kavanah*
אָבוֹת וְאִמָּהוֹת *Avot v'Imahot*
גְּבוּרוֹת *G'vurot*
וּנְתַנֶּה תֹּקֶף *Untaneh Tokef*
קְדֻשַּׁת הַשֵּׁם *K'dushat HaShem*
קְדֻשַּׁת הַיּוֹם *K'dushat HaYom*
עֲבוֹדָה *Avodah*
הוֹדָאָה **Hodaah**
שָׁלוֹם *Shalom*
תְּפִלַּת הַלֵּב *T'filat HaLev*

WHOSE GOODNESS DESERVES THANKS AND PRAISE הַטּוֹב שִׁמְךָ, וּלְךָ נָאֶה לְהוֹדוֹת. Literally, "to You, it is fitting to thank" (or "to give praise"). The Etz Yosef, a 19th-century commentary, derives from this phrase the idea that, while it is fitting to offer praise to God, it is improper to offer excessive praise of human beings, based on the Talmudic teaching (*Arachin* 16a) "Do not recount the praise of your neighbor, for it leads to disparaging remarks." The Sages tried to discourage the practice of speaking about others behind their backs, even in a positive way, since it often degenerates into malicious gossip, or prompts listeners to make negative comments. Rather than evaluating others, we are encouraged to attune our thoughts to gratitude for "all the gifts" in our own life.

TINY JOYS

שְׂשׂוֹנוֹת זְעִירִים, שְׂמָחוֹת כִּזְנַב־לְטָאָה:
הַיָּם לְפִתְאֹם בֵּין שְׁנֵי בִּנְיָנִים בַּכְּרָךְ,
זְכוּכִית הַחַלּוֹן נוֹצֶצֶת בְּשֶׁמֶשׁ שׁוֹקְעָה –
הַכֹּל מְבֹרָךְ!

הַכֹּל מְבֹרָךְ, לַכֹּל נְגִינַת נֶחָמוֹת,
בַּכֹּל רְמָזִים טְמִירִים, וְהַכֹּל יִסְכֹּן
לַחֲרֹז עַל חוּטָיו אַלְמֻגֵּי הַמִּלִּים הַנָּאווֹת.
כְּיַד הַדִּמְיוֹן.

Tiny joys, joys like a lizard's tail:
a sudden sea between two city buildings in the west,
windows glittering in the setting sun—
everything blessed!

Everything blessed.
A consoling music in everything,
in everything mysteries and hints—
and everything waiting for corals of beautiful words
to be strung by the imagination on its string.

בָּרוּךְ אַתָּה, יְיָ, הַטּוֹב שִׁמְךָ, וּלְךָ נָאֶה לְהוֹדוֹת.

Baruch atah, Adonai, hatov shimcha, ulcha na·eh l'hodot.

Blessed are You, Adonai, whose goodness deserves thanks and praise.

TINY JOYS. By Rachel Bluwstein, known as Rachel (1890–1931). Rachel was a follower of A.D. Gordon, who inspired many early Zionist pioneers with his philosophy exalting labor in the Land of Israel. Her greatest joy was participating in the physical renewal of the land. When illness forced her to leave Kibbutz Kinneret on the shore of the Sea of Galilee and move to Tel Aviv, her life and her poetry were filled with despair and nostalgia for the work she had left behind. And yet she felt gratitude for the smallest of things, and found the strength of spirit to say: "Everything blessed!"

כַּוָּנָה
Kavanah
אָבוֹת וְאִמָּהוֹת
Avot v'Imahot
גְּבוּרוֹת
G'vurot
וּנְתַנֶּה תֹּקֶף
Untaneh Tokef
קְדֻשַּׁת הַשֵּׁם
K'dushat HaShem
קְדֻשַּׁת הַיּוֹם
K'dushat HaYom
עֲבוֹדָה
Avodah
הוֹדָאָה
Hodaah
שָׁלוֹם
Shalom
תְּפִלַּת הַלֵּב
T'filat HaLev

אֱלֹהֵינוּ וֵאלֹהֵי אֲבוֹתֵינוּ וְאִמּוֹתֵינוּ,
בָּרְכֵנוּ בַּבְּרָכָה הַמְשֻׁלֶּשֶׁת
הַכְּתוּבָה בַּתּוֹרָה,
הָאֲמוּרָה מִפִּי כֹּהֲנִים
עַם קְדוֹשֶׁךָ כָּאָמוּר:
יְבָרֶכְךָ יְיָ וְיִשְׁמְרֶךָ.
כֵּן יְהִי רָצוֹן.
יָאֵר יְיָ פָּנָיו אֵלֶיךָ וִיחֻנֶּךָּ.
כֵּן יְהִי רָצוֹן.
יִשָּׂא יְיָ פָּנָיו אֵלֶיךָ
וְיָשֵׂם לְךָ שָׁלוֹם.
כֵּן יְהִי רָצוֹן.

Eloheinu v'Elohei avoteinu v'imoteinu,
bar'cheinu bab'rachah hamshuleshet
hak'tuvah baTorah,
haamurah mipi kohanim —
am k'doshecha — kaamur:
"Y'varech·cha Adonai v'yishm'recha."
Kein y'hi ratzon.
"Ya·eir Adonai panav eilecha vichuneka."
Kein y'hi ratzon.
"Yisa Adonai panav eilecha
v'yaseim l'cha shalom."
Kein y'hi ratzon.

Our God,
Divine Presence whose path our ancestors walked,
bless us now with words first bestowed on Israel
in the time of Moses and Aaron —
the threefold blessing, given us through Torah,
that joins our hopes with theirs:

May God bless you and protect you.
May it be so.
May you receive the light of God's kindness and grace.
May it be so.
May God bestow favor upon you and give you peace.
May it be so. —GO TO 292

IN THE TIME OF MOSES AND AARON הָאֲמוּרָה מִפִּי כֹּהֲנִים. Aaron and his descendants served as *kohanim* (priests) at the altar — offering the daily and festival sacrifices, and blessing the people with words that are still part of our liturgy. A midrash interprets the three parts of the blessing as follows: *May God bless you* — with material prosperity; *and protect you* — with good health. *May you receive the light of God's kindness and grace* — through the spiritual gifts of Torah knowledge, understanding, and wisdom. *May God bestow favor upon you and give you peace* — in your going out and in your coming in, with all people, in your home and everywhere (*Numbers Rabbah* 11.7; *Sifrei B'midbar, Naso*, 40–42).

MAY GOD BLESS YOU יְבָרֶכְךָ יְיָ, Numbers 6:24–26.

RABBI LEVI YITZCHAK of Berditchev taught:
The hands of the *kohanim* were a language in themselves.
Hands held out, with the palms facing up, indicate the desire to receive;
hands held up, with the palms facing down, indicate the desire to give.
So, when the *kohanim* lifted up their hands to bless,
they did not wish to pray for themselves—
but only to bestow God's bounty on the people.

Holy One, we strive to be a nation of priests,
our lives consecrated to holy work.
Help us to use our hands as instruments of divine service—
conduits of Your goodness.
May blessings flow through us to our children, our friends,
and all those whose lives we touch.

A BLESSING

May the *Shechinah*, the Holy Presence,
spread Her wings over you and protect you.
May Her light shine upon you with compassion.
And may Her countenance illumine your lives
with wholeness and peace.

BIRKAT KOHANIM

May the Divine One bless and protect you.
May She grace you with the warmth of a smile.
May She turn to you and shine into your eyes
And enfold you in a mantle of peace.

RABBI LEVI YITZCHAK OF BERDITCHEV, 1740–1809.

THE HANDS OF THE KOHANIM. When offering the Priestly Blessing, the *kohanim* would lift their hands, palms downward, their fingers forming a three-pronged shape to replicate the Hebrew letter *shin*—the first letter in *Shaddai*, a name for God connoting protection.

A BLESSING. By Rabbi Leila Gal Berner (b. 1950).

BIRKAT KOHANIM. Lyrics by Cantor Marsha Attie (b. 1957) and Rabbi Judith HaLevy (b. 1942).

כַּוָּנָה
Kavanah
אָבוֹת וְאִמָּהוֹת
Avot v'Imahot
גְּבוּרוֹת
G'vurot
וּנְתַנֶּה תֹּקֶף
Untaneh Tokef
קְדֻשַּׁת הַשֵּׁם
K'dushat HaShem
קְדֻשַּׁת הַיּוֹם
K'dushat HaYom
עֲבוֹדָה
Avodah
הוֹדָאָה
Hodaah
שָׁלוֹם
Shalom
תְּפִלַּת הַלֵּב
T'filat HaLev

שִׂים שָׁלוֹם טוֹבָה וּבְרָכָה,
חֵן וָחֶסֶד וְרַחֲמִים,
עָלֵינוּ וְעַל כָּל יִשְׂרָאֵל עַמֶּךָ.
בָּרְכֵנוּ, אָבִינוּ, כֻּלָּנוּ כְּאֶחָד
בְּאוֹר פָּנֶיךָ,
כִּי בְאוֹר פָּנֶיךָ נָתַתָּ לָּנוּ,
יְיָ אֱלֹהֵינוּ,
תּוֹרַת חַיִּים וְאַהֲבַת חֶסֶד,
וּצְדָקָה וּבְרָכָה וְרַחֲמִים וְחַיִּים
וְשָׁלוֹם.
וְטוֹב בְּעֵינֶיךָ לְבָרֵךְ אֶת עַמְּךָ יִשְׂרָאֵל,
בְּכָל עֵת וּבְכָל שָׁעָה, בִּשְׁלוֹמֶךָ.

Sim shalom tovah uvrachah,
chein vachesed v'rachamim,
aleinu v'al kol Yisrael amecha.
Bar'cheinu, Avinu — kulanu k'echad —
b'or panecha;
ki v'or panecha natata lanu,
Adonai Eloheinu,
Torat chayim v'ahavat chesed,
utzdakah uvrachah v'rachamim v'chayim
v'shalom.
V'tov b'einecha l'vareich et am'cha Yisrael,
b'chol eit uvchol shaah, bishlomecha.

בְּסֵפֶר חַיִּים, בְּרָכָה, וְשָׁלוֹם,
וּפַרְנָסָה טוֹבָה,
נִזָּכֵר וְנִכָּתֵב לְפָנֶיךָ,
אֲנַחְנוּ וְכָל עַמְּךָ בֵּית יִשְׂרָאֵל,
לְחַיִּים טוֹבִים וּלְשָׁלוֹם.

B'sefer chayim, b'rachah, v'shalom,
ufarnasah tovah,
nizacheir v'nikateiv l'fanecha —
anachnu, v'chol am'cha beit Yisrael —
l'chayim tovim ulshalom!

Let there be peace.
Grant goodness, blessing, and grace,
constancy and compassion
to us and all Israel, Your people.

Avinu —
bless and unite all human beings in the light of Your presence;
for Your light has shown us a holy path for living:
devotion to love, generosity, blessedness, mercy, life, and peace.
In Your goodness, bless Your people Israel with peace at all times.

Let us, and the whole family of Israel,
be remembered and inscribed in the Book of Life.
May it be a life of goodness, blessing, and prosperity!
May it be a life of peace!

בָּרוּךְ אַתָּה, יְיָ, עוֹשֵׂה הַשָּׁלוֹם.

Baruch atah, Adonai, oseih hashalom.

You are the Blessed One, Eternal Source of shalom.

MY CHILD WAFTS PEACE

My child wafts peace.
When I lean over him,
it is not just the smell of soap.

All the people were children
wafting peace.
(And in the whole land, not even one
millstone remained that still turned.)

Oh, the land torn like clothes
that can't be mended.
Hard, lonely fathers even in the cave
of the Machpelah.
Childless silence,

my child wafts peace.
His mother's womb promised him
what God cannot
promise us.

יַלְדִּי נוֹדֵף שָׁלוֹם.
כְּשֶׁאֲנִי רָכוּן מֵעָלָיו,
זֶה לֹא רַק רֵיחַ הַסַּבּוֹן.

כָּל הָאֲנָשִׁים הָיוּ יְלָדִים
שֶׁנָּדְפוּ שָׁלוֹם.
(וּבְכָל הָאָרֶץ לֹא נִשְׁאַר
אַף גַּלְגַּל טַחֲנָה אַחַת
שֶׁיִּסְתּוֹבֵב.)

הוֹ, הָאָרֶץ הַקְּרוּעָה כִּבְגָדִים
שֶׁאֵין לָהֶם תִּקּוּן.
אָבוֹת קָשִׁים וּבוֹדְדִים גַּם
בִּמְעָרוֹת הַמַּכְפֵּלָה.
דְּמָמָה חֲשׂוּכַת בָּנִים,

יַלְדִּי נוֹדֵף שָׁלוֹם.
רֶחֶם אִמּוֹ הִבְטִיחָה לוֹ
מַה שֶּׁאֱלֹהִים אֵינוֹ יָכוֹל
לְהַבְטִיחַ לָנוּ.

בָּרוּךְ אַתָּה, יְיָ, עוֹשֵׂה הַשָּׁלוֹם.

Baruch atah, Adonai, oseih hashalom.

You are the Blessed One, Eternal Source of shalom.

MY CHILD WAFTS PEACE. By Yehuda Amichai (1924–2000).

NOT EVEN ONE MILLSTONE. In Jeremiah 25:10, the sound of millstones grinding flour is an image of domestic peace and tranquility in ancient Judah and Jerusalem. For Jeremiah, its absence (after the Babylonian exile of 586 BCE) was a symbol of the land's ruin and desolation.

MACHPELAH. The cave in Hebron where Abraham and most other Patriarchs and Matriarchs of Israel are said to be buried.

Elohai:	אֱלֹהַי,	
N'tzor l'shoni meira;	נְצֹר לְשׁוֹנִי מֵרָע,	
usfatai midabeir mirmah.	וּשְׂפָתַי מִדַּבֵּר מִרְמָה.	
V'limkal'lai nafshi tidom;	וְלִמְקַלְלַי נַפְשִׁי תִדֹּם,	
v'nafshi ke·afar lakol tiyeh.	וְנַפְשִׁי כֶּעָפָר לַכֹּל תִּהְיֶה.	
P'tach libi b'Toratecha;	פְּתַח לִבִּי בְּתוֹרָתֶךָ,	
uvmitzvotecha tirdof nafshi.	וּבְמִצְוֹתֶיךָ תִּרְדֹּף נַפְשִׁי.	
V'chol hachoshvim alai raah —	וְכָל הַחוֹשְׁבִים עָלַי רָעָה,	
m'heirah hafeir atzatam,	מְהֵרָה הָפֵר עֲצָתָם,	
v'kalkeil machashavtam.	וְקַלְקֵל מַחֲשַׁבְתָּם.	
Aseih l'maan sh'mecha.	עֲשֵׂה לְמַעַן שְׁמֶךָ.	
Aseih l'maan y'minecha.	עֲשֵׂה לְמַעַן יְמִינֶךָ.	
Aseih l'maan k'dushatecha.	עֲשֵׂה לְמַעַן קְדֻשָּׁתֶךָ.	
Aseih l'maan Toratecha.	עֲשֵׂה לְמַעַן תּוֹרָתֶךָ.	
L'maan yeichal'tzun y'didecha,	לְמַעַן יֵחָלְצוּן יְדִידֶיךָ,	
hoshiah y'mincha vaaneini.	הוֹשִׁיעָה יְמִינְךָ וַעֲנֵנִי.	

My God:
Keep my tongue from doing harm, and my lips from lies and deceit.
Before those who wrong me with words, may silence be my practice.
Before all human beings, let humility be my stance.
Open my heart to Your Torah, that I may follow its sacred path of duty.
Shatter, at once, the malicious plans of those who would do me harm.
Act, for the sake of Your name.
Act, for the sake of Your shielding hand.
Act, for the sake of Your holiness.
Act, for the sake of Your Torah.
For the sake of those who love You — their rescue and safety —
let Your shielding hand be the answer to my prayer.

MY GOD: KEEP אֱלֹהַי, נְצֹר. The Amidah ends much as it began, with a prayer for pure and ethical speech. In our Yom Kippur confessions, the largest category of wrongdoing relates to the misuse of language. The Talmud (*Bava Batra* 165a) comments that this is a universal human failing: "Most people are guilty of dishonesty, a minority of lewd behavior, but all of improper speech (*lashon hara*)." Yet words may also create beauty, connection, and healing in our relationships. A verse in Proverbs (18:21) conveys the extraordinary significance of how we employ the gift of speech: "Death and life are in the power of the tongue."

FOR THE SAKE OF THOSE WHO LOVE YOU לְמַעַן . . . יְדִידֶיךָ, Psalm 60:7.

YOM KIPPUR

In the autumn garden,
I chop away dead yucca spires,
their white bell blossoms distant
in memory. My fingers comb ivy
and vinca for fallen leaves that crumble
in my hands. I think of crimes
against my loved ones, count my sins,
pull at spider webs and chickweed,
stubborn at the root.

I make my piles, gather the detritus
of trees into bags set against the curb.
I sweep the sidewalk, edge a trowel's
blade beneath a hardy clutch of clover.
Even in drought, the barely living cling
like runners on a fencepost, adamant.
My roses, staked and tied to the wire mesh,
wilt on the stalk, feebly pink. Still,
honeysuckle persists, fragrant, wild,
and berries will ripen in the winter to come.

IN THE AUTUMN GARDEN. By Pia Taavila-Borsheim (b. 1952).
VINCA. A flowering evergreen ornamental plant, often used as ground cover in gardens.

Yiyu l'ratzon imrei-fi

v'hegyon libi l'fanecha,

Adonai, tzuri v'go·ali.

יִהְיוּ לְרָצוֹן אִמְרֵי־פִי
וְהֶגְיוֹן לִבִּי לְפָנֶיךָ,
יְיָ, צוּרִי וְגֹאֲלִי.

May the words of my mouth
and the meditation of my heart
be acceptable to You, Soul of eternity,
my Rock and my Redeemer.

Oseh shalom bimromav,

hu yaaseh shalom aleinu,

v'al kol Yisrael,

v'al kol yoshvei teiveil.

V'imru: Amen.

עֹשֶׂה שָׁלוֹם בִּמְרוֹמָיו,
הוּא יַעֲשֶׂה שָׁלוֹם עָלֵינוּ,
וְעַל כָּל יִשְׂרָאֵל,
וְעַל כָּל יוֹשְׁבֵי תֵבֵל.
וְאִמְרוּ: אָמֵן.

May the Maker of peace above make peace for us,
all Israel, and all who dwell on earth. *Amen.*

כַּוָּנָה
Kavanah

אָבוֹת וְאִמָּהוֹת
Avot v'Imahot

גְּבוּרוֹת
G'vurot

וּנְתַנֶּה תְּקֶף
Untaneh Tokef

קְדֻשַּׁת הַשֵּׁם
K'dushat HaShem

קְדֻשַּׁת הַיּוֹם
K'dushat HaYom

עֲבוֹדָה
Avodah

הוֹדָאָה
Hodaah

שָׁלוֹם
Shalom

תְּפִלַּת הַלֵּב
T'filat HaLev

MAY THE WORDS OF MY MOUTH . . . BE ACCEPTABLE יִהְיוּ לְרָצוֹן אִמְרֵי־פִי, Psalm 19:15. In its original biblical context, this request for divine favor comes immediately after a heartfelt expression of contrition for wrongdoing and the desire to atone: "Who can discern errors? Cleanse me from hidden transgressions. . . . Then I shall be blameless and clear of grave offense" (verses 13–14). Thus, it reflects the hope that God will accept the Psalmist's prayers and thoughts, despite the serious offenses committed.

This verse, placed at the conclusion of *HaT'filah*, provide a satisfying symmetry with the verse from Psalms that introduces *HaT'filah*: "Adonai, open my lips that my mouth may declare Your praise" (Psalm 51:17). Like Psalm 19:15, that verse from Psalm 51 follows immediately after a confession of wrongdoing: "Save me from bloodguilt, O God, God, my deliverer. . ." (verse 16). Thus, *HaT'filah* is framed by verses expressing a sinner's hope for worthy thoughts, pure speech, and a renewed relationship with God.

ANTHEM

The birds they sang
at the break of day
Start again,
I heard them say,
Don't dwell on what
has passed away
or what is yet to be.

The wars they will
be fought again
The holy dove
be caught again
bought and sold
and bought again;
the dove is never free.

Ring the bells that still can ring
Forget your perfect offering
There is a crack in everything
That's how the light gets in. . . .

HOPE

אֲנִי מְקַוֶּה שֶׁאַתָּה שׁוֹמֵעַ.
אֲנִי יוֹדֵעַ
שֶׁאֵין בָּזֶה הַרְבֵּה מַמָּשׁ כָּךְ
אָמְרוּ לִי.
בְּכָל זֹאת אֲנִי רוֹצֶה עוֹד פַּעַם
לְקַוּוֹת לָזֶה
שֶׁאַתָּה שׁוֹמֵעַ אֵיךְ אֲנִי מְקַוֶּה.

תִּקְוָתִי מְחַכָּה כְּמוֹ אַיָּלָה.
הֱיֵה זָהִיר. אַל תְּחַבְּקֶנָּה.
נִפּוּץ זֶרֶד אֶחָד וְאֵינֶנָּה.
הֲיִהְיֶה לָנוּ כֹּחַ
לְעוֹד הַתְחָלָה?

אֲנִי תִּקְוָה.

My hope is: that you hear.
I know
that it holds little.
So they told me.
Even so, I want
to hope again for this.
That you hear how I hope:

My hope is like a hind, waiting.
Be careful
not to embrace it. Break one
dry shoot of a tree, and it goes.
And would we have the strength
for another beginning?

I hope and am that hope.

ANTHEM. Lyrics by Leonard Cohen (b. 1934).

HOPE. By Jechiel Mohar (b. 1921). The words "My hope is like a hind, waiting" allude to the dramatic image of spiritual thirst in Psalm 42:2: "As a hind yearns for streams of water, my soul yearns for You, God."

אָבִינוּ מַלְכֵּנוּ
Avinu Malkeinu

אָבִינוּ מַלְכֵּנוּ
Avinu Malkeinu · Almighty and Merciful

אָבִינוּ מַלְכֵּנוּ, שְׁמַע קוֹלֵנוּ.
Avinu Malkeinu, sh'ma koleinu.
Avinu Malkeinu — Almighty and Merciful — hear our voice.

אָבִינוּ מַלְכֵּנוּ, חָטָאנוּ לְפָנֶיךָ.
Avinu Malkeinu, chatanu l'fanecha.
Avinu Malkeinu, we have strayed and sinned before You.

אָבִינוּ מַלְכֵּנוּ, חֲמֹל עָלֵינוּ, וְעַל עוֹלָלֵנוּ וְטַפֵּנוּ.
Avinu Malkeinu, chamol aleinu, v'al olaleinu v'tapeinu.
Avinu Malkeinu, have compassion on us and our families.

אָבִינוּ מַלְכֵּנוּ, כַּלֵּה דֶּבֶר וְחֶרֶב וְרָעָב מֵעָלֵינוּ.
Avinu Malkeinu, kaleih dever v'cherev v'raav mei·aleinu.
Avinu Malkeinu, halt the onslaught of sickness, violence, and hunger.

אָבִינוּ מַלְכֵּנוּ, כַּלֵּה כָּל צַר וּמַשְׂטִין מֵעָלֵינוּ.
Avinu Malkeinu, kaleih kol tzar umastin mei·aleinu.
Avinu Malkeinu, halt the reign of those who cause pain and terror.

אָבִינוּ מַלְכֵּנוּ, כָּתְבֵנוּ בְּסֵפֶר חַיִּים טוֹבִים.
Avinu Malkeinu, kotveinu b'sefer chayim tovim.
Avinu Malkeinu, enter our names in the Book of Lives Well Lived.

אָבִינוּ מַלְכֵּנוּ, חַדֵּשׁ עָלֵינוּ שָׁנָה טוֹבָה.
Avinu Malkeinu, chadeish aleinu shanah tovah.
Avinu Malkeinu, renew for us a year of goodness.

אָבִינוּ מַלְכֵּנוּ, מַלֵּא יָדֵינוּ מִבִּרְכוֹתֶיךָ.
Avinu Malkeinu, malei yadeinu mibirchotecha.
Avinu Malkeinu, let our hands overflow with Your blessings.

אָבִינוּ מַלְכֵּנוּ, הָרֵם קֶרֶן מְשִׁיחֶךָ.
Avinu Malkeinu, hareim keren m'shichecha.
Avinu Malkeinu, let our eyes behold the dawn of redemption.

Avinu Malkeinu

אָבִֽינוּ מַלְכֵּֽנוּ, נָא אַל תְּשִׁיבֵֽנוּ רֵיקָם
מִלְּפָנֶֽיךָ.

Avinu Malkeinu, na al t'shiveinu reikam mil'fanecha.

Avinu Malkeinu, we pray: do not turn us away from You with nothing.

אָבִֽינוּ מַלְכֵּֽנוּ, קַבֵּל בְּרַחֲמִים
וּבְרָצוֹן אֶת תְּפִלָּתֵֽנוּ.

Avinu Malkeinu, kabeil b'rachamim uvratzon et t'filateinu.

Avinu Malkeinu, welcome our prayer with love; accept and embrace it.

אָבִֽינוּ מַלְכֵּֽנוּ, עֲשֵׂה עִמָּֽנוּ
לְמַֽעַן שְׁמֶֽךָ.

Avinu Malkeinu, aseih imanu l'maan sh'mecha.

Avinu Malkeinu, act toward us as befits Your name.

אָבִֽינוּ מַלְכֵּֽנוּ, עֲשֵׂה לְמַעַנְךָ אִם לֹא
לְמַֽעֲנֵֽנוּ.

Avinu Malkeinu, aseih l'maancha im lo l'maaneinu.

Avinu Malkeinu, act for Your sake, if not for ours.

אָבִֽינוּ מַלְכֵּֽנוּ, אֵין לָֽנוּ מֶֽלֶךְ אֶלָּא אָֽתָּה.

Avinu Malkeinu, ein lanu melech ela atah.

Avinu Malkeinu, You alone are our Sovereign.

אָבִֽינוּ מַלְכֵּֽנוּ, פְּתַח שַׁעֲרֵי שָׁמַֽיִם
לִתְפִלָּתֵֽנוּ.

Avinu Malkeinu, p'tach shaarei shamayim litfilateinu.

Avinu Malkeinu, let the gates of heaven be open to our prayer.

אָבִֽינוּ מַלְכֵּֽנוּ, שְׁמַע קוֹלֵֽנוּ, חוּס
וְרַחֵם עָלֵֽינוּ.

Avinu Malkeinu, sh'ma koleinu; chus v'racheim aleinu.

Avinu Malkeinu, hear our voice; treat us with tender compassion.

אָבִֽינוּ מַלְכֵּֽנוּ, חָנֵּֽנוּ וַעֲנֵֽנוּ,
כִּי אֵין בָּֽנוּ מַעֲשִׂים.
עֲשֵׂה עִמָּֽנוּ צְדָקָה וָחֶֽסֶד,
וְהוֹשִׁיעֵֽנוּ.

Avinu Malkeinu, choneinu vaaneinu;
ki ein banu maasim.
Aseih imanu tz'dakah vachesed,
v'hoshi·einu.

Avinu Malkeinu — Almighty and Merciful —
answer us with grace, for our deeds are wanting.
Save us through acts of justice and love.

קְרִיאַת הַתּוֹרָה

K'riat HaTorah · Reading of the Torah

Bringing the Torah into Our Midst

Let the reading of Torah be like prayer —
a meditation to remind us what we strive for,
a chant that binds us to the chain of generations

Let the reading of Torah be like prayer —
a moment of purest solidarity
with our people's hopes and history;
an invitation to affirm or dissent,
to challenge or believe,
to ask why or say amen

Let the reading of Torah be like prayer —
flowing like waters that renew the spirit,
refreshing and sweet to nourish the soul

Let the reading of Torah be like prayer —
every word a blessing,
every verse a conversation with God

READING OF THE TORAH. Participating in the Torah service drums home the wisdom of Moses' last words: "For this mitzvah . . . is neither beyond you nor far away" (Deuteronomy 30:11) — Torah is never far away from us. It is not even read far away. It is brought into the midst of the people, who choose life by welcoming it, honoring and observing its commandments. Reading Torah is an affirmation of the continuing pact between the community of Israel and God. It is a celebration of a 4000-year-old relationship that began when God chose Israel and Israel responded: *naaseh v'nishma*, "We will do and we will hear." Reading Torah is the height of the morning liturgy because, as a community, we come together "to do" the mitzvah of reading Torah and "to hear" its words together. (Rabbi Lawrence A. Hoffman, b. 1942)

Welcoming the Torah
God's Thirteen Attributes
Bringing Forth the Torah
The Torah in Our Midst
Torah Blessings
Thanksgiving Blessing
Blessing for the Aliyah
Torah Reading
Prayer for Healing
Raising the Torah
Blessing before Haftarah
Haftarah
Blessing after Haftarah
Community Blessings
Returning Torah to Ark

Ein-kamocha va·elohim, Adonai,	אֵין־כָּמְוֹךָ בָאֱלֹהִים, אֲדֹנָי,
v'ein k'maasecha.	וְאֵין כְּמַעֲשֶׂיךָ.
Malchut'cha malchut kol-olamim;	מַלְכוּתְךָ מַלְכוּת כָּל־עֹלָמִים,
umemshalt'cha b'chol-dor vador.	וּמֶמְשַׁלְתְּךָ בְּכָל־דּוֹר וָדֹר.
Adonai melech.	יְיָ מֶלֶךְ,
Adonai malach.	יְיָ מָלָךְ,
Adonai yimloch l'olam va·ed.	יְיָ יִמְלֹךְ לְעֹלָם וָעֶד.
Adonai oz l'amo yitein,	יְיָ עֹז לְעַמּוֹ יִתֵּן,
Adonai y'vareich et-amo vashalom.	יְיָ יְבָרֵךְ אֶת־עַמּוֹ בַשָּׁלוֹם.

Incomparable One —
Your deeds unsurpassed, Your sovereignty everlasting.
You guide and govern through all generations.
Adonai —
sovereign of this day.
sovereign of all days, past and future.
Adonai — sovereign of time:
Bestow strength upon our people.
Bless our people with peace.

Av harachamim,	אַב הָרַחֲמִים,
heitivah virtzoncha et-Tziyon;	הֵיטִיבָה בִרְצוֹנְךָ אֶת־צִיּוֹן,
tivneh chomot Y'rushalayim.	תִּבְנֶה חוֹמוֹת יְרוּשָׁלָיִם.
Ki v'cha l'vad batachnu —	כִּי בְךָ לְבַד בָּטָחְנוּ,
Melech El ram v'nisa,	מֶלֶךְ אֵל רָם וְנִשָּׂא,
adon olamim.	אֲדוֹן עוֹלָמִים.

Compassionate One —
let goodness in Zion be Your will,
the building of Jerusalem Your wish.
We place our faith in You alone,
in God, our Strength Eternal,
existing beyond time and space.

INCOMPARABLE אֵין־כָּמְוֹךָ, Psalm 86:8.
YOU GUIDE מַלְכוּתְךָ, Psalm 145:13.
BESTOW STRENGTH יְיָ עֹז, Psalm 29:11.
LET GOODNESS הֵיטִיבָה, Psalm 51:20.

יְיָ, יְיָ, אֵל רַחוּם וְחַנּוּן, *Adonai, Adonai — El rachum v'chanun;*
אֶרֶךְ אַפַּיִם וְרַב־חֶסֶד וֶאֱמֶת, *erech apayim, v'rav-chesed ve·emet;*
נֹצֵר חֶסֶד לָאֲלָפִים, *notzeir chesed laalafim;*
נֹשֵׂא עָוֹן וָפֶשַׁע וְחַטָּאָה וְנַקֵּה. *nosei avon vafesha v'chataah; v'nakeih.*

Adonai, Adonai —
God, compassionate, gracious, endlessly patient, loving, and true;
showing mercy to the thousandth generation;
forgiving evil, defiance, and wrongdoing; granting pardon.

שְׁמַע יִשְׂרָאֵל, *Sh'ma, Yisrael:*
יְיָ אֱלֹהֵינוּ, יְיָ אֶחָד. *Adonai Eloheinu, Adonai echad!*

Listen, Israel: Adonai is our God, Adonai is One!

אֶחָד אֱלֹהֵינוּ, גָּדוֹל אֲדוֹנֵינוּ, *Echad Eloheinu, gadol adoneinu,*
קָדוֹשׁ וְנוֹרָא שְׁמוֹ. *kadosh v'nora sh'mo.*

One and magnificent is our God; God's name is holy, inspiring awe.

גַּדְּלוּ לַייָ אִתִּי, *Gad'lu l'Adonai iti;*
וּנְרוֹמְמָה שְׁמוֹ יַחְדָּו. *unrom'mah sh'mo yachdav.*

Exalt the Eternal with me; let us extol God's name together.

לְךָ, יְיָ, הַגְּדֻלָּה וְהַגְּבוּרָה *L'cha, Adonai, hag'dulah, v'hag'vurah,*
וְהַתִּפְאֶרֶת וְהַנֵּצַח וְהַהוֹד, *v'hatiferet, v'haneitzach, v'hahod —*
כִּי־כֹל בַּשָּׁמַיִם וּבָאָרֶץ. *ki-chol bashamayim uvaaretz.*
לְךָ, יְיָ, הַמַּמְלָכָה *L'cha, Adonai, hamamlachah*
וְהַמִּתְנַשֵּׂא, לְכֹל לְרֹאשׁ. *v'hamitnasei, l'chol l'rosh.*

Yours, Adonai, are greatness, might, splendor, triumph, and majesty —
yes, all that is in heaven and earth; to You, God, belong majesty and
preeminence above all.

Hakafah Selections

רוֹמְמוּ יְיָ אֱלֹהֵינוּ,
וְהִשְׁתַּחֲווּ לַהֲדֹם רַגְלָיו,
קָדוֹשׁ הוּא.
רוֹמְמוּ יְיָ אֱלֹהֵינוּ,
וְהִשְׁתַּחֲווּ לְהַר קָדְשׁוֹ,
כִּי־קָדוֹשׁ יְיָ אֱלֹהֵינוּ.

Rom'mu Adonai Eloheinu,
v'hishtachavu lahadom raglav —
kadosh hu.
Rom'mu Adonai Eloheinu,
v'hishtachavu l'har kodsho —
ki-kadosh Adonai Eloheinu.

Exalt Adonai our God — bow to God's sovereignty;
bow toward God's holy mountain, for Adonai our God is holy.

עַל שְׁלֹשָׁה דְבָרִים הָעוֹלָם עוֹמֵד:
עַל הַתּוֹרָה,
וְעַל הָעֲבוֹדָה,
וְעַל גְּמִילוּת חֲסָדִים.

Al sh'loshah d'varim haolam omeid:
al haTorah,
v'al haavodah,
v'al g'milut chasadim.

Upon three things the world stands:
study of Torah, worship of God, and acts of human kindness.

יִשְׂרָאֵל וְאוֹרַיְתָא וְקוּדְשָׁא בְּרִיךְ הוּא
חַד הוּא.
תּוֹרָה אוֹרָה, הַלְלוּיָהּ.

Yisrael v'Oraita v'Kudsha, b'rich hu,
chad hu!
Torah orah — hal'luyah!

Israel, Torah, and our blessed, holy God
are one and unique! Torah is light — All sing God's praise!

Torah readings begin on pages 266 and 269.
Alternative Torah readings begin on pages 332 and 337.

ADONAI, ADONAI יְיָ, יְיָ (*facing page*), Exodus 34:6–7.

SH'MA שְׁמַע (*facing page*), Deuteronomy 6:4.

HAKAFAH. Literally, "encircling" the sanctuary. The Torah ritual is a dramatic reenactment of the Revelation at Sinai. As the people stood at Mount Sinai to receive Torah, so the congregation stands as the scrolls are taken from the ark. Carrying the scrolls through the congregation recalls the Israelites' journey through the wilderness. And just as Moses held aloft the stone tablets, so the Torah is lifted up after the reading. "Bow toward God's holy mountain" refers to Mount Zion, where the divine words were housed in the Temple.

UPON THREE THINGS עַל שְׁלֹשָׁה דְבָרִים, Mishnah *Avot* 1:2.

Blessing Before the Torah Reading

בָּרְכוּ אֶת יְיָ הַמְבֹרָךְ.
Bar'chu et Adonai hamvorach.

Congregation responds:

בָּרוּךְ יְיָ הַמְבֹרָךְ לְעוֹלָם וָעֶד.
Baruch Adonai hamvorach l'olam va·ed.

בָּרוּךְ יְיָ הַמְבֹרָךְ לְעוֹלָם וָעֶד.
Baruch Adonai hamvorach l'olam va·ed.
בָּרוּךְ אַתָּה, יְיָ,
Baruch atah, Adonai,
אֱלֹהֵינוּ מֶלֶךְ הָעוֹלָם,
Eloheinu melech haolam,
אֲשֶׁר בָּחַר־בָּנוּ מִכָּל הָעַמִּים
asher bachar-banu mikol haamim
וְנָתַן־לָנוּ אֶת תּוֹרָתוֹ.
v'natan-lanu et torato.

Bless the Eternal, the Blessed One.

Congregation: Blessed is the Eternal, the Blessed One, now and forever.

Blessed is the Eternal, the Blessed One, now and forever.
Blessed are You, Eternal, our God, supreme Power of the universe,
who embraced us and gave us this Teaching,
having chosen us to embody Torah among the peoples of the earth.

בָּרוּךְ אַתָּה, יְיָ, נוֹתֵן הַתּוֹרָה.
Baruch atah, Adonai, notein haTorah.
Blessed are You, God of eternity, whose gift is Torah.

Blessing After the Torah Reading

בָּרוּךְ אַתָּה, יְיָ,
Baruch atah, Adonai,
אֱלֹהֵינוּ מֶלֶךְ הָעוֹלָם,
Eloheinu melech haolam,
אֲשֶׁר נָתַן־לָנוּ תּוֹרַת אֱמֶת,
asher natan-lanu Torat emet,
וְחַיֵּי עוֹלָם נָטַע בְּתוֹכֵנוּ.
v'chayei olam nata b'tocheinu.

Blessed are You, Eternal, our God, supreme Power of the universe,
who gave us a Teaching of truth and planted within us eternal life.

בָּרוּךְ אַתָּה, יְיָ, נוֹתֵן הַתּוֹרָה.
Baruch atah, Adonai, notein haTorah.
Blessed are You, God of eternity, whose gift is Torah.

Blessing Before the Torah Reading

Source of blessing,
Your presence fills creation.
You have enlightened our path
with the wisdom of Torah,
giving it to the Jewish people
as their particular treasure.
We give You praise, Merciful One,
who gives this Torah to the Jewish people.

Blessing After the Torah Reading

Source of blessing,
Your presence fills creation.
This Torah is a teaching of truth,
and from it comes enduring life
for those who embrace it.
We give You praise, Merciful One,
who gives this Torah to the Jewish people,
for the sake of all humanity.

BLESSING BEFORE THE TORAH READING. In some congregations, people who are not Jewish come to the *bimah* to accompany their Jewish partner or as part of a group honor. The blessings above may be appropriate on such occasions.

WHO GIVES THIS TORAH. The Rabbinic sages viewed Torah as a special gift bestowed on the Jewish people, but emphasized that all people are welcome to partake of the gift and learn. Thus, one midrash explores the question of why Torah was given in the wilderness rather than in the Land of Israel, or in any nation's territory. It answers: "The Torah was given in public, openly, in a free place accessible to all. For had the Torah been given in the Land of Israel, the Israelites could have said to the nations of the world: 'You have no share in it.' But since it was given in the wilderness, publicly and openly, in a place that is free to all, anyone who wishes to accept it may come and accept it" (*M'chilta d'Rabbi Yishmael*, on Exodus 19:2).

Preparing for Birkat HaGomeil — At a Time of Profound Thanks

A teaching of our Sages:
in the presence of the sacred scroll,
we give thanks for the blessings in our lives.

Rav Judah said in the name of Rav:
"Who should offer thanksgiving?
Those who have completed an arduous voyage,
those who have recovered from an illness or injury,
and prisoners who have been set free."

In the midst of the congregation,
we honor those who have come through
times of challenge, difficulty, or danger.

Today we celebrate their survival.
Together we give thanks:
for the resilience of the body,
for the strength of the human spirit;
for the precious gift of life,
experienced with new intensity
when life has been at risk.

RAV JUDAH SAID. Adapted from a passage in the Talmud (*B'rachot* 54b), which is the basis for the blessing known as *Birkat HaGomeil* — a public declaration of thanks recited by those who have survived dangerous experiences. While the Talmud lists specific classes of people who should recite the blessing, anyone who has gone through major surgery, a frightening airplane landing, or any difficult or traumatic experience may recite it. We might also include among "prisoners who have been set free" those who have worked to overcome an addiction or have escaped an abusive relationship.

Birkat HaGomeil — Sharing Thankfulness

Individual prays:

בָּרוּךְ אַתָּה, יְיָ,
אֱלֹהֵינוּ מֶלֶךְ הָעוֹלָם,
הַגּוֹמֵל לְחַיָּבִים טוֹבוֹת,
שֶׁגְּמָלַנִי כָּל טוֹב.

Baruch atah, Adonai,
Eloheinu melech haolam,
hagomeil l'chayavim tovot,
sheg'malani kol tov.

Blessed are You, our God Eternal; Your majesty fills the universe — through Your generosity I have experienced Your goodness.

Congregation responds (for a man):

אָמֵן.
מִי שֶׁגְּמָלְךָ כָּל טוֹב,
הוּא יִגְמָלְךָ כָּל טוֹב סֶלָה.

Amen.
Mi sheg'mal'cha kol tov,
hu yigmolcha kol tov selah.

(for a woman)

אָמֵן.
מִי שֶׁגְּמָלֵךְ כָּל טוֹב,
הוּא יִגְמָלֵךְ כָּל טוֹב סֶלָה.

Amen.
Mi sheg'maleich kol tov,
hu yigmaleich kol tov selah.

(for both, or for men)

אָמֵן.
מִי שֶׁגְּמָלְכֶם כָּל טוֹב,
הוּא יִגְמָלְכֶם כָּל טוֹב סֶלָה.

Amen.
Mi sheg'molchem kol tov,
hu yigmolchem kol tov selah.

(for women)

אָמֵן.
מִי שֶׁגְּמָלְכֶן כָּל טוֹב,
הוּא יִגְמָלְכֶן כָּל טוֹב סֶלָה.

Amen.
Mi sheg'molchen kol tov,
hu yigmolchen kol tov selah.

Amen.
May the Source of goodness bring you goodness at all times.

Blessing for Those Called to the Torah

מִי שֶׁבֵּרַךְ אֲבוֹתֵינוּ וְאִמּוֹתֵינוּ	*Mi shebeirach avoteinu v'imoteinu*
אַבְרָהָם יִצְחָק וְיַעֲקֹב,	*Avraham, Yitzchak, v'Yaakov,*
שָׂרָה, רִבְקָה, רָחֵל וְלֵאָה,	*Sarah, Rivkah, Rachel, v'Leah,*
הוּא יְבָרֵךְ אֶת	*hu y'vareich et*
___ בֶּן ___ בַּעֲבוּר שֶׁעָלָה הַיּוֹם \	*___ ben ___ baavur she·alah hayom /*
___ בַּת ___ בַּעֲבוּר שֶׁעָלְתָה הַיּוֹם \	*___ bat ___ baavur she·al'tah hayom /*
___ מִבֵּית ___ בַּעֲבוּר שֶׁעָלוּ הַיּוֹם \	*___ mibeit ___ baavur she·alu hayom /*
כָּל הַקְּרוּאִים אֲשֶׁר עָלוּ הַיּוֹם	*kol hak'ruim asher alu hayom*
לִכְבוֹד הַמָּקוֹם וְלִכְבוֹד הַתּוֹרָה	*lichvod haMakom v'lichvod haTorah*
[וְלִכְבוֹד הַשַּׁבָּת]	*[v'lichvod haShabbat]*
וְלִכְבוֹד יוֹם הַזִּכָּרוֹן.	*v'lichvod Yom HaZikaron.*
הַקָּדוֹשׁ בָּרוּךְ הוּא	*HaKadosh, baruch hu,*
יִשְׁמְרֵהוּ\יִשְׁמְרֶהָ\יִשְׁמְרֵם	*yishm'reihu/yishm'reha/yishm'reim*
וְיַצִּילֵהוּ\וְיַצִּילֶהָ\וְיַצִּילֵם	*v'yatzileihu/v'yatzileha/v'yatzileim*
מִכָּל צָרָה וְצוּקָה וּמִכָּל נֶגַע וּמַחֲלָה,	*mikol tzarah v'tzukah, umikol nega umachalah,*
וְיִשְׁלַח בְּרָכָה וְהַצְלָחָה	*v'yishlach b'rachah v'hatzlachah*
בְּכָל מַעֲשֵׂה יָדָיו\יָדֶיהָ\יְדֵיהֶם,	*b'chol maaseih yadav/yadeha/y'deihem,*
וְיִכְתְּבֵהוּ\וְיִכְתְּבֶהָ\וְיִכְתְּבֵיהֶם	*v'yicht'veihu/v'yicht'veha/v'yicht'veihem*
וְיַחְתְּמֵהוּ\וְיַחְתְּמֶהָ\וְיַחְתְּמֵם	*v'yicht'meihu/v'yicht'meha/v'yicht'meim*
לְחַיִּים טוֹבִים בְּיוֹם הַזִּכָּרוֹן הַזֶּה	*l'chayim tovim b'Yom HaZikaron hazeh*
עִם כָּל יִשְׂרָאֵל. וְנֹאמַר: אָמֵן.	*im kol Yisrael. V'nomar: Amen.*

May the One who brought blessings to Abraham and Sarah;
to Isaac and Rebecca;
to Jacob, Rachel, and Leah,
bring blessings to ____________, who rise(s) today
to honor God, Torah, [this day of Shabbat,]
and the Day of Remembrance —
the blessing of safety and protection in time of trouble,
the blessing of comfort and healing in time of illness,
the blessing of success and fulfillment in all endeavors.
On this Day of Remembrance,
inscribe and seal him/her/them and all Israel for a life of goodness.
And together we say: *Amen.*

קַבָּלַת הַתּוֹרָה *Kabbalat HaTorah*
שְׁלֹשׁ עֶשְׂרֵה מִדּוֹת *Sh'losh Esreih Midot*
הוֹצָאַת הַתּוֹרָה *Hotzaat HaTorah*
הַקָּפָה *Hakafah*
בִּרְכוֹת הַתּוֹרָה *Birchot HaTorah*
בִּרְכַּת הַגּוֹמֵל *Birkat HaGomeil*
מִי שֶׁבֵּרַךְ לְעוֹלֵי הַתּוֹרָה *Mi Shebeirach L'olei HaTorah*
קְרִיאַת הַתּוֹרָה *K'riat HaTorah*
מִי שֶׁבֵּרַךְ לִרְפוּאָה *Mishebeirach Lirfuah*
הַגְבָּהָה וּגְלִילָה *Hagbahah Uglilah*
בְּרָכָה שֶׁלִּפְנֵי הַהַפְטָרָה *B'rachah Shelifnei HaHaftarah*
קְרִיאַת הַהַפְטָרָה *K'riat HaHaftarah*
בְּרָכָה שֶׁאַחֲרֵי הַהַפְטָרָה *B'rachah She-acharei HaHaftarah*
תְּפִלּוֹת הַקְּהִלָּה *T'filot HaK'hilah*
הַכְנָסַת סֵפֶר תּוֹרָה *Hachnasat Sefer Torah*

A Blessing for Menschlichkeit

May the One who showered blessings on our ancestors
rain blessings on those among us whose everyday deeds are without measure:

all who honor parents and elders with love and respect, patience and sensitivity;
all who give care to loved ones who are ill; and those who accompany the dying;
all who bring their warmth and hope to those who are confined, isolated, feeling despair;
all who say prayers for loved ones and friends; and those whose faith inspires others to pray;
all who go to *shiva minyanim*, console the bereaved, and stay to listen;
all who reach out to the widowed, the divorced, the jobless;
all who welcome guests to Shabbat and holiday tables; and those who share their bread with the hungry;
all who donate to causes that lift up the fallen, heal the sick, and heal the home we share—this earth.
All who notice others, greet newcomers, extend a hand to those with special needs;
and all who open doors to the future by caring for children —
keeping them safe, teaching them trust, helping them cultivate lives of meaning and purpose. . . .

On this Day of Atonement,
may they be inscribed for their worthy deeds;
may they be sealed for their acts of goodness and kindness.
And let us say: *Amen.*

DAY OF RIGOR יוֹם הַדִּין (*facing page*). Or "Day of Accountability" or "Day of Judgment." Nachmanides (1194–ca. 1270) calls Rosh HaShanah "the Day of Judgment with Mercy" and Yom Kippur "the Day of Mercy with Judgment."

MENSCHLICHKEIT. Human decency; a Yiddish term encompassing all the qualities that characterize a *mensch* — a person of fine character.

WHOSE EVERYDAY DEEDS ARE WITHOUT MEASURE. Based on a passage in the Mishnah (*Pei·ah* 1:1): "These are the obligations that are without measure: leaving the corners of the field for the needy; bringing first fruits, pilgrimage to the Temple, deeds of kindness, and studying Torah." The phrase "without measure" means that there is no upper limit to the obligation — these acts should be performed as much as possible, and their value is immeasurable.

THEMES OF TORAH AND HAFTARAH READINGS

We might view our readings from the Torah and Prophets as though they were mounted within a frame: on one side of the frame are the poignant words of *Untaneh Tokef*, "who will live and who will die . . . who by fire and who by water"; and on the other, *Ashamnu* and *Al Cheit*—confessions of failure and wrongdoing, defiance and sin. Seen within this frame, the Torah and haftarah readings are inseparable from the prayers that surround them, resonating with the themes of this morning's liturgy: human frailty and human strength; mortality and morality; the discoveries we make as we grow and mature; obligation and responsibility; and, above all else, the choices that are in our hands, individually and communally.

Two options are presented for the Torah reading on Yom Kippur morning.

Genesis 3–4 sets forth the Bible's story of primordial humankind, which chronicles the move from solitude to family and community. Human beings disobey God and discover good and bad, resulting in loss of innocence and banishment from the paradise of Eden. The core of the reading is the story of Cain: tensions within the family, the human propensity for violence, the first murder (which suggests that all murder is fratricide), guilt, and the impulse to atone—apt themes for reflection on Yom Kippur. In the verses that follow this Torah reading (verses 17–18), Cain marries, fathers a son, and builds a city. Five generations of descendants are named; Cain's life does not end with his crime.

In Deuteronomy 29–30 we experience a stirring moment of communal solidarity, as all Israel stands before God to make a covenantal oath that includes future generations. Reading this passage on Yom Kippur, amidst our own assembly, we ponder the meaning of mitzvah and covenant; and we discover the human power to choose between blessing and curse, life and death. We are inspired and strengthened by Moses' confidence in his people: "You can surely do it."

The haftarah (Isaiah 58)—a prophetic passage that is a later critique of the biblically prescribed observance of Yom Kippur (Leviticus 16 and 23)—comes from Second Isaiah, who both comforted and confronted his people. Dejected and disoriented, the people wonder why their performance of required ritual seems ineffective. They ask: "Why did we fast, and You do not see it?" The prophet preaches the hollowness of routinized self-affliction and fasting in the absence of a just society and righteous acts. God's question (as posed by the prophet) "Is not *this* the fast I desire?" prompts us to make our fast meaningful by sharing our bread with the hungry, freeing the oppressed, and giving shelter to the homeless.

Commentary on the Torah Reading: "You Stand This Day"

God said to Abraham: "I will establish My covenant between Me and you and your generations for an everlasting covenant" (Genesis 17:7). And again, as Moses said to the people: "I make this covenant, with its sanctions, not with you alone, but both with those who are standing here with us this day before Adonai our God and with those who are not with us here this day" (Deuteronomy 29:13–14). Creativity, adequacy, and boldness of spirit were not permitted by God only to those who participated in the founding covenantal moments; rather, they define the on-going vitality of the eternal covenant between God and God's human partners in every generation.

—Rabbi David Hartman (1931–2013)

***"I have put before you** life and death, blessing and curse. Choose life—if you and your offspring would live . . ."* (Deuteronomy 30:19).

Rabbi Eliezer Davidovits (1878–1942, Slovakia) asks the obvious question: "Is there a person who would choose death?" What kind of choice is really being offered here? Wouldn't most everyone prefer life to death, blessing to curse?

Here is his insight: There are two ways to "choose life." The first way is the "I" way. If we want, we can choose to think of ourselves first. We can worry about our needs and our desires and our wishes, and only later will we consider the needs, desires, and wishes of others.

But there is another way to "choose life," another way to live our lives. This is the "you" way. Before we act, before we decide, before we speak, we can choose to think about how our actions, decisions, and words will affect others. We can think about how our behavior will affect future generations, including our own children and grandchildren.

A real choice is in fact being offered. Do we live in a way that supports life in the broadest sense, or do we live in a way that serves only ourselves, only our own narrow interests? This narrow way, this second choice, ultimately leads not to life but to death.

—Rabbi Josh Zweiback (b. 1969)

You Stand This Day (Deuteronomy 29:9–14; 30:1–20)

9 אַתֶּם נִצָּבִים הַיּוֹם כֻּלְּכֶם לִפְנֵי
יְהוָה אֱלֹהֵיכֶם רָאשֵׁיכֶם שִׁבְטֵיכֶם
זִקְנֵיכֶם וְשֹׁטְרֵיכֶם כֹּל אִישׁ יִשְׂרָאֵל:
10 טַפְּכֶם נְשֵׁיכֶם וְגֵרְךָ אֲשֶׁר בְּקֶרֶב
מַחֲנֶיךָ מֵחֹטֵב עֵצֶיךָ עַד שֹׁאֵב
מֵימֶיךָ: 11 לְעָבְרְךָ בִּבְרִית יְהוָה
אֱלֹהֶיךָ וּבְאָלָתוֹ אֲשֶׁר יְהוָה אֱלֹהֶיךָ
כֹּרֵת עִמְּךָ הַיּוֹם: 12 לְמַעַן הָקִים־
אֹתְךָ הַיּוֹם | לוֹ לְעָם וְהוּא יִהְיֶה־לְּךָ
לֵאלֹהִים כַּאֲשֶׁר דִּבֶּר־לָךְ וְכַאֲשֶׁר
נִשְׁבַּע לַאֲבֹתֶיךָ לְאַבְרָהָם לְיִצְחָק
וּלְיַעֲקֹב: 13 וְלֹא אִתְּכֶם לְבַדְּכֶם
אָנֹכִי כֹּרֵת אֶת־הַבְּרִית הַזֹּאת
וְאֶת־הָאָלָה הַזֹּאת: 14 כִּי אֶת־אֲשֶׁר
יֶשְׁנוֹ פֹּה עִמָּנוּ עֹמֵד הַיּוֹם לִפְנֵי
יְהוָה אֱלֹהֵינוּ וְאֵת אֲשֶׁר אֵינֶנּוּ פֹּה
עִמָּנוּ הַיּוֹם:

9 You stand this day, all of you, in the
presence of Adonai your God—your
tribal heads, elders, and officials; every
man, 10 woman, and child of Israel; and
the stranger in the midst of your camp;
from the one who cuts your wood to
the one who draws your water—11 to
enter into the covenant of Adonai your
God, and the oath that Adonai your
God makes with you this day, 12 to
establish you as God's people and to
be your God, as promised to you and
sworn to your ancestors Abraham,
Isaac, and Jacob. 13 And not with you
alone do I make this covenant and this
oath, 14 but with each one who stands
here among us this day in the presence
of Adonai our God, and with each one
who is not here among us this day.

30:1 וְהָיָה כִי־יָבֹאוּ עָלֶיךָ כָּל־
הַדְּבָרִים הָאֵלֶּה הַבְּרָכָה וְהַקְּלָלָה
אֲשֶׁר נָתַתִּי לְפָנֶיךָ וַהֲשֵׁבֹתָ אֶל־
לְבָבֶךָ בְּכָל־הַגּוֹיִם אֲשֶׁר הִדִּיחֲךָ
יְהוָה אֱלֹהֶיךָ שָׁמָּה: 2 וְשַׁבְתָּ עַד־
יְהוָה אֱלֹהֶיךָ וְשָׁמַעְתָּ בְקֹלוֹ כְּכֹל
אֲשֶׁר־אָנֹכִי מְצַוְּךָ הַיּוֹם אַתָּה וּבָנֶיךָ
בְּכָל־לְבָבְךָ וּבְכָל־נַפְשֶׁךָ: 3 וְשָׁב
יְהוָה אֱלֹהֶיךָ אֶת־שְׁבוּתְךָ וְרִחֲמֶךָ
וְשָׁב וְקִבֶּצְךָ מִכָּל־הָעַמִּים אֲשֶׁר
הֱפִיצְךָ יְהוָה אֱלֹהֶיךָ שָׁמָּה: 4 אִם־
יִהְיֶה נִדַּחֲךָ בִּקְצֵה הַשָּׁמַיִם מִשָּׁם

30:1 When all these things happen
to you—the blessing and the curse that
I have set before you—and you take
them to heart, among the nations to
which Adonai your God has sent you
away, 2 and you return to Adonai your
God, listening with all your heart and
soul to God's voice, to everything I
command you this day, you and your
children—3 then Adonai your God
will bring you back from captivity and
take you back in love. Adonai your
God will return to gather you from all
the nations where you were scattered.
4 Should you be banished beyond the

קַבָּלַת הַתּוֹרָה *Kabbalat HaTorah*
שְׁלֹשׁ עֶשְׂרֵה מִדּוֹת *Sh'losh Esreih Midot*
הוֹצָאַת הַתּוֹרָה *Hotzaat HaTorah*
הַקָּפָה *Hakafah*
בִּרְכוֹת הַתּוֹרָה *Birchot HaTorah*
בִּרְכַּת הַגּוֹמֵל *Birkat HaGomeil*
מִי שֶׁבֵּרַךְ לְעוֹלֵי הַתּוֹרָה *Mi Shebeirach L'olei HaTorah*
קְרִיאַת הַתּוֹרָה *K'riat HaTorah*
מִי שֶׁבֵּרַךְ לִרְפוּאָה *Mishebeirach Lirfuah*
הַגְבָּהָה וּגְלִילָה *Hagbahah Uglilah*
בְּרָכָה שֶׁלִּפְנֵי הַהַפְטָרָה *B'rachah Shelifnei HaHaftarah*
קְרִיאַת הַהַפְטָרָה *K'riat HaHaftarah*
בְּרָכָה שֶׁאַחֲרֵי הַהַפְטָרָה *B'rachah She-acharei HaHaftarah*
תְּפִלּוֹת הַקְּהִלָּה *T'filot HaK'hilah*
הַכְנָסַת סֵפֶר תּוֹרָה *Hachnasat Sefer Torah*

horizon, even from there Adonai your God will gather you up and take you back. 5 And Adonai your God will bring you to the land of your ancestors, making it yours and giving you goodness and numbers greater than theirs. 6 Then Adonai your God will open your heart and the hearts of your children to love Adonai your God with all your heart and all your being—for the sake of your life. 7 Adonai your God will afflict your enemies and those who pursue you with hate. 8 But you, you will return, heeding the voice of Adonai, obedient to all the mitzvot I command you this day. 9 And Adonai your God will bestow abundance through the work of your hands and the fruit of your womb, through the fruit of your livestock and the fruit of your land. Once again Adonai will rejoice in your well-being, as in your ancestors' before you, 10 because you will heed the voice of Adonai your God, keep the mitzvot and the laws inscribed in this book of the Torah, and return with all your heart and all your being to Adonai your God.

11 For this mitzvah, which I command you this day, is neither beyond you nor far away. 12 It is not in heaven, causing you to say: "Who will go up to heaven on our behalf, get it for us, and let us hear it, that we may do it?" 13 And it is not across the sea, causing you to say: "Who will cross the sea on our behalf, get it for us, and let us hear it, that we may do it?" 14 No, this is so very near to you—in your mouth and

יְקַבֶּצְךָ֣ יְהֹוָ֣ה אֱלֹהֶ֔יךָ וּמִשָּׁ֖ם יִקָּחֶֽךָ׃

5 וֶהֱבִֽיאֲךָ֞ יְהֹוָ֣ה אֱלֹהֶ֗יךָ אֶל־הָאָ֛רֶץ אֲשֶׁר־יָרְשׁ֥וּ אֲבֹתֶ֖יךָ וִֽירִשְׁתָּ֑הּ וְהֵיטִֽבְךָ֥ וְהִרְבְּךָ֖ מֵאֲבֹתֶֽיךָ׃

6 וּמָ֞ל יְהֹוָ֧ה אֱלֹהֶ֛יךָ אֶת־לְבָבְךָ֖ וְאֶת־לְבַ֣ב זַרְעֶ֑ךָ לְאַהֲבָ֞ה אֶת־יְהֹוָ֧ה אֱלֹהֶ֛יךָ בְּכׇל־לְבָבְךָ֥ וּבְכׇל־נַפְשְׁךָ֖ לְמַ֥עַן חַיֶּֽיךָ׃ 7 וְנָתַן֙ יְהֹוָ֣ה אֱלֹהֶ֔יךָ אֵ֥ת כׇּל־הָאָל֖וֹת הָאֵ֑לֶּה עַל־אֹיְבֶ֥יךָ וְעַל־שֹׂנְאֶ֖יךָ אֲשֶׁ֥ר רְדָפֽוּךָ׃ 8 וְאַתָּ֣ה תָשׁ֔וּב וְשָׁמַעְתָּ֖ בְּק֣וֹל יְהֹוָ֑ה וְעָשִׂ֙יתָ֙ אֶת־כׇּל־מִצְוֺתָ֔יו אֲשֶׁ֛ר אָנֹכִ֥י מְצַוְּךָ֖ הַיּֽוֹם׃ 9 וְהוֹתִֽירְךָ֩ יְהֹוָ֨ה אֱלֹהֶ֜יךָ בְּכֹ֣ל ׀ מַעֲשֵׂ֣ה יָדֶ֗ךָ בִּפְרִ֨י בִטְנְךָ֜ וּבִפְרִ֧י בְהֶמְתְּךָ֛ וּבִפְרִ֥י אַדְמָתְךָ֖ לְטֹבָ֑ה כִּ֣י ׀ יָשׁ֣וּב יְהֹוָ֗ה לָשׂ֤וּשׂ עָלֶ֙יךָ֙ לְט֔וֹב כַּאֲשֶׁר־שָׂ֖שׂ עַל־אֲבֹתֶֽיךָ׃ 10 כִּ֣י תִשְׁמַ֗ע בְּקוֹל֙ יְהֹוָ֣ה אֱלֹהֶ֔יךָ לִשְׁמֹ֤ר מִצְוֺתָיו֙ וְחֻקֹּתָ֔יו הַכְּתוּבָ֕ה בְּסֵ֖פֶר הַתּוֹרָ֣ה הַזֶּ֑ה כִּ֤י תָשׁוּב֙ אֶל־יְהֹוָ֣ה אֱלֹהֶ֔יךָ בְּכׇל־לְבָבְךָ֖ וּבְכׇל־נַפְשֶֽׁךָ׃

11 כִּ֚י הַמִּצְוָ֣ה הַזֹּ֔את אֲשֶׁ֛ר אָנֹכִ֥י מְצַוְּךָ֖ הַיּ֑וֹם לֹֽא־נִפְלֵ֥את הִוא֙ מִמְּךָ֔ וְלֹ֥א רְחֹקָ֖ה הִֽוא׃ 12 לֹ֣א בַשָּׁמַ֖יִם הִ֑וא לֵאמֹ֗ר מִ֣י יַעֲלֶה־לָּ֤נוּ הַשָּׁמַ֙יְמָה֙ וְיִקָּחֶ֣הָ לָּ֔נוּ וְיַשְׁמִעֵ֥נוּ אֹתָ֖הּ וְנַעֲשֶֽׂנָּה׃ 13 וְלֹֽא־מֵעֵ֥בֶר לַיָּ֖ם הִ֑וא לֵאמֹ֗ר מִ֣י יַעֲבׇר־לָ֜נוּ אֶל־עֵ֤בֶר הַיָּם֙ וְיִקָּחֶ֣הָ לָּ֔נוּ וְיַשְׁמִעֵ֥נוּ אֹתָ֖הּ וְנַעֲשֶֽׂנָּה׃ 14 כִּֽי־קָר֥וֹב אֵלֶ֛יךָ הַדָּבָ֖ר מְאֹ֑ד בְּפִ֥יךָ וּבִלְבָבְךָ֖ לַעֲשֹׂתֽוֹ׃

15 רְאֵ֨ה נָתַ֤תִּי לְפָנֶ֙יךָ֙ הַיּ֔וֹם אֶת־

הַֽחַיִּ֖ים וְאֶת־הַטּ֑וֹב וְאֶת־הַמָּ֖וֶת
וְאֶת־הָרָֽע׃ 16 אֲשֶׁ֨ר אָנֹכִ֣י מְצַוְּךָ֮
הַיּוֹם֒ לְאַהֲבָ֞ה אֶת־יהוָ֤ה אֱלֹהֶ֙יךָ֙
לָלֶ֣כֶת בִּדְרָכָ֔יו וְלִשְׁמֹ֛ר מִצְוֺתָ֥יו
וְחֻקֹּתָ֖יו וּמִשְׁפָּטָ֑יו וְחָיִ֣יתָ וְרָבִ֔יתָ
וּבֵֽרַכְךָ֙ יהוָ֣ה אֱלֹהֶ֔יךָ בָּאָ֕רֶץ אֲשֶׁר־
אַתָּ֥ה בָא־שָׁ֖מָּה לְרִשְׁתָּֽהּ׃ 17 וְאִם־
יִפְנֶ֥ה לְבָבְךָ֖ וְלֹ֣א תִשְׁמָ֑ע וְנִדַּחְתָּ֗
וְהִשְׁתַּחֲוִ֛יתָ לֵאלֹהִ֥ים אֲחֵרִ֖ים
וַעֲבַדְתָּֽם׃ 18 הִגַּ֤דְתִּי לָכֶם֙ הַיּ֔וֹם כִּ֥י
אָבֹ֖ד תֹּאבֵד֑וּן לֹא־תַאֲרִיכֻ֤ן יָמִים֙
עַל־הָ֣אֲדָמָ֔ה אֲשֶׁ֨ר אַתָּ֤ה עֹבֵר֙
אֶת־הַיַּרְדֵּ֔ן לָב֥וֹא שָׁ֖מָּה לְרִשְׁתָּֽהּ׃
19 הַעִדֹ֨תִי בָכֶ֣ם הַיּוֹם֮ אֶת־הַשָּׁמַ֣יִם
וְאֶת־הָאָרֶץ֒ הַחַיִּ֤ים וְהַמָּ֙וֶת֙ נָתַ֣תִּי
לְפָנֶ֔יךָ הַבְּרָכָ֖ה וְהַקְּלָלָ֑ה וּבָֽחַרְתָּ֙
בַּֽחַיִּ֔ים לְמַ֥עַן תִּחְיֶ֖ה אַתָּ֥ה וְזַרְעֶֽךָ׃
20 לְאַהֲבָה֙ אֶת־יהוָ֣ה אֱלֹהֶ֔יךָ לִשְׁמֹ֥עַ
בְּקֹל֖וֹ וּלְדָבְקָה־ב֑וֹ כִּ֣י ה֤וּא חַיֶּ֙יךָ֙
וְאֹ֣רֶךְ יָמֶ֔יךָ לָשֶׁ֣בֶת עַל־הָאֲדָמָ֗ה
אֲשֶׁ֨ר נִשְׁבַּ֧ע יהוָ֛ה לַאֲבֹתֶ֛יךָ
לְאַבְרָהָ֛ם לְיִצְחָ֥ק וּֽלְיַעֲקֹ֖ב לָתֵ֥ת
לָהֶֽם׃

in your heart—that you can surely do
it. 15 Behold, this day I place before you
life and well-being, death and hard-
ship, 16 in that I command you this day
to love Adonai and walk in the ways
of your God—to observe the mitzvot,
laws, and judgments—so you may live
and flourish, blessed by Adonai your
God in the land that is about to be
yours. 17 But if you turn away, refusing
to listen—and, going astray, bow down
to other gods and serve them—18 I tell
you now: you will perish; yes, you will
perish. And you will not last long in
the land you are crossing the Jordan to
possess. 19 This day I call heaven and
earth to witness regarding you: life and
death I have set before you, blessing
and curse. Choose life—so that you
and your children may live—20 by
loving, obeying, and staying close to
Adonai your God. For God gives you
life and length of days to dwell upon
the land that Adonai swore to your
ancestors Abraham, Isaac, and Jacob.

The First Human Family and Its Struggles (Genesis 3:22–4:16)

22 And Adonai Elohim said: "Behold,
the human beings have become like us,
with knowledge of good and bad—and
now they might even take fruit from
the Tree of Life, eat it, and live forever."
23 So Adonai Elohim banished them
from the Garden of Eden to work the
ground from which they were taken,
24 forced them to leave, and, to the east
of Eden, stationed cherubim with a
flaming, whirling sword to guard the
way to the Tree of Life.

4:1 Now the human being knew
Chava, his wife, and she became pregnant. And she gave birth to Cain and
said: "With Adonai I have made a
human being." 2 And she went on to
give birth to his brother Abel. And
Abel shepherded flocks while Cain
tilled the soil. 3 After some time, Cain
brought to Adonai an offering from his
harvest; 4 and Abel, too, brought the
choicest and fattest of his flock. Adonai
looked favorably on Abel and his offering, 5 but not on Cain and his offering.
So Cain was furious, and crestfallen.
6 And Adonai said to Cain: "Why are
you furious, and why so downcast?
7 Would it not be better to rise above
this? And if you do not do better, sin

22 וַיֹּ֣אמֶר ׀ יְהוָ֣ה אֱלֹהִ֗ים הֵ֤ן הָֽאָדָם֙
הָיָה֙ כְּאַחַ֣ד מִמֶּ֔נּוּ לָדַ֖עַת ט֣וֹב וָרָ֑ע
וְעַתָּ֣ה ׀ פֶּן־יִשְׁלַ֣ח יָד֗וֹ וְלָקַח֙ גַּ֚ם
מֵעֵ֣ץ הַֽחַיִּ֔ים וְאָכַ֖ל וָחַ֥י לְעֹלָֽם׃
23 וַיְשַׁלְּחֵ֛הוּ יְהוָ֥ה אֱלֹהִ֖ים מִגַּן־עֵ֑דֶן
לַֽעֲבֹד֙ אֶת־הָ֣אֲדָמָ֔ה אֲשֶׁ֥ר לֻקַּ֖ח
מִשָּֽׁם׃ 24 וַיְגָ֖רֶשׁ אֶת־הָֽאָדָ֑ם וַיַּשְׁכֵּן֩
מִקֶּ֨דֶם לְגַן־עֵ֜דֶן אֶת־הַכְּרֻבִ֗ים וְאֵ֨ת
לַ֤הַט הַחֶ֙רֶב֙ הַמִּתְהַפֶּ֔כֶת לִשְׁמֹ֕ר
אֶת־דֶּ֖רֶךְ עֵ֥ץ הַֽחַיִּֽים׃

4:1 וְהָ֣אָדָ֔ם יָדַ֖ע אֶת־חַוָּ֣ה אִשְׁתּ֑וֹ
וַתַּ֙הַר֙ וַתֵּ֣לֶד אֶת־קַ֔יִן וַתֹּ֕אמֶר קָנִ֥יתִי
אִ֖ישׁ אֶת־יְהוָֽה׃ 2 וַתֹּ֣סֶף לָלֶ֔דֶת אֶת־
אָחִ֖יו אֶת־הָ֑בֶל וַֽיְהִי־הֶ֙בֶל֙ רֹ֣עֵה
צֹ֔אן וְקַ֕יִן הָיָ֖ה עֹבֵ֥ד אֲדָמָֽה׃ 3 וַֽיְהִ֖י
מִקֵּ֣ץ יָמִ֑ים וַיָּבֵ֨א קַ֜יִן מִפְּרִ֧י הָֽאֲדָמָ֛ה
מִנְחָ֖ה לַֽיהוָֽה׃ 4 וְהֶ֨בֶל הֵבִ֥יא גַם־
ה֛וּא מִבְּכֹר֥וֹת צֹאנ֖וֹ וּמֵֽחֶלְבֵהֶ֑ן
וַיִּ֣שַׁע יְהוָ֔ה אֶל־הֶ֖בֶל וְאֶל־מִנְחָתֽוֹ׃
5 וְאֶל־קַ֥יִן וְאֶל־מִנְחָת֖וֹ לֹ֣א שָׁעָ֑ה
וַיִּ֤חַר לְקַ֙יִן֙ מְאֹ֔ד וַֽיִּפְּל֖וּ פָּנָֽיו׃
6 וַיֹּ֥אמֶר יְהוָ֖ה אֶל־קָ֑יִן לָ֚מָּה חָ֣רָה
לָ֔ךְ וְלָ֖מָּה נָפְל֥וּ פָנֶֽיךָ׃ 7 הֲל֤וֹא אִם־

---

24. **CHERUBIM** הַכְּרֻבִים. These celestial creatures — part-human, part-animal, part-bird — have adorned the arks in synagogues, to symbolize "a return to the closeness with the deity that is lost here." (Richard Elliott Friedman, b. 1946)

1. **CHAVA** חַוָּה. Eve: *chavah* is the feminine form of the word *chai* (life). (Richard Elliott Friedman)

1. **CAIN**. The name (Heb. *kayin*) is a pun on "I made" (Heb. *kaniti*).

תֵּיטִיב֙ שְׂאֵ֔ת וְאִם֙ לֹ֣א תֵיטִ֔יב לַפֶּ֖תַח
חַטָּ֣את רֹבֵ֑ץ וְאֵלֶ֙יךָ֙ תְּשׁ֣וּקָת֔וֹ וְאַתָּ֖ה
תִּמְשָׁל־בּֽוֹ׃ 8 וַיֹּ֥אמֶר קַ֖יִן אֶל־הֶ֣בֶל
אָחִ֑יו וַֽיְהִי֙ בִּהְיוֹתָ֣ם בַּשָּׂדֶ֔ה וַיָּ֥קָם
קַ֛יִן אֶל־הֶ֥בֶל אָחִ֖יו וַיַּהַרְגֵֽהוּ׃
9 וַיֹּ֤אמֶר יהוה֙ אֶל־קַ֔יִן אֵ֖י הֶ֣בֶל
אָחִ֑יךָ וַיֹּ֙אמֶר֙ לֹ֣א יָדַ֔עְתִּי הֲשֹׁמֵ֥ר
אָחִ֖י אָנֹֽכִי׃ 10 וַיֹּ֖אמֶר מֶ֣ה עָשִׂ֑יתָ
ק֚וֹל דְּמֵ֣י אָחִ֔יךָ צֹעֲקִ֥ים אֵלַ֖י מִן־
הָאֲדָמָֽה׃ 11 וְעַתָּ֖ה אָר֣וּר אָ֑תָּה
מִן־הָֽאֲדָמָה֙ אֲשֶׁ֣ר פָּצְתָ֣ה אֶת־פִּ֔יהָ
לָקַ֛חַת אֶת־דְּמֵ֥י אָחִ֖יךָ מִיָּדֶֽךָ׃ 12 כִּ֤י
תַעֲבֹד֙ אֶת־הָ֣אֲדָמָ֔ה לֹֽא־תֹסֵ֥ף תֵּת־
כֹּחָ֖הּ לָ֑ךְ נָ֥ע וָנָ֖ד תִּהְיֶ֥ה בָאָֽרֶץ׃
13 וַיֹּ֥אמֶר קַ֖יִן אֶל־יהוָ֑ה גָּד֥וֹל
עֲוֺנִ֖י מִנְּשֹֽׂא׃ 14 הֵן֩ גֵּרַ֨שְׁתָּ אֹתִ֜י
הַיּ֗וֹם מֵעַל֙ פְּנֵ֣י הָאֲדָמָ֔ה וּמִפָּנֶ֖יךָ
אֶסָּתֵ֑ר וְהָיִ֜יתִי נָ֤ע וָנָד֙ בָּאָ֔רֶץ וְהָיָ֥ה
כָל־מֹצְאִ֖י יַהַרְגֵֽנִי׃
15 וַיֹּ֧אמֶר ל֣וֹ יהוה לָכֵן֙ כָּל־הֹרֵ֣ג קַ֔יִן
שִׁבְעָתַ֖יִם יֻקָּ֑ם וַיָּ֨שֶׂם יהוָ֤ה לְקַ֙יִן֙
א֔וֹת לְבִלְתִּ֥י הַכּוֹת־אֹת֖וֹ כָּל־מֹצְאֽוֹ׃
16 וַיֵּ֥צֵא קַ֖יִן מִלִּפְנֵ֣י יהוָ֑ה וַיֵּ֥שֶׁב
בְּאֶֽרֶץ־נ֖וֹד קִדְמַת־עֵֽדֶן׃

crouches like a beast at the door: you are what it craves; and yet—you can overcome it." 8 And Cain said to Abel his brother: ["Let us go out to the field."] And when they were in the field, Cain attacked Abel his brother, and killed him.

9 And Adonai said to Cain: "Where is Abel your brother?" And he said: "I do not know. Am I my brother's keeper?" 10 And Adonai said: "What have you done? Your brother's blood cries out to Me from the earth. 11 And now you are cursed by the very earth that opened its mouth to take your brother's blood from your hand. 12 When you till the soil it will no longer bring forth crops. Homeless, you will wander the earth."

13 Then said Cain to Adonai: "My punishment is more than I can bear. 14 You have driven me, this day, from the face of the earth. Hidden from Your presence, I am a homeless wanderer on the earth. Whoever finds me will kill me." 15 "Therefore," said Adonai to him, "one who kills Cain will be avenged seven times over." And Adonai gave Cain a sign to stop anyone who found him from killing him. 16 Cain left the presence of Adonai and lived in the land of nomads, east of Eden.

8. **"Let us go out to the field."** Apparently due to a scribal error, this key phrase is missing from the Masoretic text of the Hebrew Bible; but it appears in the ancient Samaritan, Greek, and Latin translations.

Welcoming the Torah
God's Thirteen Attributes
Bringing Forth the Torah
The Torah in Our Midst
Torah Blessings
Thanksgiving Blessing
Blessing for the Aliyah
Torah Reading
Prayer for Healing
Raising the Torah
Blessing before Haftarah
Haftarah
Blessing after Haftarah
Community Blessings
Returning Torah to Ark

Prayer for Healing

Mi shebeirach avoteinu v'imoteinu	מִי שֶׁבֵּרַךְ אֲבוֹתֵֽינוּ וְאִמּוֹתֵֽינוּ
Avraham, Yitzchak, v'Yaakov,	אַבְרָהָם יִצְחָק וְיַעֲקֹב,
Sarah, Rivkah, Rachel, v'Leah,	שָׂרָה רִבְקָה רָחֵל וְלֵאָה,
hu y'vareich virapei	הוּא יְבָרֵךְ וִירַפֵּא
et hacholim: ____________.	אֶת הַחוֹלִים: __________.
HaKadosh, barukh hu, yimalei rachamim aleihem,	הַקָּדוֹשׁ בָּרוּךְ הוּא יִמָּלֵא רַחֲמִים עֲלֵיהֶם,
l'hachalimam ulrapotam,	לְהַחֲלִימָם וּלְרַפֹּאתָם,
l'hachazikam ulhachayotam;	לְהַחֲזִיקָם וּלְהַחֲיוֹתָם,
v'yishlach lahem m'heirah r'fuah sh'leimah,	וְיִשְׁלַח לָהֶם מְהֵרָה רְפוּאָה שְׁלֵמָה,
b'toch sh'ar hacholim —	בְּתוֹךְ שְׁאָר הַחוֹלִים,
r'fuat hanefesh,	רְפוּאַת הַנֶּֽפֶשׁ,
urfuat haguf —	וּרְפוּאַת הַגּוּף,
hashta baagala uvizman kariv.	הַשְׁתָּא בַּעֲגָלָא וּבִזְמַן קָרִיב.
V'nomar: Amen.	וְנֹאמַר: אָמֵן.

May the One who brought blessings
to our fathers Abraham, Isaac, and Jacob,
and to our mothers Sarah, Rebecca, Rachel, and Leah,
bring the blessing of health
to those who are ill: ______________.
May the Holy One — blessed source of life and healing —
sustain and strengthen them with compassion,
and restore them to full health without delay.
For all who struggle against illness,
let renewal of spirit and renewal of body come soon.
And together we say: *Amen.*

Heal Us Now

רְפָאֵנוּ יְיָ וְנֵרָפֵא, — *R'fa·einu, Adonai, v'neirafei;*
הוֹשִׁיעֵנוּ וְנִוָּשֵׁעָה. — *hoshi·einu v'nivashei·ah.*
אֵל קָרוֹב לְכָל קֹרְאָיו. — *El karov l'chol korav.*
אַךְ קָרוֹב לִירֵאָיו יִשְׁעוֹ. — *Ach karov lirei·av yisho.*

We pray for healing of the body
we pray for healing of the soul
for strength of flesh and mind and spirit
we pray to once again be whole.

REFRAIN

אֵל נָא רְפָא נָא. — *El na r'fa na.*

Oh, please, heal us now.

רְפוּאַת הַנֶּפֶשׁ וּרְפוּאַת הַגּוּף — *R'fuat hanefesh urfuat haguf,*
רְפוּאָה שְׁלֵמָה. — *r'fuah sh'leimah.*

Heal us now, heal us now.

הוֹשִׁיעָה אֶת־עַמֶּךָ — *Hoshia et-amecha*
וּבָרֵךְ אֶת־נַחֲלָתֶךָ — *uvareich et-nachalatecha*
וּרְעֵם וְנַשְּׂאֵם עַד־הָעוֹלָם. — *ureim v'nas'eim ad haolam.*
מִי שֶׁבֵּרַךְ אֲבוֹתֵינוּ — *Mi shebeirach avoteinu*
מִי שֶׁבֵּרַךְ אִמּוֹתֵינוּ — *Mi shebeirach imoteinu*
אָנָּא יְיָ הוֹשִׁיעָה נָּא. — *ana, Adonai, hoshia na.*

We pray for healing of our people,
we pray for healing of the land
and peace for every race and nation
every child, every woman, every man.

HEAL US NOW. Lyrics by Cantor Leon Sher (b. 1958).

Hear Our Prayer

מִי שֶׁבֵּרַךְ אֲבוֹתֵינוּ אַבְרָהָם יִצְחָק וְיַעֲקֹב,
מִי שֶׁבֵּרַךְ אִמּוֹתֵינוּ שָׂרָה רִבְקָה לֵאָה וְרָחֵל . . .

Mi shebeirach avoteinu—Avraham, Yitzchak, v'Yaakov
Mi shebeirach imoteinu—Sarah, Rivkah, Leah, v'Rachel
May the One who blessed our Mothers
May the One who blessed our Fathers
Hear our prayer and bless us as well.

Bless us with the power of Your healing.
Bless us with the power of Your hope.
May our hearts be filled with understanding
And strengthened by the power of Your love!

Bless us with the vision for tomorrow.
Help us to reach out to those in pain.
May the warmth of friendship ease our sorrow,
Give us courage, give us faith, show us the way!

Mi Shebeirach

מִי שֶׁבֵּרַךְ אֲבוֹתֵינוּ
מְקוֹר הַבְּרָכָה לְאִמּוֹתֵינוּ,

Mi shebeirach avoteinu
M'kor hab'rachah l'imoteinu —
may the Source of strength who blessed the ones before us
help us find the courage to make our lives a blessing
and let us say, Amen.

מִי שֶׁבֵּרַךְ אִמּוֹתֵינוּ
מְקוֹר הַבְּרָכָה לַאֲבוֹתֵינוּ,

Mi shebeirach imoteinu
M'kor hab'rachah laavoteinu —
bless those in need of healing with *r'fuah sh'leimah*,
the renewal of body, the renewal of spirit,
and let us say, Amen.

An additional prayer for healing is on page 340.

HEAR OUR PRAYER. Lyrics by Cantor Lisa L. Levine (b. 1959).
MI SHEBEIRACH. Lyrics by Debbie Friedman (1951–2011) and Rabbi Drorah Setel (b. 1956).

Raising the Torah

We stand before the Tree of Life —
source of our strength;
our comfort, our challenge,
our call to holiness.

We stand before the Tree of Life,
our Torah —
ancient, yet ever-renewed.
Its message is for all people;
its words speak to all generations;
its truths endure and give hope.

Like those who came before us,
we carry the Torah in our midst,
and hold it close.
For those who will come after,
we preserve and cherish its teachings.

This is the Torah:
our gift, our blessing, our responsibility.
In reverence and gratitude,
we stand — all of us this day — before the Tree of Life.

וְזֹאת הַתּוֹרָה אֲשֶׁר־שָׂם מֹשֶׁה
לִפְנֵי בְּנֵי יִשְׂרָאֵל –
עַל־פִּי יְיָ, בְּיַד־מֹשֶׁה.

V'zot haTorah asher-sam Mosheh
lifnei b'nei Yisrael —
al-pi Adonai, b'yad-Mosheh.

This is the Teaching that Moses set before the people of Israel —
at the command of God, by the hand of Moses.

THIS IS THE TEACHING וְזֹאת הַתּוֹרָה, Deuteronomy 4:44.
AT THE COMMAND OF GOD עַל־פִּי יְיָ, Numbers 9:23.

Blessing Before the Haftarah

בָּרוּךְ אַתָּה, יְיָ,
אֱלֹהֵינוּ מֶלֶךְ הָעוֹלָם,
אֲשֶׁר בָּחַר בִּנְבִיאִים טוֹבִים,
וְרָצָה בְדִבְרֵיהֶם הַנֶּאֱמָרִים
בֶּאֱמֶת.

Baruch atah, Adonai,
Eloheinu melech haolam,
asher bachar binvi·im tovim,
v'ratzah v'divreihem hane·emarim
be·emet.

Blessed are You, our God Eternal, supreme Power of the universe, who called forth noble prophets to speak the truth.

בָּרוּךְ אַתָּה, יְיָ, הַבּוֹחֵר בַּתּוֹרָה, וּבְמֹשֶׁה עַבְדּוֹ,
וּבְיִשְׂרָאֵל עַמּוֹ, וּבִנְבִיאֵי הָאֱמֶת וָצֶדֶק.

Baruch atah, Adonai, habocheir baTorah, uvMosheh avdo,
uvYisrael amo, uvinvi·ei ha·emet vatzedek.

Blessed are You, God of eternity, who delights in the Torah;
in Moses, God's servant; in Israel, God's people;
and in prophets of truth and right.

BLESSING BEFORE THE HAFTARAH. Following the Torah reading, on Shabbat and festivals, it is customary to read from the Prophets, the second of the Hebrew Bible's three sections. The Hebrew word *haftarah* comes from a verb meaning "conclude" or "complete," since the prophetic reading completes the reading from the Torah. Sometimes the two are thematically linked; sometimes the haftarah reading relates to the season or festival during which it is read. Unlike the Torah, which is read from a handwritten text on a parchment scroll without vowels or punctuation, the haftarah is usually read from a printed text containing vowels and punctuation.

WHO DELIGHTS IN THE TORAH. Though the Sages viewed the prophetic literature with reverence, the highest degree of sanctity was attached to the Torah, and to Moses — teacher of Torah to the people of Israel. Thus the blessing before the haftarah seeks to link the prophets to Moses, and to see them as his successors in the transmission and interpretation of God's words. In that sense, the Rabbinic sages who composed this blessing saw themselves as continuing the work of the prophets.

Since many of the prophetic teachings date from a time before the Torah was canonized, their ideas sometimes challenge or even contradict the words of the Torah. A good example of this is Isaiah 58 (heard by many congregations on Yom Kippur morning), which makes the radical assertion that the rituals of fasting and self-affliction are not sufficient for atonement.

Commentary on Isaiah 58

Lift up your voice like the shofar! (verse 1)

Isaiah is called by God to address the people with a powerful sermon that will resound throughout the community, as the ram's horn summoned ancient Israel to battle or sacred assembly. His words are intended to be as discordant as a shofar blast, shattering complacency and disrupting the normal ceremonies of the holy day. The prophet notes, ironically, that God pays no heed to the people's ritual acts of fasting and prostration; their hypocritical displays of piety fall, as it were, on deaf ears. Only if these rituals are accompanied by humility, generosity, and care for the needy will God "hear" the worshipers and attend to their call. Thus, the entire passage plays on the theme of crying out and lifting up the voice. How does one effectively communicate with the Holy One? God, it seems, understands and responds to the language of compassion.

Do not hide yourself from your own flesh and blood. . . . (verse 7)

The Torah envisions a community that is based on a sense of social solidarity and common humanity. We are commanded to open our hands to those who are in need. Isaiah's words continue to resonate in our own day, as a warning to the prosperous: If you hide the poor and the working class from your sight, you are apt to forget about them. You become self-obsessed and callous in your personal lives. You make political decisions that suit your own interests and ignore their impact on the majority of your fellow citizens. You live in separate enclaves of privilege, rarely interacting with those who live with far less than you have. And that way of life impoverishes us all.

"Do not hide yourself from your own flesh and blood," says the prophet Isaiah. Do not turn your back on the poor; recognize your kinship with them. For the prophet, we are all one family, united in our humanity; and without one another, our community is not whole.

If you offer your compassion to the hungry. . . . (verse 10)

The verse says "if you offer your *nefesh* to the hungry," which we might translate "if you offer your life to the hungry" or "if you draw out your soul to the hungry." It suggests a profound giving of the self—not only the act of sharing food with those in need but also sharing one's attention, offering empathy, understanding, the warmth of human connection. The eleventh-century commentator Rashi explains the phrase as "offering the consolation of kind words."

קַבָּלַת הַתּוֹרָה
Kabbalat HaTorah

שְׁלֹשׁ עֶשְׂרֵה מִדּוֹת
Sh'losh Esreih Midot

הוֹצָאַת הַתּוֹרָה
Hotzaat HaTorah

הַקָּפָה
Hakafah

בִּרְכוֹת הַתּוֹרָה
Birchot HaTorah

בִּרְכַּת הַגּוֹמֵל
Birkat HaGomeil

מִי שֶׁבֵּרַךְ לְעוֹלֵי הַתּוֹרָה
Mi Shebeirach L'olei HaTorah

קְרִיאַת הַתּוֹרָה
K'riat HaTorah

מִי שֶׁבֵּרַךְ לִרְפוּאָה
Mishebeirach Lirfuah

הַגְבָּהָה וּגְלִילָה
Hagbahah Uglilah

בְּרָכָה שֶׁלִּפְנֵי הַהַפְטָרָה
B'rachah Shelifnei HaHaftarah

קְרִיאַת הַהַפְטָרָה
K'riat HaHaftarah

בְּרָכָה שֶׁאַחֲרֵי הַהַפְטָרָה
B'rachah She-acharei HaHaftarah

תְּפִלּוֹת הַקְּהִלָּה
T'filot HaK'hilah

הַכְנָסַת סֵפֶר תּוֹרָה
Hachnasat Sefer Torah

The Fast I Desire (Isaiah 58:1–14)

Cry from the depth, says God—
do not hold back, lift up your voice like the shofar!
Tell My people their transgression, and the House of Jacob their sin.
2 Yes, they seek Me daily,
as though eager to learn My ways—
as if they were a nation that does what is right
and has not abandoned God's law.
They ask of Me the right way, eager for God's nearness:
3 They say, 'Why did we fast, and You do not see it?
We afflict ourselves, and You do not know it?'
Because even on your fast day you think only of desire,
while oppressing all who work for you.
4 Because your fasting is filled with strife,
and with callous fist you strike.
No, your fasting this day will not lift up your voice before heaven.
5 Is this the fast I desire?
A day to afflict body and soul?
Bowing your head like a reed, covering yourself with sackcloth and ashes?
Do you call this a fast—a day worthy of the favor of Adonai?
6 Is not this the fast I desire—
to break the bonds of injustice and remove the heavy yoke;
to let the oppressed go free and release all those enslaved?
7 Is it not to share your bread with the hungry
and to take the homeless poor into your home,

קְרָא בְגָרוֹן אַל־תַּחְשֹׂךְ
כַּשּׁוֹפָר הָרֵם קוֹלֶךָ
וְהַגֵּד לְעַמִּי פִּשְׁעָם
וּלְבֵית יַעֲקֹב חַטֹּאתָם׃
2 וְאוֹתִי יוֹם יוֹם יִדְרֹשׁוּן
וְדַעַת דְּרָכַי יֶחְפָּצוּן
כְּגוֹי אֲשֶׁר־צְדָקָה עָשָׂה
וּמִשְׁפַּט אֱלֹהָיו לֹא עָזָב
יִשְׁאָלוּנִי מִשְׁפְּטֵי־צֶדֶק
קִרְבַת אֱלֹהִים יֶחְפָּצוּן׃
3 לָמָּה צַּמְנוּ וְלֹא רָאִיתָ
עִנִּינוּ נַפְשֵׁנוּ וְלֹא תֵדָע
הֵן בְּיוֹם צֹמְכֶם
תִּמְצְאוּ־חֵפֶץ
וְכָל־עַצְּבֵיכֶם תִּנְגֹּשׂוּ׃
4 הֵן לְרִיב וּמַצָּה תָּצוּמוּ
וּלְהַכּוֹת בְּאֶגְרֹף רֶשַׁע
לֹא־תָצוּמוּ כַיּוֹם
לְהַשְׁמִיעַ בַּמָּרוֹם קוֹלְכֶם׃
5 הֲכָזֶה יִהְיֶה צוֹם אֶבְחָרֵהוּ
יוֹם עַנּוֹת אָדָם נַפְשׁוֹ
הֲלָכֹף כְּאַגְמֹן רֹאשׁוֹ
וְשַׂק וָאֵפֶר יַצִּיעַ
הֲלָזֶה תִּקְרָא־צוֹם
וְיוֹם רָצוֹן לַיהוָה׃
6 הֲלוֹא זֶה צוֹם אֶבְחָרֵהוּ
פַּתֵּחַ חַרְצֻבּוֹת רֶשַׁע
הַתֵּר אֲגֻדּוֹת מוֹטָה
וְשַׁלַּח רְצוּצִים חָפְשִׁים
וְכָל־מוֹטָה תְּנַתֵּקוּ׃
7 הֲלוֹא פָרֹס לָרָעֵב לַחְמֶךָ
וַעֲנִיִּים מְרוּדִים תָּבִיא בָיִת

כִּֽי־תִרְאֶ֤ה עָרֹם֙ וְכִסִּית֔וֹ
וּמִבְּשָׂרְךָ֖ לֹ֥א תִתְעַלָּֽם׃
8 אָ֣ז יִבָּקַ֤ע כַּשַּׁ֙חַר֙ אוֹרֶ֔ךָ
וַאֲרֻכָתְךָ֖ מְהֵרָ֣ה תִצְמָ֑ח
וְהָלַ֤ךְ לְפָנֶ֙יךָ֙ צִדְקֶ֔ךָ
כְּב֥וֹד יהוה יַאַסְפֶֽךָ׃
9 אָ֤ז תִּקְרָא֙ וַיהוה יַעֲנֶ֔ה
תְּשַׁוַּ֖ע וְיֹאמַ֣ר הִנֵּ֑נִי
אִם־תָּסִ֤יר מִתּֽוֹכְךָ֙ מוֹטָ֔ה
שְׁלַ֥ח אֶצְבַּ֖ע וְדַבֶּר־אָֽוֶן׃
10 וְתָפֵ֤ק לָֽרָעֵב֙ נַפְשֶׁ֔ךָ
וְנֶ֥פֶשׁ נַעֲנָ֖ה תַּשְׂבִּ֑יעַ
וְזָרַ֤ח בַּחֹ֙שֶׁךְ֙ אוֹרֶ֔ךָ
וַאֲפֵלָתְךָ֖ כַּֽצָּהֳרָֽיִם׃
11 וְנָחֲךָ֣ יהוה֮ תָּמִיד֒
וְהִשְׂבִּ֤יעַ בְּצַחְצָחוֹת֙ נַפְשֶׁ֔ךָ
וְעַצְמֹתֶ֖יךָ יַחֲלִ֑יץ
וְהָיִ֙יתָ֙ כְּגַ֣ן רָוֶ֔ה
וּכְמוֹצָ֣א מַ֔יִם אֲשֶׁ֥ר
לֹא־יְכַזְּב֖וּ מֵימָֽיו׃
12 וּבָנ֤וּ מִמְּךָ֙ חָרְב֣וֹת עוֹלָ֔ם
מוֹסְדֵ֥י דוֹר־וָד֖וֹר תְּקוֹמֵ֑ם
וְקֹרָ֤א לְךָ֙ גֹּדֵ֣ר פֶּ֔רֶץ
מְשֹׁבֵ֥ב נְתִיב֖וֹת לָשָֽׁבֶת׃
13 אִם־תָּשִׁ֤יב מִשַּׁבָּת֙ רַגְלֶ֔ךָ
עֲשׂ֥וֹת חֲפָצֶ֖יךָ בְּי֣וֹם קָדְשִׁ֑י
וְקָרָ֨אתָ לַשַּׁבָּ֜ת עֹ֗נֶג
לִקְד֤וֹשׁ יהוה֙ מְכֻבָּ֔ד
וְכִבַּדְתּוֹ֙ מֵעֲשׂ֣וֹת דְּרָכֶ֔יךָ
מִמְּצ֥וֹא חֶפְצְךָ֖ וְדַבֵּ֥ר דָּבָֽר׃
14 אָ֗ז תִּתְעַנַּג֙ עַל־יהוה
וְהִרְכַּבְתִּ֖יךָ עַל־בָּ֣מֳתֵי אָ֑רֶץ
וְהַאֲכַלְתִּ֗יךָ נַחֲלַת֙ יַעֲקֹ֣ב אָבִ֔יךָ
כִּ֛י פִּ֥י יהוה דִּבֵּֽר׃

and never to neglect your own flesh and blood?
8 Then shall your light burst forth like the dawn,
and your wounds shall quickly heal,
your Righteous One leading the way before you,
the Presence of Adonai guarding you from behind.
9 Then, when you call, Adonai will answer,
and, when you cry, will respond "I am here."
If you remove the chains of oppression,
the menacing hand, the malicious word;
10 if you offer your compassion to the hungry and satisfy the suffering—
then shall your light shine through the darkness,
and your night become bright as noon;
11 Adonai will guide you always,
slake your thirst in parched places,
give strength to your bones.
You shall be like a well-watered garden,
an unfailing spring.
12 From you they will rebuild ancient ruins,
lay foundations for ages to come.
And you shall be called
"the one who mends the breach
and brings back the streets for dwelling."
13 If you cease to trample Shabbat,
stop pursuing your affairs on My holy day;
if you call Shabbat "a delight,"
the holy day of Adonai "honored";
and if you honor God by not doing business
or speaking of everyday matters—
14 then shall you take pure delight in Adonai.
I will lift up your journey on earth to the highest of places,
and nourish you from the heritage of your father Jacob.
For thus spoke Adonai!

קַבָּלַת הַתּוֹרָה *Kabbalat HaTorah*
שְׁלֹשׁ עֶשְׂרֵה מִדּוֹת *Sh'losh Esreih Midot*
הוֹצָאַת הַתּוֹרָה *Hotzaat HaTorah*
הַקָּפָה *Hakafah*
בִּרְכוֹת הַתּוֹרָה *Birchot HaTorah*
בִּרְכַּת הַגּוֹמֵל *Birkat HaGomeil*
מִי שֶׁבֵּרַךְ לְעוֹלֵי הַתּוֹרָה *Mi Shebeirach L'olei HaTorah*
קְרִיאַת הַתּוֹרָה *K'riat HaTorah*
מִי שֶׁבֵּרַךְ לִרְפוּאָה *Mishebeirach Lirfuah*
הַגְבָּהָה וּגְלִילָה *Hagbahah Uglilah*
בְּרָכָה שֶׁלִּפְנֵי הַהַפְטָרָה *B'rachah Shelifnei HaHaftarah*
קְרִיאַת הַהַפְטָרָה *K'riat HaHaftarah*
בְּרָכָה שֶׁאַחֲרֵי הַהַפְטָרָה *B'rachah She-acharei HaHaftarah*
תְּפִלּוֹת הַקְּהִלָּה *T'filot HaK'hilah*
הַכְנָסַת סֵפֶר תּוֹרָה *Hachnasat Sefer Torah*

Blessing After the Haftarah

בָּרוּךְ אַתָּה, יְיָ,	*Baruch atah, Adonai,*
אֱלֹהֵינוּ מֶלֶךְ הָעוֹלָם,	*Eloheinu melech haolam,*
צוּר כָּל הָעוֹלָמִים,	*tzur kol haolamim,*
צַדִּיק בְּכָל הַדּוֹרוֹת,	*tzadik b'chol hadorot;*
הָאֵל הַנֶּאֱמָן, הָאוֹמֵר וְעוֹשֶׂה,	*haEl hane·eman, haomeir v'oseh,*
הַמְדַבֵּר וּמְקַיֵּם,	*hamdabeir umkayeim —*
שֶׁכָּל דְּבָרָיו אֱמֶת וָצֶדֶק.	*shekol d'varav emet vatzedek.*
נֶאֱמָן אַתָּה הוּא, יְיָ אֱלֹהֵינוּ,	*Ne·eman atah hu, Adonai Eloheinu,*
וְנֶאֱמָנִים דְּבָרֶיךָ,	*v'ne·emanim d'varecha;*
וְדָבָר אֶחָד מִדְּבָרֶיךָ אָחוֹר לֹא יָשׁוּב רֵיקָם,	*v'davar echad mid'varecha achor lo yashuv reikam —*
כִּי אֵל מֶלֶךְ נֶאֱמָן וְרַחֲמָן אָתָּה.	*ki El melech ne·eman v'rachaman atah.*

Blessed are You, our God Eternal, supreme Power of the universe, Rock of all ages, Source of justice in all generations, God in whom faithfulness abides, whose word is deed, whose every utterance bespeaks truth and righteousness. Faithful are You, our God Eternal, and faithful Your words — not one of them rings hollow — for Yours is a reign of loyalty and compassion.

בָּרוּךְ אַתָּה, יְיָ, הָאֵל הַנֶּאֱמָן בְּכָל דְּבָרָיו.

Baruch atah, Adonai, haEl hane·eman b'chol d'varav.

Blessed are You, God of eternity: You are true to Your word.

רַחֵם עַל צִיּוֹן, כִּי הִיא בֵּית חַיֵּינוּ,	*Racheim al Tziyon, ki hi beit chayeinu;*
וְלַעֲלוּבַת נֶפֶשׁ תּוֹשִׁיעַ בִּמְהֵרָה בְּיָמֵינוּ.	*v'laaluvat nefesh toshia bimheirah v'yameinu.*

Have mercy on Zion, our spiritual home. And, through us, hasten Your redemption of the downcast and disheartened.

בָּרוּךְ אַתָּה, יְיָ, מְשַׂמֵּחַ צִיּוֹן בְּבָנֶיהָ.

Baruch atah, Adonai, m'samei·ach Tziyon b'vaneha.

Blessed are You, God of eternity, who brings joy to Zion through her sons and daughters.

Continued on page 282. (An alternative haftarah blessing begins on the next page.)

Alternative Haftarah Blessing

בָּרוּךְ אַתָּה, יְיָ,	*Baruch atah, Adonai,*
אֱלֹהֵינוּ מֶלֶךְ הָעוֹלָם,	*Eloheinu melech haolam,*
צוּר כָּל הָעוֹלָמִים,	*tzur kol haolamim,*
צַדִּיק בְּכָל הַדּוֹרוֹת,	*tzadik b'chol hadorot;*
הָאֵל הַנֶּאֱמָן, הָאוֹמֵר וְעוֹשֶׂה,	*haEl hane·eman, haomeir v'oseh,*
הַמְדַבֵּר וּמְקַיֵּם,	*hamdabeir umkayeim —*
שֶׁכָּל דְּבָרָיו אֱמֶת וָצֶדֶק.	*shekol d'varav emet vatzedek.*
עַל הַתּוֹרָה, וְעַל הָעֲבוֹדָה,	*Al haTorah, v'al haavodah,*
וְעַל הַנְּבִיאִים,	*v'al han'vi·im,*
[וְעַל יוֹם הַשַּׁבָּת הַזֶּה,]	*[v'al yom haShabbat hazeh,]*
וְעַל יוֹם הַכִּפּוּרִים הַזֶּה,	*v'al Yom HaKippurim hazeh,*
שֶׁנָּתַתָּ לָּנוּ, יְיָ אֱלֹהֵינוּ,	*shenatata lanu, Adonai Eloheinu,*
[לִקְדֻשָּׁה וְלִמְנוּחָה,]	*[likdushah v'limnuchah,]*
לִמְחִילָה וְלִסְלִיחָה וּלְכַפָּרָה,	*limchilah v'lislichah ulchaparah,*
לְכָבוֹד וּלְתִפְאָרֶת.	*l'chavod ultifaret.*
עַל הַכֹּל, יְיָ אֱלֹהֵינוּ,	*Al hakol, Adonai Eloheinu,*
אֲנַחְנוּ מוֹדִים לָךְ, וּמְבָרְכִים אוֹתָךְ.	*anachnu modim lach, umvar'chim otach.*
יִתְבָּרַךְ שִׁמְךָ בְּפִי כָּל חַי תָּמִיד לְעוֹלָם וָעֶד,	*Yitbarach shimcha b'fi kol chai tamid l'olam va·ed;*
וּדְבָרְךָ אֱמֶת וְקַיָּם לָעַד.	*udvar'cha emet v'kayam laad.*
בָּרוּךְ אַתָּה, יְיָ,	*Baruch atah, Adonai,*
מֶלֶךְ מוֹחֵל וְסוֹלֵחַ לַעֲוֹנוֹתֵינוּ	*melech mocheil v'solei·ach laavonoteinu*
וְלַעֲוֹנוֹת עַמּוֹ בֵּית יִשְׂרָאֵל,	*v'laavonot amo beit Yisrael,*
וּמַעֲבִיר אַשְׁמוֹתֵינוּ בְּכָל שָׁנָה וְשָׁנָה,	*umaavir ashmoteinu b'chol shanah v'shanah,*
מֶלֶךְ עַל כָּל הָאָרֶץ,	*melech al kol haaretz,*
מְקַדֵּשׁ [הַשַּׁבָּת וְ] יִשְׂרָאֵל וְיוֹם הַכִּפּוּרִים.	*m'kadeish [haShabbat v'] Yisrael v'Yom HaKippurim.*

Blessed are You, our God Eternal,
supreme Power of the universe,
Rock of all ages,
Source of justice in all generations,
God in whom faithfulness abides,
whose word is deed,
whose every utterance bespeaks truth and righteousness.

Our God Eternal,
for all of these gifts we thank You and bless You:
Torah, worship, the books of the prophets,
[this Sabbath day,] and this Day of Atonement—
given to us [for holiness and rest; and]
for the sake of pardon and forgiveness,
that we might make amends with honor and dignity.

Let all life bless Your name continually, to the end of time,
so that Your truth will endure forever.

Blessed are You, Adonai,
Sovereign who forgives our failings
and pardons the failings of Your people, the House of Israel.
You banish our guilt, from year to year;
You reign in majesty over all the earth;
You sanctify [Shabbat,] the people Israel
and the Day of Atonement.

שַׂמְּחֵנוּ, יְיָ אֱלֹהֵינוּ,
בְּאֵלִיָּהוּ הַנָּבִיא עַבְדֶּךָ,
וּבְמַלְכוּת בֵּית דָּוִד מְשִׁיחֶךָ,
בִּמְהֵרָה יָבוֹא וְיָגֵל לִבֵּנוּ,
עַל כִּסְאוֹ לֹא יֵשֶׁב זָר,
וְלֹא יִנְחֲלוּ עוֹד אֲחֵרִים אֶת כְּבוֹדוֹ.
כִּי בְשֵׁם קָדְשְׁךָ נִשְׁבַּעְתָּ לּוֹ,
שֶׁלֹּא יִכְבֶּה נֵרוֹ לְעוֹלָם וָעֶד.

Sam'cheinu, Adonai Eloheinu,
b'Eliyahu hanavi avdecha,
uvmalchut beit David m'shichecha.
Bimheirah yavo v'yageil libeinu;
al kiso lo yeishev-zar,
v'lo yinchalu od acheirim et k'vodo.
Ki v'shem kodsh'cha nishbata lo,
shelo yichbeh neiro l'olam va·ed.

Inspire joy among us, our God Eternal, through Your servant the prophet Elijah. Gladden our hearts through the House of David; and may sparks of David's reign soon grow bright enough for us to see — a beam of light in the darkness, a promise of perfection.

בָּרוּךְ אַתָּה, יְיָ, מָגֵן דָּוִד.

Baruch atah, Adonai, magein David.

Blessed are You, God of eternity, Shield of David.

INSPIRE JOY AMONG US . . . SHIELD OF DAVID שַׂמְּחֵנוּ . . . מָגֵן דָּוִד. The prophets, whose words we have just read in the haftarah, articulated both powerful social critique and inspiring visions of a better world. This *b'rachah* looks toward the messianic future which, according to biblical tradition (Malachi 3:23), will be announced by the prophet Elijah. Our Sages viewed King David and his descendants as ideal rulers of Israel, embodiments of the people's messianic hopes. Thus, the prayer harmoniously unites two different types of leaders — kings and prophets — who in actual Jewish history were often antagonists. In saying these words today, we link ourselves to the dreams and hopes of our forebears who longed for Jewish sovereignty and a just society.

Welcoming the Torah
God's Thirteen Attributes
Bringing Forth the Torah
The Torah in Our Midst
Torah Blessings
Thanksgiving Blessing
Blessing for the Aliyah
Torah Reading
Prayer for Healing
Raising the Torah
Blessing before Haftarah
Haftarah
Blessing after Haftarah
Community Blessings
Returning Torah to Ark

עַל הַתּוֹרָה, וְעַל הָעֲבוֹדָה,
וְעַל הַנְּבִיאִים,
[וְעַל יוֹם הַשַּׁבָּת הַזֶּה,]
וְעַל יוֹם הַכִּפּוּרִים הַזֶּה,
שֶׁנָּתַתָּ לָּנוּ, יְיָ אֱלֹהֵינוּ,
[לִקְדֻשָּׁה וְלִמְנוּחָה,]
לִמְחִילָה וְלִסְלִיחָה וּלְכַפָּרָה,
לְכָבוֹד וּלְתִפְאָרֶת.
עַל הַכֹּל, יְיָ אֱלֹהֵינוּ,
אֲנַחְנוּ מוֹדִים לָךְ,
וּמְבָרְכִים אוֹתָךְ.
יִתְבָּרַךְ שִׁמְךָ בְּפִי כָּל חַי תָּמִיד
לְעוֹלָם וָעֶד,
וּדְבָרְךָ אֱמֶת וְקַיָּם לָעַד.

Al haTorah, v'al haavodah,
v'al han'vi·im,
[v'al yom haShabbat hazeh,]
v'al Yom HaKippurim hazeh,
shenatata lanu, Adonai Eloheinu,
[likdushah v'limnuchah,]
limchilah v'lislichah ulchaparah,
l'chavod ultifaret —
al hakol, Adonai Eloheinu,
anachnu modim lach,
umvar'chim otach.
Yitbarach shimcha b'fi kol chai tamid
l'olam va·ed;
udvar'cha emet v'kayam laad.

Our God Eternal, for all of these gifts we thank You and bless You: Torah, worship, the books of the prophets, [this Sabbath day] and this Day of Atonement — given to us [for holiness and rest; and] for the sake of pardon and forgiveness, that we might make amends with honor and dignity.

Let all life bless Your name continually, to the end of time, so that Your truth will endure forever.

בָּרוּךְ אַתָּה, יְיָ,
מֶלֶךְ מוֹחֵל וְסוֹלֵחַ לַעֲוֹנוֹתֵינוּ
וְלַעֲוֹנוֹת עַמּוֹ בֵּית יִשְׂרָאֵל,
וּמַעֲבִיר אַשְׁמוֹתֵינוּ בְּכָל שָׁנָה
וְשָׁנָה,
מֶלֶךְ עַל כָּל הָאָרֶץ,
מְקַדֵּשׁ [הַשַּׁבָּת וְ] יִשְׂרָאֵל
וְיוֹם הַכִּפּוּרִים.

Baruch atah, Adonai —
melech mocheil v'solei·ach laavonoteinu
v'laavonot amo beit Yisrael,
umaavir ashmoteinu b'chol shanah
v'shanah —
melech al kol haaretz,
m'kadeish [haShabbat v'] Yisrael
v'Yom HaKippurim.

Blessed are You, Adonai, Sovereign who forgives our failings
and pardons the failings of Your people, the House of Israel.
You banish our guilt, from year to year;
You reign in majesty over all the earth;
You sanctify [Shabbat,] the people Israel and the Day of Atonement.

Prayer for Our Congregation

ETERNAL PRESENCE, who blessed our mothers and fathers,
bless this holy congregation — a house of study, prayer, and righteous deeds.

Together we give thanks …

For our leaders:
those who learn, teach, and uphold the Torah,
inspiring others to learn, teach, and uphold the Torah;
those who do the sacred work of building our community.
May their service bring them joy, fulfillment, and purpose;
and may they go from strength to strength.

For our members:
diverse in age, interest, and background;
Jews by birth, Jews by choice,
and those of other faiths who join with us;
all who offer their time and talent,
their love and commitment.

For all who come here, on this holy day of Yom Kippur,
to share the search for meaning and renewal:
Your presence is a blessing, your friendship a gift.

May the spirit of peace, dignity, and respect live within these walls,
inspiring us to care for one another with compassion;
and may we be a source of goodness, light, and healing for the world.

May the One who blessed the generations before us
bless us as we stand together this day:
one congregation joined with all Jewish communities of the world
through our prayers on this Day of Atonement.

Let us renew ourselves for the year ahead.
Let us honor the precious legacy that is ours.

קַבָּלַת הַתּוֹרָה
Kabbalat HaTorah

שְׁלֹשׁ עֶשְׂרֵה מִדּוֹת
Sh'losh Esreih Midot

הוֹצָאַת הַתּוֹרָה
Hotzaat HaTorah

הַקָּפָה
Hakafah

בִּרְכוֹת הַתּוֹרָה
Birchot HaTorah

בִּרְכַּת הַגּוֹמֵל
Birkat HaGomeil

מִי שֶׁבֵּרַךְ לְעוֹלֵי הַתּוֹרָה
Mi Shebeirach L'olei HaTorah

קְרִיאַת הַתּוֹרָה
K'riat HaTorah

מִי שֶׁבֵּרַךְ לִרְפוּאָה
Mishebeirach Lirfuah

הַגְבָּהָה וּגְלִילָה
Hagbahah Uglilah

בְּרָכָה שֶׁלִּפְנֵי הַהַפְטָרָה
B'rachah Shelifnei HaHaftarah

קְרִיאַת הַהַפְטָרָה
K'riat HaHaftarah

בְּרָכָה שֶׁאַחֲרֵי הַהַפְטָרָה
B'rachah She-acharei HaHaftarah

תְּפִלּוֹת הַקְּהִלָּה
T'filot HaK'hilah

הַכְנָסַת סֵפֶר תּוֹרָה
Hachnasat Sefer Torah

For All Who Teach Torah — and Their Students

May heaven grant redemption and grace,
kindness and compassion, length of days
and ample sustenance; divine support,
bodily health, and spiritual enlightenment,
and offspring who will live and endure
and never abandon the study of Torah —
to our teachers and rabbis of holy communities
in the Land of Israel and in the Diaspora;
to our religious and communal leaders,
spiritual mentors, and guides;
to all their students,
and students of their students,
and to all who engage in the study of Torah.

May the Sovereign of the universe
bless them all, prolonging their lives
with fullness of days and length of years.
May they be delivered from all trouble
and saved from serious illness.
May our heavenly Teacher be their help
on every occasion and at all times,
and let us say: *Amen.*

FOR ALL WHO TEACH — AND THEIR STUDENTS. This prayer, known by its first words, *Y'kum purkan* (May heaven grant redemption), was composed by the Babylonian *geonim*, rabbinic leaders, toward the close of the Talmudic period. Written in Aramaic, the spoken language of that period, the prayer articulates the importance of rabbis and teachers for the welfare of all Jewish communities both in Israel and in the Diaspora. It is appropriate that at the conclusion of our Torah service we affirm our support for those centers of higher Jewish learning that will provide leadership for our future. (Rabbi Ronald Aigen, b. 1948)

Prayer for Our Country (United States)

God of holiness, we hear Your message: *Justice, justice you shall pursue.* God of freedom, we hear Your charge: *Proclaim liberty throughout the land.* Inspire us through Your teachings and commandments to love and uphold our precious democracy. Let every citizen take responsibility for the rights and freedoms we cherish. Let each of us be an advocate for justice, an activist for liberty, a defender of dignity. And let us champion the values that make our nation a haven for the persecuted, a beacon of hope among the nations.

May our actions reflect compassion for all people, within our borders and abroad. May our leaders and officials embody the vision of our founders: *to form a more perfect Union, establish Justice, insure domestic Tranquility, provide for the common defense, promote the general Welfare, and secure the Blessings of Liberty to ourselves and our Posterity.*

We pray for courage and conscience as we aim to support our country's highest values and aspirations: the hard-won rights that define us as a people, the responsibilities that they entail.

We pray for all who serve our country with selfless devotion — in peace and in war, from fields of battle to clinics and classrooms, from government to the grassroots: all those whose noble deeds and sacrifice benefit our nation and our world.

We are grateful for the rights of *Life, Liberty, and the pursuit of Happiness* that our founders ascribed to You, our Creator. We pray for their wisdom and moral strength, that we may be guardians of these rights for ourselves and for the sake of all people, now and forever.

JUSTICE, JUSTICE, Deuteronomy 16:20.
PROCLAIM LIBERTY, Leviticus 25:10.
TO FORM A MORE PERFECT UNION. From the preamble to the Constitution of the United States (1787).
LIFE, LIBERTY, AND THE PURSUIT OF HAPPINESS. From the United States Declaration of Independence (July 4, 1776).

קַבָּלַת הַתּוֹרָה
Kabbalat HaTorah

שָׁלֹש עֶשְׂרֵה מִדּוֹת
Sh'losh Esreih Midot

הוֹצָאַת הַתּוֹרָה
Hotzaat HaTorah

הַקָּפָה
Hakafah

בִּרְכוֹת הַתּוֹרָה
Birchot HaTorah

בִּרְכַּת הַגּוֹמֵל
Birkat HaGomeil

מִי שֶׁבֵּרַךְ לְעוֹלֵי הַתּוֹרָה
Mi Shebeirach L'olei HaTorah

קְרִיאַת הַתּוֹרָה
K'riat HaTorah

מִי שֶׁבֵּרַךְ לִרְפוּאָה
Mishebeirach Lirfuah

הַגְבָּהָה וּגְלִילָה
Hagbahah Uglilah

בְּרָכָה שֶׁלִפְנֵי הַהַפְטָרָה
B'rachah Shelifnei HaHaftarah

קְרִיאַת הַהַפְטָרָה
K'riat HaHaftarah

בְּרָכָה שֶׁאַחֲרֵי הַהַפְטָרָה
B'rachah She-acharei HaHaftarah

תְּפִלּוֹת הַקְּהִלָּה
T'filot HaK'hilah

הַכְנָסַת סֵפֶר תּוֹרָה
Hachnasat Sefer Torah

Prayer for Our Country (Canada)

God, whose blessed dominion is everlasting,
bless our sovereign, __________;
and bless the Prime Minister of Canada, those who serve our government,
and all who labour for the good of our nation.
Inspire them to be ever more conscious of their great responsibility.
May their leadership always reflect the high ideals You place before humanity.

During this sacred time of *t'shuvah* and self-examination,
guide our efforts to become more worthy citizens —
people who work together for justice and freedom, tolerance and compassion, at home and abroad.
Enable each of us to champion the democratic values
that make our country a haven for the persecuted
and a peacemaker among the nations.
May we, by word and deed, create a national life that embodies the noble words of our national anthem:

Et ta valeur, de foi trempée, protégera nos foyers et nos droits.
Your valour, steeped in faith, will protect our homes and our rights. . . .
God keep our land glorious and free!

And may we, through our daily conduct,
bring to our national life the promise of our ancient Psalmist:
Help is near to those who revere God,
to make God's presence dwell in our land.
Kindness and truth shall meet,
justice and peace embrace.

And let us say: *Amen.*

ET TA VALEUR . . . YOUR VALOUR. From the French lyrics of "O Canada," with English translation.

GOD KEEP OUR LAND. From the English lyrics of "O Canada."

HELP IS NEAR. From Psalm 85:10–11.

Prayer for the State of Israel

אָבִינוּ שֶׁבַּשָּׁמַיִם,	*Avinu shebashamayim,*
צוּר יִשְׂרָאֵל וְגוֹאֲלוֹ,	*Tzur Yisrael v'go·alo:*
בָּרֵךְ אֶת מְדִינַת יִשְׂרָאֵל,	*bareich et m'dinat Yisrael,*
רֵאשִׁית צְמִיחַת גְּאֻלָּתֵנוּ.	*reishit tz'michat g'ulateinu.*
הָגֵן עָלֶיהָ בְּאֶבְרַת חַסְדֶּךָ,	*Hagein aleha b'evrat chasdecha;*
וּפְרֹשׂ עָלֶיהָ סֻכַּת שְׁלוֹמֶךָ.	*ufros aleha sukkat sh'lomecha.*
וּשְׁלַח אוֹרְךָ וַאֲמִתְּךָ לְרָאשֶׁיהָ,	*Ushlach orcha vaamit'cha l'rasheha,*
שָׂרֶיהָ וְיוֹעֲצֶיהָ,	*sareha, v'yo·atzeha;*
וְתַקְּנֵם בְּעֵצָה טוֹבָה מִלְּפָנֶיךָ.	*v'tak'neim b'eitzah tovah mil'fanecha.*
חַזֵּק אֶת יְדֵי מְגִנֵּי אֶרֶץ קָדְשֵׁנוּ,	*Chazeik et y'dei m'ginei eretz kodsheinu,*
וְהַנְחִילֵם, אֱלֹהֵינוּ, יְשׁוּעָה,	*v'hanchileim, Eloheinu, y'shuah;*
וַעֲטֶרֶת נִצָּחוֹן תְּעַטְּרֵם.	*vaateret nitzachon t'at'reim.*
וְנָתַתָּ שָׁלוֹם בָּאָרֶץ	*V'natata shalom baaretz,*
וְשִׂמְחַת עוֹלָם לְיוֹשְׁבֶיהָ,	*v'simchat olam l'yoshveha.*
וְנֹאמַר: אָמֵן.	*V'nomar: Amen.*

Avinu — You who are high above all nation-states and peoples —
Rock of Israel, the One who has saved us and preserved us in life,
bless the State of Israel, first flowering of our redemption.
Be her loving shield, a shelter of lasting peace.
Guide her leaders and advisors by Your light of truth;
instruct them with Your good counsel.
Strengthen the hands of those who build and protect our Holy Land.
Deliver them from danger; crown their efforts with success.
Grant peace to the land,
lasting joy to all of her people.
And together we say: *Amen.*

PRAYER FOR THE STATE OF ISRAEL. Composed in honor of the birth of the State of Israel in 1948.

FIRST FLOWERING OF OUR REDEMPTION רֵאשִׁית צְמִיחַת גְּאֻלָּתֵנוּ. S. Y. Agnon (1887–1970) added this poetic phrase (based on the language of Isaiah 11:1), which defines the establishment of the State of Israel as a spiritual as well as a political event. Thus the prayer encourages us to experience the year 1948 as a turning point in history and a moment of unprecedented hope: the dawning of a peaceful, sovereign future for the Jewish people.

GOD STILL SPEAKS TO US OF THE LAND

Strengthen the land with love
and love the land with all your being
Feel the land on your skin and in your soul
Feel the history that brings you to this moment
Set Hebrew words upon your hearts
and on your lips its poetry, its music,
the grammar of vines and fig trees—
gnarled letters like trees of knowledge before your eyes,
a forest of knowledge. . . .
Kiss the children of the land,
for they are the doorposts,
they are the gates

I HAVE NO OTHER COUNTRY

אֵין לִי אֶֽרֶץ אַחֶֽרֶת
גַּם אִם אַדְמָתִי בּוֹעֶֽרֶת,
רַק מִלָּה בְּעִבְרִית חוֹדֶֽרֶת
אֶל עוֹרְקַי אֶל נִשְׁמָתִי.
בְּגוּף כּוֹאֵב,
בְּלֵב רָעֵב,
כָּאן הוּא בֵּיתִי.

I have no other country
even if my land is burning
Just a word of Hebrew pierces
my veins, penetrates my soul
With a body that hurts
with a heart that is hungry
here is my home.

לֹא אֶשְׁתֹּק כִּי אַרְצִי שִׁנְּתָה אֶת פָּנֶֽיהָ,
לֹא אֲוַתֵּר לָהּ,
אַזְכִּיר לָהּ,
וְאָשִׁיר כָּאן בְּאָזְנֶֽיהָ,
עַד שֶׁתִּפְקַח אֶת עֵינֶֽיהָ.

I will not be silent when my country has
changed her face
I will not give in to her, I will remind her
and I will sing here in her ears
until she has opened her eyes.

I HAVE NO OTHER COUNTRY. Lyrics by Ehud Manor (b. 1941).

Returning the Torah to the Ark

יְהַלְלוּ אֶת־שֵׁם יְיָ,	*Y'hal'lu et-shem Adonai,*
כִּי־נִשְׂגָּב שְׁמוֹ לְבַדּוֹ:	*ki-nisgav sh'mo l'vado:*

All praise God's name, for God's name alone is truly sublime:

הוֹדוֹ עַל־אֶרֶץ וְשָׁמָיִם.	*hodo al-eretz v'shamayim.*
וַיָּרֶם קֶרֶן לְעַמּוֹ,	*Vayarem keren l'amo;*
תְּהִלָּה לְכָל־חֲסִידָיו,	*t'hilah l'chol-chasidav,*
לִבְנֵי יִשְׂרָאֵל עַם קְרֹבוֹ,	*livnei Yisrael am k'rovo —*
הַלְלוּ־יָהּ.	*Hal'luyah!*

Your brightness lights the earth and sky
raises us up, blares out the note
from Your people's trumpet
an exultant blast for all who struggle with You
and are close at hand —

Halleluyah!

ALL PRAISE . . . HALLELUYAH יְהַלְלוּ . . . הַלְלוּ־יָהּ, Psalm 148:13–14. These verses, like others that are sung before and after the Reading of Torah, focus on God's glory — so that we do not make an idol of the scroll itself. Torah is revered, but only as an instrument for perceiving divine wisdom.

YOUR BRIGHTNESS הוֹדוֹ. Interpretive translation by Norman Fischer (b. 1946).

YOUR PEOPLE'S TRUMPET קֶרֶן לְעַמּוֹ. Both the literal meaning of *keren* ("horn") and its metaphoric meaning in the Bible ("strength") have significance on Rosh HaShanah: there is joy in the sound of the horn; but there is a special kind of joy for those who struggle mightily with matters of faith.

Welcoming the Torah
God's Thirteen Attributes
Bringing Forth the Torah
The Torah in Our Midst
Torah Blessings
Thanksgiving Blessing
Blessing for the Aliyah
Torah Reading
Prayer for Healing
Raising the Torah
Blessing before Haftarah
Haftarah
Blessing after Haftarah
Community Blessings
Returning Torah to Ark

כִּי לֶקַח טוֹב נָתַתִּי לָכֶם:
תּוֹרָתִי. אַל־תַּעֲזֹבוּ.

עֵץ־חַיִּים הִיא לַמַּחֲזִיקִים בָּהּ,
וְתֹמְכֶיהָ מְאֻשָּׁר.
דְּרָכֶיהָ דַרְכֵי־נֹעַם,
וְכָל־נְתִיבוֹתֶיהָ שָׁלוֹם.
הֲשִׁיבֵנוּ, יְיָ, אֵלֶיךָ – וְנָשׁוּבָה.
חַדֵּשׁ יָמֵינוּ כְּקֶדֶם.

Ki lekach tov natati lachem:
Torati. Al-taazovu.

Eitz-chayim hi lamachazikim bah;
v'tom'cheha m'ushar.
D'racheha darchei-no·am,
v'chol-n'tivoteha shalom.
Hashiveinu, Adonai, elecha — v'nashuvah.
Chadeish yameinu k'kedem.

A precious teaching I have given you:
My Torah. Do not forsake it.
A Tree of Life to those who hold it fast:
all who embrace it know happiness.
Its ways are ways of pleasantness,
and all its paths are peace.
Take us back, Adonai —
let us come back to You.
Renew in our time the days of old.

A PRECIOUS TEACHING כִּי לֶקַח טוֹב, Proverbs 4:2.

A TREE OF LIFE . . . PATHS ARE PEACE עֵץ־חַיִּים הִיא . . . נְתִיבוֹתֶיהָ שָׁלוֹם, Proverbs 3:18–17. Richard Elliott Friedman (b. 1946) reminds us that the first human beings lost access to the Tree of Life in the Garden of Eden through their quest for wisdom — "knowledge of good and evil." The motifs of life and death, good and evil, recur in Moses' last words to the Israelites, found in our Torah reading for Yom Kippur. And each time the Torah is returned to the ark, we sing words from the Book of Proverbs reminding us that wisdom is now accessible to us through Torah, the "Tree of Life" that is the source of our people's continued existence.

LET US COME BACK הֲשִׁיבֵנוּ. This verse, from Lamentations 5:21, was originally a call for communal restoration and renewal after the destruction of the Jewish nation by the Babylonians. In the liturgy of the Torah service it expresses a desire for *t'shuvah*: the yearning to come closer to God by holding fast to divine wisdom through the study of Torah.

וְדּוּי וּסְלִיחוֹת
Vidui Uslichot · Confession and Forgiveness

We stand in humility, conscious of our failings:
Sh'ma koleinu — Adonai, hear our call!

True sacrifice to God is a penitent spirit;
You treasure a crushed and repentant heart.

For You are close to the brokenhearted;
and You give strength to a suffering soul.

You are the healer of shattered hearts;
You are the one who binds up their wounds.

For thus says the high and exalted One,
who lives forever, whose name is holy:

"I dwell in a high and holy place;
but also with the downcast and lowly —

to bring new life to despondent souls,
to restore and revive repentant hearts."

Return now, Israel, to Adonai your God,
for you have fallen because of your sin.

Take words with you, and return to God.
Ask the Eternal: forgive what is wrong;
accept what is good.

We stand in humility, conscious of our failings;
we set before You the wrongs we have done.

We trust in Your compassion, for You know who we are;
Sh'ma koleinu — Adonai, hear our call.

SHA MA
KOLENA
TO PG 296

TRUE SACRIFICE TO GOD . . . REPENTANT HEART. See Psalm 51:19.
FOR YOU ARE CLOSE . . . SUFFERING SOUL. See Psalm 34:19.
YOU ARE THE HEALER . . . THEIR WOUNDS. See Psalm 147:3.
FOR THUS SAYS . . . REPENTANT HEARTS. See Isaiah 57:15.
RETURN NOW . . . THE GOOD IN US. See Hosea 14:2–3.

Because I was angry
Because I didn't think
Because I was exhausted and on edge
Because I'd been drinking
Because I can be mean
Because I was reckless and selfish
Because I was worried about money
Because my marriage was dead
Because other people were doing it
Because I thought I could get away with it
Because . . .

I did something wrong.

Because I'm in pain
Because I wish I could undo it
Because I hurt him
Because I lost her trust
Because I let them down
Because I was self-destructive
Because I was foolish
Because I'm ashamed
Because that's not who I am
Because that's not who I want to be
Because . . .

I want to be forgiven.

God,
bring down my walls of defensiveness and self-righteousness.
Help me to stay in humility.
Please—
give me the strength to do what's right.

שְׁמַע קוֹלֵנוּ
Sh'ma Koleinu

וִדּוּי זוּטָא
Vidui Zuta

וִדּוּי רַבָּה
Vidui Rabbah

חֶשְׁבּוֹן הַנֶּפֶשׁ
Cheshbon HaNefesh

כִּי אָנוּ עַמֶּךָ
Ki Anu Amecha

שְׁמַע קוֹלֵנוּ
Sh'ma Koleinu

שְׁמַע קוֹלֵנוּ, יְיָ אֱלֹהֵינוּ.	*Sh'ma koleinu, Adonai Eloheinu.*
חוּס וְרַחֵם עָלֵינוּ.	*Chus v'racheim aleinu.*
וְקַבֵּל בְּרַחֲמִים וּבְרָצוֹן אֶת תְּפִלָּתֵנוּ.	*V'kabeil b'rachamim uvratzon et t'filateinu.*
הֲשִׁיבֵנוּ, יְיָ, אֵלֶיךָ וְנָשׁוּבָה,	*Hashiveinu, Adonai, eilecha — v'nashuvah;*
חַדֵּשׁ יָמֵינוּ כְּקֶדֶם.	*chadeish yameinu k'kedem.*
אֲמָרֵינוּ הַאֲזִינָה, יְיָ,	*Amareinu haazinah, Adonai,*
בִּינָה הֲגִיגֵנוּ.	*binah hagigeinu.*
יִהְיוּ לְרָצוֹן אִמְרֵי־פִינוּ וְהֶגְיוֹן לִבֵּנוּ לְפָנֶיךָ,	*Yiyu l'ratzon imrei-finu v'hegyon libeinu l'fanecha,*
יְיָ, צוּרֵנוּ וְגוֹאֲלֵנוּ.	*Adonai — tzureinu v'go·aleinu.*
אַל־תַּשְׁלִיכֵנוּ מִלְּפָנֶיךָ,	*Al-tashlicheinu mil'fanecha;*
וְרוּחַ קָדְשְׁךָ אַל־תִּקַּח מִמֶּנּוּ.	*v'ruach kodsh'cha al-tikach mimenu.*
אַל־תַּשְׁלִיכֵנוּ לְעֵת זִקְנָה,	*Al-tashlicheinu l'eit ziknah;*
כִּכְלוֹת כֹּחֵנוּ אַל־תַּעַזְבֵנוּ.	*kichlot kocheinu, al-taazveinu.*
אַל־תַּעַזְבֵנוּ, יְיָ אֱלֹהֵינוּ,	*Al-taazveinu, Adonai Eloheinu;*
אַל־תִּרְחַק מִמֶּנּוּ.	*al-tirchak mimenu.*
כִּי־לְךָ, יְיָ, הוֹחָלְנוּ,	*Ki-l'cha, Adonai, hochalnu;*
אַתָּה תַעֲנֶה, אֲדֹנָי אֱלֹהֵינוּ.	*atah taaneh, Adonai Eloheinu.*

Hear our call, Adonai our God. Show us compassion.
Accept our prayer with love and goodwill.

Take us back, Adonai; let us come back to You; renew our days as in the past.
Hear our words, Adonai; understand our unspoken thoughts.
May the speech of our mouth and our heart's quiet prayer
be acceptable to You, Adonai, our Rock and our Redeemer.

Do not cast us away from Your presence, or cut us off from Your holy spirit.
Do not cast us away when we are old; as our strength diminishes,
do not forsake us.
Do not forsake us, Adonai; be not far from us, our God.

With hope, Adonai, we await You;
surely, You, Adonai our God — You will answer.

HEAR OUR CALL שְׁמַע קוֹלֵנוּ, based on Lamentations 5:21, Psalm 5:2, 19:15, 51:13, 71:9, 38:22, 38:16.

Hear Our Call

The Short Confession

The Long Confession

Introspection and Silent Confession

We Are Your People

Hear Our Call

PRIDE

Even rocks crack, I tell you,
and not on account of age.
For years they lie on their backs in
the cold and the heat,
so many years,
it almost creates the impression
of calm.
They don't move, so the cracks can
hide.
A kind of pride.
Years pass over them as they wait.
Whoever is going to shatter them
hasn't come yet.
And so the moss flourishes, the
seaweed is cast about,
the sea bursts out and slides back,
and it seems the rocks are
perfectly still.
Till a little seal comes to rub
against them,
comes and goes.
And suddenly the stone has an
open wound.
I told you, when rocks crack, it
happens by surprise.
Not to mention people.

אֲפִלּוּ סְלָעִים נִשְׁבָּרִים,
אֲנִי אוֹמֶרֶת לָךְ,
וְלֹא מֵחֲמַת זִקְנָה.
שָׁנִים רַבּוֹת הֵם שׁוֹכְבִים
עַל גַּבָּם בַּחֹם וּבַקּוֹר,
שָׁנִים כֹּה רַבּוֹת,
כִּמְעַט נוֹצַר רֹשֶׁם שֶׁל שַׁלְוָה.
אֵין הֵם זָזִים מִמְּקוֹמָם וְכָךְ
נִסְתָּרִים הַבְּקִיעִים.
מֵעֵין גַּאֲוָה.
שָׁנִים רַבּוֹת עוֹבְרוֹת עֲלֵיהֶם בְּצִפִּיָּה.
מִי שֶׁעָתִיד לְשַׁבֵּר אוֹתָם
עֲדַיִן לֹא בָּא.
וְאָז הָאֵזוֹב מְשַׂגְשֵׂג, הָאַצּוֹת
נִגְרָשׁוֹת וְהַיָּם מֵגִיחַ וְחוֹזֵר,
וְדוֹמֶה, הֵם לְלֹא תְנוּעָה.
עַד שֶׁיָּבוֹא כֶּלֶב יָם קָטָן לְהִתְחַכֵּךְ
עַל הַסְּלָעִים
יָבוֹא וְיֵלֵךְ.
וּפִתְאֹם הָאֶבֶן פְּצוּעָה.
אָמַרְתִּי לָךְ, כְּשֶׁסְּלָעִים נִשְׁבָּרִים
זֶה קוֹרֶה בְּהַפְתָּעָה.
וּמַה גַּם אֲנָשִׁים.

PRIDE. By Dahlia Ravikovitch (1936–2005).

OUR SAGES TEACH that unwarranted pride hinders *t'shuvah*, as we cannot correct our flaws unless we are willing to admit their existence (see Maimonides, Laws of *T'shuvah* 2.5). However, self-abasement is also spiritually dangerous. "Do not regard yourself as a bad person," says Mishnah *Avot* 2:18. Rabbi Yonah Girondi (13th century) points out that a person who feels worthless will lack hope, which is essential for *t'shuvah*, and will see it as pointless to refrain from further wrongdoing, since so many sins have already been committed.

שְׁמַע קוֹלֵנוּ
Sh'ma Koleinu
וִדּוּי זוּטָא
Vidui Zuta
וִדּוּי רַבָּה
Vidui Rabbah
חֶשְׁבּוֹן הַנֶּפֶשׁ
Cheshbon HaNefesh
כִּי אָנוּ עַמֶּךָ
Ki Anu Amecha
שְׁמַע קוֹלֵנוּ
Sh'ma Koleinu

Vidui Zuta — The Short Confession

אֱלֹהֵינוּ וֵאלֹהֵי אֲבוֹתֵינוּ וְאִמּוֹתֵינוּ,
תָּבֹא לְפָנֶיךָ תְּפִלָּתֵנוּ,
וְאַל תִּתְעַלַּם מִתְּחִנָּתֵנוּ.
אֲנַחְנוּ עַזֵּי פָנִים וּקְשֵׁי עֹרֶף
לוֹמַר לְפָנֶיךָ,
יְיָ אֱלֹהֵינוּ וֵאלֹהֵי אֲבוֹתֵינוּ
וְאִמּוֹתֵינוּ:
צַדִּיקִים אֲנַחְנוּ וְלֹא חָטָאנוּ.
אֲבָל אֲנַחְנוּ חָטָאנוּ.

Eloheinu v'Elohei avoteinu v'imoteinu,
tavo l'fanecha t'filateinu;
v'al titalam mit'chinateinu.
Anachnu azei fanim ukshei oref
lomar l'fanecha,
Adonai Eloheinu v'Elohei avoteinu
v'imoteinu,
"Tzadikim anachnu, v'lo chatanu."
Aval anachnu chatanu.

Our God and God of all generations,
may our prayers reach Your presence.
And when we turn to You, do not be indifferent.
Adonai, we are arrogant and stubborn,
claiming to be blameless and free of sin.
In truth, we have stumbled and strayed.
We have done wrong.

אָשַׁמְנוּ, בָּגַדְנוּ, גָּזַלְנוּ, דִּבַּרְנוּ דֹפִי.
הֶעֱוִינוּ, וְהִרְשַׁעְנוּ, זַדְנוּ, חָמַסְנוּ,
טָפַלְנוּ שֶׁקֶר.
יָעַצְנוּ רָע, כִּזַּבְנוּ, לַצְנוּ, מָרַדְנוּ,
נִאַצְנוּ, סָרַרְנוּ, עָוִינוּ, פָּשַׁעְנוּ,
צָרַרְנוּ, קִשִּׁינוּ עֹרֶף.
רָשַׁעְנוּ, שִׁחַתְנוּ, תִּעַבְנוּ,
תָּעִינוּ, תִּעְתָּעְנוּ.

Ashamnu, bagadnu, gazalnu, dibarnu dofi.
He·evinu, v'hirshanu, zadnu, chamasnu,
tafalnu sheker.
Yaatznu ra, kizavnu, latznu, maradnu,
niatznu, sararnu, avinu, pashanu,
tzararnu, kishinu oref.
Rashanu, shichatnu, tiavnu,
ta·inu, titanu.

Of these wrongs we are guilty:
We betray. We steal. We scorn. We act perversely.
We are cruel. We scheme. We are violent. We slander.
We devise evil. We lie. We ridicule. We disobey.
We abuse. We defy. We corrupt. We commit crimes.
We are hostile. We are stubborn. We are immoral. We kill.
We spoil. We go astray. We lead others astray.

For Study and Reflection

A REPENTANT SINNER should strive to do good with the same faculties and limbs once used to commit the sin. . . . For instance, if one's feet had run to do evil, one should now run to perform mitzvot. If one's mouth had spoken falsehood, let it now be opened in wisdom and truth. Violent hands should now open to give *tzedakah*, . . . and the contentious person should now become a peacemaker.

COMMENTARY

The above teaching suggests that *t'shuvah* may be accomplished through constructive action to counteract the wrong one has done, and by channeling one's destructive energies in positive directions. For example, a person with an aggressive temperament could pursue justice and peace with vigor; a person prone to gossip and malicious tale-bearing could focus on offering kind, supportive words to others; one who has violated the law could do volunteer work of a socially responsible nature; and one who has committed adultery could atone by treating one's betrayed spouse and children with respect and honesty.

IN A CULTURE striving for permissiveness, the self-critical mood of Yom Kippur strikes a note of jarring counterpoint. The tradition's answer is that guilt in its right time and place is healthy; it is crucial to conscience. Moral maturity lies in a willingness to recognize one's own sins, not to lay upon oneself a universal or destructive guilt, a guilt that cripples all and focuses on nothing specific. Concrete acts can be corrected; bad patterns can be overcome.

Against the brokenness of guilt and the isolation of sin, Yom Kippur offers the wholeness of living, the oneness of community. To this end there is repeated confession of sins on Yom Kippur. The sins are listed alphabetically to cover the range of human behavior and to jog memory. Compassionately enough, the confessions are in the plural form (we have sinned). Everyone confesses all the sins, and each individual applies the appropriate category to herself or himself.

A REPENTANT SINNER. By Rabbi Yonah ben Avraham Girondi (13th century), author of the ethical work *Sha'arei T'shuvah* (Gates of Repentance).

IN A CULTURE. By Rabbi Irving Greenberg (b. 1933).

שְׁמַע קוֹלֵנוּ
Sh'ma Koleinu
וִדּוּי זוּטָא
Vidui Zuta
וִדּוּי רַבָּה
Vidui Rabbah
חֶשְׁבּוֹן הַנֶּפֶשׁ
Cheshbon HaNefesh
כִּי אָנוּ עַמֶּךָ
Ki Anu Amecha
שְׁמַע קוֹלֵנוּ
Sh'ma Koleinu

סַרְנוּ מִמִּצְוֹתֶיךָ וּמִמִּשְׁפָּטֶיךָ
הַטּוֹבִים, וְלֹא שָׁוָה לָנוּ.
וְאַתָּה צַדִּיק עַל כָּל הַבָּא עָלֵינוּ,
כִּי אֱמֶת עָשִׂיתָ, וַאֲנַחְנוּ הִרְשָׁעְנוּ.
מַה נֹּאמַר לְפָנֶיךָ, יוֹשֵׁב מָרוֹם,
וּמַה נְּסַפֵּר לְפָנֶיךָ, שׁוֹכֵן שְׁחָקִים.
הֲלֹא כָּל הַנִּסְתָּרוֹת וְהַנִּגְלוֹת
אַתָּה יוֹדֵעַ.

Sarnu mimitzvotecha umimishpatecha
hatovim, v'lo shavah-lanu.
V'atah tzadik al kol haba aleinu,
ki emet asita, vaanachnu hirshanu.
Mah nomar l'fanecha, yosheiv marom?
Umah n'sapeir l'fanecha, shochein sh'chakim?
Halo kol hanistarot v'haniglot
atah yodei·a.

Our turning away from Your mitzvot and laws of goodness is a hollow pursuit.
You are just, concerning all that happens in our lives.
Your way is the way of truth, while ours leads to error.
What can we say to You whose existence is beyond time and space?
What words of ours can reach Your realm
beyond the clouds, beyond heaven itself?
Every hidden mystery, every revelation — surely, You know them all.

אַתָּה יוֹדֵעַ רָזֵי עוֹלָם,
וְתַעֲלוּמוֹת סִתְרֵי כָּל חָי.
אַתָּה חוֹפֵשׂ כָּל־חַדְרֵי־בָטֶן,
וּבוֹחֵן כְּלָיוֹת וָלֵב.
אֵין דָּבָר נֶעְלָם מִמֶּךָּ,
וְאֵין נִסְתָּר מִנֶּגֶד עֵינֶיךָ.
וּבְכֵן יְהִי רָצוֹן מִלְּפָנֶיךָ,
יְיָ אֱלֹהֵינוּ וֵאלֹהֵי אֲבוֹתֵינוּ
וְאִמּוֹתֵינוּ:
שֶׁתִּסְלַח לָנוּ עַל כָּל חַטֹּאתֵינוּ,
וְתִמְחַל לָנוּ עַל כָּל עֲוֹנוֹתֵינוּ,
וּתְכַפֶּר לָנוּ עַל כָּל פְּשָׁעֵינוּ.

Atah yodei·a razei olam;
v'taalumot sitrei kol chai.
Atah chofeis kol-chadrei-vaten;
uvochein k'layot valev.
Ein davar ne·elam mimeka;
v'ein nistar mineged einecha.
Uvchein y'hi ratzon mil'fanecha,
Adonai Eloheinu v'Elohei avoteinu
v'imoteinu:
shetislach lanu al kol chatoteinu,
v'timchal lanu al kol avonoteinu,
ut·chapeir lanu al kol p'sha·einu.

You know the secrets of the universe and the secrets of the human heart.
You know and understand us, for You examine our inner lives.
Nothing is concealed from You, nothing hidden from Your sight.
Eternal One, our God and God of our ancestors,
we pray that this be Your will: forgive all our wrongs,
pardon us for every act of injustice, help us atone for all our moral failures.

FOR THE SIN we committed against You, through evading and avoiding, because we could not face the truth.
For our flight into hypocrisy and deception because we did not dare to speak it.
For the facts we dissembled, and all we glossed over, for the excuses we made.

For feeding our bodies and starving our souls.
For interfering with the souls of others, and neglecting their needs.
For shifting our responsibilities, for reproaches and recriminations.

For our foolishness, our folly and false standards.
For seeing these things only in others, never in ourselves.
For our complacency which blinds us, and our self-righteousness which lessens us.

For calculating kindness and measuring out pity.
For charity that is cold, and prayers without feeling.
For withholding our love.

For the appeals that we ignored, and the people whom we refused.
For the affection which died, and our lives that became bitter.
For the visions which faded, the ideals we neglected, and the opportunities we lost.

For the fear of change and renewal, and our unbelief.
For saying prayers aloud, but refusing to listen.
For being our own worst enemy.

FORGIVE ALL OUR WRONGS (*facing page*). The Talmud (*M'gillah* 28a) records that the Babylonian sage Mar Zutra, before going to sleep, would say, "I pardon all those who pained me." The traditional bedtime *Sh'ma* begins with a prayer in which we strive to let go of the daily accumulation of petty grievances and grudges: "I hereby forgive anyone who angered or antagonized me or who sinned against me. . . . May no one incur punishment on my account." While Jewish law does not require us to forgive those who have not repented and sought our forgiveness, it encourages us to stop clinging to anger and resentment, for these weigh down our spirit.

FOR THE SIN. By Rabbi Lionel Blue (b. 1930).

Vidui Rabbah — The Long Confession

For these sins, our God, we ask forgiveness:

Al cheit shechatanu l'fanecha
　b'ones uvratzon;
v'al cheit shechatanu l'fanecha
　b'yodim uvlo yodim.

עַל חֵטְא שֶׁחָטָאנוּ לְפָנֶיךָ
בְּאֹנֶס וּבְרָצוֹן,
וְעַל חֵטְא שֶׁחָטָאנוּ לְפָנֶיךָ
בְּיוֹדְעִים וּבְלֹא יוֹדְעִים.

The ways we have wronged You under duress and by choice;
and harm we have caused in Your world consciously and
　unconsciously.

Al cheit shechatanu l'fanecha
　bivli daat;
v'al cheit shechatanu l'fanecha
　b'ritzat raglayim l'hara.

עַל חֵטְא שֶׁחָטָאנוּ לְפָנֶיךָ
בִּבְלִי דָעַת,
וְעַל חֵטְא שֶׁחָטָאנוּ לְפָנֶיךָ
בְּרִיצַת רַגְלַיִם לְהָרַע.

The ways we have wronged You through our thoughtlessness;
and harm we have caused in Your world through impulsive acts
　of malice.

Al cheit shechatanu l'fanecha
　b'chozek yad;
v'al cheit shechatanu l'fanecha
　b'zilzul horim umorim.

עַל חֵטְא שֶׁחָטָאנוּ לְפָנֶיךָ
בְּחֹזֶק יָד,
וְעַל חֵטְא שֶׁחָטָאנוּ לְפָנֶיךָ
בְּזִלְזוּל הוֹרִים וּמוֹרִים.

The ways we have wronged You by abusing our power;
and harm we have caused in Your world through disrespect to
　parents and teachers.

שְׁמַע קוֹלֵנוּ
Sh'ma Koleinu

וִדּוּי זוּטָא
Vidui Zuta

וִדּוּי רַבָּה
Vidui Rabbah

חֶשְׁבּוֹן הַנֶּפֶשׁ
Cheshbon HaNefesh

כִּי אָנוּ עַמֶּךָ
Ki Anu Amecha

שְׁמַע קוֹלֵנוּ
Sh'ma Koleinu

FOR THESE SINS עַל חֵטְא. The original *Al Cheit* confession consisted of only six verses.
The prayer's likely author, Yose ben Yose (3rd–4th cent.), chose to focus on the underlying nature of sin by asserting that the wrongs we commit fall into six categories: those
we do under duress and those we do by choice; those we do by mistake or and those we
do deliberately; those we do secretly and those we do openly. The Sephardic *machzor*
retains Yose ben Yose's concise version, while Ashkenazic versions grew in length, over
the centuries, following Rabbi Judah ben Bava's opinion: "It is necessary to specify the
precise sin for which atonement is sought" (Talmud *Yoma* 86b).

A PERSONAL CONFESSION

I need to speak these words aloud and to know that the universe hears them.
I get caught in old patterns and paradigms; I am stubborn and hard-headed.
In the last year I have missed the mark more than I want to admit.
Forgive me, Source of all being, for the sin I have sinned before You:

by allowing my body to be an afterthought too often and too easily;
by not walking, running, leaping, climbing, or dancing although I am able;
by eating in my car and at my desk, mindlessly and without blessing;
by not embracing those who needed it, and not allowing myself to be embraced;
by not praising every body's beauty, with our quirks and imperfections;
by letting my emotions run roughshod over the needs of others;
by poking at sources of hurt like a child worrying a sore tooth;
by revealing my heart before those who neither wanted nor needed to see it;
by hiding love, out of fear of rejection, instead of giving love freely;
by dwelling on what's internal when the world is desperate for healing;
by indulging in intellectual argument without humility or consideration;
by reading words of vitriol, cultivating hot indignation;
by eschewing intellectual discomfort that might prod me into growing;
by living in anticipation, and letting anxiety rule me;
by accepting defeatist thinking and the comfortable ache of despair;
by not being awake and grateful, despite uncountable blessings;
by not being sufficiently gentle, with my actions or with my language;
by being not pliant and flexible, but obstinate, stark, and unbending;
by not being generous with my time, with my words or with my being;
by not being kind to everyone who crosses my wandering path.

For all of these, eternal Source of forgiveness:
Help me know myself to be pardoned.
Help me feel in my bones that I'm forgiven.
Remind me I'm always already at-one with You.

A PERSONAL CONFESSION. By Rabbi Rachel Barenblat (b. 1975).

MISSED THE MARK. The Hebrew word *cheit*, often translated as "sin," is from a root meaning "to miss the mark," as in archery or stone-throwing. For example, we find a reference to soldiers in Judges 20:16 who "could sling a stone at a hair and not miss (*v'lo yachati*)." Many commentators have drawn important implications from the etymology of *cheit*: As with a stone thrower or archer, our intent is to aim true and to do the right thing; wrongdoing does not cause an ineradicable stain. With practice and attention, we can improve our aim and do better in the future.

שְׁמַע קוֹלֵנוּ Sh'ma Koleinu
וִדּוּי זוּטָא Vidui Zuta
וִדּוּי רַבָּה Vidui Rabbah
חֶשְׁבּוֹן הַנֶּפֶשׁ Cheshbon HaNefesh
כִּי אָנוּ עַמֶּךָ Ki Anu Amecha
שְׁמַע קוֹלֵנוּ Sh'ma Koleinu

עַל חֵטְא שֶׁחָטָאנוּ לְפָנֶיךָ
בְּיֵצֶר הָרָע,
וְעַל חֵטְא שֶׁחָטָאנוּ לְפָנֶיךָ
בְּקַשְׁיוּת עֹרֶף.

Al cheit shechatanu l'fanecha
b'yeitzer hara;
v'al cheit shechatanu l'fanecha
b'kashyut oref.

The ways we have wronged You by giving in to our hostile impulses;
and harm we have caused in Your world through inflexibility and stubbornness.

עַל חֵטְא שֶׁחָטָאנוּ לְפָנֶיךָ
בְּכַחַשׁ וּבְכָזָב,
וְעַל חֵטְא שֶׁחָטָאנוּ לְפָנֶיךָ
בְּקַלּוּת רֹאשׁ.

Al cheit shechatanu l'fanecha
b'chachash uvchazav;
v'al cheit shechatanu l'fanecha
b'kalut rosh.

The ways we have wronged You through lies and deceit;
and harm we have caused in Your world by making light of serious matters.

עַל חֵטְא שֶׁחָטָאנוּ לְפָנֶיךָ
בְּשִׂיחַ שִׂפְתוֹתֵינוּ,
וְעַל חֵטְא שֶׁחָטָאנוּ לְפָנֶיךָ
בְּצָרוּת עָיִן.

Al cheit shechatanu l'fanecha
b'siach siftoteinu,
v'al cheit shechatanu l'fanecha
b'tzarut-ayin.

The ways we have wronged You in our routine conversations;
and harm we have caused in Your world through envy.

וְעַל כֻּלָּם, אֱלוֹהַּ סְלִיחוֹת,
סְלַח לָנוּ, מְחַל לָנוּ, כַּפֶּר־לָנוּ.

V'al kulam, Elo·ah s'lichot,
s'lach lanu, m'chal lanu, kaper-lanu.

For all these failures of judgment and will, God of forgiveness — forgive us, pardon us, lead us to atonement.

INFLEXIBILITY AND STUBBORNNESS קַשְׁיוּת עֹרֶף. Literally, "stiffness of neck." The concept of "stiff-neckedness" is drawn from the agricultural realm; it refers to an animal that refuses to bend its neck and accept the yoke of the plow. Applied to human beings, the metaphor suggests recalcitrance and resistance to authority, a quality that the prophets identify with the people of Israel. Isaiah, for instance, uses this metaphor to explain why Israel was exiled to Babylonia: "Your neck is like an iron sinew, and your forehead bronze" (48:4). As the people's resistance to God's authority led to destruction and exile, so, too, an individual's unwillingness to accept input from others or consider others' views inevitably has serious consequences.

On new year's day, next to a house being built,
a man vows not to do any wrong in it,
only to love in it.
Sins that were green in spring
have dried out in summer and now rustle and whisper.

So I washed my body and trimmed my fingernails—
the last favor
which a man does for himself
while he is still alive.

What is man? During the day
he breaks up into little words
what night has turned into a heavy lump.
What are we doing to each other?
What does a father do to his son?
What—a son to his father?

And nothing stands between
him and death
but a thin defense, like a battery
of excited lawyers,
a fence of words.

And he who uses people as handles, or as steps of a ladder,
will soon find himself
embracing a piece of wood
and holding a hand cut from its body
and wiping his tears
with a potsherd.

---

on new year's day. The poet Yehuda Amichai (1924–2000) laments the toll that wrongdoing takes on a human being. Those who began with good intentions must endure the consequences of harm done to others—treating persons as objects or means to an end. Such individuals end up embracing "a piece of wood"—surrounded by material things rather than sustained by human relationships. The reference to a potsherd recalls Job 2:8, where the man who has lost almost everything—wealth, health, and children—tries to relieve his anguish by scratching his sores with a potsherd; and, ironically, he succeeds only in increasing his pain.

שְׁמַע קוֹלֵנוּ
Sh'ma Koleinu
וִדּוּי זוּטָא
Vidui Zuta
וִדּוּי רַבָּה
Vidui Rabbah
חֶשְׁבּוֹן הַנֶּפֶשׁ
Cheshbon HaNefesh
כִּי אָנוּ עַמֶּךָ
Ki Anu Amecha
שְׁמַע קוֹלֵנוּ
Sh'ma Koleinu

עַל חֵטְא שֶׁחָטָאנוּ לְפָנֶיךָ
בַּגָּלוּי וּבַסֵּתֶר,
וְעַל חֵטְא שֶׁחָטָאנוּ לְפָנֶיךָ
בְּשִׂנְאַת חִנָּם.

Al cheit shechatanu l'fanecha
bagalui uvasater;
v'al cheit shechatanu l'fanecha
b'sinat chinam.

The ways we have wronged You openly and secretly;
and harm we have caused in Your world by hating without cause.

עַל חֵטְא שֶׁחָטָאנוּ לְפָנֶיךָ
בִּפְרִיקַת עֹל,
וְעַל חֵטְא שֶׁחָטָאנוּ לְפָנֶיךָ
בְּמַאֲכָל וּבְמִשְׁתֶּה.

Al cheit shechatanu l'fanecha
bifrikat ol;
v'al cheit shechatanu l'fanecha
b'maachal uvmishteh.

The ways we have wronged You by losing self-control;
and harm we have caused in Your world through consumption of food and drink.

עַל חֵטְא שֶׁחָטָאנוּ לְפָנֶיךָ
בְּגִלּוּי עֲרָיוֹת,
וְעַל חֵטְא שֶׁחָטָאנוּ לְפָנֶיךָ
בְּאִמּוּץ הַלֵּב.

Al cheit shechatanu l'fanecha
b'gilui arayot;
v'al cheit shechatanu l'fanecha
b'imutz halev.

The ways we have wronged You through sexual immorality;
and harm we have caused in Your world by hardening our hearts.

עַל חֵטְא שֶׁחָטָאנוּ לְפָנֶיךָ
בְּנֶשֶׁךְ וּבְמַרְבִּית,
וְעַל חֵטְא שֶׁחָטָאנוּ לְפָנֶיךָ
בְּמַשָּׂא וּבְמַתָּן.

Al cheit shechatanu l'fanecha
b'neshech uvmarbit;
v'al cheit shechatanu l'fanecha
b'masa uvmatan.

The ways we have wronged You through greed and exploitation;
and harm we have caused in Your world through dishonesty in business.

We focused inward, narrowing our vision;
we were preoccupied with ourselves.
We turned our backs on the poor and defenseless;
we were contemptuous of the weak.
We tolerated violence against children,
neglect of the old, exploitation of the innocent;
we told ourselves there was nothing we could do.
We wasted the resources of the earth;
we denied our own responsibility and put it out of our minds.
We kept silent when we should have spoken out;
we gave in to cynicism and despair.
We sought entertainment instead of enlightenment;
we were lazy, indifferent, and callous.
We forgave ourselves too easily for our failures;
we forgot that we always have a choice.

SEVEN SOCIAL SINS

Wealth without work
Pleasure without conscience
Knowledge without character
Commerce without morality
Science without humanity
Worship without sacrifice.
Politics without principle.

CONSUMPTION OF FOOD AND DRINK בְּמַאֲכָל וּבְמִשְׁתֶּה (*facing page*). Economist and Jewish scholar Meir Tamari (b. 1927) relates this to the root causes of gluttony and over-consumption: "The free market ideal of 'more is better than less' creates a search for a constantly rising standard of living, even if achieved through fraud and dishonesty. Conspicuous consumption . . . and exaggerated consumerism betray standards of self-control and exert consistent pressure to earn more money. . . . Only when the concept of 'enough' is ingrained in us do we have a benchmark for measuring the sins of consumption of food and drinks. Modest lifestyles, the moral strength won by postponing expectations, and frugality are required hallmarks of Jewish social life."

SEVEN SOCIAL SINS. By Mohandas Gandhi (1869–1948). First published in his weekly newspaper, *Young India*, on October 22, 1925. Gandhi gave the list to his grandson Arun on their last day together, shortly before his assassination.

שְׁמַע קוֹלֵנוּ
Sh'ma Koleinu

וִדּוּי זוּטָא
Vidui Zuta

וִדּוּי רַבָּה
Vidui Rabbah

חֶשְׁבּוֹן הַנֶּפֶשׁ
Cheshbon HaNefesh

כִּי אָנוּ עַמֶּךָ
Ki Anu Amecha

שְׁמַע קוֹלֵנוּ
Sh'ma Koleinu

Al cheit shechatanu l'fanecha
   b'hirhur halev;
v'al cheit shechatanu l'fanecha
   birchilut.

עַל חֵטְא שֶׁחָטָאנוּ לְפָנֶיךָ
בְּהִרְהוּר הַלֵּב,
וְעַל חֵטְא שֶׁחָטָאנוּ לְפָנֶיךָ
בִּרְכִילוּת.

The ways we have wronged You through our innermost thoughts;
and harm we have caused in Your world through gossip and rumor.

Al cheit shechatanu l'fanecha
   b'chapat shochad;
v'al cheit shechatanu l'fanecha
   b'chilul hashem.

עַל חֵטְא שֶׁחָטָאנוּ לְפָנֶיךָ
בְּכַפַּת שֹׁחַד,
וְעַל חֵטְא שֶׁחָטָאנוּ לְפָנֶיךָ
בְּחִלּוּל הַשֵּׁם.

The ways we have wronged You by offering or accepting bribes;
and harm we have caused in Your world by profaning Your name in
   public.

V'al kulam, Elo·ah s'lichot,
s'lach lanu, m'chal lanu, kaper-lanu.

וְעַל כֻּלָּם, אֱלוֹהַּ סְלִיחוֹת,
סְלַח לָנוּ, מְחַל לָנוּ, כַּפֶּר־לָנוּ.

For all these failures of judgment and will, God of forgiveness —
forgive us, pardon us, lead us to atonement.

V'AL KULAM GO BACK TO 246

FOR ALL THESE FAILURES וְעַל כֻּלָּם. In the Talmud (B'rachot 34b) we find a remark-
able claim: Said Rabbi Abbahu, "In the place where baalei t'shuvah stand, even the
perfectly righteous cannot stand." That is, the effort and dedication required to engage
in t'shuvah and overcome one's sins place the penitent at a higher spiritual level than
even the most blameless individuals. The highest degree of merit does not necessarily belong to those who have never been tempted and done wrong. Rather, struggle
for self-improvement and self-mastery seems to be more highly valued than virtuous
conduct per se.

VIDUI FOR THE TWENTY-FIRST CENTURY

We confess our sins against the earth.
We commit ourselves to saving it.

We have assaulted our planet in countless ways
We have blamed others for the spiraling, deepening crisis
We have consumed thoughtlessly and irresponsibly
We have driven myriad species to the point of extinction
We have exhausted irreplaceable resources
We have failed to transcend borders and act unselfishly
We have given in to our many appetites and our gluttony
We have harmed beyond repair the habitats of living beings
We have ignored the signs of change in our climate and our seasons
We have jeopardized the well-being of future generations
We have known the problem but left problem-solving to others
We have lost sight of our role as God's partners in creation
We have mocked, cynically, those who love creatures great and small
We have neglected the environment, most of all, in places of poverty
We have over-populated our cities and over-fished our oceans
We have polluted seashore and sky, fertile soil and freshwater springs
We have questioned and doubted solid evidence of danger
We have ravaged the old growth forests—ecosystems created over centuries
We have spewed poison into the bloodstream of our land: its rivers, lakes, and estuaries
We have transformed dazzling beauty into industrial ugliness
We have used shared resources for personal gain and corporate profit
We have violated the commandment "Do not destroy"
We have wasted precious treasures, our God-given gifts
We have exploited the weakest and most vulnerable in our midst
And yet we yearn to be better guardians of this earth and the fullness thereof
Let us be zealous now to care for this unique corner of the cosmos, this planet—our sacred home

Cheshbon HaNefesh

Introspection and Silent Confession

After each section, individuals may pause for personal reflection.

We stand together this day to confess our sins —
but these moments are mine.
In the privacy of my heart, I acknowledge the wrongs I have done;
pain I have given, intentionally and unintentionally;
my thoughtless, careless, heartless actions,
and my failure to do what was right.

I reflect on the harm I have done to myself:

through failure to care for my body and preserve my health;
through failure to develop my mind and grow in learning;
through failure to develop my spiritual life and seek God's presence;
through failure to maintain my integrity and remain faithful to my ideals;
through trying to meet my emotional needs in unhealthy ways;
through sexual irresponsibility;
through failure to manage my finances wisely;
through indulging in negative thinking, self-obsession, or self-denigration;
through closing myself off from others rather than reaching out;
through taking on too much and neglecting what matters most;
through using time in a way that does not reflect my true priorities;
through fear of change, stagnation, falling into routine. . . .

And I confess, as well, these acts of harming myself . . .

I reflect on the harm I have done to my family and friends:

through my failure to listen with care, empathy, and compassion;
through my failure to give my time, attention, and energy to sustaining important relationships;
through my failure to convey affection and respect, appreciation and gratitude;
through stubbornness, giving in to anger, or violence;
through my intolerance of imperfection in others;
through criticism, harsh judgment, and focusing on the negative;
through my failure to fulfill my responsibilities and sacred commitments;
through intrusiveness, over-involvement, or manipulation;
through gossip, tale-bearing, and failure to give the benefit of the doubt;

through withholding my deepest self, lying, and deceit;
through my failure to forgive and let go of grudges;
through neglect, impatience, or insensitivity toward my parents and other elders;
through neglect, impatience, or insensitivity toward my children and other young people. . . .

And I confess, as well, these acts of harming family and friends . . .

I reflect on the harm I have done to the world around me:

through my failure to take time to educate myself about complex social problems;
through my failure to do my part as an active citizen and make my voice heard;
through resigning myself to the way things are, rather than working for change;
through inappropriate or harmful sexual behavior;
through succumbing to racism and disdaining those different from myself;
through over-consumption, materialism, and self-indulgence;
through my failure to respond with generosity to those in need;
through my discourtesy, ill-temper, and impatience at work or in public settings;
through dishonesty in my work or financial dealings;
through breaking the law or bending the rules;
through cynicism and abandoning hope. . . .

And I confess, as well, these acts of harming the world around me . . .

I reflect on the harm I have done to the Jewish people:

through my failure to make time for Jewish learning, worship, and mitzvot;
through neglecting to do my part to carry on the tradition;
through my reluctance to keep growing in my Jewish life and deepen my Jewish practice;
through my failure to be a good Jewish role model for the children in my life;
through gossip and harmful speech about members of our community;
through taking from the community without giving back;
through my indifference to Jews in need, here and around the world;
through ignoring opportunities to visit, support, and educate myself about Israel;
through my failure to exemplify the highest Jewish values and virtues. . . .

And I confess, as well, these acts of harming the Jewish people . . .

Ki anu amecha, v'atah Eloheinu;	כִּי אָֽנוּ עַמֶּֽךָ, וְאַתָּה אֱלֹהֵינוּ,
anu vanecha, v'atah avinu.	אָֽנוּ בָנֶֽיךָ, וְאַתָּה אָבִֽינוּ.
Anu avadecha, v'atah adoneinu;	אָֽנוּ עֲבָדֶֽיךָ, וְאַתָּה אֲדוֹנֵֽנוּ,
anu k'halecha, v'atah chelkeinu.	אָֽנוּ קְהָלֶֽךָ, וְאַתָּה חֶלְקֵֽנוּ.
Anu nachalatecha, v'atah goraleinu;	אָֽנוּ נַחֲלָתֶֽךָ, וְאַתָּה גוֹרָלֵֽנוּ,
anu tzonecha, v'atah ro·einu.	אָֽנוּ צֹאנֶֽךָ, וְאַתָּה רוֹעֵֽנוּ.
Anu charmecha, v'atah notreinu;	אָֽנוּ כַרְמֶֽךָ, וְאַתָּה נוֹטְרֵֽנוּ,
anu f'ulatecha, v'atah yotzreinu.	אָֽנוּ פְעֻלָּתֶֽךָ, וְאַתָּה יוֹצְרֵֽנוּ.
Anu rayatecha, v'atah dodeinu;	אָֽנוּ רַעְיָתֶֽךָ, וְאַתָּה דוֹדֵֽנוּ,
anu s'gulatecha, v'atah k'roveinu.	אָֽנוּ סְגֻלָּתֶֽךָ, וְאַתָּה קְרוֹבֵֽנוּ.
Anu amecha, v'atah malkeinu;	אָֽנוּ עַמֶּֽךָ, וְאַתָּה מַלְכֵּֽנוּ,
anu maamirecha, v'atah maamireinu.	אָֽנוּ מַאֲמִירֶֽיךָ, וְאַתָּה מַאֲמִירֵֽנוּ.

שְׁמַע קוֹלֵֽנוּ
Sh'ma Koleinu
וִדּוּי זוּטָא
Vidui Zuta
וִדּוּי רַבָּה
Vidui Rabbah
חֶשְׁבּוֹן הַנֶּֽפֶשׁ
Cheshbon HaNefesh
כִּי אָֽנוּ עַמֶּֽךָ
Ki Anu Amecha
שְׁמַע קוֹלֵֽנוּ
Sh'ma Koleinu

Our God and God of our ancestors —

We are Your people; and You are our God.
We are Your children; and You are our father, our mother.
We are the people who serve You; and You call us to serve.
We are Your community; and You are our portion.
We are Your legacy; and You are our purpose.
We are Your flock; and You are our shepherd.
We are Your vineyard; and You watch over us.
We are Your work; and You are our maker.
We are Your beloved; and You are our lover.
We are Your treasure; and You are the one we cherish.
We are Your people; and You reign over us.
We offer You our words; and You offer us Yours.

So forgive us, pardon us, lead us to atonement.

WE ARE YOUR PEOPLE כִּי אָֽנוּ עַמֶּֽךָ. This medieval poem is based on a verse in Song of Songs, "I am my beloved's and my beloved is mine" (2:16). Its array of metaphors captures the sublime bond between human and divine; its images evoke nuances of love, loyalty, and nurturing. The language ("We . . . and You . . .") may remind us of the "I–Thou" philosophy of Martin Buber (1878–1965), which speaks of a relationship grounded in mutuality and direct address, and which, in Buber's words, "can only be spoken with the whole being." In "We Are Your People" the first-person plural replaces "I" because this prayer would have us affirm, with our whole being, the ideas of peoplehood and covenant between God and Israel. It is we, not isolated individuals, who celebrate our bond with the divine Thou.

Hear Our Call

The Short Confession

The Long Confession

Introspection and Silent Confession

We Are Your People

Hear Our Call

אל רחום

לוּ אֶחֱזֶה פָנָיו בְּלִבִּי בָיְתָה . . .

If I could see God's face within my heart . . .

I'd see the face of a Gardener —
compassionate to weed and flower alike, patiently pruning,
graciously planting,
loving the endless hours of tending and nurturing the earth —
seeds, roots, all that grows;
and true to the essence of the gardener's work:
forgiving the fallen branches, the withered petals, the cracked stones,
the broken stems

לוּ אֶחֱזֶה פָנָיו בְּלִבִּי בָיְתָה . . .

If I could see God's face within my heart . . .

I'd see the human face in a thousand acts of mercy —
the one who gives bread to the hungry and shelters the lost,
who hears the voice of grief
and makes room for the stranger;
who brings relief to the blind, the bent, the unjustly imprisoned;
and is true to the essence of holy work:
resisting evil, healing brokenness, easing pain;
and, in the end, forgiving ourselves as God forgives us.

יְיָ יְיָ, אֵל רַחוּם וְחַנּוּן, — *Adonai, Adonai — El rachum v'chanun;*
אֶרֶךְ אַפַּיִם, וְרַב־חֶסֶד וֶאֱמֶת. — *erech apayim, v'rav-chesed ve·emet;*
נֹצֵר חֶסֶד לָאֲלָפִים, — *notzeir chesed laalafim;*
נֹשֵׂא עָוֹן וָפֶשַׁע וְחַטָּאָה, וְנַקֵּה. — *nosei avon vafesha v'chataah; v'nakeih.*

Adonai, Adonai —
God, compassionate, gracious, endlessly patient, loving, and true;
showing mercy to the thousandth generation;
forgiving evil, defiance, and wrongdoing; granting pardon.

IF I COULD SEE GOD'S FACE WITHIN MY HEART. This refrain is adapted from the poem "Vision of God" by Yehudah Halevi (ca. 1075–1141).

ADONAI, ADONAI יְיָ, יְיָ, Exodus 34:6–7.

HAKARAT HATOV — RECOGNIZING THE GOOD

Throughout the year
regard yourself as equally balanced
between merit and sin.
With one act, you can tip the balance
for yourself, and for the world.
Every good deed
makes a difference.
And so it is written:
"A righteous person
is the foundation of the world"—
for one who does good
tips the balance of the scales
and can save the world.

Rabbi Nachman of Breslov taught:
Always look for the good
in yourself.

And remember:
Joy is not incidental to your spiritual quest;
it is vital.

For so it is written (Isaiah 55:12):
"You will go out through joy,
and be led forth in peace."
Focus on the good in yourself;
take joy in what is good,
and you will be led forth from inner darkness.

THROUGHOUT THE YEAR . . . SAVE THE WORLD. Based on Talmud *Kiddushin* 40b and Maimonides, *Mishneh Torah*, Laws of *T'shuvah* 3.4.

A RIGHTEOUS PERSON, Proverbs 10:25.

RABBI NACHMAN OF BRESLOV, 1772–1810.

FOR SO IT IS WRITTEN. Rabbi Nachman creatively interprets this verse in Isaiah ("You shall go out in joy," the prophet's promise of deliverance from the Babylonian exile) as a message that one may find a personal exodus from sadness by learning to focus on the good and to cultivate joy.

FOR EVERY ACT OF GOODNESS

Let us affirm the good we have done;
let us acknowledge our acts of healing and repair . . .

For the good we have done
by acting with self-restraint and self-control;

For the good we have done
through acts of generosity and compassion;

For the good we have done
by offering children our love and support;

For the good we have done
by honoring our parents with care and respect;

For the good we have done
through acts of friendship and hospitality;

For the good we have done
through acts of forgiveness and reconciliation;

For the good we have done
by keeping promises and honoring commitments;

For the good we have done
through the work of our hands, and by serving others;

For the good we have done
by caring for the earth and sustaining its creatures;

For the good we have done
by housing the homeless, feeding the hungry, and welcoming the stranger;

For the good we have done
by acting with integrity and honesty;

For the good we have done
through thoughtful and encouraging words;

For the good we have done
by caring for our health and that of our loved ones;

For the good we have done
by strengthening our Jewish community;

For the good we have done
through acts of civic engagement and *tikkun olam*;

All these have brought light and healing into the world.
May these acts inspire us to renew our efforts in the year to come.

Open your heart, he said
Open your eyes, see the truth
and forgive.
I can't, I said
through clenched teeth.
It's this way, he said
The Endless One made a world
wild and chaotic—
light and darkness, birthing and dying,
joy and sorrow.
All of us are enmeshed in good and evil,
caught by forces beyond our control.
We act in ignorance and confusion, blindly lashing out.
But I'm hurt, I said.
Listen, he said:
You expect order; you think you can exert control—
this is the source of your pain.
The one who hurt you is trapped,
as you are trapped
in compulsion and fear.
Know this, he said:
All of life—*haveil havalim*,
a breath of air, a bubble that bursts in an instant.
So learn to live with impermanence;
accept uncertainty, and your suffering will ease.
You cannot guarantee security, he said,
But you can hold fast to wisdom.
Look at the world with new eyes, he said.
Let go of expectations
and you will relinquish anger.
In their place, love and compassion will blossom.
And then the clenched fist of your heart will open
and you will forgive.

Open your heart. Based on the writings of Rabbi Rami Shapiro (b. 1951).

Endless One. In Hebrew, *Ein Sof*, a kabbalistic name for God.

Haveil havalim. A key phrase in the Book of Ecclesiastes, sometimes translated "vanity of vanities" or "utter futility." This phrase is based on the noun *hevel* (a breath of air), conveying that life is fleeting and evanescent—or in the words of the *Untaneh Tokef* prayer, "like a shadow moving on, a cloud passing by, mere dust in the wind, a dream that flies away."

שְׁמַע קוֹלֵנוּ
Sh'ma Koleinu

וִדּוּי זוּטָא
Vidui Zuta

וִדּוּי רַבָּה
Vidui Rabbah

חֶשְׁבּוֹן הַנֶּפֶשׁ
Cheshbon HaNefesh

כִּי אָנוּ עַמֶּךָ
Ki Anu Amecha

שְׁמַע קוֹלֵנוּ
Sh'ma Koleinu

God, God, open unto me:

Open unto me—
light for my darkness
Open unto me—
courage for my fear
Open unto me—
hope for my despair
Open unto me—
peace for my turmoil
Open unto me—
joy for my sorrow
Open unto me—
strength for my weakness
Open unto me—
wisdom for my confusion
Open unto me—
forgiveness for my sins
Open unto me—
tenderness for my toughness
Open unto me—
love for my hates
Open unto me—
Your Self for my self
God, God, open unto me!

GOD, GOD. By Howard Thurman (1899–1981).

שְׁמַע קוֹלֵנוּ, יְיָ אֱלֹהֵינוּ.
חוּס וְרַחֵם עָלֵינוּ.
וְקַבֵּל בְּרַחֲמִים וּבְרָצוֹן אֶת
  תְּפִלָּתֵנוּ.
הֲשִׁיבֵנוּ, יְיָ, אֵלֶיךָ וְנָשׁוּבָה,
חַדֵּשׁ יָמֵינוּ כְּקֶדֶם.
אֲמָרֵינוּ הַאֲזִינָה, יְיָ,
בִּינָה הֲגִיגֵנוּ.
יִהְיוּ לְרָצוֹן אִמְרֵי־פִינוּ וְהֶגְיוֹן
  לִבֵּנוּ לְפָנֶיךָ,
יְיָ, צוּרֵנוּ וְגוֹאֲלֵנוּ.
אַל־תַּשְׁלִיכֵנוּ מִלְּפָנֶיךָ,
וְרוּחַ קָדְשְׁךָ אַל־תִּקַּח מִמֶּנּוּ.
אַל־תַּשְׁלִיכֵנוּ לְעֵת זִקְנָה,
כִּכְלוֹת כֹּחֵנוּ אַל־תַּעַזְבֵנוּ.
אַל־תַּעַזְבֵנוּ, יְיָ אֱלֹהֵינוּ,
אַל־תִּרְחַק מִמֶּנּוּ.
כִּי־לְךָ, יְיָ, הוֹחָלְנוּ,
אַתָּה תַעֲנֶה, אֲדֹנָי אֱלֹהֵינוּ.

Sh'ma koleinu, Adonai Eloheinu.
Chus v'racheim aleinu.
V'kabeil b'rachamim uvratzon et
  t'filateinu.
Hashiveinu, Adonai, eilecha — v'nashuvah;
chadeish yameinu k'kedem.
Amareinu haazinah, Adonai,
binah hagigeinu.
Yiyu l'ratzon imrei-finu v'hegyon
  libeinu l'fanecha,
Adonai — tzureinu v'go·aleinu.
Al-tashlicheinu mil'fanecha;
v'ruach kodsh'cha al-tikach mimenu.
Al-tashlicheinu l'eit ziknah;
kichlot kocheinu, al-taazveinu.
Al-taazveinu, Adonai Eloheinu;
al-tirchak mimenu.
Ki-l'cha, Adonai, hochalnu;
atah taaneh, Adonai Eloheinu.

Hear our call, Adonai our God. Show us compassion.
Accept our prayer with love and goodwill.

Take us back, Adonai; let us come back to You; renew our days as in the past.
Hear our words, Adonai; understand our unspoken thoughts.
May the speech of our mouth and our heart's quiet prayer
be acceptable to You, Adonai, our Rock and our Redeemer.

Do not cast us away from Your presence, or cut us off from Your holy spirit.
Do not cast us away when we are old; as our strength diminishes,
  do not forsake us.
Do not forsake us, Adonai; be not far from us, our God.

With hope, Adonai, we await You;
surely, You, Adonai our God — You will answer.

HEAR OUR CALL שְׁמַע קוֹלֵנוּ, based on Lamentations 5:21; Psalm 5:2, 19:15, 51:13, 71:9, 38:22, 38:16.

שְׁמַע קוֹלֵנוּ, יְיָ אֱלֹהֵינוּ . . .

Sh'ma koleinu—
Hear our call, *Adonai Eloheinu*.
And may we hear Yours
in our apologies and confessions,
in the meditations of our heart,
in the accountings of our soul.

Hear our call,
and may we hear Yours
in words of counsel and consolation,
in the silence of one who listens,
in the strength of a hand that upholds.

Hear our call, *Adonai Eloheinu*,
as we strive to hear Yours
on this day of the heart,
this day of repair and healing.

THE MYSTERY OF THE NECESSITY TO INFORM YOU

אֲנִי יוֹדֵעַ, אֲנִי מְשֻׁכְנָע וּכְבָר הוֹכַחְתִּי לְעַצְמִי אֶלֶף וְאַחַת –
שֶׁאֵינְךָ קַיָּם,
שֶׁאַתָּה אַיִן, שֶׁאַתָּה בְּלִי, שֶׁאַתָּה חוּט תָּלוּי עַל תֹּהוּ.
מַה שֶּׁמַּטְרִיד וּמַקְנִיט וּמֵבִיךְ אוֹתִי כָּל פַּעַם מֵחָדָשׁ
הֵם הַמִּסְתּוֹרִין שֶׁבַּכֹּרַח לְהוֹדִיעֲךָ כָּל זֹאת יוֹם יוֹם
וּלְשַׁתֵּף אוֹתְךָ בַּמַּסְקָנוֹת הָאִישִׁיּוֹת שֶׁלִּי.

I know, I am certain and have already proven to myself a thousand and one times—
that you do not exist,
that you are nothingness, that you are without, that you are a thread hung over the abyss.
What disturbs and annoys me and embarrasses me time and time again
is the mystery of the necessity I feel to inform you of this every day,
and to share with you my personal conclusions.

THE MYSTERY. By Yaakov Orland (1914–2002).

סִיּוּם הַשַּׁחֲרִית
Siyum HaShacharit · Concluding Prayers

1.
Infinite Source of goodness,
help us to see the good
in ourselves, in others, and in the world around us.
Teach us to cultivate a discerning mind
to know right from wrong;
and a listening heart
open to love and forgiveness.

Guide us to walk in Your ways with integrity,
ever faithful to the promises our forebears made.
And may Your goodness inspire us to do what is just and right.

Hayom t'am'tzeinu! Amen.	הַיּוֹם תְּאַמְּצֵנוּ, אָמֵן.
Hayom t'var'cheinu! Amen.	הַיּוֹם תְּבָרְכֵנוּ, אָמֵן.
Hayom t'gad'leinu! Amen.	הַיּוֹם תְּגַדְּלֵנוּ, אָמֵן.
Hayom tidr'sheinu l'tovah! Amen.	הַיּוֹם תִּדְרְשֵׁנוּ לְטוֹבָה, אָמֵן.
Hayom ticht'veinu l'chayim tovim! Amen.	הַיּוֹם תִּכְתְּבֵנוּ לְחַיִּים טוֹבִים, אָמֵן.
Hayom tishma shavateinu! Amen.	הַיּוֹם תִּשְׁמַע שַׁוְעָתֵנוּ, אָמֵן.
Hayom titm'cheinu bimin tzidkecha! Amen.	הַיּוֹם תִּתְמְכֵנוּ בִּימִין צִדְקֶךָ, אָמֵן.

Strengthen us this day! Amen.
Bless us this day! Amen.
This day, exalt us! Amen.
Show us kindness this day! Amen.
Inscribe us this day for a life of goodness! Amen.
This day, hear our cry! Amen.
Now and always, support us with the strength of
Your righteousness! Amen.

DISCERNING MIND . . . LISTENING HEART. Both phrases echo Solomon's prayer in I Kings 3:9. The young king, when asked by God what he seeks for himself, requests "*lev shomei·a* (a discerning mind — literally: a listening heart) . . . to distinguish between good and bad."

WALK IN YOUR WAYS . . . WHAT IS JUST AND RIGHT. Based on God's words to Abraham in Genesis 17:1 and 18:19.

Concluding Prayers

2.

In humble linen garments the priests once stood at the altar;
so we stand now, in humility, to lift up our offering to You.

It is written in the Torah:
Each morning the *kohein* shall take up the ashes left from
the night's offering,
and remove them from the altar;
thus begins the service of a new day.

And our Sages teach:
Clear away the debris of the past — begin anew.
Complacency and despair are the enemies of hope;
each day summons us to start again.

The fire on the altar must never die out —
tend it with care; keep the sacred flame alive.

So also should the spirit be sustained and preserved.
This day we nourish ourselves with Torah and prayer,
and tomorrow return to the world.

Our energies replenished, our commitments renewed,
tomorrow we go forth to serve the Most High.
In small ways, in all ways, let us align ourselves with the good —
our minds and hearts and hands devoted to *tikkun*.

In humility we stand here this day, hoping to lift up our lives
and persevere through life's trials.
Let us gain strength from one another.
Let us gain strength from the tradition we share.

EACH MORNING. Based on Leviticus 6:3.

OUR SAGES TEACH. Based on the commentary of Rabbi Samson Raphael Hirsch (1808–1888), who wrote: "The past must recede into the background; it must not clothe us in pride as we set out upon the new task to which each new day summons us." Similarly, Amy Hill Shevitz (b. 1953) writes: "The ashes are disposed of in 'a clean place.' But when the camp moves on, they are left behind. . . . When we do not clear out the ashes of the old . . . we cannot proceed with our own service to God."

FIRE ON THE ALTAR. Based on Leviticus 6:5–6.

TIKKUN. Acts of healing and repair.

מנחה ליום כיפור

Yom Kippur Afternoon Service

You shall be holy.

—LEVITICUS 19:2

הֲכָנָה
Hachanah

הֲכָנָה לַמִּנְחָה
Hachanah LaMinchah · Preparing for Minchah

Our Sages taught:
Isaac established the *Minchah* (Afternoon) prayer, as the Torah says: "Isaac went out walking (*lasuach*) in the field toward evening." The word *lasuach* also refers to prayer, as the Psalmist says: "A prayer of the lowly person when he is faint and pours forth his plea (*sichah*)."

Late in the afternoon, tired and faint, Isaac wandered in the fields and he opened his heart to God. "Do you remember," he asked, "how I lay upon the altar of Moriah, long ago?"

Said Rabbi Yehudah:
When the knife touched Isaac's neck, his soul flew out of his body in terror. But when the heavenly Voice commanded: "Do not stretch out your hand to hurt the youth . . ." his soul returned, and Isaac stood upon his feet, restored to life. At that moment he declared: "Blessed be Adonai, who brings life to the dead."

At the waning of the day, our father Isaac found himself in prayer.
So may we find ourselves, and You, as we approach the Afternoon Prayer.
As Isaac rose up from death, restored to life, may we come forth from this day of Yom Kippur touched by remembrance of mortality, but full of the joy of life.

For those who wear a tallit (no blessing is said):
Holy One, Your light wraps me in beauty,
as I wrap myself in a tallit and enter the *Minchah* service of this holy day.

For those who do not wear a tallit:
Holy One, Your light enfolds me in beauty
as I enter the *Minchah* service of this holy day.

OUR SAGES TAUGHT. Based on Talmud *B'rachot* 26b, citing Genesis 24:63 and Psalm 102:1. The Talmud plays on the shared Hebrew root of the words *lasuach* (walking) and *sichah* (plea, prayer).

SAID RABBI YEHUDAH. Based on Midrash *Pirkei d'Rabbi Eliezer* 30.

Preparation

From Psalm 34

מִי־הָאִישׁ הֶחָפֵץ חַיִּים,
אֹהֵב יָמִים לִרְאוֹת טוֹב.
נְצֹר לְשׁוֹנְךָ מֵרָע,
וּשְׂפָתֶיךָ מִדַּבֵּר מִרְמָה.
סוּר מֵרָע וַעֲשֵׂה־טוֹב,
בַּקֵּשׁ שָׁלוֹם וְרָדְפֵהוּ.

Mi-ha·ish hechafeitz chayim,
oheiv yamim, lirot tov?
N'tzor l'shon'cha meira,
usfatecha midabeir mirmah.
Sur meira vaaseih-tov;
bakeish shalom v'rodfeihu.

What is the way of a person who delights in life,
who loves each day and yearns to see goodness?
Guard your tongue from evil,
your lips from cunning speech.
Turn your back on immorality
and do good without delay.
Seek shalom and pursue it.

A Very Narrow Bridge

כָּל הָעוֹלָם כֻּלּוֹ גֶּשֶׁר צַר מְאֹד,
וְהָעִקָּר לֹא לְפַחֵד כְּלָל.

Kol haolam kulo gesher tzar m'od,
v'ha·ikar lo l'facheid k'lal.

All the world is a very narrow bridge;
and the most important thing is not to be afraid.

From Psalm 118

עָזִּי וְזִמְרָת יָהּ,
וַיְהִי־לִי לִישׁוּעָה.

Ozi v'zimrat Yah;
vaihi li lishuah.

Adonai is my strength, my song of praise,
for God has saved my life.

WHAT IS THE WAY, Psalm 34:13–15.

A VERY NARROW BRIDGE. Adapted from a teaching by the Chasidic master Nachman of Breslov (1772–1810).

ADONAI IS MY STRENGTH, Psalm 118:14; Exodus 15:2; Isaiah 12:2.

הֲכָנָה
Hachanah

We Stand as One

At this hour, Israel stands as one in prayer;
all Jews on earth unite through memory and hope.

A people unafraid, unvanquished, says to God:
This people You have formed still lives to tell Your praise.

Still lives—to share this teaching with our youth:
Our ancient journey has not reached its end.
The faith implanted at our people's birth
is realized from age to age—our sacred covenant.
This people, few in number, ventured forth
to carve a lonely path through wilderness;
with dreams of vines and fig trees,
justice in the gates, the land at peace.

And still we make our way across the desert—
this people You have formed still lives to walk before You.

Exiled once, to Babylon, we learned the unity of God;
a second time, dispersed by Rome, we learned that humankind is one.
Hear, O Israel—
the call still sounds:
Eternity is ever present in your midst;
a heritage of sacred purpose in your heart.
Your past tells a story for all peoples;
your future holds a promise still unfolding.

At this hour, Israel stands as one in prayer;
all Jews on earth unite through memory and hope.
We look at one another, and we know who we are;
we look to our Creator and we know our strength.

In pursuit of truth this people lives,
to serve the Most High, for the sake of life.
Behind us, pain and glory; before us, holy work.
Timeless words command us; toward eternity we gaze.

AT THIS HOUR, ISRAEL STANDS AS ONE. This statement is based on the opening line of a prayer by Rabbi Leo Baeck (1873–1956) "for all Jewish communities in Germany" on the eve of Yom Kippur, October 6, 1935.

THIS PEOPLE YOU HAVE FORMED. Based on Isaiah 43:21.

Preparation

JACOB HAD a dream:
a ladder, set on the ground, with its top reaching the sky—
and angels of God were ascending and descending the ladder.

Our Sages taught:
The Holy One said, "Jacob, *you* must climb, as well."
But Jacob was afraid, and he did not climb up.

We want to climb higher
but we're tired
and there's so much to do
and we don't know how to rise.

God of Becoming,
whose name means "I Will Be What I Will Be,"
You are the Unfinished One,
ever-unfolding, evolving with Your creation.
Made in Your image,
we too are fluid,
ever-becoming who we will be.

Keep us alive to possibilities;
show us a path to grow in mind, heart and spirit;
help us find the strength to ascend.

JEWISH THOUGHT pays little attention to inner tranquility and peace of mind. . . . In fact, the very concept of the Divine as infinite implies an activity that is endless, of which one must never grow weary. . . . The Jewish approach to life considers the person who has stopped going—one who has a feeling of completion, of peace, of a great light from above that has brought him or her to rest—to be someone who has lost the way.

JACOB HAD A DREAM . . . DESCENDING THE LADDER, Genesis 28:12.
THE HOLY ONE SAID . . . DID NOT CLIMB UP. From the ca. 6th-century midrashic collection called *P'sikta d'Rav Kahana* 23.2.
I WILL BE WHAT I WILL BE, Exodus 3:14 (in Hebrew: *Eyeh Asher Eyeh*).
JEWISH THOUGHT. By Rabbi Adin Steinsaltz (b. 1937), adapted.

קְרִיאַת הַתּוֹרָה

K'riat HaTorah · Reading of the Torah

Bringing the Torah into Our Midst

It shall come to pass, in the fullness of time, that the mountain of the House of God shall be established as the highest mountain, and raised above the hills; and all nations shall flow to it. Then many peoples shall say: Come, let us go up to the mountain of the Eternal, to the House of the God of Jacob. And they shall say:

Teach us Your ways, that we may walk in Your paths.

We give thanks today for a Torah of life — the way of kindness, mercy, and truth.
May compassion be our source of sustenance now, as in our people's past.
May our souls withstand times of crisis, and our hearts the inclination to evil.
May the covenant of Abraham and Sarah strengthen our will to do what is right.
May the qualities of mercy and goodness, love and forgiveness flow through our lives.
And let us be strong in a perilous world; let us open our hearts to the path of Torah.

וַיְהִי בִּנְסֹעַ הָאָרֹן, וַיֹּאמֶר מֹשֶׁה:
קוּמָה, יְיָ, וְיָפֻצוּ אֹיְבֶיךָ,
וְיָנֻסוּ מְשַׂנְאֶיךָ מִפָּנֶיךָ.

Vaihi binsoa haaron, vayomer Mosheh:
"Kumah, Adonai! V'yafutzu oivecha;
v'yanusu m'sanecha mipanecha."

When the Ark set out in the wilderness, Moses would say:
"Go forward, Adonai! May Your enemies be scattered;
may Your enemies flee before You."

IT SHALL COME TO PASS, Isaiah 2:2–3.

WE GIVE THANKS. Based, in part, on the prayer *Av Harachamim, hu y'racheim* (May the Source of Compassion Have Mercy on Us), a 12th-century prayer before the Torah reading.

WHEN THE ARK SET OUT וַיְהִי בִּנְסֹעַ, Numbers 10:35. It is customary to rise at these words, as the ark is opened.

כִּי מִצִּיּוֹן תֵּצֵא תוֹרָה,
וּדְבַר־יְיָ מִירוּשָׁלָיִם.

Ki mitziyon teitzei Torah,
udvar-Adonai miYrushalayim.

For Torah shall come forth from Zion,
the word of Adonai from Jerusalem.

בָּרוּךְ שֶׁנָּתַן תּוֹרָה לְעַמּוֹ יִשְׂרָאֵל
בִּקְדֻשָּׁתוֹ.

Baruch shenatan Torah l'amo Yisrael
bikdushato.

Blessed is the One whose holiness brought Torah to the people Israel.

שְׁמַע יִשְׂרָאֵל,
יְיָ אֱלֹהֵינוּ, יְיָ אֶחָד.

Sh'ma, Yisrael:
Adonai Eloheinu, Adonai echad!

Listen, Israel: Adonai is our God, Adonai is One!

אֶחָד אֱלֹהֵינוּ, גָּדוֹל אֲדוֹנֵינוּ,
קָדוֹשׁ וְנוֹרָא שְׁמוֹ.

Echad eloheinu, gadol adoneinu,
kadosh v'nora sh'mo.

One and magnificent is our God; God's name is holy, **inspiring awe.**

גַּדְּלוּ לַייָ אִתִּי,
וּנְרוֹמְמָה שְׁמוֹ יַחְדָּו.

Gad'lu l'Adonai iti;
unrom'mah sh'mo yachdav.

לְךָ, יְיָ, הַגְּדֻלָּה וְהַגְּבוּרָה
וְהַתִּפְאֶרֶת וְהַנֵּצַח וְהַהוֹד,
כִּי־כֹל בַּשָּׁמַיִם וּבָאָרֶץ.
לְךָ, יְיָ, הַמַּמְלָכָה
וְהַמִּתְנַשֵּׂא, לְכֹל לְרֹאשׁ.

L'cha, Adonai, hag'dulah, v'hag'vurah,
v'hatiferet, v'haneitzach, v'hahod —
ki-chol bashamayim uvaaretz.
L'cha, Adonai, hamamlachah
v'hamitnasei, l'chol l'rosh.

Exalt the Eternal with me; let us extol God's name together.

Yours, Adonai, are greatness, might, splendor, triumph, and majesty — yes, all that is in heaven and earth; to You, God, belong majesty and preeminence above all.

FOR TORAH כִּי מִצִּיּוֹן, Isaiah 2:3. We enact these words as we sing them, taking the Torah from the ark to bring it forth — as though "from Zion."

HEAR שְׁמַע, Deuteronomy 6:4.

EXALT גַּדְּלוּ, Psalm 34:4.

YOURS, ADONAI לְךָ, יְיָ, I Chronicles 29:11.

Blessing Before the Torah Reading

בָּרְכוּ אֶת יְיָ הַמְבֹרָךְ.
Bar'chu et Adonai hamvorach.

Congregation responds:

בָּרוּךְ יְיָ הַמְבֹרָךְ לְעוֹלָם וָעֶד.
Baruch Adonai hamvorach l'olam va·ed.

בָּרוּךְ יְיָ הַמְבֹרָךְ לְעוֹלָם וָעֶד.
בָּרוּךְ אַתָּה, יְיָ,
אֱלֹהֵינוּ מֶלֶךְ הָעוֹלָם,
אֲשֶׁר בָּחַר־בָּנוּ מִכָּל הָעַמִּים
וְנָתַן־לָנוּ אֶת תּוֹרָתוֹ.

Baruch Adonai hamvorach l'olam va·ed.
Baruch atah, Adonai,
Eloheinu melech haolam,
asher bachar-banu mikol haamim
v'natan-lanu et torato.

Bless the Eternal, the Blessed One.

Congregation: Blessed is the Eternal, the Blessed One, now and forever.

Blessed is the Eternal, the Blessed One, now and forever.
Blessed are You, Eternal, our God, supreme Power of the universe,
who embraced us and gave us this Teaching,
having chosen us to embody Torah among the peoples of the earth.

בָּרוּךְ אַתָּה, יְיָ, נוֹתֵן הַתּוֹרָה.
Baruch atah, Adonai, notein haTorah.
Blessed are You, God of eternity, whose gift is Torah.

The Torah portions are on pages 332–33 or pages 337–39.

Blessing After the Torah Reading

בָּרוּךְ אַתָּה, יְיָ,
אֱלֹהֵינוּ מֶלֶךְ הָעוֹלָם,
אֲשֶׁר נָתַן־לָנוּ תּוֹרַת אֱמֶת,
וְחַיֵּי עוֹלָם נָטַע בְּתוֹכֵנוּ.

Baruch atah, Adonai,
Eloheinu melech haolam,
asher natan-lanu Torat emet,
v'chayei olam nata b'tocheinu.

Blessed are You, Eternal, our God, supreme Power of the universe,
who gave us a Teaching of truth and planted within us eternal life.

בָּרוּךְ אַתָּה, יְיָ, נוֹתֵן הַתּוֹרָה.
Baruch atah, Adonai, notein haTorah.
Blessed are You, God of eternity, whose gift is Torah.

Genesis 50

Forgiveness and Continuity

For at least three reasons, the reading of Genesis 50 can be especially poignant on Yom Kippur. (1) The Day of Atonement begins with a sacred chant to annul vows and oaths that cannot be kept (*Kol Nidrei*); here we turn to a dramatic chapter of the Torah that is framed by promises that are kept: Joseph's promise to bury Jacob in the land of Canaan; and the promise that Joseph elicits from his brothers to carry his bones to the Promised Land. (2) The chapter is framed, as well, by the deaths of Jacob and Joseph—appropriate to this day of the solemn *Yizkor* prayer. (3) Genesis 50 bears witness to the power of forgiveness to heal emotional wounds.

Indeed, Joseph's tears of forgiveness in chapter 50 are fraught with memories of the events recounted in Genesis 37—his assault, kidnapping, and sale into slavery. According to a retelling of the story in the Book of Jubilees, his brothers' heinous crime against Joseph occurred on the tenth day of the seventh month—the very date of Yom Kippur—which suggests a connection between the Joseph narrative and this holy day, on which forgiveness is sought and offered.

In the end, Joseph consoles his brothers, which leaves us with a consummate lesson for Yom Kippur. "Deceptions and hurts within a family can go on in a perpetual cycle," writes Richard Elliot Friedman (b. 1946). "In order to bring it to an end, one member of the family who is entitled to retribution must stop the cycle and forgive instead. That is what Joseph does here."

And perhaps that is precisely why this chapter is framed by promises that are kept. Genesis 50 is an atonement tale of a family now healed of intergenerational wounds—cleansed of jealousy, resentment, and deceit—a family whose continuity is assured by the promise to carry Joseph's bones to the land of his ancestors.

JUBILEES. In 34:10–18. Probably written in the mid-2nd century BCE, the Book of Jubilees retells the stories of Genesis and Exodus, from Creation to Sinai. It is one of many Jewish religious texts of the late biblical period that were not included in the Hebrew Bible.

HIS BROTHERS' HEINOUS CRIME. Joseph's ten brothers were never punished for their violation of Exodus 21:16, which states: "One who kidnaps a person—whether having sold or still holding the victim—shall be put to death." The Book of Jubilees understands our annual observance of Yom Kippur, on the anniversary of this violation, as an ongoing ritual of collective repentance for the crime committed by Joseph's brothers.

Forgiveness and Continuity (Genesis 50:14–26)

14 After burying his father, Joseph returned to Egypt—he, his brothers, and all who had gone up with him to bury his father.

15 Seeing that their father was dead, Joseph's brothers said: "If Joseph carries a grudge against us, he will surely pay us back for all the evil we caused him." 16 So they sent instructions to Joseph: "Before his death your father gave these instructions: 17 Tell Joseph this: 'Please forgive your brothers' transgression and their sin, for they caused you harm.' So now, please forgive the crime of the servants of your father's God." And Joseph wept when they spoke to him.

18 His brothers proceeded to fling themselves before him and said: "Here we are—servants to you." 19 But Joseph said to them: "Do not be afraid—for am I in God's place? 20 Though your intentions toward me were evil, God intended it for good—so as to bring about the current situation: the survival of many people. 21 So now, do not be afraid. I will provide for you and for those who depend on you." And thus he comforted them, and spoke to their hearts.

22 And Joseph made his home in Egypt, he and his father's household. And Joseph lived one hundred and ten years. 23 And Joseph saw the third generation of Ephraim's children; and, moreover, the children of Machir, son of Manasseh, were born on Joseph's knees.

14 וַיָּ֨שָׁב יוֹסֵ֤ף מִצְרַ֨יְמָה֙ ה֣וּא
וְאֶחָ֔יו וְכָל־הָעֹלִ֥ים אִתּ֖וֹ לִקְבֹּ֣ר
אֶת־אָבִ֑יו אַחֲרֵ֖י קָבְר֥וֹ אֶת־אָבִֽיו׃
15 וַיִּרְא֤וּ אֲחֵֽי־יוֹסֵף֙ כִּי־מֵ֣ת
אֲבִיהֶ֔ם וַיֹּ֣אמְר֔וּ ל֥וּ יִשְׂטְמֵ֖נוּ
יוֹסֵ֑ף וְהָשֵׁ֤ב יָשִׁיב֙ לָ֔נוּ אֵ֚ת כָּל־
הָ֣רָעָ֔ה אֲשֶׁ֥ר גָּמַ֖לְנוּ אֹתֽוֹ׃ 16 וַיְצַוּ֕וּ
אֶל־יוֹסֵ֖ף לֵאמֹ֑ר אָבִ֣יךָ צִוָּ֔ה לִפְנֵ֥י
מוֹת֖וֹ לֵאמֹֽר׃ 17 כֹּֽה־תֹאמְר֣וּ
לְיוֹסֵ֗ף אָ֣נָּ֡א שָׂ֣א נָ֠א פֶּ֣שַׁע אַחֶ֤יךָ
וְחַטָּאתָם֙ כִּי־רָעָ֣ה גְמָל֔וּךָ וְעַתָּה֙
שָׂ֣א נָ֔א לְפֶ֥שַׁע עַבְדֵ֖י אֱלֹהֵ֣י אָבִ֑יךָ
וַיֵּ֥בְךְּ יוֹסֵ֖ף בְּדַבְּרָ֥ם אֵלָֽיו׃
18 וַיֵּלְכוּ֙ גַּם־אֶחָ֔יו וַֽיִּפְּל֖וּ
לְפָנָ֑יו וַיֹּ֣אמְר֔וּ הִנֶּ֥נּֽוּ לְךָ֖ לַעֲבָדִֽים׃
19 וַיֹּ֧אמֶר אֲלֵהֶ֛ם יוֹסֵ֖ף אַל־תִּירָ֑אוּ
כִּ֛י הֲתַ֥חַת אֱלֹהִ֖ים אָֽנִי׃ 20 וְאַתֶּ֕ם
חֲשַׁבְתֶּ֥ם עָלַ֖י רָעָ֑ה אֱלֹהִים֙
חֲשָׁבָ֣הּ לְטֹבָ֔ה לְמַ֗עַן עֲשֹׂ֛ה כַּיּ֥וֹם
הַזֶּ֖ה לְהַחֲיֹ֥ת עַם־רָֽב׃ 21 וְעַתָּה֙
אַל־תִּירָ֔אוּ אָנֹכִ֛י אֲכַלְכֵּ֥ל אֶתְכֶ֖ם
וְאֶת־טַפְּכֶ֑ם וַיְנַחֵ֣ם אוֹתָ֔ם
וַיְדַבֵּ֖ר עַל־לִבָּֽם׃
22 וַיֵּ֤שֶׁב יוֹסֵף֙ בְּמִצְרַ֔יִם ה֖וּא
וּבֵ֣ית אָבִ֑יו וַיְחִ֣י יוֹסֵ֔ף מֵאָ֥ה
וָעֶ֖שֶׂר שָׁנִֽים׃ 23 וַיַּ֤רְא יוֹסֵף֙
לְאֶפְרַ֔יִם בְּנֵ֖י שִׁלֵּשִׁ֑ים גַּ֗ם בְּנֵ֤י
מָכִיר֙ בֶּן־מְנַשֶּׁ֔ה יֻלְּד֖וּ עַל־בִּרְכֵּ֥י

הוֹצָאַת הַתּוֹרָה
Hotzaat HaTorah
בִּרְכוֹת הַתּוֹרָה
Birchot HaTorah
קְרִיאַת הַתּוֹרָה
K'riat HaTorah
מִי שֶׁבֵּרַךְ
Mi Shebeirach
הַגְבָּהָה
Hagbahah
בְּרָכָה שֶׁלִּפְנֵי הַהַפְטָרָה
B'rachah Shelifnei HaHaftarah
קְרִיאַת הַהַפְטָרָה
K'riat HaHaftarah
בְּרָכָה שֶׁאַחֲרֵי הַהַפְטָרָה
B'rachah She-acharei HaHaftarah
הַכְנָסַת סֵפֶר תּוֹרָה
Hachnasat Sefer Torah

Bringing the Torah into Our Midst

Torah Blessings

Torah Reading

Prayer for Healing

Raising the Torah

Blessing before Haftarah

Haftarah

Blessing after Haftarah

Returning the Torah to the Ark

24 And Joseph said to his brothers: "I am dying. But God will surely remember you and bring you up from this land to the land sworn to Abraham, Isaac, and Jacob." 25 And Joseph made the sons of Israel swear, saying: "When God remembers you, bring up my bones from here."

26 And Joseph died at the age of one hundred and ten years. And they embalmed him and he was placed in a coffin in Egypt.

יוֹסֵף׃ 24 וַיֹּאמֶר יוֹסֵף֙ אֶל־אֶחָ֔יו
אָנֹכִ֖י מֵ֑ת וֵֽאלֹהִ֞ים פָּקֹ֧ד יִפְקֹ֣ד
אֶתְכֶ֗ם וְהֶעֱלָ֤ה אֶתְכֶם֙ מִן־הָאָ֣רֶץ
הַזֹּ֔את אֶל־הָאָ֕רֶץ אֲשֶׁ֥ר נִשְׁבַּ֛ע
לְאַבְרָהָ֥ם לְיִצְחָ֖ק וּֽלְיַעֲקֹֽב׃
25 וַיַּשְׁבַּ֣ע יוֹסֵ֔ף אֶת־בְּנֵ֥י יִשְׂרָאֵ֖ל
לֵאמֹ֑ר פָּקֹ֨ד יִפְקֹ֤ד אֱלֹהִים֙ אֶתְכֶ֔ם
וְהַעֲלִתֶ֥ם אֶת־עַצְמֹתַ֖י מִזֶּֽה׃
26 וַיָּ֣מָת יוֹסֵ֔ף בֶּן־מֵאָ֥ה וָעֶ֖שֶׂר
שָׁנִ֑ים וַיַּחַנְט֣וּ אֹת֔וֹ וַיִּ֥ישֶׂם בָּאָר֖וֹן
בְּמִצְרָֽיִם׃

---

23. **BORN ON JOSEPH'S KNEES** יֻלְּדוּ עַל־בִּרְכֵּי יוֹסֵף. The 11th-century commentator Rashi, quoting the Aramaic translation of the Torah (the *Targum*), understands this phrase to mean that Joseph himself raised and educated the children of Machir. Many contemporary scholars assert that it refers to a ritual of adoption or legitimation. Perhaps Joseph adopted Machir's children, his great-grandchildren, just as Jacob adopted Ephraim and Manasseh, his grandchildren (see Genesis 48:12). Perhaps a special bond existed between Joseph, who was sold by his brothers, and Machir, whose name means "sold."

24. **GOD WILL SURELY REMEMBER YOU** וֵאלֹהִים פָּקֹד יִפְקֹד אֶתְכֶם. Joseph's dying words offer a hopeful promise to his survivors: God's care for them will endure, and they will someday return to the Land of Israel. The patriarch's promise (using the doubled verb *pakod yifkod*) comes to fruition in Exodus 3:16–17, when Moses is instructed to gather the elders of Israel and report to them God's words: "I have remembered (*pakod pakadti*) you . . . and I will take you out of the misery of Egypt . . . to a land flowing with milk and honey."

25. **BRING UP MY BONES** וְהַעֲלִתֶם אֶת־עַצְמֹתַי. In fact, it is none other than Moses himself who carries out Joseph's charge. The Mishnah finds in this an illustration of the important Rabbinic principle of "measure for measure." Because "Joseph went up to bury his father" (Genesis 50:7), Moses, generations later (as reported in Exodus 13:19) "took with him the bones of Joseph" (Mishnah *Sotah* 1:7, 9). Ultimately, those bones were buried in Shechem (Joshua 24:32), the very city to which Jacob had sent Joseph, then a brash teenager, at the beginning of this astonishing tale of discord and reconciliation in the family that bears God's promise (Genesis 37:13). (Jon D. Levenson, b. 1949; adapted)

Leviticus 16 and 19

Chapters of Origin

In Leviticus 16 we encounter the origin of the Day of Atonement; and in Leviticus 19 we experience the origin of *k'dushah*—the Jewish idea that human beings must strive for a life of holiness. This afternoon Torah reading begins with the last six verses of chapter 16, from the traditional portion for Yom Kippur morning, describing the essential elements of the holy day—self-denial, atonement, and purification. The reading continues with selections from chapter 19, chosen years ago by the Reform movement as a substitute for Leviticus 18 (the traditional reading for Yom Kippur afternoon, which focuses on illicit sexual relations).

Reform Jews have long found meaning in the ethical ideals of Leviticus 19. But why read Leviticus 16, as well, with its description of priests, vestments, and sacrificial altars? Perhaps because each section is incomplete without the other: chapter 16 teaches us about Israel's spiritual past, while chapter 19 encourages us to embark, this very moment, on a path of holiness.

At the heart of these chapters is the nature of our relationship with God—a relationship made manifest through both religious ritual and ethical behaviors such as fairness, generosity, and justice. Both chapters depict this relationship as overwhelmingly communal and dependent upon a spirit and energy that are unmistakably collective. Chapter 16 declares that the expiation of sin through sacrifice is performed by the priests for "the whole congregation of Israel"; and chapter 19 makes the attainment of holiness the goal of "the whole Israelite community." Leviticus 16 reminds us why our prayers, to this day, are so often couched in the first-person plural; and Leviticus 19 may surprise us with its assertion that holiness is primarily the aim and concern of a society, not the spiritual gift of some extraordinary individuals.

Can I believe in a God who participates in my life? The "Chapters of Origin" that we read on Yom Kippur frame the issue differently. For these sacred passages, personal faith is not the central concern. Individual faith is unpredictable, perhaps based on variables we cannot understand; but when we attach ourselves to the whole congregation of Israel, a God-inspired history and a God-infused way of life can become ours.

On Leviticus 19:1–2

Adonai spoke to Moses, saying: "Speak to the whole Israelite community and say to them: You shall be holy. . . ." (Leviticus 19:1–2)

COMMENTARY

No station in life, no sex, no age, no state of personal fortune is excluded from this call to strive for the heights of absolute morality, nor is the call addressed to any one individual apart from all others. We must all be *k'doshim* (holy).

—Rabbi Samson Raphael Hirsch (1808–1888)

COMMENTARY

The Hebrew command is in the second-person plural, suggesting that individuals cannot attain holiness alone—we can rise to this level only in community, supported by the efforts of those around us. Holiness is not a private affair; it is not a one-to-one encounter with Divinity. Rather, holiness describes a society in which relationships are grounded in eternal values. The Hebrew term for a synagogue—*k'hilah k'doshah* (holy congregation)—derives from this communal notion of sanctity.

Jews are not a holy people—we are a people commanded to strive for holiness. Leviticus 19 should not elicit pride or self-satisfaction; it is intended to set before us a powerful aspiration for the future.

Rabbi Ovadia Sforno (16th century) suggests that the commandment to "be holy" teaches us the notion of *imitatio Dei*, emulating the ways of God. To be made in the image of God imposes an obligation to model ourselves on the divine ideal—for example, by caring for the poor and vulnerable. Thus, "you shall be holy" directs us to make God's presence felt in our human communities.

Classical commentators often define *kadosh* as "set apart" or "separate." A midrash depicts God saying to the Israelites, "Just as I am set apart, so you must be set apart." Thus, holiness is linked to the notion of distinctiveness, the Jewish obligation to practice a way of life different from those of surrounding peoples.

But does this concept of spirituality, based on separation and division, have meaning for all Jews? Those who experience a heightened sense of the holy through connections with others may wish to seek a new understanding of what it means to be *am kadosh* (a holy people).

A midrash depicts. From Midrash *Sifra* 91.4 on Leviticus 19:2.

On Leviticus 19:17

Regarding the verse "You shall not hate your kin in your heart" (Leviticus 19:17), our Sages taught: Perhaps this means that one should not hit them or curse them? [Are only physical and verbal violence condemned?] No—the Torah teaches: "in your heart"; it is speaking here even of hatred in the heart.

From where [in Scripture] do we learn that if we see ugly behavior in another, we are required to reprove that person? The Torah says (Leviticus 19:17): "Reprove your neighbor." If we offer reproof and the other does not respond, how do we know whether we should reprove again? The Torah says: "You shall surely reprove." Shall we do so even if our reproof causes the other's face to change (that is, to flush or turn pale with embarrassment)? The Torah says: "incur no guilt on their account." Hence, if we offer reproof in a way that humiliates the other person, the guilt is ours.

—Midrash *Tanchuma, Mishpatim* 7, adapted

Instead of harboring resentment and rage, we are instructed by the Torah to communicate directly with another to address a wrong. Reproof (*tochachah*) must be offered respectfully and sensitively, and not as an expression of anger, wounded ego, or the desire to give pain. Maimonides teaches that when offering reproof we should speak to the other in private, in a soft and gentle voice, without sarcasm or scorn, conveying our genuine concern for the other's welfare. We should consider the capacity of the other to hear and accept our reproof, and our own ability to deliver it properly. Delivering and receiving *tochachah* can be very challenging! Our Sages were not sure that it could ever be done correctly, as indicated by this passage in the Talmud (*Arachin* 16b):

> Rabbi Tarfon said: "I wonder if there is anyone in this generation who is capable of accepting reproof. . . ." Rabbi Eleazar ben Azariah said: "I wonder whether there is anyone in this generation who knows how to reprove [properly]."

FOR REFLECTION

Is there someone in my life from whom I accept reproof? Do I welcome it as a way to help me grow and improve? Is this a reciprocal relationship?

You shall surely reprove. Since the Hebrew repeats the same verb twice (*hochei·ach tochiach*), the midrash concludes that we must offer reproof twice.

Tanchuma. A compilation of midrashic material edited no later than the 8th century.

Maimonides teaches. In *Mishneh Torah, Hilchot Dei·ot* 6.7–8.

A Chapter of Origin (Leviticus 16:29–34)

29 וְהָיְתָה לָכֶם לְחֻקַּת עוֹלָם בַּחֹדֶשׁ
הַשְּׁבִיעִי בֶּעָשׂוֹר לַחֹדֶשׁ תְּעַנּוּ אֶת־
נַפְשֹׁתֵיכֶם וְכׇל־מְלָאכָה לֹא תַעֲשׂוּ
הָאֶזְרָח וְהַגֵּר הַגָּר בְּתוֹכְכֶם: 30 כִּי־
בַיּוֹם הַזֶּה יְכַפֵּר עֲלֵיכֶם לְטַהֵר
אֶתְכֶם מִכֹּל חַטֹּאתֵיכֶם לִפְנֵי
יְהֹוָה תִּטְהָרוּ: 31 שַׁבַּת שַׁבָּתוֹן הִיא
לָכֶם וְעִנִּיתֶם אֶת־נַפְשֹׁתֵיכֶם חֻקַּת
עוֹלָם: 32 וְכִפֶּר הַכֹּהֵן אֲשֶׁר־יִמְשַׁח
אֹתוֹ וַאֲשֶׁר יְמַלֵּא אֶת־יָדוֹ לְכַהֵן
תַּחַת אָבִיו וְלָבַשׁ אֶת־בִּגְדֵי הַבָּד
בִּגְדֵי הַקֹּדֶשׁ: 33 וְכִפֶּר אֶת־מִקְדַּשׁ
הַקֹּדֶשׁ וְאֶת־אֹהֶל מוֹעֵד וְאֶת־
הַמִּזְבֵּחַ יְכַפֵּר וְעַל הַכֹּהֲנִים וְעַל־
כׇּל־עַם הַקָּהָל יְכַפֵּר: 34 וְהָיְתָה־
זֹּאת לָכֶם לְחֻקַּת עוֹלָם לְכַפֵּר
עַל־בְּנֵי יִשְׂרָאֵל מִכׇּל־חַטֹּאתָם
אַחַת בַּשָּׁנָה וַיַּעַשׂ כַּאֲשֶׁר צִוָּה
יְהֹוָה אֶת־מֹשֶׁה:

29 "And it shall be an eternal law for you:
in the seventh month, on the tenth day
of the month, you shall practice self-
denial; and you shall not do any work—
the citizen and the stranger who dwells
among you. 30 For on this day atonement shall be made for you to purify
you from all your wrongs. And pure you
shall be in the presence of Adonai. 31 It is
for you a Sabbath, a cessation. And you
shall practice self-denial—an eternal
law. 32 And the priest, the one anointed
to fulfill the role of priest in his father's
place, will make atonement; and he will
dress in linen: garments of the holy.
33 And he will atone for the holy sanctuary and for the tent of meeting, and he
will atone for the altar, and he will atone
for the priests; and for all the people of
the community he will atone. 34 And
this shall become for you an eternal law:
to atone, once a year, for the Israelites
for all their wrongs." And Moses did as
Adonai had commanded him.

---

29. **IN THE SEVENTH MONTH, ON THE TENTH DAY OF THE MONTH** בַּחֹדֶשׁ הַשְּׁבִיעִי בֶּעָשׂוֹר לַחֹדֶשׁ. Leviticus 16 contains the first biblical reference to Yom Kippur. Earlier verses in the chapter describe a complex ritual of "purging the Shrine" — an annual purification rite designed to remove the contamination of sin from the Tabernacle, in which the Divine Presence was thought to dwell. The ritual included the sacrifice of a bull (an offering on behalf of the High Priest and his household); the sacrifice of a goat (an offering on behalf of the Israelite community); and the sending of a live goat into the wilderness to remove (symbolically) the people's sins. William Tyndale, 16th-century English translator of the Bible, coined the term "scapegoat" to designate "the goat that departs or escapes."

Following the destruction of the Temple in 70 CE, sacrificial offerings ceased. They were replaced by more personal and introspective practices: repentance, prayer, fasting, and other forms of self-denial.

29. **PRACTICE SELF-DENIAL** תְּעַנּוּ אֶת־נַפְשֹׁתֵיכֶם. Rabbi Lauren Eichler Berkun (b. 1972) writes: "On Pesach, we ingest the 'Bread of Affliction.' On Yom Kippur, we 'afflict our souls' by abstaining from all food or drink. This striking parallel suggests an important Jewish value. Through our sufferings and our self-discipline, we can achieve greatness."

הוֹצָאַת הַתּוֹרָה
Hotzaat HaTorah
בִּרְכוֹת הַתּוֹרָה
Birchot HaTorah
קְרִיאַת הַתּוֹרָה
K'riat HaTorah
מִי שֶׁבֵּרַךְ
Mi Shebeirach
הַגְבָּהָה
Hagbahah
בְּרָכָה שֶׁלִּפְנֵי הַהַפְטָרָה
B'rachah Shelifnei HaHaftarah
קְרִיאַת הַהַפְטָרָה
K'riat HaHaftarah
בְּרָכָה שֶׁאַחֲרֵי הַהַפְטָרָה
B'rachah She-acharei HaHaftarah
הַכְנָסַת סֵפֶר תּוֹרָה
Hachnasat Sefer Torah

A Chapter of Origin (Leviticus 19:1–18, 32–37)

1 And Adonai spoke to Moses, saying:
2 "Speak to all the community of Israel,
and say to them: You shall be holy for I,
Adonai your God, am holy.
3 "Revere, each of you, your mother and
your father; and keep My Sabbaths. I am
Adonai your God. 4 You shall not turn to
idols and you shall not fashion for yourselves molten gods. I am Adonai your God.
5 "And when you make a sacrifice of
well-being to Adonai, you shall offer it so
that it will be acceptable for you. 6 It shall
be eaten on the day of your sacrifice and
on the next day, but what remains until
the third day shall be burned in fire. 7 And
if, nevertheless, it is eaten on the third
day, it will be a foul thing—unacceptable.
8 And one who eats it shall bear guilt for
profaning the holiness of Adonai; and that
person will be cut off from the people.
9 "And when you reap the harvest of
your land, you shall not finish by reaping
the corners of your field; and you shall
not gather the gleanings of your harvest.
10 And you shall not pick your vineyard
bare; and you shall not gather the fallen
fruits of your vineyard: leave them for
the poor and for the stranger. I am Adonai
your God.
11 "You shall not steal; and you shall not
deceive; and you shall not lie to one another, 12 nor swear falsely in My name, profaning the name of your God. I am Adonai.
13 "You shall not exploit your neighbor,
and you shall not rob. You shall not keep a
worker's wage with you overnight, until
morning.

1 וַיְדַבֵּר יהוָה אֶל־מֹשֶׁה לֵּאמֹר׃
2 דַּבֵּר אֶל־כָּל־עֲדַת בְּנֵי־יִשְׂרָאֵל
וְאָמַרְתָּ אֲלֵהֶם קְדֹשִׁים תִּהְיוּ כִּי
קָדוֹשׁ אֲנִי יהוָה אֱלֹהֵיכֶם׃
3 אִישׁ אִמּוֹ וְאָבִיו תִּירָאוּ
וְאֶת־שַׁבְּתֹתַי תִּשְׁמֹרוּ אֲנִי
יהוָה אֱלֹהֵיכֶם׃ 4 אַל־תִּפְנוּ אֶל־
הָאֱלִילִם וֵאלֹהֵי מַסֵּכָה לֹא
תַעֲשׂוּ לָכֶם אֲנִי יהוָה אֱלֹהֵיכֶם׃
5 וְכִי תִזְבְּחוּ זֶבַח שְׁלָמִים
לַיהוָה לִרְצֹנְכֶם תִּזְבָּחֻהוּ׃ 6 בְּיוֹם
זִבְחֲכֶם יֵאָכֵל וּמִמָּחֳרָת וְהַנּוֹתָר
עַד־יוֹם הַשְּׁלִישִׁי בָּאֵשׁ יִשָּׂרֵף׃
7 וְאִם הֵאָכֹל יֵאָכֵל בַּיּוֹם הַשְּׁלִישִׁי
פִּגּוּל הוּא לֹא יֵרָצֶה׃ 8 וְאֹכְלָיו
עֲוֹנוֹ יִשָּׂא כִּי־אֶת־קֹדֶשׁ יהוָה חִלֵּל
וְנִכְרְתָה הַנֶּפֶשׁ הַהִוא מֵעַמֶּיהָ׃
9 וּבְקֻצְרְכֶם אֶת־קְצִיר אַרְצְכֶם
לֹא תְכַלֶּה פְּאַת שָׂדְךָ לִקְצֹר וְלֶקֶט
קְצִירְךָ לֹא תְלַקֵּט׃ 10 וְכַרְמְךָ לֹא
תְעוֹלֵל וּפֶרֶט כַּרְמְךָ לֹא תְלַקֵּט
לֶעָנִי וְלַגֵּר תַּעֲזֹב אֹתָם אֲנִי יהוָה
אֱלֹהֵיכֶם׃
11 לֹא תִּגְנֹבוּ וְלֹא־תְכַחֲשׁוּ
וְלֹא־תְשַׁקְּרוּ אִישׁ בַּעֲמִיתוֹ׃
12 וְלֹא־תִשָּׁבְעוּ בִשְׁמִי לַשָּׁקֶר
וְחִלַּלְתָּ אֶת־שֵׁם אֱלֹהֶיךָ אֲנִי
יהוָה׃
13 לֹא־תַעֲשֹׁק אֶת־רֵעֲךָ וְלֹא
תִגְזֹל לֹא־תָלִין פְּעֻלַּת שָׂכִיר
אִתְּךָ עַד־בֹּקֶר׃

14 "You shall not curse a person who
is deaf, nor put a stumbling-block before
a person who is blind. Rather, you shall
revere your God. I am Adonai.
15 "You shall not do injustice in judgment: you shall not favor one who is
weak, and you shall not defer to one who
is powerful. You shall judge your kin with
justice. 16 You shall not spread slander
among your people. You shall not stand
idly by the blood of your neighbor. I am
Adonai.
17 "You shall not hate your kin in your
heart. Reprove your friend; thus, you will
not bear guilt because of a friend. 18 You
shall not seek vengeance or bear a grudge
against members of your people—but love
your neighbor as yourself. I am Adonai."

14 לֹא־תְקַלֵּל חֵרֵשׁ וְלִפְנֵי עִוֵּר
לֹא תִתֵּן מִכְשֹׁל וְיָרֵאתָ מֵּאֱלֹהֶיךָ
אֲנִי יְהוָה׃
15 לֹא־תַעֲשׂוּ עָוֶל בַּמִּשְׁפָּט לֹא־
תִשָּׂא פְנֵי־דָל וְלֹא תֶהְדַּר פְּנֵי
גָדוֹל בְּצֶדֶק תִּשְׁפֹּט עֲמִיתֶךָ׃
16 לֹא־תֵלֵךְ רָכִיל בְּעַמֶּיךָ לֹא
תַעֲמֹד עַל־דַּם רֵעֶךָ אֲנִי יְהוָה׃
17 לֹא־תִשְׂנָא אֶת־אָחִיךָ בִּלְבָבֶךָ
הוֹכֵחַ תּוֹכִיחַ אֶת־עֲמִיתֶךָ וְלֹא־
תִשָּׂא עָלָיו חֵטְא׃ 18 לֹא־תִקֹּם
וְלֹא־תִטֹּר אֶת־בְּנֵי עַמֶּךָ וְאָהַבְתָּ
לְרֵעֲךָ כָּמוֹךָ אֲנִי יְהוָה׃

32 "Rise before the one whose head
is white with age, and regard an elder
with respect; and revere your God. I am
Adonai.
33 "And when strangers dwell with you
in your land, you shall not wrong them.
34 The stranger who dwells with you
shall be like a citizen among you; and you
shall love that person as yourself, for you
were strangers in the land of Egypt. I am
Adonai your God.
35 "You shall not act unjustly in judgment: in the measurement of weight and
in liquid measure, 36 you shall have honest
scales, honest weights, an honest *eifah*,
and an honest *hin*.
"I am Adonai your God who brought
you forth from the land of Egypt. 37 And
you shall keep all My laws and all My
judgments—and do them. I am Adonai."

32 מִפְּנֵי שֵׂיבָה תָּקוּם וְהָדַרְתָּ
פְּנֵי זָקֵן וְיָרֵאתָ מֵּאֱלֹהֶיךָ אֲנִי
יְהוָה׃
33 וְכִי־יָגוּר אִתְּךָ גֵּר בְּאַרְצְכֶם
לֹא תוֹנוּ אֹתוֹ׃ 34 כְּאֶזְרָח מִכֶּם
יִהְיֶה לָכֶם הַגֵּר ׀ הַגָּר אִתְּכֶם
וְאָהַבְתָּ לוֹ כָּמוֹךָ כִּי־גֵרִים הֱיִיתֶם
בְּאֶרֶץ מִצְרָיִם אֲנִי יְהוָה אֱלֹהֵיכֶם׃
35 לֹא־תַעֲשׂוּ עָוֶל בַּמִּשְׁפָּט
בַּמִּדָּה בַּמִּשְׁקָל וּבַמְּשׂוּרָה׃
36 מֹאזְנֵי צֶדֶק אַבְנֵי־צֶדֶק אֵיפַת
צֶדֶק וְהִין צֶדֶק יִהְיֶה לָכֶם
אֲנִי יְהוָה אֱלֹהֵיכֶם אֲשֶׁר־
הוֹצֵאתִי אֶתְכֶם מֵאֶרֶץ מִצְרָיִם׃
37 וּשְׁמַרְתֶּם אֶת־כָּל־חֻקֹּתַי
וְאֶת־כָּל־מִשְׁפָּטַי וַעֲשִׂיתֶם אֹתָם
אֲנִי יְהוָה׃

A Prayer for Those Who Are Ill and for Givers of Care

May the Eternal One who blesses all life,
bless and strengthen all of us
who struggle against illness.

May we whose lives are touched by illness
be blessed with faith, courage, love, and caring.

May we experience the support and sustenance
of family, friends, companions, and community.

May we be granted restful nights and days of comfort.
We pray for *r'fuah sh'leimah* — precious moments of healing —
and a sense of wholeness in body and soul.

May those who care for the sick
with their hands, their voices, and their hearts
be blessed with courage and stamina.

May those who pursue healing
through medical skill and knowledge
be blessed with insight, patience, and compassion.

May all of us,
the sick and the well together,
find courage and hope.

And let us say: *Amen.*

More prayers for healing are on pages 271–73.

Raising the Torah

וְזֹאת הַתּוֹרָה אֲשֶׁר־שָׂם מֹשֶׁה	*V'zot haTorah asher-sam Mosheh*
לִפְנֵי בְּנֵי יִשְׂרָאֵל –	*lifnei b'nei Yisrael —*
עַל־פִּי יְיָ, בְּיַד־מֹשֶׁה.	*al-pi Adonai, b'yad-Mosheh.*

This is the Teaching that Moses set before the people Israel —
at the command of God, by the hand of Moses.

A PRAYER FOR THOSE WHO ARE ILL. Inspired by Rabbi Leila Gal Berner (b. 1950).
THIS IS THE TEACHING וְזֹאת הַתּוֹרָה, Deuteronomy 4:44.
AT THE COMMAND OF GOD עַל־פִּי יְיָ, Numbers 9:23.

Introduction to the Haftarah

Jonah's Journey—and Ours

Jonah, famously swallowed by a huge fish, prayed from deep inside its belly:

> I called to Adonai in my distress,
> and God answered me;
> I cried out from the belly of the netherworld,
> and You heard my voice. . . .
> And I thought to myself:
> "I was banished from before Your eyes—
> Will I ever again gaze
> upon Your holy Temple?"
> The waters closed in over me;
> the deep engulfed me. . . .

Yom Kippur worshipers might well identify with Jonah and his descent to solitude in the belly of the fish. By afternoon, we find ourselves deep inside a cavernous day of fasting, prayer, and penitence—a day that "swallows" us up, and draws us in, through powerful music, ritual, and the unnerving awareness of our moral frailty and physical vulnerability.

Cries Jonah: "I was banished from before Your eyes." The Day of Atonement places before us a similar problem: our wrongs, errors, and sins alienate us from our noble purposes. Intentional or not, they threaten to distance us from the sacred. Immersed in litanies of confession, we ask ourselves, "Where am I?" and "What kind of a life have I been leading?" We wonder if we, like Jonah, are "banished" from the holiness that gives life its meaning. Are we morally adrift and spiritually at sea?

In the spaciousness of afternoon prayer, there is unhurried time for reflection and meditation; time to contemplate things that matter to us most; and time to consider the direction our lives might take in the year before us.

Jonah is the story of a journey at sea, the tale of a hapless prophet who fled the sacred purpose of his life. The issues raised and the lessons drawn from our study of this text can be an anchor for the soul in the rough waters that always threaten to engulf us. Delve into this text on the Day of Atonement and find there tools for the work of *t'shuvah* (repentance) and *cheshbon hanefesh* (taking account of the soul). With its multiple meanings and its questions about faith and repentance, the Book of Jonah offers a narrative both thought-provoking and spiritually challenging for the inner journey of Yom Kippur.

Blessing Before the Haftarah

בָּרוּךְ אַתָּה, יְיָ,
אֱלֹהֵינוּ, מֶלֶךְ הָעוֹלָם,
אֲשֶׁר בָּחַר בִּנְבִיאִים טוֹבִים,
וְרָצָה בְדִבְרֵיהֶם הַנֶּאֱמָרִים
בֶּאֱמֶת.

Baruch atah, Adonai,
Eloheinu melech haolam,
asher bachar binvi·im tovim,
v'ratzah v'divreihem hane·emarim
be·emet.

Blessed are You, our God Eternal, supreme Power of the universe, who called forth noble prophets to speak the truth.

בָּרוּךְ אַתָּה, יְיָ, הַבּוֹחֵר בַּתּוֹרָה, וּבְמשֶׁה עַבְדּוֹ,
וּבְיִשְׂרָאֵל עַמּוֹ, וּבִנְבִיאֵי הָאֱמֶת וָצֶדֶק.

Baruch atah, Adonai, habocheir baTorah, uvMosheh avdo,
uvYisrael amo, uvinvi·ei ha·emet vatzedek.

Blessed are You, God of eternity, who delights in the Torah;
in Moses, God's servant; in Israel, God's people;
and in prophets of truth and right.

TO SPEAK THE TRUTH הַנֶּאֱמָרִים בֶּאֱמֶת. How can we pray if there are things in prayer we do not believe? Many people treat prayer like a treatise, picking through the book for doctrinal points. While we should not assert things we do not believe, prayer is not philosophy. Prayer is poetry. The sound of the words, the rhythm and cadence, are integral to prayer. . . . When we say "This is the Torah God gave to Moses" as we hold the Torah aloft, we can recite that declaration even if we have doubts that the Torah is the literal, verbatim word of God. The declaration is deeper than the definition. It is a current carried from the past into the future. "Beauty is truth and truth beauty — that is all ye know on earth and all ye need to know" famously declared Keats. Clearly not if you have to balance a checkbook. But we do not read poetry for information and we do not pray from the newspaper. (Rabbi David Wolpe, b. 1958)

For Reflection on the Book of Jonah

The sailors, as representatives of all humanity, are ready to consider new truths, fearing a previously unknown God and ultimately worshiping God. As suggested by his patronymic "Amittai," derived from the Hebrew word for truth, *emet*, Jonah stays rooted to truth as he defines it. He lives his life as "the son of Amittai," the offspring and purveyor of his own inexorable truths.

It is in this light that we might best understand Jonah's objection to delivering God's warning to the people of Nineveh. Jonah reasons that if human nature is fixed, if truths once learned are never questioned, then repentance is impossible. To offer a second chance to the people of Nineveh would be to indulge in an illusion. . . . The sailors act as God's messengers to Jonah, demonstrating humanity's capacity for self-transformation. These anonymous "men" respond to God's word, delivered by Jonah, with alacrity and sincerity. Yet Jonah himself remains firmly attached to his implacable "truth," the immutable nature of the human psyche.

—Judy Klitsner (b. 1957)

The book of Jonah is full of anomalies. Other biblical books contain the words of prophets sent to influence the people of Israel; Jonah is sent, instead, to speak to the people of Nineveh, capital of Assyria, Israel's arch-enemy. Other prophets fear that the people will not believe them; Jonah is afraid that they *will* believe. Other prophets expend thousands of words to warn or exhort the people without apparent results; Jonah speaks just five Hebrew words (3:4) and achieves instant success. Other prophets stand as exemplars of courage and integrity in a corrupt society; Jonah is a rigid, narrow-minded malcontent who exhibits less compassion and moral concern than the non-Jews around him. Other prophetic books reflect a mood of impassioned solemnity; Jonah is replete with irony and comic elements—animals who fast and wear sackcloth; a prophet who flees in the opposite direction from God's command; who sleeps through a major storm at sea; who spends three days in the belly of a fish; who frets and fumes when a great city is saved from destruction; and is more attached to a plant than to his fellow human beings.

Why, then, do we read the Book of Jonah on Yom Kippur? Because, despite its farcical elements, it eloquently conveys themes appropriate to the holiest day of the year: universalism—the intrinsic worth of all human beings; our responsibility for one another; God's compassionate care for all living things; the power of *t'shuvah* (repentance); and the human capacity for change.

Jonah, chapter 1

1 וַיְהִי דְּבַר־יהוה אֶל־יוֹנָה בֶן־
אֲמִתַּי לֵאמֹר: 2 קוּם לֵךְ אֶל־נִינְוֵה
הָעִיר הַגְּדוֹלָה וּקְרָא עָלֶיהָ כִּי־
עָלְתָה רָעָתָם לְפָנָי:
3 וַיָּקָם יוֹנָה לִבְרֹחַ תַּרְשִׁישָׁה
מִלִּפְנֵי יהוה וַיֵּרֶד יָפוֹ וַיִּמְצָא
אָנִיָּה | בָּאָה תַרְשִׁישׁ וַיִּתֵּן שְׂכָרָהּ
וַיֵּרֶד בָּהּ לָבוֹא עִמָּהֶם תַּרְשִׁישָׁה
מִלִּפְנֵי יהוה:
4 וַיהוה הֵטִיל רוּחַ־גְּדוֹלָה אֶל־
הַיָּם וַיְהִי סַעַר־גָּדוֹל בַּיָּם וְהָאֳנִיָּה
חִשְּׁבָה לְהִשָּׁבֵר: 5 וַיִּירְאוּ הַמַּלָּחִים
וַיִּזְעֲקוּ אִישׁ אֶל־אֱלֹהָיו וַיָּטִלוּ
אֶת־הַכֵּלִים אֲשֶׁר בָּאֳנִיָּה אֶל־הַיָּם
לְהָקֵל מֵעֲלֵיהֶם וְיוֹנָה יָרַד אֶל־
יַרְכְּתֵי הַסְּפִינָה וַיִּשְׁכַּב וַיֵּרָדַם:
6 וַיִּקְרַב אֵלָיו רַב הַחֹבֵל וַיֹּאמֶר
לוֹ מַה־לְּךָ נִרְדָּם קוּם קְרָא אֶל־
אֱלֹהֶיךָ אוּלַי יִתְעַשֵּׁת הָאֱלֹהִים
לָנוּ וְלֹא נֹאבֵד:
7 וַיֹּאמְרוּ אִישׁ אֶל־רֵעֵהוּ לְכוּ
וְנַפִּילָה גוֹרָלוֹת וְנֵדְעָה בְּשֶׁלְּמִי
הָרָעָה הַזֹּאת לָנוּ וַיַּפִּלוּ גּוֹרָלוֹת
וַיִּפֹּל הַגּוֹרָל עַל־יוֹנָה: 8 וַיֹּאמְרוּ
אֵלָיו הַגִּידָה־נָּא לָנוּ בַּאֲשֶׁר לְמִי־
הָרָעָה הַזֹּאת לָנוּ מַה־מְּלַאכְתְּךָ
וּמֵאַיִן תָּבוֹא מָה אַרְצֶךָ וְאֵי־מִזֶּה
עַם אָתָּה: 9 וַיֹּאמֶר אֲלֵיהֶם עִבְרִי

1 And the word of Adonai came to
Jonah son of Amittai: 2 "Get up! Go to
the great city of Nineveh, and proclaim
against it—for their evil deeds have
risen up before Me."

3 But Jonah got up to flee to Tarshish—away from the presence of
Adonai. And he went down to Jaffa and
found there a ship heading for Tarshish,
and he paid its fare and went down into
it, to head with them to Tarshish—
away from the presence of Adonai.
4 But Adonai hurled a great wind upon
the sea, a storm at sea so great that
the ship was in danger of being shattered to pieces. 5 And the sailors were
frightened, cried out, each to his own
god; and flung the ship's cargo into the
sea to lighten their load. But Jonah had
gone down into the hold, the lower
deck of the vessel, and he lay down and
fell into a deep sleep. 6 And the cap-
tain approached him and said to him:
"What are you doing sound asleep?
Get up! Call to your god. Perhaps the
god will be kind to us and we will not
perish."

7 And they said, each man to his
companion: "Let us cast lots, that we
might know on whose account this evil
event has come to us." So they cast lots
and the lot fell on Jonah. 8 And they
said to him: "Tell us, you who have
brought this evil upon us: What is your
trade, and where have you come from?
What is your country, and who are
your people?" 9 And he said to them:

Bringing the Torah into Our Midst
Torah Blessings
Torah Reading
Prayer for Healing
Raising the Torah
Blessing before Haftarah
Haftarah
Blessing after Haftarah
Returning the Torah to the Ark

"I am a Hebrew. I revere Adonai, God
of heaven, who made sea and dry land."
10 The men felt great fear, and they asked
him: "What have you done?"—because
the men knew he was fleeing from
Adonai, for so he had told them. 11 And
they asked him: "What should we do
to you to bring calm to the sea around
us?"—for the sea was growing more and
more stormy. 12 So he said to them: "Lift
me up and hurl me into the sea, and the
sea will calm down for you, for I know
that this great storm came upon you
because of me."
13 And the crew rowed hard to return
to the dry land; but they could not do
it, for the sea was raging more and more
fiercely around them. 14 And they called
out to Adonai, saying: "Please, Adonai,
please do not let us perish because of
the life of this man. And do not hold us
guilty of shedding innocent blood. For
You, Adonai—that which You desired
You have brought about." 15 And they
lifted Jonah and hurled him into the sea.
Then the sea stopped raging.
16 The men revered Adonai; great was
their reverence. So they offered to
Adonai a sacrifice, and made vows.

אָנֹכִי וְאֶת־יהוה אֱלֹהֵי הַשָּׁמַיִם
אֲנִי יָרֵא אֲשֶׁר־עָשָׂה אֶת־הַיָּם
וְאֶת־הַיַּבָּשָׁה׃ 10 וַיִּירְאוּ הָאֲנָשִׁים
יִרְאָה גְדוֹלָה וַיֹּאמְרוּ אֵלָיו מַה־
זֹּאת עָשִׂיתָ כִּי־יָדְעוּ הָאֲנָשִׁים כִּי־
מִלִּפְנֵי יהוה הוּא בֹרֵחַ כִּי הִגִּיד
לָהֶם׃ 11 וַיֹּאמְרוּ אֵלָיו מַה־נַּעֲשֶׂה
לָּךְ וְיִשְׁתֹּק הַיָּם מֵעָלֵינוּ כִּי הַיָּם
הוֹלֵךְ וְסֹעֵר׃ 12 וַיֹּאמֶר אֲלֵיהֶם
שָׂאוּנִי וַהֲטִילֻנִי אֶל־הַיָּם וְיִשְׁתֹּק
הַיָּם מֵעֲלֵיכֶם כִּי יוֹדֵעַ אָנִי כִּי
בְשֶׁלִּי הַסַּעַר הַגָּדוֹל הַזֶּה עֲלֵיכֶם׃
13 וַיַּחְתְּרוּ הָאֲנָשִׁים לְהָשִׁיב אֶל־
הַיַּבָּשָׁה וְלֹא יָכֹלוּ כִּי הַיָּם הוֹלֵךְ
וְסֹעֵר עֲלֵיהֶם׃ 14 וַיִּקְרְאוּ אֶל־יהוה
וַיֹּאמְרוּ אָנָּה יהוה אַל־נָא נֹאבְדָה
בְּנֶפֶשׁ הָאִישׁ הַזֶּה וְאַל־תִּתֵּן
עָלֵינוּ דָּם נָקִיא כִּי־אַתָּה יהוה
כַּאֲשֶׁר חָפַצְתָּ עָשִׂיתָ׃ 15 וַיִּשְׂאוּ
אֶת־יוֹנָה וַיְטִלֻהוּ אֶל־הַיָּם
וַיַּעֲמֹד הַיָּם מִזַּעְפּוֹ׃
16 וַיִּירְאוּ הָאֲנָשִׁים יִרְאָה גְדוֹלָה
אֶת־יהוה וַיִּזְבְּחוּ־זֶבַח לַיהוה
וַיִּדְּרוּ נְדָרִים׃

Jonah, chapter 2

1 And Adonai provided a great fish to swallow
Jonah. And Jonah was in the belly of the fish
three days and three nights. 2 Jonah prayed
to Adonai his God from the belly of the fish.
3 And he said:

1 וַיְמַן יהוה דָּג גָּדוֹל לִבְלֹעַ
אֶת־יוֹנָה וַיְהִי יוֹנָה בִּמְעֵי הַדָּג
שְׁלֹשָׁה יָמִים וּשְׁלֹשָׁה לֵילוֹת׃
2 וַיִּתְפַּלֵּל יוֹנָה אֶל־יהוה
אֱלֹהָיו מִמְּעֵי הַדָּגָה׃ 3 וַיֹּאמֶר

I called to Adonai in my distress,
and God answered me;
I cried out from the belly of the netherworld,
and You heard my voice.

4 Into the depths You cast me,
into the heart of the sea—
and the floods engulfed me;
all Your billowing, breaking waves
swept over me.

5 And I thought to myself:
"I was banished from before Your eyes—
Will I ever again gaze
upon Your holy Temple?"

6 The waters closed in over me,
the deep engulfed me—
rushes wrapped around my head.

7 I descended to the low-point of the
mountains;
the gates of the earth closed upon me
forever.
Yet You, Adonai my God,
raised up my life from the pit.

8 When my life fainted away,
I called Adonai to mind;
and my prayer came to You,
to Your holy Temple.

9 They who cling to empty folly
forsake their own welfare;

10 but I—with a shout of
thanksgiving,
I will sacrifice to You.
What I have vowed I will fulfill.
Rescue comes from Adonai.

קָרָ֤אתִי מִצָּ֥רָה לִ֖י אֶל־יְהֹוָ֖ה
וַֽיַּעֲנֵ֑נִי
מִבֶּ֥טֶן שְׁא֛וֹל שִׁוַּ֖עְתִּי
שָׁמַ֥עְתָּ קוֹלִֽי:

4 וַתַּשְׁלִיכֵ֤נִי מְצוּלָה֙
בִּלְבַ֣ב יַמִּ֔ים
וְנָהָ֖ר יְסֹֽבְבֵ֑נִי
כָּל־מִשְׁבָּרֶ֥יךָ וְגַלֶּ֖יךָ
עָלַ֥י עָבָֽרוּ:

5 וַאֲנִ֣י אָמַ֔רְתִּי
נִגְרַ֖שְׁתִּי מִנֶּ֣גֶד עֵינֶ֑יךָ
אַ֚ךְ אוֹסִ֣יף לְהַבִּ֔יט
אֶל־הֵיכַ֖ל קָדְשֶֽׁךָ:

6 אֲפָפ֤וּנִי מַ֙יִם֙ עַד־נֶ֔פֶשׁ
תְּה֖וֹם יְסֹבְבֵ֑נִי
ס֖וּף חָב֥וּשׁ לְרֹאשִֽׁי:

7 לְקִצְבֵ֤י הָרִים֙ יָרַ֔דְתִּי
הָאָ֛רֶץ בְּרִחֶ֥יהָ בַעֲדִ֖י לְעוֹלָ֑ם
וַתַּ֧עַל מִשַּׁ֛חַת חַיַּ֖י
יְהֹוָ֥ה אֱלֹהָֽי:

8 בְּהִתְעַטֵּ֤ף עָלַי֙ נַפְשִׁ֔י
אֶת־יְהֹוָ֖ה זָכָ֑רְתִּי
וַתָּב֤וֹא אֵלֶ֙יךָ֙ תְּפִלָּתִ֔י
אֶל־הֵיכַ֖ל קָדְשֶֽׁךָ:

9 מְשַׁמְּרִ֖ים הַבְלֵי־שָׁ֑וְא
חַסְדָּ֖ם יַעֲזֹֽבוּ:

10 וַאֲנִ֗י בְּק֤וֹל תּוֹדָה֙
אֶזְבְּחָה־לָּ֔ךְ
אֲשֶׁ֥ר נָדַ֖רְתִּי אֲשַׁלֵּ֑מָה
יְשׁוּעָ֖תָה לַֽיהֹוָֽה:

Bringing the Torah into Our Midst
Torah Blessings
Torah Reading
Prayer for Healing
Raising the Torah
Blessing before Haftarah
Haftarah
Blessing after Haftarah
Returning the Torah to the Ark

11 Adonai commanded the fish, and
it spewed Jonah out upon dry land.

וַיֹּאמֶר יהוָה לַדָּג וַיָּקֵא אֶת־ 11
יוֹנָה אֶל־הַיַּבָּשָׁה׃

Jonah, chapter 3

1 And the word of Adonai came to
Jonah a second time: 2 "Get up! Go to
the great city of Nineveh, and call out
to it the proclamation that I tell you."
3 So Jonah got up and went to Nineveh
according to the word of Adonai. Now
Nineveh was a great city of God—three
days' journey across. 4 And Jonah started out and made his way into the city
the distance of a one-day walk. And he
called out and said: "Forty more days
and Nineveh shall be overturned!"

5 The people of Nineveh trusted in
God, and they proclaimed a fast; and
they put on sackcloth, from the richest
to the poorest. 6 And word reached the
king of Nineveh, and he got up from his
throne, took off his robe, put on sackcloth, and sat in ashes. 7 And he cried
out and said in Nineveh: "By decree
of the king and his nobles: No person
or beast—of flock or herd—shall taste
anything! They shall not graze and they
shall not drink water! 8 They shall be
covered with sackcloth—person and
beast—and shall call loudly to God.
Let all turn back from their evil ways
and from the violence which is in their

1 וַיְהִי דְבַר־יהוָה אֶל־יוֹנָה שֵׁנִית
לֵאמֹר׃ 2 קוּם לֵךְ אֶל־נִינְוֵה הָעִיר
הַגְּדוֹלָה וּקְרָא אֵלֶיהָ אֶת־הַקְּרִיאָה
אֲשֶׁר אָנֹכִי דֹּבֵר אֵלֶיךָ׃ 3 וַיָּקָם יוֹנָה
וַיֵּלֶךְ אֶל־נִינְוֶה כִּדְבַר יהוָה וְנִינְוֵה
הָיְתָה עִיר־גְּדוֹלָה לֵאלֹהִים מַהֲלַךְ
שְׁלֹשֶׁת יָמִים׃ 4 וַיָּחֶל יוֹנָה לָבוֹא
בָעִיר מַהֲלַךְ יוֹם אֶחָד וַיִּקְרָא
וַיֹּאמַר עוֹד אַרְבָּעִים יוֹם וְנִינְוֵה
נֶהְפָּכֶת׃

5 וַיַּאֲמִינוּ אַנְשֵׁי נִינְוֵה בֵּאלֹהִים
וַיִּקְרְאוּ־צוֹם וַיִּלְבְּשׁוּ שַׂקִּים
מִגְּדוֹלָם וְעַד־קְטַנָּם׃ 6 וַיִּגַּע הַדָּבָר
אֶל־מֶלֶךְ נִינְוֵה וַיָּקָם מִכִּסְאוֹ
וַיַּעֲבֵר אַדַּרְתּוֹ מֵעָלָיו וַיְכַס שַׂק
וַיֵּשֶׁב עַל־הָאֵפֶר׃ 7 וַיַּזְעֵק וַיֹּאמֶר
בְּנִינְוֵה מִטַּעַם הַמֶּלֶךְ וּגְדֹלָיו
לֵאמֹר הָאָדָם וְהַבְּהֵמָה הַבָּקָר
וְהַצֹּאן אַל־יִטְעֲמוּ מְאוּמָה אַל־
יִרְעוּ וּמַיִם אַל־יִשְׁתּוּ׃ 8 וְיִתְכַּסּוּ
שַׂקִּים הָאָדָם וְהַבְּהֵמָה וְיִקְרְאוּ
אֶל־אֱלֹהִים בְּחָזְקָה וְיָשֻׁבוּ אִישׁ
מִדַּרְכּוֹ הָרָעָה וּמִן־הֶחָמָס אֲשֶׁר

---

8. **THE VIOLENCE** הֶחָמָס. The sin that the people of Nineveh commit is called in Hebrew *chamas*—violence, oppression, ruthlessness—the same sin associated with the generation of the Flood (Genesis 6:2). In that story, God responded to the people's cruel and lawless behavior with an act of wholesale destruction. The Book of Jonah, by contrast, presents a merciful and hopeful God who intervenes by sending a prophetic messenger so as to inspire the people of Nineveh to change their behavior and live.

בְּכַפֵּיהֶם: 9 מִי־יוֹדֵעַ יָשׁוּב וְנִחַם
הָאֱלֹהִים וְשָׁב מֵחֲרוֹן אַפּוֹ וְלֹא
נֹאבֵד:
10 וַיַּרְא הָאֱלֹהִים אֶת־מַעֲשֵׂיהֶם
כִּי־שָׁבוּ מִדַּרְכָּם הָרָעָה וַיִּנָּחֶם
הָאֱלֹהִים עַל־הָרָעָה אֲשֶׁר־דִּבֶּר
לַעֲשׂוֹת־לָהֶם וְלֹא עָשָׂה:

hands. 9 Who knows? God may turn
and relent—turn back from the heat of
anger—so that we do not perish."
10 God saw what they did—how
they were turning back from their evil
ways; and God relented from the evil
planned for them, and did not carry it
out.

1 וַיֵּרַע אֶל־יוֹנָה רָעָה גְדוֹלָה וַיִּחַר
לוֹ: 2 וַיִּתְפַּלֵּל אֶל־יהוה וַיֹּאמַר
אָנָּה יהוה הֲלוֹא־זֶה דְבָרִי עַד־
הֱיוֹתִי עַל־אַדְמָתִי עַל־כֵּן קִדַּמְתִּי
לִבְרֹחַ תַּרְשִׁישָׁה כִּי יָדַעְתִּי כִּי
אַתָּה אֵל־חַנּוּן וְרַחוּם אֶרֶךְ אַפַּיִם
וְרַב־חֶסֶד וְנִחָם עַל־הָרָעָה:
3 וְעַתָּה יהוה קַח־נָא אֶת־נַפְשִׁי
מִמֶּנִּי כִּי טוֹב מוֹתִי מֵחַיָּי: 4 וַיֹּאמֶר
יהוה הַהֵיטֵב חָרָה לָךְ:
5 וַיֵּצֵא יוֹנָה מִן־הָעִיר וַיֵּשֶׁב
מִקֶּדֶם לָעִיר וַיַּעַשׂ לוֹ שָׁם סֻכָּה
וַיֵּשֶׁב תַּחְתֶּיהָ בַּצֵּל עַד אֲשֶׁר יִרְאֶה
מַה־יִּהְיֶה בָּעִיר: 6 וַיְמַן יהוה־
אֱלֹהִים קִיקָיוֹן וַיַּעַל | מֵעַל לְיוֹנָה
לִהְיוֹת צֵל עַל־רֹאשׁוֹ לְהַצִּיל לוֹ
מֵרָעָתוֹ וַיִּשְׂמַח יוֹנָה עַל־הַקִּיקָיוֹן
שִׂמְחָה גְדוֹלָה: 7 וַיְמַן הָאֱלֹהִים
תּוֹלַעַת בַּעֲלוֹת הַשַּׁחַר לַמָּחֳרָת
וַתַּךְ אֶת־הַקִּיקָיוֹן וַיִּיבָשׁ: 8 וַיְהִי |
כִּזְרֹחַ הַשֶּׁמֶשׁ וַיְמַן אֱלֹהִים
רוּחַ קָדִים חֲרִישִׁית וַתַּךְ הַשֶּׁמֶשׁ

Jonah, chapter 4

1 But to Jonah this was a great evil, and
it made him angry. 2 So he prayed to
Adonai, saying, "Please, Adonai, is
this not what I said when I was still in
my own country? This is why I fled to
Tarshish to begin with. For I knew that
You are a gracious and compassionate
God, endlessly patient and abounding
in steadfast love, ready to repent of evil.
3 And now, Adonai, please, take my life
from me—for it is better for me to die
than to live." 4 And Adonai said: "Is it
good for you to be angry?"
5 Then Jonah left the city, found a
place east of the city, made himself a
shelter there, and sat under it in the
shade until he might see what would
become of the city. 6 And Adonai
Elohim provided a gourd, and made
it rise up over Jonah to give shade for
his head and rescue him from his evil
situation. And Jonah rejoiced—with
great joy—because of the gourd. 7 But
at dawn the next day God provided a
worm that attacked the gourd, and it
withered. 8 And as the sun rose, God
provided an oppressive wind from the

הוֹצָאַת הַתּוֹרָה
Hotzaat HaTorah
בִּרְכוֹת הַתּוֹרָה
Birchot HaTorah
קְרִיאַת הַתּוֹרָה
K'riat HaTorah
מִי שֶׁבֵּרַךְ
Mi Shebeirach
הַגְבָּהָה
Hagbahah
בְּרָכָה שֶׁלִּפְנֵי הַהַפְטָרָה
B'rachah Shelifnei HaHaftarah
קְרִיאַת הַהַפְטָרָה
K'riat HaHaftarah
בְּרָכָה שֶׁאַחֲרֵי הַהַפְטָרָה
B'rachah She-acharei HaHaftarah
הַכְנָסַת סֵפֶר תּוֹרָה
Hachnasat Sefer Torah

east; and the sun beat down on Jonah's
head, making him faint. He begged for
death, saying: "It is better for me to die
than to live." 9 Then God said to Jonah:
"Are you good and angry about the
gourd?" And he said: "I am good and
angry to the point of death."

10 Then Adonai said: "You pitied the
gourd, which you neither worked for
nor grew, which appeared overnight
and perished overnight. 11 Should I,
then, not have compassion for the great
city of Nineveh, a place of more than a
hundred and twenty thousand human
beings unable to tell their right hand
from their left—and many beasts?"

עַל־רֹאשׁ יוֹנָה וַיִּתְעַלָּף וַיִּשְׁאַל
אֶת־נַפְשׁוֹ לָמוּת וַיֹּאמֶר טוֹב
מוֹתִי מֵחַיָּי׃ 9 וַיֹּאמֶר אֱלֹהִים אֶל־
יוֹנָה הַהֵיטֵב חָרָה־לְךָ עַל־הַקִּיקָיוֹן
וַיֹּאמֶר הֵיטֵב חָרָה־לִי עַד־מָוֶת׃
10 וַיֹּאמֶר יהוה אַתָּה חַסְתָּ עַל־
הַקִּיקָיוֹן אֲשֶׁר לֹא־עָמַלְתָּ בּוֹ וְלֹא
גִדַּלְתּוֹ שֶׁבִּן־לַיְלָה הָיָה וּבִן־לַיְלָה
אָבָד׃ 11 וַאֲנִי לֹא אָחוּס עַל־נִינְוֵה
הָעִיר הַגְּדוֹלָה אֲשֶׁר יֶשׁ־בָּהּ הַרְבֵּה
מִשְׁתֵּים־עֶשְׂרֵה רִבּוֹ אָדָם אֲשֶׁר
לֹא־יָדַע בֵּין־יְמִינוֹ לִשְׂמֹאלוֹ
וּבְהֵמָה רַבָּה׃

JONAH INVERTS God's world. Death becomes life. Curse becomes blessing. The attributes of God—reverently celebrated in the Torah, and recited again and again on these holidays, *Adonai, Adonai—El rachum v'hanun* (God—compassionate, kind, forgiving), the attributes of God's love—are derisively and sarcastically dismissed. They are rejected. He'd rather die than live in a world governed by a loving God.

God is astonished and asks him, "Are you so angry?" The Hebrew is more powerful: "*Haheiteiv charah lach*—Is your anger so dear to you?" *Heiteiv* comes from *tov*. Literally, the question is: Has anger become your goodness? Has hate displaced the good in you? . . .

The book ends with God's frustration, God's distress. It ends with God's question. But it isn't God's question to Jonah anymore. It is God's question to us: Why can't you love?

The question isn't asked out of rage, or disapproval. It is asked in tears, in divine tears of sadness—when God looks into the world and sees what we do to one another. How many genocides since the Holocaust? Cambodia, Biafra, Rwanda, Darfur. . . . God cries and asks: "*Haheitev charah lach*? Where is your compassion? Why can't you love?" (Rabbi Edward Feinstein, b. 1954)

Micah 20–7:18

18 Is there another God like You—
pardoning iniquity,
annulling transgression,
for the remnant of this people?
God does not hold fast to endless anger,
for God desires steadfast love.
19 God will take us back,
will have compassion for us,
and will subdue our iniquities.
Into the depths of the sea
You will cast all our sins.
20 You will be true and faithful to Jacob,
granting steadfast love to Abraham—
as You swore to our ancestors
in days of old.

18 מִי־אֵל כָּמוֹךָ
נֹשֵׂא עָוֹן
וְעֹבֵר עַל־פֶּשַׁע
לִשְׁאֵרִית נַחֲלָתוֹ
לֹא־הֶחֱזִיק לָעַד אַפּוֹ
כִּי־חָפֵץ חֶסֶד הוּא:
19 יָשׁוּב יְרַחֲמֵנוּ
יִכְבֹּשׁ עֲוֺנֹתֵינוּ
וְתַשְׁלִיךְ בִּמְצֻלוֹת יָם
כָּל־חַטֹּאותָם:
20 תִּתֵּן אֱמֶת לְיַעֲקֹב
חֶסֶד לְאַבְרָהָם
אֲשֶׁר־נִשְׁבַּעְתָּ לַאֲבֹתֵינוּ
מִימֵי קֶדֶם:

18. **IS THERE ANOTHER GOD LIKE YOU** מִי־אֵל כָּמוֹךָ. The Rabbinic sages appended these three verses from the prophet Micah to the end of the Yom Kippur haftarah to reinforce the message of God's mercy and forgiveness. The phrase "You will cast (*v'tashlich*) all our sins into the depths of the sea" (verse 19) links Micah's words to the prayer Jonah utters in the belly of the fish (2:4): "Into the depths You cast me, into the heart of the sea." By juxtaposing the words of these two prophets, our Sages highlight a central lesson of the haftarah: Jonah's spiritual journey "into the depths" was necessary to teach him the fathomless depths of God's compassion.

These verses from Micah are also recited during the *Tashlich* ceremony on Rosh HaShanah afternoon, when we symbolically cast our sins into a body of flowing water, expressing our desire to start the new year afresh, with a clean conscience.

19. **OUR SINS** חַטֹּאותָם. The word *chatotam* in the biblical text means "their sins" but is emended for meaning, as if it had been written *chatoteinu*.

Blessing After the Haftarah

For transliteration of this blessing, see page 279. Another version is on page 280.

Blessed are You, our God Eternal,
supreme Power of the universe,
Rock of all ages,
Source of justice in all generations,
God in whom faithfulness abides,
whose word is deed,
whose every utterance bespeaks truth and righteousness.

בָּרוּךְ אַתָּה, יְיָ,
אֱלֹהֵינוּ, מֶלֶךְ הָעוֹלָם,
צוּר כָּל הָעוֹלָמִים,
צַדִּיק בְּכָל הַדּוֹרוֹת,
הָאֵל הַנֶּאֱמָן, הָאוֹמֵר וְעוֹשֶׂה,
הַמְדַבֵּר וּמְקַיֵּם,
שֶׁכָּל דְּבָרָיו אֱמֶת וָצֶדֶק.

Our God Eternal,
for all of these gifts we thank You and bless You:
Torah, worship, the books of the prophets,
[this Sabbath day,] and this Day of Atonement—
given to us [for holiness and rest; and]
for the sake of pardon and forgiveness,
that we might make amends with honor and dignity.

עַל הַתּוֹרָה, וְעַל הָעֲבוֹדָה,
וְעַל הַנְּבִיאִים,
[וְעַל יוֹם הַשַּׁבָּת הַזֶּה,]
וְעַל יוֹם הַכִּפּוּרִים הַזֶּה,
שֶׁנָּתַתָּ לָּנוּ, יְיָ אֱלֹהֵינוּ,
[לִקְדֻשָּׁה וְלִמְנוּחָה,]
לִמְחִילָה וְלִסְלִיחָה וּלְכַפָּרָה,
לְכָבוֹד וּלְתִפְאָרֶת.
עַל הַכֹּל, יְיָ אֱלֹהֵינוּ,
אֲנַחְנוּ מוֹדִים לָךְ, וּמְבָרְכִים אוֹתָךְ.

Let all life bless Your name continually, to the end of time,
so that Your truth will endure forever.

יִתְבָּרַךְ שִׁמְךָ בְּפִי כָּל חַי תָּמִיד
לְעוֹלָם וָעֶד,
וּדְבָרְךָ אֱמֶת וְקַיָּם לָעַד.

Blessed are You, Adonai,
Sovereign who forgives our failings
and pardons the failings of Your people, the House of Israel.
You banish our guilt, from year to year;
You reign in majesty over all the earth;
You sanctify [Shabbat,] the people Israel
and the Day of Atonement.

בָּרוּךְ אַתָּה, יְיָ,
מֶלֶךְ מוֹחֵל וְסוֹלֵחַ לַעֲוֹנוֹתֵינוּ
וְלַעֲוֹנוֹת עַמּוֹ בֵּית יִשְׂרָאֵל,
וּמַעֲבִיר אַשְׁמוֹתֵינוּ בְּכָל שָׁנָה
וְשָׁנָה,
מֶלֶךְ עַל כָּל הָאָרֶץ,
מְקַדֵּשׁ [הַשַּׁבָּת וְ] יִשְׂרָאֵל
וְיוֹם הַכִּפּוּרִים.

Returning the Torah to the Ark

יְהַלְלוּ אֶת־שֵׁם יְיָ, — *Y'hal'lu et-shem Adonai,*
כִּי־נִשְׂגָּב שְׁמוֹ לְבַדּוֹ: — *ki-nisgav sh'mo l'vado:*

All praise God's name, for God's name alone is truly sublime:

הוֹדוֹ עַל־אֶרֶץ וְשָׁמָיִם. — *hodo al-eretz v'shamayim.*
וַיָּרֶם קֶרֶן לְעַמּוֹ, — *Vayarem keren l'amo;*
תְּהִלָּה לְכָל־חֲסִידָיו, — *t'hilah l'chol-chasidav,*
לִבְנֵי יִשְׂרָאֵל עַם קְרֹבוֹ, הַלְלוּ־יָהּ. — *livnei Yisrael am k'rovo — hal'lu-Yah!*

Your brightness lights the earth and sky
raises us up, blares out the note
from Your people's trumpet
an exultant blast for all who struggle with You
and are close at hand — Halleluyah!

From Psalm 24

מִי־יַעֲלֶה בְהַר־יְיָ, — *Mi-yaaleh v'har-Adonai,*
וּמִי־יָקוּם בִּמְקוֹם קָדְשׁוֹ. — *umi-yakum bimkom kodsho?*
נְקִי כַפַּיִם וּבַר־לֵבָב, — *N'ki chapayim uvar-leivav,*
אֲשֶׁר לֹא־נָשָׂא לַשָּׁוְא נַפְשִׁי, — *asher lo-nasa lashav nafshi,*
וְלֹא נִשְׁבַּע לְמִרְמָה. — *v'lo nishba l'mirmah.*
יִשָּׂא בְרָכָה מֵאֵת יְיָ, — *Yisa v'rachah mei·eit Adonai,*
וּצְדָקָה מֵאֱלֹהֵי יִשְׁעוֹ. — *utzdakah mei·Elohei yisho.*

Who may ascend the mountain of the Eternal?
And who may rise up to the place where holiness abides?
A person of clean hands and pure heart,
who has neither taken a false oath
nor sworn deceitfully —
such a person shall receive God's blessing,
and kindness from the Well of salvation.

ALL PRAISE יְהַלְלוּ, Psalm 148:13.
YOUR BRIGHTNESS הודו. Adaptation of Psalm 148:14 by Norman Fischer (b. 1946).
WHO MAY ASCEND מִי־יַעֲלֶה, Psalm 24:3–5.

הוֹצָאַת הַתּוֹרָה
Hotzaat HaTorah
בִּרְכוֹת הַתּוֹרָה
Birchot HaTorah
קְרִיאַת הַתּוֹרָה
K'riat HaTorah
מִי שֶׁבֵּרַךְ
Mi Shebeirach
הַגְבָּהָה
Hagbahah
בְּרָכָה שֶׁלִּפְנֵי הַהַפְטָרָה
B'rachah Shelifnei HaHaftarah
קְרִיאַת הַהַפְטָרָה
K'riat HaHaftarah
בְּרָכָה שֶׁאַחֲרֵי הַהַפְטָרָה
B'rachah She-acharei HaHaftarah
הַכְנָסַת סֵפֶר תּוֹרָה
Hachnasat Sefer Torah

Bringing the Torah into Our Midst
Torah Blessings
Torah Reading
Prayer for Healing
Raising the Torah
Blessing before Haftarah
Haftarah
Blessing after Haftarah
Returning the Torah to the Ark

Take Us Back

כִּי לֶֽקַח טוֹב נָתַֽתִּי לָכֶם:
תּוֹרָתִי. אַל־תַּעֲזֹֽבוּ.

Ki lekach tov natati lachem:
Torati. Al-taazovu.

עֵץ־חַיִּים הִיא לַמַּחֲזִיקִים בָּהּ,
וְתֹמְכֶֽיהָ מְאֻשָּׁר.
דְּרָכֶֽיהָ דַרְכֵי־נֹֽעַם,
וְכָל־נְתִיבוֹתֶֽיהָ שָׁלוֹם.
הֲשִׁיבֵֽנוּ, יְיָ, אֵלֶֽיךָ – וְנָשֽׁוּבָה.
חַדֵּשׁ יָמֵֽינוּ כְּקֶֽדֶם.

Eitz-chayim hi lamachazikim bah;
v'tom'cheha m'ushar.
D'racheha darchei-no·am,
v'chol-n'tivoteha shalom.
Hashiveinu, Adonai, elecha — v'nashuvah.
Chadeish yameinu k'kedem.

A precious teaching I have given you:
My Torah. Do not forsake it.
A Tree of Life to those who hold it fast:
all who embrace it know happiness.
Its ways are ways of pleasantness,
and all its paths are peace.
Take us back, Adonai —
let us come back to You.
Renew in our time the days of old.

Return Again

Return again, return again, return to the land of your soul.
Return to who you are, return to what you are, return to where you are
Born and reborn again.

A PRECIOUS TEACHING כִּי לֶֽקַח טוֹב, Proverbs 4:2.
A TREE OF LIFE עֵץ־חַיִּים הִיא, Proverbs 3:18.
ITS WAYS דְּרָכֶֽיהָ, Proverbs 3:17.
LET US COME BACK הֲשִׁיבֵֽנוּ, Lamentations 5:21.
RETURN AGAIN. Lyrics by Rabbi Shlomo Carlebach (1924–1994).

The Heart of Yom Kippur: Tikkun Midot HaNefesh

HaT'filah for the afternoon (seven benedictions also known as the *Amidah* or "Standing Prayer") differs from its counterparts in other services. The waning hours of Yom Kippur provide an extended opportunity for quiet reflection and introspection. Thus, these seven core prayers, which speak to the deepest issues in our lives, set forth a framework for this work of the soul.

The heart of Yom Kippur afternoon is *tikkun midot hanefesh*, often called *tikkun midot*: repairing and strengthening the personal qualities and traits that enable us to fulfill our urge to be good—virtues such as love, self-discipline, gratitude, and forgiveness. Each of the seven blessings of *HaT'filah* is supplemented by a creative prayer that focuses on one of these qualities; and each blessing is preceded by two pages of ideas for reflection, in the form of sacred Jewish text, poetry, philosophy, and literature. Included, as well, are questions related to the *midot*, which may be addressed quietly and privately or shared with others. In the tradition of *musar* (the ethical way), *HaT'filah* for the afternoon aims to place righteousness and goodness at the center of our everyday lives.

MUSAR (THE ETHICAL WAY). *Musar* means "instruction, correction, and ethics." The modern Musar movement began in 19th-century Lithuania, under the leadership of Rabbi Yisrael Salanter (1810–1883), as a spiritual path for self-improvement and character development. The discipline of *musar* is based on close study of important texts; systematic evaluation of one's behavior; and the diligent practice of new habits of thought and action.

To walk in God's ways . . . (Deuteronomy 11:22)

COMMENTARY

How is it possible for a human being *to walk in God's ways*? As God is called compassionate, so too, you should be compassionate. As God is called gracious, so too, you should be gracious and give freely. As God is called just, so too, you should be just. As the Holy Blessed One is called kind and loving, be kind and loving as well. And thus for all the qualities ascribed to the Holy Blessed One. To walk in God's ways is to emulate God.

—From Midrash *Sifrei D'varim, Eikev* 49

I have labored twenty-one years to discover truth—
seven years to recognize what truth is;
seven years to drive out falsehood;
seven years to fill my inner self with truth.

—Rabbi Pinchas of Koretz (1728–1790)

Fixing the world entails a never-ending process of actions that contribute to the moral uplifting of society, such as building a home for the homeless and offering hope to the hopeless. Rooted in Jewish mysticism, acts of *tikkun olam* have a cosmic effect; they change the balance of good and evil in the universe.

But the practice of *tikkun olam* does not stand alone. It is necessary, but not sufficient to live up to the ethics of Judaism. Some of us may be so drawn to fixing the outside world that we neglect the inner world of our being. And so Jewish tradition offers us a partner to *tikkun olam*, a partner that has too often been neglected—the process of internal mending called *tikkun midot*. Whereas acts of *tikkun olam* are social and public, acts of *tikkun midot* are personal and private. As *tikkun olam* confronts the incompleteness and imperfection of the world around us, *tikkun midot* addresses the incompleteness and imperfection of our inner self. . . .

Tikkun midot and *tikkun olam* are not mutually exclusive; they are mutually dependent and inextricably intertwined; both are necessary to uplift the world. The moral whole is more than the sum of the moral parts. Spiritual awareness and social justice are two sides of the same coin: *tikkun midot* looks at the moral life from the inside out; *tikkun olam* approaches the same domain from the outside in. *Tikkun midot* starts with me; *tikkun olam* starts with us.

—Rabbi Jan Katzew (b. 1956)

SIFREI D'VARIM. Collection of *midrashim* (interpretive commentaries) on the Book of Deuteronomy, probably compiled at the end of the 4th century CE in the Land of Israel.

הַתְּפִלָּה
HaT'filah · Standing before God

Ultimately the goal of prayer is not to translate a word but to translate the self; not to render an ancient vocabulary in modern terminology, but to transform our lives into prayers.

—RABBI ABRAHAM JOSHUA HESCHEL

כַּוָּנָה
Kavanah

אָבוֹת וְאִמָּהוֹת
Avot v'Imahot

גְּבוּרוֹת
G'vurot

קְדֻשַּׁת הַשֵּׁם
K'dushat HaShem

קְדֻשַּׁת הַיּוֹם
K'dushat HaYom

עֲבוֹדָה
Avodah

הוֹדָאָה
Hodaah

שָׁלוֹם
Shalom

תְּפִלַּת הַלֵּב
T'filat HaLev

Horeini, Adonai, darkecha —
ahaleich baamitecha.
Yacheid l'vavi l'yirah sh'mecha.

הוֹרֵנִי, יְיָ, דַּרְכֶּךָ,
אֲהַלֵּךְ בַּאֲמִתֶּךָ.
יַחֵד לְבָבִי לְיִרְאָה שְׁמֶךָ.

God, teach me Your path;
Your truth will guide my steps.
Point my heart toward awe —
Your name the center of my devotion.

Adonai, s'fatai tiftach,
ufi yagid t'hilatecha.

אֲדֹנָי, שְׂפָתַי תִּפְתָּח,
וּפִי יַגִּיד תְּהִלָּתֶךָ.

Adonai, open my lips,
that my mouth may declare Your praise.

STANDING BEFORE GOD. I am always in awe at the sight and sound of our sacred community on the High Holy Days. For example, when we all stand or all sit down and I hear the sound of each seat. When I hear the sound of the seats, I feel a rush of emotion — both excitement that everyone is together praying and sadness when I think that most of the people don't realize they could have this feeling every Shabbat. (Louise Stirpe-Gill, b. 1953)
GOD, TEACH ME הוֹרֵנִי יְיָ, Psalm 86:11.
ADONAI ... MY LIPS אֲדֹנָי, שְׂפָתַי, Psalm 51:17.

SAID THE HOLY ONE to Israel:
I asked you to pray in the synagogue of your city
but if you cannot pray in the synagogue,
pray outdoors in an open field;
and if you cannot pray in the field,
pray in the shelter of your home;
and if you cannot pray in your home,
pray in the dark on your bed;
and if you cannot pray on your bed,
meditate in your heart without words.

I AM ISRAEL
All the generations before
exist within me.
All are present at this moment—
dwellers in tents and tenements;
weavers, tailors, bankers, physicians;
beggars dozing in a sunny corner;
fruit-sellers freezing in the market square.
Mothers and fathers in a tangled chain—
all those who studied the Torah;
all those who settled the Land;
all those who were crammed into steerage;
who broke the glass and circumcised their sons.
Six hundred thousand who stood at Sinai;
six million souls who perished.
Abraham my father
Sarah my mother
Joseph my brother
Miriam my sister
Moses my teacher—
their voices speak in me;
I am Israel.

SAID THE HOLY ONE. Based on *Midrash T'hilim* on Psalm 4:9.

Steadfast Love: The Virtue of Chesed

WHAT IS CHESED?

The word *chesed*, as used in the Bible, does not refer to a single, one-way expression of kindness or mercy. The essence of *chesed* is mutual loyalty and allegiance—between human beings, or between human beings and God. It is best understood within the context of reciprocal rights, responsibilities, and duties.

GOD'S LOVING-KINDNESS is that sure love which will not let Israel go. Not all Israel's persistent waywardness could ever destroy it. Though Israel be faithless, yet God remains faithful still. This steady, persistent refusal of God to "wash his hands" of wayward Israel is the essential meaning of the Hebrew word [*chesed*].

—Norman H. Snaith (1898–1982)

WHAT IS CHESED? It is usually translated as "kindness" but it also means "love"—not love as emotion or passion, but love expressed as deed. Theologians define *chesed* as covenant love. Covenant is the bond by which two parties pledge themselves to one another, agreeing to join their separate destinies into a single journey that they will travel together. . . .

Chesed is the love that is loyalty, and the loyalty that is love. It is born in the generosity of faithfulness, the love that means being ever-present for the other, in hard times as well as good; love that grows stronger, not weaker, over time. Those who know it experience the world differently from those who do not. It is not for them a threatening and dangerous place. It is one where trust is rewarded precisely because it does not seek reward. *Chesed* is the gift of love that begets love.

—Rabbi Jonathan Sacks (b. 1948)

LEARNING THE MEANING OF *CHESED* FROM THE HEBREW ALPHABET

ג ד (*Gimmel–dalet*): This stands for גְּמוֹל דַּלִּים (*g'mol dalim*), "show kindness to the poor." Why is the foot of the ג (*gimmel*) stretched toward the ד (*dalet*)? Because those who do *chesed* should seek out [literally: "run after"] the poor [rather than simply wait until they encounter a poor person]. . . . And why is the face of the ד (*dalet*) turned away from the ג (*gimmel*)? Because those who do *chesed* should help the poor in secret, lest they be embarrassed.

—Talmud *Shabbat* 104a

כַּוָּנָה
Kavanah

אָבוֹת וְאִמָּהוֹת
Avot v'Imahot

גְּבוּרוֹת
G'vurot

קְדֻשַּׁת הַשֵּׁם
K'dushat HaShem

קְדֻשַּׁת הַיּוֹם
K'dushat HaYom

עֲבוֹדָה
Avodah

הוֹדָאָה
Hodaah

שָׁלוֹם
Shalom

תְּפִלַּת הַלֵּב
T'filat HaLev

Moses said to God: "Now, if I have been granted favor in Your eyes, enable me, I pray, to recognize the unity of purpose in the diversity of Your ways, so that I may know You." . . . And God said: "I will let all My goodness pass before you . . ."

(Exodus 33:13, 19)

And God passed by before [Moses] and proclaimed: "God always remains God... loving Creation and ready to bestow favor, long-suffering and abundant in *chesed* and truth, preserving *chesed* for a thousand generations. . . ."

(Exodus 34:6–7)

COMMENTARY

Moses sought to discern the ways of God: diverse and multifaceted, but always directed toward one single purpose. This unity of purpose, this basic principle that is realized in every aspect of God's ways—even as the spectrum of seven colors unites to form one single ray of white light—is "My goodness" (טוּבִי *tuvi*). Goodness, kindness, generosity, and compassion—all elements of *chesed*—are the essence of the Divine.

—Based on Rabbi Samson Raphael Hirsch (1808–1888)

Our guiding principle is *Imitatio Dei*—the imitation of God, our attempt to incorporate divine acts and virtues into our own life. Thus, we seek to model our own acts of *chesed* on the ideal, infinite *chesed* we associate with God. As Rabbi Abraham Joshua Heschel (1907–1972) writes:

"We live by the conviction that acts of goodness reflect the hidden light of His holiness. His light is above our minds but not above our will. It is within our power to mirror His unending love in deeds of kindness, like brooks that hold the sky."

FOR REFLECTION

From the Psalms: "The world is built with *chesed*" (89:3).

How has the *chesed* that I have experienced shaped the person I am and the life that I lead?

From the Psalms: "Your *chesed* is before my eyes; I have set my course by it" (26:3).

Who are my own models of *chesed*? How have I sought to emulate them during this past year?

כַּוָּנָה
Kavanah
אָבוֹת וְאִמָּהוֹת
Avot v'Imahot
גְּבוּרוֹת
G'vurot
קְדֻשַּׁת הַשֵּׁם
K'dushat HaShem
קְדֻשַּׁת הַיּוֹם
K'dushat HaYom
עֲבוֹדָה
Avodah
הוֹדָאָה
Hodaah
שָׁלוֹם
Shalom
תְּפִלַּת הַלֵּב
T'filat HaLev

בָּרוּךְ אַתָּה, יְיָ,	*Baruch atah, Adonai,*
אֱלֹהֵינוּ וֵאלֹהֵי אֲבוֹתֵינוּ וְאִמּוֹתֵינוּ:	*Eloheinu v'Elohei avoteinu v'imoteinu:*
אֱלֹהֵי אַבְרָהָם, אֱלֹהֵי יִצְחָק,	*Elohei Avraham, Elohei Yitzchak,*
וֵאלֹהֵי יַעֲקֹב,	*v'Elohei Yaakov;*
אֱלֹהֵי שָׂרָה, אֱלֹהֵי רִבְקָה,	*Elohei Sarah, Elohei Rivkah,*
אֱלֹהֵי רָחֵל, וֵאלֹהֵי לֵאָה,	*Elohei Rachel, v'Elohei Leah;*
הָאֵל הַגָּדוֹל הַגִּבּוֹר וְהַנּוֹרָא,	*haEl hagadol hagibor v'hanora,*
אֵל עֶלְיוֹן,	*El elyon,*
גּוֹמֵל חֲסָדִים טוֹבִים, וְקוֹנֵה הַכֹּל –	*gomeil chasadim tovim, v'koneih hakol —*
וְזוֹכֵר חַסְדֵי אָבוֹת וְאִמָּהוֹת,	*v'zocheir chasdei avot v'imahot,*
וּמֵבִיא גְאֻלָּה לִבְנֵי בְנֵיהֶם,	*umeivi g'ulah livnei v'neihem,*
לְמַעַן שְׁמוֹ בְּאַהֲבָה.	*l'maan sh'mo b'ahavah.*
זָכְרֵנוּ לְחַיִּים,	***Zochreinu l'chayim,***
מֶלֶךְ חָפֵץ בַּחַיִּים.	***Melech chafeitz bachayim.***
וְכָתְבֵנוּ בְּסֵפֶר הַחַיִּים,	***V'chotveinu b'sefer hachayim,***
לְמַעַנְךָ אֱלֹהִים חַיִּים.	***l'maancha, Elohim chayim.***
מֶלֶךְ עוֹזֵר וּמוֹשִׁיעַ וּמָגֵן –	*Melech ozeir umoshia umagein —*

You are the Source of blessing, Adonai, our God
and God of our fathers and mothers:
God of Abraham, God of Isaac, and God of Jacob;
God of Sarah, God of Rebecca, God of Rachel, and God of Leah;
exalted God, dynamic in power, inspiring awe,
God sublime, Creator of all —
yet You offer us kindness,
recall the loving deeds of our fathers and mothers,
and bring redemption to their children's children,
acting in love for the sake of Your name.

Remember us for life, sovereign God who treasures life.
Inscribe us in the Book of Life, for Your sake, God of life.

Sovereign of salvation, Pillar of protection —

בָּרוּךְ אַתָּה, יְיָ, מָגֵן אַבְרָהָם וְעֶזְרַת שָׂרָה.

Baruch atah, Adonai, magein Avraham v'ezrat Sarah.

Blessed are You in our lives, Adonai, Shield of Abraham, Sustainer of Sarah.

AVOT V'IMAHOT:
Kindness of Heart and Hand: The Blessing of Chesed

זוֹכֵר חַסְדֵי אָבוֹת וְאִמָּהוֹת
Zocheir chasdei avot v'imahot . . .
Remember the *chesed* of those who came before us:
a desert tent furled on every side—the home of Abraham and Sarah—
wide open to welcome travelers from all directions;
an open hand, to offer bread to strangers in need;
an open heart, a bold voice lifted up in defense of others.

נֹצֵר חֶסֶד לָאֲלָפִים
Notzeir chesed laalafim . . .
Hold fast these memories of *chesed*. Show mercy in a thousand ways.
Weave threads of kindness from generation to generation.

And so our Sages teach:
Why call God *Magein Avraham* (the Shield of Abraham)?
Through this name, we ask God to protect the "Abraham" within each of us—
our spark of generosity and kindness,
the impulse to open our circle and widen our horizon of concern.
And when we call God *Ezrat Sarah*—the One who intervened on Sarah's behalf—
we seek to awaken within ourselves a spirit of generous activism;
to inspire life-sustaining deeds,
selfless moments of giving to others.

Descendants of compassionate ancestors,
may we cultivate the instinct to love and serve.
Blessed is the open heart, blessed the open hand.

FURLED ON EVERY SIDE. A midrash teaches that Job's tent was also open on all sides, but Abraham reached an even higher level of hospitality, for he would go out in search of guests. (*Avot d'Rabbi Natan* 7)

A VOICE LIFTED UP. Referring to Abraham's plea on behalf of the people of Sodom (Genesis 18).

NOTZEIR CHESED LAALAFIM. "Keeping mercy to the thousandth generation" (Exodus 34:7). The 11th-century commentator Rashi teaches that this phrase denotes "the *chesed* that a person performs before God"—not God's kindness, but human kindness. That is, when a person performs a kind deed, God treasures and preserves it.

WHY CALL GOD MAGEIN AVRAHAM. A teaching of Rabbi Judah Aryeh Leib Alter (1847–1905), also known as the *S'fat Emet* (Language of Truth), the title of his most famous work.

DESCENDANTS OF COMPASSIONATE ANCESTORS. Based on a traditional description of the Jewish people as *rachamanim b'nei rachamanim* (compassionate children of compassionate parents). Talmud *Y'vamot* 79a states: "Jews are distinguished by three characteristics: they are merciful, they are modest, and they perform acts of loving kindness."

Strength, Discipline, and Restraint: The Virtue of G'vurah

Like a ravaged city without walls is a person whose spirit lacks self-restraint.

—Proverbs 25:28

Ben Zoma said: Who is mighty (*eizeh hu gibor*)? One who conquers one's impulses; as Scripture says (Proverbs 16:32): "A person who is slow to anger is better than a mighty hero; one who controls one's temper (*mosheil b'rucho*), than one who conquers a city."

—Mishnah *Avot* 4:1

How should we discipline our children? There must be a combination of caring and compassion on the one hand and of firmness and strength on the other hand. As the Talmud puts it, "pushing away with the left hand while drawing closer with the right hand" (*Sanhedrin* 107b). Love, represented by the stronger right hand, should always be the most powerful force.

—Wendy Mogel (b. 1951)

The quality of *g'vurah* may be understood as strength, justice, severity, discipline, and will. Reflecting on *g'vurah* offers us an opportunity to contemplate the way in which we set limits for ourselves and the way we judge ourselves and others. Like many people, I tend to be quite hard on myself. Love and strength, *chesed* and *g'vurah*, are partners when I keep them in balance with each other, allowing me to be both critical and kind to myself and others.

FOR REFLECTION

Is my self-criticism and severity helpful or harmful?

Do I reflect on my own behavior in a way that is both strict and loving?

Is my judgment of other people harsh and without compassion?

How do I use my strength and self-discipline to reach the highest within me?

THE QUALITY OF G'VURAH . . . HIGHEST WITHIN ME. By Rabbi Jeff Goldwasser (b. 1963), adapted.

כַּוָּנָה
Kavanah

אָבוֹת וְאִמָּהוֹת
Avot v'Imahot

גְּבוּרוֹת
G'vurot

קְדֻשַּׁת הַשֵּׁם
K'dushat HaShem

קְדֻשַּׁת הַיּוֹם
K'dushat HaYom

עֲבוֹדָה
Avodah

הוֹדָאָה
Hodaah

שָׁלוֹם
Shalom

תְּפִלַּת הַלֵּב
T'filat HaLev

Whoever exercises mercy where strictness is required,
will eventually be cruel where kindness is required.

—Midrash *Ecclesiastes Rabbah* 7:33

COMMENTARY: WHEN KINDNESS IS MISGUIDED

What is "enabling"? "Enabling" refers to the behavior of people in close contact with a person who is acting destructively toward himself and/or others. The concept was initially developed in regard to alcoholism, but is applicable not only to other addictions, but to many other types of destructive behavior. . . .

Let us follow the pattern of the alcoholic as an example to illustrate the phenomenon of "enabling." Excessive use of alcohol invariably results in unpleasant consequences including physical distress, loss of mental acuity, absenteeism, impaired work performance, aggression, anti-social behavior, and frank violation of the law. These consequences can result in so much distress that the drinker may conclude that the pleasurable effects of the drinking are just not worth it. When the misery resulting from the drinking exceeds the pleasure it provides, the drinking may stop, or the person may seek help to stop the drinking.

It follows that anyone who in any way relieves the alcoholic of the unpleasant consequences of his drinking is eliminating the only thing that could cause him to stop. The one who tries to be benevolent by "helping" the drinker is inadvertently, but very effectively, promoting continuation of the drinking. . . . The same is true of the compulsive overeater, the compulsive gambler, the drug-dependent person, and even other types of destructive behavior which are not addictive. . . .

"Enabling" can apply to parents who cover up for their children's dereliction and blame others for things that are really the child's responsibility. . . . When this happens, parents are fostering an attitude of finding fault in others for one's own dereliction, and this trait may persist well through adult life.

Effective treatment of destructive behavior requires elimination of the "oxygen," i.e., whatever is enabling it. . . . The father, wife, or doctor may think s/he is being kind, helpful and considerate. This is where the Talmudic prediction comes into play: misguided "kindness" ultimately leads to cruelty.

—Rabbi Abraham Twerski (b. 1930)

כַּוָּנָה
Kavanah

אָבוֹת וְאִמָּהוֹת
Avot v'Imahot

גְּבוּרוֹת
G'vurot

קְדֻשַּׁת הַשֵּׁם
K'dushat HaShem

קְדֻשַּׁת הַיּוֹם
K'dushat HaYom

עֲבוֹדָה
Avodah

הוֹדָאָה
Hodaah

שָׁלוֹם
Shalom

תְּפִלַּת הַלֵּב
T'filat HaLev

In Hebrew, choose either hakol *or* meitim.

Atah gibor l'olam, Adonai —	אַתָּה גִּבּוֹר לְעוֹלָם, אֲדֹנָי –
m'chayeih hakol/meitim atah,	מְחַיֵּה הַכֹּל\מֵתִים אַתָּה,
rav l'hoshia.	רַב לְהוֹשִׁיעַ.
Morid hatal.	מוֹרִיד הַטָּל.
M'chalkeil chayim b'chesed,	מְכַלְכֵּל חַיִּים בְּחֶסֶד,
m'chayeih hakol/meitim	מְחַיֵּה הַכֹּל\מֵתִים
b'rachamim rabim —	בְּרַחֲמִים רַבִּים –
someich noflim,	סוֹמֵךְ נוֹפְלִים,
v'rofei cholim umatir asurim;	וְרוֹפֵא חוֹלִים וּמַתִּיר אֲסוּרִים,
umkayeim emunato lisheinei afar.	וּמְקַיֵּם אֱמוּנָתוֹ לִישֵׁנֵי עָפָר.
Mi chamocha, baal g'vurot;	מִי כָמְוֹךָ, בַּעַל גְּבוּרוֹת,
umi domeh-lach? —	וּמִי דְוֹמֶה לָּךְ,
melech meimit umchayeh	מֶלֶךְ מֵמִית וּמְחַיֶּה
umatzmiach y'shuah.	וּמַצְמִיחַ יְשׁוּעָה.
Mi chamocha, El harachamim? —	מִי כָמְוֹךָ, אֵל הָרַחֲמִים,
zocheir y'tzurav l'chayim b'rachamim.	זוֹכֵר יְצוּרָיו לְחַיִּים בְּרַחֲמִים.
V'ne·eman atah l'hachayot hakol/meitim.	וְנֶאֱמָן אַתָּה לְהַחֲיוֹת הַכֹּל\מֵתִים.

Your life-giving power is forever, Adonai — with us in life and in death.
You liberate and save, cause dew to descend;
and with mercy abundant, lovingly nurture all life.
From life to death, You are the force that flows without end —
You support the falling, heal the sick, free the imprisoned and confined;
You are faithful, even to those who rest in the dust.

Power-beyond-Power, from whom salvation springs,
Sovereign over life and death — who is like You?
    Merciful God, who compares with You?
    With tender compassion You remember all creatures for life.
Faithful and true, worthy of our trust —
You sustain our immortal yearnings; in You we place our undying hopes.

בָּרוּךְ אַתָּה, יְיָ, מְחַיֵּה הַכֹּל\וְהַמֵּתִים.

Baruch atah, Adonai, m'chayeih hakol/hameitim.

Wellspring of blessing, Power eternal, You are the One who gives and renews all life.

G'vurot:
The Blessing of Strength

אַתָּה גִּבּוֹר לְעוֹלָם, אֲדֹנָי

Atah gibor l'olam, Adonai . . .
You are the Power that never diminishes and never subsides.
From You we draw *g'vurah*—our inner core of strength:
Strength to rise at dawn when hungry babies cry;
Strength to rise before the aged parent, to bring care and dignity;
Strength to give patience to a child whose needs overwhelm us;
Strength to hold and heal a spouse in pain, to give love without losing hope;
Strength to survive a job that is stressful and unrewarding;
Strength to endure months or years without work and purpose;
Strength to face crises and strength to surmount everyday hurdles;
Strength to keep practicing and exercising, trying mightily in spite of failure;
Strength to do what is called for, even when it is hard;
Strength to do what is right, especially when others do not.

אַתָּה גִּבּוֹר לְעוֹלָם, אֲדֹנָי

Atah gibor l'olam, Adonai . . .
Your power is with us always:
in our human stamina and resilience;
in our determination to persevere;
in the discipline to set limits and make choices;
in the fortitude to be true to our principles.
Blessed is *g'vurah*—
the will to act with courage, the gift of inner strength.

THE DISCIPLINE TO SET LIMITS. Rabbi Meir Leib ben Yechiel Michel (called Malbim; 1809–1879) taught: "Parents who cannot bear to discipline a child actually care more for themselves—their own tender feelings—than they do for their child's ultimate good. Indulgence is not love." Similarly, we find this critique of Abraham's parenting skills in a midrash: by neglecting to correct Ishmael's objectionable behavior, Abraham allowed his son to become a disagreeable person (*Exodus Rabbah* 1.1).

Holy Living: The Virtue of K'dushah

Speak to the whole Israelite community and say to them:
You shall be holy, for I, the Eternal your God, am holy. (Leviticus 19:2)

COMMENTARY

What is the difference between that which we scientifically call morality and the religious expression of holiness? The difference is to be derived from the difference of the tense and the verb in the sentence in which holiness is used with regard to God and the human being. With God, it is being: "For I am holy." With regard to the human being, however, it says: "You shall be holy." Hence one may translate: "You shall *become* holy." Holiness thus means for the human being a task, whereas for God it designates being.

—Hermann Cohen (1842–1918)

In the name of the daybreak
and the eyelids of morning
and the wayfaring moon
and the night when it departs,

I swear I will not dishonor
my soul with hatred,
but offer myself humbly
as a guardian of nature,
as a healer of misery,
as a messenger of wonder,
as an architect of peace.

In the name of the sun and its mirrors
and the day that embraces it
and the cloud veils drawn over it
and the uttermost night
and the male and the female
and the plants bursting with seed
and the crowning seasons
of the firefly and the apple,

I will honor all life
—wherever and in whatever form
it may dwell—on Earth my home,
and in the mansions of the stars.

—Diane Ackerman (b. 1948)

CHAPTERS 18–20 OF LEVITICUS [known as the Holiness Code] give a clear account of holiness in life. The prime emphasis is ethical. And the moral laws of these chapters are not mere injunctions of conformity. They call for just, humane, and sensitive treatment of others. The aged, the handicapped, and the poor are to receive consideration and courtesy. The laborer is to be promptly paid. The stranger is to be accorded the same love we give our fellow citizens. The law is concerned not only with overt behavior, but also with motive; vengefulness and the bearing of grudges are condemned. . . .

In holy living, the ethical factor is primary, but it is not the only one. In combining moral and ceremonial commandments, the authors of the Holiness Code displayed sound understanding.

Such are the components of the way of life called *kadosh* (holy). Leviticus 19 begins with the startling declaration that by these means we can and should try to be holy like God. The same Torah that stresses the distance between God's sublime perfection and our earthly limitations urges us to strive to reduce that distance. The task is endless, but it is infinitely rewarding. Rabbi Tarfon said: "Do not avoid an undertaking that has no limit or a task that cannot be completed. It is like the case of a fellow who was hired to take water from the sea and pour it out on the land. But, as the sea was not emptied out nor the land filled with water, he became downhearted. Then someone said to him, 'Fool! Why should you be downhearted as long as you receive a dinar of gold every day as your wage?'" (*Avot d'Rabbi Natan* 27) The pursuit of the unattainable can be a means of fulfillment.

The Law of Holiness is not addressed to selected individuals. It is addressed to the entire community of Israel. Its objective is not to produce a few saints withdrawn from the world in contemplative or ascetic practices. Rather, the Torah aims to create a holy people which displays its consecration to God's service in the normal day-to-day relations of farming, commerce, family living, and communal affairs.

—Rabbi Bernard Bamberger (1904–1980)

FOR REFLECTION

As I consider the most fulfilling activities of my life, in what ways do they provide me with opportunities to strive for holiness?

Have I created a spiritual practice that includes ethical and ritual elements?

What might be preventing me from developing a richer practice that encourages "holy living"?

נְקַדֵּשׁ אֶת שִׁמְךָ בָּעוֹלָם,
כְּשֵׁם שֶׁמַּקְדִּישִׁים אוֹתוֹ
בִּשְׁמֵי מָרוֹם,
כַּכָּתוּב עַל יַד נְבִיאֶךָ:
וְקָרָא זֶה אֶל־זֶה וְאָמַר:

קָדוֹשׁ, קָדוֹשׁ, קָדוֹשׁ יְיָ צְבָאוֹת,
מְלֹא כָל־הָאָרֶץ כְּבוֹדוֹ.

אַדִּיר אַדִּירֵנוּ, יְיָ אֲדֹנֵינוּ —
מָה־אַדִּיר שִׁמְךָ בְּכָל־הָאָרֶץ.

בָּרוּךְ כְּבוֹד־יְיָ מִמְּקוֹמוֹ.

אֶחָד הוּא אֱלֹהֵינוּ, הוּא אָבִינוּ,
הוּא מַלְכֵּנוּ, הוּא מוֹשִׁיעֵנוּ —
וְהוּא יַשְׁמִיעֵנוּ בְּרַחֲמָיו
לְעֵינֵי כָּל חָי:
אֲנִי יְיָ אֱלֹהֵיכֶם.

N'kadeish et shimcha baolam,
k'shem shemakdishim oto
bishmei marom;
kakatuv al yad n'vi·echa:
V'kara zeh el-zeh v'amar:

"Kadosh, kadosh, kadosh Adonai tz'vaot,
m'lo chol-haaretz k'vodo."

Adir adireinu, Adonai adoneinu —
mah-adir shimcha b'chol haaretz.

"Baruch k'vod-Adonai mim'komo."

Echad hu eloheinu, hu avinu,
hu malkeinu, hu moshi·einu —
v'hu yashmi·einu b'rachamav
l'einei kol chai:
"Ani Adonai Eloheichem."

We sanctify Your name in the world,
as celestial song sanctifies You in realms beyond our world,
in the words of Your prophet:

Holy Holy Holy is the God of heaven's hosts.
The fullness of the whole earth is God's glory.

God of Strength who gives us strength,
God of Might who gives us might —
how magnificent the signs of Your Being throughout the earth.

Blessed is the God of eternity who comes forth in splendor.

Our God is one —
Avinu and *Malkeinu*, sovereign Source of life and liberation —
revealing with mercy to all who live: "I am Adonai your God."

כַּוָּנָה *Kavanah*
אָבוֹת וְאִמָּהוֹת *Avot v'Imahot*
גְּבוּרוֹת *G'vurot*
קְדֻשַּׁת הַשֵּׁם *K'dushat HaShem*
קְדֻשַּׁת הַיּוֹם *K'dushat HaYom*
עֲבוֹדָה *Avodah*
הוֹדָאָה *Hodaah*
שָׁלוֹם *Shalom*
תְּפִלַּת הַלֵּב *T'filat HaLev*

HOLY קָדוֹשׁ, Isaiah 6:3.
GOD OF MIGHT יְיָ אֲדֹנֵינוּ, Psalm 8:2, 10.
BLESSED בָּרוּךְ, Ezekiel 3:12.
I AM אֲנִי, Exodus 15:10.

K'dushat HaShem: The Blessing of Holiness

נְקַדֵּשׁ אֶת שִׁמְךָ בָּעוֹלָם

N'kadeish et shimcha baolam . . .
Let us sanctify Your name in this world
as celestial song sanctifies Your name on high.

Asked the *Chofetz Chayim*:
Is it not presumptuous for us to compare ourselves to angels?
One might think it is like a pauper dressed in rags who appears before the king,
pretending to be one of the royal ministers!

And he answered:
In truth, we have as much right to stand before God as the angels.
For it is written in the Torah:
"God blew into Adam's nostrils the breath of life, and he became a living soul."
Holy One, You breathed into the human soul something of Yourself;
a spark of You is within us, yearning to rise up and unite with its Source.

And so we hunger for holiness;
we long to lift up mundane acts and make them beautiful.
Let us re-imagine our tables as holy altars where each day we offer up our best—
through blessings and mindful eating,
thoughtful conversation and care for one another.
Let us make marriages that are truly *kiddushin*—
holy partnerships of intimacy, faithfulness, and love.
Let us sanctify time, preserve and remember Shabbat,
and keep the holy days of our people.
In a world that can be cruel, let us create holy communities—
oases of compassion.

The Torah teaches:
"Do not profane My holy name—
that I may be sanctified amidst the people of Israel."

We sanctify Your name in this world
when we bring Your spirit into all our deeds.

THE CHOFETZ CHAYIM. Yisrael Meir Kagan Poupko (1838–1933) was a Lithuanian rabbi popularly known by the title of his most famous work, *Chofetz Chayim* (The One Who Desires Life), a discussion of the laws of gossip and ethical speech.

GOD BLEW INTO ADAM'S NOSTRILS, Genesis 2:7.

HOLY ONE, YOU BREATHED. Adapted from the *Zohar* ("Splendor" or "Radiance"), the central text of Jewish mysticism.

LET US RE-IMAGINE OUR TABLES. See Talmud *B'rachot* 55a.

DO NOT PROFANE MY HOLY NAME, Leviticus 22:32.

יִמְלֹךְ יְיָ לְעוֹלָם,
אֱלֹהַיִךְ, צִיּוֹן, לְדֹר וָדֹר,
הַלְלוּ־יָהּ.

"Yimloch Adonai l'olam;
Elohayich, Tziyon, l'dor vador —
hal'lu-Yah!"

לְדוֹר וָדוֹר נַגִּיד גָּדְלֶךָ.
וּלְנֵצַח נְצָחִים קְדֻשָּׁתְךָ נַקְדִּישׁ.
וְשִׁבְחֲךָ, אֱלֹהֵינוּ, מִפִּינוּ לֹא יָמוּשׁ
לְעוֹלָם וָעֶד,
כִּי אֵל מֶלֶךְ גָּדוֹל וְקָדוֹשׁ אָתָּה.

L'dor vador nagid godlecha.
Ulneitzach n'tzachim k'dushat'cha nakdish.
V'shivchacha, Eloheinu, mipinu lo yamush
l'olam va·ed,
ki El melech gadol v'kadosh atah.

"The Eternal shall reign for all time,
your God for all generations, Zion — Halleluyah!"

We will teach Your greatness
l'dor vador — from generation to generation.
And to the end of time
we will affirm Your holiness.
Our God, Your praise shall ever be on our lips,
for Your power is boundless — sovereign and holy.

THE ETERNAL SHALL REIGN יִמְלֹךְ יְיָ, Psalm 146:10.

YOUR PRAISE SHALL EVER BE ON OUR LIPS וְשִׁבְחֲךָ . . . מִפִּינוּ לֹא יָמוּשׁ לְעוֹלָם וָעֶד. The liturgy has us utter a multitude of praises of God. Why this unrelenting repetition of God's praises? Surely, if God is as powerful as we say, God does not need all this flattery. One answer is that God does not need these praises; *we* do. We need to bless God repeatedly in order to extricate our focus from ourselves. We are, by nature, egocentric. If we are going to be able to get out of ourselves sufficiently to have a relationship with God, we must learn to put aside our self-centered feelings and thoughts. (Rabbi Elliot Dorff, b. 1943; adapted)

From Generation to Generation: Two Ethical Wills

1

Be careful to visit the sick, for sympathy lightens pain.
Comfort the bereaved, and speak tenderly to them.

Treat the poor with respect, and give to them anonymously.

Kindle a light. Do not leave it to others who come after you,
lest they be unable to kindle it, and it be left unlit forever.

Do not turn a deaf ear to those who seek your help.

Never storm into your house, or cause those who live with you to be afraid of you.
Rid your soul of anger, for "anger lodges in the bosom of fools."

Never fail to greet a fellow human being;
always speak the truth.

2

Judaism, my child, is the struggle to bring God down to earth, a struggle for the sanctification of the human heart. This struggle your people wages not with physical force but with spirit, with sincere, heartfelt prayers, and by constant striving for peace and justice.

So do you understand, my child, how we are distinct from others and wherein lies the secret of our existence on earth?

Knowing this, will your heart still be heavy, my child? Will you still say you cannot stand your fate? But you must, my child, for so were you commanded; it is your calling. This is your mission, your purpose on earth.

You must go to work alongside people of other nations . . . and you will teach them that they must come to a brotherhood of nations and to a union of all nations with God.

You may ask, "How does one speak to them?" This is how: "Thou shalt not murder; thou shalt not steal; thou shalt not covet; love thy neighbor as thyself . . ."

Do these things and through their merit, my child, you will be victorious.

BE CAREFUL TO VISIT. From the earliest known Jewish ethical will, attributed to Rabbi Eleazar the Great (Eleazar ben Isaac of Worms, 11th century).

ANGER LODGES, Ecclesiastes 7:9.

JUDAISM, MY CHILD. Published in the ghetto newspaper of Warsaw-Krakow in 1940, this ethical will was signed only "Your Mother."

How Do We Sense God's Holiness?
Through Awe

Uvchein tein pachd'cha, Adonai Eloheinu,	וּבְכֵן תֵּן פַּחְדְּךָ, יְיָ אֱלֹהֵינוּ,
al kol maasecha;	עַל כָּל מַעֲשֶׂיךָ,
v'eimat'cha al kol mah shebarata.	וְאֵימָתְךָ עַל כָּל מַה שֶּׁבָּרָאתָ.
V'yira·ucha kol hamaasim;	וְיִירָאוּךָ כָּל הַמַּעֲשִׂים,
v'yishtachavu l'fanecha kol hab'ruim.	וְיִשְׁתַּחֲווּ לְפָנֶיךָ כָּל הַבְּרוּאִים.
V'yei·asu chulam agudah echat,	וְיֵעָשׂוּ כֻלָּם אֲגֻדָּה אֶחָת,
laasot r'tzoncha b'leivav shaleim —	לַעֲשׂוֹת רְצוֹנְךָ בְּלֵבָב שָׁלֵם,
k'mo sheyadanu, Adonai Eloheinu,	כְּמוֹ שֶׁיָּדַעְנוּ, יְיָ אֱלֹהֵינוּ,
shehasholtan l'fanecha,	שֶׁהַשָּׁלְטָן לְפָנֶיךָ,
oz b'yad'cha, ugvurah biminecha,	עֹז בְּיָדְךָ, וּגְבוּרָה בִּימִינֶךָ,
v'shimcha nora al kol mah shebarata.	וְשִׁמְךָ נוֹרָא עַל כָּל מַה שֶּׁבָּרָאתָ.

And so, in Your holiness,
give all creation the gift of awe.
Turn our fear to reverence;
let us be witnesses of wonder —
perceiving all nature as a prayer come alive.
We bow to the sovereignty of Your strength,
the primacy of Your power.
We yearn for connection with all that lives,
doing Your will with wholeness of heart.
Awe-inspiring is Your creation,
all-encompassing Your transcendent name.

WE YEARN FOR CONNECTION WITH ALL THAT LIVES וְיֵעָשׂוּ כֻלָּם אֲגֻדָּה אֶחָת. This prayer, the first of a three-part insertion in the High Holy Day liturgy, expresses a universalistic vision in which all living beings unite in reverence for their Creator. Inherent in this vision is a humble appreciation of all forms of life, regardless of their usefulness to human beings. "Our Sages taught: Even those things that you may regard as completely superfluous to Creation — such as fleas, gnats, and flies — even they were included in Creation; and God's purpose is carried through everything — even through a snake, a scorpion, a gnat, a frog" (Midrash *Genesis Rabbah* 10.7). Awe and reverence remove humanity from the center of the universe. We learn instead to become "witnesses of wonder" — admiring observers of God's magnificent world.

The Gift of Awe

Come to the woods, for here is rest.
There is no repose like that of the deep green woods. . . .

The clearest way into the Universe is through a forest wilderness.

The winds will blow their own freshness into you and the storms their energy, while cares will drop off like autumn leaves. As age comes on, one source of enjoyment after another is closed, but nature's sources never fail.

The poetry of earth is never dead.

Study nature, love nature,
stay close to nature. It will never fail you.

Nature is the living, visible garment of God.

Nature never hurries: atom by atom, little by little,
she achieves her work.

What seems to be a stone is a drama.

The joy of looking and comprehending
is nature's most beautiful gift.

When I behold Your heavens, the work of Your fingers,
the moon and stars that You set in place . . .

Replete is the world with a spiritual radiance, replete with sublime and marvelous secrets. But a small hand held against the eye hides it all.

The heavens declare the glory of God;
the sky proclaims God's handiwork.

What we lack is not a will to believe,
but a will to wonder.

THE GIFT OF AWE. Compiled from the words of John Muir (1838–1914), John Keats (1795–1821), Frank Lloyd Wright (1867–1959), Johann von Goethe (1749–1832), Ralph Waldo Emerson (1803–1882), Rabbi Abraham Joshua Heschel (1907–1972), Albert Einstein (1879–1955), Psalm 8:4, Rabbi Israel ben Eliezer ("the Baal Shem Tov," 1698–1760), Psalm 19:2, and Rabbi Abraham Joshua Heschel, respectively.

How Do We Sense God's Holiness?
Through Honor

Uvchein tein kavod, Adonai, l'amecha;	וּבְכֵן תֵּן כָּבוֹד, יְיָ, לְעַמֶּךָ,
t'hilah lirei·echa;	תְּהִלָּה לִירֵאֶיךָ
v'tikvah tovah l'dorshecha;	וְתִקְוָה טוֹבָה לְדוֹרְשֶׁיךָ,
ufit·chon peh lamyachalim lach,	וּפִתְחוֹן פֶּה לַמְיַחֲלִים לָךְ,
simchah l'artzecha,	שִׂמְחָה לְאַרְצֶךָ,
v'sason l'irecha;	וְשָׂשׂוֹן לְעִירֶךָ,
utzmichat keren l'David avdecha;	וּצְמִיחַת קֶרֶן לְדָוִד עַבְדֶּךָ,
vaarichat ner l'ven Yishai m'shichecha,	וַעֲרִיכַת נֵר לְבֶן יִשַׁי מְשִׁיחֶךָ,
bimheirah v'yameinu.	בִּמְהֵרָה בְיָמֵינוּ.

And so, in Your holiness,
give Your people the gift of honor.
Bless with praise those who praise You.
Bless with hope those who seek You.
Give Your believers a basis for faith:
true happiness for the Land of Israel,
true joy in Jerusalem.
May the sparks of David, Your servant,
soon grow bright enough for us to see
a beam of light in the darkness,
a promise of perfection.

כַּוָּנָה *Kavanah*
אָבוֹת וְאִמָּהוֹת *Avot v'Imahot*
גְּבוּרוֹת *G'vurot*
קְדֻשַּׁת הַשֵּׁם *K'dushat HaShem*
קְדֻשַּׁת הַיּוֹם *K'dushat HaYom*
עֲבוֹדָה *Avodah*
הוֹדָאָה *Hodaah*
שָׁלוֹם *Shalom*
תְּפִלַּת הַלֵּב *T'filat HaLev*

THE GIFT OF HONOR כָּבוֹד. Honor [in Hebrew, *kavod*; literally "weight"] is of two sorts. There is the honor that depends upon status, and is inherently scarce. It puffs up ego, precludes humility, seeks a name for self rather than the name of God. Exodus 14–15 plays on usages of the Hebrew root *k-b-d* in this sense. Pharaoh's heart is not only hardened but made heavy, swollen with self-importance; God, by making the chariots sink heavily in the mud, will be honored, raised in stature in the eyes of those who witness this event. Eyes are crucial to this kind of *kavod*. It has to be seen to exist; it exists in the seeing of it. It is external, the result of rank or achievement.

There is, however, an inner weightiness, a character so deeply engraved that it is not easily washed away, a rootedness of self secure against prevailing winds. No human being is totally immune to the loss of this honor. We need each other's confirmations of self. But the core is within, a function of who we are and what we stand for. (Arnold M. Eisen, b. 1951)

Focusing Prayer
God of All Generations
God's Powers
God's Holiness
The Day's Holiness
Our Offering
Thanksgiving
Peace
Prayer of the Heart

"True joy in Jerusalem . . ."

יְרוּשָׁלַיִם עִיר נָמָל עַל שְׂפַת הַנֵּצַח.
הַר־הַבַּיִת אֳנִיָּה גְּדוֹלָה, סְפִינַת שַׁעֲשׁוּעִים
מְפֹאֶרֶת. מֵאֶשְׁנַבֵּי כָּתְלָהּ הַמַּעֲרָבִי מִסְתַּכְּלִים קְדוֹשִׁים
עַלִּיזִים, נוֹסְעִים. חֲסִידִים בָּרָצִיף מְנַפְנְפִים
לְשָׁלוֹם, צוֹעֲקִים הֵידָד לְהִתְרָאוֹת. הִיא
תָּמִיד מַגִּיעָה, תָּמִיד מַפְלִיגָה. וְהַגְּדֵרוֹת וְהָרְצִיפִים
וְהַשּׁוֹטְרִים וְהַדְּגָלִים וְהַתְּרָנִים הַגְּבֹהִים שֶׁל כְּנֵסִיּוֹת
וּמִסְגָּדִים וְהָאֲרֻבּוֹת שֶׁל בָּתֵּי הַכְּנֶסֶת וְהַסִּירוֹת
שֶׁל הַלֵּל וְגַלֵּי הָרִים. קוֹל שׁוֹפָר נִשְׁמַע: עוֹד
אַחַת הִפְלִיגָה. מַלָּחֵי יוֹם־כִּפּוּר בְּמַדִּים לְבָנִים
מְטַפְּסִים בֵּין סֻלָּמוֹת וַחֲבָלִים שֶׁל תְּפִלּוֹת בְּדוּקוֹת.

וְהַמַּשָּׂא וּמַתָּן וְהַשְּׁעָרִים וְכִפּוֹת הַזָּהָב:
יְרוּשָׁלַיִם הִיא וֶנֶצְיָה שֶׁל אֱלֹהִים.

Jerusalem port city on the shores of eternity.
The Holy Mount is a huge ship, a luxurious pleasure
liner. From the portholes of her Western Wall happy
saints look out, travelers. Hasidim on the dock wave
good-bye, shout hurrah till we meet again. She's
always arriving, always sailing. And the gates and the docks
and the policemen and the flags and the high masts of churches
and mosques and the smokestacks of synagogues and the boats
of praise and waves of mountains. The sound of the ram's horn
is heard: still another sailed. Day of Atonement sailors in white
uniforms climb among ladders and ropes of seasoned prayers.

And the trade and the gates and the gold domes:
Jerusalem is the Venice of God.

JERUSALEM PORT CITY. By Yehuda Amichai (1924–2000). This 1967 poem offers a vision of a Jerusalem that is spiritually cosmopolitan—a city whose main "commodity" is piety, but where the secular (for example, police and flags) has an easy relationship with the religious (Hasidim and the sound of the ram's horn); a place whose skyline defines an ethos of interfaith coexistence, and whose Western Wall affords a view that brings joy. It is a dream-like vision of beauty: the purity of the white-garbed "sailors," the gold of the domes. Amichai's poem is a prayer.

How Do We Sense God's Holiness?
Through Righteousness

וּבְכֵן צַדִּיקִים יִרְאוּ וְיִשְׂמָחוּ,	*Uvchein tzadikim yiru v'yismachu,*
וִישָׁרִים יַעֲלֹזוּ,	*visharim yaalozu,*
וַחֲסִידִים בְּרִנָּה יָגִילוּ,	*vachasidim b'rinah yagilu;*
וְעוֹלָתָה תִּקְפָּץ־פִּיהָ,	*v'olatah tikpotz-piha,*
וְכָל הָרִשְׁעָה כֻּלָּהּ כְּעָשָׁן תִּכְלֶה,	*v'chol harishah kulah k'ashan tichleh,*
כִּי תַעֲבִיר מֶמְשֶׁלֶת זָדוֹן מִן הָאָרֶץ.	*ki taavir memshelet zadon min haaretz.*

And so, in Your holiness,
give the righteous the gift of a vision bright with joy:
a world where evil has no voice
and the rule of malevolence fades like wisps of smoke.
Good people everywhere will celebrate
the stunning sight of arrogance gone from the earth.

GIVE THE RIGHTEOUS THE GIFT OF A VISION BRIGHT WITH JOY צַדִּיקִים יִרְאוּ וְיִשְׂמָחוּ. This prayer looks toward a day when righteous people will see a world in which their ideals are fulfilled and their adherence to goodness vindicated. In our own world, too often good people are the victims of others' cruelty and oppression. A particularly challenging biblical verse (Psalm 37:25) says: "I was young; now I am old; yet I have never seen the righteous forsaken or their children begging for bread" — a statement that seems to contradict our own experience of reality.

Rabbi Joseph B. Soloveitchik (1903–1993) suggested that in this verse, the verb "seen" (Hebrew *ra·iti*) has a meaning similar to that in Esther 8:6, when Esther says "How can I bear to see (*ra·iti*) disaster fall upon my people?" That is, *ra·iti* here means "to stand still and watch." Thus Rabbi Soloveitchik read the verse from Psalms as follows: "I was young, now I am old; yet I have never stood still and watched while the righteous were forsaken or their children begging for bread." Another possible reading: "By the time my youth is over and I am ripened with age, may I never see the righteous forsaken or their children begging for bread."

Rava taught: When we are led in for Judgment in the next world,
we will be asked these questions:

1. Did you conduct your business honestly?
2. Did you set a time to study?
3. Did you leave a legacy for future generations?
4. Did you have hope in your heart?
5. Did you get your priorities straight?
6. Did you enjoy this world?
7. Were you the best you could be?

Among the Righteous of the Nations: Wallenberg

Wallenberg—
no smaller than his myth.
Real, ideal, handsome,
big-hearted, pushy-for-Life, tireless—
all of those.

At long last
I don't have to expect
someone will write a book before I die
tearing apart his Image
like they did to the Kennedys and King.

Hype and wishful thinking, exaggeration won't touch him.
He was, indeed, what he was.

The beggar who has been sitting and sleeping
on the same bench in the park
day after day,
surrounded by paper bags stuffed with her belongings,
has now become a donor:
feeding with crumbs the pigeons and sparrows
in a broad circle about her.

---

rava taught. Adapted from Ron Wolfson (b. 1949), based on Talmud *Shabbat* 31a.

among the righteous of the nations. By Danny Siegel (b. 1944). Raoul Wallenberg (1912–1947?) was a Swedish diplomat and humanitarian who served in Nazi-occupied Budapest during World War II. By issuing protective passes and hiding Jews in "safe houses" designated as Swedish territory, Wallenberg saved tens of thousands of Hungarian Jews from deportation and death.

the beggar. By Charles Reznikoff (1894–1976).

כַּוָּנָה
Kavanah
אָבוֹת וְאִמָּהוֹת
Avot v'Imahot
גְּבוּרוֹת
G'vurot
קְדֻשַּׁת הַשֵּׁם
K'dushat HaShem
קְדֻשַּׁת הַיּוֹם
K'dushat HaYom
עֲבוֹדָה
Avodah
הוֹדָאָה
Hodaah
שָׁלוֹם
Shalom
תְּפִלַּת הַלֵּב
T'filat HaLev

וְתִמְלֹךְ, אַתָּה, יְיָ, לְבַדֶּךָ
עַל כָּל מַעֲשֶׂיךָ,
בְּהַר צִיּוֹן מִשְׁכַּן כְּבוֹדֶךָ,
וּבִירוּשָׁלַיִם עִיר קָדְשֶׁךָ,
כַּכָּתוּב בְּדִבְרֵי קָדְשֶׁךָ:
יִמְלֹךְ יְיָ לְעוֹלָם,
אֱלֹהַיִךְ, צִיּוֹן, לְדֹר וָדֹר,
הַלְלוּ־יָהּ.

V'timloch — atah, Adonai — l'vadecha
al kol maasecha,
b'Har Tziyon, mishkan k'vodecha,
uviYrushalayim, ir kodshecha —
kakatuv b'divrei kodshecha:
"Yimloch Adonai l'olam;
Elohayich, Tziyon, l'dor vador —
hal'lu-Yah!"

You, and You alone, Adonai, will reign over Creation,
upon Mount Zion, home of Your Presence,
and in Jerusalem, a city set apart by You —
as the Psalmist believed:
"The Eternal shall reign for all time,
your God for all generations, Zion — Halleluyah!"

קָדוֹשׁ אַתָּה, וְנוֹרָא שְׁמֶךָ,
וְאֵין אֱלוֹהַּ מִבַּלְעָדֶיךָ, כַּכָּתוּב:
וַיִּגְבַּהּ יְיָ צְבָאוֹת בַּמִּשְׁפָּט,
וְהָאֵל הַקָּדוֹשׁ נִקְדַּשׁ בִּצְדָקָה.

Kadosh atah, v'nora sh'mecha;
v'ein elo·ah mibaladecha, kakatuv:
"Vayigbah Adonai tz'vaot bamishpat;
v'haEl hakadosh nikdash bitzdakah."

You are holy.
Your name is Awe.
There is nothing divine beyond You —
as the prophet Isaiah taught:
"The Source of all might is exalted through justice,
the God of holiness made holy through righteousness."

בָּרוּךְ אַתָּה, יְיָ, הַמֶּלֶךְ הַקָּדוֹשׁ.

Baruch atah, Adonai, haMelech hakadosh.

Blessed are You, Adonai, holy Sovereign.

THE ETERNAL SHALL REIGN יִמְלֹךְ יְיָ, Psalm 146:10.
THE SOURCE OF ALL MIGHT IS EXALTED וַיִּגְבַּהּ יְיָ צְבָאוֹת, Isaiah 5:16.

The Gathering

Past the gates of the city
with the cattle, the wind,
between the mountains and the sea,
with the tent, with the faces.

You, an everywhere, like air.
They called You by different names,
none of them Yours,
all of them Yours.

You knew the hunger of open beaks
high in the cedar.
You watched the infant goats
sway to their feet.

You, an everywhere, like air.
I called You by different names,
all of them Yours,
none of them Yours.

A gust of wind parted the grass.
There was the bread I ate,
the heart of the bread,
the bread of the heart.

בָּרוּךְ אַתָּה, יְיָ, הַמֶּלֶךְ הַקָּדוֹשׁ.

Baruch atah, Adonai, haMelech hakadosh.

Blessed are You, Adonai, holy Sovereign.

THE GATHERING. By Jennifer Barber (b. 1956). This contemporary work offers a counterpoint to the image of God celebrated in *K'dushat HaShem* (the prayer on the facing page in praise of God's holiness). Rather than the holy Sovereign who "will reign over Creation," the poet evokes God as the One who nourishes and provides for all beings. This image, too, is drawn from the tradition, especially the Psalms, as in "God gives the animals their food, the young ravens what they cry for" (147:9); "All of them look to You with hope, to provide their food in its proper time" (104:27). The poet, too, ponders the nature of spiritual hunger and nourishment.

Forgiveness: The Virtue of S'lichah

The most basic kind of forgiveness is "forgoing the other's indebtedness" (*m'chilah*). If the offender has done *t'shuvah*, and is sincere in his or her repentance, the offended person should offer *m'chilah*; that is, the offended person should forgo the debt of the offender, relinquish his or her claim against the offender. This is not a reconciliation of heart or an embracing of the offender; it is simply reaching the conclusion that the offender no longer owes me anything for whatever it was that he or she did. *M'chilah* is like a pardon granted to a criminal by the modern state. The crime remains; only the debt is forgiven.

The tradition, however, is quite clear that the offended person is not obliged to offer *m'chilah* if the offender is not sincere in his or her repentance and has not taken concrete steps to correct the wrong done. *M'chilah* is, thus, an expectation of the offended person but only if the sinner is actually repentant. For example, a woman who has been battered by her husband, or abused by her father, is not obliged to grant such a person *m'chilah* unless he has, first, desisted from all abusive activity; second, reformed his character through analysis of sin, remorse, restitution, and confession; and third, actually asked for forgiveness several times. Only then, after ascertaining that he is sincere in his repentance, would a woman in such a situation be morally bound, though not legally obligated, to offer the offender *m'chilah*.

The principle that *m'chilah* ought to be granted only if deserved is the great Jewish "No" to easy forgiveness. It is core to the Jewish view of forgiveness, just as desisting from sin is core to the Jewish view of repentance. Without good grounds, the offended person should not forgo the indebtedness of the sinner; otherwise, the sinner may never truly repent and evil will be perpetuated. And, conversely, if there are good grounds to waive the debt or relinquish the claim, the offended person is morally bound to do so. This is the great Jewish "Yes" to the possibility of repentance for every sinner.

The second kind of forgiveness is "forgiveness" (*s'lichah*). It is an act of the heart. It is reaching a deeper understanding of the sinner. It is achieving an empathy for the troubledness of the other. *S'lichah*, too, is not a reconciliation or an embracing of the offender; it is simply reaching the conclusion that the offender, too, is human, frail, and deserving of sympathy. It is closer to an act of mercy than to an act of grace. A woman abused by a man may never reach this level of forgiveness; she is not obliged, nor is it morally necessary for her, to do so.

The third kind of forgiveness is "atonement" (*kapparah*) or "purification" (*tohorah*). This is a total wiping away of all sinfulness. It is an existential cleansing. *Kapparah* is the ultimate form of forgiveness, but it is only granted by God. No human can "atone" the sin of another; no human can "purify" the spiritual pollution of another.

—Rabbi David R. Blumenthal (b. 1938)

In the words of *The Fathers According to Rabbi Nathan*: "Who is a hero among heroes? One who turns an enemy into a friend" (chapter 23). A strong person is not one who takes pride in holding a grudge, but one who relinquishes it. A strong person fights the inclination toward vengefulness—trying instead to find a way to reconcile.

Go out of your way to offer those who have hurt you the opportunity to repent. For example, don't avoid the person by not returning phone calls (unless the wrong done to you was so extreme that you are not required to forgive it, and/or it would be emotionally unhealthy for you to be in contact).

Strive to let your forgiveness be wholehearted. One way to achieve this is to reflect on some unintended good that resulted from the wrong done to you. When others harm us, it frequently forces us to grow in ways we would otherwise not have done. Therefore, if you find it very hard to forgive someone—particularly somebody who has asked for forgiveness—see whether you can find any personal growth or other good that came about because of what happened. On the basis of that, find it in your heart to forgive the person who hurt you, or at least to stop bearing a grudge.

Take into account any psychological problems the ones who offended you might suffer from or any abuse they experienced, and ask yourself whether those factors might have made them more liable to do the evil they did to you. While those factors do not excuse their behavior, your thinking about them with some sympathy will probably make it easier for you to forgive them.

—Rabbi Joseph Telushkin (b. 1948), adapted

FOR REFLECTION

Have I forgiven someone who wronged me in a significant way? Did I achieve *m'chilah*, or *s'lichah*? How was I able to forgive?

Against whom am I harboring feelings of anger and resentment now?

What is holding me back from being a more forgiving person?

Atah v'chartanu mikol haamim;	אַתָּה בְחַרְתָּנוּ מִכָּל הָעַמִּים,
ahavta otanu, v'ratzita banu.	אָהַבְתָּ אוֹתָנוּ וְרָצִיתָ בָּנוּ.
V'romamtanu mikol hal'shonot,	וְרוֹמַמְתָּנוּ מִכָּל הַלְּשׁוֹנוֹת,
v'kidashtanu b'mitzvotecha.	וְקִדַּשְׁתָּנוּ בְּמִצְוֹתֶיךָ.
V'keiravtanu, Malkeinu, laavodatecha;	וְקֵרַבְתָּנוּ, מַלְכֵּנוּ, לַעֲבוֹדָתֶךָ,
v'shimcha hagadol v'hakadosh aleinu karata.	וְשִׁמְךָ הַגָּדוֹל וְהַקָּדוֹשׁ עָלֵינוּ קָרָאתָ.

You chose us, with love, to be messengers of mitzvot;
and through us You made known Your aspirations.

Among all the many peoples,
You gave us a pathway to holiness.
Among all the great nations,
You uplifted us and made Yourself our Sovereign —
and so we seek You and serve You
and celebrate our nearness to Your presence.

Your great and sacred name has become our calling.

Vatiten-lanu, Adonai Eloheinu, b'ahavah et	וַתִּתֶּן־לָנוּ, יְיָ אֱלֹהֵינוּ, בְּאַהֲבָה אֶת
[Yom haShabbat hazeh	[יוֹם הַשַּׁבָּת הַזֶּה
likdushah v'limnuchah, v'et]	לִקְדֻשָּׁה וְלִמְנוּחָה, וְאֶת]
Yom HaKippurim hazeh —	יוֹם הַכִּפּוּרִים הַזֶּה,
limchilah v'lislichah ulchaparah —	לִמְחִילָה וְלִסְלִיחָה וּלְכַפָּרָה,
v'limchol-bo et kol avonoteinu [b'ahavah],	וְלִמְחָל־בּוֹ אֶת כָּל עֲוֹנוֹתֵינוּ [בְּאַהֲבָה],
mikra-kodesh,	מִקְרָא קֹדֶשׁ,
zeicher litziat Mitzrayim.	זֵכֶר לִיצִיאַת מִצְרָיִם.

In Your love, Eternal our God,
You have given us this [Shabbat — for holiness and rest —
and this] Yom Kippur:
a day on which our wrongs are forgiven [with love];
a day of sacred assembly;
a day to be mindful of our people's going-out from Egypt.

HAS BECOME OUR CALLING עָלֵינוּ קָרָאתָ. Rabbi Mordecai Kaplan (1881–1983), founder of Reconstructionist Judaism, proposed, as an alternative to the concept of "the Chosen People," that Jews "live with a sense of vocation or calling" — a notion that he believed implied neither exclusivity nor Jewish superiority. The vocation of the Jewish people is that work to which we have felt summoned by a Power beyond ourselves, and for which we have both passion and aptitude.

"A DAY ON WHICH OUR WRONGS ARE FORGIVEN . . ."

ADONAI, ADONAI – God, compassionate, gracious, endlessly patient, loving, and true; showing mercy to the thousandth generation; forgiving evil, defiance, and wrongdoing; granting pardon.

RAVA SAID: Those who forego their right to demand punishment are forgiven all their sins.

AS I WISH to be forgiven for what I've done wrong,
viewed with leniency and understanding,
my good intentions acknowledged,
even when I fall short—
so I commit myself to follow the model of the Holy One:
giving others the benefit of the doubt,
perceiving their virtues as keenly as I see their flaws,
offering them the chance to begin anew,
relinquishing the need to punish.

DO NOT SEEK VENGEANCE or bear a grudge against your people.
Love your neighbor as yourself; I am Adonai.

EVEN IF one has a genuine grievance toward a neighbor, one ought not to respond with hatred. The Talmud cited the case of a man cutting with one hand and inadvertently hurting the other hand. "Shall he in retaliation cut the hand that wielded the knife?" We are all part of one another and the hurts we inflict on others really strike at ourselves, since our lives are interdependent.

ADONAI, ADONAI, Exodus 34:6–7.
RAVA SAID, Talmud *Rosh HaShanah* 17a.
DO NOT SEEK VENGEANCE, Leviticus 19:18.
EVEN IF ONE HAS. By Rabbi Ben Zion Bokser (1907–1984).
THE TALMUD CITED, Jerusalem Talmud *N'darim* 9:4.

אֱלֹהֵינוּ וֵאלֹהֵי אֲבוֹתֵינוּ וְאִמּוֹתֵינוּ,
יַעֲלֶה וְיָבֹא וְיַגִּיעַ, וְיֵרָאֶה וְיֵרָצֶה
וְיִשָּׁמַע וְיִפָּקֵד וְיִזָּכֵר
זִכְרוֹנֵנוּ וּפִקְדוֹנֵנוּ,
וְזִכְרוֹן אֲבוֹתֵינוּ וְאִמּוֹתֵינוּ,
וְזִכְרוֹן יְרוּשָׁלַיִם עִיר קָדְשֶׁךָ,
וְזִכְרוֹן כָּל עַמְּךָ בֵּית יִשְׂרָאֵל,
לְפָנֶיךָ לִפְלֵיטָה לְטוֹבָה,
לְחֵן וּלְחֶסֶד וּלְרַחֲמִים,
לְחַיִּים וּלְשָׁלוֹם,
בְּיוֹם הַכִּפּוּרִים הַזֶּה.

Eloheinu v'Elohei avoteinu v'imoteinu,
yaaleh v'yavo v'yagia, v'yeira·eh v'yeiratzeh
v'yishama, v'yipakeid, v'yizacheir
zichroneinu ufikdoneinu —
v'zichron avoteinu v'imoteinu,
v'zichron Y'rushalayim ir kodshecha,
v'zichron kol am'cha beit Yisrael
l'fanecha — lifleitah l'tovah,
l'chein ulchesed ulrachamim,
l'chayim ulshalom,
b'Yom HaKippurim hazeh.

Our God, and God of the generations before us,
may a memory of us ascend and come before You.
May it be heard and seen by You,
winning Your favor and reaching Your awareness —
together with the memory of our ancestors,
the memory of Your sacred city, Jerusalem,
and the memory of Your people, the family of Israel.
May we be remembered —
for safety, well-being, and favor,
for love and compassion,
for life,
and for peace —
on this Day of Atonement.

MAY A MEMORY OF US ASCEND יַעֲלֶה וְיָבֹא. In the days of the Temple, the sound of trumpets (*chatzotz'rot*) accompanied communal offerings, dramatically symbolizing the people's cry for God's intervention. This prayer's poetry takes the place of our ancestors' instruments. Opening with a series of eight strong Hebrew verbs, the prayer, like the ancient trumpet itself, communicates immediacy and urgency: ascend, come, reach, appear; be favored, heard, regarded, and remembered (*yaaleh v'yavo v'yagia v'yeiraeh v'yeiratzeh v'yishama v'yipakeid v'yizacheir*). The language transports us to the ancient rite.

"May we be remembered . . . for love and compassion . . ."

Rabbi Shimon taught: Do not regard yourself as worthless.

HaRachaman, Source of mercy,
teach me the art of a compassionate gaze.
Show me how to be patient and forgiving,
kind and encouraging, loving and understanding,
generous in spirit when faced with imperfection.
Help me to extend love and compassion
to my own imperfect soul.
Help me to embrace these truths:
I share the lot of all human beings;
I am not alone in my failings.
Whatever I have done,
I am loved and valued by You,
worthy of love, capable of goodness.
Do not let me slip into self-loathing or despair.
As I ask for Your remembrance, I commit myself to remember:
Self-compassion is not self-indulgence.
It is not an excuse for bad behavior or an impediment to my growth.
Harsh self-rebuke will not make me more gentle with others.
On this holy day I hold fast to these words of Torah:
"Be loving to your neighbor, as you are to yourself."

Forgiving Yourself

Feel bad. It won't kill you. Use these feelings as a catalyst to make amends, so long as doing so doesn't inflict more pain. Do something positive that will help offset the damage you have caused. After you have done all you can by way of making amends, and have learned all you can from what you did, make a solemn vow not to repeat the act.

Assuming you have done all this, let it go. How? The next time the memory arises, don't give yourself over to the drama. "Yes, I did that. I won't do that again. There is no point in dwelling on it, and doing so simply feeds my narcissism. Better to do something constructive with my time and energy."

RABBI SHIMON TAUGHT, Mishnah *Avot* 2:18.
BE LOVING, Leviticus 19:18.
FEEL BAD. By Rabbi Rami Shapiro (b. 1951).

זָכְרֵנוּ, יְיָ אֱלֹהֵינוּ, בּוֹ לְטוֹבָה. אָמֵן.
וּפָקְדֵנוּ בוֹ לִבְרָכָה. אָמֵן.
וְהוֹשִׁיעֵנוּ בוֹ לְחַיִּים. אָמֵן.

Zochreinu, Adonai Eloheinu, bo l'tovah. Amen.
Ufokdeinu vo livrachah. Amen.
V'hoshi·einu vo l'chayim. Amen.

Eternal our God,
remember us, *Amen*
be mindful of us, *Amen*
and redeem us
for a life of goodness and blessing. *Amen*

וּבִדְבַר יְשׁוּעָה וְרַחֲמִים חוּס וְחָנֵּנוּ,
וְרַחֵם עָלֵינוּ וְהוֹשִׁיעֵנוּ,
כִּי אֵלֶיךָ עֵינֵינוּ,
כִּי אֵל מֶלֶךְ חַנּוּן וְרַחוּם אָתָּה.

Uvidvar y'shuah v'rachamim chus v'choneinu;
v'racheim aleinu v'hoshi·einu —
ki elecha eineinu;
ki El melech chanun v'rachum atah.

Favor us with words of deliverance and mercy.
Show us the depth of Your care.
God, we await Your redemption,
for You reign with grace and compassion.

GRACE AND COMPASSION חַנּוּן וְרַחוּם. Many people think of "grace" as a Christian idea, not a Jewish one. But *chanun* (gracious) is paired with *rachum* (compassionate) in the Torah's presentation of God's qualities (the Thirteen Attributes, Exodus 34:6–7, which are prominent in the Yom Kippur "Songs of Forgiveness"). A verse in the Book of Isaiah points toward the traditional Jewish understanding of grace: "Surely God will show you grace, in response to the sound of your cry" (30:19).

The Talmud (*B'rachot* 7a) associates the word *chanun* with the root *chinam* ("free" or "undeserved"). Thus the Sages understood grace as an "undeserved gift" — unpredictable and surprising, bestowed even on those who are unworthy of compassion. Why would the Sages believe that God acts with grace toward those who do not deserve it? The Jewish answer — an answer that is especially meaningful during the ten days of confession, forgiveness, and repentance — says more about us than it says about God: we hope for a God who cannot ignore the sound of our cry, the voice of human suffering.

A Prayer for Goodness and Blessing

Oneness at the heart of all life,
may I let go of the pettiness within myself,
and transform myself into a conduit of love.
Let me be healing and comfort
for those who are tired and ill.
Let me be nourishment for the hungry.
Let me be a shield for those who are helpless and afraid.
Let me be a lamp to those who dwell in the dark.
May I be a haven for the troubled,
a guide for the lost,
a voice for those who cannot speak.
Let all those I meet
come away feeling better for having encountered me.

The Depth of Your Care

God called to Israel in a vision by night: "Jacob! Jacob!"
And Jacob answered: "*Hineini*—I am here."
Said the Holy One: "I am Adonai, the God of your ancestors.
Do not be afraid to descend into Egypt,
for there I will make you into a great nation.
I myself will go down with you to Egypt,
and I myself will bring you up again."

Jacob our father, weary and frightened,
in the last years of his life came to see:
God's love and care had been with him all his days—
even when he did not know.
Said the Holy One:
"Fear not—
for even in the darkness of your struggle I am with you.
I descend with you, and I will help you to rise again."

GOD CALLED TO ISRAEL, Genesis 46:2–4.

I MYSELF WILL BRING YOU UP AGAIN. Taught Rabbi Levi Yitzchak of Berditchev (1740–1809): This also may be understood as "I will make you ascend and ascend" (*anochi aalcha gam aloh*). And so we learn that all our life we must strive to ascend. Our primary purpose is not to attain a high spiritual level, but to keep climbing from wherever we are.

EVEN WHEN HE DID NOT KNOW. As when Jacob said, "Surely God is in this place, and I did not know" (Genesis 28:16).

כַּוָּנָה
Kavanah
אָבוֹת וְאִמָּהוֹת
Avot v'Imahot
גְּבוּרוֹת
G'vurot
קְדֻשַּׁת הַשֵּׁם
K'dushat HaShem
קְדֻשַּׁת הַיּוֹם
K'dushat HaYom
עֲבוֹדָה
Avodah
הוֹדָאָה
Hodaah
שָׁלוֹם
Shalom
תְּפִלַּת הַלֵּב
T'filat HaLev

אֱלֹהֵינוּ וֵאלֹהֵי אֲבוֹתֵינוּ וְאִמּוֹתֵינוּ,
מְחַל
לַעֲוֹנוֹתֵינוּ בְּיוֹם
[הַשַּׁבָּת הַזֶּה וּבְיוֹם]
הַכִּפּוּרִים הַזֶּה.
מְחֵה וְהַעֲבֵר פְּשָׁעֵינוּ וְחַטֹּאתֵינוּ
מִנֶּגֶד עֵינֶיךָ, כָּאָמוּר:
אָנֹכִי אָנֹכִי הוּא מֹחֶה פְשָׁעֶיךָ
לְמַעֲנִי,
וְחַטֹּאתֶיךָ לֹא אֶזְכֹּר.
וְנֶאֱמַר: מָחִיתִי כָעָב פְּשָׁעֶיךָ,
וְכֶעָנָן חַטֹּאתֶיךָ,
שׁוּבָה אֵלַי כִּי גְאַלְתִּיךָ.
וְנֶאֱמַר: כִּי־בַיּוֹם הַזֶּה יְכַפֵּר
עֲלֵיכֶם לְטַהֵר אֶתְכֶם,
מִכֹּל חַטֹּאתֵיכֶם לִפְנֵי יְיָ תִּטְהָרוּ.

Eloheinu v'Elohei avoteinu v'imoteinu,
m'chal
laavonoteinu b'Yom
[haShabbat hazeh uvYom]
HaKippurim hazeh.
M'cheih v'haaveir p'sha·einu v'chatoteinu
mineged einecha, kaamur:
"Anochi, anochi hu mocheh f'sha·echa
l'maani;
v'chatotecha lo ezkor."
V'ne·emar: "Machiti kaav p'sha·echa,
v'che·anan chatotecha —
shuvah eilai, ki g'alticha."
V'ne·emar: "Ki-vayom hazeh y'chapeir
aleichem l'taheir et·chem;
mikol chatoteichem lifnei Adonai tit·haru."

Our God and God of our forebears,
pardon
our failings on [this day of Shabbat, and] this Day of Atonement;
erase our misdeeds; see beyond our defiance.

For Isaiah said in Your name: "It is I, I alone
who wipe away your defiant acts — this is My essence.
I shall pay no heed to your errors."

And the prophet said: "As a cloud fades away, as mist dissolves into air,
so your wrongs and mistakes shall be gone; I will wipe them away —
come back to Me, that I may redeem you."

As You said to Moses: "For on this day atonement shall be made for you
to purify you from all your wrongs.
And pure you shall be in the presence of Adonai."

IT IS I אָנֹכִי אָנֹכִי, Isaiah 43:25.
AS A CLOUD FADES AWAY מָחִיתִי כָעָב, Isaiah 44:22.
FOR ON THIS DAY כִּי־בַיּוֹם הַזֶּה, Leviticus 16:30.

My God

אֶת אֱלֹהַי רָאִיתִי בַּקָּפֶה.
הוּא נִתְגַּלָּה לִי בַּעֲשַׁן סִיגָרִיּוֹת.
נְכֵה־רוּחַ, מִסְתַּלֵּחַ וְרָפֶה
רָמַז לִי: "עוֹד אֶפְשָׁר לִחְיוֹת!"

הוּא לֹא הָיָה דוֹמֶה לַאֲהוּבִי:
קָרוֹב מִמֶּנּוּ – וְאֻמְלָל,
כְּצֵל שָׁקוּף שֶׁל אוֹר הַכּוֹכָבִים
הוּא לֹא מִלֵּא אֶת הֶחָלָל.

לְאוֹר שְׁקִיעָה חִוֵּר וַאֲדַמְדַּם,
כְּמִתְוַדֶּה עַל חֵטְא לִפְנֵי מוֹתוֹ,
יָרַד לְמַטָּה לְנַשֵּׁק רַגְלֵי אָדָם
וּלְבַקֵּשׁ אֶת סְלִיחָתוֹ.

In the café I saw my God
revealed to me in the smoke of cigarettes.
Disheartened, sheepish, and weak
he hinted to me: "Living is yet possible!"

He was nothing like my beloved:
nearer than he—and far from happy.
Like starlight's transparent shadow
he did not fill the space.

By the fading light of a pale red sunset,
as if to confess a sin before death,
he fell down to kiss our human feet
and to ask of us forgiveness.

MY GOD. By Lea Goldberg (1911–1970). The poet, who made *aliyah* from Germany to Tel Aviv in 1935, evokes a disturbing image: God as feeble, weary, and barely present—perhaps reflecting her generation's loss of faith. The "revelation" takes place in a café, emblematic of sophisticated western culture; the cigarette smoke plays on the biblical imagery of incense clouds in the Sanctuary. Rather than the All-powerful to whom we confess sins, this God begs our forgiveness—a God who admits to failure in the face of modernity.

כַּוָּנָה
Kavanah

אָבוֹת וְאִמָּהוֹת
Avot v'Imahot

גְּבוּרוֹת
G'vurot

קְדֻשַּׁת הַשֵּׁם
K'dushat HaShem

קְדֻשַּׁת הַיּוֹם
K'dushat HaYom

עֲבוֹדָה
Avodah

הוֹדָאָה
Hodaah

שָׁלוֹם
Shalom

תְּפִלַּת הַלֵּב
T'filat HaLev

אֱלֹהֵינוּ וֵאלֹהֵי אֲבוֹתֵינוּ וְאִמּוֹתֵינוּ,
[רְצֵה בִמְנוּחָתֵנוּ,]
קַדְּשֵׁנוּ בְּמִצְוֹתֶיךָ,
וְתֵן חֶלְקֵנוּ בְּתוֹרָתֶךָ.
שַׂבְּעֵנוּ מִטּוּבֶךָ,
וְשַׂמְּחֵנוּ בִּישׁוּעָתֶךָ.
[וְהַנְחִילֵנוּ, יְיָ אֱלֹהֵינוּ,
בְּאַהֲבָה וּבְרָצוֹן שַׁבַּת קָדְשֶׁךָ,
וְיָנוּחוּ בָהּ יִשְׂרָאֵל,
מְקַדְּשֵׁי שְׁמֶךָ.]

Eloheinu v'Elohei avoteinu v'imoteinu,
[r'tzeih vimnuchateinu,]
kad'sheinu b'mitzvotecha;
v'tein chelkeinu b'Toratecha.
Sab'einu mituvecha;
v'sam'cheinu bishuatecha.
[V'hanchileinu, Adonai Eloheinu,
b'ahavah uvratzon Shabbat kodshecha;
v'yanuchu vah Yisrael,
m'kad'shei sh'mecha.]

God who is ours
and God of our fathers and mothers:
[may our rest on this Shabbat bring You pleasure;]
lead us to holiness through Your mitzvot;
and may each of us find a portion of Torah that is ours.
You bestow such goodness — teach us to be satisfied,
and to know the joy of Your salvation.
[Let Your holy Shabbat be our heritage,
embraced freely and with love;
and may all our people bring holiness to Your name
by resting on this day.]

MAY EACH OF US FIND A PORTION OF TORAH THAT IS OURS וְתֵן חֶלְקֵנוּ בְּתוֹרָתֶךָ. Literally, "Give us our portion in Your Torah." Rabbi Lawrence Kushner (b. 1943) writes: "Each person has a Torah, unique to that person, his or her innermost teaching. Some seem to know their Torahs very early in life and speak and sing them in a myriad of ways. Others spend their whole lives stammering, shaping, and rehearsing them. Some are long, some short. Some are intricate and poetic, others are only a few words, and still others can only be spoken through gesture and example. But every soul has a Torah. . . . For each soul, by the time of his or her final hour, the Torah is complete, the teaching done."

THE JOY OF YOUR SALVATION וְשַׂמְּחֵנוּ בִּישׁוּעָתֶךָ. The English word "salvation" is used by many Christians to reference a personal relationship with God, deliverance from sin, and the afterlife implications of both. But in Hebrew, salvation (*y'shuah*) means peace among nations, and an end to tyranny and oppression. In Jewish tradition, salvation is experienced communally — as in the Exodus from Egypt, or the airlift of Ethiopian Jews to Israel in the 1980s. And when Jews pray for salvation, it is a prayer for the perfection of this world. In the words of the *Kaddish*: "May God's majestic reign prevail soon in your lives, in your days, and in the life of the whole House of Israel."

V'taheir libeinu l'ovd'cha be·emet —	וְטַהֵר לִבֵּנוּ לְעָבְדְּךָ בֶּאֱמֶת,
ki atah solchan l'Yisrael,	כִּי אַתָּה סָלְחָן לְיִשְׂרָאֵל,
umocholan l'shivtei Y'shurun	וּמָחֳלָן לְשִׁבְטֵי יְשֻׁרוּן
b'chol dor vador;	בְּכָל דּוֹר וָדוֹר,
umibaladecha ein lanu melech mocheil	וּמִבַּלְעָדֶיךָ אֵין לָנוּ מֶלֶךְ מוֹחֵל
v'solei·ach ela atah.	וְסוֹלֵחַ אֶלָּא אָתָּה.

Make our hearts pure, so that we may be of true service to You —
for You are the Forgiver of Israel,
in every generation granting pardon to the tribes of Yeshurun.
We have no God of forgiveness and pardon but You, You alone.

Baruch atah, Adonai —	בָּרוּךְ אַתָּה, יְיָ,
melech mocheil v'solei·ach laavonoteinu	מֶלֶךְ מוֹחֵל וְסוֹלֵחַ לַעֲוֹנוֹתֵינוּ
v'laavonot amo beit Yisrael,	וְלַעֲוֹנוֹת עַמּוֹ בֵּית יִשְׂרָאֵל,
umaavir ashmoteinu b'chol shanah	וּמַעֲבִיר אַשְׁמוֹתֵינוּ בְּכָל שָׁנָה
v'shanah —	וְשָׁנָה,
melech al kol haaretz,	מֶלֶךְ עַל כָּל הָאָרֶץ,
m'kadeish [haShabbat v'] Yisrael	מְקַדֵּשׁ [הַשַּׁבָּת וְ] יִשְׂרָאֵל
v'Yom HaKippurim.	וְיוֹם הַכִּפּוּרִים.

You are blessed, Adonai, Sovereign who forgives our failings
and pardons the failings of Your people, the House of Israel.
You banish our guilt, from year to year,
You reign in majesty over all the earth;
You sanctify [Shabbat,] the people Israel and the Day of Atonement.

MAKE OUR HEARTS PURE וְטַהֵר לִבֵּנוּ. A prayer for personal integrity, so that we may align our thoughts, words, and deeds in pursuing good purposes. The Talmud cautions us against hypocrisy and duplicity in our personal interactions. "Abbaye said: One must never speak one thing with the mouth and intend another thing in the heart" (*Bava M'tzia* 49a).

YOU REIGN מֶלֶךְ. This blessing began on page 382 by recounting the Jewish people's redemptive role: "You chose us . . . to be messengers of mitzvot." It now ends by proclaiming God's rule over the entire world. The Sages quote the prophet Zechariah but alter his meaning; he had said that God would be the universal Sovereign only in a messianic future: "Adonai shall reign over all the earth; on that day Adonai shall be one. . . ." (14:9). Rabbi Reuven Kimelman (b. 1944) notes that the Sages do not hope for a time when all people will embrace Judaism. Rather, they envision "the universal acceptance of God's authority. The goal is not the incorporating of humanity into Israel, but the extending of divine sovereignty to all humanity."

Love of Zion: The Virtue of Ahavat Tziyon

When I go to Israel every stone and every tree is a reminder of hard labor and glory, of prophets and psalmists, of loyalty and holiness. The Jews go to Israel not only for physical security for themselves and their children; they go to Israel for renewal, for the experience of resurrection. . . . Israel enables us to bear the agony of Auschwitz without a radical despair, to sense a ray of God's radiance in the jungles of history.

—Rabbi Abraham Joshua Heschel (1907–1972)

My heart, homeland, is with your dews,
at night on fields of bramble,
and to the cypress's scent, and moist thistle,
I will extend a hidden wing.
Your paths are soft cradles of sand
stretching between acacia hedges,
as though on a surface of pure silk
I'll move forever upon them
held by some unfathomable charm,
and transparent skies whisper over
the dark—a frozen sea of trees.

—Esther Raab (1894–1981)

A great adventure. I wouldn't have missed it for the world.

There's been nothing like it in human history. A small and ancient people loses its land and forgets how to speak its language; wanders defenselessly for hundreds, thousands, of years throughout the world with its God and its sacred books; meets with contumely, persecution, violence, dispossession, banishment, mass murder; refuses to give up; refuses to surrender its faith; continues to believe that it will one day be restored to the land it lost; manages in the end, by dint of its own efforts, against all odds, to gather itself from the four corners of the earth and return to that land; learns again to speak the language of its old books; learns again to bear arms and defend itself; wrests its new-old home from the people who had replaced it; entrenches itself; builds; fructifies; fortifies; repulses the enemies surrounding it; grows and prospers in the face of all threats.

Had it not happened, could it have been imagined? Would anyone have believed it possible?

—Hillel Halkin (b. 1939)

כַּוָּנָה
Kavanah
אָבוֹת וְאִמָּהוֹת
Avot v'Imahot
גְּבוּרוֹת
G'vurot
קְדֻשַּׁת הַשֵּׁם
K'dushat HaShem
קְדֻשַּׁת הַיּוֹם
K'dushat HaYom
עֲבוֹדָה
Avodah
הוֹדָאָה
Hodaah
שָׁלוֹם
Shalom
תְּפִלַּת הַלֵּב
T'filat HaLev

THUS SAYS the Eternal God: This is Jerusalem! I have set her in the midst of the nations, and countries are round about her. (Ezekiel 5:5)

As the navel is in the center of the human body,
so is the Land of Israel the navel of the world,
as Scripture says: "that dwell in the navel of the earth" (Ezekiel 38:12).
The Land of Israel is located in the center of the world,
Jerusalem in the center of the Land of Israel,
the Temple in the center of Jerusalem,
the Holy of Holies in the center of the Temple,
the Ark in the center of the Holy of Holies,
and in front of the Holy of Holies is the Foundation Stone,
from which the world was founded.

—Midrash *Tanchuma, K'doshim*, adapted

COMMENTARY

The concept of Israel as "the navel of the world" is less geographic than religious; it conveys the spiritual and cultural centrality of *Eretz Yisrael*. By reminding us of the umbilical cord, the metaphor also suggests the primacy of the land: it is, as James Michener called it, "the source"—the place where the Jewish people began. The metaphor of "navel" expresses motherly love and intimacy, as well: *Eretz Yisrael* "birthed" and nurtured the Jews, sustained their physical and spiritual life, rejoiced and suffered with them over the millennia. For the Sages who created this midrash, the Land of Israel, and Jerusalem in particular, are not only precious to the Jews; they also possess cosmic significance. For they believed that from this sacred place, the universe expanded. For billions of people around the world, Zion remains the place where heaven and earth touch.

AS A RESULT of the historic catastrophe in which Titus of Rome destroyed Jerusalem and Israel was exiled from its land, I was born in one of the cities of the Exile. But always I regarded myself as one who was born in Jerusalem.

—S. Y. Agnon (1888–1970)

HOLY OF HOLIES. Inner sanctuary of the Temple, entered only by the High Priest on Yom Kippur.

FOUNDATION STONE. Hebrew: *even sh'tiyah*. According to Talmud *Yoma* 54b, it was from this rock that the world was created. The *Zohar* (*Vay'chi* 1:231a) calls the Foundation Stone "the center of the world."

רְצֵה, יְיָ אֱלֹהֵינוּ, בְּעַמְּךָ יִשְׂרָאֵל.
וּתְפִלָּתָם בְּאַהֲבָה תְקַבֵּל בְּרָצוֹן,
וּתְהִי לְרָצוֹן תָּמִיד עֲבוֹדַת
יִשְׂרָאֵל עַמֶּךָ.
אֵל קָרוֹב לְכָל קֹרְאָיו,
פְּנֵה אֶל עֲבָדֶיךָ וְחָנֵּנוּ.
שְׁפֹךְ רוּחֲךָ עָלֵינוּ,
וְתֶחֱזֶינָה עֵינֵינוּ בְּשׁוּבְךָ לְצִיּוֹן
בְּרַחֲמִים.

R'tzeih, Adonai Eloheinu, b'am'cha Yisrael.
Utfilatam b'ahavah t'kabeil b'ratzon,
ut·hi l'ratzon tamid avodat
Yisrael amecha.
El karov l'chol korav,
p'neih el avadecha v'choneinu.
Sh'foch ruchacha aleinu,
v'techezenah eineinu b'shuvcha l'Tziyon
b'rachamim.

Eternal, our God, Your people Israel yearns for Your favor.
Receive their prayer with loving acceptance,
and may You always desire Your people's worship.
Divine One, close to all who call upon You,
bring Your grace and presence near to those who serve You.
Pour forth Your spirit on us,
and may our eyes see Your merciful return to Zion.

בָּרוּךְ אַתָּה, יְיָ, הַמַּחֲזִיר שְׁכִינָתוֹ לְצִיּוֹן.
Baruch atah, Adonai, hamachazir Sh'chinato l'Tziyon.
Blessed are You whose Divine Presence is felt again in Zion.

כַּוָּנָה *Kavanah*
אָבוֹת וְאִמָּהוֹת *Avot v'Imahot*
גְּבוּרוֹת *G'vurot*
קְדֻשַּׁת הַשֵּׁם *K'dushat HaShem*
קְדֻשַּׁת הַיּוֹם *K'dushat HaYom*
עֲבוֹדָה *Avodah*
הוֹדָאָה *Hodaah*
שָׁלוֹם *Shalom*
תְּפִלַּת הַלֵּב *T'filat HaLev*

MAY OUR EYES SEE YOUR MERCIFUL RETURN TO ZION וְתֶחֱזֶינָה עֵינֵינוּ בְּשׁוּבְךָ לְצִיּוֹן בְּרַחֲמִים. The word *shuvcha* (Your return) reminds us that the days from Rosh HaShanah to Yom Kippur are called *Aseret Y'mei T'shuvah* (the Ten Days of Return or Repentance). Our personal *t'shuvah* may take the form of return to healthy relationships with people in our lives; return to faith, to our people, or to our better selves. But what does it mean for us to see God's "return to Zion"? The Talmud (*M'gillah* 29a) says: "We find that wherever Israel went into exile the *Shechinah* (Divine Presence) went with them . . . and when they return, the *Shechinah* will return with them." In the Jewish imagination, God experiences our comings and goings, our wanderings and misfortunes. When we suffer, God suffers; when we lose our place in the world, God is *with* us, wherever we happen to be. It is a theology of purest empathy. To see God's return to Zion is to see *our* return to Zion — the Jewish people's place in the world.

To the Father
Fifty years on the land of Petach Tikvah

Blessed are the hands
that sowed
red-soil fields
on winter mornings,
amid the swoop and swirl of starlings.
They made the vine kneel with humility,
and, by the waters of Yarkon,
they planted eucalyptus like perfumed pennants.
They bridled the horse
and nuzzled rifle to cheek
to fend off an enemy from a ramshackle hut—
a shelter of peace ruling
over sand dune and sweet bean.
And with a fierce green eye
he would keep watch over the young birds:
soft acreage seeded with grass for grazing,
as a few oxen lower themselves into the marsh. . . .
He plows the furrow in spite of the rough earth,
makes a first parting in virgin soil.
Blessed are the hands!

א
The Hebrew of your poets, Zion,
is like oil upon a burn,
cool as oil;
after work,
the smell in the street at night
of the hedge in flower.
Like Solomon,
I have married and married the speech of strangers;
none are like you, Shulamite.

ב
How difficult for me is Hebrew:
even the Hebrew for *mother*, for *bread*, for *sun*
is foreign. How far I have been exiled, Zion.

TO THE FATHER. By Esther Raab (1894–1981).
THE HEBREW . . . EXILED, ZION. By Charles Reznikoff (1894–1976).

Gratitude: The Virtue of Hodaah

Though all sacrifices may be discontinued in the future—
for, in the messianic age, there will be no sin—
the offering of thanksgiving will never cease.
Though all prayers may be discontinued,
the prayer of thanksgiving will never cease.

—Midrash *Leviticus Rabbah* 9.7

"It Is Good to Give Thanks"

The Psalmist exclaims, *It is good to give thanks to God* (92:2)—good for whom? Do we know what God gains from our thanksgiving? We can only guess that God is pleased to have our thanksgiving, as we are pleased to receive thanks from anyone to whom we showed favor. But this is projecting our mentality upon God. Considering that each of us is less than a speck of dust in the universe, it is difficult to imagine that God gains anything from our words of thanksgiving. What good there is in thanksgiving to God goes entirely to the person who gives thanks.

Gratitude opens the door to contentment, and contentment induces happiness. The American poet John Greenleaf Whittier made the keen observation that gratitude focuses on the good we enjoy in the present:

> No longer forward nor behind
> I look in hope or fear,
> But grateful, take the good I find,
> The best of now and here.

To put yourself in a better mood, all you need to do is to count the things you appreciate. Gratitude is the twin of appreciation. Whether you give thanks to God or to human beings, you will be the first to benefit from thanksgiving.

—Rabbi Joshua Haberman (b. 1919)

Insights from the 23rd Psalm

My version of the psalm's second line would read, *The Lord is my shepherd; I shall often want.* I shall yearn, I shall long, I shall aspire. I shall continue to miss the people and the abilities that are taken from my life as loved ones die and skills diminish. I shall probe the empty spaces in my life like a tongue probing a missing tooth. But I will never feel deprived or diminished if I don't get what I yearn for, because I know how blessed I am by what I have.

My cup runneth over.... Our ability to receive God's blessings with thanksgiving will never outstrip God's ability to bless us. For those who have cultivated the habit of gratitude, no matter how large a bowl we set out to receive God's blessings, it will always overflow.

—Rabbi Harold Kushner (b. 1935)

The Urge to Give Thanks

The older we get, the greater becomes our inclination to give thanks, especially heavenward. We feel more strongly than we could have ever felt before that life is a free gift. Our hands reach out gratefully to receive the unexpected gift of each good hour.

But we also feel, again and again, an urge to thank a friend, even if he or she has not done anything special for us. For what, then? For really meeting me when we meet; for opening her eyes, and not mistaking me for someone else; for opening her ears, and listening carefully to what I had to say; indeed, for opening up to me what I really wanted to address—her securely locked heart.

—Martin Buber (1878–1965), adapted

FOR REFLECTION

What has happened in my life, since last Yom Kippur, that makes me thankful?

Have I grown during the past year in my ability to experience and express gratitude?

Am I consistent in expressing gratitude to loved ones and friends? Do I look for things to feel grateful for, or things to complain about?

Do I feel appreciated by others? What have I done during the past year that has earned someone else's gratitude?

What blessings have nourished me in recent years? What are some miracles that greet me every day?

Modim anachnu lach,	מוֹדִים אֲנַחְנוּ לָךְ,	כַּוָּנָה *Kavanah*
shaatah hu Adonai Eloheinu v'Elohei	שָׁאַתָּה הוּא יְיָ אֱלֹהֵינוּ וֵאלֹהֵי	אָבוֹת וְאִמָּהוֹת *Avot v'Imahot*
avoteinu v'imoteinu l'olam va·ed.	אֲבוֹתֵינוּ וְאִמּוֹתֵינוּ לְעוֹלָם וָעֶד.	
Tzur chayeinu, magein yisheinu,	צוּר חַיֵּינוּ, מָגֵן יִשְׁעֵנוּ,	גְּבוּרוֹת *G'vurot*
atah hu l'dor vador.	אַתָּה הוּא לְדוֹר וָדוֹר.	
Nodeh l'cha unsapeir t'hilatecha:	נוֹדֶה לְּךָ וּנְסַפֵּר תְּהִלָּתֶךָ:	קְדֻשַּׁת הַשֵּׁם *K'dushat HaShem*
al chayeinu ham'surim b'yadecha,	עַל חַיֵּינוּ הַמְּסוּרִים בְּיָדֶךָ,	קְדֻשַּׁת הַיּוֹם *K'dushat HaYom*
v'al nishmoteinu hap'kudot lach,	וְעַל נִשְׁמוֹתֵינוּ הַפְּקוּדוֹת לָךְ,	
v'al nisecha sheb'chol yom imanu,	וְעַל נִסֶּיךָ שֶׁבְּכָל יוֹם עִמָּנוּ,	עֲבוֹדָה *Avodah*
v'al nifl'otecha v'tovotecha sheb'chol eit,	וְעַל נִפְלְאוֹתֶיךָ וְטוֹבוֹתֶיךָ שֶׁבְּכָל עֵת,	**הוֹדָאָה** ***Hodaah***
erev vavoker v'tzohorayim.	עֶרֶב וָבֹקֶר וְצָהֳרָיִם.	
Hatov — ki lo chalu rachamecha;	הַטּוֹב, כִּי לֹא כָלוּ רַחֲמֶיךָ,	שָׁלוֹם *Shalom*
v'hamracheim — ki lo tamu chasadecha:	וְהַמְרַחֵם, כִּי לֹא תַמּוּ חֲסָדֶיךָ,	תְּפִלַּת הַלֵּב *T'filat HaLev*
mei·olam kivinu lach.	מֵעוֹלָם קִוִּינוּ לָךְ.	

God who is ours,
God of all generations,
to You we are grateful forever.

Rock and Protector of our lives,
Your saving power endures from age to age.

We thank You and tell the tale of Your praise:
Your power in our lives,
Your caring for our souls,
the constant miracle of Your kindness.

Morning, noon, and night
we call You Goodness — for Your compassion never ends;
we call You Mercy — for Your love has no limit;
we call You Hope, now and for all time.

WE ARE GRATEFUL מוֹדִים. The Hebrew verb *modim* conveys both gratitude and acknowledgment. Hence this prayer seeks to awaken an intense awareness of the wonder of existence itself, so that we might experience life as "a constant miracle" bestowed on us by the One whose essence is kindness and goodness.

Hodaah: The Blessing of Gratitude

מוֹדִים אֲנַחְנוּ לָךְ

Modim anachnu lach . . .
For miracles and wonders are with us always;
And goodness is woven through our lives.

Our Sages teach that miracles are astounding acts—they shake us to the core.
And wonders? These, they say, are the miracles of which we are unaware.
Well-hidden in the laws of nature, great wonders reside:
the rhythm of our breathing, the rise and fall of tides,
the wing-beats of a hummingbird, the choreography of bees,
the cycles of the heavens, the seasons of the sky,
and sunlight on leaves transmuted into energy.
How wondrously fixed and predictable—
migration of birds, circulation of blood.
How utterly extraordinary is the ordinary.

But goodness—is it with us always? Can we feel it even now?
Consider this: the eye is narrow in its gaze.
For, at this very moment, some lives are bathed in miracle:
a newborn child in the arms of parents who were past the point of hope;
the happiness of improbable love after many years alone;
recovery from surgery; the easing of grief;
food for the hungry, rain after drought,
the first light of peace in a war-darkened land.
May I look up from my dark places and be glad:
Somewhere, even now, wondrous goodness blossoms forth.

MIRACLES AND WONDERS. The distinction between "miracles" as supernatural acts and "wonders" as "hidden miracles" manifest in the laws of nature is based on the teaching of Nachmanides (1194–1270), a Spanish philosopher and kabbalist.

OUR STORY tells of the sacredness of life, of the astonishing complexity of cells and organisms, of the vast lengths of time it took to generate their splendid diversity, of the enormous improbability that any of it happened at all. Reverence is the religious emotion elicited when we perceive the sacred. (Ursula Goodenough, b. 1943)

PRAYER IS the contemplation of the facts of life from the highest point of view. It is the soliloquy of a beholding and jubilant soul. (Ralph Waldo Emerson, 1803–1882)

כַּוָּנָה
Kavanah

אָבוֹת וְאִמָּהוֹת
Avot v'Imahot

גְּבוּרוֹת
G'vurot

קְדֻשַּׁת הַשֵּׁם
K'dushat HaShem

קְדֻשַּׁת הַיּוֹם
K'dushat HaYom

עֲבוֹדָה
Avodah

הוֹדָאָה
Hodaah

שָׁלוֹם
Shalom

תְּפִלַּת הַלֵּב
T'filat HaLev

וְעַל כֻּלָּם יִתְבָּרַךְ וְיִתְרוֹמַם שִׁמְךָ,
מַלְכֵּנוּ, תָּמִיד לְעוֹלָם וָעֶד.

וּכְתֹב לְחַיִּים טוֹבִים
כָּל בְּנֵי בְרִיתֶךָ.

וְכֹל הַחַיִּים יוֹדוּךָ סֶּלָה,
וִיהַלְלוּ אֶת שִׁמְךָ בֶּאֱמֶת,
הָאֵל יְשׁוּעָתֵנוּ וְעֶזְרָתֵנוּ סֶּלָה.

V'al kulam yitbarach v'yitromam shimcha,
Malkeinu, tamid l'olam va·ed.

Uchtov l'chayim tovim
kol b'nei v'ritecha.

V'chol hachayim yoducha selah,
vihal'lu et shimcha be·emet —
haEl y'shuateinu v'ezrateinu selah.

And for all these gifts, God of majesty,
may Your name come to be blessed and praised —
our gratitude a daily offering until the end of time.

Inscribe Your covenant partners
for a life of goodness.

And may all life resound with gratitude and faith
in praise of Your name.
God, You sustain us and help us.

בָּרוּךְ אַתָּה, יְיָ, הַטּוֹב שִׁמְךָ, וּלְךָ נָאֶה לְהוֹדוֹת.

Baruch atah, Adonai, hatov shimcha, ulcha na·eh l'hodot.
Blessed are You, Adonai, whose goodness
deserves thanks and praise.

FOR ALL THESE GIFTS וְעַל כֻּלָּם. In the end, living a life of gratitude means choosing to see the blessings in life rather than focusing on the curses. Choosing to see the good that people do for us, rather than focusing on the complaints we have about them; choosing to focus on the goodness in life rather than the inevitable struggles. (Robert Emmons, b. 1958)

OUR GRATITUDE A DAILY OFFERING תָּמִיד. A hundred times every day I remind myself that my inner and outer life are based on the labors of others, living and dead, and that I must exert myself in order to give in the same measure as I have received and am still receiving. (Albert Einstein, 1879–1955)

MAY ALL LIFE RESOUND WITH GRATITUDE AND FAITH וְכֹל הַחַיִּים יוֹדוּךָ סֶּלָה. This prayer, which concludes the *Hodaah* (Gratitude) blessing of *HaT'filah*, does not merely give thanks to God. It also expresses a poignant yearning found in many Jewish prayers — that all living beings might know gratitude and render thanks to their Creator. The liturgy imagines a time when even animals might experience a kind of religious consciousness — a joyous awareness of the blessing of life and a sense of overwhelming indebtedness to the Source of all being. Perhaps the poet believes that gratitude itself is a kind of blessing, as it enriches the experience of being alive.

Hodaah: We Give Thanks for the Covenant

וּכְתֹב לְחַיִּים טוֹבִים כָּל בְּנֵי בְרִיתֶךָ.

Uchtov l'chayim tovim kol b'nei v'ritecha. . . .

Inscribe Your covenant partners for a life of goodness. . . .

Holy One,
the mystics had names for You—
Atik Yomin, Ancient of Days; *Yotzeir Ruchot*, Creator of Winds—
to capture Your grandeur in words.
In covenant with You we glimpse ineffable forces:
invisible time, inscrutable nature, infinite challenge.
We are grateful for the gift of life;
we respond by ennobling our lives through service and healing.
We are grateful for the beauty of creation;
we respond by guarding and preserving forest, sea, and air.
We are grateful that Your love has blessed our lives;
we respond with our own acts of kindness, care, and love.
In a universe we can never fully grasp, we are Your partners for all generations.

בָּרוּךְ אַתָּה, יְיָ, הַטּוֹב שִׁמְךָ, וּלְךָ נָאֶה לְהוֹדוֹת.

Baruch atah, Adonai, hatov shimcha, ulcha naeh l'hodot.

Blessed are You, Adonai, whose goodness
deserves thanks and praise.

Ten thousand flowers in spring, the moon in autumn,
a cool breeze in summer, snow in winter.
If your mind isn't clouded by unnecessary things,
this is the best season of your life.

ANCIENT OF DAYS. A name for God that is associated with divine eternality, appearing several times in the Book of Daniel (chapter 7), and in a mystical hymn for the special meal eaten on Shabbat afternoon, by the 16th-century kabbalist Rabbi Isaac Luria.

CREATOR OF WINDS. From a prayer for forgiveness for the Fast of 17 Tammuz.

TEN THOUSAND FLOWERS. By Wu-Men Hui-k'ai (1183–1260).

Peace at Home: The Virtue of Sh'lom Bayit

Better a piece of dry bread and tranquility with it,
than a house full of feasting with strife. (Proverbs 17:1)

The prosperity and success of the wicked, however impressive, is only illusion. Far better is the fortune of those who are *tzadikim* (righteous ones), even if they have only a crust of bread, because they have peace in their homes, while the wicked are in a state of discord, either with their families or with other people. Family harmony and peace are the essence of true success in life, and can be attained even with a piece of dry bread.

—Malbim (Rabbi Meir Leibush ben Yehiel Michel Weiser, 1809–1879)

Parents and Children

Start softly. A discussion that begins with accusation or criticism triggers the natural inclination to fight back, drastically reducing the chances of resolution. A soft start, by contrast, invites constructive conversation. The importance of a soft start and soft reply is established in Jewish tradition. In Proverbs 15:1, we read: "A soft answer turns away wrath"; and in *Pirkei Avot* 1:15: "Receive everyone with a cheerful expression." Beginning softly does not mean abandoning a parent's responsibility to set limits or to discipline the child; it means only that we do not begin with blame.

When problem-solving in the context of an unequal relationship like parent–child, the *principle of justice* still applies. The rule is that inequalities in authority should be justified by the purpose and function of the relationship. In other words, parental authority is justified by the responsibility to care for, keep safe, and raise children properly. It would be grossly unfair to grant such a major responsibility without the authority to carry it out. At the same time, the person with more power should not take advantage of it in a self-serving or cruel way. Such advantage-taking is known in Rabbinic parlance as *honaat rei·a*—a serious moral violation and one of the sins in the Yom Kippur confession.

Being a kind and just parent during their early years helps build a foundation of respect that will endure through the difficult teen years. Agreeing to abide by *a covenant of respect* can help keep parent–teenager discussions on track. The covenant of respect means that teens follow the biblical commandment to honor their parents—which includes accepting parental authority and parental rights to set appropriate limits (Talmud, *Kiddushin* 29–32). Parents, in turn, would follow the Rabbinic injunction to honor all people (*Pirkei Avot* 4:1), which involves listening to their child's point of view with an open mind.

—William K. Berkson (b. 1944), adapted

If your wife is short, bend over to hear her whisper.

—Talmud *Bava M'tzia* 59a

When his disciples asked Rabbi Adda bar Ahavah, "To what do you attribute your long life?" he replied, "I never lost my temper in the midst of my family."

—Talmud *Taanit* 20b

Diversity is built into the human condition; our tradition regards it as a blessing. Says the Talmud (*B'rachot* 58a): "Just as the faces of human beings are different, so their minds and personalities are different." Disagreements are inevitable in any close relationship. But the prophet Zechariah taught, "Love truth and peace" (8:19). In other words: balance the quest for truth with the striving for peace. Don't let brutal honesty lead you to hurt the ones you love. Don't insist on being right at the expense of a loving, harmonious relationship with your partner or spouse.

When the Temple was destroyed, it was replaced not by another Temple but by the home, later named a *mikdash m'at*, a sanctuary in miniature. The Rabbis established an extraordinary equivalence:

Temple = home	priests = us around the table
altar = table	sacrifice = bread

And because the altar could not be built from hewn stones (it would take a tool of violence to shape them), so, too, a tool of violence is not used to cut the bread on the Shabbat table. How many of us tear the challah with our hands (instead of using a knife) at the Friday night dinner?

Just as the Temple had to be a place of peace and wholeness, it is our hope that our home will also be a place of peace, not a place of hurt, competition, or violence. We reinforce these wonderful principles not only through grand gestures and statements but also through the regular practice of law and ritual.

—Rabbi Shira Milgrom (b. 1951)

FOR REFLECTION

Sh'lom bayit does not mean a "quiet house" but a home in which people are at peace with one another. How can I bring more peace into my home and into my relationships? Am I refraining from discussing important matters in order to maintain peace in my home?

כּוָּנָה
Kavanah

אָבוֹת וְאִמָּהוֹת
Avot v'Imahot

גְּבוּרוֹת
G'vurot

קְדֻשַּׁת הַשֵּׁם
K'dushat HaShem

קְדֻשַּׁת הַיּוֹם
K'dushat HaYom

עֲבוֹדָה
Avodah

הוֹדָאָה
Hodaah

שָׁלוֹם
Shalom

תְּפִלַּת הַלֵּב
T'filat HaLev

אֱלֹהֵינוּ וֵאלֹהֵי אֲבוֹתֵינוּ וְאִמּוֹתֵינוּ,
בָּרְכֵנוּ בַּבְּרָכָה הַמְשֻׁלֶּשֶׁת
הַכְּתוּבָה בַּתּוֹרָה,
הָאֲמוּרָה מִפִּי כֹהֲנִים
עַם קְדוֹשֶׁךָ כָּאָמוּר:
יְבָרֶכְךָ יְיָ וְיִשְׁמְרֶךָ.
כֵּן יְהִי רָצוֹן.
יָאֵר יְיָ פָּנָיו אֵלֶיךָ וִיחֻנֶּךָּ.
כֵּן יְהִי רָצוֹן.
יִשָּׂא יְיָ פָּנָיו אֵלֶיךָ
וְיָשֵׂם לְךָ שָׁלוֹם.
כֵּן יְהִי רָצוֹן.

Eloheinu v'Elohei avoteinu v'imoteinu,

bar'cheinu bab'rachah hamshuleshet

hak'tuvah baTorah,

haamurah mipi kohanim —

am k'doshecha — kaamur:

"Y'varech·cha Adonai v'yishm'recha."

    Kein y'hi ratzon.

"Ya·eir Adonai panav eilecha vichuneka."

    Kein y'hi ratzon.

"Yisa Adonai panav eilecha

v'yaseim l'cha shalom."

    Kein y'hi ratzon.

Our God,
Divine Presence whose path our ancestors walked,
bless us now with words first bestowed on Israel
in the time of Moses and Aaron —
the threefold blessing, given us through Torah,
that joins our hopes with theirs:

May God bless you and protect you.
    May it be so.
May you receive the light of God's kindness and grace.
    May it be so.
May God bestow favor upon you and give you peace.
    May it be so.

MAY GOD BLESS YOU יְבָרֶכְךָ יְיָ, Numbers 6:24–26.

RECEIVE THE LIGHT. Hebrew *ya·eir panav*, literally "make His face to shine," that is, illumine. The anthropomorphic expression indicates God's friendly concern. (Rabbi Jacob Milgrom, 1923–2010; adapted)

BESTOW FAVOR. The Hebrew idiom *nasa panim*, literally "lift the face," can mean "to look with favor." (Rabbi Jacob Milgrom, adapted)

Focusing Prayer

God of All Generations

God's Powers

God's Holiness

The Day's Holiness

Our Offering

Thanksgiving

Peace

Prayer of the Heart

FACE

אֶת פָּנֶיךָ, מִסִּדְקִית
מִנִּסִּים שֶׁאֵינָם עוֹצְרִים נְשִׁימָה
מֵחֲשֵׁכָה לַחָה בְּגֻמְחוֹת הַבְּרוּאִים
מֵאֵפֶר אָדָם נִטְרָד בָּרוּחוֹת
בְּרַחֲמִים גְּדוֹלִים אֲקַבֵּץ

Your face, from finery
from miracles that do not stop one's breath
from moist darkness in the niches of all creatures
from the ash of humanity stirred up in the winds
with great mercy I will gather

אֶת פָּנֶיךָ, מֵחֲסָדִים קְבוּעִים
מֵאִישׁ עוֹטֵף לִי בַּלַּיְלָה
מִבִּתִּי נִרְדֶּמֶה עַל שְׂפַת נְהַר הֶחָלָב
אֲבַקֵּשׁ

Your face, from constant kindnesses
from the man who envelops me at night
from my daughter falling asleep at the shore of the milk river
I'll seek

אֶת פָּנֶיךָ,
כִּי פְּנֵי הַחַיָּל הִתְעַוְּתוּ
פְּנֵי אָבִי הִתְפַּזְּרוּ
וּפְנֵי תְּרָפִים בְּאַמְתַּחְתִּי

Your face,
for the face of the soldier has become distorted
the face of my father has dispersed
and my face is an idol in my sack

וְאַתָּה הוּא וּפָנֶיךָ

but You exist as does Your face.

FACE. By Sivan Har-Shefi (b. 1978). On the facing page, the threefold blessing of ancient Israel's priests (Numbers 6:24–26) refers literally to God's "face" illumined and lifted up in blessing.

YOUR FACE. A seeker of God's face, our poet knows well the Psalmist's cry, "How long will You hide Your face from me?" (Psalm 13:2). Here she first describes the experience of seeing God's face almost everywhere: in fine clothing and acts of kindness, in the ordinary "miracles" of daily life, in her husband's embrace and in her daughter nursing at her breast. She gathers these "sightings" together as though creating a composite sketch of God's multifaceted presence. But then we hear urgent echoes of Psalm 13 as the poet notes the places where she has felt threats to God and perhaps even God's absence: the face of war, the face of a parent no longer available to her, her own face (that is, vanity and the modern cult of self-worship). In the end, like the author of Psalm 13, the poet affirms the truth of her experience: God exists and God's face exists—both the idea of God and, more important, the living reality of God in the world: source of protection, grace, and peace.

Sim shalom tovah uvrachah,	שִׂים שָׁלוֹם טוֹבָה וּבְרָכָה,	כַּוָּנָה *Kavanah*
chein vachesed v'rachamim,	חֵן וָחֶסֶד וְרַחֲמִים,	אָבוֹת וְאִמָּהוֹת *Avot v'Imahot*
aleinu v'al kol Yisrael amecha.	עָלֵינוּ וְעַל כָּל יִשְׂרָאֵל עַמֶּךָ.	גְּבוּרוֹת *G'vurot*
Bar'cheinu, Avinu — kulanu k'echad — b'or panecha;	בָּרְכֵנוּ, אָבִינוּ, כֻּלָּנוּ כְּאֶחָד בְּאוֹר פָּנֶיךָ,	קְדֻשַּׁת הַשֵּׁם *K'dushat HaShem*
ki v'or panecha natata lanu,	כִּי בְאוֹר פָּנֶיךָ נָתַתָּ לָּנוּ,	קְדֻשַּׁת הַיּוֹם *K'dushat HaYom*
Adonai Eloheinu,	יְיָ אֱלֹהֵינוּ,	עֲבוֹדָה *Avodah*
Torat chayim v'ahavat chesed,	תּוֹרַת חַיִּים וְאַהֲבַת חֶסֶד,	הוֹדָאָה *Hodaah*
utzdakah uvrachah v'rachamim v'chayim v'shalom.	וּצְדָקָה וּבְרָכָה וְרַחֲמִים וְחַיִּים וְשָׁלוֹם.	שָׁלוֹם *Shalom*
V'tov b'einecha l'vareich et am'cha Yisrael,	וְטוֹב בְּעֵינֶיךָ לְבָרֵךְ אֶת עַמְּךָ יִשְׂרָאֵל,	תְּפִלַּת הַלֵּב *T'filat HaLev*
b'chol eit uvchol shaah, bishlomecha.	בְּכָל עֵת וּבְכָל שָׁעָה, בִּשְׁלוֹמֶךָ.	
B'sefer chayim, b'rachah, v'shalom,	בְּסֵפֶר חַיִּים, בְּרָכָה, וְשָׁלוֹם,	
ufarnasah tovah,	וּפַרְנָסָה טוֹבָה,	
nizacheir v'nikateiv l'fanecha —	נִזָּכֵר וְנִכָּתֵב לְפָנֶיךָ,	
anachnu, v'chol am'cha beit Yisrael —	אֲנַחְנוּ וְכָל עַמְּךָ בֵּית יִשְׂרָאֵל,	
l'chayim tovim ulshalom!	לְחַיִּים טוֹבִים וּלְשָׁלוֹם.	

Let there be peace.
Grant goodness, blessing, and grace,
constancy and compassion
to us and all Israel, Your people.

Avinu —
bless and unite all human beings in the light of Your presence;
for Your light has shown us a holy path for living:
devotion to love, generosity, blessedness, mercy, life, and peace.
In Your goodness, bless Your people Israel with peace at all times.

Let us and the whole family of Israel
be remembered and inscribed in the Book of Life.
May it be a life of goodness, blessing, and prosperity!
May it be a life of peace!

בָּרוּךְ אַתָּה, יְיָ, עוֹשֵׂה הַשָּׁלוֹם.

Baruch atah, Adonai, oseih hashalom.

You are the Blessed One, Eternal Source of shalom.

Sim Shalom: The Blessing of Peace

שִׂים שָׁלוֹם טוֹבָה וּבְרָכָה,
חֵן וָחֶסֶד וְרַחֲמִים . . .

Sim shalom tovah uvrachah,
chein vachesed v'rachamim . . .
Let there be peace. Grant goodness and blessing, grace, constancy, and compassion. . . .

Rabbi Joshua ben Levi taught:
Great is peace; peace is to the world as leaven is to dough.

And thus we learn: Peace is not passivity, a state of restful inertia.
Peace is the fermenting energy, the source of creative and expansive growth.
When there is peace in the world, human talents may blossom and all are enriched.
When there is peace in a family, all members may grow to fulfill their potential.
When there is peace in our soul, we are free to express all the gifts within us.

Our sages teach: Humility is the pathway to peace.
Strive to purify yourself of jealousy, resentment, and competition for honor.
These lead to arguments and strife between people.
A quiet, contented spirit—rooted in gratitude for what we possess—will be at peace.
Thus, after our prayer for peace, we ask:
"Before all human beings, let humility be my stance."

Sang the psalmist: Seek peace, and pursue it!
Seek it in your own place; pursue it everywhere.
Seek peace for our people; pursue it for all who dwell on earth.
Even when it seems distant, do not let go of peace.

RABBI JOSHUA BEN LEVI TAUGHT. In tractate *Derekh Eretz Zuta, Perek Hashalom* 1.
HUMILITY IS THE PATHWAY TO PEACE. Based on the teachings of Rabbi Yitzchak Meltzan (1854–1916), a student of Rabbi Yisrael Salanter, founder of the Musar (moral education) movement.
BEFORE ALL HUMAN BEINGS. From the conclusion of the *T'filah* (see next page).
SEEK PEACE, AND PURSUE IT, Psalm 34:15.
IN YOUR OWN PLACE. Based on the 11th-century commentator Rashi, who cites midrashim.
DO NOT LET GO. Based on Rabbi Samson Raphael Hirsch (1808–1888), commentary on Psalm 34:15.

כַּוָּנָה
Kavanah
אָבוֹת וְאִמָּהוֹת
Avot v'Imahot
גְּבוּרוֹת
G'vurot
קְדֻשַּׁת הַשֵּׁם
K'dushat HaShem
קְדֻשַּׁת הַיּוֹם
K'dushat HaYom
עֲבוֹדָה
Avodah
הוֹדָאָה
Hodaah
שָׁלוֹם
Shalom
תְּפִלַּת הַלֵּב
T'filat HaLev

אֱלֹהַי,	*Elohai:*
נְצֹר לְשׁוֹנִי מֵרָע,	*N'tzor l'shoni meira;*
וּשְׂפָתַי מִדַּבֵּר מִרְמָה.	*usfatai midabeir mirmah.*
וְלִמְקַלְלַי נַפְשִׁי תִדֹּם,	*V'limkal'lai nafshi tidom;*
וְנַפְשִׁי כֶּעָפָר לַכֹּל תִּהְיֶה.	*v'nafshi ke·afar lakol tiyeh.*
פְּתַח לִבִּי בְּתוֹרָתֶךָ,	*P'tach libi b'Toratecha;*
וּבְמִצְוֹתֶיךָ תִּרְדֹּף נַפְשִׁי.	*uvmitzvotecha tirdof nafshi.*
וְכָל הַחוֹשְׁבִים עָלַי רָעָה,	*V'chol hachoshvim alai raah —*
מְהֵרָה הָפֵר עֲצָתָם,	*m'heirah hafeir atzatam,*
וְקַלְקֵל מַחֲשַׁבְתָּם.	*v'kalkeil machashavtam.*
עֲשֵׂה לְמַעַן שְׁמֶךָ.	*Aseih l'maan sh'mecha.*
עֲשֵׂה לְמַעַן יְמִינֶךָ.	*Aseih l'maan y'minecha.*
עֲשֵׂה לְמַעַן קְדֻשָּׁתֶךָ.	*Aseih l'maan k'dushatecha.*
עֲשֵׂה לְמַעַן תּוֹרָתֶךָ.	*Aseih l'maan Toratecha.*
לְמַעַן יֵחָלְצוּן יְדִידֶיךָ,	*L'maan yeichal'tzun y'didecha,*
הוֹשִׁיעָה יְמִינְךָ וַעֲנֵנִי.	*hoshiah y'mincha vaaneini.*

My God:
Keep my tongue from doing harm, and my lips from lies and deceit.
Before those who wrong me with words, may silence be my practice.
Before all human beings, let humility be my stance.
Open my heart to Your Torah, that I may follow its sacred path of duty.
Shatter, at once, the malicious plans of those who would do me harm.
Act, for the sake of Your name.
Act, for the sake of Your shielding hand.
Act, for the sake of Your holiness.
Act, for the sake of Your Torah.
For the sake of those who love You — their rescue and safety —
let Your shielding hand be the answer to my prayer.

MY GOD — KEEP אֱלֹהַי, נְצֹר, based on Psalm 34:14.

THOSE WHO WRONG ME WITH WORDS. *HaT'filah* concludes as it began — by focusing our thoughts on the ethical use of language. We pray that our own words do no harm, and that we may resist the impulse to respond angrily to the insults of others.

FOR THE SAKE OF THOSE WHO LOVE YOU לְמַעַן יֵחָלְצוּן, Psalm 60:7.

"LET HUMILITY BE MY STANCE . . ."

UPON GIVING BIRTH to her fourth son, our matriarch Leah named him *Y'hudah*, a name derived from the verb *l'hodot*—to thank, praise, or acknowledge. Thanks and praise are essential to our identity as Jews (*Y'hudim*); indeed, we might translate the word *Y'hudim* as "grateful people—those who acknowledge with praise."

But our Sages ask: Why did Leah wait until she had her fourth child to express gratitude? Did she not feel thankful for the birth of the first three? They answer: Leah knew that her husband *Yaakov* was destined to father twelve sons who would become the Twelve Tribes of Israel. Since there were four matriarchs, she assumed that each woman would give birth to three sons. Thus, at the birth of her fourth son, she exclaimed: "I have received more than my share—thus I must offer thanks."

A sense of entitlement destroys our joy in what we receive. To know that we are blessed beyond what we deserve—this is true gratitude.

I POSE THIS CHALLENGE to my spirit:
To receive with open mind and heart what is offered to me.
May I learn to embrace as easily as I evaluate.
May I quiet the ever-present instinct to judge and critique.
May I cultivate the gift of listening without framing a reply.
May I learn to accept help from those who care for me.
May I grow less insistent that life bend to my will and expectations.
May generosity of spirit find a home within me.

OUR SAGES ASK. Based on the 11th-century commentary of Rashi to Genesis 29:35, where he cites Midrash *Genesis Rabbah* 7.14.

A SENSE OF ENTITLEMENT. Gratitude is a function not of how much we have, but rather of how much we have relative to how much we feel we deserve. When you have worked hard at your job, you usually do not feel flooded with gratitude when you pick up your paycheck. Even a holiday bonus may come to be expected as your just deserts and not elicit a great surge of gratitude—unless it is a far bigger sum than you feel you deserve. The opposite of gratitude is a feeling of entitlement. The attitude of "I deserve it" turns every gift into a paycheck. (Sara Yoheved Rigler, b. 1948)

יִהְיוּ לְרָצוֹן אִמְרֵי־פִי — *Yiyu l'ratzon imrei-fi*
וְהֶגְיוֹן לִבִּי לְפָנֶיךָ, — *v'hegyon libi l'fanecha,*
יְיָ, צוּרִי וְגֹאֲלִי. — *Adonai, tzuri v'go·ali.*

May the words of my mouth
and the meditation of my heart
be acceptable to You, Soul of eternity,
my Rock and my Redeemer.

עֹשֶׂה שָׁלוֹם בִּמְרוֹמָיו, — *Oseh shalom bimromav,*
הוּא יַעֲשֶׂה שָׁלוֹם עָלֵינוּ, — *hu yaaseh shalom aleinu,*
וְעַל כָּל יִשְׂרָאֵל, — *v'al kol Yisrael,*
וְעַל כָּל יוֹשְׁבֵי תֵבֵל. — *v'al kol yoshvei teiveil.*
וְאִמְרוּ: אָמֵן. — *V'imru: Amen.*

May the Maker of peace above make peace for us,
all Israel, and all who dwell on earth. *Amen.*

MAY THE WORDS OF MY MOUTH AND THE MEDITATION OF MY HEART יִהְיוּ לְרָצוֹן אִמְרֵי־פִי וְהֶגְיוֹן לִבִּי. Though it is a closing prayer for *HaT'filah* also on weekdays and Shabbat, Psalm 19:15 has special resonance on Yom Kippur — for on this day we confess the "harm we have caused in Your world through the words of our mouth" (*b'dibur peh*) and "the ways we have wronged You through our innermost thoughts" (*b'hirhur halev*, literally, "meditation of the heart"). In the *Al Cheit* confession, the mouth (*peh*) and the heart (*lev*) stand out as sources of wrongdoing. In Psalm 19:15 we declare that our words and thoughts may also help us reach the Source of holiness.

"May the Words of My Mouth and the Meditation of My Heart . . ."

I have spoken words of tradition,
but this silence belongs to me.
To whatever is Eternal amid ceaseless ebb and flow;
To the Root of goodness—
to Being itself, ever-present, ever-emerging,
expressed in the bodies of all living things;
to the Indwelling Presence
that powers my own pulse-beat;
to the Giver of life, who is with me all my days—
I address myself in reverence:
Hineini
I set before You this day
all that I am and wish to be.
Hineini—
receive the offering of my heart.

"Acceptable to You . . ."

God paid heed to Abel and his offering,
but to Cain and his offering God paid no heed.

Our Sages teach: Cain's offering was of inferior quality,
but Abel brought his best, as it is written:
Abel brought the choicest of the firstlings of his flock.

Do I bring my best energies to those I cherish most?
Or do I offer them too little—a shadow of myself:
tired, distracted, taciturn, short-tempered?

Do I bring passion to the work I have chosen,
my finest talents to tasks of true significance?
Or do I let my powers dissipate, wasting precious time on trivia?

On this, the altar of my life,
I want to offer my best,
using all my gifts in service to the good.

HINEINI. May be translated "here I am," "behold, I am present," "ready," or "at your service."
GOD PAID HEED TO ABEL, Genesis 4:4–5.
OUR SAGES TEACH. Based on the 11th-century commentary of Rashi.
ABEL BROUGHT THE CHOICEST, Genesis 4:4.

סְלִחוֹת וּוִדּוּי

S'lichot Uvidui · Forgiveness and Confession

כְּרַחֵם אָב
K'racheim Av

כִּי אָנוּ עַמֶּךָ
Ki Anu Amecha

וִדּוּי זוּטָא
Vidui Zuta

וִדּוּי רַבָּה
Vidui Rabbah

כְּרַחֵם אָב עַל־בָּנִים,
רַחֵם יְיָ עַל־יְרֵאָיו.
כִּי כִגְבֹהַּ שָׁמַיִם עַל־הָאָרֶץ,
גָּבַר חַסְדּוֹ עַל־יְרֵאָיו.
לַייָ הַיְשׁוּעָה,
עַל־עַמְּךָ בִרְכָתֶךָ סֶּלָה.
יְיָ צְבָאוֹת עִמָּנוּ,
מִשְׂגָּב־לָנוּ אֱלֹהֵי יַעֲקֹב, סֶלָה.
יְיָ צְבָאוֹת, אַשְׁרֵי אָדָם בֹּטֵחַ בָּךְ.
יְיָ הוֹשִׁיעָה,
הַמֶּלֶךְ יַעֲנֵנוּ בְיוֹם־קָרְאֵנוּ.

סְלַח־נָא לַעֲוֹן הָעָם הַזֶּה
כְּגֹדֶל חַסְדֶּךָ,
וְכַאֲשֶׁר נָשָׂאתָה לָעָם הַזֶּה
מִמִּצְרַיִם וְעַד־הֵנָּה.

K'racheim av al-banim,
richam Adonai al-y'rei·av.
Ki chigvo·ah shamayim al-haaretz,
gavar chasdo al-y'rei·av.
L'Adonai haishuah,
al-am'cha virchatecha selah.
Adonai Tz'vaot imanu;
misgav-lanu Elohei Yaakov, selah.
Adonai Tz'vaot, ashrei adam botei·ach bach.
Adonai, hoshiah!
HaMelech yaaneinu v'yom-koreinu.

"S'lach na laavon haam hazeh
k'godel chasdecha,
v'chaasher nasata laam hazeh
miMitzrayim v'ad heinah."

As parents show tenderness to their children,
may You show mercy to those who worship You.
Like the heavens that tower above the earth,
Your love is powerful for those who revere You.
Liberation is a gift from God — a blessing upon Your people.
You are the God of all we can perceive, our haven, the God of *Yaakov*.
And You are the God of all that is beyond our perception;
the one who has faith in You is fortunate.
Sovereign God, show us the way to freedom!
Answer us on this day of our calling out to You.

Moses prayed to God:
"As You have been faithful to this people ever since Egypt,
please forgive their failings now, in keeping with Your boundless love."

AS PARENTS SHOW TENDERNESS כְּרַחֵם אָב. The prayer is built around biblical verses: Psalms 103:13 and 11; 3:9; 46:8; 84:13; 20:10; Numbers 14:19–20.

I DO NOT WANT to beg forgiveness
or seek absolution: a poor petitioner before the throne.
If a power flows through the universe,
if some force or higher consciousness infuses all of life—
it does not notice my misdeeds.

Said Elisha, the heretic rabbi:
"There is no justice; there is no Judge."
No one to hear my confession. No one to grant me mercy. No one to seal my fate.

Still the words of prayer
are in my mouth.
Still the wrongs I commit
are on my mind.
And still this yearning in my heart:
to make things right, breathe free, be clean again.

אֵיךְ אָבוֹא לְפָנֶיךָ הַיּוֹם
וְאַתָּה עָסוּק בְּחֶשְׁבּוֹנוֹת רַבִּים.

HOW SHALL I COME before You today,
You're busy with so many matters.

אֵיךְ אֲבַקֵּשׁ קִצְבַּת חַיִּים
וַאֲנִי אוֹרֵחַ שֶׁנָּטָה לָלוּן.

How shall I plead for a measure of life
while I am but a guest for the night.

מוּטָב וְאָבוֹא בְּפַעַם אַחֶרֶת,
יְחִידִי –
עִם דְּמְמַת עֲוֹנוֹתַי.

It's better if I come another time,
alone—
with the silence of my sins.

אַל תַּרְעִיל אֶת אוֹר הַחַלּוֹנוֹת
אַל תַּגִּיף אֶת הַתְּרִיסִים,

Don't veil the windows' light
don't close the shutters.

חַ כֵּ ה !

Wait!

הֲרֵי אָשׁוּב אֵלֶיךָ
בְּיוֹם מִן הַיָּמִים.

For I'll return to You
one of these days.

THERE IS NO JUSTICE. Words uttered by Rabbi Elisha ben Abuyah (ca. 100 CE) after witnessing the sudden death of a child who was performing a mitzvah (Talmud *Kiddushin* 30b).
HOW SHALL I COME. By Asher Reich (b. 1937).

וְשָׁם נֶאֱמַר:
וַיֹּאמֶר יְיָ: סָלַחְתִּי כִּדְבָרֶךָ.

V'sham ne·emar:
"Vayomer Adonai: 'Salachti, kidvarecha.'"

And God responded: "I forgive, as you have asked."

כִּי אָנוּ עַמֶּךָ, וְאַתָּה אֱלֹהֵינוּ,
אָנוּ בָנֶיךָ, וְאַתָּה אָבִינוּ.
אָנוּ עֲבָדֶיךָ, וְאַתָּה אֲדוֹנֵנוּ,
אָנוּ קְהָלֶךָ, וְאַתָּה חֶלְקֵנוּ.
אָנוּ נַחֲלָתֶךָ, וְאַתָּה גוֹרָלֵנוּ,
אָנוּ צֹאנֶךָ, וְאַתָּה רוֹעֵנוּ.
אָנוּ כַרְמֶךָ, וְאַתָּה נוֹטְרֵנוּ,
אָנוּ פְעֻלָּתֶךָ, וְאַתָּה יוֹצְרֵנוּ.
אָנוּ רַעְיָתֶךָ, וְאַתָּה דוֹדֵנוּ,
אָנוּ סְגֻלָּתֶךָ, וְאַתָּה קְרוֹבֵנוּ.
אָנוּ עַמֶּךָ, וְאַתָּה מַלְכֵּנוּ,
אָנוּ מַאֲמִירֶיךָ, וְאַתָּה מַאֲמִירֵנוּ.

Ki anu amecha, v'atah Eloheinu;
anu vanecha, v'atah avinu.
Anu avadecha, v'atah adoneinu;
anu k'halecha, v'atah chelkeinu.
Anu nachalatecha, v'atah goraleinu;
anu tzonecha, v'atah ro·einu.
Anu charmecha, v'atah notreinu;
anu f'ulatecha, v'atah yotzreinu.
Anu rayatecha, v'atah dodeinu;
anu s'gulatecha, v'atah k'roveinu.
Anu amecha, v'atah malkeinu;
anu maamirecha, v'atah maamireinu.

Our God and God of our ancestors—

We are Your people; and You are our God.
We are Your children; and You are our father, our mother.
We are the people who serve You; and You call us to serve.
We are Your community; and You are our portion.
We are Your legacy; and You are our purpose.
We are Your flock; and You are our shepherd.
We are Your vineyard; and You watch over us.
We are Your work; and You are our maker.
We are Your beloved; and You are our lover.
We are Your treasure; and You are the one we cherish.
We are Your people; and You reign over us.
We offer You our words; and You offer us Yours.

So forgive us, pardon us, lead us to atonement.

כְּרַחֵם אָב
K'racheim Av

כִּי אָנוּ עַמֶּךָ
Ki Anu Amecha

וִדּוּי זוּטָא
Vidui Zuta

וִדּוּי רַבָּה
Vidui Rabbah

WE ARE YOUR LEGACY . . . OUR PURPOSE אָנוּ נַחֲלָתֶךָ, וְאַתָּה גוֹרָלֵנוּ. Part of a poem celebrating the multidimensional relationship between God and Israel, this verse identifies the Jewish people as carrying forward the divine purpose from generation to generation.

"We are Your beloved; and You are our lover . . ."

Truly, my life is one long hearkening unto my self and unto others, unto God. And if I say that I hearken, it is really God who hearkens inside me. The most essential and the deepest in me hearkening unto the most essential and deepest in the other. God to God.

How great are the needs of Your creatures on this earth, oh God. They sit there, talking quietly and quite unsuspecting, and suddenly their need erupts in all its nakedness. Then, there they are, bundles of human misery, desperate and unable to face life. And that's when my task begins. It is not enough simply to proclaim You, God, to commend You to the hearts of others. One must also clear the path towards You in them, God, and to do that one has to be a keen judge of the human soul. A trained psychologist. Ties to father and mother, youthful memories, dreams, guilt feelings, inferiority complexes and all the rest block the way.

I embark on a slow voyage of exploration with everyone who comes to me. And I thank You for the great gift of being able to read people. Sometimes they seem to me like houses with open doors. I walk in and roam through passages and rooms, and every house is furnished a little differently and yet they are all of them the same, and every one must be turned into a dwelling dedicated to You, oh God. And I promise You, yes, I promise that I shall try to find a dwelling and a refuge for You in as many houses as possible. There are so many empty houses, and I shall prepare them all for You, the most honored lodger. Please forgive this poor metaphor.

—Etty Hillesum (1914–1943), diary entry of 17 September 1942

DIARY ENTRY. Written between 1941 and 1943, when the author perished in Auschwitz, the diaries of Etty Hillesum reflect a religious sensibility in harmony with the spiritual outpourings of the High Holy Days.

כְּרַחֵם אָב
K'racheim Av
כִּי אָֽנוּ עַמֶּֽךָ
Ki Anu Amecha
וִדּוּי זוּטָא
Vidui Zuta
וִדּוּי רַבָּה
Vidui Rabbah

Vidui Zuta — The Short Confession

אֱלֹהֵֽינוּ וֵאלֹהֵי אֲבוֹתֵֽינוּ וְאִמּוֹתֵֽינוּ,
תָּבֹא לְפָנֶֽיךָ תְּפִלָּתֵֽנוּ,
וְאַל תִּתְעַלַּם מִתְּחִנָּתֵֽנוּ.
אֲנַֽחְנוּ עַזֵּי פָנִים וּקְשֵׁי עֹֽרֶף
לוֹמַר לְפָנֶֽיךָ,
יְיָ אֱלֹהֵֽינוּ וֵאלֹהֵי אֲבוֹתֵֽינוּ
וְאִמּוֹתֵֽינוּ:
צַדִּיקִים אֲנַֽחְנוּ וְלֹא חָטָֽאנוּ.
אֲבָל אֲנַֽחְנוּ חָטָֽאנוּ.

Eloheinu v'Elohei avoteinu v'imoteinu,
tavo l'fanecha t'filateinu;
v'al titalam mit'chinateinu.
Anachnu azei fanim ukshei oref
lomar l'fanecha,
Adonai Eloheinu v'Elohei avoteinu
v'imoteinu:
Tzadikim anachnu, v'lo chatanu.
Aval anachnu chatanu.

Our God and God of all generations,
may our prayers reach Your presence.
And when we turn to You, do not be indifferent.
Adonai, we are arrogant and stubborn,
claiming to be blameless and free of sin.
In truth, we have stumbled and strayed.
We have done wrong.

אָשַֽׁמְנוּ, בָּגַֽדְנוּ, גָּזַֽלְנוּ, דִּבַּֽרְנוּ דֹֽפִי.
הֶעֱוִֽינוּ, וְהִרְשַֽׁעְנוּ, זַֽדְנוּ, חָמַֽסְנוּ,
טָפַֽלְנוּ שֶֽׁקֶר. יָעַֽצְנוּ רָע, כִּזַּֽבְנוּ,
לַֽצְנוּ, מָרַֽדְנוּ, נִאַֽצְנוּ, סָרַֽרְנוּ, עָוִֽינוּ,
פָּשַֽׁעְנוּ, צָרַֽרְנוּ, קִשִּֽׁינוּ עֹֽרֶף. רָשַֽׁעְנוּ,
שִׁחַֽתְנוּ, תִּעַֽבְנוּ, תָּעִֽינוּ, תִּעְתָּֽעְנוּ.

Ashamnu, bagadnu, gazalnu, dibarnu dofi.
He·evinu, v'hirshanu, zadnu, chamasnu,
tafalnu sheker. Yaatznu ra, kizavnu,
latznu, maradnu, niatznu, sararnu, avinu,
pashanu, tzararnu, kishinu oref. Rashanu,
shichatnu, tiavnu, ta·inu, titanu.

Of these wrongs we are guilty:
We betray. We steal. We scorn. We act perversely.
We are cruel. We scheme. We are violent. We slander.
We devise evil. We lie. We ridicule. We disobey.
We abuse. We defy. We corrupt. We commit crimes.
We are hostile. We are stubborn. We are immoral. We kill.
We spoil. We go astray. We lead others astray.

Sarnu mimitzvotecha umimishpatecha	סַרְנוּ מִמִּצְוֹתֶיךָ וּמִמִּשְׁפָּטֶיךָ
hatovim, v'lo shavah-lanu.	הַטּוֹבִים, וְלֹא שָׁוָה לָנוּ.
V'atah tzadik al kol haba aleinu,	וְאַתָּה צַדִּיק עַל כָּל הַבָּא עָלֵינוּ,
ki emet asita, vaanachnu hirshanu.	כִּי אֱמֶת עָשִׂיתָ, וַאֲנַחְנוּ הִרְשָׁעְנוּ.
Mah nomar l'fanecha, yosheiv marom?	מַה נֹּאמַר לְפָנֶיךָ, יוֹשֵׁב מָרוֹם,
Umah n'sapeir l'fanecha, shochein sh'chakim?	וּמַה נְּסַפֵּר לְפָנֶיךָ, שׁוֹכֵן שְׁחָקִים.
Halo kol hanistarot v'haniglot	הֲלֹא כָּל הַנִּסְתָּרוֹת וְהַנִּגְלוֹת
atah yodei·a.	אַתָּה יוֹדֵעַ.

Our turning away from Your mitzvot and laws of goodness is a hollow pursuit.
You are just, concerning all that happens in our lives.
Your way is the way of truth, while ours leads to error.
What can we say to You whose existence is beyond time and space?
What words of ours can reach Your realm
beyond the clouds, beyond heaven itself?
Every hidden mystery, every revelation — surely, You know them all.

Atah yodei·a razei olam;	אַתָּה יוֹדֵעַ רָזֵי עוֹלָם,
v'taalumot sitrei kol chai.	וְתַעֲלוּמוֹת סִתְרֵי כָּל חָי.
Atah chofeis kol-chadrei-vaten;	אַתָּה חוֹפֵשׂ כָּל־חַדְרֵי־בָטֶן,
uvochein k'layot valev.	וּבוֹחֵן כְּלָיוֹת וָלֵב.
Ein davar ne·elam mimeka;	אֵין דָּבָר נֶעְלָם מִמֶּךָּ,
v'ein nistar mineged einecha.	וְאֵין נִסְתָּר מִנֶּגֶד עֵינֶיךָ.
Uvchein y'hi ratzon mil'fanecha,	וּבְכֵן יְהִי רָצוֹן מִלְּפָנֶיךָ,
Adonai Eloheinu v'Elohei avoteinu	יְיָ אֱלֹהֵינוּ וֵאלֹהֵי אֲבוֹתֵינוּ
v'imoteinu:	וְאִמּוֹתֵינוּ:
shetislach lanu al kol chatoteinu,	שֶׁתִּסְלַח לָנוּ עַל כָּל חַטֹּאתֵינוּ,
v'timchal lanu al kol avonoteinu,	וְתִמְחַל לָנוּ עַל כָּל עֲוֹנוֹתֵינוּ,
ut·chapeir lanu al kol p'sha·einu.	וּתְכַפֶּר לָנוּ עַל כָּל פְּשָׁעֵינוּ.

You know the secrets of the universe and the secrets of the human heart.
You know and understand us, for You examine our inner lives.
Nothing is concealed from You, nothing hidden from Your sight.
Eternal One, our God and God of our ancestors,
we pray that this be Your will: forgive all our wrongs,
pardon us for every act of injustice, help us atone for all our moral failures.

Vidui Rabbah — The Long Confession

כְּרַחֵם אָב
K'racheim Av

כִּי אָֽנוּ עַמֶּֽךָ
Ki Anu Amecha

וִדּוּי זוּטָא
Vidui Zuta

וִדּוּי רַבָּה
Vidui Rabbah

For these sins, our God, we ask forgiveness:

עַל חֵטְא שֶׁחָטָֽאנוּ לְפָנֶֽיךָ
בְּזָדוֹן וּבִשְׁגָגָה,
וְעַל חֵטְא שֶׁחָטָֽאנוּ לְפָנֶֽיךָ
בִּשְׁבוּעַת שָׁוְא.

Al cheit shechatanu l'fanecha
b'zadon uvishgagah;
v'al cheit shechatanu l'fanecha
bishvuat shav.

The ways we have wronged You deliberately and by mistake;
and harm we have caused in Your world through insincere promises.

עַל חֵטְא שֶׁחָטָֽאנוּ לְפָנֶֽיךָ
בִּפְלִילוּת,
וְעַל חֵטְא שֶׁחָטָֽאנוּ לְפָנֶֽיךָ
בְּקַלּוּת רֹאשׁ.

Al cheit shechatanu l'fanecha
biflilut;
v'al cheit shechatanu l'fanecha
b'kalut rosh.

The ways we have wronged You by judging others unfairly;
and harm we have caused in Your world by making light of serious matters.

עַל חֵטְא שֶׁחָטָֽאנוּ לְפָנֶֽיךָ
בְּיֵֽצֶר הָרָע,
וְעַל חֵטְא שֶׁחָטָֽאנוּ לְפָנֶֽיךָ
בְּעֵינַֽיִם רָמוֹת.

Al cheit shechatanu l'fanecha
b'yeitzer hara;
v'al cheit shechatanu l'fanecha
b'einayim ramot.

The ways we have wronged You by giving in to our hostile impulses;
and harm we have caused in Your world through condescension.

FOR THESE SINS. In biblical Hebrew there are three main terms for sin — *pesha, avon,* and *cheit. Pesha* means rebellion. *Avon* comes from a root meaning "to be twisted," "to be crooked." *Cheit* is the weakest of the three terms. It comes from a root meaning "to miss." The word is used, for example, of an archer whose arrows fail to hit the target. *Cheit* denotes failure to follow the good path, the lack of character or staying power that prevents a person from arriving at a set goal. (Rabbi Louis Jacobs, 1920–2006; adapted)

עַל חֵטְא שֶׁחָטָאנוּ לְפָנֶיךָ
בְּהִרְהוּר הַלֵּב,
וְעַל חֵטְא שֶׁחָטָאנוּ לְפָנֶיךָ
בְּדִבּוּר פֶּה.

Al cheit shechatanu l'fanecha
b'hirhur halev;
v'al cheit shechatanu l'fanecha
b'dibur peh.

The ways we have wronged You through our innermost thoughts;
and harm we have caused in Your world through the words of our mouths.

עַל חֵטְא שֶׁחָטָאנוּ לְפָנֶיךָ
בְּכַחַשׁ וּבְכָזָב,
וְעַל חֵטְא שֶׁחָטָאנוּ לְפָנֶיךָ
בְּהוֹנָאַת רֵעַ.

Al cheit shechatanu l'fanecha
b'chachash uvchazav;
v'al cheit shechatanu l'fanecha
b'honaat rei·a.

The ways we have wronged You through lies and deceit;
and harm we have caused in Your world by mistreating a friend or neighbor.

עַל חֵטְא שֶׁחָטָאנוּ לְפָנֶיךָ
בְּשִׂנְאַת חִנָּם,
וְעַל חֵטְא שֶׁחָטָאנוּ לְפָנֶיךָ
בְּוִדּוּי פֶּה.

Al cheit shechatanu l'fanecha
b'sinat chinam;
v'al cheit shechatanu l'fanecha
b'vidui peh.

The ways we have wronged You by hating without cause;
and harm we have caused in Your world through hypocrisy.

וְעַל כֻּלָּם, אֱלוֹהַּ סְלִיחוֹת, סְלַח
לָנוּ, מְחַל לָנוּ, כַּפֶּר־לָנוּ.

V'al kulam, Elo·ah s'lichot, s'lach
lanu, m'chal lanu, kapper-lanu.

For all these failures of judgment and will —
God of forgiveness, forgive us, pardon us, lead us to atonement.

OUR INNERMOST THOUGHTS בְּהִרְהוּר הַלֵּב. What harm could be caused by private thoughts and fantasies? Thoughts shape our feelings, which in turn guide our actions. For example, indulging in harsh self-criticism, ruminating over the ways we have been slighted, or aggressive fantasies may lead to damaging ourselves or others. Jewish tradition encourages us to discipline our thoughts as well as our behavior.

THROUGH LIES AND DECEIT בְּכַחַשׁ וּבְכָזָב. Falsehood is the common characteristic of deceptive advertising, exploiting another's ignorance or naivete, and providing substandard work or services. (Meir Tamari, b. 1927)

עַל חֵטְא שֶׁחָטָאנוּ לְפָנֶיךָ
בַּגָּלוּי וּבַסָּתֶר,
וְעַל חֵטְא שֶׁחָטָאנוּ לְפָנֶיךָ
בִּבְלִי דָעַת.

Al cheit shechatanu l'fanecha
bagalui uvasater;
v'al cheit shechatanu l'fanecha
bivli daat.

The ways we have wronged You openly and secretly;
and harm we have caused in Your world through our thoughtlessness.

עַל חֵטְא שֶׁחָטָאנוּ לְפָנֶיךָ
בְּחִלּוּל הַשֵּׁם,
וְעַל חֵטְא שֶׁחָטָאנוּ לְפָנֶיךָ
בְּטֻמְאַת שְׂפָתָיִם.

Al cheit shechatanu l'fanecha
b'chilul hashem;
v'al cheit shechatanu l'fanecha
b'tumat s'fatayim.

The ways we have wronged You by profaning Your name in public;
and harm we have caused in Your world through offensive speech.

עַל חֵטְא שֶׁחָטָאנוּ לְפָנֶיךָ
בִּרְכִילוּת,
וְעַל חֵטְא שֶׁחָטָאנוּ לְפָנֶיךָ
בְּזִלְזוּל הוֹרִים וּמוֹרִים.

Al cheit shechatanu l'fanecha
birchilut;
v'al cheit shechatanu l'fanecha
b'zilzul horim umorim.

The ways we have wronged You through gossip and rumor;
and harm we have caused in Your world through disrespect to parents and teachers.

עַל חֵטְא שֶׁחָטָאנוּ לְפָנֶיךָ
בְּצָרוּת עָיִן,
וְעַל חֵטְא שֶׁחָטָאנוּ לְפָנֶיךָ
בְּמַשָּׂא וּבְמַתָּן.

Al cheit shechatanu l'fanecha
b'tzarut-ayin;
v'al cheit shechatanu l'fanecha
b'masa uvmatan.

The ways we have wronged You through narrow-mindedness;
and harm we have caused in Your world through dishonesty in business.

כְּרַחֵם אָב
K'racheim Av
כִּי אָנוּ עַמֶּךָ
Ki Anu Amecha
וִדּוּי זוּטָא
Vidui Zuta
וִדּוּי רַבָּה
Vidui Rabbah

God's Tenderness
We Are Your People
The Short Confession
The Long Confession

עַל חֵטְא שֶׁחָטָֽאנוּ לְפָנֶֽיךָ
בְּגִלּוּי עֲרָיוֹת,
וְעַל חֵטְא שֶׁחָטָֽאנוּ לְפָנֶֽיךָ
בְּמַאֲכָל וּבְמִשְׁתֶּה.

Al cheit shechatanu l'fanecha
b'gilui arayot;
v'al cheit shechatanu l'fanecha
b'maachal uvmishteh.

The ways we have wronged You through sexual immorality;
and harm we have caused in Your world through consumption of food and drink.

עַל חֵטְא שֶׁחָטָֽאנוּ לְפָנֶֽיךָ
בִּתְשׂוּמֶת יָד,
וְעַל חֵטְא שֶׁחָטָֽאנוּ לְפָנֶֽיךָ
בְּרִיצַת רַגְלַֽיִם לְהָרַע.

Al cheit shechatanu l'fanecha
bitsumet yad;
v'al cheit shechatanu l'fanecha
b'ritzat raglayim l'hara.

The ways we have wronged You by betraying trust;
and harm we have caused in Your world through impulsive acts of malice.

וְעַל כֻּלָּם, אֱלֽוֹהַּ סְלִיחוֹת, סְלַח
לָֽנוּ, מְחַל לָֽנוּ, כַּפֶּר־לָֽנוּ.

V'al kulam, Elo·ah s'lichot, s'lach
lanu, m'chal lanu, kapper-lanu.

For all these failures of judgment and will —
God of forgiveness, forgive us, pardon us, lead us to atonement.

DISHONESTY IN BUSINESS בְּמַשָּׂא וּבְמַתָּן (*facing page*). Several of the underlying principles of Jewish business ethics are found in Leviticus, two of them in the Yom Kippur afternoon Torah portion, *K'doshim tiyu* (You shall be holy): "You shall not deceive, and you shall not lie to one another. . . . In the measurement of weight and in liquid measure, you shall have honest scales, honest weights" (19:11, 35); and later in the book we find: "And when you sell anything to your neighbor, or when you buy anything from your neighbor, you shall not oppress one another" (25:14).

From these biblical commandments sprang an ethos of honesty, fairness, and integrity so strong that, when the Sages described a person standing in judgment before the heavenly court, they imagined that God's first question would be: "Did you transact your business honestly?" (Talmud, *Shabbat* 31a). Among numerous expressions of ethical business behavior in Jewish law codes, these are emblematic: "If one has something to sell, it is forbidden to make it appear better than it is in reality, in order to deceive"; "Measuring and weighing must be performed with a generous eye."

IMPULSIVE ACTS OF MALICE בְּרִיצַת רַגְלַֽיִם לְהָרַע. Or, "running to do evil." The expression suggests rash or instinctive behavior. To counteract our malicious impulses, Rabbi Yehudah ben Tema teaches in the Mishnah, "Run like a deer . . . to do the will of your Creator in heaven" (*Avot* 5:20). That is, develop the habit of eagerly and promptly doing mitzvot, so that your instinct will be to help and not to harm others.

Failures of Integrity

We wrong You when we wrong ourselves.
For our failures of integrity, Adonai, we seek forgiveness.

For passing judgment without knowledge of the facts,
and for distorting facts to suit our purposes.

For succumbing in silence to social pressure,
and for acquiescing in beliefs we find offensive.

For using others' bad behavior to excuse our own,
and for blaming others for our mistakes and poor decisions.

For pretending to emotions we do not feel,
and for appearing to be other than what we are.

For condemning in our children the faults we tolerate in ourselves,
and for tolerating in ourselves the faults we condemn in our parents.

Failures of Justice

We dishonor You when we dishonor our society.
For our failures of justice, Adonai, we seek forgiveness.

For being indifferent to deprivation and hunger,
while accepting a culture of self-indulgence and greed.

For abuse of power in board rooms, court rooms and classrooms,
and for accepting the neglect of children and elders, the ill and the weak.

For permitting social inequalities to prevail,
and for lacking the vision to transcend our selfishness.

For glorifying violence and turning hastily to war,
and for allowing history to repeat itself.

For behaviors that risk the future of our planet,
and for wreaking havoc on our only true inheritance—God's Creation.

Failures of Love

We sin against You when we hurt one another.
For our failures of love, Adonai, we seek forgiveness.

For exploiting another for our own pleasure,
and for the wounds we cause through betrayal and deception.

For withholding affection from those we claim to love,
and for using love to control our spouses and partners, our children and parents.

For abandoning friends and siblings whose love has sustained us,
and for neglecting those who love us when they need us most.

For harboring in our relationships mistrust, boredom, and disloyalty,
and for rejecting our partner's efforts at repair and renewal.

For possessiveness, jealousy, and avarice,
and for lashing out in anger at those who are closest to us.

Who among us is blameless? Who shall say: "I have not erred;
I have not wronged or sinned"?

We **a**buse, we **b**rutalize, we **c**ovet, we **d**eceive, we **e**nslave, we **f**eud,
we **g**ossip, we **h**umiliate, we **i**njure, we **j**udge unfairly, we **k**ill, we **l**ie,
we **m**anipulate, we **n**eglect, we **o**stracize, we **p**lagiarize, we **q**uarrel,
we **r**age, we **s**hame, we **t**urn away, we **u**ndermine, we **v**ilify, we **w**aste,
we e**x**ploit the earth, we **y**earn too much for yesterday—and too easily forget **Z**ion.

Our sins are an alphabet of woe.

Help us, Holy One, to follow Your ways of integrity, justice, and love.
Teach us to seek forgiveness with humility and an open heart.

Said Rabbi Adda son of Rabbi Hanina: If the people Israel had not sinned, only the Torah and the Book of Joshua would have been given to them, but the books of prophetic rebukes would have been unnecessary. Thus, the people's wrongdoing led to additional teaching. So, too, do we learn and grow from our misdeeds. What text teaches this lesson? The words of Kohelet: *For much wisdom may proceed from anger* (Ecclesiastes 1:18). (Talmud *N'darim* 22b, adapted)

For Acts of Healing and Repair

God our Creator and Guide,
let us reflect on the healing acts by which we bring You into our lives,
the acts of repair that make You a living presence in our words
and deeds:

acts of healing we have done by judging others with compassion,
and acts of repair we have done through rigorous self-judgment;

acts of healing we have done through kindness to parents and children,
and acts of repair we have done through loyalty to spouses, partners,
and friends;

acts of healing we have done through self-discipline and self-restraint,
and acts of repair we have done by ridding ourselves of destructive
behavior;

acts of healing we have done by seeing the holy in the ordinary,
and acts of repair we have done by taking upon ourselves sacred
obligations;

acts of healing we have done by seeking forgiveness,
and acts of repair we have done by forgiving others;

acts of healing we have done by turning in love toward Zion,
and acts of repair we have done by supporting the State of Israel;

acts of healing we have done by receiving life as a blessing and a gift,
and acts of repair we have done by expressing gratitude and
appreciation;

acts of healing we have done by listening with an open mind to those
we love,
and acts of repair we have done by making our homes shelters
of safety and peace—

for all of these bring nearer the day when You shall be one and Your name shall be one.

God's Tenderness

We Are Your People

The Short Confession

The Long Confession

Hakarat Hatov — Recognizing the Good

הַכָּרַת הַטּוֹב . . .
What gives us strength to pursue goodness?

Awareness of the good that is around us—
decent, generous acts that remind us of what is possible,
here and now, in this world of moral ambiguity.
So our Sages taught: one mitzvah inspires another.

Thus we acknowledge and celebrate:

Those who do their best on the job, whatever their level or pay;
and those who run an honest business, who don't cut corners, falsify, or lie.

Those who labor in obscurity to help others, or advance the frontiers of truth;
those who add beauty to the world through the arts, or through unselfish deeds.

Patient teachers who see the potential in shy or "difficult" students;
students who focus on learning, not just good marks, and earn their grades fairly without cheating.

Athletes who exemplify good sportsmanship and self-discipline;
all those who use their wealth to benefit society and the greater good.

Those in high places who resist the corruption of power;
whistle-blowers, alert to malfeasance, who bravely sound the alarm.

Public servants who do the people's business with integrity;
politicians who place conscience above popularity.

Those who travel far from home to defend our country from foes;
those who keep our communities safe, who run into fires to save lives.

Parents who care selflessly for ill or troubled children;
children who give time and love to frail and aging parents.

Loving spouses who remain faithful;
loyal friends who stand fast in times of trouble.

May their mitzvot inspire our own.
May we find the strength to emulate their honor.
Let us take joy in remembering that goodness still abides.

HAKARAT HATOV. A Hebrew term for gratitude, literally "recognizing the good." The expression conveys a moral lesson: that we find blessing not in receiving something beneficial, but in noticing and appreciating the good that is already ours.

ONE MITZVAH INSPIRES ANOTHER. Based on *Pirkei Avot* 4:2.

אָבִֽינוּ מַלְכֵּֽנוּ
Avinu Malkeinu · Almighty and Merciful

Before the Open Ark

Avinu Malkeinu —
As Joseph wept and opened a forgiving heart to his brothers,
let our hearts be open to those who ask our forgiveness.

Avinu Malkeinu —
As the High Priest entered the innermost Shrine to atone,
let our acts of *t'shuvah* touch our innermost life.

Avinu Malkeinu —
As Jonah cried out to God, "I thought I was driven away,"
let us reach for the Divine from the depths of our being.

Avinu Malkeinu —
As You said to Moses and Israel, "You shall be holy, for I am holy,"
let us affirm today: "We shall pursue holiness in our everyday lives —
revering mother and father,
providing for the poor,
rising before the aged,
loving neighbor and stranger as ourselves."

Avinu Malkeinu —
Hear our voice. . . .

AS JOSEPH WEPT AND OPENED A FORGIVING HEART. See Genesis 45 and 50.
AS THE PRIEST ENTERED THE INNERMOST SHRINE. See Leviticus 16.
AS JONAH CRIED OUT TO GOD. See Jonah 2:5.
AS YOU SAID TO MOSES AND ISRAEL. See Leviticus 19.

Avinu Malkeinu

אָבִינוּ מַלְכֵּנוּ *Avinu Malkeinu,*
We join generations of Jews who have sought your compassion

שְׁכִינָה אִמֵּנוּ *Sh'chinah Imeinu:* Nurturing Presence
מְקוֹר בִּינָתֵנוּ *M'kor Binateinu:* Source of insight and understanding
צוּר חַיֵּינוּ *Tzur Chayeinu:* Unweathered Stone, steadying strength beneath us
יְדִיד נַפְשׁוֹתֵינוּ *Y'did Nafshoteinu:* Intimate Soul-Companion

חָנֵּנוּ וַעֲנֵנוּ *Choneinu vaaneinu,*
We open to You in self-examination . . .

Grace us and answer us.
Be present with us and inspire us.
Accompany us.
Assure us we are not alone.

כִּי אֵין בָּנוּ מַעֲשִׂים *Ki ein banu maasim,*
We approach you empty-handed . . .

Our accomplishments set aside —
rather than defend ourselves, we confess
We are broken-hearted at our failures
and our world remains unrepaired

עֲשֵׂה עִמָּנוּ צְדָקָה וָחֶסֶד *Aseih imanu tz'dakah v'chesed,*
Embrace us generously as we expose our errors . . .

Be our example.
Hold us with abundant love.
Turn us to face the world
with justice and compassion.

וְהוֹשִׁיעֵנוּ *V'hoshi·einu,*
Save us . . .

We join our strength to Yours
as we offer ourselves fully to life ahead.

אָבִינוּ מַלְכֵּנוּ
Avinu Malkeinu

אָבִינוּ מַלְכֵּנוּ, חָטָאנוּ לְפָנֶיךָ.
Avinu Malkeinu, chatanu l'fanecha.

Avinu Malkeinu — Almighty and Merciful — we have strayed and sinned before You.

אָבִינוּ מַלְכֵּנוּ, אֵין לָנוּ מֶלֶךְ אֶלָּא אָתָּה.
Avinu Malkeinu, ein lanu melech ela atah.

Avinu Malkeinu, You alone are our Sovereign.

אָבִינוּ מַלְכֵּנוּ, עֲשֵׂה עִמָּנוּ לְמַעַן
שְׁמֶךָ.
Avinu Malkeinu, aseih imanu l'maan
sh'mecha.

Avinu Malkeinu, act toward us as befits Your name.

אָבִינוּ מַלְכֵּנוּ, חַדֵּשׁ עָלֵינוּ שָׁנָה
טוֹבָה.
Avinu Malkeinu, chadeish aleinu shanah
tovah.

Avinu Malkeinu, renew for us a year of goodness.

אָבִינוּ מַלְכֵּנוּ, זְכֹר כִּי עָפָר אֲנַחְנוּ.
Avinu Malkeinu, zachor ki afar anachnu.

Avinu Malkeinu, remember: we are but dust of the earth.

אָבִינוּ מַלְכֵּנוּ, תְּהֵא הַשָּׁעָה הַזֹּאת
שְׁעַת רַחֲמִים וְעֵת רָצוֹן מִלְּפָנֶיךָ.
Avinu Malkeinu, t'hei hashaah hazot
sh'at rachamim v'eit ratzon mil'fanecha.

Avinu Malkeinu, let this hour in Your presence be a time of compassion and acceptance.

אָבִינוּ מַלְכֵּנוּ, חֲמֹל עָלֵינוּ, וְעַל
עוֹלָלֵינוּ וְטַפֵּנוּ.
Avinu Malkeinu, chamol aleinu, v'al
olaleinu v'tapeinu.

Avinu Malkeinu, have compassion on us and our families.

WE HAVE STRAYED AND SINNED חָטָאנוּ לְפָנֶיךָ. The verb *chatanu*, often translated "we have sinned," derives from a root meaning "to miss the mark," usually in relation to archery or slinging a stone (see Judges 20:16). The implication is that one has gone off course, departing from the proper path. There is no sense of being permanently tainted; with effort, one can return to the right way.

REMEMBER: WE ARE BUT DUST זְכֹר כִּי עָפָר אֲנַחְנוּ. Based on Psalm 103:14: "God knows how we are formed; God remembers that we are dust." *Avinu Malkeinu* centers on the contrast between the ephemeral frailty of human beings and the lasting power and mercy of God. This line also echoes Genesis 3:19: "For dust you are, and to dust you shall return." In full awareness that life and death are not in our hands — conscious of our dependence on a power greater than ourselves — we lift our voices in shared humility.

Avinu Malkeinu

אָבִינוּ מַלְכֵּנוּ, עֲשֵׂה לְמַעַן טְבוּחִים
עַל יִחוּדֶךָ.

Avinu Malkeinu, aseih l'maan t'vuchim
al yichudecha.

Avinu Malkeinu, act for the sake of those slain for their devotion to You.

אָבִינוּ מַלְכֵּנוּ, עֲשֵׂה לְמַעַן הֲרוּגִים
עַל שֵׁם קָדְשֶׁךָ.

Avinu Malkeinu, aseih l'maan harugim
al shem kodshecha.

Avinu Malkeinu, act for the sake of those killed because they were Jews.

אָבִינוּ מַלְכֵּנוּ, עֲשֵׂה לְמַעַן בָּאֵי
בָאֵשׁ וּבַמַּיִם עַל קִדּוּשׁ שְׁמֶךָ.

Avinu Malkeinu, aseih l'maan ba·ei
va·eish uvamayim al kiddush sh'mecha.

Avinu Malkeinu, act for the sake of those who suffered fire and water to sanctify Your name.

אָבִינוּ מַלְכֵּנוּ, חָנֵּנוּ וַעֲנֵנוּ,
כִּי אֵין בָּנוּ מַעֲשִׂים.
עֲשֵׂה עִמָּנוּ צְדָקָה וָחֶסֶד,
וְהוֹשִׁיעֵנוּ.

Avinu Malkeinu, choneinu vaaneinu;
ki ein banu maasim.
Aseih imanu tz'dakah vachesed,
v'hoshi·einu.

Avinu Malkeinu — Almighty and Merciful —
answer us with grace, for our deeds are wanting.
Save us through acts of justice and love.

FIRE AND WATER בָּאֵשׁ וּבַמַּיִם. This phrase, which echoes the wording of *Untaneh Tokef* ("Who by fire and who by water?"), may refer to Jews who were drowned or burned at the stake in medieval Europe.

TO SANCTIFY YOUR NAME עַל קִדּוּשׁ שְׁמֶךָ. This verse and the previous two verses (added in the Middle Ages) refer to Jews who were willing, in times of persecution, to give their lives rather than violate the mitzvot. Tradition calls these martyrs "those who died to sanctify God's name (*al kiddush HaShem*)." The duty to sanctify God's name through holy acts derives from this biblical verse: "You shall not profane My holy name, that I may be sanctified in the midst of the Israelite people — I, Adonai, who sanctifies you" (Leviticus 22:32).

סִיּוּם הַמִּנְחָה
Siyum HaMinchah
Conclusion of Afternoon Prayers

Ours Is the Duty

Aleinu —
ours the duty to listen and ours the duty to praise;
ours is the duty to respond to what we hear;
to raise questions
and build houses of study in which to ask them;
to praise the Creator for creating;
to praise the Creator for rest;
to praise the God of Torah for the challenge of Torah;
to praise the God of eternity for every hour, every day;
to plant and build, to seek peace and pursue it;
ours the duty to do justice; ours the duty to be Israel:
to fix the broken, to open doors of hope;
to bow before a commanding Power that speaks to us
from Sinai, from history, from deep within the heart.

Hear, O Israel:
it is not your duty to complete the work,
but you may not turn away.

IT IS NOT YOUR DUTY TO COMPLETE THE WORK. Based on Mishnah *Avot* 2:16.

Try to Praise the Mutilated World

Try to praise the mutilated world.
Remember June's long days,
and wild strawberries, drops of wine, the dew.
The nettles that methodically overgrow
the abandoned homesteads of exiles.
You must praise the mutilated world.
You watched the stylish yachts and ships;
one of them had a long trip ahead of it,
while salty oblivion awaited others.
You've seen the refugees heading nowhere,
you've heard the executioners sing joyfully.
You should praise the mutilated world.
Remember the moments when we were together
in a white room and the curtain fluttered.
Return in thought to the concert where music flared.
You gathered acorns in the park in autumn
and leaves eddied over the earth's scars.
Praise the mutilated world
and the gray feather a thrush lost,
and the gentle light that strays and vanishes
and returns.

Give yourself to the dream:
The lion and the lamb, the vine and the fig tree.
Build it from the stones of earth.
Like the slow accretion of coral reef,
and the mountains that rise by inches,
knowledge of the Good shall fill up the earth
as the sea overflows with water.
Lift up your eyes and look to the stars.
None shall hurt and none shall destroy;
and great shall be the peace of your children.

TRY TO PRAISE THE MUTILATED WORLD. By Adam Zagajewski (b. 1945).
LION . . . LAMB, Isaiah 11:6.
VINE . . . FIG TREE, Micah 4:4.
KNOWLEDGE OF THE GOOD, based on Habbakuk 2:14.
LIFT UP YOUR EYES, based on God's words to Abraham in Genesis 15:5.
NONE SHALL HURT, Isaiah 11:9.
GREAT SHALL BE THE PEACE, Isaiah 54:13.

עָלֵינוּ
Aleinu

קַדִּישׁ דְּרַבָּנָן
Kaddish D'Rabanan

עָלֵינוּ לְשַׁבֵּחַ לַאֲדוֹן הַכֹּל,
לָתֵת גְּדֻלָּה לְיוֹצֵר בְּרֵאשִׁית,
שֶׁלֹּא עָשָׂנוּ כְּגוֹיֵי הָאֲרָצוֹת,
וְלֹא שָׂמָנוּ כְּמִשְׁפְּחוֹת הָאֲדָמָה,
שֶׁלֹּא שָׂם חֶלְקֵנוּ כָּהֶם,
וְגֹרָלֵנוּ כְּכָל הֲמוֹנָם.
וַאֲנַחְנוּ כּוֹרְעִים
וּמִשְׁתַּחֲוִים וּמוֹדִים
לִפְנֵי מֶלֶךְ מַלְכֵי הַמְּלָכִים,
הַקָּדוֹשׁ בָּרוּךְ הוּא.

Aleinu l'shabei·ach laAdon hakol,
lateit g'dulah l'Yotzeir b'reishit —
shelo asanu k'goyei haaratzot,
v'lo samanu k'mishp'chot haadamah;
shelo sam chelkeinu kahem,
v'goraleinu k'chol hamonam.
Vaanachnu korim,
umishtachavim, umodim
lifnei melech malchei ham'lachim:
HaKadosh, baruch hu,

Ours is the duty to praise the All-Sovereign, to honor the Artist of Creation, who made us unique in the human family, with a destiny all our own. For this we bend our knees and bow with gratitude before the Sovereign Almighty — Monarch of All — the Wellspring of holiness and blessing,

שֶׁהוּא נוֹטֶה שָׁמַיִם וְיוֹסֵד אָרֶץ,
וּמוֹשַׁב יְקָרוֹ בַּשָּׁמַיִם מִמַּעַל,
וּשְׁכִינַת עֻזּוֹ בְּגָבְהֵי מְרוֹמִים.
הוּא אֱלֹהֵינוּ, אֵין עוֹד.
אֱמֶת מַלְכֵּנוּ, אֶפֶס זוּלָתוֹ,
כַּכָּתוּב בְּתוֹרָתוֹ:
וְיָדַעְתָּ הַיּוֹם וַהֲשֵׁבֹתָ אֶל־לְבָבֶךָ,
כִּי יְיָ הוּא הָאֱלֹהִים
בַּשָּׁמַיִם מִמַּעַל
וְעַל־הָאָרֶץ מִתָּחַת, אֵין עוֹד.

shehu noteh shamayim v'yoseid aretz,
umoshav y'karo bashamayim mimaal,
ush·chinat uzo b'govhei m'romim.
Hu Eloheinu; ein od.
Emet Malkeinu, efes zulato —
kakatuv b'Torato:
"V'yadata hayom v'hasheivota el-l'vavecha,
ki Adonai hu haElohim
bashamayim mimaal
v'al-haaretz mitachat. Ein od."

who spread out the sky and fashioned the land, who dwells in beauty far beyond sight, whose powerful presence is the loftiest height. You are our God; there is none else. We take as true Your sovereignty; there is no other — as Torah teaches: "Embrace and carry in your heart this day: In heaven above, on earth below, the Eternal is God. There is no other."

EMBRACE וְיָדַעְתָּ, Deuteronomy 4:39.
SPREAD OUT . . . THE LAND אָרֶץ . . . נוֹטֶה, Isaiah 51:13; Zechariah 12:1.

Our Duty to Praise

Rabbis' Kaddish

עַל כֵּן נְקַוֶּה לְּךָ, יְיָ אֱלֹהֵינוּ,
לִרְאוֹת מְהֵרָה בְּתִפְאֶרֶת עֻזֶּךָ,
לְהַעֲבִיר גִּלּוּלִים מִן הָאָרֶץ,
וְהָאֱלִילִים כָּרוֹת יִכָּרֵתוּן.
לְתַקֵּן עוֹלָם בְּמַלְכוּת שַׁדַּי,
וְכָל בְּנֵי בָשָׂר יִקְרְאוּ בִשְׁמֶךָ,
לְהַפְנוֹת אֵלֶיךָ כָּל רִשְׁעֵי אָרֶץ.

Al kein n'kaveh l'cha, Adonai Eloheinu,
lirot m'heirah b'tiferet uzecha,
l'haavir gilulim min haaretz;
v'ha·elilim karot yikareitun.
L'takein olam b'malchut Shaddai,
v'chol b'nei vasar yikr'u vishmecha;
l'hafnot eilecha kol rishei aretz.

And so, Adonai our God, we look to You,
hoping soon to behold the splendor of Your power revealed:
a world free of idolatry and false gods;
a world growing more perfect through divine governance;
a world in which all human beings make known Your name,
while those who do evil turn toward You instead.

וְנֶאֱמַר:
וְהָיָה יְיָ לְמֶלֶךְ עַל־כָּל־הָאָרֶץ,
בַּיּוֹם הַהוּא יִהְיֶה יְיָ אֶחָד,
וּשְׁמוֹ אֶחָד.

V'ne·emar:
"V'hayah Adonai l'melech al-kol-haaretz,
bayom hahu yiyeh Adonai echad,
ushmo echad."

As the prophet announced,
"The Eternal shall be sovereign over all the earth.
On that day the Eternal shall be one, and God's name shall be one."

WE BEND OUR KNEES AND BOW וַאֲנַחְנוּ כּוֹרְעִים וּמִשְׁתַּחֲוִים (*facing page*). What distinguishes the Days of Awe from all other festivals is that here and only here does the Jew kneel. Here we do what we refused to do before the king of Persia, what no power on earth can compel us to do, and what we need not do before God on any other day of the year, or in any other situation we may face during our lifetime. And we do not kneel to confess a fault or to pray for forgiveness of sins, acts to which this festival is primarily dedicated. We kneel only in beholding the immediate nearness of God, hence on an occasion which transcends the earthly needs of today. (Franz Rosenzweig, 1886–1929; adapted)

THE ETERNAL SHALL BE וְהָיָה יְיָ, Zechariah 14:9.

The Task That Awaits Us

What is the Jewish way to God? It is not a way of ascending the ladder of speculation. Our understanding of God is not the triumphant outcome of an assault upon the riddles of the universe or a donation we receive in return for intellectual surrender. Our understanding comes by the way of *mitzvah*.

By living as Jews we attain our faith as Jews. We do not have faith in deeds; we attain faith through deeds.

When Moses recounted to the people the laws of the covenant with God, the people responded: "We will do and we will hear." This statement was interpreted to mean: *In doing we perceive*. A Jew is asked to take a *leap of action* rather than a *leap of thought*.

What is a mitzvah? A prayer in the form of a deed.

Genuine religiosity is *doing*. It wants to sculpt the unconditioned out of the matter of this world. The countenance of God reposes, invisible, in an earthen block; it must be wrought, carved, out of it. To be engaged in this work is to be religious—nothing else.

Multiplicity is given into our hands, to be transformed into unity; a vast, formless mass, to be given form by us with the Divine.

The human community is as yet only a projected opus that is waiting for us—a chaos that we must put in order; a Diaspora that we must gather in; a conflict to which we must bring reconciliation.

But this we can accomplish only if . . . each of us, each in our own place, will perform the just, the unifying, the "in-forming" deed.

For God does not want to be believed in, to be debated and defended by us, but simply to be realized through us.

WHAT IS THE JEWISH WAY TO GOD . . . IN THE FORM OF A DEED. By Rabbi Abraham Joshua Heschel (1907–1972).

GENUINE RELIGIOSITY . . . REALIZED THROUGH US. By Martin Buber (1878–1965).

We stand before God who calls forth our strength.

The nobility and truth of our history is in God;
in God—the source of our survival,
our firm stand through trial and change.

Ours is a history of spiritual greatness,
a legacy of spiritual dignity.
We turn to it when we are besieged by insult and attack.
We look to it when need and suffering press in upon us.

From generation to generation, the Eternal led our ancestors.
The One who leads us through all our days
will lead our children through theirs.

We stand before our God—
strengthened by reverence for the sacred obligations of Torah,
ennobled by a commitment to do what is just and right.

We bow before God,
stand upright before all people.
In a world of tumultuous change, we are steadfast:
we serve the Eternal.

With humility we say:
our faith is in God whose call is compelling.
Our response will shape our future.

**Thinking of My Death
—An Affirmation**

Love is forever.
Goodness goes on.
These two things
Comfort my heart
As death approaches.
These the lasting songs
In the lasting silence.

WE STAND BEFORE GOD. Based on part of a prayer for the eve of Yom Kippur by Rabbi Leo Baeck (1873–1956) "for all Jewish communities in Germany," October 6, 1935.
COMMITMENT TO DO WHAT IS JUST AND RIGHT. See Genesis 18:19.
THINKING OF MY DEATH. By Rabbi Norman Hirsh (b. 1930).

עָלֵינוּ
Aleinu

קַדִּישׁ דְּרַבָּנָן
Kaddish D'Rabanan

It is written: "Know before whom you stand"—
but in truth we do not know.

Perhaps we stand before our history—
a chronicle of stubbornness,
quiet heroism and the will to live.

Perhaps it is the memory of those who struggled to be human
in a world that was dark and cold.

Perhaps it is Torah that summons us to rise:
the golden chain of tradition;
a reverence for learning;
permission to question and doubt.

Perhaps we stand before ideals that call us
to do justice, to love kindness, to walk humbly on this earth.

Perhaps it is awe at the kinship of all that live,
or the Unknowable, Unnamable mystery that brought us here.

We stand together:
seekers, doubters, and those who are firm in their faith.
And this we know:

The day is short;
the work immense;
the laborers are reluctant;
the reward is great;
and the need is urgent.

KNOW BEFORE WHOM YOU STAND. The Talmud (*B'rachot* 28b) states: "When you pray, know before whom you stand." This phrase, often inscribed above the *aron kodesh* (the ark in which the sacred Torah scrolls are kept), summons the worshiper to a reverent and focused attention in the presence of the holy. It may be related to Exodus 3:5, in which Moses is told to remove his sandals because "the ground on which you stand is holy."

WHO STRUGGLED TO BE HUMAN. Based on *Pirkei Avot* 2:5: "Hillel taught: . . . In a place where there are no human beings, strive to be human."

TO DO JUSTICE . . . WALK HUMBLY. See Micah 6:8.

THE DAY IS SHORT. Adapted from *Pirkei Avot* 2:20: "Rabbi Tarfon used to say: The day is short, the task is great, the laborers are lazy, the reward is abundant, and the Master is urgent."

Our Duty to Praise

Rabbis' Kaddish

Kadish D'Rabanan

For our teachers and their students,
And the students of the students,
We ask for peace and loving-kindness,
And let us say, Amen.

And for those who study Torah
Here and everywhere,
May they be blessed with all they need,
And let us say, Amen.

We ask for peace and loving-kindness,
And let us say, Amen.

Amar Rabbi Yehudah

אָמַר רַבִּי יְהוּדָה:
אַל תִּסְתַּכֵּל בַּקַּנְקַן,
אֶלָּא בְּמַה שֶׁיֵּשׁ־בּוֹ.

Amar Rabbi Yehudah:
Al tistakeil bakankan,
ela b'mah sheyesh-bo.

Rabbi Yehudah said: Look not at the vessel, but at what it contains.

Amar Rabbi Akiva

אָמַר רַבִּי עֲקִיבָא:
וְאָהַבְתָּ לְרֵעֲךָ כָּמוֹךָ –
זֶה כְּלָל גָּדוֹל בַּתּוֹרָה.

Amar Rabbi Akiva:
"V'ahavta l'rei·acha kamocha" —
zeh k'lal gadol baTorah.

Rabbi Akiva said:
"Love your neighbor as yourself"—
this is the essence of the Torah.

KADDISH D'RABANAN. Lyrics by Debbie Friedman (1951–2011).
AMAR RABBI YEHUDAH, Mishnah *Avot* 4:20.
AMAR RABBI AKIVA, Midrash *Sifra*, *K'doshim* 4.12.
LOVE YOUR NEIGHBOR, Leviticus 19:18.

Kaddish D'Rabanan

עָלֵינוּ
Aleinu

קַדִּישׁ דְּרַבָּנָן
Kaddish D'Rabanan

יִתְגַּדַּל וְיִתְקַדַּשׁ שְׁמֵהּ רַבָּא,
בְּעָלְמָא דִּי בְרָא כִרְעוּתֵהּ.
וְיַמְלִיךְ מַלְכוּתֵהּ בְּחַיֵּיכוֹן
וּבְיוֹמֵיכוֹן,
וּבְחַיֵּי דְכָל בֵּית יִשְׂרָאֵל,
בַּעֲגָלָא וּבִזְמַן קָרִיב. וְאִמְרוּ: אָמֵן.

Yitgadal v'yitkadash sh'meih raba,
b'alma di v'ra chiruteih.
V'yamlich malchuteih b'chayeichon
uvyomeichon,
uvchayei d'chol beit Yisrael —
baagala uvizman kariv; v'imru: Amen.

May God's great name come to be magnified and sanctified
in the world God brought into being.
May God's majestic reign prevail soon in your lives, in your days,
and in the life of the whole House of Israel; and let us say: *Amen.*

יְהֵא שְׁמֵהּ רַבָּא מְבָרַךְ
לְעָלַם וּלְעָלְמֵי עָלְמַיָּא.

Y'hei sh'meih raba m'varach
l'alam ul·almei almaya.

יִתְבָּרַךְ וְיִשְׁתַּבַּח וְיִתְפָּאַר
וְיִתְרוֹמַם וְיִתְנַשֵּׂא וְיִתְהַדָּר
וְיִתְעַלֶּה וְיִתְהַלָּל שְׁמֵהּ
דְּקֻדְשָׁא, בְּרִיךְ הוּא,
לְעֵלָּא וּלְעֵלָּא מִכָּל בִּרְכָתָא וְשִׁירָתָא,
תֻּשְׁבְּחָתָא וְנֶחֱמָתָא
דַּאֲמִירָן בְּעָלְמָא. וְאִמְרוּ: אָמֵן.

Yitbarach v'yishtabach v'yitpaar
v'yitromam v'yitnasei v'yit·hadar
v'yitaleh v'yit·halal sh'meih
d'kudsha — b'rich hu —
l'eila ul·eila mikol birchata v'shirata,
tushb'chata v'nechemata
daamiran b'alma; v'imru: Amen.

May God's great name be blessed to the end of time.

May God's holy name come to be blessed, acclaimed, and glorified;
revered, raised, and beautified; honored and praised.
Blessed is the One who is entirely beyond
all the blessings and hymns,
all the praises and words of comfort
that we speak in the world; and let us say: *Amen.*

THE RABBIS' KADDISH (*Kaddish d'Rabanan*) was born in the ancient Study House (*beit midrash*), where it became customary to end the learning of Rabbinic teachings with an expression of hope for a world growing in peace, life, compassion, sustenance, and salvation. Thus, the Rabbis' *Kaddish* concludes this service, which is largely devoted to the study of sacred text, poetry, and literature about *tikkun midot* (repairing and strengthening personal qualities). But the Rabbis' *Kaddish* is not only for rabbis! It is a prayer that embraces "all who engage in the study of Torah here and everywhere."

Our Duty to Praise

Rabbis' Kaddish

Al Yisrael v'al rabanan,	עַל יִשְׂרָאֵל וְעַל רַבָּנָן,
v'al talmideihon	וְעַל תַּלְמִידֵיהוֹן
v'al kol talmidei talmideihon,	וְעַל כָּל תַּלְמִידֵי תַלְמִידֵיהוֹן,
di v'atra hadein	דִּי בְּאַתְרָא הָדֵין
v'di v'chol atar v'atar:	וְדִי בְכָל אֲתַר וַאֲתַר,
y'hei l'hon ulchon sh'lama raba,	יְהֵא לְהוֹן וּלְכוֹן שְׁלָמָא רַבָּא,
chinna v'chisda v'rachamin,	חִנָּא וְחִסְדָּא וְרַחֲמִין,
v'chayin arichin,	וְחַיִּין אֲרִיכִין,
umzonei r'vichei, ufurkana,	וּמְזוֹנֵי רְוִיחֵי, וּפֻרְקָנָא,
min kodam avuhon d'vishmaya v'ara;	מִן קֳדָם אֲבוּהוֹן דְּבִשְׁמַיָּא וְאַרְעָא.
v'imru: Amen.	וְאִמְרוּ: אָמֵן.

God of heaven and earth,
grant abundant peace
to our people Israel and their rabbis,
to our teachers and their disciples,
and to all who engage in the study of Torah here and everywhere.
Let there be for them and for us all, grace, love, and compassion,
a full life, ample sustenance, and salvation from God; and let us say:
Amen.

Y'hei sh'lama raba min sh'maya,	יְהֵא שְׁלָמָא רַבָּא מִן שְׁמַיָּא,
v'chayim tovim aleinu v'al kol Yisrael;	וְחַיִּים טוֹבִים עָלֵינוּ וְעַל כָּל יִשְׂרָאֵל.
v'imru: Amen.	וְאִמְרוּ: אָמֵן.
Oseh shalom bimromav,	עֹשֶׂה שָׁלוֹם בִּמְרוֹמָיו
hu yaaseh v'rachamav shalom aleinu,	הוּא יַעֲשֶׂה בְרַחֲמָיו שָׁלוֹם עָלֵינוּ
v'al kol Yisrael	וְעַל כָּל יִשְׂרָאֵל
v'al kol yoshvei teiveil; v'*imru: Amen.*	וְעַל כָּל יוֹשְׁבֵי תֵבֵל. וְאִמְרוּ: אָמֵן.

Let perfect peace abound;
let there be abundant life for us and for all Israel.
May the One who makes peace in the high heavens
make peace for us, all Israel, and all who dwell on earth; and let us say:
Amen.

סדר העבודה

Seder HaAvodah

Discovering the Holy

May we ascend toward the holy.

—LITURGY

הַקְדָּמָה

Hakdamah

Introduction: A Life of Purpose

הַקְדָּמָה
Hakdamah

מַסָּע קָדוֹשׁ
Masa Kadosh

אַנְעִים זְמִירוֹת
Anim Z'mirot

Faith does not spring out of nothing.
It comes with the discovery
of the holy dimension
of our existence.

—Rabbi Abraham Joshua Heschel (1902–1972)

Shimon HaTzadik hayah mish'yarei Ch'neset HaG'dolah.	שִׁמְעוֹן הַצַּדִּיק הָיָה מִשְּׁיָרֵי כְּנֶסֶת הַגְּדוֹלָה.
Hu hayah omeir:	הוּא הָיָה אוֹמֵר:
"Al sh'loshah d'varim haolam omeid:	עַל שְׁלֹשָׁה דְבָרִים הָעוֹלָם עוֹמֵד:
al haTorah,	עַל הַתּוֹרָה,
v'al vaavodah,	וְעַל הָעֲבוֹדָה,
v'al g'milut chasadim."	וְעַל גְּמִילוּת חֲסָדִים.

Shimon HaTzadik was one of the last of the Great Assembly.
He used to say:
"Upon three things the world stands:
Torah, holy service, and acts of human kindness."

Ki veiti beit t'filah yikarei l'chol haamim.	כִּי בֵיתִי בֵּית־תְּפִלָּה יִקָּרֵא לְכָל־הָעַמִּים.

My House shall be called a house of prayer for all people.

SHIMON HATZADIK שִׁמְעוֹן הַצַּדִּיק, *Pirkei Avot* 1:2. Simon the Righteous, a High Priest during the time of the Second Temple (ca. 200 BCE). This, his best-known maxim, identifies three essential ways of seeking the holy dimension of existence: study of sacred texts (intellectual acts), the Temple service (spiritual acts), and loving deeds (interpersonal acts).

HOLY SERVICE עֲבוֹדָה. The Hebrew word *avodah* has a rich repertoire of possible meanings; it may be translated as "service," "work," "labor," or "worship." In Rabbinic literature, it refers specifically to the sacrificial offerings in the Jerusalem Temple. The human act of connecting with God originally implied significant effort on behalf of the Divine. The ancient idea that worship means "serving God" lives on in our term for communal worship: "services."

MY HOUSE, Isaiah 56:7.

Avodah in the Ancient Temple

What Does This Service Mean to Us?

For more than a millennium—from the time of Moses and Aaron until Rome's destruction of the Second Temple—the Day of Atonement was marked by rites of purification. Leviticus, chapter 16, depicts Yom Kippur as a day when priests cleansed the Sanctuary from all that defiled it. Later reimagined by Sages who created the Mishnah, Yom Kippur became "The Day" (*Yoma*): an annual purification from sin for the entire community of Israel.

In Leviticus and in the Mishnah's tractate *Yoma*, the priests burn incense in fire-pans, slaughter bulls and lambs as offerings to God, and send a goat into the wilderness to banish the people's sins. The climax of the ritual is the High Priest's entry into the Holy of Holies, the innermost chamber of the Sanctuary, to pronounce aloud the name of God. When the Temple fell, the Sages ruled that atonement would no longer require sacrificial offerings (*korbanot*). Instead, God would respond to sincere confession (*Vidui*) and prayers for forgiveness (*S'lichot*), accompanied by good deeds. As one prophet had taught in the eighth century BCE (Hosea 14:3):

Bring words with you
and come back to the Eternal.
Say to God:
"Forgive all guilt,
and accept the good;
our 'bulls' will be the offerings of our lips."

A midrash declares that in the absence of *korbanot*, God accepts our verbal recitation of *Avodah*—a description of the ancient Yom Kippur ritual in the Temple. The heart of the traditional *Avodah* service is a poetic composition written in the Land of Israel by Yose ben Yose (fourth or fifth century CE). His poetry recounts the history of Israel from the six days of Creation to the time of the Temple; the priestly rites of atonement form the spiritual center of this history. Thus, with Creation as his starting point, the poet weaves the holiness of Yom Kippur into the very fabric of the universe.

WHAT DOES THIS SERVICE MEAN. This question recalls the one posed by the wicked child at the Passover seder: "What does this service mean to you?" (Exodus 12:26). In the Haggadah, the question implies skepticism and alienation, yet it also reflects an effort to find relevance in ancient rituals.

A MIDRASH DECLARES. In Midrash *Song of Songs Rabbah* 4.3.

The Enduring Treasure of Avodah

In ancient Israel, the priests performed ceremonies that brought forth blood from animals, rituals in which we cannot imagine ourselves participating; yet our forebears believed in their efficacy and found them spiritually uplifting. What meaning can those rites and words have for us—Jews of a different time and sensibility? Some see them as artifacts from a bygone era. But they have a deeper meaning if we think of them not as remote and inaccessible—objects in a museum—but as something close to our hearts: *family heirlooms.*

Heirlooms: we treasure them; we preserve them for posterity. Their beauty is in the heart and eye of the beholder. A family heirloom has the power to tell us who we are, by showing us where we came from. It reminds us of a cherished past; it adorns special occasions in our lives. An heirloom's meaning transcends the historical moment.

What is the enduring meaning of *Avodah* for us? What do we have in common with the Jews of antiquity who hallowed the rituals of Yom Kippur?

- *We have a hunger for the spiritual.* Like our ancestors, we long to transcend the limits of our personal existence and connect to our Source.
- *We have the capacity to grow in spirit.* Like our ancestors, we sense that our own words and actions can bring us closer to God or distance us from the Divine Presence.
- *We yearn to express our gratitude and confess our sins.* Though God does not need our gifts, the generous act of offering thanks to God makes us better human beings. Though God does not need our words, we feel the need to articulate our moral failures and our commitment to *t'shuvah*.
- *We have a longing to begin again.* Like our ancestors, we yearn to wipe the slate clean and start our lives afresh, with renewed energy and determination.

We, who gather on the Day of Atonement, are not visitors to a museum; we come together as members of a family. And our family's traditions—its stories and beliefs, its ceremonies and collective memories—go back more generations than we can count. We are blessed: our heirlooms bind us, teach us, and remind us; they draw us near to those who came before us; and they pave the way to a life of purpose.

The Sacred Journey of Life

The ark is opened.

Let us rise to this call:
"*Kadosh* shall you be. . . ."

Dulled by routine, awash in trivia,
assaulted by noise —
can we still hear the ancient voice?

"*Kadosh* shall you be
for *kadosh* am I, the Eternal. . . ."

Within us, beyond us,
the still small voice
urgent, insistent,
summons the soul.

"*K'doshim tiyu*
for *kadosh* am I, the Eternal. . . ."

Lift up your deeds
Awaken to awe
Strive for the good
Hold fast to the truth.

Listen well, family of Israel; the voice still speaks:
Become a holy people — *am kadosh.*
Bring holiness to earth — and live.

Here and now,
bind yourselves to this journey:
make your life a pilgrimage of service,
a sacred ascent.

Eternity dwells within you.
Join yourselves to the Eternal.

The ark is closed.

KADOSH SHALL YOU BE, Leviticus 19:2. From one of the Torah readings in the Yom Kippur Afternoon Service (pages 338–39).

הַקְדָּמָה
Hakdamah

מַסַּע קָדוֹשׁ
Masa Kadosh

אַנְעִים זְמִירוֹת
Anim Z'mirot

A Song of Yearning for the Sacred — Anim Z'mirot

אַנְעִים זְמִירוֹת וְשִׁירִים אֶאֱרֹג
כִּי אֵלֶיךָ נַפְשִׁי תַעֲרֹג.
נַפְשִׁי חִמְּדָה בְּצֵל יָדֶךָ
לָדַעַת כָּל רָז סוֹדֶךָ.
מִדֵּי דַּבְּרִי בִּכְבוֹדֶךָ
הוֹמֶה לִבִּי אֶל דּוֹדֶיךָ.
עַל כֵּן אֲדַבֵּר בְּךָ נִכְבָּדוֹת
וְשִׁמְךָ אֲכַבֵּד בְּשִׁירֵי יְדִידוֹת.

Anim z'mirot v'shirim e·erog
ki eilecha nafshi taarog.
Nafshi chim'dah b'tzeil yadecha
Ladaat kol raz sodecha.
Midei dab'ri bichvodecha
homeh libi el dodecha.
Al kein adabeir b'cha nichbadot
v'shimcha achabeid b'shirei y'didot.

To make You sweet music I weave psalm-songs together;
so deeply for You my soul aches from desire.
My heart's greatest wish is the gift of Your shelter —
to know, to embrace what Your secrets inspire.

When I speak the words to spell out Your radiance,
my verses of love to honor Your name —
I long to be near You, I yearn for Your Presence.
Your glory, Your grandeur is mine to proclaim.

Though I have not known You, about You I have written.
Though I have not seen You, Your splendor I praise.
Your servants, the prophets, reveal what is hidden —
Your beauty evoked by their powerful gaze.

With elegance and grace, in prophecy and poem,
we praise Your compassion, the wonders You have done.
The acts and the attributes by which You are known
are far beyond counting, and yet — You are One.

ANIM Z'MIROT אַנְעִים זְמִירוֹת. Initial words of a poem ascribed to Rabbi Judah the Pious of Regensburg, Germany (d. 1271). Because of its references to God's glory, the poem is often known as *Shir HaKavod* (The Song of Glory). This excerpt conveys an intense longing to forge a connection with the Eternal through the power of language and the creative imagination. Even in the absence of what moderns would call empirical evidence, the poet passionately asserts his capacity to sing of the Divine.

MY SOUL ACHES FROM DESIRE נַפְשִׁי תַעֲרֹג. The language of this *piyut* conveys a sense of erotic desire — for example, the biblical words *dodecha* (literally "Your love") and *ladaat* ("to know; to embrace"). These terms point to the poet's longing for radical spiritual intimacy — a vision of the sacred infused with sensuality.

וְטַעֲמָא דְבֵית הִלֵּל
דְּמַעֲלִין בַּקֹּדֶשׁ
וְאֵין מוֹרִידִין.

V'taama d'veit Hillel
d'maalin bakodesh
v'ein moridin.

According to the Academy of Hillel:
In matters of holiness, we ascend and increase;
we do not descend or diminish.

Life in the presence of God — or the cultivation of a life in the ordinary world bearing the holiness once associated with sacred space and time, with Temple and with holy days — is perhaps as close as one can come to a definition of "spirituality" that is native to the Jewish tradition.

To say God is one means that I must do my best to make God primary to what I value — and in so doing to make God and God's will, as best I can understand them, the criterion of everything else that seems important. Since I have not been blessed with a congenitally pious or mystical soul, gaining and maintaining a living sense of God's primacy in my existence is a constant effort for me, a not unproblematic one but also one not without its joys and rewards. I take it that is what the Jewish religious life, the life of study, commandments, prayer and good deeds is all about, to take the ordinary human stuff most of us are made of and turn it into something very much more noble — dare I say holy?

ACCORDING TO THE ACADEMY OF HILLEL. Talmud *Shabbat* 21b. The Academy of Hillel refers to the school of Jewish law and religious thought founded by Hillel the Elder (ca. 32 BCE–ca. 7 CE).

LIFE IN THE PRESENCE OF GOD. By Rabbi Arthur Green (b. 1941).

TO SAY GOD IS ONE. By Rabbi Eugene B. Borowitz (b. 1924).

מַסַּע אֶל הַקְּדֻשָּׁה
Masa el HaK'dushah · A Journey to Holiness

חֲמֵשׁ־עֶשְׂרֵה עֲלִיּוֹת
Chameish-Esreih Aliyot

שִׁיר הַמַּעֲלוֹת
Shir HaMaalot

עֲלִיָּה א׳ *Aliyah 1*
עֲלִיָּה ב׳ *Aliyah 2*
עֲלִיָּה ג׳ *Aliyah 3*
עֲלִיָּה ד׳ *Aliyah 4*
עֲלִיָּה ה׳ *Aliyah 5*
עֲלִיָּה ו׳ *Aliyah 6*
עֲלִיָּה ז׳ *Aliyah 7*
עֲלִיָּה ח׳ *Aliyah 8*
עֲלִיָּה ט׳ *Aliyah 9*
עֲלִיָּה י׳ *Aliyah 10*
עֲלִיָּה י״א *Aliyah 11*
עֲלִיָּה י״ב *Aliyah 12*
עֲלִיָּה י״ג *Aliyah 13*
עֲלִיָּה י״ד *Aliyah 14*
עֲלִיָּה ט״ו *Aliyah 15*

Fifteen Steps

Fifteen Songs of Ascent in the Book of Psalms —
to what do they correspond?

Our Sages used to teach: Fifteen steps led up to the holy Temple in Jerusalem.
And on these steps, the Levites stood with trumpets and drums:
an orchestra of holiness for the singers of David's psalms.

But others say: The exiles sang the fifteen songs on their journey home.
Step by step, they ascended —
from the rivers of Babylon to the land of Abraham and Sarah.

Another view: The fifteen psalms were songs the pilgrims chanted
as they climbed the hills of Zion —
to celebrate sacred seasons with matzah, first fruits, lulav-and-etrog.

Or perhaps these fifteen songs are timeless —
speaking to the innermost self, tracing the ascent to God of every soul.

Our bodies dwell upon the earth; our souls thirst for the living God.
Like those who came before us, we too seek the holy dimension.

Then and now, fifteen steps mark the ascent —
song and prayer, speech and silence.

Through *Avodah*, our act of sacred service,
let us reach for the Holy One.

FIFTEEN SONGS OF ASCENT. Namely, Psalms 120–134, which all begin with the phrase *Shir HaMaalot* or *Shir LaMaalot* (A Song of Ascents).

OUR SAGES USED TO TEACH. Based on Mishnah *Sukkah* 5:2; Talmud *Sukkah* 51b.

THE EXILES. The Judeans who returned from Babylonian exile, beginning in 538 BCE. Ezra 7:9 refers to "the journey up from Babylon" (*hamaalah miBavel*).

PILGRIMS. Many contemporary scholars believe that the Songs of Ascent were sung by those making the journey up to Jerusalem for the three major festivals: Sukkot, Pesach, and Shavuot.

ASCENT TO GOD OF EVERY SOUL. Philo, a Jewish philosopher of the 1st century CE, understood these psalms allegorically: a description of the soul's ascent from the material world to spiritual union with God.

OUR SOULS THIRST. Based on Psalm 42:3.

A Pilgrimage Song — Psalm 122

Fifteen Steps

Psalm 122
First Step
Second Step
Third Step
Fourth Step
Fifth Step
Sixth Step
Seventh Step
Eighth Step
Ninth Step
Tenth Step
Eleventh Step
Twelfth Step
Thirteenth Step
Fourteenth Step
Fifteenth Step

Shir hamaalot l'David.	שִׁיר הַמַּעֲלוֹת לְדָוִד.
Samachti b'om'rim li: Beit Adonai neileich.	שָׂמַחְתִּי בְּאֹמְרִים לִי: בֵּית יְיָ נֵלֵךְ.
Om'dot hayu ragleinu bisharayich,	עֹמְדוֹת הָיוּ רַגְלֵינוּ בִּשְׁעָרַיִךְ,
Y'rushalayim.	יְרוּשָׁלָיִם.
Y'rushalayim hab'nuyah —	יְרוּשָׁלַיִם הַבְּנוּיָה,
k'ir shechub'rah-lah yachdav.	כְּעִיר שֶׁחֻבְּרָה־לָּהּ יַחְדָּו.
Shesham alu sh'vatim shivtei-Yah	שֶׁשָּׁם עָלוּ שְׁבָטִים שִׁבְטֵי־יָהּ
eidut l'Yisrael l'hodot l'shem Adonai.	עֵדוּת לְיִשְׂרָאֵל לְהֹדוֹת לְשֵׁם יְיָ.
Ki shamah yash'vu chisot l'mishpat	כִּי שָׁמָּה יָשְׁבוּ כִסְאוֹת לְמִשְׁפָּט
kisot l'veit David.	כִּסְאוֹת לְבֵית דָּוִד.
Shaalu sh'lom Y'rushalayim;	שַׁאֲלוּ שְׁלוֹם יְרוּשָׁלָיִם
yishlayu ohavayich.	יִשְׁלָיוּ אֹהֲבָיִךְ.
Y'hi-shalom b'cheileich	יְהִי־שָׁלוֹם בְּחֵילֵךְ
shalvah b'arm'notayich.	שַׁלְוָה בְּאַרְמְנוֹתָיִךְ.
L'maan achai v'rei·ai, adab'rah-na	לְמַעַן אַחַי וְרֵעָי אֲדַבְּרָה־נָּא
shalom bach.	שָׁלוֹם בָּךְ.
L'maan beit-Adonai Eloheinu	לְמַעַן בֵּית־יְיָ אֱלֹהֵינוּ
avakshah tov lach.	אֲבַקְשָׁה טוֹב לָךְ.

A Song of Ascent for David

Jerusalem,
place where each is welcome
all belong

For this is the place
toward which people ascend. . . .

A PILGRIMAGE SONG. This psalm recalls the joy of gathering in the holy city, where all the tribes of Israel would assemble for the festivals. Interpretive translation by Norman Fischer (b. 1946).

Ascending toward the Holiness of God

בְּרֵאשִׁית...

B'reishit

"In the Beginning..." (Genesis 1:1)

Fourth Step
Holy space

Third Step
Holy time

Second Step
The holiness of Creation

First Step
The holiness of God

א First Step
The Holiness of God

Shir HaMaalot — A Song of Ascents

Eilecha nasati et-einai. אֵלֶיךָ נָשָׂאתִי אֶת־עֵינַי.

Unto You
I lift my eyes.

(Psalm 123:1)

May our eyes be opened to the Presence of the One in all things.
Through contemplating the Divine, may we ascend toward the holy.

Holiness —
it begins with the Divine.

The mystics of the Kabbalah teach:
God encompasses all that exists, everything we can ever know.
Every being the eye discerns, every phenomenon hidden from mind —
all dwell within the Infinite, the One we call *Ein Sof.*

No separate selves, no "You," no "I";
all divisions are illusion.
For all are one within the One
and everything is God.

So it is written:
No holiness compares with God;
apart from You, there is nothing. . . .

קָדוֹשׁ קָדוֹשׁ קָדוֹשׁ

Kadosh Kadosh Kadosh — Holy Holy Holy

Holy — in the highest heaven
Holy — upon the earth
Holy — forever and ever

EIN SOF. Literally, "Without End" or "Infinity," a kabbalistic term for God.
NO HOLINESS COMPARES. A mystical reading of I Samuel 2:2.
HOLY . . . HOLY . . . HOLY. Commentary on Isaiah 6:3 from Targum Jonathan.

חֲמֵשׁ־עֶשְׂרֵה עֲלִיּוֹת
Chameish-Esreih Aliyot

שִׁיר הַמַּעֲלוֹת
Shir HaMaalot

עֲלִיָּה א׳
Aliyah 1

עֲלִיָּה ב׳
Aliyah 2

עֲלִיָּה ג׳
Aliyah 3

עֲלִיָּה ד׳
Aliyah 4

עֲלִיָּה ה׳
Aliyah 5

עֲלִיָּה ו׳
Aliyah 6

עֲלִיָּה ז׳
Aliyah 7

עֲלִיָּה ח׳
Aliyah 8

עֲלִיָּה ט׳
Aliyah 9

עֲלִיָּה י׳
Aliyah 10

עֲלִיָּה י״א
Aliyah 11

עֲלִיָּה י״ב
Aliyah 12

עֲלִיָּה י״ג
Aliyah 13

עֲלִיָּה י״ד
Aliyah 14

עֲלִיָּה ט״ו
Aliyah 15

A Dudele

רבונו של עולם, רבונו של עולם,
רבונו של עולם, רבונו של עולם,
רבונו של עולם!
כ׳וועל דיר אַ דודעלע זינגען:
דו, דו, דו, דו, דו!

איה אמצאך, ואיה לא אמצאך?
ווּ קאָן איך דיך יאָ געפֿינען,
און ווּ קאָן איך דיך נישט געפֿינען?
דו, דו, דו, דו, דו!

אַז ווּ איך גיי – דו!
און ווּ איך שטיי – דו!
רק דו, נאָר דו, ווידער דו, אָבער דו!
דו, דו, דו, דו, דו!

איז עמעצן גוט – דו!
חלילה שלעכט – איַי, דו!
אוי, דו, דו, דו, דו, דו – דו!

מזרח – דו, מער – דו,
צפֿון – דו, דרום – דו,
דו, דו, דו, דו, דו!

שמים – דו, ארץ – דו,
מעלה – דו, מטה – דו,
דו, דו, דו, דו, דו!

ווּ איך קער מיך
און ווּ איך ווענד מיך –
דו, דו!

Riboyno shel oylom, Riboyno shel oylom,
Riboyno shel oylom, Riboyno shel oylom,
Riboyno shel oylom!
Ch'vel Dir a dudele zingen:
Du, Du, Du, Du, Du!

Ayeh emtzo·echo, v'ayeh lo emtzo·echo?
Vu kon ich dich yo gefinen,
Un vu kon ich Dich nisht gefinen?
Du, Du, Du, Du, Du!

Az vu ich gey — Du!
Un vu ich shtey — Du!
Rak Du, nor Du, vider Du, ober Du!
Du, Du, Du, Du, Du!

Iz emetz'n gut — Du!
Chalilo shlecht — ay, Du!
Oy, Du, Du, Du, Du, Du — Du!

Mizrech — Du, mer — Du
Tsofun — Du, dorem — Du
Du, Du, Du, Du, Du!

Shamayim — Du, oretz — Du,
Mayle — Du, matah — Du
Du, Du, Du, Du, Du!

Vu ich ker mich
Un vu ich vend mich —
Du, Du!

Ruler of the World,
I will sing You a song!
Where shall I find You?
And where shall I not find You?

Where I wander — You are there.
Where I sojourn — You are there.
Only You, always You.
You! You! You!

When I am joyful — it is You.
When I am woeful — it is You.
Only You, always You.
You! You! You!

East and west, north and south,
In all directions — to and fro,
In the sky and on the earth,
You above and You below —
Only You, always You.
You! You! You!

RULER OF THE WORLD רבונו של עולם. This Yiddish song, by the Chasidic rabbi Levi Yitzchak of Berditchev (1740–1809), uses the intimate form of "you" (*du*) as well as the more formal Talmudic name "Ruler/Master of the World" (*Riboyno shel oylom*) to address God. The song alludes to Hebrew lines by the medieval poet Yehudah Halevi (d. 1141): "Where shall I find You? Your place is high and hidden. And where shall I not find You? Your glory fills the world."

אֲדוֹן עוֹלָם אֲשֶׁר מָלַךְ,
בְּטֶרֶם כָּל יְצִיר נִבְרָא.
לְעֵת נַעֲשָׂה בְחֶפְצוֹ כֹּל,
אֲזַי מֶלֶךְ שְׁמוֹ נִקְרָא.

Adon olam asher malach,
b'terem kol y'tzir nivra.
L'eit naasah v'cheftzo kol,
azai Melech sh'mo nikra.

Eternal God, who reigned before the earth was formed and life appeared,
when all came forth as You desired, You ruled supreme, Your name revered.

And after all shall fade away, alone our God of Awe remains;
You were, You are, shall always be; Your presence shines; Your glory reigns.

Our God is One, beyond compare; through You we glimpse pure unity.
Unbound by words like "first" and "last," our Moment of eternity.

My living God, my Rock, my Help, in times of grief I seek Your face;
my sign of hope, my cup of life — my prayer reveals Your sheltering place.

My soul entrusted to Your care, both when I sleep and when I rise.
My body, too, will rest in You. I have no fear — for God is mine.

בָּרוּךְ אַתָּה, יְיָ, מְקוֹר הַקְּדֻשָּׁה.

Baruch atah, Adonai, m'kor hak'dushah.

Blessed are You, Eternal Presence,
the holiness at the heart of existence.

חֲמֵשׁ־עֶשְׂרֵה עֲלִיּוֹת *Chameish-Esreih Aliyot*
שִׁיר הַמַּעֲלוֹת *Shir HaMaalot*
עֲלִיָּה א׳ *Aliyah 1*
עֲלִיָּה ב׳ *Aliyah 2*
עֲלִיָּה ג׳ *Aliyah 3*
עֲלִיָּה ד׳ *Aliyah 4*
עֲלִיָּה ה׳ *Aliyah 5*
עֲלִיָּה ו׳ *Aliyah 6*
עֲלִיָּה ז׳ *Aliyah 7*
עֲלִיָּה ח׳ *Aliyah 8*
עֲלִיָּה ט׳ *Aliyah 9*
עֲלִיָּה י׳ *Aliyah 10*
עֲלִיָּה י״א *Aliyah 11*
עֲלִיָּה י״ב *Aliyah 12*
עֲלִיָּה י״ג *Aliyah 13*
עֲלִיָּה י״ד *Aliyah 14*
עֲלִיָּה ט״ו *Aliyah 15*

ETERNAL GOD, WHO REIGNED אֲדוֹן עוֹלָם אֲשֶׁר מָלַךְ. Attributed to the 11th–century Spanish poet and philosopher Rabbi Solomon ibn Gabirol. The poet imagines a primordial time when God's holiness was all that existed in the cosmos. Only after other conscious beings were summoned forth to life was God acknowledged as Sovereign.

MY LIVING GOD . . . FOR GOD IS MINE. In the first three stanzas of this song, the poet's voice is that of a theologian and philosopher. We notice, however, that the more the poet sings about God, the more personal he becomes. Indeed, in the last two stanzas the philosopher-poet turns from the world of ideas to an inner world of personal faith and belief. Wrote Rabbi Abraham Joshua Heschel (1907–1972): "The power of worship is song. First we sing, then we understand." The singable English translation on this page allows one to put Rabbi Heschel's assertion to the test.

Fifteen Steps
Psalm 122
First Step
Second Step
Third Step
Fourth Step
Fifth Step
Sixth Step
Seventh Step
Eighth Step
Ninth Step
Tenth Step
Eleventh Step
Twelfth Step
Thirteenth Step
Fourteenth Step
Fifteenth Step

ב

Second Step
The Holiness of Creation

Shir HaMaalot — A Song of Ascents

Esa einai el-heharim: mei·ayin yavo ezri? אֶשָּׂא עֵינַי אֶל־הֶהָרִים: מֵאַיִן יָבֹא עֶזְרִי.
Ezri mei·im Adonai, oseih shamayim vaaretz. עֶזְרִי מֵעִם יְיָ, עֹשֵׂה שָׁמַיִם וָאָרֶץ.

I lift my eyes to the mountains: from where will my help come?
My help comes from the Eternal, Maker of heaven and earth.

(Psalm 121:1–2)

We marvel at the abiding miracle of our existence,
the primordial explosion of Being and light, our origins in Oneness.
Through contemplating the mystery of Creation, may we ascend toward the holy.

בְּרֵאשִׁית בָּרָא אֱלֹהִים אֵת הַשָּׁמַיִם וְאֵת הָאָרֶץ. וְהָאָרֶץ הָיְתָה תֹהוּ וָבֹהוּ,
וְחֹשֶׁךְ עַל־פְּנֵי תְהוֹם, וְרוּחַ אֱלֹהִים מְרַחֶפֶת עַל־פְּנֵי הַמָּיִם.
וַיֹּאמֶר אֱלֹהִים יְהִי אוֹר, וַיְהִי־אוֹר.

WHEN GOD BEGAN to create heaven and earth — the earth being unformed and void, with darkness over the surface of the deep and a wind from God sweeping over the water — God said, "Let there be light," and there was light.

Oneness is grounded in scientific reality.
We are made of the same stuff as all of creation.
Everything that is, was, or will be
started off together as one infinitesimal point:
the cosmic seed.

Life has since branched out, but this should not blind us to its underlying unity.

Said the Neshkizer Rebbe:
To every one of us creation comes as a new thing, again and again,
and so we are bound to acknowledge the Creator again and again.

WHEN GOD BEGAN, Genesis 1:1–3.
GOD SAID. The philosopher and rabbi Moses Maimonides (1135–1204) teaches in his *Guide of the Perplexed* (1:65) that such anthropomorphic terms for God are never to be taken literally.
ONENESS IS GROUNDED . . . UNDERLYING UNITY. By Daniel Matt (b. 1951).
NESHKIZER REBBE. Rabbi Mordechai of Neshkiz (d. 1800) or his son, Rabbi Yitzchak (d. 1868).

In Praise

Hail the hand that scattered space with stars,
Wrapped whirling world in bright blue blanket, air,
Made worlds within worlds, elements in earth,
Souls within skins, every one a teeming universe,
Every tree a system of semantics, and pushed
Beyond probability to place consciousness
On this cooling crust of burning rock.

Oh praise that hand, mind, heart, soul, power or force
That so inclosed, separated, limited planets, trees, humans
Yet breaks all bounds and borders
To lavish on us light, love, life
This trembling glory.

Psalm 8

Unnamable God, how measureless
   is your power on all the earth
   and how radiant in the sky!
When I look up at your heavens,
   the work of your fingers,
   the moon and the multitude of stars,
what is man, that you love him,
   and woman, that you gladden her heart?
Yet you made us almost like the angels
   and crowned us with understanding.
You put us in charge of all creatures
   and placed your whole earth in our hands:
all animals, tame and wild,
   all forests, fields, and deserts,
even the pure air of the sky,
   even the depths of the ocean.
Unnamable God, how terrible
   is our power on all the earth!

חֲמֵשׁ־עֶשְׂרֵה עֲלִיוֹת
Chameish-Esreih Aliyot

שִׁיר הַמַּעֲלוֹת
Shir HaMaalot

עֲלִיָּה א׳
Aliyah 1

עֲלִיָּה ב׳
Aliyah 2

עֲלִיָּה ג׳
Aliyah 3

עֲלִיָּה ד׳
Aliyah 4

עֲלִיָּה ה׳
Aliyah 5

עֲלִיָּה ו׳
Aliyah 6

עֲלִיָּה ז׳
Aliyah 7

עֲלִיָּה ח׳
Aliyah 8

עֲלִיָּה ט׳
Aliyah 9

עֲלִיָּה י׳
Aliyah 10

עֲלִיָּה י״א
Aliyah 11

עֲלִיָּה י״ב
Aliyah 12

עֲלִיָּה י״ג
Aliyah 13

עֲלִיָּה י״ד
Aliyah 14

עֲלִיָּה ט״ו
Aliyah 15

IN PRAISE. By Ruth Brin (1921–2009).
PSALM 8. Adapted by Stephen Mitchell (b. 1943).

Primary Wonder

Days pass when I forget the mystery.
Problems insoluble and problems offering
their own ignored solutions
jostle for my attention, they crowd its antechamber
along with a host of diversions, my courtiers, wearing
their colored clothes; cap and bells.
And then
once more the quiet mystery
is present to me, the throng's clamor
recedes: the mystery
that there is anything, anything at all,
let alone cosmos, joy, memory, everything,
rather than void: and that, O Lord,
Creator, Hallowed One, You still,
hour by hour sustain it.

From Psalm 66

Hariu l'Elohim, kol haaretz.	הָרִיעוּ לֵאלֹהִים כָּל־הָאָרֶץ.
Zam'ru ch'vod sh'mo;	זַמְּרוּ כְבוֹד־שְׁמוֹ,
simu chavod t'hilato.	שִׂימוּ כָבוֹד תְּהִלָּתוֹ.
Imru l'Elohim:	אִמְרוּ לֵאלֹהִים:
"Mah nora maasecha."	מַה־נּוֹרָא מַעֲשֶׂיךָ.

Raise a shout, all creation, to God
To the Name of glory sing out
To the Praise of glory give voice
To God you shall say:
"How great the awe Your works inspire."

בָּרוּךְ אַתָּה, יְיָ, יוֹצֵר מַעֲשֵׂה בְרֵאשִׁית.
Baruch atah, Adonai, yotzeir maaseih v'reishit.

Blessed are You, Eternal Presence,
creative force at the heart of existence.

PRIMARY WONDER. By Denise Levertov (1923–1997).
PSALM 66, verses 1–3.

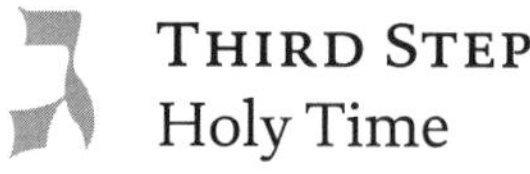

Third Step
Holy Time

חֲמֵשׁ־עֶשְׂרֵה עֲלִיּוֹת
Chameish-Esreih Aliyot

שִׁיר הַמַּעֲלוֹת
Shir HaMaalot

עֲלִיָּה א׳ *Aliyah 1*
עֲלִיָּה ב׳ *Aliyah 2*
עֲלִיָּה ג׳ *Aliyah 3*
עֲלִיָּה ד׳ *Aliyah 4*
עֲלִיָּה ה׳ *Aliyah 5*
עֲלִיָּה ו׳ *Aliyah 6*
עֲלִיָּה ז׳ *Aliyah 7*
עֲלִיָּה ח׳ *Aliyah 8*
עֲלִיָּה ט׳ *Aliyah 9*
עֲלִיָּה י׳ *Aliyah 10*
עֲלִיָּה י״א *Aliyah 11*
עֲלִיָּה י״ב *Aliyah 12*
עֲלִיָּה י״ג *Aliyah 13*
עֲלִיָּה י״ד *Aliyah 14*
עֲלִיָּה ט״ו *Aliyah 15*

Shir HaMaalot — A Song of Ascents

Nafshi l'Adonai mishom'rim laboker נַפְשִׁי לַאדֹנָי מִשֹּׁמְרִים לַבֹּקֶר

I am more eager for the Eternal
than watchmen for the morning.

(Psalm 130:6)

Through celebration of Shabbat and festivals, may we ascend toward the holy.

וַיְכֻלּוּ הַשָּׁמַיִם וְהָאָרֶץ וְכָל־צְבָאָם. וַיְכַל אֱלֹהִים בַּיּוֹם
הַשְּׁבִיעִי מְלַאכְתּוֹ אֲשֶׁר עָשָׂה . . . וַיְבָרֶךְ אֱלֹהִים
אֶת־יוֹם הַשְּׁבִיעִי, וַיְקַדֵּשׁ אֹתוֹ . . .

The heaven and the earth were finished, and all their array.
On the seventh day, God finished the work that had been done. . . .
And God blessed the seventh day and declared it holy. . . .

Holiness entered the world as God's final gift of Creation:
Shabbat,
first taste of sacred time.
A festival whose name is "Cessation" —
renewing the body,
restoring the soul.

Island of stillness . . .
a day of detachment from things, instruments, and practical affairs . . .
a day of attachment to the spirit.

Remember the Sabbath day, to keep it holy.
Six days shall you labor and do all your work.
But the seventh day is a Sabbath for the Eternal your God.

THE HEAVEN AND THE EARTH, Genesis 2:1–3.
CESSATION. Literal meaning of the word *shabbat*. It may also be translated as "Stopping."
ISLAND OF STILLNESS. By Rabbi Abraham Joshua Heschel (1907–1972).
REMEMBER THE SABBATH DAY. The fourth commandment, Exodus 20:7–9.

Fifteen Steps
Psalm 122
First Step
Second Step
Third Step
Fourth Step
Fifth Step
Sixth Step
Seventh Step
Eighth Step
Ninth Step
Tenth Step
Eleventh Step
Twelfth Step
Thirteenth Step
Fourteenth Step
Fifteenth Step

At the time of Creation, Shabbat said to the Holy One:
"Ruler of the universe, every living thing has its mate,
and each day has its companion — save for me; I am alone."
Said the Holy One: "The people of Israel will be your mate."

So when the Israelites came to Sinai, the Holy One instructed them:
"Recall My words — Shabbat will be your mate."
Thus we are commanded: *Remember the Sabbath day, to keep it holy.*
Shabbat is yours, to guard and protect, to cherish and hold sacred.

Meditation

For our ancestors, the Seventh Day was a sign of their covenant with God.
They kept it faithfully.
When their lives were torn by violence from without,
Shabbat made them whole within.
When their lives were embittered, Shabbat brought them sweetness.
When their lives were peaceful, Shabbat deepened their joy.

Our ways are not like theirs.
We have leisure time, retreats and vacations, idle days —
but few Sabbaths.
We speak many words —
but few that remind us of the covenant.
We praise proficiency at time management —
but forget the holiness of the moment.

Let us emerge from this Sabbath of Sabbaths renewed in our quest for wholeness —
reawakened to the urgent beauty of being present in a God-filled world.
Let us crown the Seventh Day
by living it —
by tasting its sweetness,
by feeling its joy,
by opening ourselves to it in awe.

AT THE TIME OF CREATION . . . HOLD SACRED. Based on Midrash *Genesis Rabbah* 11.8.

חֲמֵשׁ־עֶשְׂרֵה עֲלִיּוֹת
Chameish-Esreih Aliyot

שִׁיר הַמַּעֲלוֹת
Shir HaMaalot

עֲלִיָּה א׳ *Aliyah 1* · עֲלִיָּה ב׳ *Aliyah 2* · עֲלִיָּה ג׳ *Aliyah 3* · עֲלִיָּה ד׳ *Aliyah 4* · עֲלִיָּה ה׳ *Aliyah 5* · עֲלִיָּה ו׳ *Aliyah 6* · עֲלִיָּה ז׳ *Aliyah 7* · עֲלִיָּה ח׳ *Aliyah 8* · עֲלִיָּה ט׳ *Aliyah 9* · עֲלִיָּה י׳ *Aliyah 10* · עֲלִיָּה י״א *Aliyah 11* · עֲלִיָּה י״ב *Aliyah 12* · עֲלִיָּה י״ג *Aliyah 13* · עֲלִיָּה י״ד *Aliyah 14* · עֲלִיָּה ט״ו *Aliyah 15*

Judaism teaches us to be attached to *holiness in time*, to be attached to sacred events, to learn how to consecrate sanctuaries that emerge from the magnificent stream of a year.

אֵלֶּה מוֹעֲדֵי יְיָ, מִקְרָאֵי קֹדֶשׁ אֲשֶׁר־תִּקְרְאוּ אֹתָם בְּמוֹעֲדָם.

These are the set times of the Eternal, the sacred occasions you shall celebrate, each at its appointed time.

The Sabbaths are our great cathedrals; and our Holy of Holies is a shrine that neither the Romans nor the Germans were able to burn; a shrine that even apostasy cannot easily obliterate: the Day of Atonement.

The festivals act as lodgings for travelers making their way through the year.
These festival inns are special accommodations
not solely for rest or retreat from the world,
but also places to halt and take our bearings
to make sure we are traveling
and not just going around in circles.
These are inns not for sleeping
but rather for awakening from obliviousness.

This is the gift of holy time:
a year adorned with *mo·adim* —
festivals and hallowed assemblies
sanctified and set apart from the steady flow of our days.

Sheltered in these sacred meeting-times,
we see our lives afresh —
small chapters in a greater story.

בָּרוּךְ אַתָּה, יְיָ, אֱלֹהֵינוּ מֶלֶךְ הָעוֹלָם,
אֲשֶׁר בִּקְדֻשָּׁתוֹ נָתַן־לָנוּ מוֹעֲדֵי קֹדֶשׁ.

Baruch atah, Adonai, Eloheinu melech haolam,
asher bikdushato natan-lanu mo·adei kodesh.

Blessed are You, Eternal Presence, by whose power we experience the holiness of Israel's sacred times and seasons.

JUDAISM TEACHES . . . DAY OF ATONEMENT. By Rabbi Abraham Joshua Heschel (1907–1972).
THESE ARE THE SET TIMES, Leviticus 23:4.
THE SABBATHS. By Rabbi Abraham Joshua Heschel.
THE FESTIVALS . . . AWAKENING FROM OBLIVIOUSNESS. By Rabbi Michael Strassfeld (b. 1950).

ד

FOURTH STEP
Holy Space

Shir HaMaalot — A Song of Ascents

S'u-y'deichem kodesh, uvar'chu et-Adonai. שְׂאוּ־יְדֵכֶם קֹדֶשׁ, וּבָרְכוּ אֶת־יְיָ.

Lift up your hands to the sanctuary
and bless the Eternal.

(Psalm 134:2)

By remembering the Mishkan and the Temple,
may we ascend toward the holy.

HOLINESS —
It entered the life of the Jewish people through the priests
and their sacred service at God's altar.

V'asu li mikdash, v'shachanti b'tocham. וְעָשׂוּ לִי מִקְדָּשׁ, וְשָׁכַנְתִּי בְּתוֹכָם.

Said the Holy One to Moses:
"Let them make Me a sanctuary,
that I may dwell among them."

Long ago — in a Tent in the wilderness, in the Temples of Jerusalem —
our ancestors reached for God through sacrificial offerings:
with bulls and goats and sheep, with grains and wine and oil.

וְאָמַרְתָּ לָהֶם: זֶה הָאִשֶּׁה אֲשֶׁר תַּקְרִיבוּ לַייָ.

Say to the Israelite people:
"These are the offerings by fire
that you shall present to the Eternal."

HOLY SPACE. When history began, there was only one holiness in the world, holiness in time. . . . It was only after the people had succumbed to the temptation of worshiping a thing, a golden calf, that the erection of a Tabernacle, of holiness in space, was commanded. The sanctity of time came first . . . and the sanctity of space last. Time was hallowed by God; space, the Tabernacle, was consecrated by Moses. (Rabbi Abraham Joshua Heschel)

MISHKAN. Literally, "dwelling place"; a biblical name for the Tabernacle, the temporary sanctuary in the wilderness.

LET THEM MAKE ME A SANCTUARY, Exodus 25:8.

SAY TO THE ISRAELITE PEOPLE, Numbers 28:3.

חֲמֵשׁ־עֶשְׂרֵה עֲלִיּוֹת
Chameish-Esreih Aliyot

שִׁיר הַמַּעֲלוֹת
Shir HaMaalot

עֲלִיָּה א׳ *Aliyah 1*
עֲלִיָּה ב׳ *Aliyah 2*
עֲלִיָּה ג׳ *Aliyah 3*
עֲלִיָּה ד׳ *Aliyah 4*
עֲלִיָּה ה׳ *Aliyah 5*
עֲלִיָּה ו׳ *Aliyah 6*
עֲלִיָּה ז׳ *Aliyah 7*
עֲלִיָּה ח׳ *Aliyah 8*
עֲלִיָּה ט׳ *Aliyah 9*
עֲלִיָּה י׳ *Aliyah 10*
עֲלִיָּה י״א *Aliyah 11*
עֲלִיָּה י״ב *Aliyah 12*
עֲלִיָּה י״ג *Aliyah 13*
עֲלִיָּה י״ד *Aliyah 14*
עֲלִיָּה ט״ו *Aliyah 15*

Bring All That I Command You

וַעֲבַרְתֶּם אֶת־הַיַּרְדֵּן וִישַׁבְתֶּם בָּאָרֶץ אֲשֶׁר־יְיָ אֱלֹהֵיכֶם מַנְחִיל אֶתְכֶם, וְהֵנִיחַ לָכֶם מִכָּל־אֹיְבֵיכֶם מִסָּבִיב וִישַׁבְתֶּם־בֶּטַח. וְהָיָה הַמָּקוֹם אֲשֶׁר־יִבְחַר יְיָ אֱלֹהֵיכֶם בּוֹ לְשַׁכֵּן שְׁמוֹ שָׁם, שָׁמָּה תָבִיאוּ אֵת כָּל־אֲשֶׁר אָנֹכִי מְצַוֶּה אֶתְכֶם, עוֹלֹתֵיכֶם וְזִבְחֵיכֶם מַעְשְׂרֹתֵיכֶם וּתְרֻמַת יֶדְכֶם וְכֹל מִבְחַר נִדְרֵיכֶם אֲשֶׁר תִּדְּרוּ לַייָ.

When you cross the Jordan and settle in the land that the Eternal your God is granting you as a legacy, God will give you safety from all your surrounding enemies and you will live in security. Then you shall bring all that I command you to the place where the Eternal your God will choose to establish the Divine Name: your burnt offerings and your sacrifices, your tithes and the gift of your hand, and all your choice votive offerings that you vow to the Eternal.

My Tithe: A Psalm

How to explain this impulse to bring to an altar some gift or tithe?
I am, by now, so settled into my land of uncertainty,
reticent about religion, ambivalent about faith.
And yet, I cannot help but wonder —
Is it too late to turn my place of doubt into a sanctuary of hope?
Find within myself a song of praise, a few plain words of thanks?
For what?
For the freedom to think my own thoughts.
For the feeling of awe when I gaze at the night sky.
For the capacity of the human mind to reflect on the universe.
Perhaps, then, there is no need to explain —
let my thoughts be my gift;
let the search for truth be my tithe;
and let awe bring me to places where holiness dwells.

WHEN YOU CROSS THE JORDAN, Deuteronomy 12:10–11.
GOD WILL GIVE YOU SAFETY וְהֵנִיחַ לָכֶם. These verses reflect the centralization of worship in the Jerusalem Temple sometime between the late 8th century BCE and the late 7th century — an era framed by two periods of reform under Kings Hezekiah and Josiah, respectively. The centralization of worship could only happen when pilgrims felt that they could leave their homes unprotected for a time, sure that their journey to Jerusalem (for Pesach, Shavuot, and Sukkot) would be safe. The success of the Temple as a spiritual institution depended on physical safety and security.

Fifteen Steps
Psalm 122
First Step
Second Step
Third Step
Fourth Step
Fifth Step
Sixth Step
Seventh Step
Eighth Step
Ninth Step
Tenth Step
Eleventh Step
Twelfth Step
Thirteenth Step
Fourteenth Step
Fifteenth Step

וְעָשׂוּ לִי מִקְדָּשׁ, וְשָׁכַנְתִּי בְּתוֹכָם.

V'asu li mikdash, v'shachanti b'tocham.

Let them make Me a sanctuary,
that I may dwell among them.

What gave the Tabernacle and the Temple their holiness?

They were created through heartfelt generosity. . . .

And everyone who excelled in ability and all whose spirits moved them came, bringing to the Eternal their offerings for the work of the Tent of Meeting and for all its service and for the sacral vestments. Men and women, all whose hearts moved them, all who would make an elevation offering of gold to the Eternal, came bringing brooches, earrings, rings, and pendants—gold objects of all kinds. And all who had in their possession blue, purple, and crimson yarns, fine linen, goats' hair, tanned ram skins, and dolphin skins, brought them; everyone who would make gifts of silver or copper brought them as gifts for the Eternal; and all who had in their possession acacia wood for any work of the service brought that.

And all the skilled women spun with their own hands, and brought what they had spun, in blue, purple, and crimson yarns, and in fine linen. And all the women who excelled in that skill spun the goats' hair. And the chieftains brought lapis lazuli and other stones for setting, for the ephod and for the breastpiece; and spices and oil for lighting, for the anointing oil, and for the aromatic incense. Thus the Israelites, all the men and women whose hearts moved them to bring anything for the work that the Eternal, through Moses, had commanded to be done, brought it as a freewill offering to the Eternal.

LET THEM MAKE וְעָשׂוּ, Exodus 25:8.

AND EVERYONE. Exodus 35:21–29.

HEARTFELT GENEROSITY. *T'rumah* ("gift, donation, offering") comes from a verb that means "to elevate." Not only is the offering lifted up to God and priest; by dedicating our gifts to a sacred purpose our lives are uplifted, as well. Rabbinic commentators on the Torah, both medieval and modern, note that this passage is highly unusual because of its repeated description of women and men as equal partners in the creation of the *Mishkan* (Tabernacle). We see in Exodus 35:21–29 a spiritual community in which men and women are depicted as equal in their enthusiasm and generosity. And further, their gifts are equally valued. This adds immeasurably to the holiness of Israel's meeting-place with the Divine.

What gave the Tabernacle and the Temple their holiness?

Each was created as a place to bear witness to the Divine.... עֵדוּת

On this our faith is founded: God is boundless, ever-present, unseen by the eye — a still, small voice having neither body, form, nor image. God can be praised in all places, encountered anywhere. Yet we have built sanctuaries to praise the Ineffable and contain our experience of the Uncontainable.

"You are My witnesses (*atem eidai*)," declares Adonai. Through Tabernacle and Temple our people witnessed God's presence. There they testified to a divine reality and affirmed that a meeting-place with God is possible. There they created holy space in which to ground and give structure to their spiritual yearnings and insights. And there they expressed, through signs and symbols, their belief that human beings can create in this world a direct connection with God.

They were created to bring light into the world.... אוֹר

When human beings build a house, they make it with windows that are narrow on the outside and broad within, so that the light may enter from outside and illuminate the interior. King Solomon, however, who built the Temple, did not do it in this manner, but made windows that were narrow on the inside and broad on the outside, so that the light might go forth from the Temple and shine outside.

בָּרוּךְ אַתָּה, יְיָ, הַשּׁוֹכֵן בְּתוֹכֵנוּ בִּקְדֻשָּׁה.

Baruch atah, Adonai, hashochein b'tocheinu bikdushah.

Blessed are You, Eternal Presence,
who dwells among us in holiness.

STILL, SMALL VOICE, I Kings 19:12.
NEITHER BODY, FORM, OR IMAGE. From the hymn *Yigdal*.
YOU ARE MY WITNESSES, Isaiah 43:10.
WHEN HUMAN BEINGS, Midrash *Numbers Rabbah* VI:642–43.
BRING LIGHT INTO THE WORLD. According to the Midrash, the *Mishkan* (Tabernacle) was an extraordinary structure: its physical design was intended to fulfill the words of the Priestly Blessing: "May God's face shine upon you...." (Numbers 6:25). Through the symbolism of its windows, the *Mishkan* is understood as a source of light for the entire world, illuminating the world with the radiance of God's presence.

חֲמֵשׁ־עֶשְׂרֵה עֲלִיּוֹת
Chameish-Esreih Aliyot

שִׁיר הַמַּעֲלוֹת
Shir HaMaalot

עֲלִיָּה א'
Aliyah 1

עֲלִיָּה ב'
Aliyah 2

עֲלִיָּה ג'
Aliyah 3

עֲלִיָּה ד'
Aliyah 4

עֲלִיָּה ה'
Aliyah 5

עֲלִיָּה ו'
Aliyah 6

עֲלִיָּה ז'
Aliyah 7

עֲלִיָּה ח'
Aliyah 8

עֲלִיָּה ט'
Aliyah 9

עֲלִיָּה י'
Aliyah 10

עֲלִיָּה י"א
Aliyah 11

עֲלִיָּה י"ב
Aliyah 12

עֲלִיָּה י"ג
Aliyah 13

עֲלִיָּה י"ד
Aliyah 14

עֲלִיָּה ט"ו
Aliyah 15

Ascending toward the Holiness of Yom Kippur

יְכַפֵּר עֲלֵיכֶם...

Y'chapeir aleichem . . .

"Atonement shall be made for you . . ." (Leviticus 16:30)

Seventh Step
The holy act of sacrificial offering

Sixth Step
The holy act of confession

Fifth Step
The holy day: Yom Kippur

Fifth Step
The Holy Day: Yom Kippur

חֲמֵשׁ־עֶשְׂרֵה עֲלִיּוֹת
Chameish-Esreih Aliyot

שִׁיר הַמַּעֲלוֹת
Shir HaMaalot

עֲלִיָּה א׳
Aliyah 1

עֲלִיָּה ב׳
Aliyah 2

עֲלִיָּה ג׳
Aliyah 3

עֲלִיָּה ד׳
Aliyah 4

עֲלִיָּה ה׳
Aliyah 5

עֲלִיָּה ו׳
Aliyah 6

עֲלִיָּה ז׳
Aliyah 7

עֲלִיָּה ח׳
Aliyah 8

עֲלִיָּה ט׳
Aliyah 9

עֲלִיָּה י׳
Aliyah 10

עֲלִיָּה י״א
Aliyah 11

עֲלִיָּה י״ב
Aliyah 12

עֲלִיָּה י״ג
Aliyah 13

עֲלִיָּה י״ד
Aliyah 14

עֲלִיָּה ט״ו
Aliyah 15

Shir HaMaalot — A Song of Ascents

אֶל־יְיָ בַּצָּרָתָה לִּי קָרָאתִי וַיַּעֲנֵנִי.

El-Adonai batzaratah li karati vayaaneini.

To the Eternal I called
in my distress;
and God responded to me.

(Psalm 120:1)

By recalling our people's ancient rites of Yom Kippur, may we ascend toward the holy.

Dawn: The Holy Day

The morning horizon glowed before the gaze of the watchman.
As they spread a curtain of linen, to give the High Priest privacy,
he removed his clothing and immersed in the *mikveh* — the first of five baths —
then dressed himself in garments of gold.
He stood, in a state of holiness, to begin the first offering;
he kindled incense and lamps, brought forth sacrifice and libation. . . .
Having bathed again, he wore a white robe —
an exquisite garment to serve the Sovereign of Glory.

THE MORNING HORIZON. This description of the ancient Yom Kippur ritual in the Jerusalem Temple is drawn from *Amitz Ko·ach*, a *piyut* (religious poem) composed by Rabbi Meshulam ben Kalonymus (10th century CE). The *piyut* consists of three sections: 1) a history of the world from Creation through the time of the Patriarchs; 2) a description of the Yom Kippur rite, primarily drawn from Mishnah *Yoma*; 3) an account of the celebration following the High Priest's completion of the Temple service.

SACRIFICE AND LIBATION. Numbers 29:7–11 sets forth the sacrificial offering for Yom Kippur: "On the tenth day of the seventh month you shall observe a sacred occasion. . . . You shall present to the Eternal a burnt offering of pleasing odor: one bull of the herd, one ram, seven yearling lambs; see that they are without blemish. The meal offering with them — of choice flour with oil mixed in — shall be: three-tenths of a measure for a bull, two-tenths for the one ram, one-tenth for each of the seven lambs. And there shall be one goat for a sin offering, in addition to the sin offering of expiation and the regular burnt offering with its meal offering, each with its libation."

Fifteen Steps
Psalm 122
First Step
Second Step
Third Step
Fourth Step
Fifth Step
Sixth Step
Seventh Step
Eighth Step
Ninth Step
Tenth Step
Eleventh Step
Twelfth Step
Thirteenth Step
Fourteenth Step
Fifteenth Step

Our Sages teach:

There are seventy peoples in the world.
Among these holy peoples is the people of Israel.
The holiest of the people of Israel was the tribe of Levi.
The holiest in the tribe of Levi were the priests.
The holiest among the priests was the High Priest.

The world God made is holy.
Among the holy lands in the world is the holy Land of Israel.
The holiest city in the Land of Israel is Jerusalem.
The holiest place in Jerusalem was the Temple.
And the holiest place in the Temple was the Holy of Holies.

Among the days of the year, the festivals are holy.
Higher than the festivals is the Holy Sabbath.
The holiest Sabbath — the Sabbath of Sabbaths — is Yom Kippur.

There are seventy languages in the world.
Among the holy languages is Hebrew.
The holiest words in Hebrew are the words of the Torah.
The holiest utterances in the Torah are the Ten Commandments,
and the holiest word in the Ten Commandments is the Name of God.

One word
on the lips of one person
in one place
at one moment
brought together these four dimensions of the holy:
when the High Priest would enter the Holy of Holies on Yom Kippur
and utter the Name of God.

בָּרוּךְ אַתָּה, יְיָ, הַמְכַפֵּר לָנוּ בְּיוֹם הַכִּפּוּרִים.

Baruch atah, Adonai, hamchaper lanu b'Yom HaKippurim.

Blessed are You, Eternal Presence,
who leads us to atonement on this holy day.

OUR SAGES TEACH. Adapted from a Jewish folktale in *The Dybbuk* by S. An-Ski (1863–1920).

ו

Sixth Step
The Holy Act of Confession

חֲמֵשׁ־עֶשְׂרֵה עֲלִיּוֹת
Chameish-Esreih Aliyot

שִׁיר הַמַּעֲלוֹת
Shir HaMaalot

עֲלִיָּה א׳ *Aliyah 1*
עֲלִיָּה ב׳ *Aliyah 2*
עֲלִיָּה ג׳ *Aliyah 3*
עֲלִיָּה ד׳ *Aliyah 4*
עֲלִיָּה ה׳ *Aliyah 5*
עֲלִיָּה ו׳ *Aliyah 6*
עֲלִיָּה ז׳ *Aliyah 7*
עֲלִיָּה ח׳ *Aliyah 8*
עֲלִיָּה ט׳ *Aliyah 9*
עֲלִיָּה י׳ *Aliyah 10*
עֲלִיָּה י״א *Aliyah 11*
עֲלִיָּה י״ב *Aliyah 12*
עֲלִיָּה י״ג *Aliyah 13*
עֲלִיָּה י״ד *Aliyah 14*
עֲלִיָּה ט״ו *Aliyah 15*

Shir HaMaalot — A Song of Ascents

וְהוּא יִפְדֶּה אֶת־יִשְׂרָאֵל מִכֹּל עֲוֺנֹתָיו.

V'hu yifdeh et-Yisrael mikol avonotav.

The Eternal will redeem us
from all our moral failures.

(Psalm 130:8)

Through sincere confession, offered in humility, may we ascend toward the holy.

Within the Holy of Holies the High Priest spoke words of confession —
first, for himself and his family;
then, for the priests who served at his side;
and, finally, for the whole community.

His hands on the head of a bull, he confessed all their sins and his own.
Nothing was concealed in his heart.

Quietly he spoke the four letters that form God's name.
Quietly — so none would hear.

For the holiest name was known only to him.
Clear and pure were the High Priest's confessions —
a ladder
for the soul
seeking
atonement

WITHIN THE HOLY OF HOLIES. The poets of Israel have woven a tapestry that gives the worshiper, centuries and continents removed from the Temple, a feeling of immediacy and of being, even now, a participant in those moments of spiritual grandeur. (Rabbi Berel Wein, b. 1934)

HIS HANDS . . . IN HIS HEART. Adapted from *Amitz Ko·ach*, a *piyut* (religious poem) composed by Rabbi Meshulam ben Kalonymus (10th century CE).

Fifteen Steps
Psalm 122
First Step
Second Step
Third Step
Fourth Step
Fifth Step
Sixth Step
Seventh Step
Eighth Step
Ninth Step
Tenth Step
Eleventh Step
Twelfth Step
Thirteenth Step
Fourteenth Step
Fifteenth Step

The High Priest's Confession

God, I plead before You:
We have sinned.
We have done wrong.
We have rebelled against You —
my family and I,
the community of priests,
and the whole House of Israel.
I beseech You by Your name:
grant atonement for the sins, the wrongs, and the acts of rebellion
that we have committed against You —
my family and I,
the community of priests,
and the whole House of Israel.
As it is written in the Torah of Your servant Moses:
For on this day atonement shall be made for you
to purify you from all your wrongs.
And pure you shall be in the presence of the Eternal.

After the High Priest pronounced the name of God,
the people bowed and knelt and touched their heads to the ground, saying:

בָּרוּךְ שֵׁם כְּבוֹד מַלְכוּתוֹ לְעוֹלָם וָעֶד.

Baruch shem k'vod malchuto l'olam va·ed.

Blessed is God's glorious majesty forever and ever.

FOR ON THIS DAY, Leviticus 16:30.

BLESSED IS GOD'S GLORIOUS MAJESTY בָּרוּךְ שֵׁם כְּבוֹד מַלְכוּתוֹ. This affirmation of God's sovereignty was the response to the High Priest's confession — a congregational "amen," as it were. According to Mishnah *Yoma* (6:2): "The priests and the people, hearing the Ineffable Name come forth from the mouth of the High Priest, would kneel, prostrate themselves, fall down on their faces, and say: *Blessed is God's glorious majesty forever and ever.*" The custom of saying these words in synagogue (as part of the *Sh'ma*) arose after the destruction of the Temple in 70 CE, when the Ineffable Name and the voice of the High Priest were no longer heard.

A New Confession — Ours

We confess —

In our generation, faith is partial and frayed.
Like an old *tallis*, threadbare and torn,
faith has been worn thin by doubts,
torn by ambivalence.
What do we see when we look at its knotted fringe?
Reminders of mitzvot?
Or something tangled, coming apart — a reminder of all our misgivings?

We confess —

In our generation, love of Torah is tenuous;
indifference to communal obligation profound.
We allow our differences to divide us;
resentments fester; and a small people is made smaller by disunity and strife.

We fail to notice the signs of Your presence in our world,
and we forget to lament Your absence from our lives.
Uncertainty too easily turns to skepticism;
we allow hard questions to consign religion to irrelevance.

Our forebears called You *Tzur Yisrael, Tzur Olamim* —
Rock of Israel, Rock of All Time and Space.
We confess our longing for the faith that sustained them.
We confess our need and desire to attach our hopes to theirs.

בָּרוּךְ אַתָּה, יְיָ, אֱלֹהֵינוּ מֶלֶךְ הָעוֹלָם,
אֲשֶׁר קִדְּשָׁנוּ בְּמִצְוֹתָיו, וְצִוָּנוּ לְהִתְוַדּוֹת.

Baruch atah, Adonai, Eloheinu melech haolam,
asher kid'shanu b'mitzvotav, v'tzivanu l'hitvadot.

Blessed are You, Eternal Presence,
by whose power we sanctify life
through the mitzvah of
confessing the wrongs we have done.

חֲמֵשׁ־עֶשְׂרֵה עֲלִיּוֹת
Chameish-Esreih Aliyot

שִׁיר הַמַּעֲלוֹת
Shir HaMaalot

עֲלִיָּה א׳
Aliyah 1

עֲלִיָּה ב׳
Aliyah 2

עֲלִיָּה ג׳
Aliyah 3

עֲלִיָּה ד׳
Aliyah 4

עֲלִיָּה ה׳
Aliyah 5

עֲלִיָּה ו׳
Aliyah 6

עֲלִיָּה ז׳
Aliyah 7

עֲלִיָּה ח׳
Aliyah 8

עֲלִיָּה ט׳
Aliyah 9

עֲלִיָּה י׳
Aliyah 10

עֲלִיָּה י״א
Aliyah 11

עֲלִיָּה י״ב
Aliyah 12

עֲלִיָּה י״ג
Aliyah 13

עֲלִיָּה י״ד
Aliyah 14

עֲלִיָּה ט״ו
Aliyah 15

ז

Seventh Step
The Holy Act of Sacrificial Offering

Shir HaMaalot — A Song of Ascents

Yacheil Yisrael el-Adonai;	יַחֵל יִשְׂרָאֵל אֶל־יְיָ
ki-im-Adonai hachesed,	כִּי־עִם־יְיָ הַחֶסֶד
v'harbeih imo f'dut.	וְהַרְבֵּה עִמּוֹ פְדוּת׃

Let Israel put its hope in God,
for with You is a storehouse of kindness,
and with the Holy One redemption abounds.
(Psalm 130:7)

Through generous acts of self-sacrifice, may we ascend toward the holy.

The Ritual of the Two Goats

After the first confession, the High Priest walked to the east,
where two goats, alike in height and appearance,
stood bound together in the Temple courtyard —
bound there for the sake of atonement. . . .
The priest cast golden lots, lifted one from the box,
and lowered it to destine one goat for God high above
and the other for the high mountain cliff.
"A sin offering to God!" he cried.
Then he tied crimson wool to the head of the goat to be sent into the wilderness.

Our gift to God is neither scapegoat nor sin offering,
but an offering of heart and soul.
Our gift is a vision of how life should be lived.
Our offerings are unselfishness and strength, generosity and service to others.

THE RITUAL OF THE TWO GOATS. On the Day of Atonement, the High Priest dispatched a goat deep into the heart of the desert — the "scapegoat" — and sacrificed another. Did our ancestors believe this would remove sin from their midst? Perhaps this ritual drama expressed their fervent wish to make their world safe from every harmful force, to create a pure and worthy society in which God's presence would be manifest.

AFTER THE FIRST CONFESSION . . . THE WILDERNESS. Reciting this description of the Yom Kippur ritual fulfills the concept set forth in a verse from the prophet Hosea: "Let [the words of] our lips replace the [sacrificial] bulls" (14:3). That is, according to the Midrash, when we are no longer able to perform the sacrificial offerings, God accepts our verbal offerings in their stead (Midrash *Song of Songs Rabbah* 4.3).

In the Temple

אֱלֹהַי, מִשְׁכְּנוֹתֶיךָ יְדִידוֹת,
וְקִרְבָתְךָ בְּמַרְאֶה, לֹא בְחִידוֹת.
הֱבִיאַנִי חֲלוֹמִי מִקְדְּשֵׁי אֵל,
וְשַׁרְתִּי מַלְאֲכוֹתָיו הַחֲמוּדוֹת,
וְהָעוֹלָה וּמִנְחָתָהּ וְנִסְכָּהּ,
וְסָבִיב תִּימְרוֹת עָשָׁן כְּבֵדוֹת.
וְנָעַמְתִּי בְּשָׁמְעִי שִׁיר לְוִיִּם
בְּסוֹדֵיהֶם לְסֵדֶר הָעֲבוֹדוֹת.
הֱקִיצוֹתִי, וְעוֹדִי עִמְּךָ, אֵל,
וְהוֹדֵיתִי, וְלָךְ נָאֶה לְהוֹדוֹת.

Elohai, mishk'notecha y'didut;
v'kirvat'cha b'mareh, lo v'chidot.
Heviani chalomi mikd'shei El,
v'sharti malachotav hachamudot,
v'haolah uminchatah v'niskah;
v'saviv timrot ashan k'veidot.
V'naamti b'shomi shir l'viyim
b'sodeihem l'seder haavodot.
Hekitzoti, v'odi im'cha, El,
v'hodeiti, v'lach na·eh l'hodot.

Your dwellings, my God, are places of love,
And Your nearness is clear as things seen, not guessed of.
My dream took me to Your Temple's mount to sing
In all its lovely worshiping and bring
My offerings with their libations.
Around me swirled thick smoke and ministrations,
Sweet to my ears, of Levites at their stations.
I woke, but when I did You still were there
For me to thank You as befits my prayer.

IN THE TEMPLE אֱלֹהַי, מִשְׁכְּנוֹתֶיךָ. By Yehudah Halevi (ca. 1075–1141). The poet sees himself in a dream among the Levites in Jerusalem, taking part in their rituals of song and sacrifice. For Halevi — a Levite and singer/poet himself — this intense experience of God's nearness remains even when he awakens to find himself in exile, far from Zion, the spiritual home for which he yearns. In old age, Halevi journeyed from Spain to the Land of Israel, where, as legend has it, he died upon reaching Jerusalem.

חֲמֵשׁ־עֶשְׂרֵה עֲלִיּוֹת
Chameish-Esreih Aliyot

שִׁיר הַמַּעֲלוֹת
Shir HaMaalot

עֲלִיָּה א׳
Aliyah 1

עֲלִיָּה ב׳
Aliyah 2

עֲלִיָּה ג׳
Aliyah 3

עֲלִיָּה ד׳
Aliyah 4

עֲלִיָּה ה׳
Aliyah 5

עֲלִיָּה ו׳
Aliyah 6

עֲלִיָּה ז׳
Aliyah 7

עֲלִיָּה ח׳
Aliyah 8

עֲלִיָּה ט׳
Aliyah 9

עֲלִיָּה י׳
Aliyah 10

עֲלִיָּה י״א
Aliyah 11

עֲלִיָּה י״ב
Aliyah 12

עֲלִיָּה י״ג
Aliyah 13

עֲלִיָּה י״ד
Aliyah 14

עֲלִיָּה ט״ו
Aliyah 15

Fifteen Steps
Psalm 122
First Step
Second Step
Third Step
Fourth Step
Fifth Step
Sixth Step
Seventh Step
Eighth Step
Ninth Step
Tenth Step
Eleventh Step
Twelfth Step
Thirteenth Step
Fourteenth Step
Fifteenth Step

וַהֲבִיאוֹתִים אֶל־הַר קָדְשִׁי,
וְשִׂמַּחְתִּים בְּבֵית תְּפִלָּתִי.
עוֹלֹתֵיהֶם וְזִבְחֵיהֶם
לְרָצוֹן עַל־מִזְבְּחִי,
כִּי בֵיתִי בֵּית־תְּפִלָּה יִקָּרֵא
לְכָל־הָעַמִּים.

Vahaviotim el-har kodshi;
v'simachtim b'veit t'filati.
Oloteihem v'zivcheihem
l'ratzon al-mizb'chi —
ki veiti beit-t'filah yikarei
l'chol haamim.

I will bring them to My holy mountain
and grant them happiness in My house of prayer.
Their burnt offerings and their sacrifices
shall be welcome on My altar —
for My House shall be called a house of prayer for all people.

The Nearness of God

The nearness of God —

Priests and Levites felt it when offering a *korban* —
nearness came through sacrifice and a thanksgiving psalm.
And our people's poets felt it in their dreams of return —
the ones who crafted songs of exile,
far from the sweet city for which they longed.

And what of us?
When do we feel that nearness?
What is our *korban*?

The nearness of God —

It comes through acts of goodness, deeds of self-sacrifice —
when we give of ourselves in selfless ways.
It comes when we hear — truly hear — those who cry out . . .

I WILL BRING THEM וַהֲבִיאוֹתִים, Isaiah 56:7.

KORBAN. The biblical word for an offering to God — *korban* — comes from a Hebrew root that means "come near; approach." The ancient idea that human beings approach God through the ritual of sacrificial offerings suggests the modern notion that self-sacrifice — behavior that is ethical, even altruistic, in nature — is a way to draw closer to the Divine.

These Cry Out to Us

חֲמֵשׁ־עֶשְׂרֵה עֲלִיּוֹת
Chameish-Esreih Aliyot

שִׁיר הַמַּעֲלוֹת
Shir HaMaalot

Let now a Generous Presence teach us gentleness
that melts our hardness of heart.
Then shall we be more sensitive to the needs of others,
and responsive to their pleas —

עֲלִיָּה א׳ *Aliyah 1*

All who struggle to be heard;
and those who live behind walls of illness, poverty, and injustice.

עֲלִיָּה ב׳ *Aliyah 2*

All whose faces are forgotten from one encounter to the next;
and those who never find a place of shelter and safety.

עֲלִיָּה ג׳ *Aliyah 3*

All whose skills and talents go unnoticed;
and those whose bright promise has dimmed for want of attention.

עֲלִיָּה ד׳ *Aliyah 4*

All whose bodies are burdened with pain;
and those whose minds are clouded by confusion.

עֲלִיָּה ה׳ *Aliyah 5*

All whose voices tremble with a cry of absence;
and those whose only season is the winter of the heart.

עֲלִיָּה ו׳ *Aliyah 6*

All who die alone in spiritual darkness;
and those whose isolation is a living death.

עֲלִיָּה ז׳ *Aliyah 7*

All who are abandoned, neglected, or abused;
and those who have been driven from their homes by violence and war.

עֲלִיָּה ח׳ *Aliyah 8*

All who wait for love that never comes;
and those who long for a word, a touch, a friend.

עֲלִיָּה ט׳ *Aliyah 9*

To all these,
let us respond with open hearts.

עֲלִיָּה י׳ *Aliyah 10*

עֲלִיָּה י״א *Aliyah 11*

עֲלִיָּה י״ב *Aliyah 12*

עֲלִיָּה י״ג *Aliyah 13*

עֲלִיָּה י״ד *Aliyah 14*

עֲלִיָּה ט״ו *Aliyah 15*

בָּרוּךְ אַתָּה, יְיָ, אֱלֹהֵינוּ מֶלֶךְ הָעוֹלָם,
אֲשֶׁר קִדְּשָׁנוּ בְּמִצְוֹתָיו, וְצִוָּנוּ עַל מִצְוַת קָרְבָּנוֹת.

Baruch atah, Adonai, Eloheinu melech haolam,
asher kid'shanu b'mitzvotav, v'tzivanu al mitzvat korbanot.

Blessed are You, Eternal Presence,
by whose power we sanctify life
through acts of generosity and self-sacrifice.

Ascending toward the Holiness of Jewish Spirituality

וְעָשׂוּ לִי מִקְדָּשׁ, וְשָׁכַנְתִּי בְּתוֹכָם.

V'asu li mikdash, v'shachanti b'tocham.

"Let them make Me a sanctuary,
that I may dwell among them." (Exodus 25:8)

ELEVENTH STEP
Finding holiness through prayer

TENTH STEP
Finding holiness through Torah study

NINTH STEP
Building a world of holy places — small sanctuaries

EIGHTH STEP
The holiness of Jewish memory

ח EIGHTH STEP
The Holiness of Jewish Memory

חֲמֵשׁ־עֶשְׂרֵה עֲלִיּוֹת
Chameish-Esreih Aliyot

שִׁיר הַמַּעֲלוֹת
Shir HaMaalot

עֲלִיָּה א׳
Aliyah 1

עֲלִיָּה ב׳
Aliyah 2

עֲלִיָּה ג׳
Aliyah 3

עֲלִיָּה ד׳
Aliyah 4

עֲלִיָּה ה׳
Aliyah 5

עֲלִיָּה ו׳
Aliyah 6

עֲלִיָּה ז׳
Aliyah 7

עֲלִיָּה ח׳
Aliyah 8

עֲלִיָּה ט׳
Aliyah 9

עֲלִיָּה י׳
Aliyah 10

עֲלִיָּה י״א
Aliyah 11

עֲלִיָּה י״ב
Aliyah 12

עֲלִיָּה י״ג
Aliyah 13

עֲלִיָּה י״ד
Aliyah 14

עֲלִיָּה ט״ו
Aliyah 15

Shir HaMaalot — A Song of Ascents

Az yom'ru vagoyim:

Higdil Adonai laasot im-eileh.

אָז יֹאמְרוּ בַגּוֹיִם:
הִגְדִּיל יְיָ לַעֲשׂוֹת עִם־אֵלֶּה.

Then they shall say among the nations:
"The Eternal has done great things for them!"

(Psalm 126:2)

Inspired by Jewish memory, and rooted in the history of our people,
may we ascend toward the holy.

PRECIOUS IS THE LIGHT by which we gaze upon the past,
and blessed are the journeys of those who came before us.

Abraham and Sarah left familiar ways —
went forth to places they did not know.
Moses and Miriam led their people from fear to faith
through a wilderness of doubt.

Blessed is the wisdom of sages and prophets,
who taught our ancestors the life of holiness —

You shall not oppress a stranger,
for you know the stranger's heart . . .

Let justice well up like water,
righteousness like an unfailing stream . . .

You must not remain indifferent . . .

Love your neighbor as yourself . . .

Out of violence and brokenness came prayers of healing;
a religion of renewal, joy, and compassion.

WISDOM OF SAGES AND PROPHETS. Citing Exodus 23:9, Amos 5:24, Deuteronomy
22:3, and Leviticus 19:18.

Through centuries of longing —
their hearts in the East when they were in the West —
those who came before us prayed: Next year in Jerusalem!

They bless us —
the ones sustained on their journeys by righteousness and love;
the ones who built lives from words of Torah, memory, and hope.

Blessed is the Light that makes their hope ours,
and their memory our sacred path.

Our Gratitude for Jewish Memory

Ashrei ayin raatah kol eileh. אַשְׁרֵי עַיִן רָאֲתָה כָּל אֵלֶּה.

Happy the eye that witnessed the ways of old:
the majesty of the Temple,
the joyful shouts of pilgrims in Jerusalem.

Grateful are we for the gift of memory come alive.

Happy the eye that witnessed the celebrations of our people's soul;
blessed the ear that heard the hush,
when the High Priest entered the Holy of Holies.

Grateful are we for the blessing of memory come alive.

Happy the eye that witnessed the piety of priests
who made offerings by fire;
blessed the ear that heard the fiery words
and the searing cries of prophets.

Grateful are we for the miracle of memory come alive.

Happy the eye that witnessed the throngs at the gates of the holy city;
blessed the ear that heard the Psalms —
the ancient songs that renew our days as of old.

THEIR HEARTS . . . JERUSALEM. An allusion to a poem of Zion by Yehudah Halevi (1075–1141) that begins: "My heart is in the East and I am at the edge of the West." The expression "Next year in Jerusalem" ends both *N'ilah* (the closing of Yom Kippur) and the Passover seder.

HAPPY THE EYE. A contemporary poem based on a *piyut* (religious poem) for *Avodah*. The original evokes the joy of seeing the Temple and laments its loss.

MEMORY COME ALIVE. "I am a memory come alive." (Franz Kafka, 1883–1924)

Reading and Memory: The Holiness of Books

What kept the Jews going were the books.

Of course the books were considered holy; but turn this around, and you will see a people who loved the books so much that they consecrated them. So what came first, sanctity or scroll? . . . Driven from Jerusalem, bereft of Tabernacles and Menorah, only the books remained. . . .

Bialik salutes the decaying old scrolls in the abandoned synagogue of his childhood shtetl, or in the deserted yeshiva of his youth: "ancients of dust," "eternally dead." Incessant reading, whether purely repetitive or freshly interpretive, was the only act that retained, rebooted, and reconsecrated the texts. There was collective reading and individual reading, wielding the scroll-pointer and orally reciting, knowing-by-heart and reading-in-the-heart, *nigun*-humming and melody-chanting and voice-raising and soundless lip-moving. There was reading as prayer, reading as ritual, reading as messaging, and reading as reasoning.

In Jewish households, fathers and mothers, grandfathers and grandmothers, prayed and blessed and narrated, recited and sang. They went through a fairly large corpus of texts over and over again. The children ate and drank and watched and listened. . . .

This piece of social history is . . . the single most important fact about the survival of the Jews. At the youngest age, when words can be magical and stories spellbinding, a unique vocabulary came along with the sweet and savory Sabbath-meal offerings. . . .

Of course, not only in the Jewish hippocampus do texts and tastes inhabit neighboring neurons. Other cultures mixed verse and lore, food and festivities. Perhaps all human traditions were formed in much the same way. But as we imagine these bookish tables and those verbal meals, we seem to understand how they must have imprinted a particularly strong connectivity on infant minds.

חֲמֵשׁ־עֶשְׂרֵה עֲלִיּוֹת
Chameish-Esreih Aliyot
שִׁיר הַמַּעֲלוֹת
Shir HaMaalot
עֲלִיָּה א׳
Aliyah 1
עֲלִיָּה ב׳
Aliyah 2
עֲלִיָּה ג׳
Aliyah 3
עֲלִיָּה ד׳
Aliyah 4
עֲלִיָּה ה׳
Aliyah 5
עֲלִיָּה ו׳
Aliyah 6
עֲלִיָּה ז׳
Aliyah 7
עֲלִיָּה ח׳
Aliyah 8
עֲלִיָּה ט׳
Aliyah 9
עֲלִיָּה י׳
Aliyah 10
עֲלִיָּה י״א
Aliyah 11
עֲלִיָּה י״ב
Aliyah 12
עֲלִיָּה י״ג
Aliyah 13
עֲלִיָּה י״ד
Aliyah 14
עֲלִיָּה ט״ו
Aliyah 15

WHAT KEPT THE JEWS GOING. By Amos Oz (b. 1939) and Fania Oz-Salzberger (b. 1960).
BIALIK. Hebrew poet Chaim Nachman Bialik (1873–1934; see page 494).

Fifteen Steps
Psalm 122
First Step
Second Step
Third Step
Fourth Step
Fifth Step
Sixth Step
Seventh Step
Eighth Step
Ninth Step
Tenth Step
Eleventh Step
Twelfth Step
Thirteenth Step
Fourteenth Step
Fifteenth Step

Years Since We Have Traveled

Years since we have traveled but when I hear
through the open windows
of the backyards
plates being collected, and silverware being
gathered up, two glasses laughing
when knocked into each other
like friends jostled on a bus ride
I think of all those towns of narrow streets
how just when we made it outside
with our extra shirt and guide book
the shops and the museums closed
and outside of time we heard
the families setting places for their lunch
and then clearing them, each apartment with its own
set of bells, and the lovely stones
we could walk at any time, and didn't leave
the seedlings that floated through May
air, and how the walls of the ghetto
remained, and made me dance
I just heard the singing there
and was never more present anywhere else.

YEARS SINCE WE HAVE TRAVELED. By Jessica Greenbaum (b. 1957). In this poem a traveler's sublime reverie exceeds the commonplace offerings of guide books. We are reminded that travel has many dimensions, including a spiritual one in which personal and collective memory meet.

Deep Are the Waters

Deep are the waters of time.

To search their darkness
for glimmers of the ancient radiance,
sparks of inspiration and guidance —
this is our *Avodah*, the sacred service of this holy day.

Deep are the waters of our people's past.

To plumb their depth,
to see our reflections
in the living stream of history —
this is our *Avodah*, the sacred service of this holy day.

Deep are the waters of memory.

To drink from this well,
to remember our past
and make it come alive —
this is our *Avodah*, the sacred service of this holy day.

Deep are these waters. Are they not the source of our salvation?

Civilization Hangs Suspended

Civilization hangs suspended, from generation to generation, by the gossamer strand of memory. If only one cohort of mothers and fathers fails to convey to its children what it has learned from its parents, then the great chain of learning and wisdom snaps. If the guardians of human knowledge stumble only one time, in their fall collapses the whole edifice of knowledge and understanding.

בָּרוּךְ אַתָּה, יְיָ, אֱלֹהֵינוּ מֶלֶךְ הָעוֹלָם,
אֲשֶׁר קִדְּשָׁנוּ בְּמִצְוֹתָיו, וְצִוָּנוּ עַל הַזִּכָּרוֹן.

Baruch atah, Adonai, Eloheinu melech haolam,
asher kid'shanu b'mitzvotav, v'tzivanu al hazikaron.

Blessed are You, Eternal Presence,
by whose power we sanctify life
through the mitzvah of Jewish memory.

חֲמֵשׁ־עֶשְׂרֵה עֲלִיּוֹת
Chameish-Esreih Aliyot

שִׁיר הַמַּעֲלוֹת
Shir HaMaalot

עֲלִיָּה א׳
Aliyah 1

עֲלִיָּה ב׳
Aliyah 2

עֲלִיָּה ג׳
Aliyah 3

עֲלִיָּה ד׳
Aliyah 4

עֲלִיָּה ה׳
Aliyah 5

עֲלִיָּה ו׳
Aliyah 6

עֲלִיָּה ז׳
Aliyah 7

עֲלִיָּה ח׳
Aliyah 8

עֲלִיָּה ט׳
Aliyah 9

עֲלִיָּה י׳
Aliyah 10

עֲלִיָּה י״א
Aliyah 11

עֲלִיָּה י״ב
Aliyah 12

עֲלִיָּה י״ג
Aliyah 13

עֲלִיָּה י״ד
Aliyah 14

עֲלִיָּה ט״ו
Aliyah 15

CIVILIZATION HANGS. By Rabbi Jacob Neusner (b. 1932).

Fifteen Steps
Psalm 122
First Step
Second Step
Third Step
Fourth Step
Fifth Step
Sixth Step
Seventh Step
Eighth Step
Ninth Step
Tenth Step
Eleventh Step
Twelfth Step
Thirteenth Step
Fourteenth Step
Fifteenth Step

ט

NINTH STEP
Building a World of Holy Places — Small Sanctuaries

Shir HaMaalot — A Song of Ascents

Hineih mah-tov umah-na·im: הִנֵּה מַה־טּוֹב וּמַה־נָּעִים
shevet achim gam-yachad. שֶׁבֶת אַחִים גַּם־יָחַד.

Behold! How sweet and pleasant
is a dwelling of brothers and sisters
who live together as one.

(Psalm 133:1)

With every Jewish home we create, with every synagogue we build and sustain, may we ascend toward the holy.

וְעָשׂוּ לִי מִקְדָּשׁ, וְשָׁכַנְתִּי בְּתוֹכָם.
כִּי הַאֻמְנָם יֵשֵׁב אֱלֹהִים עַל־הָאָרֶץ.
הִנֵּה הַשָּׁמַיִם וּשְׁמֵי הַשָּׁמַיִם לֹא יְכַלְכְּלוּךָ,
אַף כִּי־הַבַּיִת הַזֶּה אֲשֶׁר בָּנִיתִי.

AND LET THEM MAKE ME a sanctuary that I may dwell among them.
But will God really dwell on earth?
Even the heavens to the uttermost reaches cannot contain You,
how much less this House that I have built!

King Solomon's Temple ended long ago —
left in ruins by the army of Babylon.
The Second Temple, burned by Rome, is now a distant memory.

Where is God's dwelling place now?

Said the prophet Ezekiel: God has become for Israel a *mikdash m'at* — a diminished sanctity — after the fall of Jerusalem and the scattering of our people.

AND LET THEM MAKE ME, Exodus 25:8.
BUT WILL GOD, I Kings 8:27.
SAID THE PROPHET EZEKIEL. Based on Ezekiel 11:16.

But our Sages taught:

Every synagogue is *mikdash m'at* (a small sanctuary) —

each carries a spark of *Beit HaMikdash*, the Holy Temple in Jerusalem.

Asked Rashi:

Why did they call the Temple *the House of the God of Jacob*?

And he answered:

for Abraham, the abode of the Divine was a mountain;

for Isaac, an open field;

but Jacob said: *How wondrous is this place! This must be the House of God.*

Jacob discovered the Divine in the vision of a house;

and so the Temple is forever linked with his name.

Mountains and fields inspire us with nature's beauty,

but houses are built by human hands.

Every Jewish home is now a sanctuary

where goodness is nurtured and brought to life.

And God's altar? Now the altar is our table,

where we gather to offer our best and share what we have.

חֲמֵשׁ־עֶשְׂרֵה עֲלִיּוֹת
Chameish-Esreih Aliyot

שִׁיר הַמַּעֲלוֹת
Shir HaMaalot

עֲלִיָּה א׳
Aliyah 1

עֲלִיָּה ב׳
Aliyah 2

עֲלִיָּה ג׳
Aliyah 3

עֲלִיָּה ד׳
Aliyah 4

עֲלִיָּה ה׳
Aliyah 5

עֲלִיָּה ו׳
Aliyah 6

עֲלִיָּה ז׳
Aliyah 7

עֲלִיָּה ח׳
Aliyah 8

עֲלִיָּה ט׳
Aliyah 9

עֲלִיָּה י׳
Aliyah 10

עֲלִיָּה י״א
Aliyah 11

עֲלִיָּה י״ב
Aliyah 12

עֲלִיָּה י״ג
Aliyah 13

עֲלִיָּה י״ד
Aliyah 14

עֲלִיָּה ט״ו
Aliyah 15

BUT OUR SAGES TAUGHT. Based on Talmud *M'gillah* 29a.

RASHI. Rabbi Shlomo Yitzchaki (d. 1105), author of the best-known commentary on the Torah and on the Talmud.

THE HOUSE OF THE GOD OF JACOB, Isaiah 2:3.

ABRAHAM . . . ISAAC . . . JACOB. Abraham encountered God on Mount Moriah (Genesis 22:14); Isaac "meditated in the field" (Genesis 24:63); and Jacob had a vision of God's angels at *Beit El*, the House of God (Genesis 28:17).

To Devotion

To devotion God set no limits
and to dedication of the spirit
God set no bounds.

But great quantities of tribute God did not demand,
and the people were restrained from bringing
too much gold for the Tabernacle.

Though the Temples of Solomon and Herod
were far more costly,
it is written that the Divine Presence was found
more constantly in the humbler structure.

To dedicate the spirit to God is more difficult
than to give money,
to devote the whole heart to the Eternal
is more difficult than bringing gifts.

Not because of the gold on the walls
does the light of the sanctuary shine forth,
but because of the spirit within.

Those who worship carry away with them
more than they bring
for they find there the light to illumine
their lives.

בָּרוּךְ אַתָּה, יְיָ, אֱלֹהֵינוּ מֶלֶךְ הָעוֹלָם,
אֲשֶׁר קִדְּשָׁנוּ בְּמִצְוֹתָיו, וְצִוָּנוּ לִבְנוֹת מִקְדָּשׁ מְעַט.

Baruch atah, Adonai, Eloheinu melech haolam,
asher kid'shanu b'mitzvotav, v'tzivanu livnot mikdash m'at.

Blessed are You, Eternal Presence,
by whose power we sanctify life
when we build "small sanctuaries"—
Jewish homes and synagogues.

TO DEVOTION GOD SET NO LIMITS. By Ruth Brin (1921–2009).

י

Tenth Step
The Holiness of Torah Study

חֲמֵשׁ־עֶשְׂרֵה עֲלִיּוֹת
Chameish-Esreih Aliyot

שִׁיר הַמַּעֲלוֹת
Shir HaMaalot

עֲלִיָּה א׳ *Aliyah 1*
עֲלִיָּה ב׳ *Aliyah 2*
עֲלִיָּה ג׳ *Aliyah 3*
עֲלִיָּה ד׳ *Aliyah 4*
עֲלִיָּה ה׳ *Aliyah 5*
עֲלִיָּה ו׳ *Aliyah 6*
עֲלִיָּה ז׳ *Aliyah 7*
עֲלִיָּה ח׳ *Aliyah 8*
עֲלִיָּה ט׳ *Aliyah 9*
עֲלִיָּה י׳ ***Aliyah 10***
עֲלִיָּה י״א *Aliyah 11*
עֲלִיָּה י״ב *Aliyah 12*
עֲלִיָּה י״ג *Aliyah 13*
עֲלִיָּה י״ד *Aliyah 14*
עֲלִיָּה ט״ו *Aliyah 15*

Shir HaMaalot — A Song of Ascents

וְלֹא־הִלַּכְתִּי בִּגְדֹלוֹת וּבְנִפְלָאוֹת מִמֶּנִּי. *V'lo-hilachti bigdolot uvniflaot mimeni.*
אִם־לֹא שִׁוִּיתִי וְדוֹמַמְתִּי נַפְשִׁי. *Im-lo shiviti v'domamti nafshi.*

I do not aspire to great things or to what is beyond me;
I have taught myself to be contented.

(Psalm 131:1–2)

Through words of Torah, through deeds of Torah, may we ascend toward the holy.

Our Sages teach:
So bright was the light of the first day of Creation
that it shone from one end of the world to the other.
Such light could not co-exist with the darkness of evil,
so God concealed this holy light and hid it away.
Where is the light today?
The Holy One concealed it in the Holy Book —
and those who study Torah will bring forth its radiant sparks.

Rabban Yochanan ben Zakkai received the tradition from Hillel and Shammai. He used to say: If you have learned much Torah, do not hold yourself in high esteem, because that is what you were created to do.

OUR SAGES TEACH. Based on the 11th-century commentary of Rashi to Genesis 1:4, and Talmud *Chagigah* 12a.

THE HOLY BOOK. Based on the teaching of Rabbi Dov Baer of Mezeritch (d. 1772), the successor of the Baal Shem Tov, who founded Chasidism.

RABBAN YOCHANAN BEN ZAKKAI, *Pirkei Avot* 2:9.

DO NOT HOLD YOURSELF. In Hebrew, *Al tachazik tovah l'atzmach* — literally "do not hold yourself good." The commentary *Lev Avot* (1990) understands this to mean: "If you have learned much Torah, do not hoard the good for yourself." One who has knowledge must share it with others, for that is the purpose for which we are created—both to learn and to teach Torah.

IN HIGH ESTEEM. Others: Do not take credit or flatter yourself.

In Praise of Torah

תּוֹרַת יְיָ תְּמִימָה, מְשִׁיבַת נָפֶשׁ.
עֵדוּת יְיָ נֶאֱמָנָה, מַחְכִּימַת פֶּתִי.
פִּקּוּדֵי יְיָ יְשָׁרִים, מְשַׂמְּחֵי־לֵב.
מִצְוַת יְיָ בָּרָה, מְאִירַת עֵינָיִם.

Torat Adonai t'mimah; m'shivat nafesh.
Eidut Adonai ne·emanah; machkimat peti.
Pikudei Adonai y'sharim; m'sam'chei lev.
Mitzvat Adonai barah; m'irat einayim.

The Torah of the Eternal is perfect —
renewing the soul.

The testimony of the Eternal is enduring —
making the simple wise.

The precepts of the Eternal are just —
rejoicing the heart.

The instruction of the Eternal is lucid —
giving light to the eyes.

Rabbi Meir said: If you study Torah in order to learn and do God's will, you acquire many merits; and not only that, but the whole world is indebted to you. You will be cherished as a friend, a lover of God and of people. It clothes you with humility and reverence; it enables you to become righteous and saintly, upright and faithful. It keeps you far from sin, and brings you near to virtue. You benefit humanity with counsel and knowledge, wisdom and strength. You become like a never-failing fountain, like a river that grows ever mightier as it flows. You are modest, slow to anger, and forgiving of insults; and it magnifies and exalts you above all things.

THE TORAH OF THE ETERNAL, Psalm 19:8–9.

RABBI MEIR SAID. *Pirkei Avot* 6:1. This is the first in a series of sayings that is attached to the end of Mishnah *Avot* and became chapter 6. These sayings were added to the first five chapters to facilitate the study of *Avot* on the six Shabbatot between Passover and Shavuot. Chapter 6 celebrates and venerates the study of Torah, making it an ideal prelude to the holy day that commemorates the Giving of Torah to Israel.

IF YOU STUDY TORAH IN ORDER TO LEARN. Literally, "All who occupy themselves with Torah for its own sake (*lishmah*)." Maimonides (1135–1204), among others, defines Torah *lishmah* not only as study that leads to proper action, but also as Torah study that is "for the sake of God" — in other words, study that has spiritual but no worldly instrumental purpose (*Mishneh Torah, Hilchot T'shuvah* 10.5).

חֲמֵשׁ־עֶשְׂרֵה עֲלִיּוֹת
Chameish-Esreih Aliyot

שִׁיר הַמַּעֲלוֹת
Shir HaMaalot

עֲלִיָּה א׳
Aliyah 1

עֲלִיָּה ב׳
Aliyah 2

עֲלִיָּה ג׳
Aliyah 3

עֲלִיָּה ד׳
Aliyah 4

עֲלִיָּה ה׳
Aliyah 5

עֲלִיָּה ו׳
Aliyah 6

עֲלִיָּה ז׳
Aliyah 7

עֲלִיָּה ח׳
Aliyah 8

עֲלִיָּה ט׳
Aliyah 9

עֲלִיָּה י׳
Aliyah 10

עֲלִיָּה י״א
Aliyah 11

עֲלִיָּה י״ב
Aliyah 12

עֲלִיָּה י״ג
Aliyah 13

עֲלִיָּה י״ד
Aliyah 14

עֲלִיָּה ט״ו
Aliyah 15

Give ear, O heavens, let me speak;
let the earth hear the words I utter!
May my discourse come down as the rain,
my speech distill as the dew,
like showers on young growth,
like droplets on the grass.

Rain exists forever;
so too, words of Torah endure.

Dew delights the earth;
so too, words of Torah delight those who study.

Showers give young plants their special traits —
color, height, and blossoms.
So too, words of Torah cultivate human virtues —
kindness, compassion, and piety.

Tiny droplets revive a fading flower;
so too, words of Torah refresh the soul,
awakening mind and heart.

No one knows when rain will come
until it falls upon the earth;
so too, no one knows a Torah teacher's skill
until the student's life unfolds.

Rain bestows upon each fruit its own specific taste —
olive, carob, grape, and fig;
so too, each Torah-teaching is unique in form —
codes and commandments, legend and lore.

Rain is pure and washes everything on which it falls;
so too, words of Torah wash away sin
and make atonement for our errors and our wrongs.

בָּרוּךְ אַתָּה, יְיָ, נוֹתֵן הַתּוֹרָה.
Baruch atah, Adonai, notein haTorah.

Blessed are You, Eternal Presence,
who places Torah at the heart of existence.

GIVE EAR. Deuteronomy 32:1–2.
RAIN EXISTS. Based on a midrash in *Sifrei D'varim, Haazinu* 306.

י״א

ELEVENTH STEP
Finding Holiness through Prayer

Shir HaMaalot — A Song of Ascents

Yacheil, Yisrael, el-Adonai, יַחֵל יִשְׂרָאֵל אֶל־יְיָ,
mei·atah v'ad-olam. מֵעַתָּה וְעַד־עוֹלָם.

Israel, yearn for God,
from now until the end of time.

(Psalm 131:3)

Through prayers of praise and thanks, and when we humbly ask for Your help, may we ascend toward the holy.

Avodah SheBaLev—Service of the Heart

וְהָיָה אִם־שָׁמֹעַ תִּשְׁמְעוּ אֶל־מִצְוֹתַי אֲשֶׁר אָנֹכִי מְצַוֶּה אֶתְכֶם הַיּוֹם
לְאַהֲבָה אֶת־יְיָ אֱלֹהֵיכֶם וּלְעָבְדוֹ בְּכָל־לְבַבְכֶם וּבְכָל־נַפְשְׁכֶם.

If, then, you obey the mitzvot that I enjoin upon you this day,
loving the Eternal your God and serving God with all your heart . . .

What is the service of the heart? It is prayer.

When a person, overwhelmed by the impact of a specific experience, seeks the nearness of God or bursts forth in halleluyah or bows down in gratitude, it is prayer but not service of God yet; it is a human response to a potent stimulus. But when we pray without the stimulus of a specific occasion, acknowledging that we are always dependent on God, that independently of all personal experiences God is always to be praised and to be thanked, then — and only then — is prayer divine service of the heart.

IF, THEN, Deuteronomy 11:13.

WHAT IS THE SERVICE OF THE HEART. Talmud *Taanit* 2a. Usually the word *avodah* (service) implies bodily action. "Service of the heart" is therefore a puzzling phrase. The Talmud concludes that it refers to the heartfelt work of prayer — the form of worship that replaced Temple sacrifice.

WHEN A PERSON. By Rabbi Eliezer Berkovits (1908–1992).

OUR PRAYERS take aim at eternity —
we bless the Mystery of life.
Our prayers are the birth mothers of hope —
we bless the Giver of life.
Our prayers teach us to make distinctions —
we bless the Wisdom of life.
Our prayers are the currents of the soul —
we bless the Breath of life.
Our prayers are a clearing in the forest —
we bless the Stillness of life.
Our prayers ebb and flow like the tides —
we bless the Ocean of life.
Our prayers carry us in loving arms —
we bless the Goodness of life.

אֲנִי אוֹמֵר בֶּאֱמוּנָה שְׁלֵמָה
שֶׁהַתְּפִלּוֹת קָדְמוּ לֵאלֹהִים.
הַתְּפִלּוֹת יָצְרוּ אֶת הָאֱלֹהִים,
הָאֱלֹהִים יָצַר אֶת הָאָדָם.
וְהָאָדָם יוֹצֵר תְּפִלּוֹת
שֶׁיּוֹצְרוֹת אֶת הָאֱלֹהִים שֶׁיּוֹצֵר אֶת הָאָדָם.

I say with perfect faith
that prior to God there was prayer.
Prayer created God,
God created people,
and people create prayers
which create God who creates people.

I SAY WITH PERFECT FAITH. By Yehuda Amichai (1924–2000). The Thirteen Principles of Faith by Maimonides (1135–1204) are enshrined in both poetry (the hymn *Yigdal*) and prose in the Jewish prayer book. In the prose version, each principle is introduced by the statement: "I believe with perfect faith" (*ani maamin be-emunah sh'leimah*). A poet who often subverts tradition and rebels against it, Amichai nevertheless grounds his own theological ideas in the pious language of Maimonides.

Fifteen Steps
Psalm 122
First Step
Second Step
Third Step
Fourth Step
Fifth Step
Sixth Step
Seventh Step
Eighth Step
Ninth Step
Tenth Step
Eleventh Step
Twelfth Step
Thirteenth Step
Fourteenth Step
Fifteenth Step

SPONTANEOUS PRAYER is born out of the need of the moment. Prescribed prayer teaches us to feel a need we might not otherwise feel.

Whether our prayers are rooted in ancient tradition or arise as outpourings of the heart, they reveal a world of wonders.

Prayer is meaningless unless it is subversive, unless it seeks to overthrow and ruin the pyramids of callousness, hatred, opportunism, falsehoods.

How is it that those who pray and those who do not pray live thoroughly different lives?

It is because the time devoted to prayer makes an impression upon every aspect of the day.

To be able to pray is to know how to stand still and to dwell upon a word. This is how some worshipers of the past would act: they would repeat the same word many times, because they loved and cherished it so much that they could not part with it.

בָּרוּךְ אַתָּה, יְיָ, אֱלֹהֵינוּ מֶלֶךְ הָעוֹלָם,
אֲשֶׁר קִדְּשָׁנוּ בְּמִצְוֹתָיו, וְצִוָּנוּ עַל הַתְּפִלָּה.

Baruch atah, Adonai, Eloheinu melech haolam,
asher kid'shanu b'mitzvotav, v'tzivanu al hat'filah.

Blessed are You, Eternal Presence,
by whose power we experience holiness through prayer.

SPONTANEOUS PRAYER. Adapted from Franz Rosenzweig (1886–1929).
WHETHER OUR PRAYERS. Adapted from Rabbi Abraham Isaac Kook (1865–1935).
PRAYER IS MEANINGLESS. By Rabbi Abraham Joshua Heschel (1907–1972).
HOW IS IT. Adapted from Rabbi Abraham Isaac Kook.
TO BE ABLE TO PRAY. By Rabbi Abraham Joshua Heschel.

Ascending toward the Holiness of the Human Spirit

חֲמֵשׁ־עֶשְׂרֵה עֲלִיּוֹת
Chameish-Esreih Aliyot

שִׁיר הַמַּעֲלוֹת
Shir HaMaalot

עֲלִיָּה א׳
Aliyah 1

עֲלִיָּה ב׳
Aliyah 2

עֲלִיָּה ג׳
Aliyah 3

עֲלִיָּה ד׳
Aliyah 4

עֲלִיָּה ה׳
Aliyah 5

עֲלִיָּה ו׳
Aliyah 6

עֲלִיָּה ז׳
Aliyah 7

עֲלִיָּה ח׳
Aliyah 8

עֲלִיָּה ט׳
Aliyah 9

עֲלִיָּה י׳
Aliyah 10

עֲלִיָּה י״א
Aliyah 11

עֲלִיָּה י״ב
Aliyah 12

עֲלִיָּה י״ג
Aliyah 13

עֲלִיָּה י״ד
Aliyah 14

עֲלִיָּה ט״י
Aliyah 15

קְדֹשִׁים תִּהְיוּ...

K'doshim tiyu.

"You shall be holy . . ." (Leviticus 19:2)

FIFTEENTH STEP
Seeing ourselves as vessels of holiness

FOURTEENTH STEP
The holiness of joy

THIRTEENTH STEP
The holiness of children, the holiness of hope

TWELFTH STEP
Finding holiness in nature

Fifteen Steps
Psalm 122
First Step
Second Step
Third Step
Fourth Step
Fifth Step
Sixth Step
Seventh Step
Eighth Step
Ninth Step
Tenth Step
Eleventh Step
Twelfth Step
Thirteenth Step
Fourteenth Step
Fifteenth Step

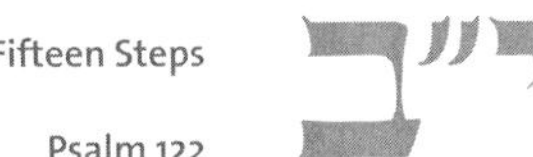

Twelfth Step
Finding Holiness in Nature

Shir HaMaalot — A Song of Ascents

K'tal-Chermon sheyoreid al-har'rei Tziyon, כְּטַל־חֶרְמוֹן שֶׁיֹּרֵד עַל־הַרְרֵי צִיּוֹן
ki sham tzivah Adonai et hab'rachah כִּי שָׁם צִוָּה יְיָ אֶת־הַבְּרָכָה
chayim ad-haolam. חַיִּים עַד־הָעוֹלָם.

Like the dew of Hermon that falls upon Zion —
there the Eternal ordained blessing,
everlasting life.

(Psalm 133:3)

We contemplate the sacred depths of nature — its elegant designs, its intricate patterns. Through the mystery and beauty of the natural world, may we ascend toward the holy.

Y'iruni s'ipai lachazotecha: יְעִירוּנִי שְׂעִפַּי לַחֲזוֹתֶךָ,
v'yaruni b'ein lev norotecha; וְיַרְאוּנִי בְּעֵין לֵב נוֹרְאוֹתֶיךָ,
v'yoruni l'hagid nifl'otecha — וְיוֹרוּנִי לְהַגִּיד נִפְלְאוֹתֶיךָ –
ki ereh shamecha, maaseih etzb'otecha. כִּי אֶרְאֶה שָׁמֶיךָ, מַעֲשֵׂה אֶצְבְּעוֹתֶיךָ.

EXCITED, my thoughts give rise to a vision:
Your marvels — which I see with the eye of my heart;
Your wonders — when toward heaven I gaze,
inspired to speak of Your handiwork.

THE SACRED DEPTHS OF NATURE. This phrase is the title of a book by biologist Ursula Goodenough, a meditation on the spiritual meaning and beauty that can be found in contemplating nature's complexity.

EXCITED. By Rabbi Moses ibn Ezra (ca. 1055–after 1135).

מָה־רַבּוּ מַעֲשֶׂיךָ, יְיָ.
כֻּלָּם בְּחָכְמָה עָשִׂיתָ,
מָלְאָה הָאָרֶץ קִנְיָנֶךָ.

Mah-rabu maasecha, Adonai!
Kulam b'chochmah asita;
mal·ah haaretz kinyanecha.

How manifold are Your works, Eternal One!
In wisdom You have made them all.
The earth is full of Your creatures.

הָיִיתִי מַפְלִיג לִי כְּחֹם יוֹם קַיִץ
אֶל־מַמְלְכוּת הַשַּׁלְוָה הַנֶּאְדָּרָה –
לַעֲבִי הַיָּעַר.
וְשָׁם, בֵּין עֲצֵי־אֵל לֹא שָׁמְעוּ בַּת קוֹל קַרְדֹּם,
בִּשְׁבִיל יָדְעוּ רַק הַזְּאֵב וְגִבּוֹר צַיִד,
הָיִיתִי תוֹעֶה לִי לְבַדִּי שָׁעוֹת שְׁלֵמוֹת,
מִתְיַחֵד עִם לְבָבִי וֵאלֹהַי עַד־בֹּאִי,
פָּסוֹחַ וַעֲבוֹר בֵּין מוֹקְשֵׁי זָהָב,
אֶל־קֹדֶשׁ הַקֳּדָשִׁים שֶׁבַּיַּעַר – אֶל־בַּת עֵינוֹ.

I used to journey at the heat of a summer's day
To the kingdom of magnificent tranquility —
To the forest's dense thickets.
There between God's trees which had not heard the ax's echo,
On a path known only to the wolf and mighty hunter,
I used to wander whole hours by myself,
Uniting with my heart and with my God until I came,
Stepping over, passing between golden snares,
To the Holy of Holies in the forest — the pupil of its eye.

חֲמֵשׁ־עֶשְׂרֵה עֲלִיּוֹת
Chameish-Esreih Aliyot

שִׁיר הַמַּעֲלוֹת
Shir HaMaalot

עֲלִיָּה א׳
Aliyah 1

עֲלִיָּה ב׳
Aliyah 2

עֲלִיָּה ג׳
Aliyah 3

עֲלִיָּה ד׳
Aliyah 4

עֲלִיָּה ה׳
Aliyah 5

עֲלִיָּה ו׳
Aliyah 6

עֲלִיָּה ז׳
Aliyah 7

עֲלִיָּה ח׳
Aliyah 8

עֲלִיָּה ט׳
Aliyah 9

עֲלִיָּה י׳
Aliyah 10

עֲלִיָּה י״א
Aliyah 11

עֲלִיָּה י״ב
Aliyah 12

עֲלִיָּה י״ג
Aliyah 13

עֲלִיָּה י״ד
Aliyah 14

עֲלִיָּה ט״ו
Aliyah 15

HOW MANIFOLD מָה־רַבּוּ, Psalm 104:24. These joyful words of awe and praise are recited daily in the morning prayer called *Yotzeir Or* (Shaper of Light).

I USED TO JOURNEY הָיִיתִי מַפְלִיג לִי. Excerpted from *Hab'reichah* (The Pool) by Chaim Nachman Bialik (1873–1934). In a poem that explores the spirituality of nature, the poet reflects on a memory from childhood: his experience of solitude and awe by a small pool hidden deep in the woods. With the power of a mystical revelation, nature awakens the boy and sets him on his life's journey.

Fifteen Steps
Psalm 122
First Step
Second Step
Third Step
Fourth Step
Fifth Step
Sixth Step
Seventh Step
Eighth Step
Ninth Step
Tenth Step
Eleventh Step
Twelfth Step
Thirteenth Step
Fourteenth Step
Fifteenth Step

God's Acrostic

What if the universe is God's acrostic?
He's sneaking bits of proverbs into seismic variations;
Abbreviating psalms in flecks of snow.
Try to read them, says a comet,

If you dare.
Fine print. What you've been waiting for.

Twisted in the DNA of marmosets:
Hermetic feedback to your tight-lipped prayer.
Examine indentations left by hailstones in the grass;

Unearth their parallel soliloquies;
Note, too, the shifting patterns of cuneiform
Initiating each communication.
Verify them. Don't take my word.
Eavesdrop on the planets in the outer spheres; they can
Reverse the letters' previous direction.
Silence, as you might imagine, has no bearing here.
Episodes of stillness—however brief—must be

Interpreted as unheard
Sounds,

Gaps that, with any luck, you'll fill in later—
Or so you tell yourself, acknowledging
Delusion's primal status in this enterprise.
Still, that's no reason to slow down.

Abandonments are howling out around you:
Cast off lamentations from the thwarted drops of rain
Reduced to vapor on their struggle down;
Observe, at the very least, their passing.
Sanctify them. Don't succumb
To anything less vivid than a spelled-out
Invitation to a not yet formulated nebula.
Calm yourself. Come quickly. Welcome home.

GOD'S ACROSTIC. By Jacqueline Osherow (b. 1956).

The Delicate Light of My Peace

פַּרְפַּר יָמָיו בְּגַן־עֵדֶן
דָּבַק בַּפֶּרַח שֶׁזָּרַעְתִּי
בַּסְּתָו
אוֹתִיּוֹת שֶׁל מַעְלָה בִּכְנָפָיו הַכְּתֻמּוֹת
סִימָנִים שֶׁל יָהּ.

בַּסִּימָנִים הָאֵלֶּה
שֶׁנֶּגֶד עֵינַי טָבְעוּ בֶּחָלָל
רִפְרֵף הָאוֹר הַדַּק
שֶׁל שְׁלוֹמִי.

A butterfly hailing from paradise
clung to the flower I planted
in autumn
letters from on high on its golden wings
signs of God.

In these signs
that before my eyes sank into space
fluttered the delicate light
of my peace.

בָּרוּךְ אַתָּה, יְיָ, הַפּוֹקֵחַ עֵינֵינוּ לְנִפְלָאוֹת הַטֶּבַע.
Baruch atah, Adonai, hapokei·ach eineinu l'niflaot hateva.

Blessed are You, Eternal Presence,
who opens our eyes to the wonder and power of nature.

THE DELICATE LIGHT OF MY PEACE. By Zelda Schneurson Mishkowsky (1914–1984), known as Zelda to readers of Hebrew poetry.

Thirteenth Step
The Holiness of Children, the Holiness of Hope

Shir HaMaalot — A Song of Ascents

Esht'cha k'gefen poriyah b'yark'tei veitecha; אֶשְׁתְּךָ כְּגֶפֶן פֹּרִיָּה בְּיַרְכְּתֵי בֵיתֶךָ,
banecha kishtilei zeitim saviv l'shulchanecha. בָּנֶיךָ כִּשְׁתִלֵי זֵיתִים סָבִיב לְשֻׁלְחָנֶךָ.

Your beloved shall be like a fruitful vine
at the center of your home;
your children, like young olive trees,
planted about your table.

(Psalm 128:3)

Our love and devotion to the next generation inspire us with hope for the future. Through nurturing the young, may we ascend toward the holy.

The holiness of children —
a gift to us all, a treasure to celebrate, a responsibility we share.
Each of us —
a spiritual parent, a giver of Torah, a source of love and nurture.

How beautiful are your tents, O Jacob,
your dwellings, O Israel!
Like palm groves that stretch out,
Like gardens beside a river . . .

Asks the Midrash:
What is the meaning of the verse *like gardens beside a river*?
These are the teachers of young children,
who bring forth wisdom and understanding from their hearts.

All who share learning and love,
and cultivate generations to come,
bring beauty to the places where Israel dwells.

HOW BEAUTIFUL, Numbers 24:5–6.
WHAT IS THE MEANING . . . UNDERSTANDING FROM THEIR HEARTS. Adapted from *Tanna d'Vei Eliyahu*, a midrashic work compiled at the end of the 10th century CE.

A Mother's Prayer before Dawn

חֲמֵשׁ־עֶשְׂרֵה עֲלִיּוֹת
Chameish-Esreih Aliyot

שִׁיר הַמַּעֲלוֹת
Shir HaMaalot

עֲלִיָּה א׳
Aliyah 1

עֲלִיָּה ב׳
Aliyah 2

עֲלִיָּה ג׳
Aliyah 3

עֲלִיָּה ד׳
Aliyah 4

עֲלִיָּה ה׳
Aliyah 5

עֲלִיָּה ו׳
Aliyah 6

עֲלִיָּה ז׳
Aliyah 7

עֲלִיָּה ח׳
Aliyah 8

עֲלִיָּה ט׳
Aliyah 9

עֲלִיָּה י׳
Aliyah 10

עֲלִיָּה י״א
Aliyah 11

עֲלִיָּה י״ב
Aliyah 12

עֲלִיָּה י״ג
Aliyah 13

עֲלִיָּה י״ד
Aliyah 14

עֲלִיָּה ט״ו
Aliyah 15

בְּשָׁעָה שֶׁאֲנִי עוֹמֶדֶת לְבַשֵּׁל דַּיְסַת סֹלֶת
הָסֵר מִמֶּנִּי כָּל מִינֵי מַחֲשָׁבוֹת זָרוֹת
וּכְשֶׁאֲנִי נוֹגַעַת בְּגוּ הַתִּינוֹק וּמָדָה חֻמּוֹ
שֶׁיֵּלְכוּ מִמֶּנִּי כָּל מִינֵי טְרָדוֹת
שֶׁלֹּא יְבַלְבְּלוּ מַחְשְׁבוֹתַי.
וְתֶן לִי אֹמֶץ לְזַכֵּךְ פָּנַי
שֶׁיּוּכַל כָּל אֶחָד מִילָדַי
לִרְאוֹת פָּנָיו בְּתוֹךְ פָּנַי
כְּמוֹ בְּמַרְאָה רְחוּצָה לִקְרַאת חַג

As I stand cooking fine-grained cereal
remove from me all manner of forbidden thoughts
and as I touch my baby's body to measure his fever
may all manner of cares leave me
and not trouble my thoughts.
And give me the courage to purify my face
so that all my children
can see their faces in my face
as a face washed for the holiday in a mirror.

וְאֶת הַחֹשֶׁךְ הַמֻּשְׁקָע מִפְּנִים
פָּנַי – כַּסֵּה בָאוֹר.
שֶׁלֹּא תִּפָּקַע סַבְלָנוּתִי וְלֹא יֵחַר גְּרוֹנִי
מִצְּעָקָה מִתְחַבֶּטֶת וּמִתְעַבָּה
שֶׁלֹּא יִהְיֶה לִי רִפְיוֹן יָדַיִם
מוּל הַבִּלְתִּי נוֹדָע
וְשֶׁלֹּא יִפָּסֵק אַף לֹא לְרֶגַע
מַגָּע בָּשָׂר בְּבָשָׂר בֵּינִי לְבֵין יְלָדַי

And the darkness deep within
my face — cover with light.
So that I don't lose patience and my throat is never hoarse
from a struggling and thickening cry
so that I'm not helpless
before the unknown
and so that nothing will prevent even for a moment
the contact of flesh between me and my children.

Fifteen Steps
Psalm 122
First Step
Second Step
Third Step
Fourth Step
Fifth Step
Sixth Step
Seventh Step
Eighth Step
Ninth Step
Tenth Step
Eleventh Step
Twelfth Step
Thirteenth Step
Fourteenth Step
Fifteenth Step

תֵּן בִּי אַהֲבָתְךָ שֶׁיְּהֵא בִּי דַּי לַעֲמֹד בְּפֶתַח הַבַּיִת וּלְחַלְּקָהּ
בְּפַשְׁטוּת בָּהּ פּוֹרְסִים לֶחֶם וּמוֹרְחִים חֶמְאָה כָּל בֹּקֶר
מֵחָדָשׁ בִּיחוֹחַ חָלָב רוֹתֵחַ וְגוֹלֵשׁ וְרֵיחַ הַקָּפֶה מְכַסִּים
עַל קָרְבַּן תּוֹדָה וְקָרְבַּן תָּמִיד
שֶׁאֵינִי יוֹדַעַת אֵיךְ נוֹתְנִים.

Instill in me Your love so that I can stand at the entrance of my home
and distribute it
as simply as one slices bread and spreads the butter each morning
anew, the aroma of boiling, flowing milk and the smell of coffee
covering over
the thanksgiving and daily sacrifices
that I know not how to offer.

A MOTHER'S PRAYER BEFORE DAWN. By Hava Pinchas-Cohen (b. 1955). This modern *piyut* begins with the mundane morning ritual of making hot cereal. But the poet then boldly encourages us to ponder the ways in which a parent is like a priest — an intermediary who brings God's love into her children's lives. The cereal, the bread, the milk, and the smell of coffee remind us that our kitchen tables have taken on the holiness of the ancient altar, even as the home has become a *mikdash m'at* (small sanctuary) with family now in the role of priests and worshipers.

Through her every thought, deed, and desire, the parent-priest of this poem embodies the words that open the Thirteenth Step of *Avodah*: *Through nurturing the young, may we ascend toward the holy.*

חֲמֵשׁ־עֶשְׂרֵה עֲלִיּוֹת
Chameish-Esreih Aliyot

שִׁיר הַמַּעֲלוֹת
Shir HaMaalot

עֲלִיָּה א׳ *Aliyah 1*

עֲלִיָּה ב׳ *Aliyah 2*

עֲלִיָּה ג׳ *Aliyah 3*

עֲלִיָּה ד׳ *Aliyah 4*

עֲלִיָּה ה׳ *Aliyah 5*

עֲלִיָּה ו׳ *Aliyah 6*

עֲלִיָּה ז׳ *Aliyah 7*

עֲלִיָּה ח׳ *Aliyah 8*

עֲלִיָּה ט׳ *Aliyah 9*

עֲלִיָּה י׳ *Aliyah 10*

עֲלִיָּה י״א *Aliyah 11*

עֲלִיָּה י״ב *Aliyah 12*

עֲלִיָּה י״ג *Aliyah 13*

עֲלִיָּה י״ד *Aliyah 14*

עֲלִיָּה ט״ו *Aliyah 15*

On the Day My Daughter Was Born

בַּיּוֹם שֶׁבּוֹ נוֹלְדָה בִּתִּי לֹא מֵת
אַף אִישׁ בְּבֵית הַחוֹלִים וְעַל שַׁעַר הַכְּנִיסָה
הָיָה כָּתוּב: ״הַיּוֹם הַכְּנִיסָה לַכֹּהֲנִים מֻתֶּרֶת.״
וְזֶה הָיָה בַּיּוֹם הָאָרֹךְ בְּיוֹתֵר שֶׁל הַשָּׁנָה.
וּמֵרֹב שִׂמְחָה
נָסַעְתִּי עִם יְדִידִי אֶל גִּבְעוֹת שַׁעַר הַגַּיְא.

רָאִינוּ עֵץ אֹרֶן חוֹלֶה וְחָשׂוּף מְכֻסֶּה רַק אִצְטְרֻבָּלִים אֵין סְפֹר. וּצְבִי אָמַר שֶׁעֵצִים הָעוֹמְדִים לָמוּת מַצְמִיחִים יוֹתֵר אִצְטְרֻבָּלִים מִן הַחַיִּים. וְאָמַרְתִּי לוֹ: זֶה הָיָה שִׁיר וְלֹא יָדַעְתָּ. אַף עַל פִּי שֶׁאַתָּה אִישׁ הַמַּדָּעִים הַמְדֻיָּקִים, עָשִׂיתָ שִׁיר. וְהֵשִׁיב לִי: וְאַתָּה, אַף עַל פִּי שֶׁאַתָּה אִישׁ חֲלוֹמוֹת עָשִׂיתָ יַלְדָּה מְדֻיֶּקֶת עִם כָּל הַמִּתְקָנִים הַמְדֻיָּקִים לְחַיֶּיהָ.

On the day my daughter was born no one
in the hospital died. So at the gate
a sign was posted: "*Kohanim* may enter today."
And it was the longest day of the year.
So great was my joy that
off I went with my good friend to the hills of *Shaar HaGai*.

We saw a bare and sickly pine tree covered only with countless cones. And Zvi said that trees on the verge of death yield more pine cones than the living. And I said to him: that was a poem — and you did not know it. Although you are a man of the exact sciences, you made a poem. And he responded: And you, although you are a man of dreams — you made an exact little girl with all the exact machinery for her life.

בָּרוּךְ אַתָּה, יְיָ, הַנּוֹטֵעַ בְּתוֹכֵנוּ אַהֲבָה וְתִקְוָה.
Baruch atah, Adonai, hanotei·a b'tocheinu ahavah v'tikvah.

Blessed are You, Eternal Presence,
who implants within us love and hope for the future.

ON THE DAY MY DAUGHTER WAS BORN. By Yehuda Amichai (1924–2000).

KOHANIM MAY ENTER TODAY. Descendants of the ancient priests are forbidden by laws of ritual purity to be near the dead. In this poem about life and death, the poet "receives a sign," which leads to a moment of illumination: this is a day of pure, unrestrained joy, hope, and holiness.

SHAAR HAGAI. Literally, "Gate of the Valley," a forested area near Jerusalem.

י״ד

FOURTEENTH STEP
Finding Holiness through Joy

Shir HaMaalot — A Song of Ascents

Hazorim b'dimah, b'rinah yiktzoru. הַזֹּרְעִים בְּדִמְעָה, בְּרִנָּה יִקְצֹרוּ.

Those who sow in tears
shall reap in joy.

(Psalm 126:5)

Through joy and exultation, may we ascend toward the holy.

עִבְדוּ אֶת־יְיָ בְּשִׂמְחָה, בֹּאוּ לְפָנָיו בִּרְנָנָה.

Ivdu et-Adonai b'simchah; bo·u l'fanav birnanah.

Serve the Eternal through celebration;
Encounter God's presence in joyful song.

Each of us is called to a life of service (*avodah*) that is rooted in joy and celebration; and leads to thanksgiving, praise, and loving-kindness. Jewish tradition teaches that such a life is the source of true *simchah*: the feeling of constant spiritual and moral growth, which endures in spite of external events and circumstances.

Serving God with our very lives should not be a burden. We are summoned to serve with gladness — not fear; and to serve beyond the walls of the synagogue: in our homes and in the street, in work-place and marketplace — in all of our encounters. When we serve God in our everyday lives, a steady joy dwells in our hearts — and will accompany us when we enter the House of the Eternal.

SERVE THE ETERNAL, Psalm 100:2.
EACH OF US. Based on Rabbi Samson Raphael Hirsch (1808–1888).

Joy as "Holy Deed" — Mitzvah Shel Simchah

1

וְשִׁבַּחְתִּי אֲנִי אֶת־הַשִּׂמְחָה,
אֲשֶׁר אֵין־טוֹב לָאָדָם תַּחַת הַשֶּׁמֶשׁ
כִּי אִם־לֶאֱכוֹל וְלִשְׁתּוֹת וְלִשְׂמוֹחַ.
וְהוּא יִלְוֶנּוּ בַעֲמָלוֹ,
יְמֵי חַיָּיו אֲשֶׁר־נָתַן־לוֹ הָאֱלֹהִים
תַּחַת הַשָּׁמֶשׁ.

V'shibachti ani et-hasimchah,
asher ein-tov laadam tachat hashemesh
ki im-le·echol v'lishtot v'lismo·ach.
V'hu yilvenu vaamalo,
y'mei chayav asher-natan-lo haElohim
tachat hashamesh.

I celebrate joy!
For under the sun there is nothing better
than to eat, drink, and rejoice.
Joy is the companion we earn with our toil
in the days God gives us life —
under the sun.

2

רַבִּי חִזְקִיָּה רַבִּי כֹּהֵן בְּשֵׁם רַב:
עָתִיד אָדָם לִיתֵּן דִּין וְחֶשְׁבּוֹן עַל כָּל שֶׁרָאֲתָה עֵינוֹ
וְלֹא אָכַל.

Rabbi Chizkiyah said in the name of Rav:
You will one day give reckoning for everything your eyes saw
that you did not enjoy.

חֲמֵשׁ־עֶשְׂרֵה עֲלִיּוֹת
Chameish-Esreih Aliyot

שִׁיר הַמַּעֲלוֹת
Shir HaMaalot

עֲלִיָּה א׳
Aliyah 1

עֲלִיָּה ב׳
Aliyah 2

עֲלִיָּה ג׳
Aliyah 3

עֲלִיָּה ד׳
Aliyah 4

עֲלִיָּה ה׳
Aliyah 5

עֲלִיָּה ו׳
Aliyah 6

עֲלִיָּה ז׳
Aliyah 7

עֲלִיָּה ח׳
Aliyah 8

עֲלִיָּה ט׳
Aliyah 9

עֲלִיָּה י׳
Aliyah 10

עֲלִיָּה י״א
Aliyah 11

עֲלִיָּה י״ב
Aliyah 12

עֲלִיָּה י״ג
Aliyah 13

עֲלִיָּה י״ד
Aliyah 14

עֲלִיָּה ט״ו
Aliyah 15

I CELEBRATE, Ecclesiastes 8:15.
RABBI CHIZKIYAH, Jerusalem Talmud *Kiddushin* 4:12. The text is understood to mean: "Every pleasure your eyes saw which, although permissible, you did not enjoy."

Fifteen Steps
Psalm 122
First Step
Second Step
Third Step
Fourth Step
Fifth Step
Sixth Step
Seventh Step
Eighth Step
Ninth Step
Tenth Step
Eleventh Step
Twelfth Step
Thirteenth Step
Fourteenth Step
Fifteenth Step

3

Rabbi Samson Raphael Hirsch surprised his followers one day by announcing his intention to travel to Switzerland. "When I stand shortly before the Almighty," he explained, "I will be held accountable to many questions.... But what will I say when ... I'm sure to be asked, 'Shimshon, did you see My Alps?'"

4

We fulfill the "mitzvah of joy" in both material and spiritual ways: when we buy something we enjoy — the purchase of food or clothing, for example; or when we bring happiness to other people on holy days — especially those in need. But if one enjoys oneself in excess, while ignoring the poor, it is considered *simchat hakareis* (שִׂמְחַת הַכָּרֵס, "happiness of the stomach" — purely physical gratification). The mitzvah of joy is an expression of holiness, for it brings the realization that we are in God's presence. The Talmud uses the same language to describe the state of mind of the prophets: "The Divine Presence is not found where there is a state of sorrow ... but rather through *simchah shel mitzvah*."

בָּרוּךְ אַתָּה, יְיָ, אֱלֹהֵינוּ מֶלֶךְ הָעוֹלָם,
אֲשֶׁר קִדְּשָׁנוּ בְּמִצְוֹתָיו, וְצִוָּנוּ עַל הַשִּׂמְחָה.

Baruch atah, Adonai, Eloheinu melech haolam,
asher kid'shanu b'mitzvotav, v'tzivanu al hasimchah.

Blessed are You, Eternal Presence,
by whose power we experience holiness through joy.

RABBI SAMSON RAPHAEL HIRSCH, 1808–1888.

WE FULFILL. Maimonides, *Mishneh Torah: Hilchot Yom Tov* 6.17–18; *Hilchot Y'sodei HaTorah* 7.3; *Hilchot Lulav* 8.15.

DIVINE PRESENCE IS NOT FOUND, Talmud *P'sachim* 117a.

Fifteenth Step
Seeing Ourselves as Vessels of Holiness

חֲמֵשׁ־עֶשְׂרֵה עֲלִיּוֹת
Chameish-Esreih Aliyot

שִׁיר הַמַּעֲלוֹת
Shir HaMaalot

עֲלִיָּה א׳ *Aliyah 1*
עֲלִיָּה ב׳ *Aliyah 2*
עֲלִיָּה ג׳ *Aliyah 3*
עֲלִיָּה ד׳ *Aliyah 4*
עֲלִיָּה ה׳ *Aliyah 5*
עֲלִיָּה ו׳ *Aliyah 6*
עֲלִיָּה ז׳ *Aliyah 7*
עֲלִיָּה ח׳ *Aliyah 8*
עֲלִיָּה ט׳ *Aliyah 9*
עֲלִיָּה י׳ *Aliyah 10*
עֲלִיָּה י״א *Aliyah 11*
עֲלִיָּה י״ב *Aliyah 12*
עֲלִיָּה י״ג *Aliyah 13*
עֲלִיָּה י״ד *Aliyah 14*
עֲלִיָּה ט״ו *Aliyah 15*

Shir HaMaalot — A Song of Ascents

Im-etein sh'nat l'einai,	אִם־אֶתֵּן שְׁנַת לְעֵינָי
l'afapai t'numah,	לְעַפְעַפַּי תְּנוּמָה,
ad-emtza makom l'Adonai —	עַד־אֶמְצָא מָקוֹם לַייָ
mishkanot laAvir Yaakov.	מִשְׁכָּנוֹת לַאֲבִיר יַעֲקֹב.

I will not allow my eyes to sleep . . . until I find a place for You,
a tabernacle for the Invincible Strength of Jacob.

(Psalm 132:4–5)

Seeing ourselves as vessels of holiness, performing acts of courage and compassion, may we ascend toward the holy.

וְאַתֶּם תִּהְיוּ־לִי מַמְלֶכֶת כֹּהֲנִים וְגוֹי קָדוֹשׁ.
YOU SHALL BE to Me a community of priests, a holy people.

Bamah akadeim Adonai,	בַּמָּה אֲקַדֵּם יְיָ
ikaf l'Elohei marom?	אִכַּף לֵאלֹהֵי מָרוֹם
Haakad'menu v'olot,	הַאֲקַדְּמֶנּוּ בְעוֹלוֹת
baagalim b'nei shanah?	בַּעֲגָלִים בְּנֵי שָׁנָה.
Hayirtzeh Adonai b'alfei eilim,	הֲיִרְצֶה יְיָ בְּאַלְפֵי אֵילִים
b'riv'vot nachalei-shamen?	בְּרִבְבוֹת נַחֲלֵי־שָׁמֶן
Ha·etein b'chori pishi,	הַאֶתֵּן בְּכוֹרִי פִּשְׁעִי
p'ri vitni chatat nafshi?	פְּרִי בִטְנִי חַטַּאת נַפְשִׁי.

How shall I meet the Eternal,
 bow in worship before God on high?
Shall I approach God with burnt offerings,
 with calves a year old?
Would the Eternal be pleased with thousands of rams,
 with ten thousand rivers of oil?
Shall I give my firstborn for my transgression,
 the fruit of my body for the sins of my soul?

YOU SHALL BE TO ME, Exodus 19:6.

Fifteen Steps
Psalm 122
First Step
Second Step
Third Step
Fourth Step
Fifth Step
Sixth Step
Seventh Step
Eighth Step
Ninth Step
Tenth Step
Eleventh Step
Twelfth Step
Thirteenth Step
Fourteenth Step
Fifteenth Step

הִגִּיד לְךָ אָדָם מַה־טּוֹב
וּמָה־יְיָ דּוֹרֵשׁ מִמְּךָ
כִּי אִם־עֲשׂוֹת מִשְׁפָּט
וְאַהֲבַת חֶסֶד
וְהַצְנֵעַ לֶכֶת עִם־אֱלֹהֶיךָ.

Higid l'cha, adam, mah-tov,
umah-Adonai doreish mim'cha.
Ki im-asot mishpat,
v'ahavat chesed,
v'hatznei·a lechet im-Elohecha.

You who are mortal —
God has taught you what is good,
and what the Eternal requires of you.
Only this: to do justice, to love goodness,
and to walk humbly with your God.

To do justice, to love goodness, and to walk humbly with your God.
What does this verse imply?
Taught Rabbi Eleazar: *To do justice* means:
act in accordance with the principles of justice.
To love goodness means:
let your actions be guided by principles of loving-kindness.
To walk humbly with your God means:
assist needy families with their funerals and weddings
And Rashi taught further:
by giving modestly, in private, to help them meet their expenses.

כׇּל הָעוֹשֶׂה צְדָקָה וּמִשְׁפָּט,
כְּאִלּוּ מִלֵּא כׇל הָעוֹלָם
כֻּלּוֹ חֶסֶד.

Kol haoseh tz'dakah umishpat,
k'ilu milei kol haolam
kulo chesed.

Whoever performs deeds of righteous giving (*tzedakah*)
and justice is considered as having filled the entire world,
all of it, with loving-kindness.

HOW SHALL I MEET THE ETERNAL . . . HUMBLY WITH YOUR GOD (*starting on the facing page*), Micah 6:6–8. Even while the Temple stood, the prophet Micah (8th century BCE) taught his people that the offering most desired by God is moral behavior, not ritual sacrifice. The Talmudic sage Rabbi Eleazar interpreted "walk humbly" in specific and concrete ways, applying them to generous deeds done quietly, without publicity or ostentation.

WHOEVER PERFORMS, Talmud *Sukkah* 49b.

ONCE, as Rabban Yochanan ben Zakkai was leaving Jerusalem, Rabbi Yehoshua, who was following him, looked back, saw the Temple in ruins, and remarked in despair, "How terrible for us! The place that atoned for the sins of all the people Israel lies in ruins!" Then Rabban Yochanan ben Zakkai said: "My friend, do not grieve. There is another way to gain atonement, equal to it. And what is that? Performing deeds of kindness and love, as the prophet Hosea declared: 'I desire deeds of kindness and love, not burnt offerings.'"

WHEN EVIL darkens our world, let us be the bearers of light.
When fists are clenched in self-righteous rage, let our hands be open for the sake of peace.
When injustice slams doors on the ill, the poor, the old, and the stranger, let us pry the doors open.

Where shelter is lacking, let us be builders.
Where food and clothing are needed, let us be providers.
Where knowledge is denied, let us be champions of learning.

When dissent is stifled, let our voices speak truth to power.
When the earth and its creatures are threatened, let us be their guardians.
When bias, greed, and bigotry erode our country's values,
let us proclaim liberty throughout the land.

In the places where no one acts like a human being,
let us bring courage;
let us bring compassion;
let us bring humanity.

ONCE, AS RABBI YOCHANAN. From *Avot d'Rabbi Natan* 4:5 (compiled 700–900 CE), a commentary to the Mishnah tractate *Avot.* Rabbi Yochanan (ca. 30–90 CE) moved the center of Torah study from Jerusalem to Yavneh during the siege of Jerusalem, enabling Judaism to survive the destruction of the Second Temple by the Romans (70 CE). In this midrash, he teaches that holiness is not limited to Temple and priesthood; rather, each person is a vessel of holiness who can gain atonement through deeds — that is to say, our deeds have transformative power.

I DESIRE DEEDS OF KINDNESS AND LOVE, Hosea 6:6.

PROCLAIM LIBERTY THROUGHOUT THE LAND, Leviticus 25:10. The words are inscribed on one of the icons of modern democracy, the Liberty Bell in Independence Hall, Philadelphia.

IN THE PLACES WHERE NO ONE ACTS LIKE A HUMAN BEING. Based on Mishnah *Avot* 2:6.

Fifteen Steps
Psalm 122
First Step
Second Step
Third Step
Fourth Step
Fifth Step
Sixth Step
Seventh Step
Eighth Step
Ninth Step
Tenth Step
Eleventh Step
Twelfth Step
Thirteenth Step
Fourteenth Step
Fifteenth Step

RABBI YOCHANAN and Resh Lakish taught:
At the time when the Temple stood,
the altar used to make atonement for us;
now our tables make atonement for us.

And Rashi taught further:
Our tables make atonement for us when we welcome guests to our tables
through the mitzvah of hospitality (*hachnasat orchim*).

OUR TRADITION TEACHES:
"All who are hungry — let them come and eat.
All who are needy — let them come and find a place at our table."

Why distinguish between the two?
Are the hungry and the needy not the same?

There are many kinds of hunger, many dimensions of need.

Some hunger for companionship —
they crave respect, affection, a sense of belonging;
many souls starve for lack of meaning and purpose.

Some speak without being heard —
they need strength of spirit in their isolation.
Others are in pain that goes unnoticed, unseen —
they need kindness and attention from one who understands them.

Let us give nourishment according to the hunger.
Let us give sustenance according to the need.
So may we see ourselves as vessels of holiness.
May every place we find ourselves be an altar where we serve.

בָּרוּךְ אַתָּה, יְיָ, אֱלֹהֵינוּ מֶלֶךְ הָעוֹלָם,
אֲשֶׁר קִדְּשָׁנוּ בְּמִצְוֹתָיו, וְצִוָּנוּ לִרְאוֹת אֶת עַצְמֵנוּ כִּכְלֵי קֹדֶשׁ.

Baruch atah, Adonai, Eloheinu melech haolam,
asher kid'shanu b'mitzvotav, v'tzivanu lirot et atzmeinu kichlei kodesh.

Blessed are You, Eternal Presence, by whose power we sanctify life
when we see ourselves as vessels of holiness.

RABBI YOCHANAN AND RESH LAKISH TAUGHT, Talmud *Chagigah* 27a (adapted).
AND RASHI TAUGHT. The 11th-century commentator expands on the ancient teaching.
OUR TRADITION TEACHES. In the Haggadah for Passover ("This is the bread of affliction").

אֱמֶת מַה נֶּהְדָּר
Emet Mah Nedar

בְּרָכָה אַחֲרוֹנָה
B'rachah Acharonah

סִיּוּם
Siyum
Conclusion: Renewal and Blessing

Renew Us This Day

אֱמֶת מַה נֶּהְדָּר הָיָה כֹּהֵן גָּדוֹל
בְּצֵאתוֹ מִבֵּית קָדְשֵׁי הַקֳּדָשִׁים
בְּשָׁלוֹם בְּלִי פֶגַע.

Emet mah nedar hayah kohein gadol
b'tzeito mibeit kodshei hakodashim
b'shalom b'li fega.

Truly —
how splendid a sight it was
when the High Priest came forth in peace
from the Holy of Holies!

Renew us this day through memory, the gift of imagination.

Like a tent stretched out across the sky —
So too the robe of the *Kohein Gadol*

Renew us to praise with song and prayer — reverent service of the heart.

Like a rainbow wrapped in a cloth of cloud —
So too the light of the *Kohein Gadol*

Open our eyes to nature's mosaic, our ears to music of amazement.

Like a rose when it opens to the light —
So too the outstretched hands of the *Kohein Gadol*

Renew us each day with wonder, infinite wellspring of the soul.

TRULY — HOW SPLENDID. A contemporary *piyut* (liturgical poem) that draws on the imagery of one of the traditional poems for the *Avodah* Service. The original *piyut*, whose author is unknown, is based on chapter 50 in the apocryphal Book of Ben Sirach (Ecclesiasticus), where a poem describes the radiance of the High Priest's face as he emerged from the Holy of Holies in the Temple. Ben Sirach is the only detailed Hebrew source of the Temple ritual by an eyewitness from the Second Temple period.

CAME FORTH IN PEACE. The High Priest's solitary encounter with the power of the Divine on Yom Kippur was considered not only a solemn ritual, but also a perilous one.

KOHEIN GADOL. High Priest.

Renew Us

Closing Blessing

Like the brightness of stars in the eastern sky —
So too the face of the *Kohein Gadol*

Open us up to realms beyond — to worlds of insight and discovery.

Like glimmering lamplight through curtained pane —
So too the glow of the *Kohein Gadol*

Renew us with the warmth of home, the bonds of love,
the shelter of belonging.

Like a tender lily surrounded by thorns —
So too the spirit of the *Kohein Gadol*

Renew us like dew in the morning, fresh leaves in the spring.

Like radiant sunrise on dark horizon —
So too the heart of the *Kohein Gadol*

Renew us with freedom from strife: shalom — the dawning of peace.

IN EACH HUMAN HAND and heart is the power to renew life:

To see dignity where there is brokenness and defeat;
to know and cherish the image of God in every human face;

To open eyes that have closed in despair;
to shelter the weak and shield the helpless;

To give strength to the weary,
hope and comfort to those who feel pain;

To care for the earth like an old friend;
to give to its oceans, rivers, and forests our selfless love;
to treat ponds and tide pools, the sky and the mountains
as sacred living beings.

In each of us is the power to renew life.

Closing Blessing

אֱמֶת מַה נֶּהְדָּר
Emet Mah Nedar

בְּרָכָה אַחֲרוֹנָה
B'rachah Acharonah

Long ago,
one word
on the lips of one person
in one place
at one moment
brought together four dimensions of the holy:
when the High Priest would enter the Holy of Holies on Yom Kippur
and utter the Name of God.

And now,
every place where we lift our eyes to God is a Holy of Holies.
Created in the image of God, we are all High Priests.
Every day of our life lived in love is a Yom Kippur.
Every word that we speak in truth is the Name of God.

We pray from the Holy of Holies in our hearts:
our God and God of all generations before us,
may it be Your will in the coming year to grant us:

a year of Abundance and atonement
a year of Blessings bestowed and received
a year of Community and compassion
a year of Delight and exultation
a year of Enlightenment
a year of Friendship and forgiveness
a year of Going-up in gladness to the Land of Israel
a year of Health and healing and humor
a year of Inner strength and well-being
a year of Joy and Jewish celebration
a year of Knowledge and learning for its own sake
a year of Love — between parents and children, friends and spouses, brothers and sisters
a year of Mitzvot and moments of sweetness
a year of Nature protected and enjoyed

AND NOW. Inspired by a Jewish folktale in the play *The Dybbuk* by S. An-ski, pseudonym of Shloyme Zanvyl Rappoport (1863–1920).

MAY IT BE YOUR WILL. Inspired by a passage in Jerusalem Talmud *Yoma* 42c: "the prayer of the High Priest going forth in peace from the house of the Holy of Holies."

Renew Us

Closing Blessing

a year of Optimism and hope
a year of Peace — pursued with perseverance
a year of Quiet and tranquility
a year of Rain in its season
a year of Song and spiritual growth
a year of Torah study and *tikkun olam*
a year of Understanding and unity
a year of Vows fulfilled and violence overcome
a year of Wisdom acquired and shared
a year of co-eXistence among the families of the earth
a year of Young and old reaching out to one another
a year of Zion aglow with light for us and all the world.

אֱלֹהֵֽינוּ וֵאלֹהֵי דוֹרוֹתֵֽינוּ,
בִּפְרֹס שָׁנָה חֲדָשָׁה עַל עוֹלָמֶֽךָ,
אָנָּא תֵּן בְּלִבֵּֽנוּ לְהוֹדוֹת וּלְהַלֵּל
לְשֵׁם קָדְשֶֽׁךָ,
עַל הַגְּדֻלָּה בְּבִרְכוֹתֶֽיךָ,
עַל מַתְּנַת הַחַיִּים שֶׁנָּטַֽעְתָּ בְּקִרְבֵּֽנוּ.

Eloheinu v'Elohei doroteinu,
bifros shanah chadasha al olamecha,
ana tein b'libeinu l'hodo ulhaleil
l'shem kodshecha,
al hag'dulah b'virchotecha,
al matanat hachayim shenatata b'kirbeinu.

Our God and God of the generations before us,
grant us a year of gratitude to You for the most
profound of blessings — Your gift of life.

Faith does not spring out of nothing.
It comes with the discovery
of the holy dimension
of our existence.

FAITH DOES NOT SPRING. By Rabbi Abraham Joshua Heschel (1907–1972).

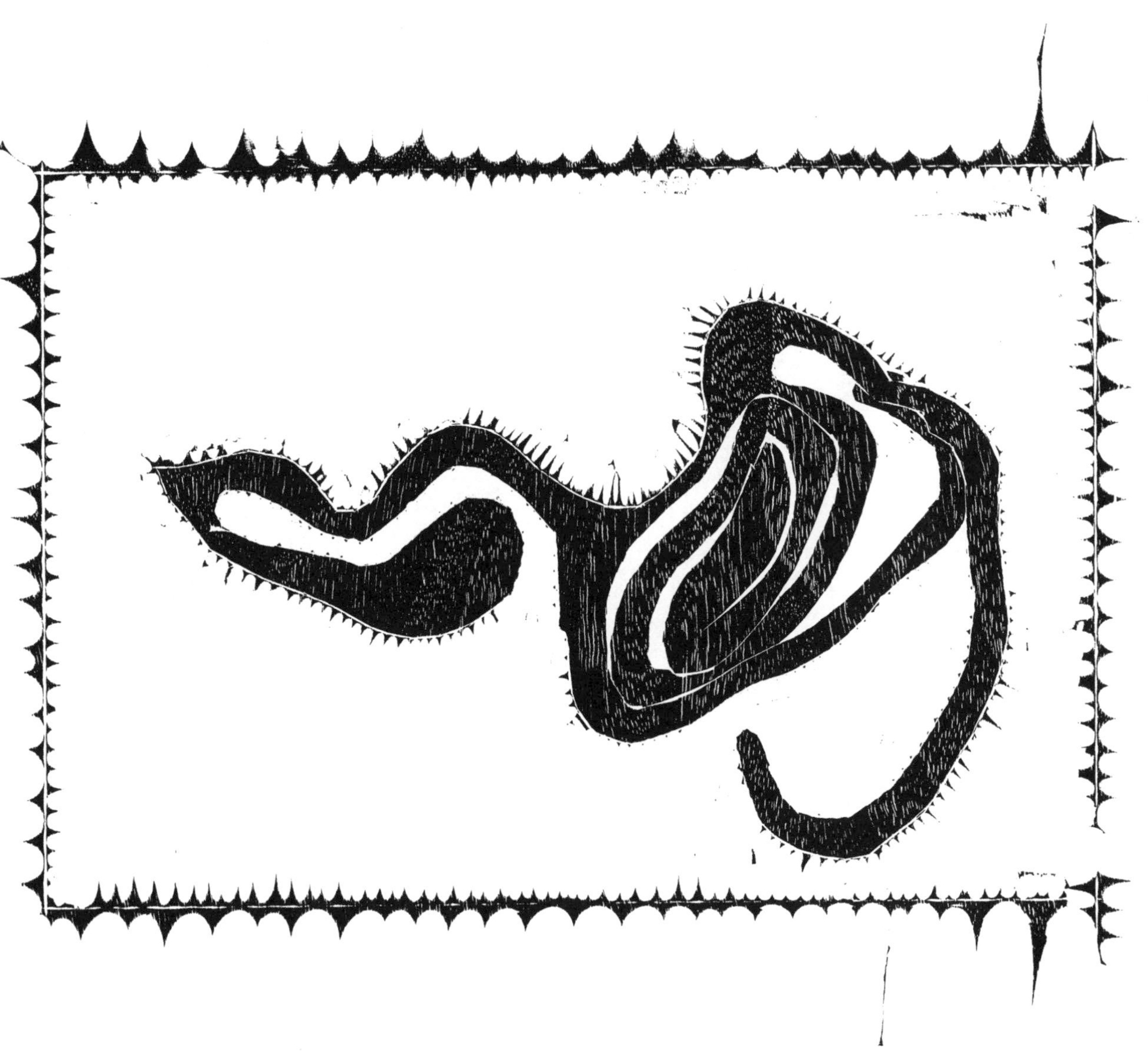

Eileh Ezk'rah

These I Remember

For these I weep.

—LAMENTATIONS 1:16

אֵלֶּה אֶזְכְּרָה
Eileh Ezk'rah
These I Remember: Stories of Repairing the World

INTRODUCTION: In the prayer book of the High Holy Days, which evolved during the Middle Ages, *Eileh Ezk'rah* is a moment of poignant identification with Jews of the past. Through the poetry of lament ("For these I weep") it recalls the martyrdom of ten rabbis executed by Rome in the first and second centuries of the Common Era; and it venerates those who were martyred. The legend of the ten rabbis entered the Yom Kippur *machzor* of Western European Jews during the Crusades, when waves of Crusaders cut a path of destruction across Europe en route to the Holy Land. The Jews who survived found spiritual meaning in the stories of ancestors who had perished under Rome a thousand years earlier in the Land of Israel.

Our ancestors believed that death atones for sin. Thus they saw a connection between martyrdom and the Day of Atonement. But the traditional *Eileh Ezk'rah* of the Middle Ages might also be read as a crisis of faith, presented annually as a challenge to God: Why do we, the innocent, suffer? What has become of the covenant? Where are You?

Every generation tells the story in its own way. The *Eileh Ezk'rah* in this *machzor* frames the themes of life, death, and remembrance differently from that of our forebears. From the account of Rabbi Akiva's spiritual resistance against the evil of Rome, we turn to human beings who lived in the more familiar, but no less treacherous, terrain of modernity and responded to extraordinary events in ways worthy of sacred remembrance. In *Eileh Ezk'rah* we recall men and women who responded "*Hineini* (Here I am)": they gave their lives while struggling to right wrongs, make peace, and save others from humiliation, harm, or death.

We remember them today not as martyrs and not as saints, but as human beings defined by their moral choices, their sacrifices, their sense of responsibility. Theirs are stories of repairing the world: *tikkun olam*.

TEN RABBIS EXECUTED BY ROME. The list of ten Sages in the service that follows reflects the order in which the executions are recounted in the traditional *Eileh Ezk'rah* liturgy. The order, however, is not historically accurate; the liturgical poem that tells the story of martyrdom telescopes the history of Roman persecution for dramatic purpose.

For These I Weep

עַל־אֵלֶּה אֲנִי בוֹכִיָּה.
עֵינִי עֵינִי יֹרְדָה מַּיִם,
כִּי־רָחַק מִמֶּנִּי מְנַחֵם –
מֵשִׁיב נַפְשִׁי.

Al-eileh ani vochiyah.
Eini eini yor'dah-mayim,
ki-rachak mimeni m'nacheim —
meishiv nafshi.

For these I weep.
My eyes, my eyes flow like streams of water,
for a comforting presence is far from me —
the one who restores my soul.

Therefore Choose Life

הַעִידֹתִי בָכֶם הַיּוֹם
אֶת־הַשָּׁמַיִם וְאֶת־הָאָרֶץ,
הַחַיִּים וְהַמָּוֶת נָתַתִּי
לְפָנֶיךָ –
הַבְּרָכָה וְהַקְּלָלָה.
וּבָחַרְתָּ בַּחַיִּים
לְמַעַן תִּחְיֶה
אַתָּה וְזַרְעֶךָ.

Ha·idoti vachem hayom
et hashamayim v'et haaretz;
hachayim v'hamavet natati
l'fanecha —
hab'rachah v'hak'lalah.
Uvarcharta bachayim —
l'maan tichyeh,
atah v'zarecha.

Therefore choose life. Therefore choose life,
that you and your children may live.
(Therefore choose life. Therefore choose life,
that you and your children may live.)
By loving the Eternal God and heeding God's
commands
and holding fast (and holding fast and holding fast) to God
(and holding fast and holding fast and holding fast to God).

FOR THESE I WEEP, Lamentations 1:16.
THEREFORE CHOOSE LIFE, Deuteronomy 30:19. Lyrics by Aviva Rosenbloom (b. 1947) and Alan Weiner (b. 1948).

These I remember —

The ones whose lives were shaped by a mitzvah:
"You must not remain indifferent."

The ones who lost their lives through devotion to a mitzvah:
"Justice, justice you shall pursue."

The ones who embodied, through deed and dedication, a mitzvah:
"Choose life."

And these I remember . . .

The ones who mended the broken, brought healing to the wounded,
fought back despair with the solace of faith.

The ones who breathed life into a prayer: *L'takein olam b'malchut
Shaddai*: to establish in the world the sovereignty of High and Noble
Purpose.

I remember these . . .

Artists of the soul, architects of redemption —

the activists and advocates of justice and beauty, exemplars of *tikkun
olam*: repairing the world.

On this holy day, we remember . . .

מָבוֹא
Mavo

הָעֲשָׂרָה
HaAsarah

שְׁמוּאֵל
זַייגֶלבּוֹים
Shmuel Zygelboym

גֵּיימְס צֵ׳יינִי
James Chaney

אַנְדְרוּ גוּדְמַן
Andrew Goodman

מַייקֶל שׁוֹאוֹרְנֶר
Michael Schwerner

אֶתִי הִילֶסוּם
Etty Hillesum

יוֹסֵף רוֹמָנוֹ
Yosef Romano

חַנָה סֶנֶשׁ
Hana Senesh

דָנִיאֵל פֶּרְל
Daniel Pearl

רַבִּינֶר רְגִינָה יוֹנַס
Rabbi Regina Jonas

יִצְחָק רַבִּין
Yitzhak Rabin

סִיּוּם
Siyum

YOU MUST NOT REMAIN INDIFFERENT, Deuteronomy 22:3.

JUSTICE, JUSTICE, Deuteronomy 16:20.

CHOOSE LIFE, Deuteronomy 30:19.

SHADDAI . . . HIGH AND NOBLE PURPOSE. Some scholars connect Shaddai (a
  biblical name of God) with an ancient Semitic word for "mountain." It thus suggests an image of the Divine as that which is lofty and noble — elevated above all
  else in our lives.

Ten Sages . . .

. . . known as the Ten Martyrs, were executed by Rome in the uprisings of the first and second centuries of the Common Era, in the Land of Israel. Though many other Jews lost their lives as well, the courage of these ten has been recalled for centuries in a Yom Kippur poem of lament, "*Eileh Ezk'rah* (These I Remember)," which reflected the experience of Jewish communities devastated by the Crusades, which began in 1096.

And these are their names . . .
Rabbi Yishmael the High Priest
Rabban Shimon ben Gamliel, Prince of Israel
Rabbi Akiva
Rabbi Chananya ben Teradyon
Rabbi Chutzpit
Rabbi Elazar ben Shamua
Rabbi Chanina ben Chachinai
Rabbi Yeshevav the Scribe
Rabbi Yehudah ben Dama
Rabbi Yehudah ben Bava

PRINCE OF ISRAEL. In the first centuries of the Common Era, *Nasi* was the title given to the president of the Sanhedrin, the Jewish governing body under Roman rule. The Romans recognized the *Nasi* as the political head, the Patriarch, of the Jewish people. The office, always held by a descendant of Hillel the Elder, encompassed political, religious, and judicial leadership.

Rabbi Akiva . . .

. . . was one of "The Ten," a man of piety and humility, spiritual leader of the Jewish community in the Land of Israel; supporter of the Bar Kochba revolt against Rome that began in 132 CE, who openly defied the Roman decree against assembling in synagogues and teaching Torah. Of Akiva ben Yosef we are told:

When the time came to say the morning *Sh'ma*, the Roman executioners were combing Akiva's flesh with iron. And he said:

"Hear, O Israel: Adonai is our God, Adonai is One." Akiva's students asked him: "Rabbi, even now?" And he said: "All my life, I have been troubled that I could not obey this verse — 'Love Adonai *with all your soul*' — which is to say: 'Love God, even when God takes your soul.' And I have wondered: 'When will I be able to fulfill this mitzvah?' Now that the moment has come, how can I not obey?" Akiva stretched out the affirmation of Divine unity, the word *echad*, until the departure of his soul. And he died with *echad* upon his lips.

Rabbi Akiva would teach:

חָבִיב אָדָם שֶׁנִּבְרָא בְּצֶלֶם.

Chaviv adam shenivra v'tzelem.

Human beings were made in God's
image as an act of love.

מָבוֹא
Mavo

הָעֲשָׂרָה
HaAsarah

שְׁמוּאֵל זִייגֶלְבּוֹים
Shmuel Zygelboym

גֵ׳יימְס צֵ׳יינִי
James Chaney

אַנְדְרוּ גוּדְמַן
Andrew Goodman

מַייקְל שׁוֹאוֹרְנֶר
Michael Schwerner

אֶתִּי הִילֶסוּם
Etty Hillesum

יוֹסֵף רוֹמֶנוּ
Yosef Romano

חַנָּה סֶנֶשׁ
Hana Senesh

דָּנִיֵּאל פֶּרְל
Daniel Pearl

רַבִּינֶר רֶגִינָה יוֹנַס
Rabbi Regina Jonas

יִצְחָק רַבִּין
Yitzhak Rabin

סִיּוּם
Siyum

WHEN THE TIME CAME, *Avot d'Rabbi Natan* A, 38:3 (adapted).
RABBI AKIVA WOULD TEACH, *Pirkei Avot* 3:14.

And These Ten We Remember . . .

Shmuel Zygelboym, James Chaney, Andrew Goodman, Michael Schwerner, Etty Hillesum, Yosef Romano, Hana Senesh, Daniel Pearl, Rabbi Regina Jonas, Yitzchak Rabin . . .

. . . men and women of the modern era who embodied the essence of *tikkun olam*: offering hands and hearts to a world in need of repair. Their rich lives and their tragic deaths remind us that every human life has the power to shape history.

The prayers of Yom Kippur set us on the path
to becoming better human beings.
Today let us learn from the lives of those
who walked that path before us.

Shifchi Kamayim

שִׁפְכִי כַמַּ֫יִם לִבֵּךְ
Shifchi kamayim, kamayim libeich
And pour out your hearts like water.
Pour out your hearts.
And remember.

To Choose One's Own Way

We who lived in concentration camps can remember the people who walked through the huts comforting others, giving away their last piece of bread. They may have been few in number, but they offer sufficient proof that everything can be taken from a person but one thing: the last of the human freedoms — to choose one's attitude in any given set of circumstances, to choose one's own way.

AND THESE TEN. Like the narratives of the traditional *Eileh Ezk'rah* liturgy, the modern stories are not told chronologically. Rather, the order here is meant to create cross-currents and echoes of theme and place, generation and gender, background and deed.

SHIFCHI KAMAYIM. Lyrics by Cantor Linda Hirschhorn, from Lamentations 2:19.

WE WHO LIVED. By Viktor E. Frankl (1905–1997); adapted.

Shmuel Zygelboym . . .

. . . was a leader of the General Jewish Workers' Union, known as the Polish Bund.

Upon entering Warsaw in 1939, the Germans demanded from the city government twelve hostages. Zygelboym, who had taken part in the defense of the city, offered himself as one of the twelve in place of another hostage. In 1940 he escaped to Belgium and then America, settling in London in 1942. When he received information about Nazi Germany's "Final Solution," he campaigned passionately for international aid to rescue European Jewry. Depressed by the lack of response to his pleas, and by German ruthlessness during the Warsaw Ghetto revolt, Zygelboym took his own life on May 12, 1943, at the age of forty-eight, to protest the world's indifference to the impending destruction of his people.

Zygelboym's "suicide note" took the form of a letter to the president and premier of the Polish Government-in-Exile.
These are his words:

> I cannot be silent and I cannot live while the remnants of the Jewish people of Poland, of whom I am representative, are perishing. . . . By my death I wish to express my strongest protest against the inactivity with which the world is looking on and permitting the extermination of the Jewish people. I know how little human life is worth, especially today. But as I was unable to do anything during my life, perhaps by my death I shall contribute to destroying the indifference. . . . My life belongs to the Jewish people in Poland and therefore I give it to them.

Hillel teaches:

וּבִמְקוֹם שֶׁאֵין אֲנָשִׁים, הִשְׁתַּדֵּל לִהְיוֹת אִישׁ.

Uvimkom she·ein anashim, hishtadeil liyot ish.

In a place where there are no human beings,
strive to be human.

HILLEL TEACHES, *Pirkei Avot* 2:6.

James Chaney, Andrew Goodman, and Michael Schwerner . . .

. . . were civil rights activists who met in 1964, anticipating a summer of voter registration among African-Americans in Neshoba County, Mississippi. They disappeared together one night in June.

A hundred years after the Civil War, the denial of civil rights based on race was still pervasive — especially in the American South. Time and again, the nonviolent struggle for equality was met with violence that shocked the nation. Speaking before 250,000 people at the historic March on Washington for Jobs and Freedom (August 28, 1963), Rabbi Joachim Prinz — once the Rabbi of Berlin Jews under Nazi rule — placed a challenge before the marchers and before the collective conscience of America itself: "The most urgent, the most disgraceful, the most shameful, and the most tragic problem is silence. . . . America must not become a nation of onlookers. American must not remain silent."

James Chaney, an African-American native of Mississippi, had been a Freedom Rider at age fifteen. His mother recalled James telling her why he joined the civil rights movement: "I can probably do something for myself and help somebody else." Chaney's work with Michael and Rita Schwerner began in 1963; they helped establish a community center in Neshoba County — to house day care for children, Freedom School classes, and the headquarters of the voting rights movement.

Schwerner, raised in a Jewish home in New York City, worked with his wife, Rita, for the Congress of Racial Equality in Mississippi. Their lives were threatened from the time they arrived there, but they persisted.

When Andrew Goodman volunteered to register African-American voters in the South, he was a student at New York's Queens College, with a major in anthropology and an interest in theater. Like Schwerner, Goodman was raised in a Jewish home. Like Chaney, he had been involved in desegregation efforts before the three met in Neshoba County.

Goodman was 20, Chaney 21, and Schwerner 25 years old when they were murdered by members of the Ku Klux Klan on the night of June 21–22, 1964 — Goodman's first day in Mississippi. Their bodies were found in early August, nearly a year after the March on Washington.

continued next page

THE MOST URGENT. By Rabbi Joachim Prinz (1902–1988).

After the murders, Rita Schwerner said:

> It's tragic, as far as I'm concerned, that white northerners have to be caught up in the machinery of injustice and indifference in the South before the American people register concern. I personally suspect that if Mr. Chaney, who is a native Mississippian Negro, had been alone at the time of the disappearance, that this case, like so many others that have come before, would have gone completely unnoticed.

וְשַׁבְתִּי אֲנִי וָאֶרְאֶה אֶת־כָּל־הָעֲשֻׁקִים
אֲשֶׁר נַעֲשִׂים תַּחַת הַשָּׁמֶשׁ,
וְהִנֵּה דִּמְעַת הָעֲשֻׁקִים,
וְאֵין לָהֶם מְנַחֵם.

V'shavti ani va·ereh et-kol-haashukim
asher naasim tachat hashamesh.
V'hineih dimat haashukim —
v'ein lahem m'nacheim.

Again I saw all the oppressions
that are practiced under the sun.
And behold, the tears of the oppressed,
and they had no one to comfort them!

I have a *dream* today!
I have a dream that one day every valley shall be exalted, and every hill and mountain shall be made low, the rough places will be made plain, and the crooked places will be made straight; "and the glory of the LORD shall be revealed, and all flesh shall see it together."

צֶדֶק צֶדֶק תִּרְדֹּף.

Tzedek, tzedek tirdof.

Justice, justice you shall pursue.

IT'S TRAGIC. By Rita Schwerner.
AGAIN I SAW, Ecclesiastes 4:1.
I HAVE A DREAM. From Rev. Martin Luther King, Jr.'s speech at the March on Washington for Jobs and Freedom, August 28, 1963; quoting Isaiah 40:4–5.
JUSTICE, JUSTICE, Deuteronomy 16:20.

Etty Hillesum . . .

. . . bravely served the Jews of Holland during the Shoah.

Hillesum was a volunteer social worker at Westerbork — a German transit camp for Jews and other "foreigners" who were sent to Auschwitz in freight cars that left the camp every Tuesday beginning in 1942. After traveling for a year between Amsterdam and Westerbork, advocating for her people and offering them comfort and material support, she herself was imprisoned in Westerbork in 1943. The diaries and letters Hillesum wrote during her last two years of life document her courage, empathy, and spiritual depth.

Dutch farmers found a postcard she threw from the train as it left Westerbork. It read: "We left the camp singing." She died in Auschwitz in November 1943 at the age of 29.

> It is sometimes hard to take in and comprehend, oh God, what those created in Your likeness do to each other in these disjointed days. But I no longer shut myself away in my room, God, I try to look things straight in the face, even the worst crimes. . . . I try to face up to Your world, God, not to escape from reality into beautiful dreams — though I believe that beautiful dreams can exist beside the most horrible reality — and I continue to praise Your creation, God, despite everything.

וּבָחַרְתָּ בַּחַיִּים, לְמַעַן תִּחְיֶה, אַתָּה וְזַרְעֶךָ.

Uvacharta bachayim, l'maan tichyeh — atah v'zarecha.

Choose life — so that you and your children may live.

SHOAH. This Hebrew term, which literally means "disaster, catastrophe, destruction," refers to the murder of six million Jews during World War II.

IT IS SOMETIMES HARD. Hillesum's diary entry for Tuesday, May 26, 1942.

CHOOSE LIFE, Deuteronomy 30:19.

Yosef Romano...

...represented the State of Israel and the Jewish people on the world stage, as an Olympic athlete.

Born in Benghazi, Libya in 1940, Romano immigrated with his family to British Mandatory Palestine at age six — amidst the terror caused by Muslim massacres against the Jews of Tripoli and five other Libyan communities in July 1945 and January 1946. Two decades later, Romano fought on the Golan Heights in the Six-Day War; and, in Munich, he fought back against Palestinian terrorists who had taken Israeli wrestlers and weightlifters hostage.

Romano, a weightlifter, was a member of the Israeli team in the 1972 Summer Olympics in Munich. "This is my last competition," he said of his athletic career on September 4 of that year. "I don't have enough time for my children."

Eleven members of the Israeli Olympic team were taken hostage and murdered in the massacre by Black September terrorists on September 5, 1972. Though suffering from a ruptured tendon of the knee, Yosef Romano resisted the assailants in an effort to save the lives of his teammates. He was murdered early in the siege. "Courage," according to a friend, "was his religion."

לֹא תוּכַל לְהִתְעַלֵּם.

Lo tuchal l'hitalem.

You must not remain indifferent.

מָבוֹא
Mavo

הָעֲשָׂרָה
HaAsarah

שְׁמוּאֵל זַיגֶלְבּוֹים
Shmuel Zygelboym

גֵ׳יימְס צֵ׳ייני
James Chaney

אַנְדְרוּ גוֹדְמַן
Andrew Goodman

מַייקְל שׁוֹאוֹרְנֶר
Michael Schwerner

אֶתִּי הִילְסוּם
Etty Hillesum

יוֹסֵף רוֹמָנוֹ
Yosef Romano

חַנָּה סֶנֶשׁ
Hana Senesh

דָּנִיאֵל פֶּרְל
Daniel Pearl

רַבִּינֶר רֶגִינָה יוֹנַס
Rabbi Regina Jonas

יִצְחָק רַבִּין
Yitzhak Rabin

סִיוּם
Siyum

THIS IS MY LAST COMPETITION. Cited by journalist Giulio Meotti.

BLACK SEPTEMBER. A terrorist organization (1970–1973), initially formed by Palestinians seeking revenge against King Hussein of Jordan for the deaths and expulsions of thousands of Palestinians in a conflict that followed an attempted coup d'état in September 1970.

COURAGE. Cited by journalist Giulio Meotti.

YOU MUST NOT REMAIN INDIFFERENT, Deuteronomy 22:3.

Hana Senesh . . .

. . . was a native of Budapest, Hungary, who made aliyah to British Mandatory Palestine in 1939.

Five years later, having trained as a paratrooper, Senesh was one of thirty-seven Jews who parachuted behind German lines in an attempt to rescue Hungarian Jews destined for Auschwitz. During her three months in Europe with partisan resistance fighters, she wrote the prayerful poem "Blessed Is the Match" (*Ashrei HaGafrur*). It was her last.

Captured and tortured — and having refused a blindfold — Hana Senesh was executed by Nazi firing squad in 1944 at the age of twenty-three. She is buried in a special section of the military cemetery on Mount Herzl in Jerusalem, where the gravestones are arranged in the shape of a parachute.

Ashrei hagafrur shenisraf	אַשְׁרֵי הַגַּפְרוּר שֶׁנִּשְׂרַף
v'hitzit l'havot.	וְהִצִּית לְהָבוֹת,
Ashrei halehavah shebaarah	אַשְׁרֵי הַלֶּהָבָה שֶׁבָּעֲרָה
b'sitrei l'vavot.	בְּסִתְרֵי לְבָבוֹת.
Ashrei hal'vavot sheyad'u	אַשְׁרֵי הַלְּבָבוֹת שֶׁיָּדְעוּ
lachdol b'chavod.	לַחְדֹּל בְּכָבוֹד . . .
Ashrei hagafrur shenisraf	אַשְׁרֵי הַגַּפְרוּר שֶׁנִּשְׂרַף
v'hitzit l'havot.	וְהִצִּית לְהָבוֹת.

Blessed is the match consumed in a kindling flame.
Blessed is the flame that softly burns in a heart's
secret place.
Blessed the hearts that, like flickering lights,
knew to flutter and die without shame.
Blessed is the match consumed in a kindling flame.

Hillel teaches:

וּבִמְקוֹם שֶׁאֵין אֲנָשִׁים, הִשְׁתַּדֵּל לִהְיוֹת אִישׁ.

Uvimkom she·ein anashim, hishtadeil liyot ish.

In a place where there are no human beings,
strive to be human.

HILLEL TEACHES, *Pirkei Avot* 2:6.

Daniel Pearl . . .

. . . put himself in harm's way to inform the world of turbulent events.

Pearl was an American journalist who covered ethnic strife and war in the Balkans, in Sudan, and in Iran. He was also a citizen of Israel. By 2002 Pearl was the *Wall Street Journal*'s bureau chief in South Asia. While investigating Islamic terrorism in Karachi, Pakistan, he was abducted and executed by Al Qaeda terrorists. A videotape of his murder, at the age of 38, preserves his last words:

> My father is Jewish, my mother is Jewish, I am Jewish. Back in the town of Bnei Brak, there is a street named after my great-grandfather, Chayim Pearl, who was one of the founders of the town.

South African writer and political activist Nadine Gordimer later reflected:

> I am a Jew. To be a Jew, to be black — it is simply something you *are*. There is no pride in belonging to one particular race, color, or designation, and no denigration whatever in your identity. . . . I was asked in a questionnaire what wish I would want to leave behind me in the world. My answer is: recognize yourself in others.
>
> That would be the end of racism, which we know in all its pain and despicable horror. I believe that Daniel Pearl's last words "I am a Jew" were an assertion of his inalienable right to recognition of the human oneness in his specific identity. His was the ultimate judgment on the senseless brutality that took his young life.

צֶדֶק צֶדֶק תִּרְדֹּף.

Tzedek, tzedek tirdof.

Justice, justice you shall pursue.

NADINE GORDIMER, 1923–2014.
JUSTICE, JUSTICE, Deuteronomy 16:20.

Rabbi Regina Jonas . . .

. . . saw life as a journey of faith and service to people:

> God has placed abilities and callings in our hearts, without regard to gender. Thus each of us has the duty, whether man or woman, to realize those gifts God has given.

Born in Berlin in 1902 and ordained in 1935, Jonas was a religious pioneer — the first woman in Jewish history to hold the title of rabbi. But her rabbinic studies and ordination occurred just as the darkness of Nazism overshadowed the greatness of achievements like hers.

Reared in poverty, Jonas gravitated to those in need — the poor, the ill, the elderly. Perhaps because of her empathy, and her belief in the intrinsic value of every life, she clung to an optimistic worldview that integrated spirituality, theology, and service to others, even in the midst of the gathering storm.

Jonas chose to remain in Germany to serve her people. Subjected to forced labor by the Nazis in 1941 and imprisoned in the Theresienstadt concentration camp in 1942, her calling as a rabbi grew stronger under duress. Of Regina Jonas it has been said: "Her synagogue was everywhere. . . . She wanted to stay where her people were, just like [Rabbi] Leo Baeck."

Regina Jonas came to the rabbinate for two reasons: "My belief in the godly calling and my love for people." She served the Jews of Germany as a teacher, pastoral caregiver, and interpreter of Jewish tradition until she was murdered in Auschwitz in October 1944.

וּבָחַרְתָּ בַּחַיִּים, לְמַעַן תִּחְיֶה, אַתָּה וְזַרְעֶךָ.

Uvacharta bachayim, l'maan tichyeh — atah v'zarecha.

Choose life — so that you and your children may live.

GOD HAS PLACED ABILITIES. From the German newspaper *Central-Verein-Zeitung*, June 23, 1938.

HER SYNAGOGUE WAS EVERYWHERE. Gad Beck, who worked in a slave-labor factory with Jonas.

MY BELIEF IN THE GODLY CALLING. From the German newspaper *Central-Verein-Zeitung*, June 23, 1938.

CHOOSE LIFE, Deuteronomy 30:19.

Yitzhak Rabin . . .

. . . born in Jerusalem in 1922, served as an Israeli military leader and twice as prime minister.

As a statesman, he worked assiduously for peace between Israel and the Palestinians, for which he received the Nobel Peace Prize in 1994. Upon signing the Oslo Accords on the White House lawn on September 13, 1993, he said:

> Let me say to you, the Palestinians: We are destined to live together, on the same soil in the same land. We, the soldiers who have returned from battle stained with blood, we who have seen our relatives and friends killed before our eyes, we who have attended their funerals and cannot look into the eyes of their parents, we who have come from a land where parents bury their children, we who have fought against you, the Palestinians — we say to you today in a loud and clear voice: Enough of blood and tears. Enough!
>
> We have no desire for revenge. We harbor no hatred toward you. We, like you, are people who want to build a home, to plant a tree, to love, live side by side with you — in dignity, in empathy, as human beings, as free people. We are today giving peace a chance and again saying to you: Let us pray that a day will come when we will say, enough, farewell to arms.

On July 26, 1994 Rabin spoke before the United States Congress:

> I, serial number 30743, Lieutenant General in reserves Yitzhak Rabin, a soldier in the Israeli Defense Forces and in the army of peace, I, who have sent armies into fire and soldiers to their death, say today: We sail onto a war which has no casualties, no wounded, no blood nor suffering. It is the only war which is a pleasure to participate in — the war for peace.

On November 4, 1995, at a peace rally in Tel Aviv, Yitzhak Rabin was assassinated by a radical, Jewish opponent of his plan for peace. A blood-stained photocopy of the song *Shir LaShalom* (A Song for Peace) was found in his pocket.

לֹא תוּכַל לְהִתְעַלֵּם.

Lo tuchal l'hitalem.

You must not remain indifferent.

YOU MUST NOT REMAIN INDIFFERENT, Deuteronomy 22:3.

Shir LaShalom

T'nu lashemesh laalot	תְּנוּ לַשֶּׁמֶשׁ לַעֲלוֹת
laboker l'ha·ir,	לַבֹּקֶר לְהָאִיר,
hazakah shebat'filot	הַזַּכָּה שֶׁבַּתְּפִלּוֹת
otanu lo tachzir.	אוֹתָנוּ לֹא תַחֲזִיר.
Al tagidu "yom yavo"	אַל תַּגִּידוּ יוֹם יָבוֹא –
Haviu et hayom!	הָבִיאוּ אֶת הַיּוֹם!
Ki lo chalom hu —	כִּי לֹא חֲלוֹם הוּא
uvchol hakikarot	וּבְכָל הַכִּכָּרוֹת
hariu rak shalom!	הָרִיעוּ רַק שָׁלוֹם!
Lachein rak shiru shir lashalom	לָכֵן, רַק שִׁירוּ שִׁיר לַשָּׁלוֹם
al tilchashu t'filah.	אַל תִּלְחֲשׁוּ תְּפִלָּה
Mutav tashiru shir lashalom	מוּטָב תָּשִׁירוּ שִׁיר לַשָּׁלוֹם
bitzakah g'dolah.	בִּצְעָקָה גְדוֹלָה.

Let the sun rise up
Let dawn be lit in radiance —
The purest of prayers
Will not restore us

So do not say, "There will come a day"
But bring that day yourselves —
For it is no dream
And in every town and city square
Raise a shout — just the shout of shalom!

So sing —
Not a hushed, whispered prayer —
Just a song for shalom
How good —
How much better to sing
To be boisterous and loud
For the sake of a song,
A song for shalom!

Eileh ezk'rah . . . אֵלֶּה אֶזְכְּרָה
On Yom Kippur the voice of sacred history calls to us:

These you shall remember — their lives, their deaths, their legacy.
Their legacy is in your hands.

SHIR LASHALOM שִׁיר לַשָּׁלוֹם. Hebrew lyrics by Yaacov Rotblit (b. 1945) and Yair Rosenblum.

Kaddish

Upon Israel and upon the rabbis
and upon the disciples and upon all the disciples of their disciples
and upon all who study the Torah in this place and in every place,
to them and to you
peace;

upon Israel and upon all who meet with unfriendly glances, sticks
    and stones and names —
on posters, in newspapers, or in books to last,
chalked on asphalt or in acid on glass,
shouted from a thousand thousand windows by radio;
who are pushed out of class-rooms and rushing trains,
whom the hundred hands of a mob strike,
and whom jailers strike with bunches of keys, with revolver butts;
to them and to you
in this place and in every place
safety;

upon Israel and upon all who live
as the sparrows of the streets
under the cornices of the houses of others,
and as rabbits
in the fields of strangers
on the grace of the seasons
and what the gleaners leave in the corners;
you children of the wind —
birds
that feed on the tree of knowledge
in this place and in every place,
to them and to you
a living;

upon Israel
and upon their children and upon all the children of their children
in this place and in every place,
to them and to you
life.

מָבוֹא
Mavo

הָעֲשָׂרָה
HaAsarah

שְׁמוּאֵל זַייגֶלבּוֹים
Shmuel Zygelboym

גֵ׳יימְס צֵ׳ייני
James Chaney

אַנְדְרוּ גוּדְמַן
Andrew Goodman

מַייקל שְׁוָאוֹרְנֶר
Michael Schwerner

אֶתִּי הִילֶסוֹם
Etty Hillesum

יוֹסֵף רוֹמַנוֹ
Yosef Romano

חַנָּה סֶנֶשׁ
Hana Senesh

דָּנִיאֵל פֶּרְל
Daniel Pearl

רְבִּינֶר רֶגִינָה יוֹנַס
Rabbi Regina Jonas

יִצְחָק רַבִּין
Yitzhak Rabin

סִיּוּם
Siyum

KADDISH. By Charles Reznikoff (1894–1976). Based on the prayer *Kaddish d'Rabanan* (Rabbis' Kaddish), which asks for abundant peace, grace, loving-kindness, mercy, long life, ample sustenance, and salvation for teachers, disciples, and all who engage in the study of Torah.

Kaddish D'Rabanan

For our teachers and their students,
And the students of the students,
We ask for peace and loving-kindness,
And let us say, Amen.
And for those who study Torah
Here and everywhere,
May they be blessed with all they need,
And let us say, Amen
We ask for peace and loving-kindness,
And let us say, Amen.

We need not build monuments for the righteous.
We shall remember them for their deeds.

KADDISH D'RABANAN. Lyrics by Debbie Friedman (1951–2011).
WE NEED NOT BUILD. Based on Jerusalem Talmud *Sh'kalim* 2:5.

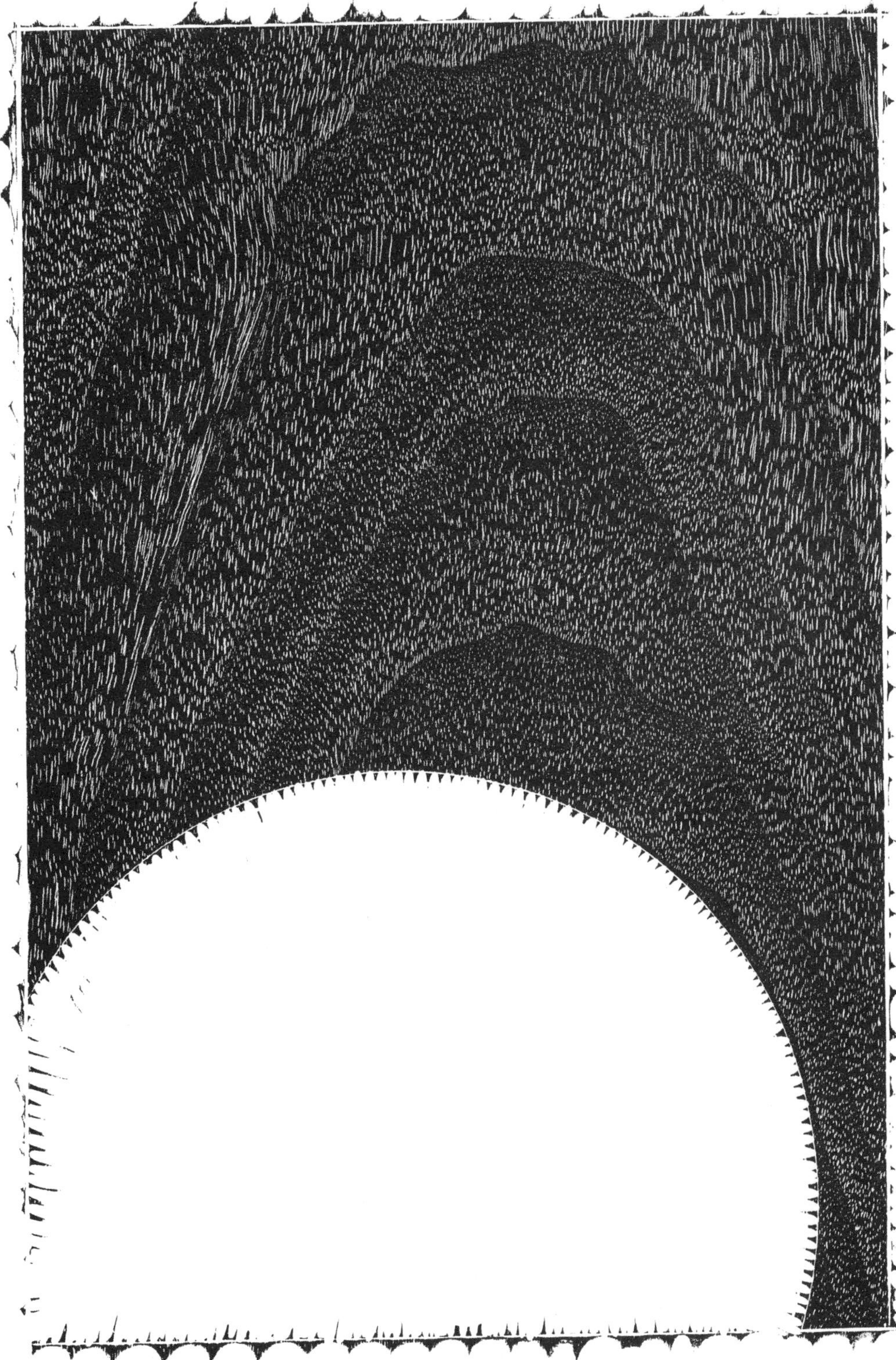

יזכור

Yizkor · Memorial Service

These are the lights that guide us . . .
These are the ways we remember.

—HANA SENESH (1921–1944)

יִזְכֹּר
Yizkor

מָבוֹא
Mavo

Opening Words

The Wisdom of Our Tradition

Our tradition shows great wisdom in teaching us to gather for services of remembrance on Yom Kippur and on the three pilgrimage festivals (Pesach, Shavuot, and Sukkot). These moments that mark the seasons of the year — and the seasons of our lives — awaken strong memories of relationships that shaped us, sustained us, and sometimes challenged us; and of holy days we shared with loved ones and cherished friends.

When they are gone, we can still affirm the beautiful and lasting values we learned from them, and remember them in all their humanness. One of the ways we do that is by coming together as a community of comfort and care.

From its inception a thousand years ago, when it was prayed by Ashkenazic Jews on the morning of Yom Kippur, *Yizkor* has had two profound themes: God's embrace of the loved ones who are beyond our reach; and our commitment to do the good deeds that are within our reach by giving *tzedakah* in their memory. When we say *Yizkor* (May God remember . . .) we proclaim our faith that those who have died have significance now and forever.

A word about leading this service . . .

This *Yizkor* service empowers both leaders and worshipers to make choices. It is not meant to be read in its entirety — though that could be a meaningful experience. The main elements are: music and silence; poetry, prayer, and personal reflections that center on relationships, loss, and healing. There are passages that may be read alone in silence (particularly in the section called Fourth Candle); passages that may be read aloud (by a single reader; by two readers; or responsively — for example: pages 548, 561, or 586); and passages that may be read in unison (for example: the selections from Psalms).

The service may open with a musical selection, perhaps *Eli, Eli* or *Shiviti*, followed by a poem from the section called "Entering *Yizkor*."

Introduction

In each of the Seven Candles (the main body of the service), choices may be made from the opening "Words of Faith and Tradition" (sung or read in unison), and likewise from the closing "Words of Healing." In between, time for silent meditation can be offered, as well as one or two passages read by all or led by one or two readers.

If desired, seven *Yizkor* candles may be lit in the course of the service.

A word about praying this service . . .

Through traditional texts and modern poems, this *Yizkor* service encourages silence and song; personal reflection and communal prayer. Its hope is that worshipers will find meaning within and derive strength from the shared voice of the congregation.

APPROACHING GRIEF THROUGH POETRY: Robert Frost liked to distinguish between *grievances* (complaints) and *griefs* (sorrows). He even suggested that grievances, which are propagandistic, should be restricted to prose, "leaving poetry free to go its way in tears." Implicit in poetry is the notion that we are deepened by heartbreaks, that we are not so much diminished as enlarged by grief, by our refusal to vanish — to let others vanish — without leaving a verbal record. Poetry is a stubborn art. The poet is one who will not be reconciled, who is determined to leave a trace in words, to transform oceanic depths of feeling into the faithful nuances of art. (Edward Hirsch, b. 1950)

כַּוָּנוֹת לִיְזְכֹּר
Entering Yizkor
Prayers of Remembrance, Words of Hope

Like the stars by day, our beloved dead are not seen with mortal eyes,
but they shine on in the untroubled firmament of endless time.

—Rabbi Edward N. Calisch

To ask of death that it never come is futile, but it is not futility to pray
that when death comes for us, it may take us from a world one corner
of which is a little better because we were there.

—Rabbi Jacob P. Rudin

פֶּתַח דָּבָר
Peitach Davar

כַּוָּנוֹת
Kavanot

Eli, Eli

Eli, Eli,
shelo yigameir l'olam:
hachol v'hayam,
rishrush shel hamayim,
b'rak hashamayim,
t'filat haadam.

אֵלִי, אֵלִי,
שֶׁלֹּא יִגָּמֵר לְעוֹלָם
הַחוֹל וְהַיָּם,
רִשְׁרוּשׁ שֶׁל הַמַּיִם,
בְּרַק הַשָּׁמַיִם,
תְּפִלַּת הָאָדָם.

Eli, Eli, I pray that these things
    never end —
the sand and the sea,
the rush of the waters,
the crash of the heavens,
the prayer of the heart.

ELI, ELI אֵלִי, אֵלִי. By Hana Senesh (1921–1944).

Opening Words

Meditations

THIS IS the hour of memory —
and this is our house of comfort.
Wounded by loss, we retreat from life;
our synagogue gathers us in.
Into this place we bring stories and prayers,
unanswered questions,
tears that need to be shed.
Lives recollected and carried within us —
moments of courage and laughter and pain —
this day embraces them all;
this place embraces us all.
Now the heart opens in sorrow,
for we are time's subjects,
and all that we love we must lose.
So let us hold fast to the love that remains,
and cherish the light of the sun.
Today all of us walk the mourner's path;
together may we find strength.

ETERNAL GOD, we ask Your help, for our need is great.
Our days fly past in quick succession,
and we cannot look back without regret, or ahead without misgiving.
We seek to understand the mystery of our own lives,
but our effort is in vain.
And when suffering and death strike those we love,
our faith all but fails us, and we forget that we are Your children.
God, help us now to feel Your presence.
When our own weaknesses and the storms of life
hide You from our sight,
help us to know that You are with us still.
Uphold us with the comfort of Your love.

WE ARE TIME'S SUBJECTS. William Shakespeare, from *Henry IV, Part II.*

פֶּתַח דָּבָר
Peitach Davar

כַּוָּנוֹת
Kavanot

Meditations

At the moment of our departure
from this world,
neither silver nor gold nor precious
stones accompany us —
only learning and good deeds.

Mishnah *Avot* 6:9

A voice says: Cry out!
And I say: What shall I cry?
All flesh is grass, all its goodness like
flowers of the field.
Grass withers, flowers fade, when
from Beyond the wind blows.
Indeed we are but grass.
It withers, and the flowers
fade — but the word of our
God abides forever.

Isaiah 40:6–8 (adapted)

The dust returns to
the earth as it was;
the spirit returns to
God, who gave it.

Ecclesiastes 12:7

נֵר יְיָ נִשְׁמַת אָדָם
Ner Adonai nishmat adam
The spirit within is the
lamp of God Eternal.

Proverbs 20:27

By the sweat of your brow shall you
get bread to eat,
until you return to the ground — for
from it were you taken:
for dust you are, and to dust you
shall return.

Genesis 3:19

Human beings are like a cord tied at two ends: bound to the earth through their bodies and to heaven through their souls. They are partly animal through the physical aspect of their being and partly angel through the spiritual aspect of their being. They are mortal yet immortal, transient yet eternal, filled at once with misery and grandeur.

Rabbi Samuel H. Dresner (adapted)

How precious Your loving-kindness —
We take refuge in the shadow of Your
wings.
How abundant the feast in Your
house —
You give us drink from the river of
Your delights.
For You are the fountain of life;
in Your light shall we see light.

Psalm 36:8–10 (adapted)

In reverence, suffering, and humility
we discover our existence and find
the bridge that leads from existence
to God.

Rabbi Abraham Joshua Heschel

Where Does It End?

I look out upon the far horizon. Where does it end? The line drawn by my eye is only imaginary. It will recede as I come near it. Space, like time, is continuous, and there are no sharp interruptions to differentiate one thing from another.

And is it not likewise with my life? I look back into my past. I cannot tell where it began. I am familiar with some of my ancestors, but my life did not begin with them. It stretches far back into time beyond my reckoning. A long line of generations labored to produce me.

The peculiarity of my walk, of my smile, may go back to one, and the bent of my mind to another. The sound of my voice may carry an echo of some unknown benefactor who passed something of himself on to me. The seed that develops in me was planted in a faraway past, and as I reap the harvest I know that other hands made it possible.

Equally long is the line of my spiritual ancestors. The love of life and the sense of kinship I feel for my fellow human beings are but simple expressions of my spirit, but human beings achieved it after groping and suffering. The first person who rubbed two stones to produce fire is my ancestor, and so is the first person who discovered the glow of friendship in the clasp of two hands. The people who explored the seas and the mountains and who brought up the hidden riches of the earth are my ancestors. They enriched me with the fruit of their discoveries, as well as with the spirit of their daring.

I am what I am because of the first amoeba that developed into a more complex form, impelled by the divine imperative to grow. A thousand sunsets have shaped my sense of beauty, and a thousand soft voices have taught me to be kind. Waters from a thousand springs have quenched my thirst. I look out upon my world and act in it with all that is mine, with every past experience, and with everything that entered into it.

As I think of the long line stretching far into the past, I also cast my glance forward. The line into the future is just as unbroken. It moves through me into generations yet unborn. And as I think of this, I am comforted. For I am a point in that line, and the course of existence travels through me. I have inherited from all the past and I will bequeath to all the future. In the movement of that line lies the secret of immortality, and I am a part of it.

Rabbi Ben Zion Bokser

From Psalm 16: Secure in the Presence of God

שִׁוִּיתִי, יְיָ, לְנֶגְדִּי תָמִיד	*Shiviti Adonai l'negdi tamid;*
כִּי מִימִינִי בַּל־אֶמּוֹט.	*ki mimini: bal-emot.*
לָכֵן שָׂמַח לִבִּי וַיָּגֶל כְּבוֹדִי	*Lachein samach libi, vayagel k'vodi;*
אַף־בְּשָׂרִי יִשְׁכֹּן לָבֶטַח.	*af-b'sari yishkon lavetach.*
כִּי לֹא־תַעֲזֹב נַפְשִׁי לִשְׁאוֹל	*Ki lo-taazov nafshi lish·ol;*
לֹא־תִתֵּן חֲסִידְךָ לִרְאוֹת שָׁחַת.	*lo-titein chasid'cha lirot shachat.*
תּוֹדִיעֵנִי אֹרַח חַיִּים	*Todi·eini orach chayim,*
שֹׂבַע שְׂמָחוֹת אֶת־פָּנֶיךָ	*sova s'machot et panecha,*
נְעִמוֹת בִּימִינְךָ נֶצַח.	*n'imot bimin'cha netzach.*

Keep me, Eternal One, for in You I find refuge,
and in You my soul finds its peace.
Guardian of all my days,
You are my cup from which I drink,
and the portion of my life.
I thank You for guiding my steps,
for the inner voice that instructs me.

I have set You before me always;
with You beside me I cannot fail.
So my heart is glad, my soul rejoices,
and all of me can rest secure:
for You will not abandon me in death.
You show me the path of life,
and Your presence is fullness of joy.

KEEP ME, ETERNAL ONE שִׁוִּיתִי, יְיָ. This psalm, one of ten designated by Rabbi Nachman of Breslov (1772–1810) for their special healing qualities, radiates a sense of quiet confidence, serenity, and joy. The capacity to discern God's presence in ordinary things — to experience the Divine "close at hand" at all times — helps us heal from grief and restores us to the path of life.

A Woodpecker Taps

First day
of the year you did not
live to see
foothills shrouded
lightly in fog.

Winter rain:
waiting at the station
for the tram
that goes where you
no longer are.

These trees
you photographed . . .
why do I see only
empty branches?

So warm
this winter of your death;
beneath
our chestnut tree
a clump of snowdrops.

Cold rain
this first day of spring;
I discard
can after can of old paint,
the plaid shirt you never wore.

Soft rain
high above the path
we walked
a woodpecker taps
and taps again.

Whitman wrote:
Look for me under
your boot soles.
And I do.
And you are.

Pamela Miller Ness

שֶׁבַע נֵרוֹת יִזְכֹּר
The Seven Lights of Yizkor

THE TRADITIONAL *Yizkor* prayer asks God to remember the souls of our loved ones and to shelter them for eternity. But the Yizkor Service on Yom Kippur has significance beyond the prayer itself. This is a moment set apart for solitary reflection; an opportunity to fulfill a sacred obligation; and it is a time to feel the physical and emotional closeness of community — the presence of other people who know what we have been through because they have been through it, too. At *Yizkor* we see the sorrow in one another's eyes.

As the number seven is a Jewish symbol of wholeness and holiness, our Yizkor Service offers seven ways to reflect on loss and memory, grief and healing. We choose, alone and together, from among these diverse lights.

<table>
<tr><td>

מָבוֹא
Mavo

</td></tr>
<tr><td>

נֵר א'
אָבְדַן אֲהוּבִים
Ner 1:
Ovdan Ahuvim

</td></tr>
<tr><td>

נֵר ב'
כֹּחוֹת הַנֶּפֶשׁ
Ner 2:
Kochot HaNefesh

</td></tr>
<tr><td>

נֵר ג'
קְדֻשַּׁת הַזִּכָּרוֹן
Ner 3:
K'dushat HaZikaron

</td></tr>
<tr><td>

נֵר ד'
הַיְחָסִים הַמְקֻדָּשִׁים
שֶׁלָּנוּ
Ner 4:
Ha-Y'chasim
Hamkudashim
Shelanu

</td></tr>
<tr><td>

נֵר ה'
עַל אָבְדַן וְעַל קַבָּלָה
Ner 5:
Al Ovdan V'al
Kabbalah

</td></tr>
<tr><td>

נֵר ו'
הוֹדָאָה
Ner 6:
Hodaah

</td></tr>
<tr><td>

נֵר ז'
שָׁלוֹם
Ner 7:
Shalom

</td></tr>
</table>

Enosh kechatzir yamav,	אֱנוֹשׁ כֶּחָצִיר יָמָיו,
k'tzitz hasadeh kein yatzitz.	כְּצִיץ הַשָּׂדֶה כֵּן יָצִיץ.
Ki ruach av'rah-bo v'einenu,	כִּי רוּחַ עָבְרָה־בּוֹ וְאֵינֶנּוּ,
v'lo-yakirenu od m'komo.	וְלֹא־יַכִּירֶנּוּ עוֹד מְקוֹמוֹ.
V'chesed Adonai mei·olam	וְחֶסֶד יְיָ מֵעוֹלָם
v'ad olam al-y'rei·av;	וְעַד־עוֹלָם עַל־יְרֵאָיו,
v'tzidkato livnei vanim —	וְצִדְקָתוֹ לִבְנֵי בָנִים,
l'shom'rei v'rito.	לְשֹׁמְרֵי בְרִיתוֹ.

Our days —
Like the grass of the field, like flowers in the meadow
vanish in a momentary gust of wind,
gone, never to be seen again.
But God's love is infinite and with us forever.
God's goodness reaches far into the future —
This is the gift of the covenant.

Psalm 103:15–18

From "Yom Kippur"

יוֹם כִּפּוּר בְּלִי אָבִי וּבְלִי אִמִּי
הוּא לֹא יוֹם כִּפּוּר.

מִבִּרְכַּת יְדֵיהֶם עַל רֹאשִׁי
נִשְׁאַר רַק הָרַעַד, כְּמוֹ רַעַד מָנוֹעַ
שֶׁלֹּא פָּסַק גַּם אַחַר מוֹתָם.

Yom Kippur without my father and without my mother
Is not Yom Kippur.

From the blessing of their hands on my head
Just the tremor has remained like the tremor of an engine
That didn't stop even after their death . . .

Yehuda Amichai

At David's Grave

Yes, he is here in this
open field, in sunlight, among
the few young trees set out
to modify the bare facts —

he's here, but only
because we are here.
When we go, he goes with us

to be your hands that never
do violence, your eyes
that wonder, your lives

that daily praise life
by living it, by laughter.

He is never alone here,
never cold in the field of graves.

Denise Levertov

YOUR LIVES. The dead live on in the lives of those who remember, cherish, and emulate the life now lost. Perhaps, through the use of the plural, the poet also suggests the many dimensions of each person's life — a concept implicit in the Hebrew word for life, *chayim*, which is, grammatically speaking, a plural form.

AT BIRTH, a miracle:
You light the spark in every human soul.

Emerging into light, we breathe it in —
the n'shamah, Your sacred gift of life.

And every day, every breath
comes to us as a miracle.

The light within us — unique and precious,
is with us always, while we live.

When breath has ceased and life has gone,
the n'shamah returns to You.

And the spark that lived inside the ones we love,
unique and precious, beautiful and good,
is theirs no more.

Their light is ours; their radiance now burns in us,
eternal flame of memory.

So we light candles, to keep our love alive,
to bring their light into the world;

A light unique and precious,
ours to treasure, while we live;

A ner tamid that lights our days
and gives us strength to journey through the nights.

מָבוֹא
Mavo

נֵר א'
אֲבְדַן אֲהוּבִים
Ner 1:
Ovdan Ahuvim

נֵר ב'
כֹּחוֹת הַנֶּפֶשׁ
Ner 2:
Kochot HaNefesh

נֵר ג'
קְדֻשַּׁת הַזִּכָּרוֹן
Ner 3:
K'dushat HaZikaron

נֵר ד'
הַיְחָסִים הַמְקֻדָּשִׁים שֶׁלָּנוּ
Ner 4:
Ha-Y'chasim
Hamkudashim
Shelanu

נֵר ה'
עַל אֲבְדַן וְעַל קַבָּלָה
Ner 5:
Al Ovdan V'al
Kabbalah

נֵר ו'
הוֹדָאָה
Ner 6:
Hodaah

נֵר ז'
שָׁלוֹם
Ner 7:
Shalom

MORE PRECIOUS was the light in your eyes than all
the roses in the world.

Edna St. Vincent Millay

כִּי יְיָ יִהְיֶה־לָּךְ לְאוֹר עוֹלָם, וְשָׁלְמוּ יְמֵי אֶבְלֵךְ.

Adonai shall be your everlasting light,
and your days of mourning shall be ended.

Isaiah 60:20

First Candle
On the Loss of Loved Ones

Words of Faith and Tradition

As a deer yearns for streams of water,
so I yearn for You, O God.
My whole being thirsts for God,
for the living God.

Psalm 42:2

Hear my prayer.
Let my cry come before You.
Do not hide from me in my time of sorrow.
Turn Your ear to me.
When I cry, answer me soon.

Psalm 102:2–3

My God,
my soul is downcast.
Therefore I think of You.

Psalm 42:7

The death of a loved one is the most profound of all sorrows. The grief that comes with such a loss is intense and multifaceted, affecting our emotions, our bodies, and our lives. Grief is preoccupying and depleting. Emotionally, grief is a mixture of raw feelings such as sorrow, anguish, anger, regret, longing, fear, and deprivation. Grief may be experienced physically as exhaustion, emptiness, tension, sleeplessness, or loss of appetite.

Grief invades our daily lives in many sudden gaps and changes, like that empty place at the dinner table, or the sudden loss of affection and companionship, as well as in many new apprehensions, adjustments, and uncertainties.

The loss of a loved one throws every aspect of our lives out of balance. The closer we were to the person who died, the more havoc the loss creates. Love does not die quickly. Hence to grieve is also "to celebrate the depth of the union. Tears are then the jewels of remembrance, sad but glistening with the beauty of the past. So grief in its bitterness marks the end . . . but it also is praise to the one who is gone."

Judy Tatelbaum

We Die

I

We die despite appointments and feuds,
while our toddler,
who has recently learned to say No,
opens and shuts drawers
a hundred times a day
and our teen braces
for the rapids of romance.

We die despite the contracts
and business trips we planned,
when our desk is untidy,
despite a long list of things to do
which we keep simmering
like a rich broth.

We die despite work we cherish,
marrying whom we love,
piling up a star-spangled fortune,
basking on the Riviera of fame,
and achieving, that human participle
with no known object.

II

Life is not fair, the old saw goes.
We know, we know, but the saw glides slow,
one faint rasp, and then at length another.
When you died, I felt its jagged teeth rip.
Small heartwounds opened and bled,
closing as new ones opened ahead.
Horror welled, not from the how but the when.

You died at the top of your career,
happy, blessed by love, still young.
Playing by evolution's rules, you won:
prospered, bred, rose in your tribe,
did what the parent gods and society prized.

continued next page

מָבוֹא
Mavo

נֵר א'
אָבְדַן אֲהוּבִים
Ner 1:
Ovdan Ahuvim

נֵר ב'
כֹּחוֹת הַנֶּפֶשׁ
Ner 2:
Kochot HaNefesh

נֵר ג'
קְדֻשַּׁת הַזִּכָּרוֹן
Ner 3:
K'dushat HaZikaron

נֵר ד'
הַיְחָסִים הַמְקֻדָּשִׁים
שֶׁלָּנוּ
Ner 4:
Ha-Y'chasim
Hamkudashim
Shelanu

נֵר ה'
עַל אָבְדַן וְעַל קַבָּלָה
Ner 5:
Al Ovdan V'al
Kabbalah

נֵר ו'
הוֹדָאָה
Ner 6:
Hodaah

נֵר ז'
שָׁלוֹם
Ner 7:
Shalom

Yet it didn't save you, love or dough.
Even when it happens slow, it happens fast,
and then there's no tomorrow.
Time topples, the castle of cards collapses,
thoughts melt, the subscription lapses.
What a waste of life we spend in asking,
in wish and worry and want and sorrow.

A tall man, you lie low, now and forever,
complete, your brilliant star eclipsed.
. . . . Lost friend, you taught me lessons
I longed to learn, and this final one I've learned
against my will: the one spoken in silence,
warning us to love hard and deep,
clutch dear ones tighter, ransom each day,
the horror lesson I saw out of the corner of my eye
but refused to believe until now: we die.

Diane Ackerman

שִׁיר הַמַּעֲלוֹת:
מִמַּעֲמַקִּים קְרָאתִֽיךָ, יְיָ.
אֲדֹנָי, שִׁמְעָה בְקוֹלִי
תִּהְיֶֽינָה אָזְנֶֽיךָ קַשֻּׁבוֹת
לְקוֹל תַּחֲנוּנָי.

Shir hamaalot:
Mimaamakim k'raticha, Adonai.
Adonai, shimah v'koli.
Tiyenah oznecha kashuvot
l'kol tachanunai.

A poem for reaching up

Out of the depths, I cry to You:
Hear me, hear my voice.
Let my plea reach Your ear.

Psalm 130:1–2

My Dead

הֵם בִּלְבַד נוֹתְרוּ לִי, רַק בָּהֶם בִּלְבַד
לֹא יִנְעַץ הַמָּוֶת סַכִּינוֹ הַחַד.

בְּמִפְנֵה הַדֶּרֶךְ, בַּעֲרֹב הַיּוֹם
יַקִּיפוּנִי חֶרֶשׁ, יְלַוּוּנִי דֹּם.

בְּרִית אֱמֶת הִיא לָנוּ, קֶשֶׁר לֹא נִפְרָד
רַק אֲשֶׁר אָבַד לִי – קִנְיָנִי לָעַד.

They alone are left me; they alone still faithful,
for now death can do no more to them.

At the bend of the road, at the close of day,
they gather around me silently, and walk by my side.

This is a bond nothing can ever loosen.
What I have lost: what I possess forever.

Rachel

Together

Together
We were like
two guy wires
supporting a fragile
sapling.

Our tenuous lives,
dreams, fantasies
entwined as one.

Slowly, the sapling
flourished, rooted,
produced two sons.

One day, after forty-two years,
without warning,
you let go.

Dora Kushner

The Death of a Parent

Move to the front
of the line
a voice says, and suddenly
there is nobody
left standing between you
and the world, to take
the first blows
on their shoulders.
This is the place in books
where part one ends, and part two begins,
and there is no part three.
The slate is wiped
not clean but like a canvas
painted over in white
so that a whole new landscape
must be started,
bits of the old
still showing underneath —
those colors sadness lends
to a certain hour of evening.
Now the line of light
at the horizon
is the hinge between earth
and heaven, only visible
a few moments
as the sun drops
its rusted padlock
into place.

Linda Pastan

Separation

Your absence has gone through me
Like thread through a needle.
Everything I do is stitched with its color.

W. S. Merwin

Lo Ira (Psalm 3:7)

לֹא־אִירָא מֵרִבְבוֹת עָם
אֲשֶׁר סָבִיב שָׁתוּ עָלָי

Lo-ira meiriv·vot am
asher saviv shatu alai.

I have no fear of the myriad forces
arrayed against me on every side.

Words of Healing

Adonai is my shepherd; I shall not want.

Psalm 23:1

For personal reflection . . .

For whom do I grieve?
In my grief, what is it that I need?
What kinds of moments make me most aware of what I have lost?

Blessed are those who give meaning to our lives;
holy and precious is the example they leave behind.
We pray:
May our sorrows diminish as we recall their strength.
May their wisdom protect us and help us to live.
Let our grief be transformed into tenderness toward those
who are still with us.

בָּרוּךְ אַתָּה, יְיָ, מְקוֹר הַחַיִּים.

Baruch atah, Adonai, m'kor hachayim.

Blessed are You, Holy One, who gives and renews life.

FORCES ARRAYED AGAINST ME. The righteous are called living even in death; the wicked are called dead even when alive. (Talmud *B'rachot* 18a)

DIE WHEN I MAY, I want it said of me, by those who knew me best, that I always plucked a thistle and planted a flower, when I thought a flower would grow. (Abraham Lincoln, 1809–1865)

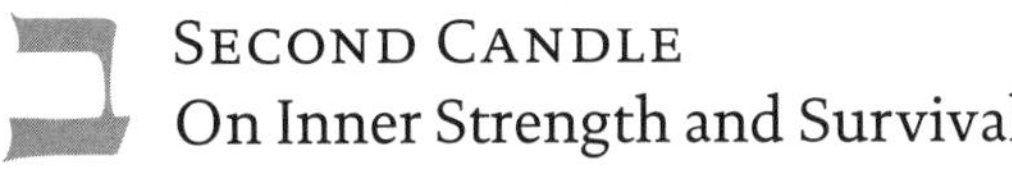

Second Candle
On Inner Strength and Survival

Words of Faith and Tradition

Adonai, mah-adam vateida·eihu;	יְיָ, מָה־אָדָם וַתֵּדָעֵהוּ,
ben-enosh vat'chash'veihu?	בֶּן־אֱנוֹשׁ וַתְּחַשְּׁבֵהוּ.
Adam lahevel damah;	אָדָם לַהֶבֶל דָּמָה,
yamav k'tzeil oveir.	יָמָיו כְּצֵל עוֹבֵר.

Adonai, how hard to fathom that we are worthy of Your care!
How astonishing — Your awareness of us!
For we are like the morning mist; our days — a passing shadow.

At dawn we flourish anew; by dusk we wither and fade.
Sending us back to earth's dust,
You tell us: "Return, you who belong to humanity."
If only we were wise and understood what lies ahead —
for when we die we carry nothing away;
we leave our possessions behind.
So mark the whole-hearted, take note of the upright —
for there is purpose in a life of integrity.
Adonai, You replenish the lives of all who revere You;
and those who trust in You will never despair.

based on Psalms 144:3–4; 90:6, 3; Deuteronomy 32:29; Psalms 49:18; 37:37; 34:23

From the prison of my grief I called You —
and You led me to open spaces.

based on Psalm 118:5

Happy is the one who draws strength from God,
whose heart is on a path to You.

based on Psalm 84:6

Send forth Your light and Your truth —
they will guide me.

Psalm 43:3

Psalm 121

Shir lamaalot:

Esa einai el-heharim:

mei·ayin yavo ezri?

Ezri mei-im Adonai —

oseih shamayim vaaretz.

Al-yitein lamot raglecha;

al-yanum shom'recha.

Hineih: lo-yanum v'lo yishan

shomeir Yisrael.

Adonai shom'recha;

Adonai tzil'cha al-yad y'minecha.

Yomam hashemesh lo-yakeka,

v'yarei-ach balailah.

Adonai yishmorcha mikol-ra —

yishmor et-nafshecha.

Adonai yishmor-tzeit'cha uvo·echa,

mei·atah v'ad-olam.

שִׁיר לַמַּעֲלוֹת:
אֶשָּׂא עֵינַי אֶל־הֶהָרִים,
מֵאַיִן יָבֹא עֶזְרִי.
עֶזְרִי מֵעִם יְיָ,
עֹשֵׂה שָׁמַיִם וָאָרֶץ.
אַל־יִתֵּן לַמּוֹט רַגְלֶךָ
אַל־יָנוּם שֹׁמְרֶךָ.
הִנֵּה לֹא־יָנוּם וְלֹא יִישָׁן
שׁוֹמֵר יִשְׂרָאֵל.
יְיָ שֹׁמְרֶךָ
יְיָ צִלְּךָ עַל־יַד יְמִינֶךָ.
יוֹמָם הַשֶּׁמֶשׁ לֹא־יַכֶּכָּה
וְיָרֵחַ בַּלָּיְלָה.
יְיָ יִשְׁמָרְךָ מִכָּל־רָע
יִשְׁמֹר אֶת־נַפְשֶׁךָ.
יְיָ יִשְׁמָר־צֵאתְךָ וּבוֹאֶךָ
מֵעַתָּה וְעַד־עוֹלָם.

A song for reaching up

I turn my eyes to the mountains;
from where will my help come?
My help comes from the Eternal,
maker of heaven and earth.
God will not let your foot give way;
your guardian will not slumber.
See, the guardian of Israel
neither slumbers nor sleeps!
The Eternal is your guardian,
The Eternal is your protection
at your right hand.
By day the sun will not strike you,
nor the moon by night.
The Eternal will guard you from all harm;
God will guard your soul.
The Eternal will guard your going and coming now and forever.

מָבוֹא
Mavo

נֵר א׳
אָבְדַן אֲהוּבִים
Ner 1:
Ovdan Ahuvim

נֵר ב׳
כֹּחוֹת הַנֶּפֶשׁ
Ner 2:
Kochot HaNefesh

נֵר ג׳
קְדֻשַּׁת הַזִּכָּרוֹן
Ner 3:
K'dushat HaZikaron

נֵר ד׳
הַיְחָסִים הַמְקֻדָּשִׁים שֶׁלָּנוּ
Ner 4:
Ha-Y'chasim Hamkudashim Shelanu

נֵר ה׳
עַל אָבְדַן וְעַל קַבָּלָה
Ner 5:
Al Ovdan V'al Kabbalah

נֵר ו׳
הוֹדָאָה
Ner 6:
Hodaah

נֵר ז׳
שָׁלוֹם
Ner 7:
Shalom

IN THE morning I said to myself:
Life's magic will never come back.
It won't come back.
All at once the sunshine in my house
is alive for me
and the table with its bread
is gold
and the cups on the table and the flower —
all gold.
And what of the sorrow?
Even in the sorrow, radiance.

Zelda

בַּבֹּקֶר הִרְהַרְתִּי:
לֹא יָשׁוּב עוֹד קֶסֶם הַחַיִּים
לֹא יָשׁוּב.
פִּתְאֹם בְּבֵיתִי הַשֶּׁמֶשׁ
יֵשׁוּת חַיָּה לִי
וְהַשֻּׁלְחָן אֲשֶׁר עָלָיו לֶחֶם
זָהָב
וְהַפֶּרַח אֲשֶׁר עַל הַשֻּׁלְחָן וְהַסְּפָלִים
זָהָב
וּמֶה הָיָה לָעֶצֶב
גַּם בָּעֶצֶב נֹגַהּ.

The Courage That My Mother Had

The courage that my mother had
Went with her, and is with her still.
Rock from New England quarried,
Now granite on a granite hill.

The golden brooch my mother wore
She left behind for me to wear;
I have no thing I treasure more:
Yet, it is something I could spare.

Oh, if instead she'd left me
The thing she took into the grave! —
That courage like a rock, which she
Has no more need of, and I have.

Edna St. Vincent Millay

White Apples

when my father had been dead a week
I woke
with his voice in my ear
    I sat up in bed
and held my breath
and stared at the pale closed door

white apples and the taste of stone

if he called again
I would put on my coat and galoshes

Donald Hall

A prayer for those who mourn the suicide of a loved one . . .

Let there be rest.
And let it be, at last, the perfect rest —
Oh, Merciful God Most High.

Let there be light:
heaven's radiance, gleaming light of the holy and pure
for my holy and pure one
whose corner was lit only by broken shards of light —
not nearly enough to see by.

Let there be, in my life, a shelter
against the storms of guilt, anger, grief, and pain.
When dark clouds gather above me —
may I find a warm shelter of peace.

And let there be a circle of souls around me —
patient, persistent, filled with Your compassion;
and let us be bound up in a loving bond that will not break.

Rest.
  Light.
    Shelter of peace.
      Circle of souls.

And give me the strength to praise.

PERFECT REST. The language of this prayer echoes "El Malei Rachamim" (page 598).

מָבוֹא
Mavo

נֵר א׳
אָבְדַן אֲהוּבִים
Ner 1:
Ovdan Ahuvim

נֵר ב׳
כֹּחוֹת הַנֶּפֶשׁ
Ner 2:
Kochot HaNefesh

נֵר ג׳
קְדֻשַּׁת הַזִּכָּרוֹן
Ner 3:
K'dushat HaZikaron

נֵר ד׳
הַיְחָסִים הַמְקֻדָּשִׁים שֶׁלָּנוּ
Ner 4:
Ha-Y'chasim Hamkudashim Shelanu

נֵר ה׳
עַל אָבְדַן וְעַל קַבָּלָה
Ner 5:
Al Ovdan V'al Kabbalah

נֵר ו׳
הוֹדָאָה
Ner 6:
Hodaah

נֵר ז׳
שָׁלוֹם
Ner 7:
Shalom

IN MY DARKNESS, be a light to me,
in my loneliness help me to find
a soul akin to my own.
Give me strength
to live with courage;
and give me courage
to draw blessing from life,
even in the midst of suffering;
to hold fast against the storm,
and to smile at a loved one's glance.

Rabbi Chaim Stern

THEY SAID in the name of Rabbi Meir:
With clenched fists an infant enters this world,
as if to say:
The whole world is mine to acquire.
With hands wide open we leave the world,
as if to say:
I have acquired nothing in this world.
For so it is said:
Naked came I from my mother's womb,
and naked shall I return.

Midrash *Ecclesiastes Rabbah* 5.20

DO NOT GRIEVE for me too much. I am a spirit confident of my rights. Death is only an incident, and not the most important which happens to us in this state of being. On the whole, especially since I met you, my darling one, I have been happy; and you have taught me how noble a woman's heart can be. If there is anywhere else, I shall be on the look out for you. Meanwhile look forward, feel free, rejoice in Life, cherish the children, guard my memory. God bless you.

Winston Churchill, from a letter to his wife: "In the event of my death . . ."

UNNAMABLE GOD, I feel You
  with me at every moment.
You are my food, my drink,
  my sunlight, and the air I breathe.
You are the ground I have built on
  and the beauty that rejoices my heart.

Psalm 16:8–9 (adapted)

Words of Healing

God makes me lie down in green pastures,
leads me beside the still waters.

Psalm 23:2

I SAT DOWN in the middle of the garden . . . and leaned my
back against a warm yellow pumpkin. . . . The earth was warm
under me, and warm as I crumbled it through my fingers. . . .
I kept as still as I could. Nothing happened. I did not expect
anything to happen. I was something that lay under the sun
and felt it, like the pumpkins, and I did not want to be anything more. I was entirely happy. Perhaps we feel like that
when we die and become a part of something entire, whether
it is sun and air, or goodness and knowledge. At any rate, that
is happiness; to be dissolved into something complete and
great. When it comes to one, it comes as naturally as sleep.

For personal reflection . . .

What are my sources of inner strength?
How have I survived loss and its pain?
Where do I find "green pastures" and "still waters"?

Blessed is the life force within us even in the worst of times.
Like dew on the grass, it renews and restores.
We pray:
May courage come.
Let dark fears be gone with morning's light.
Let grief give way to confidence and new hope.

בָּרוּךְ אַתָּה, יְיָ, מְקוֹר הַחַיִּים.

Baruch atah, Adonai, m'kor hachayim.

Blessed are You, Holy One, who gives and renews life.

I SAT DOWN. By Willa Cather (1873–1947). In Cather's novel *My Antonia,* a boy
in his grandmother's garden is surrounded by tall prairie grass. As in Psalm 23,
it is an image of lying down to rest outdoors: an expression of peace, abiding in
the whole — the deepest longing of humanity.

מָבוֹא
Mavo

נֵר א׳
אְבְדַּן אֲהוּבִים
Ner 1:
Ovdan Ahuvim

נֵר ב׳
כֹּחוֹת הַנֶּפֶשׁ
Ner 2:
Kochot HaNefesh

נֵר ג׳
קְדֻשַּׁת הַזִּכָּרוֹן
Ner 3:
K'dushat HaZikaron

נֵר ד׳
הַיְחָסִים הַמְקֻדָּשִׁים
שֶׁלָּנוּ
Ner 4:
Ha-Y'chasim
Hamkudashim
Shelanu

נֵר ה׳
עַל אְבְדַּן וְעַל קַבָּלָה
Ner 5:
Al Ovdan V'al
Kabbalah

נֵר ו׳
הוֹדָאָה
Ner 6:
Hodaah

נֵר ז׳
שָׁלוֹם
Ner 7:
Shalom

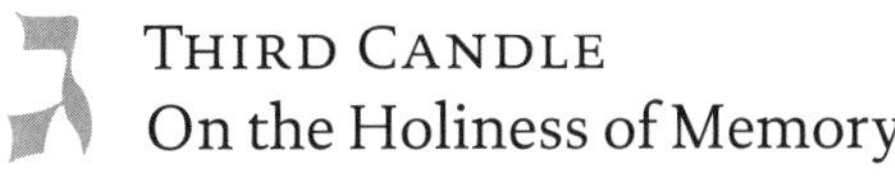

Third Candle
On the Holiness of Memory

Words of Faith and Tradition

I will preserve your memory forever. . . .

Psalm 45:18

The Echo of Your Promise

Based on Psalm 77

When I cry my voice trembles with fear
When I call out it cracks with anger

How can I greet the dawn with song
when darkness eclipses the rising sun

To whom shall I turn
when the clouds of the present eclipse the rays of tomorrow

Turn me around to yesterday
that I may be consoled by its memories

Were not the seas split asunder
Did we not once walk together through the waters to the dry side

Did we not bless the bread
that came forth from the heavens

Did your voice not reach my ears
and direct my wanderings

The waters, the lightning, the thunder
remind me of yesterday's triumphs

Let the past offer proof of tomorrow
Let it be my comforter and guarantor

I have been here before
known the fright and found your companionship

I enter the sanctuary again
to await the echo of your promise

Rabbi Harold Schulweis

HaN'shamah Lach

הַנְּשָׁמָה לָךְ וְהַגּוּף פָּעֳלָךְ,
חוּסָה עַל עֲמָלָךְ.

Han'shamah lach, v'haguf po·olach:
chusah al amalach.

The soul is Yours, the body is Your work;
have mercy on Your creation.

My Father

זֵכֶר אָבִי עָטוּף בִּנְיָר לָבָן
כִּפְרוּסוֹת לְיוֹם עֲבוֹדָה.

כְּקוֹסֵם, הַמּוֹצִיא מִכּוֹבָעוֹ אַרְנָבוֹת וּמִגְדָּלִים,
הוֹצִיא מִתּוֹךְ גּוּפוֹ הַקָּטָן – אַהֲבָה.

נַהֲרוֹת יָדָיו
נִשְׁפְּכוּ לְתוֹךְ מַעֲשָׂיו הַטּוֹבִים.

The memory of my father is wrapped up in white paper,
like sandwiches taken for a day at work.

Just as a magician takes towers and rabbits out of his hat,
he drew love from his small body,

and the rivers of his hands
overflowed with good deeds.

Yehuda Amichai

My Mother

In her last sickness, my mother took my hand in hers
tightly: for the first time I knew
how calloused a hand it was, and how soft was mine.

Charles Reznikoff

HAN'SHAMAH LACH. These lines, excerpted from a medieval poem for Yom Kippur, declare that both the soul and the body are God's handiwork. Both are precious and worthy of care. At this moment — aware of our physical exhaustion, weakness of will, and mortality — we do not celebrate body and soul; rather, we ask for compassion, simply because we belong to God.

I Needed to Talk to My Sister

I needed to talk to my sister
talk to her on the telephone   I mean
just as I used to every morning
in the evening too whenever the
grandchildren said a sentence that
clasped both our hearts
I called   her phone rang four times
you can imagine my breath stopped   then
there was a terrible telephonic noise
a voice said   this number is no
longer in use   how wonderful I
thought   I can
call again they have not yet assigned
her number to another person despite
two years of absence due to death

Grace Paley

Prayer for the Dead

The light snow started late last night and continued
all night long while I slept and could hear it occasionally
enter my sleep, where I dreamed my brother
was alive again and possessing the beauty of youth, aware
that he would be leaving again shortly and that is the lesson
of the snow falling and of the seeds of death that are in everything
that is born: we are here for a moment
of a story that is longer than all of us and few of us
remember, the wind is blowing out of someplace
we don't know, and each moment contains rhythms
within rhythms, and if you discover some old piece
of your own writing, or an old photograph,
you may not remember that it was you and even if it was once you,
it's not you now, not this moment that the synapses fire
and your hands move to cover your face in a gesture
of grief and remembrance.

Stuart Kestenbaum

I DREAMED MY BROTHER / WAS ALIVE. The author's brother, Howard, died in the destruction of the twin towers of the World Trade Center on September 11, 2001.

A Candle in a Glass

When you died, it was time to light the first
candle of the eight. The dark tidal shifts
of the Jewish calendar of waters and the moon
that grows like a belly and starves like a rabbit
in winter have carried that holiday forward
and back since then. I light only your candle
at sunset, as the red wax of the sun melts
into the rumpled waters of the bay.

The ancient words pass like cold water
out of stone over my tongue as I say kaddish.
When I am silent and the twilight drifts
in on skeins of unraveling woolly snow
blowing over the hill dark with pitch pines,
I have a moment of missing that pierces
my brain like sugar stabbing a cavity
till the nerve lights its burning wire.

Grandmother Hannah comes to me at Pesach
and when I am lighting the sabbath candles.
The sweet wine in the cup has her breath.
The challah is braided like her long, long hair.
She smiles vaguely, nods, is gone like a savor
passing. You come oftener when I am putting
up pears or tomatoes, baking apple cake.
You are in my throat laughing or in my eyes.

When someone dies, it is the unspoken words
that spoil in the mind and ferment to wine
and to vinegar. I obey you still, going
out in the saw toothed wind to feed the birds
you protected. When I lie in the arms of my love,
I know how you climbed like a peavine twining,
lush, grasping for the sun, toward love
and always you were pinched back, denied.

continued next page

It's a little low light the yahrtzeit candle
makes, you couldn't read by it or even warm
your hands. So the dead are with us only
as the scent of fresh coffee, of cinnamon,
of pansies excites the nose and then fades,
with us as the small candle burns in its glass.
We lose and we go on losing as long as we live,
a little winter no spring can melt.

Marge Piercy

Footprints

Everything will remember that I was here.
The ships will be the color of my clothing.
The birds will use my voice for singing.
The fisherman on the rock will ponder my poem.
The river will follow my footprints.

Rajzel Zychlinsky

My Father

That every night my father
shone like the window in the ark.

That every night I was like a shadow
clinging to the wings of his light.

Tonight my father sweeps over me
as over a candle the dark.

שֶׁבְּכָל הַלֵּילוֹת הָיָה אֲבִי
מֵאִיר כְּצֹהַר בַּתֵּבָה.

שֶׁבְּכָל הַלֵּילוֹת הָיִיתִי כְּצֵל
נֶאֱחָז בְּכַנְפֵי אוֹרוֹ.

הַלַּיְלָה הַזֶּה גּוֹהֵר מֵעָלַי
אֲבִי כַּחֹשֶׁךְ עַל נֵר.

Tuvia Rubner

Promised Land

At the edge
Of a world
Beyond my eyes
Beautiful
I know Exile
Is Always
Green with hope —
The river
We cannot cross
Flows forever.

Samuel Menashe

Words of Healing

God restores my soul. . . .

Psalm 23:3

For personal reflection . . .

What memories of my loved one(s) do I cherish most?
Do some of my memories still hurt?
How do my memories help me to live a better life?

Blessed are the memories,
holy and cherished the love they reveal.
We pray —
May our sorrows soften and diminish in strength.
May the pains of past bereavements grow gentler with time.
Let memory bring us nearer to the loved ones in our midst.

בָּרוּךְ אַתָּה, יְיָ, מְקוֹר הַחַיִּים.
Baruch atah, Adonai, m'kor hachayim.
Blessed are You, Holy One, who gives and renews life.

מָבוֹא
Mavo

נֵר א׳
אָבְדַן אֲהוּבִים
Ner 1:
Ovdan Ahuvim

נֵר ב׳
כֹּחוֹת הַנֶּפֶשׁ
Ner 2:
Kochot HaNefesh

נֵר ג׳
קְדֻשַּׁת הַזִּכָּרוֹן
Ner 3:
K'dushat HaZikaron

נֵר ד׳
הַיְחָסִים הַמְקֻדָּשִׁים
שֶׁלָּנוּ
Ner 4:
Ha-Y'chasim
Hamkudashim
Shelanu

נֵר ה׳
עַל אָבְדַן וְעַל קַבָּלָה
Ner 5:
Al Ovdan V'al
Kabbalah

נֵר ו׳
הוֹדָאָה
Ner 6:
Hodaah

נֵר ז׳
שָׁלוֹם
Ner 7:
Shalom

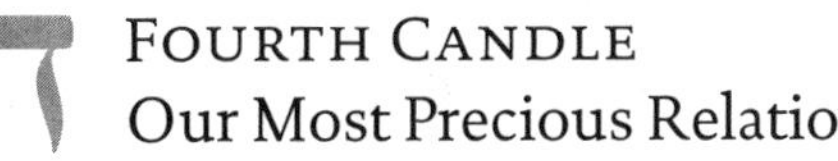

Fourth Candle
Our Most Precious Relationships

Words of Faith and Tradition

Yeish kochavim she·oram magia artzah	יֵשׁ כּוֹכָבִים שֶׁאוֹרָם מַגִּיעַ אַרְצָה
rak kaasher hem atzmam	רַק כַּאֲשֶׁר הֵם עַצְמָם
av'du v'einam.	אָבְדוּ וְאֵינָם.
Yeish anashim sheziv zichram mei·ir	יֵשׁ אֲנָשִׁים שֶׁזִּיו זִכְרָם מֵאִיר
kaasher hem atzmam einam od	כַּאֲשֶׁר הֵם עַצְמָם אֵינָם עוֹד
b'tocheinu.	בְּתוֹכֵנוּ.
Orot eileh hamavhikim	אוֹרוֹת אֵלֶּה הַמַּבְהִיקִים
b'cheshkat halayil.	בְּחֶשְׁכַּת הַלַּיִל.
Heim heim shemarim laadam et	הֵם הֵם שֶׁמַּרְאִים לָאָדָם אֶת
haderech.	הַדֶּרֶךְ.

There are stars up above,
so far away we only see their light
long, long after the star itself is gone.
And so it is with people that we loved —
their memories keep shining ever brightly
though their time with us is done.
But the stars that light up the darkest night,
these are the lights that guide us.
As we live our days, these are the ways we remember.

Hana Senesh

my uncle

my grandmother

my father-in-law

I miss

my loved one

I am sorry

my grandfather

I promise

I ask forgiveness

my aunt

I wish

my grandchild

my niece

I regret

my mother

my spouse

my child

I cherish

my brother

my father

my wife

my daughter

May God Remember

I remember

my brother-in-law

my teacher

I forgive

I honor

my friend

my companion

I hold close

I hope

my nephew

my mother-in-law

my sister-in-law

I grieve

I mourn

I am grateful

my sister

my husband

my son

Yizkor Elohim

The Yizkor Prayer

"Love is strong as death." Song of Songs 8:6

For a Man or Boy

Yizkor Elohim et nishmat	יִזְכֹּר אֱלֹהִים אֶת נִשְׁמַת . . . . .
shehalach l'olamo.	שֶׁהָלַךְ לְעוֹלָמוֹ.
Hin'ni nodev/nodevet tz'dakah	הִנְנִי נוֹדֵב\נוֹדֶבֶת צְדָקָה
b'ad hazkarat nishmato.	בְּעַד הַזְכָּרַת נִשְׁמָתוֹ.
Ana t'hi nafsho	אָנָּא תְּהִי נַפְשׁוֹ
tz'rurah bitzror hachayim	צְרוּרָה בִּצְרוֹר הַחַיִּים
ut·hi m'nuchato kavod —	וּתְהִי מְנוּחָתוֹ כָּבוֹד,
sova s'machot et panecha,	שֹׂבַע שְׂמָחוֹת אֶת פָּנֶיךָ,
n'imot bimincha netzach.	נְעִימוֹת בִּימִינְךָ נֶצַח.

May God remember the soul of . . . . .
who has gone to his eternal home.
For the sake of *tikkun olam*, I freely give *tzedakah* in his memory.
For the sake of his precious soul, let my memories, my prayers,
and my acts of goodness bind him to the bond of life.
May I bring honor to his memory by word and deed.
May he be at one with the One who is life eternal;
and may the beauty of his life shine forevermore.

Introduction

First Candle: The Loss of Loved Ones

Second Candle: Inner Strength and Survival

Third Candle: The Holiness of Memory

Fourth Candle: Our Most Precious Relationships

Fifth Candle: Acceptance

Sixth Candle: Gratitude

Seventh Candle: Finding Peace

For a Woman or Girl

Yizkor Elohim et nishmat	יִזְכֹּר אֱלֹהִים אֶת נִשְׁמַת . . . . .
shehal'chah l'olamah.	שֶׁהָלְכָה לְעוֹלָמָהּ.
Hin'ni nodev/nodevet tz'dakah	הִנְנִי נוֹדֵב\נוֹדֶבֶת צְדָקָה
b'ad hazkarat nishmatah.	בְּעַד הַזְכָּרַת נִשְׁמָתָהּ.
Ana t'hi nafshah	אָנָּא תְּהִי נַפְשָׁהּ
tz'rurah bitzror hachayim	צְרוּרָה בִּצְרוֹר הַחַיִּים
ut·hi m'nuchatah kavod —	וּתְהִי מְנוּחָתָהּ כָּבוֹד,
sova s'machot et panecha,	שֹׂבַע שְׂמָחוֹת אֶת פָּנֶיךָ,
n'imot bimincha netzach.	נְעִימוֹת בִּימִינְךָ נֶצַח.

May God remember the soul of . . . . .
who has gone to her eternal home.
For the sake of *tikkun olam*, I freely give *tzedakah* in her memory.
For the sake of her precious soul, let my memories, my prayers,
and my acts of goodness bind her to the bond of life.
May I bring honor to her memory by word and deed.
May she be at one with the One who is life eternal;
and may the beauty of her life shine forevermore.

Yizkor Meditations

WHEN WE ASK GOD to remember the souls of our departed at *Yizkor*, we request more than a mere mental act. We pray implicitly that by focusing on our loved ones' souls, God will take action on their behalf and save them from whatever pain they may be suffering, wherever they may be. At the same time, the implication is that this act of remembrance also constitutes a guarantee of Jewish continuity — well beyond just those we remember, and far beyond us as well. In remembering and in asking for God's remembrance, we request divine help in continuing our people's trajectory beyond ourselves, to achieve the ultimate aims of our people's history.

Yizkor is, in the end, not a prayer for the dead, but a promise by the living.

Rabbi Aaron Panken

MAY THESE MOMENTS of meditation link me more strongly with my closest companion in life — my soulmate, my friend, my confidant, my helping hand, my listening heart, my compass, my shining light.

In spite of death, our deep bonds of love are strong.
May I always be worthy of that love.
May the memory of our companionship lead me out of loneliness;
may it awaken in me gratitude for that which still endures.
And may you rest forever in dignity and peace.

BLESSED IS THE ONE who is far beyond all the blessings and hymns, all the praises and words of comfort that we speak in the world. And blessed are those who are now far beyond my words, my praise, my voice — even my silence.

מָבוֹא
Mavo

נֵר א׳
אָבְדַן אֲהוּבִים
Ner 1: Ovdan Ahuvim

נֵר ב׳
כֹּחוֹת הַנֶּפֶשׁ
Ner 2: Kochot HaNefesh

נֵר ג׳
קְדֻשַּׁת הַזִּכָּרוֹן
Ner 3: K'dushat HaZikaron

נֵר ד׳
הַיְחָסִים הַמְקֻדָּשִׁים שֶׁלָּנוּ
Ner 4: Ha-Y'chasim Hamkudashim Shelanu

נֵר ה׳
עַל אָבְדַן וְעַל קַבָּלָה
Ner 5: Al Ovdan V'al Kabbalah

נֵר ו׳
הוֹדָאָה
Ner 6: Hodaah

נֵר ז׳
שָׁלוֹם
Ner 7: Shalom

Introduction

First Candle: The Loss of Loved Ones

Second Candle: Inner Strength and Survival

Third Candle: The Holiness of Memory

Fourth Candle: Our Most Precious Relationships

Fifth Candle: Acceptance

Sixth Candle: Gratitude

Seventh Candle: Finding Peace

For an Infant or Child

God of hope, God of strength —
As my heart aches in silence
I turn to You on this holy day for healing and comfort.
I pray to You, God of life, for renewal of spirit.
I long for the shelter of Your love.

May the soul of my beloved .....
be embraced by You forever with love and tenderness.
May the promise of this innocent young life
teach me to cherish sweetness and beauty,
and not give in to the bitterness I have tasted.
May the gift of memory bless each of my days.

Weep with me, God, Creator of life,
for the precious life whose songs were left unsung.
Weep with me, God, for the loss of my child —
a loss that is like no other.
Shelter me,
that I may be a source of care and shelter for those who need me.
Strengthen me,
that I may be a source of strength.
Be with me
in sorrow and joy, in moments of emptiness, and in the fullness of life.

REFLECTING ON THE DEATH of his 20-year-old son Uri, an Israeli soldier who died in the final hours of the 2006 Lebanon War, novelist David Grossman (b. 1954) said: "You have to understand that when something like this happens to you, you feel exiled from every part of your life. Nothing is home again, not even your body."

For One Who Died by Violence

קוֹל דְּמֵי אָחִיךָ צֹעֲקִים אֵלַי מִן־הָאֲדָמָה.

"Your brother's blood cries to Me from the ground." Genesis 4:10

Creator of life, Source of healing,
grant peace in Your great shelter of peace
to my loved one .....
whose life ended abruptly through an act of senseless violence.

With sadness I recall the joy that ..... brought into the world;
that voice and face I will never forget.
May these precious memories console me.
Let there be light —
to guide my way through the shadow of loss.

I long with all my being
for an end to baseless hatred, war, and violence.
May a time come soon
when no one will suffer or die at the hands of another.

May my loved one's soul be embraced by You —
free of pain now, held in tenderness and love.
I will cherish forever this life now lost:
a blessing in the bond of life everlasting,
a blessing here and now.

מָבוֹא
Mavo

נֵר א׳
אָבְדַן אֲהוּבִים
Ner 1: Ovdan Ahuvim

נֵר ב׳
כֹּחוֹת הַנֶּפֶשׁ
Ner 2: Kochot HaNefesh

נֵר ג׳
קְדֻשַּׁת הַזִּכָּרוֹן
Ner 3: K'dushat HaZikaron

נֵר ד׳
הַיְחָסִים הַמְקֻדָּשִׁים שֶׁלָּנוּ
Ner 4: Ha-Y'chasim Hamkudashim Shelanu

נֵר ה׳
עַל אָבְדַן וְעַל קַבָּלָה
Ner 5: Al Ovdan V'al Kabbalah

נֵר ו׳
הוֹדָאָה
Ner 6: Hodaah

נֵר ז׳
שָׁלוֹם
Ner 7: Shalom

In Memory of a Parent Who Was Hurtful

Dear God,

You know my heart. Indeed, You know me better than I know myself, so I turn to You in these quiet moments of Yizkor.

My emotions swirl as I recite this prayer. The parent I remember was not kind to me. His/her death left me with a legacy of unhealed wounds, of anger and of dismay that a parent could hurt a child as I was hurt.

I do not want to pretend to love, or to grief that I do not feel, but I do want to do what is right as a Jew and as a son/daughter.

Help me, God, to subdue my bitter emotions that do me no good, and to find that place in myself where happier memories may lie hidden, and where grief for all that could have been, all that should have been, may be calmed by forgiveness, or at least soothed by the passage of time.

I pray that You, who raise up slaves to freedom, will liberate me from the oppression of my hurt and anger, and that You will lead me from this desert to Your holy place.

Rabbi Robert Saks

אַל־תַּסְתֵּר פָּנֶיךָ מִמֶּנִּי, אַל־תַּט־בְּאַף עַבְדֶּךָ, עֶזְרָתִי הָיִיתָ.
אַל־תִּטְּשֵׁנִי, וְאַל־תַּעַזְבֵנִי, אֱלֹהֵי יִשְׁעִי.
כִּי־אָבִי וְאִמִּי עֲזָבוּנִי, וַייָ יַאַסְפֵנִי.

Don't hide your face from me —
Don't push me away;
I depend on you.
I've looked to you for help —
please don't abandon me.

Adonai, may I find safety in You.
Though my mother and father forsake me,
the Eternal will take me in.

DON'T HIDE YOUR FACE, Psalm 27:9–10, with an interpretive translation.

Psalm

I am still on a rooftop in Brooklyn on your holy day.
The harbor is before me, Governor's Island, the Verrazano Bridge
and the Narrows.
I keep in my head
what Rabbi Nachman said about the world being a narrow bridge
and that the important thing is not to be afraid.
So on this day
I bless my mother and father,
that they be not fearful where they wander.
And I ask you to bless them,
and before you close your Book of Life, your Sefer Hachayim,
remember that I always praised your world and your splendor
and that my tongue tried to say your name on Court Street in Brooklyn.
Take me safely through the Narrows to the sea.

Harvey Shapiro

YOU ARE NOT beautiful, exactly.
You are beautiful, inexactly.
You let a weed grow by the mulberry
and a mulberry grow by the house.
So close, in the personal quiet
of a windy night, it brushes the wall
and sweeps away the day till we sleep.

A child said it, and it seemed true:
"Things that are lost are all equal."
But it isn't true. If I lost you,
the air wouldn't move, nor the tree grow.
Someone would pull the weed, my flower.
The quiet wouldn't be yours. If I lost you,
I'd have to ask the grass to let me sleep.

Marvin Bell

מָבוֹא
Mavo

נֵר א׳
אָבְדַן אֲהוּבִים
Ner 1: Ovdan Ahuvim

נֵר ב׳
כֹּחוֹת הַנֶּפֶשׁ
Ner 2: Kochot HaNefesh

נֵר ג׳
קְדֻשַּׁת הַזִּכָּרוֹן
Ner 3: K'dushat HaZikaron

נֵר ד׳
הַיְחָסִים הַמְקֻדָּשִׁים שֶׁלָּנוּ
Ner 4: Ha-Y'chasim Hamkudashim Shelanu

נֵר ה׳
עַל אָבְדַן וְעַל קַבָּלָה
Ner 5: Al Ovdan V'al Kabbalah

נֵר ו׳
הוֹדָאָה
Ner 6: Hodaah

נֵר ז׳
שָׁלוֹם
Ner 7: Shalom

What Happens after Death?

I find it hard to believe that all we are simply vanishes. I don't think we go to a physical place. After all, the essence, the soul, is not physical. As the Israeli scholar Adin Steinsaltz once remarked, to ask "where the soul goes is a nonsense question. The soul is not physical. Where does a dream go once it has been dreamt? Where does love go when it disappears?"

We cannot conceive of what life might be like if it is not material like this life. In this life we are tied to the tangible, except our deepest experiences tend to be things that are not really physical, like love, like memory. We cannot imagine what happens after death, but the poverty of our imagination does not prove that the world is not more creative than we know.

It is lovely to think that the loss of this world is a ticket price to the inheritance of the next. Maybe we step through this world as if through a corridor. A beautiful comment by Bronson Alcott, friend of Emerson and father of Louisa May Alcott, ties together the themes of failing memory and the world to come. As he grew older, Emerson started to lose his memory. He tried to get around it—once, forgetting the term "umbrella," he called it "the thing that strangers take away" — but it troubled him. He was consoled by Alcott, who made reference to the Platonic legend that human beings know all about this world but lose that knowledge the moment we are born. Likewise, he said that as we get older, we start to lose knowledge of this world in the form of failing memory, to prepare us for the next one. Each time we cannot remember something about this world, it is not a failing but a letting go.

Rabbi David Wolpe

Words of Healing

. . . and guides me in straight paths
   for the sake of God's name.

Psalm 23:3

For personal reflection . . .

How do my feelings of grief differ for each person I have lost?

What is my personal prayer for each one?

What would I like each of them to know about me now?

Blessed is the life of every soul,

pure and bright the breath of God within us.

We pray —

Help us know the Infinite Wisdom that gives life and takes
   it away.

Forgive us for anger, bitterness, and selfishness.

Teach us the language of healing.

בָּרוּךְ אַתָּה, יְיָ, מְקוֹר הַחַיִּים.

Baruch atah, Adonai, m'kor hachayim.

Blessed are You, Holy One, who gives and renews life.

מָבוֹא
Mavo

נֵר א׳
אָבְדַן אֲהוּבִים
Ner 1:
Ovdan Ahuvim

נֵר ב׳
כֹּחוֹת הַנֶּפֶשׁ
Ner 2:
Kochot HaNefesh

נֵר ג׳
קְדֻשַּׁת הַזִּכָּרוֹן
Ner 3:
K'dushat HaZikaron

נֵר ד׳
הַיְחָסִים הַמְקֻדָּשִׁים שֶׁלָּנוּ
Ner 4:
Ha-Y'chasim Hamkudashim Shelanu

נֵר ה׳
עַל אָבְדָן וְעַל קַבָּלָה
Ner 5:
Al Ovdan V'al Kabbalah

נֵר ו׳
הוֹדָאָה
Ner 6:
Hodaah

נֵר ז׳
שָׁלוֹם
Ner 7:
Shalom

TEACH US THE LANGUAGE OF HEALING.
How shall the heart be reconciled
to its feast of losses?
   (Stanley Kunitz, 1905–2006)

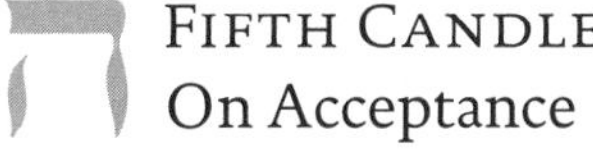

Fifth Candle
On Acceptance

Words of Faith and Tradition

I have taught myself to be contented. . . .

Psalm 131:2

Psalm 90

Adonai, through all generations, we have found our home in You.
Before the mountains rose up, before the birth-pangs of the earth,
You alone have been with us, steadfast and constant for all time.

In the end You return us to dust, saying: "Come home now,
daughters and sons of Adam and Eve — you are mortal."
In Your sight a thousand years pass in an instant,
like a fleeting watch in the night. But how brief the span of our lives!
Our years flow by in a dream; we sleep away our days.
In the morning we blossom in beauty; in the evening we wither away.
Burnt like grass in the blasting heat of summer,
we perish like chaff on the wind.

A human life may be three score years and ten;
or four score years, for those who are blessed with strength.
So many days consumed by toil and troubles —
then our time is cut short; and too soon we go into the dark.
So teach us to number our days,
that we may bring home a heart of wisdom.
Give us a sense of Your presence; nourish us with Your compassion.
Knowing Your love at the dawn of our life, let us live our days in contentment.
May our moments of joy surpass the times of struggle.
May we taste the sweetness of each precious day.
May the work of our hands bring fulfillment.

STEADFAST AND CONSTANT FOR ALL TIME. Based on the commentary of Rabbi Samson Raphael Hirsch (1808–1888) on Psalm 90:1.

GO INTO THE DARK. T. S. Eliot, "East Coker," from *Four Quartets.*

TEACH US . . . BRING HOME A HEART OF WISDOM. From the translation by Rabbi Samson Raphael Hirsch of Psalm 90:12.

The Five Stages of Grief

The night I lost you
someone pointed me towards
the Five Stages of Grief.
Go that way, they said,
it's easy, like learning to climb
stairs after the amputation.
And so I climbed.
Denial was first.
I sat down at breakfast
carefully setting the table
for two. I passed you the toast —
you sat there. I passed
you the paper — you hid
behind it.
Anger seemed more familiar.
I burned the toast, snatched
the paper and read the headlines myself.
But they mentioned your departure,
and so I moved on to
Bargaining. What could I exchange
for you? The silence
after storms? My typing fingers?
Before I could decide, *Depression*
came puffing up, a poor relation
its suitcase tied together
with string. In the suitcase
were bandages for the eyes
and bottles of sleep. I slid
all the way down the stairs
feeling nothing.
And all the time Hope
flashed on and off
in defective neon.
Hope was a signpost pointing
straight in the air.
Hope was my uncle's middle name,
he died of it.
After a year I am still climbing,
though my feet slip
on your stone face.
The treeline
has long since disappeared;
green is a color
I have forgotten.
But now I see what I am climbing
towards: *Acceptance*
written in capital letters,
a special headline:
Acceptance,
its name is in lights.
I struggle on,
waving and shouting.
Below, my whole life spreads its surf,
all the landscapes I've ever known
or dreamed of. Below
a fish jumps: the pulse
in your neck.
Acceptance. I finally
reach it.
But something is wrong.
Grief is a circular staircase.
I have lost you.

Linda Pastan

מָבוֹא
Mavo

נֵר א׳
אָבְדַן אֲהוּבִים
Ner 1: Ovdan Ahuvim

נֵר ב׳
כֹּחוֹת הַנֶּפֶשׁ
Ner 2: Kochot HaNefesh

נֵר ג׳
קְדֻשַּׁת הַזִּכָּרוֹן
Ner 3: K'dushat HaZikaron

נֵר ד׳
הַיְחָסִים הַמְקֻדָּשִׁים שֶׁלָּנוּ
Ner 4: Ha-Y'chasim Hamkudashim Shelanu

נֵר ה׳
עַל אָבְדַן וְעַל קַבָּלָה
Ner 5: Al Ovdan V'al Kabbalah

נֵר ו׳
הוֹדָאָה
Ner 6: Hodaah

נֵר ז׳
שָׁלוֹם
Ner 7: Shalom

Forgiveness and the Afterlife

I do have an ongoing relationship with the dead, and I do think about the afterlife — my afterlife, that is — after someone I know dies: what happens to me afterwards, in my life.

Some deaths come too soon; some deaths are unexpected; some deaths we think we are prepared for, but really we are rarely ready: we don't usually know when a conversation is the last conversation, with so much that may be left unsaid, unresolved.

So in this afterlife of mine I am still in relationship with people who have died. I miss them, I talk to them in my mind, I ask them questions about our relationship that I wasn't ready to ask them when they were still alive. I show off my accomplishments, and wish they could witness them; and yes, I still have some of the same old arguments, still trying to prove my point of view. What helps me go forward? How do I resolve these lingering feelings?

Here is what makes the Yom Kippur *Yizkor* so special — this forgiveness prayer devoted exclusively to those no longer with us, that comes late in the afternoon when we are tired, hungry, vulnerable, and open. During this *Yizkor* I am given the opportunity to forgive myself for cutting off that last phone conversation with my father — I was always in a hurry; he always wanted to chat longer; and then he died. It's during this *Yizkor* that I have the opportunity to forgive my mother for her harsh ways; to let go of being angry — for my sake in this world, if not for her sake in the world-to-come.

For this *Yizkor* to feel honest and meaningful, I don't want to sentimentalize those relationships. I don't just want to remember the ideals and gifts they may or may not have passed down. I want to remember those relationships exactly as they were, and then be able to forgive myself and them for our failings, for what we never got a chance to repair or finish.

Cantor Linda Hirschhorn (adapted)

SO I HAVE SPENT my life watching, not to see beyond the world, merely to see, great mystery, what is plainly before my eyes. I think the concept of transcendence is based on a misreading of creation. With all respect to heaven, the scene of miracle is here, among us. (Marilynne Robinson, b. 1943)

Bright Mariner

Had I known that you were going
I could have given you
At least, good speed.
But you slipped away so suddenly
That I was left standing on the shore
Watching into space.
Not knowing that you would never come back,
Till I felt the waters of the incoming tide
Cold about my heart.
I do not ask for you again,
I know the sea you sail
Does not touch these shores,
I only look for a distant "All hail"
Like the white crest of a wave against the horizon
Or a signal light flashing once,
Far against the Sky.
Sail on, my bright sturdy mariner!
Let out a full sheet to your new winds,
Taste the clear spray of your new waters.
You were made for flight and swiftness,
And eternal freedom.
Nothing shall weigh you down
Or call you back to the warm earth,
Or the shape we knew,
Or the place that held you so very dear.
I have cut the anchor chain that bound you to me,
and the great strength of my love,
And the heavy ache of my loneliness,
Which might bear upon you and hold you back,
I have fashioned into a shining, silken fabric
To the highest, and strongest of your new sails.

Katherine Garrison Chapin

מָבוֹא
Mavo

נֵר א'
אָבְדַן אֲהוּבִים
Ner 1:
Ovdan Ahuvim

נֵר ב'
כֹּחוֹת הַנֶּפֶשׁ
Ner 2:
Kochot HaNefesh

נֵר ג'
קְדֻשַּׁת הַזִּכָּרוֹן
Ner 3:
K'dushat HaZikaron

נֵר ד'
הַיְחָסִים הַמְקֻדָּשִׁים
שֶׁלָּנוּ
Ner 4:
Ha-Y'chasim
Hamkudashim
Shelanu

נֵר ה'
עַל אָבְדָן וְעַל קַבָּלָה
Ner 5:
Al Ovdan V'al
Kabbalah

נֵר ו'
הוֹדָאָה
Ner 6:
Hodaah

נֵר ז'
שָׁלוֹם
Ner 7:
Shalom

BRIGHT MARINER. An elegy, composed about three years after the death
of the author's young son, Garrison Chapin Biddle (1923–1930).

Let Evening Come

Let the light of late afternoon
shine through chinks in the barn, moving
up the bales as the sun moves down.

Let the cricket take up chafing
as a woman takes up her needles
and her yarn. Let evening come.

Let dew collect on the hoe abandoned
in long grass. Let the stars appear
and the moon disclose her silver horn.

Let the fox go back to its sandy den.
Let the wind die down. Let the shed
go black inside. Let evening come.

To the bottle in the ditch, to the scoop
in the oats, to air in the lung
let evening come.

Let it come, as it will, and don't
be afraid. God does not leave us
comfortless, so let evening come.

Jane Kenyon

B'yado Afkid Ruchi (from Adon Olam)

B'yado afkid ruchi,	בְּיָדוֹ אַפְקִיד רוּחִי,
b'eit ishan v'a·irah.	בְּעֵת אִישַׁן וְאָעִירָה.
V'im ruchi g'viyati,	וְעִם רוּחִי גְּוִיָּתִי,
Adonai li v'lo ira.	יְיָ לִי וְלֹא אִירָא.

My soul entrusted to Your care,
both when I sleep and when I rise.
My body, too, will rest in You.
I have no fear — for God is mine.

GOD OF PITY AND LOVE, return to this earth.
Go not so far away, leaving us to grief.
Return, Eternal One, return. Come back with the day.
Come with the light, that we may see once more
across this earth's unsettled floor
the kindly path, the old and living way.
Let us not give way to evil in the night.
Let there be God again.
Let there be light.

The Union Prayerbook (adapted)

Words of Healing

Yea, though I walk through the valley of the shadow of death,
I will fear no evil, for You are with me;
Your rod and Your staff, they comfort me.

Psalm 23:4

For personal reflection . . .
As I try to accept my losses, what helps me? What stands in my
way?
What have I learned?

Blessed is the path to acceptance —
very near and sometimes distant as the horizon.
We pray —
that our moments of joy surpass the times of struggle,
that we taste the sweetness of each precious day,
that the work of our hands brings fulfillment.

בָּרוּךְ אַתָּה, יְיָ, מְקוֹר הַחַיִּים.
Baruch atah, Adonai, m'kor hachayim.
Blessed are You, Holy One, who gives and renews life.

מָבוֹא
Mavo

נֵר א'
אָבְדַן אֲהוּבִים
Ner 1:
Ovdan Ahuvim

נֵר ב'
כֹּחוֹת הַנֶּפֶשׁ
Ner 2:
Kochot HaNefesh

נֵר ג'
קְדֻשַּׁת הַזִּכָּרוֹן
Ner 3:
K'dushat HaZikaron

נֵר ד'
הַיְחָסִים הַמְקֻדָּשִׁים
שֶׁלָּנוּ
Ner 4:
Ha-Y'chasim
Hamkudashim
Shelanu

נֵר ה'
עַל אָבְדַן וְעַל קַבָּלָה
Ner 5:
Al Ovdan V'al
Kabbalah

נֵר ו'
הוֹדָאָה
Ner 6:
Hodaah

נֵר ז'
שָׁלוֹם
Ner 7:
Shalom

ו

Sixth Candle
On Gratitude

Words of Faith and Tradition

הַזֹּרְעִים בְּדִמְעָה, בְּרִנָּה יִקְצֹרוּ.

Hazorim b'dimah — b'rinah yiktzoru.

Those who sow in tears shall reap in joy.

Psalm 126:5

It is good to praise,
to sing hymns at daybreak,
psalms of faith each night. . . .
How great is Your creation, God Most High —
How subtle the beauty of Your designs!

Psalm 92 (adapted)

I shall not die but live
and proclaim the works of the living God.

Psalm 118:17

Gratitude for the Next Generation

If some messenger were to come to us with the offer that death should be overthrown, but with the one inseparable condition that birth should also cease; if the existing generation were given the chance to live forever, but on the clear understanding that never again would there be a child, or a youth, or first love, never again new persons with new hopes, new ideas, new achievements; ourselves for always and never any others — could the answer be in doubt?

When we fear death's decree, let these bring us solace: the memory of loved ones who have gone before us; a vision of generations to come, through whom we reach far into the future — beyond our own lives.

IF LIFE is a pilgrimage, death is an arrival, a celebration. The last word should be neither craving nor bitterness, but gratitude and peace.

> We have been given so much. Why is the outcome of our lives, the sum of our achievements, so little?

Our embarrassment is like an abyss. Whatever we give away is so much less than what we receive.

> Perhaps this is the meaning of dying: to give one's whole self away.

Death is the end of what we can do as God's partners in redemption. The life that follows must be earned while we are here.

> It does not come out of nothing; it is an ingathering, the harvest of eternal moments achieved while on earth.

Unless we cultivate sensitivity to the glory while we are here, unless we learn how to experience a foretaste of heaven while on earth, what can there be in store for us in the life to come?

> The seed of life eternal is planted within us here and now. But a seed is wasted when placed on stone, into souls that die while the body is still alive.

How can I repay the Eternal for all God's bountiful gifts to me? When life is an answer, death is a homecoming.

> The deepest wisdom we can attain is to know that our destiny is to aid and to serve.

This is the meaning of death: the ultimate self-dedication to the divine. Death so understood will not be distorted by the craving for immortality, for this act of giving away is reciprocity on our part for God's gift of life.

> For the pious person, it is a privilege to die.

Rabbi Abraham Joshua Heschel

מָבוֹא
Mavo

נֵר א׳
אָבְדַן אֲהוּבִים
Ner 1:
Ovdan Ahuvim

נֵר ב׳
כֹּחוֹת הַנֶּפֶשׁ
Ner 2:
Kochot HaNefesh

נֵר ג׳
קְדֻשַּׁת הַזִּכָּרוֹן
Ner 3:
K'dushat HaZikaron

נֵר ד׳
הַיְחָסִים הַמְקֻדָּשִׁים
שֶׁלָּנוּ
Ner 4:
Ha-Y'chasim
Hamkudashim
Shelanu

נֵר ה׳
עַל אָבְדַן וְעַל קַבָּלָה
Ner 5:
Al Ovdan V'al
Kabbalah

נֵר ו׳
הוֹדָאָה
Ner 6:
Hodaah

נֵר ז׳
שָׁלוֹם
Ner 7:
Shalom

HOW CAN I REPAY THE ETERNAL, Psalm 116:12.

Leisure

הָיָה לָנוּ אוֹצָר סָמוּי שֶׁל פְּנַאי
עָדִין כַּאֲוִיר הַבֹּקֶר,
פְּנַאי שֶׁל סִפּוּרִים, דְּמָעוֹת, נְשִׁיקוֹת
וְחַגִּים.
פְּנַאי שֶׁל אִמָּא, סַבְתָּא, וְהַדּוֹדוֹת
יוֹשְׁבוֹת בְּנַחַת בְּסִירָה
שֶׁל זִיו,
שָׁטוֹת אַט־אַט
בְּדוּגִית הַשָּׁלוֹם
עִם הַיָּרֵחַ וְעִם הַמַּזָּלוֹת.

Ours was a secret treasure of unhurried time
gentle as the morning air,
a leisurely time of tales and tears, kisses
and holy days.
Leisure of Mama, Grandma, and the Aunts
quietly sitting in a boat
of heavenly light,
drifting ever so slowly
in a small boat of contentment
with the constellations and with the moon.

Zelda

ONE LEAF LEFT on a branch
and not a sound of sadness
or despair. One leaf left
on a branch and no unhappiness.
One leaf left all by itself
in the air and it does not speak
of loneliness or death.
One leaf and it spends itself
in swaying mildly in the breeze.

David Ignatow

Day Three
and the coral peony
on the kitchen counter
has opened into

another life —

last night, flower
now, half-bird, how

did it cross over, how
does it keep opening —

layer upon layer
of petals feathering
fan-like,
deckle-edged,

a ragged softness
with veins
of Floridian color
running through —

if, in three days,
a cut peony
can turn itself

from fist
to flower
to flamingo,

what isn't possible
for this balled up heart?

Judy Katz

מָבוֹא
Mavo

נֵר א'
אָבְדַן אֲהוּבִים
Ner 1:
Ovdan Ahuvim

נֵר ב'
כֹּחוֹת הַנֶּפֶשׁ
Ner 2:
Kochot HaNefesh

נֵר ג'
קְדֻשַּׁת הַזִּכָּרוֹן
Ner 3:
K'dushat HaZikaron

נֵר ד'
הַיְחָסִים הַמְקֻדָּשִׁים
שֶׁלָּנוּ
Ner 4:
Ha-Y'chasim
Hamkudashim
Shelanu

נֵר ה'
עַל אָבְדַן וְעַל קַבָּלָה
Ner 5:
Al Ovdan V'al
Kabbalah

נֵר ו'
הוֹדָאָה
Ner 6:
Hodaah

נֵר ז'
שָׁלוֹם
Ner 7:
Shalom

Father

Today you would be ninety-seven
if you had lived, and we would all be
miserable, you and your children,
driving from clinic to clinic,
an ancient fearful hypochondriac
and his fretful son and daughter,
asking directions, trying to read
the complicated, fading map of cures.
But with your dignity intact
you have been gone for twenty years,
and I am glad for all of us, although
I miss you every day—the heartbeat
under your necktie, the hand cupped
on the back of my neck, Old Spice
in the air, your voice delighted with stories.
On this day each year you loved to relate
that at the moment of your birth
your mother glanced out the window
and saw lilacs in bloom. Well, today
lilacs are blooming in side yards
all over Iowa, still welcoming you.

Ted Kooser

OUR ABILITY to receive God's blessings with thanksgiving will never exceed God's ability to bless us. For those who have cultivated the habit of gratitude, no matter how large a bowl we set out to receive God's blessings, it will always overflow.

Rabbi Harold Kushner

Rabbi Judah taught:

There are ten strong things:
Iron is strong, but fire melts it.
Fire is strong, but water quenches it.
Water is strong, but the clouds evaporate it.
Clouds are strong, but wind drives them away.
Wind is strong, but the human body bears it.
Human beings are strong, but fear casts them down.
Fear is strong, but wine allays it.
Wine is strong, but sleep overcomes it.
Sleep is strong, but death is stronger.
And loving-kindness survives death.

Remember Me

Every weekend your mother & I tour cemetery plots,
Father said, the way most people visit model homes.
We have different tastes. I like jutting hills
overlooking traffic, whereas she prefers a bed
of flowers. She desires a plot away from traffic noise.
I let her have her way in death to avoid a life of Hell.
But when you light memorial candles for us, arrange hers
in the center of a flowery tablecloth, but place mine
on the windowsill. Don't say any prayers for me,
just wet your finger, & pass it through the flame.
Remember me by the tricks I have taught you.

Hal Sirowitz

מָבוֹא
Mavo

נֵר א׳
אָבְדַן אֲהוּבִים
Ner 1:
Ovdan Ahuvim

נֵר ב׳
כֹּחוֹת הַנֶּפֶשׁ
Ner 2:
Kochot HaNefesh

נֵר ג׳
קְדֻשַּׁת הַזִּכָּרוֹן
Ner 3:
K'dushat HaZikaron

נֵר ד׳
הַיְחָסִים הַמְקֻדָּשִׁים שֶׁלָּנוּ
Ner 4:
Ha-Y'chasim Hamkudashim Shelanu

נֵר ה׳
עַל אָבְדַן וְעַל קַבָּלָה
Ner 5:
Al Ovdan V'al Kabbalah

נֵר ו׳
הוֹדָאָה
Ner 6:
Hodaah

נֵר ז׳
שָׁלוֹם
Ner 7:
Shalom

RABBI JUDAH TAUGHT. Based on Talmud *Bava Batra* 10a. The last line in the original text quotes Proverbs 10:2, "Righteousness (*tz'dakah*) saves from death."

Words of Healing

You prepare a table before me in the presence of my enemies;
You have anointed my head with oil;
my cup overflows.

Psalm 23:5

For personal reflection . . .

What blessings were bestowed on me by the loved one(s) whom I have lost?
In what ways have I been cared for and sustained by others?
Who deserves my gratitude? Who is a blessing in my life today?

Blessed is the pilgrimage from grief to gratitude;
precious are the sights along the way.
We pray —
for humility: to see in all things the great Artist of Eternity;
for generosity: to respond to the gift of life by giving of ourselves;
for strength: to hold on to life — and let it go.

בָּרוּךְ אַתָּה, יְיָ, מְקוֹר הַחַיִּים.

Baruch atah, Adonai, m'kor hachayim.

Blessed are You, Holy One, who gives and renews life.

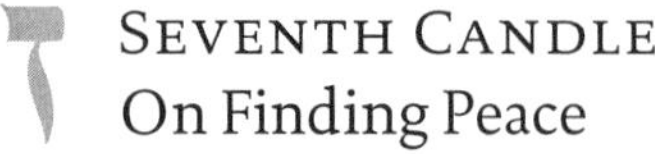

Seventh Candle
On Finding Peace

Words of Faith and Tradition

There is a future for one who finds peace and wholeness.

Psalm 37:37

One morning shortly after my mother died, a hesitant tap on the shoulder stopped me as I left the synagogue where I had just finished saying the mourner's *Kaddish.* I turned to face a fellow morning-service "regular" — a tall, gray-haired gentleman with a football player's thick build. "I don't mean to be presumptuous," he said in a soft voice. "I know you're very sad right now. But I wanted to tell you that I went through that, too, when my father died several years ago. And here's the thing: Believe it or not, I am as close to my father now as when he was alive! Maybe even closer, because I have come to understand him better. He is inside me, I hear his voice. We are still that close." Then he smiled and waved goodbye, leaving me to ponder words that I began to understand only years later.

What he meant, I think, was that our dead inhabit us like ghosts. The trick, as he knew then and I have learned since, is to befriend them rather than have them haunt us. They will greet us on sad anniversaries as well as in joy. We will imagine a deceased parent's response to her grandchild's arrival; or we will call back from memory the words or actions of the one person to whom we would have turned were he or she still there. And eventually, when we hear that voice again, it will bring not just pain but comfort and resolution.

Diane Cole

Introduction

First Candle: The Loss of Loved Ones

Second Candle: Inner Strength and Survival

Third Candle: The Holiness of Memory

Fourth Candle: Our Most Precious Relationships

Fifth Candle: Acceptance

Sixth Candle: Gratitude

Seventh Candle: Peace

The 23rd Psalm

No other psalm—perhaps no other prayer but the *Kaddish* itself—is as inseparable from our experience of grief and mourning as the twenty-third. One phrase, so simple and direct yet emotionally profound, has made it so: *ki atah imadi* ("For You are with me"). Or in the language of an earlier age: "for Thou art with me." To arrive at those words after passing through "the valley of the shadow of death" is to know, in the words of Rabbi Joshua Loth Liebman, that God "contains and supports us as a mighty ocean contains and supports the infinitesimal drops of every wave." To arrive at those words is to feel at home in the cosmos—held and comforted, cared for and serene.

The twenty-third Psalm does not make promises that cannot be kept: the end of all evil; the eradication of suffering and pain; sunshine instead of shadows. It makes but one promise—only this: you are not alone.

Mizmor l'David.	מִזְמוֹר לְדָוִד.
Adonai ro·i; lo echsar.	יְיָ רֹעִי, לֹא אֶחְסָר.
Binot deshe yarbitzeini;	בִּנְאוֹת דֶּשֶׁא יַרְבִּיצֵנִי,
al-mei m'nuchot y'nahaleini.	עַל מֵי מְנֻחוֹת יְנַהֲלֵנִי.
Nafshi y'shoveiv;	נַפְשִׁי יְשׁוֹבֵב,
yancheini v'mag'lei-tzedek l'maan sh'mo.	יַנְחֵנִי בְמַעְגְּלֵי־צֶדֶק לְמַעַן שְׁמוֹ.
Gam ki-eileich b'gei tzalmavet,	גַּם כִּי אֵלֵךְ בְּגֵיא צַלְמָוֶת
lo-ira ra, ki-atah imadi.	לֹא אִירָא רָע כִּי אַתָּה עִמָּדִי.
Shivt'cha umishantecha — heimah y'nachamuni.	שִׁבְטְךָ וּמִשְׁעַנְתֶּךָ הֵמָּה יְנַחֲמֻנִי.
Taaroch l'fanai shulchan neged tzor'rai.	תַּעֲרֹךְ לְפָנַי שֻׁלְחָן נֶגֶד צֹרְרָי,
Dishanta vashemen roshi;	דִּשַּׁנְתָּ בַשֶּׁמֶן רֹאשִׁי,
kosi r'vayah.	כּוֹסִי רְוָיָה.
Ach tov vachesed yird'funi kol-y'mei chayai;	אַךְ טוֹב וָחֶסֶד יִרְדְּפוּנִי כָּל־יְמֵי חַיָּי,
v'shavti b'veit-Adonai l'orech yamim.	וְשַׁבְתִּי בְּבֵית יְיָ לְאֹרֶךְ יָמִים.

I

A Psalm of David.
The Lord is my shepherd; I shall not want.
He maketh me to lie down in green pastures;
He leadeth me beside the still waters.
He restoreth my soul;
He guideth me in straight paths for His name's sake.
Yea, though I walk through the valley of the shadow of death,
I will fear no evil, for Thou art with me;
Thy rod and Thy staff, they comfort me.
Thou preparest a table before me in the presence of mine enemies;
Thou hast anointed my head with oil; my cup runneth over.
Surely goodness and mercy shall follow me all the days of my life;
and I shall dwell in the house of the Lord forever.

II

With God as my shepherd I shall not want.
The Eternal makes me lie down in green pastures,
leads me beside the still waters,
restores my soul,
guides me in straight paths for the sake of God's name.
Yea, though I walk through the valley of the shadow of death,
I will fear no evil, for You are with me;
Your rod and Your staff — they comfort me.
You prepare a table before me in the presence of my enemies;
You have anointed my head with oil; my cup overflows.
Surely goodness and mercy shall follow me all the days of my life;
and I shall dwell in the house of the Eternal forever.

מָבוֹא
Mavo

נֵר א׳
אָבְדַן אֲהוּבִים
Ner 1:
Ovdan Ahuvim

נֵר ב׳
כֹּחוֹת הַנֶּפֶשׁ
Ner 2:
Kochot HaNefesh

נֵר ג׳
קְדֻשַּׁת הַזִּכָּרוֹן
Ner 3:
K'dushat HaZikaron

נֵר ד׳
הַיְחָסִים הַמְקֻדָּשִׁים שֶׁלָּנוּ
Ner 4:
Ha-Y'chasim Hamkudashim Shelanu

נֵר ה׳
עַל אָבְדַן וְעַל קַבָּלָה
Ner 5:
Al Ovdan V'al Kabbalah

נֵר ו׳
הוֹדָאָה
Ner 6:
Hodaah

נֵר ז׳
שָׁלוֹם
Ner 7:
Shalom

III

The Shechinah, a sheltering presence, makes me whole . . .
causing me to rest in green fields,
leading me to calming waters,
replenishing my soul,
and empowering me to make life-affirming choices
in celebration of God's name.
Even though I have walked in darkness and known loss,
I have not despaired for you are with me.
Your guidance and your nurturing spirit have sustained me.
You have set a full table for me when I have been hurt and alienated.
You have conferred upon me unique potential, which I strive to realize.
From the deep core of my being I am overflowing with gratitude.
I know that your goodness and loving-kindness will continue to abide within me,
and I will live out my days in God's house.

IV

God is my shepherd, I shall not want.
God gives me rest in green pasture,
guides me by the restful waters,
refreshes my soul,
directs me along straight trails for the sake of God's name.
Even when I pass through the valley of ominous shadows,
I am not frightened for You are with me.
Your rod and Your staff calm me.
You provide for me even if there are enemies about.
Your care exceeds all expectation.
My cup overflows.
Truly, a generous goodness will pursue me all the days of my life
and I shall be with God as long as I live.

MY VERSION of the psalm's second line would read, "The Lord is my shepherd; I shall often want." I shall yearn, I shall long, I shall aspire. I shall continue to miss the people and the abilities that are taken from my life as loved ones die and skills diminish. I shall probe the empty spaces in my life like a tongue probing a missing tooth. But I will never feel deprived or diminished if I don't get what I yearn for, because I know how blessed I am by what I have.

Rabbi Harold Kushner

מָבוֹא
Mavo

נֵר א'
אֲבְדַן אֲהוּבִים
Ner 1:
Ovdan Ahuvim

נֵר ב'
כֹּחוֹת הַנֶּפֶשׁ
Ner 2:
Kochot HaNefesh

נֵר ג'
קְדֻשַּׁת הַזִּכָּרוֹן
Ner 3:
K'dushat HaZikaron

נֵר ד'
הַיְחָסִים הַמְקֻדָּשִׁים שֶׁלָּנוּ
Ner 4:
Ha-Y'chasim Hamkudashim Shelanu

נֵר ה'
עַל אֲבְדַן וְעַל קַבָּלָה
Ner 5:
Al Ovdan V'al Kabbalah

נֵר ו'
הוֹדָאָה
Ner 6:
Hodaah

נֵר ז'
שָׁלוֹם
Ner 7:
Shalom

Words of Healing

Surely goodness and mercy shall follow me all the days of
   my life;
and I shall dwell in the house of Adonai forever.

Psalm 23:6

For personal reflection . . .
What fills me with shalom?
What makes me feel like a whole person?
How has my community been a source of renewal and strength
   for me?

Blessed is peace, for all blessings flow from it.
Precious is peace, for without it no blessing is complete.
We pray —
for inner serenity,
for peace of mind,
for the feeling of at-homeness in the universe
and in our hearts.

בָּרוּךְ אַתָּה, יְיָ, מְקוֹר הַחַיִּים.

Baruch atah, Adonai, m'kor hachayim.
Blessed are You, Holy One, who gives and renews life.

דִּבְרֵי קֹדֶשׁ לַדֶּרֶךְ
Prayers for the Journey
A Broken Heart, a Narrow Bridge

Rabbi Menachem Mendel of Kotzk would say:
אֵין דָּבָר שָׁלֵם יוֹתֵר מִלֵּב שָׁבוּר.
Ein davar shaleim yoteir milev shavur.
"There is nothing more whole than a broken heart."

Says Rabbi Nachman of Breslov:
כָּל הָעוֹלָם כֻּלּוֹ גֶּשֶׁר צַר מְאֹד, וְהָעִקָּר לֹא לְפַחֵד כְּלָל.
Kol haolam kulo gesher tzar m'od; v'ha·ikar lo l'facheid k'lal.
"We travel through this world on a very narrow bridge,
and what matters most is this: Do not be afraid."

All that live must die, passing through nature to eternity.
William Shakespeare

Recitation of Names

Our loved ones live in our broken hearts — and, at times, that brings some measure of healing. Their acts of kindness and generosity are the inheritance they leave behind. We feel their absence; but the beauty of their lives abides among us. As it is said, *The name of one who has died shall not disappear.* Our loved ones' names — and their memories — will endure among us. And these are the names — on our lips and in our hearts. . . .

THE NAME OF ONE WHO HAS DIED, Ruth 4:10.

הַזְכָּרַת נְשָׁמוֹת
Hazkarat N'shamot

אֵל מָלֵא רַחֲמִים
El Malei Rachamim

כַּוָּנוֹת לַקַּדִּישׁ
Kavanot LaKaddish

קַדִּישׁ יָתוֹם
Kaddish Yatom

Memorial Prayer

El malei rachamim,	אֵל מָלֵא רַחֲמִים,
shochein bam'romim,	שׁוֹכֵן בַּמְּרוֹמִים.
hamtzei m'nuchah n'chonah	הַמְצֵא מְנוּחָה נְכוֹנָה
tachat kanfei hash'chinah —	תַּחַת כַּנְפֵי הַשְּׁכִינָה
im k'doshim ut·horim	עִם קְדוֹשִׁים וּטְהוֹרִים
k'zohar harakia mazhirim—	כְּזֹהַר הָרָקִיעַ מַזְהִירִים
l'nishmot yakireinu	לְנִשְׁמוֹת יַקִּירֵינוּ
shehal'chu l'olamam.	שֶׁהָלְכוּ לְעוֹלָמָם.
Baal harachamim yastireim	בַּעַל הָרַחֲמִים יַסְתִּירֵם
b'seiter k'nafav l'olamim;	בְּסֵתֶר כְּנָפָיו לְעוֹלָמִים,
v'yitzror bitzror hachayim	וְיִצְרוֹר בִּצְרוֹר הַחַיִּים
et nishmatam.	אֶת נִשְׁמָתָם.
Adonai — hu nachalatam.	יְיָ הוּא נַחֲלָתָם.
V'yanuchu b'shalom al mishkavam.	וְיָנוּחוּ בְּשָׁלוֹם עַל מִשְׁכָּבָם.
V'nomar: Amen.	וְנֹאמַר: אָמֵן.

Merciful God,
God Most High:
Let there be perfect rest
for the souls of our loved ones who have gone into eternity.
May they find shelter in Your presence among the holy and pure
whose light shines like the radiance of heaven.
Compassionate God, hold them close to You forever.
May their souls be bound up in the bond of life eternal.
May they find a home in You.
And may they rest in peace.
Together we say: *Amen.*

For Those Who Died for the Sake of Your Name

May God remember
the souls of those slain for their devotion to You —
all who died *al Kiddush HaShem* —
our brothers and sisters, in every generation,
killed because they were Jews:
the ones who suffered fire
and the ones who suffered water
to sanctify Your name.

May God remember those — in our own time — killed in acts of hate,
acts of terror against the Jewish people, against the Jewish state,
and against human beings of every nation.
Though holiness was diminished by their deaths,
may their memories be turned to good,
their legacies a sanctification of Your name.

Let us honor their memory
by word, by deed, by acts of hope and kindness.
Let us honor them through the study of history
and by working against bigotry and bias.
As we cling to their memory,
so may God embrace their souls
and give them everlasting peace.
Together we say: *Amen.*

For the Six Million and for All Who Died in the Shoah

Avinu Malkeinu:
Let there be perfect rest for the souls of the six million
who died as Jews in the flames of the Shoah.
Let there be perfect rest for the countless millions
who died because of race, religion or nationality,
political affiliation or sexual orientation.
Hold them close to You forever.
Seal their souls for everlasting life in the shelter of Your presence,
for You are their eternal home.
Together we say: *Amen.*

A Prayer for the Righteous of the Nations — Chasidei Umot HaOlam

Creator of all:
Let there be perfect rest for the souls of the righteous,
whose hands and hearts were open,
whose self-sacrifice was limitless.
They risked all they had
to hide and rescue our brothers and sisters during the Shoah.
As they gave shelter and care to others,
shelter them in Your presence — for they are the holy and pure,
and their light shines like the radiance of heaven.
Hold them close to You forever. May they find a home in You.
And may they rest in peace.
Together we say: *Amen.*

For Those Who Died for Our Country

Merciful God, God Most High,
may there be perfect rest in Your presence
for all who placed themselves in peril
and died protecting our country, our citizens,
and our highest principles.
With gratitude we honor their bravery and devotion.
With love we pray:
hold them close to You forever among the holy and pure
whose light shines like the radiance of heaven.

Let the words of the prophet Isaiah be their timeless memorial:

> *The work of righteousness shall be peace,*
> *yielding quietness and confidence forever.*
> *Nation shall not lift up sword against nation,*
> *neither shall they learn war any more.*
> *Then the glory of God Eternal shall be revealed,*
> *and all life, as one, shall behold it.*

Merciful God,
shelter those who served and died for the sake of peace;
shelter them forever among the souls of the righteous. *Amen.*

THE WORK OF RIGHTEOUSNESS, Isaiah 32:17; 2:4; 40:5.

WHAT IS the correct way to stand at a memorial ceremony?
Erect or stooped, pulled taut as a tent or in the slumped posture
of mourning, head bowed like the guilty or held high
in a collective protest against death,
eyes gaping frozen like the eyes of the dead
or shut tight, to see stars inside?
And what is the best time for remembering? At noon
when shadows are hidden beneath our feet, or at twilight
when shadows lengthen like longings
that have no beginning, no end, like God?

Yehuda Amichai

A Remembrance for Those Who Fell on the Battlefields of Israel

Kadosh Yisrael — Holy One of Israel:
Remember, on this holy day, the courage and devotion
of Your daughters and sons:
remember the ones who stood for independence in 1948,
and those, in every generation since, who served in the Israel Defense Forces,
placed their lives in mortal danger, and fell in battle.
Remember them all — Your sons, Your daughters —
all who died for the sake of Israel's rebirth in our time.

Am Yisrael — People of Israel:
May we be blessed with strength as we remember
and mourn over the beauty of their youth,
the glory of their gifts, their sacred willingness to serve,
their self-sacrifice on fields of honor.
Above all, let these be their crowning victory: a lasting peace;
the memory of their undying hope forever sealed in Israel's heart.
Together we say: *Amen.*

Preparing for Kaddish

1

May God's name be sanctified and praised.
May God's design for this world, for us and our people, lead us to justice and good.
May God, who decreed that all who live must die, teach us to accept death, yet with all our hearts desire life.
May God, whose plan for us is sometimes hidden, reveal the way to become stronger, having faced the trials of life —
and may God, *Oseh Hashalom*, be for us a source of comfort, strength, and peace.
Together we say: *Amen.*

Rabbi James Kaufman and Rabbi David Frank (adapted)

2

We miss them at celebrations,
when there's an empty seat at the table.
We miss them when the community gathers,
and there's an empty place beside us.
We miss them today, and every today,
with every year that passes,
as our life goes on without them.
Their faces, their voices, the feel of our arms around them —
these are with us forever.
For so it is written:
Love is strong as death.
The love that we gave, the love we received —
these endure amid the pain of loss.

LOVE IS STRONG AS DEATH, Song of Songs 8:6.

3

Strange now to think of you, gone . . .
your beauty, fading into the earth.
From the depth of my being
I summon the strength to stand before sorrow.
From where will my help come?

4

If every life were like a drop of rain —
each of us a small, solitary self —
then death would be for us return,
back to the ocean whence we came . . .

Some raindrops soft and gentle as the showers of spring;
others hard and raging like summer storms of hail and thunder.
Each life a separate journey back to the beginning, and back to God.

Picture God as a great ocean,
teeming with life in the ebb tide and flow,
where each raindrop begins and ends
and begins again
and again . . .

In the dance of waves we dance forever —
not I as I, nor you as you,
and yet together
rising and falling,
soft and peaceful, hard and raging —
a dance we only dimly see
to music we but faintly hear,
together and forever . . .

And if all this were so —
if God were like the ocean
and each of us like rain and mist —

Would my heart not break at losing you?
Could the ocean contain my tears?

Rabbi Donald Rossoff (adapted)

STRANGE . . . GONE. The opening words of "Kaddish" (1961), written by American Jewish poet Allen Ginsberg in memory of his mother, Naomi Ginsberg.

FROM WHERE WILL MY HELP COME, Psalm 121:1.

5

Deep contemplation of death can elevate the soul; it may even lead to peace of mind. Above all, it helps us see our lives in a truer light. For all things that appear trivial in light of death are already without significance in themselves. Annoyance that someone has slighted us, envy over others' achievements — how inconsequential it all seems when viewed from the perspective of our mortality.

To pass each day solely in pursuit of material success — this is life lived in what the poet calls "the shadow of a shadow." Rather, when death is near, may each of us carry this truth in our hearts: "I have contributed to the work of *tikkun olam*; I have done my part in the struggle for goodness." No act of kindness is too small to count; no act of love is without power. The world needs every heart and every hand; and, though we can never know the final outcome of our deeds, the fruit of our service will be gathered in by those who come after us.

At this sacred moment, reflecting on the impermanence of our lives, let these words serve as affirmation of the quiet ways in which each of us joins the great quest of humankind: "The growing good of the world is partly dependent on unhistoric acts; and that things are not so ill with you and me as they might have been, is half owing to the number who lived faithfully a hidden life and rest in unvisited tombs."

Based on Claude Montefiore

THE SHADOW OF A SHADOW. William Shakespeare, *Hamlet* (ca. 1600).
THE GROWING GOOD OF THE WORLD. George Eliot, *Middlemarch* (1871).

6

All who mourn the loss of loved ones, and, at this hour, remember the sweet companionship and the cherished hopes that have passed away with them, give ear to the word of comfort spoken in the name of God. Only the body has died and has returned to the dust. The spirit lives in the shelter of God's love and mercy. Our loved ones live on, as well, in the remembrance of those to whom they were precious. Their deeds of loving kindness, the true and beautiful words they spoke, are treasured as inspiration for deeds by which the living honor the dead.

And when we ask in our grief: from where will our help come? then in the strength of faith let us answer with the Psalmist: Our help will come from God. God will not forsake us or leave us in our grief. Upon the Holy One we cast our burden, and God will grant us strength to live out the days apportioned to us. All life comes from God; all souls are in God's keeping. Come then, all who share in this community of sympathy and support: let us rise and hallow the name of God.

The Union Prayerbook (adapted)

Our thoughts turn to loved ones
whom death has taken from us in recent days,
and those who died at this season in years past.
Our hearts open, as well, to the wider circles of loss
in our community and wherever grief touches
the human family. . . .
Zichronam livrachah — זִכְרוֹנָם לִבְרָכָה
May their memories be a blessing in this new year — and always.

הַזְכָּרַת נְשָׁמוֹת
Hazkarat N'shamot

אֵל מָלֵא רַחֲמִים
El Malei Rachamim

כַּוָּנוֹת לַקַּדִּישׁ
Kavanot LaKaddish

קַדִּישׁ יָתוֹם
Kaddish Yatom

Mourner's Kaddish

יִתְגַּדַּל וְיִתְקַדַּשׁ שְׁמֵהּ רַבָּא,	*Yitgadal v'yitkadash sh'meih raba,*
בְּעָלְמָא דִּי בְרָא כִרְעוּתֵהּ.	*b'alma di v'ra chiruteih.*
וְיַמְלִיךְ מַלְכוּתֵהּ בְּחַיֵּיכוֹן וּבְיוֹמֵיכוֹן,	*V'yamlich malchuteih b'chayeichon uvyomeichon,*
וּבְחַיֵּי דְכָל בֵּית יִשְׂרָאֵל,	*uvchayei d'chol beit Yisrael —*
בַּעֲגָלָא וּבִזְמַן קָרִיב.	*baagala uvizman kariv;*
וְאִמְרוּ: אָמֵן.	*v'imru: Amen.*

יְהֵא שְׁמֵהּ רַבָּא מְבָרַךְ	*Y'hei sh'meih raba m'varach*
לְעָלַם וּלְעָלְמֵי עָלְמַיָּא.	*l'alam ul·almei almaya.*
יִתְבָּרַךְ וְיִשְׁתַּבַּח וְיִתְפָּאַר	*Yitbarach v'yishtabach v'yitpaar*
וְיִתְרוֹמַם וְיִתְנַשֵּׂא וְיִתְהַדָּר	*v'yitromam v'yitnasei v'yit·hadar*
וְיִתְעַלֶּה וְיִתְהַלָּל שְׁמֵהּ	*v'yitaleh v'yit·halal sh'meih*
דְּקֻדְשָׁא, בְּרִיךְ הוּא,	*d'kudsha — b'rich hu —*
לְעֵלָּא וּלְעֵלָּא מִכָּל בִּרְכָתָא וְשִׁירָתָא,	*l'eila ul·eila mikol birchata v'shirata,*
תֻּשְׁבְּחָתָא וְנֶחֱמָתָא דַּאֲמִירָן בְּעָלְמָא.	*tushb'chata v'nechemata daamiran b'alma;*
וְאִמְרוּ: אָמֵן.	*v'imru: Amen.*

יְהֵא שְׁלָמָא רַבָּא מִן שְׁמַיָּא,	*Y'hei sh'lama raba min sh'maya,*
וְחַיִּים עָלֵינוּ וְעַל כָּל יִשְׂרָאֵל.	*v'chayim aleinu v'al kol Yisrael;*
וְאִמְרוּ: אָמֵן.	*v'imru: Amen.*

עֹשֶׂה שָׁלוֹם בִּמְרוֹמָיו	*Oseh shalom bimromav,*
הוּא יַעֲשֶׂה שָׁלוֹם עָלֵינוּ	*Hu yaaseh shalom aleinu,*
וְעַל כָּל יִשְׂרָאֵל	*v'al kol Yisrael*
וְעַל כָּל יוֹשְׁבֵי תֵבֵל.	*v'al kol yoshvei teiveil;*
וְאִמְרוּ: אָמֵן.	*v'imru: Amen.*

May God's great name come to be magnified and sanctified
in the world God brought into being.
May God's majestic reign prevail soon in your lives, in your days,
and in the life of the whole House of Israel;
and let us say: *Amen.*

May God's great name be blessed to the end of time.

May God's holy name come to be blessed, acclaimed, and glorified;
revered, raised, and beautified; honored and praised.
Blessed is the One who is **entirely** beyond
all the blessings and hymns,
all the praises and words of comfort
that we speak in the world;
and let us say: *Amen.*

Let perfect peace abound;
let there be abundant life for us and for all Israel.
May the One who makes peace in the high heavens
make peace for us, all Israel, and all who dwell on earth;
and let us say: *Amen.*

Words of Hope

שִׂימֵנִי כַחוֹתָם עַל־לִבֶּךָ . . . כִּי־עַזָּה כַמָּוֶת אַהֲבָה.

Simeini chachotam al-libecha . . . ki-azah chamavet ahavah.

Set me as a seal upon your heart, for love is strong as death. Song of Songs 8:6

הַזֹּרְעִים בְּדִמְעָה, בְּרִנָּה יִקְצֹרוּ.

Hazorim b'dimah — b'rinah yiktzoru.

Those who sow in tears shall reap in joy. Psalm 126:5

נֵר יְיָ נִשְׁמַת אָדָם.

Ner Adonai nishmat adam.

The spirit within is the lamp of God Eternal. Proverbs 20:27

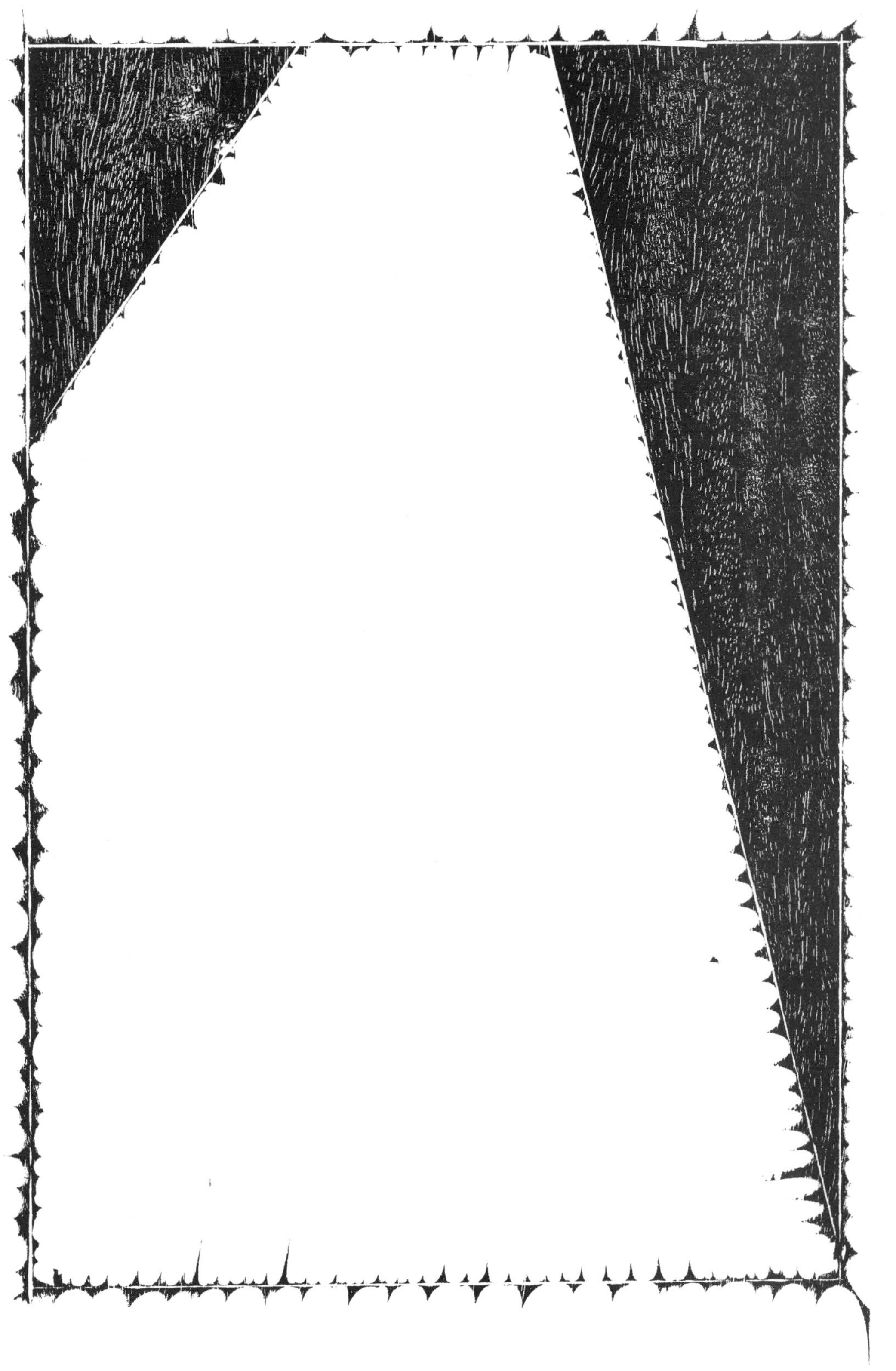

N'ilah · Closing of the Gates

You hold out Your hand.

—LITURGY

בִּשְׁעֲרֵי הַנְּעִילָה
B'shaarei HaN'ilah · Entering N'ilah

The long day
is over and the gates are closing.
Slowly day fades into dusk;
soon the earth will darken.
Our bodies weak and weary,
our inner strength undiminished.

This day has been a gift —
uncluttered time, free from hurry and routine,
appointments or assignments;
a time to face our sins and imperfections,
our dreams and yearnings for the life we want to live;
a time to leave the clamor of the world
and attend to the voice within.

Long ago, the Temple gates were locked at dusk;
so too, at this hour, the gates of Yom Kippur begin to close.
Have we done all that needed to be done,
said everything that needed to be said?

The gates of God's compassion never close;
but, soon enough, our lives close in on us.
Now, in the silence of the soul —
now, before the holy day comes to an end —
release the unshed tears,
the deepest prayers locked in our hearts.

THE TEMPLE GATES WERE LOCKED. Why should this prayer of the synagogue be timed to the closing of the Temple gates? It makes more sense to say that the prayer refers to the gates of our hearts, which are about to close up because we have reached the end of our ability to keep them open. . . . In this final hour, as we realize the inner gates will have to close, we begin to turn from supplication toward making peace. We start on the road to accepting the new year, whatever our fate in it will be. (Rabbi Arthur Green, b. 1941)

פְּתַח לָנוּ שַׁעַר,	*P'tach lanu shaar,*
בְּעֵת נְעִילַת שַׁעַר,	*b'eit n'ilat shaar —*
כִּי פָנָה יוֹם.	*ki fanah yom.*
הַיּוֹם יִפְנֶה,	*Hayom yifneh;*
הַשֶּׁמֶשׁ יָבֹא וְיִפְנֶה,	*hashemesh yavo v'yifneh —*
נָבוֹאָה שְׁעָרֶיךָ.	*navo·ah sh'arecha!*

Open a gate for us when the gates are being closed,
for the day is about to fade.
The day shall end, the sun shall set.
Let us enter Your gates!

Akeidah for Yom Kippur

After Sarah died, Abraham went to Isaac—
his son, his only one, whom he loved.
And he said:
"Is it too late, my son? Forgive me. Please, forgive me."

N'ilah

Again the day rolls
into darkness; the sky
spills its pinks and purples,
draining to blackness. Deep
inside there is a closing,
a small gate
swinging shut in the mind.
Those few last thoughts
rush through, and a life
is sealed. Outside the temple
a lone bird sounds its call,
waits for response.

OPEN A GATE . . . FORGIVE ME. These two poems (one medieval, based on Psalm 118:19; and the other contemporary, based on Genesis 22–23) capture the urgent mood of *N'ilah*. Time flows inexorably; the sunset cannot be halted. So, too, our days will come to an end; the time for meaningful action is now.

AGAIN THE DAY ROLLS. By Lucille Day (b. 1947).

פֵּתַח דָּבָר
Peitach Davar

אֵל נוֹרָא עֲלִילָה
El Nora Alilah

בִּתְהִלָּה
Bit·hilah

חֲצִי קַדִּישׁ
Chatzi Kaddish

El Nora Alilah

אֵל נוֹרָא עֲלִילָה, אֵל נוֹרָא עֲלִילָה,
הַמְצֵא לָנוּ מְחִילָה, בִּשְׁעַת הַנְּעִילָה.

El nora alilah, El nora alilah,
hamtzei lanu m'chilah, bishat han'ilah.

מְתֵי מִסְפָּר קְרוּאִים, לְךָ עַיִן נוֹשְׂאִים,
וּמְסַלְדִים בְּחִילָה, בִּשְׁעַת הַנְּעִילָה. אֵל נוֹרָא עֲלִילָה . . .

M'tei mispar k'ruim, l'cha ayin nosim,
umsal'dim b'chilah, bishat han'ilah. El nora alilah . . .

שׁוֹפְכִים לְךָ נַפְשָׁם, מְחֵה פִּשְׁעָם וְכַחֲשָׁם,
הַמְצִיאֵם מְחִילָה, בִּשְׁעַת הַנְּעִילָה. אֵל נוֹרָא עֲלִילָה . . .

Shofchim l'cha nafsham, m'cheih fisham v'chachasham,
hamtzi·eim m'chilah, bishat han'ilah. El nora alilah . . .

הֱיֵה לָהֶם לְסִתְרָה, וְהַלְּצֵם מִמְּאֵרָה,
וְחָתְמֵם לְהוֹד וּלְגִילָה, בִּשְׁעַת הַנְּעִילָה. אֵל נוֹרָא עֲלִילָה . . .

Heyeih lahem l'sitrah, v'hal'tzeim mim'eirah,
v'chotmeim l'hod ulgilah, bishat han'ilah. El nora alilah . . .

חוֹן אוֹתָם וְרַחֵם, וְכָל לוֹחֵץ וְלוֹחֵם,
עֲשֵׂה בָהֶם פְּלִילָה, בִּשְׁעַת הַנְּעִילָה. אֵל נוֹרָא עֲלִילָה . . .

Chon otam v'racheim, v'chol locheitz v'locheim,
aseih vahem f'lilah, bishat han'ilah. El nora alilah . . .

זְכֹר צִדְקַת אֲבִיהֶם, וְחַדֵּשׁ אֶת יְמֵיהֶם,
כְּקֶדֶם וּתְחִלָּה, בִּשְׁעַת הַנְּעִילָה. אֵל נוֹרָא עֲלִילָה . . .

Z'chor tzidkat avihem, v'chadeish et y'meihem,
k'kedem ut·chilah, bishat han'ilah. El nora alilah . . .

קְרָא נָא שְׁנַת רָצוֹן, וְהָשֵׁב שְׁאָר הַצֹּאן,
לְאָהֳלִיבָה וְאָהֳלָה, בִּשְׁעַת הַנְּעִילָה. אֵל נוֹרָא עֲלִילָה . . .

K'ra na sh'nat ratzon, v'hasheiv sh'ar hatzon,
l'Oholivah v'Oholah, bishat han'ilah. El nora alilah . . .

תִּזְכּוּ לְשָׁנִים רַבּוֹת, הַבָּנִים וְהַבָּנוֹת,
בְּדִיצָה וּבְצָהֳלָה, בִּשְׁעַת הַנְּעִילָה. אֵל נוֹרָא עֲלִילָה . . .

Tizku l'shanim rabot, habanim v'habanot,
b'ditzah uvtzoholah, bishat han'ilah. El nora alilah . . .

EL NORA ALILAH אֵל נוֹרָא עֲלִילָה. Composed by Rabbi Moses Ibn Ezra (ca. 1055–1138), this *piyut* (religious poem) from the Sephardic tradition resounds with urgency, hope, and faith in the special power of prayers uttered in this closing hour of Yom Kippur.

Our Creator, God of awe,
God sublime, whose deeds are true,
have compassion, grant us pardon,
as we enter *N'ilah.*

"Small in Number," we are called—
we who lift our eyes to seek You,
and with trembling hearts, beseech You,
in this hour of *N'ilah.*

For You our very life pours forth:
free us of falsehood, rid us of sin;
Fount of forgiveness, show us Your mercy,
as we enter *N'ilah.*

Be our true and faithful shelter;
embrace us in grief, console us in pain;
seal us for honor, contentment, and joy,
in this hour of *N'ilah.*

With grace and compassion
oppose the oppressors, bring judgment to foes;
oust the ones who war against us,
as we enter *N'ilah.*

Recall our mothers, remember our fathers;
renew their righteousness in our days.
Be near to us as You were to them,
in this hour of *N'ilah.*

Proclaim for us a year of favor;
restore the unity to Your flock.
Return this remnant to its glory,
as we enter *N'ilah.*

Daughters and sons, be worthy of your years —
may they be many, and filled with joy!
Bless us, *Avinu*, bless us with gladness,
in this hour of *N'ilah.*

Reflections on a Day of Fasting

When we refrain from indulging our physical appetites for a limited period, in order to devote ourselves for a time more exclusively to demands that rank higher in our hierarchy of values, we are not denying the physical appetites their just place in life; we are simply recognizing the need of putting them in their place.

—Rabbi Mordecai Kaplan (1881–1983)

This is the fast I chose:
it reminds me that I can master the appetites of my body
and decide when and how I will satisfy them.
This is the fast I chose:
lifting me, for this one holy day, above my animal nature.
This is the fast I chose:
it teaches me that I am a human being
capable of reflection, self-discipline and moral behavior.

I chose this fast as an act of purification;
I rededicate myself to a life of purpose.
I chose this fast as an act of solidarity;
I link myself to my Jewish brothers and sisters everywhere.
I chose this fast as a spur to compassion;
I will not forget those who hunger and suffer all over the earth.

As my ancestors once drew near to You
by making an offering on the altar,
so I have made an offering of myself—
my bodily strength diminished, my pride brought low.

Willingly and intentionally, I chose this fast.
May I carry its lessons with me when I leave this place.

As my ancestors . . . brought low. Based on a passage in Talmud *B'rachot* 17a: Upon completing his fast, Rav Sheishet would say: "Master of the universe, You know that when the Temple stood, one who sinned would bring a sacrifice—offering only the fat and the blood, and yet gaining atonement. As my fat and blood have been diminished [through fasting], may You accept them as my offering and grant me favor."

A Meditation for Those Unable to Fast

I was not able to fast on this Holy Day—and this I regret.
But I am thankful for all that I am able to do,
and for everything that brings me to this moment.

I am grateful to parents and grandparents, teachers and friends,
who have taught me and encouraged me to live a Jewish life.

I am grateful to the Jews of other times and places
who shaped Yom Kippur
into a spiritual peak that calls out:
"You can climb higher than you think."

I am grateful for the rich spiritual tapestry of this day:
the multifaceted wisdom of *machzor* and Torah,
a symphony of melodies,
the radiance of our sanctuary draped in white,
the piercing cry of shofar.

I am grateful for traditions that awaken within me
the beauty and majesty of the Sublime,
and guide me on the arduous path of *t'shuvah*.

I am grateful for *t'shuvah*,
which makes the Days of Awe a turning point in my life:
a time of return, a time of change, a season of response.

I am grateful for my bond with the House of Israel,
the great family of Jews throughout the world:
those who stand with me this day and those who do not—
the companions who surround me here,
and those whose presence I feel
when I hear the sound of Torah
and the vibrant notes of *t'ruah–sh'varim–t'kiah*.

I was not able to fast on this Holy Day.
But my gratitude is deep beyond words.

In Praise of God's Hands

When I consider the heavens, the work of Your hands; when I gaze at the sea of space and its endless array of stars; when I set out to understand this marvel and its Maker — Your greatness overwhelms me. Your majesty makes me tremble with awe. What are we, that You have given us eyes to glimpse Your truth? What am I, that You have given me a mind to fathom hints of Your purpose?

We are witnesses to nature's repeated refrains — forests dancing with life, mountains rising like prayers, oceans bursting forth with hymns. In the midst of this beauty, You have placed within humanity two worlds: mortal flesh and immortal soul; finite matter and infinite spirit. You have taught us to live at peace with the earth and with all living beings, and to care for the works of Your hands. But something deep within us darkens the soul.

In nature, spring follows winter; but human behavior is far less certain. Called to a life of righteousness, we rebel, possessed by arrogance and unrestrained ambition. Again and again we speak of the struggle between good and evil, love and hate, forgetting that the power to choose is the greatness and glory of our humanity. In our forgetfulness, life loses its beauty and we hear a voice of judgment: Where are you? How you have fallen!

In this hour of *N'ilah*, as day fades into dusk, we hear another voice. It says:

אַתָּה נוֹתֵן יָד לְפוֹשְׁעִים, וִימִינְךָ פְּשׁוּטָה לְקַבֵּל שָׁבִים.

Atah notein yad l'foshim, vimincha f'shutah l'kabeil shavim.

You hold out Your hand to those who do wrong;
Your right hand opens wide to receive those who return.
The gates of Your forgiveness are open wide.

WHEN I CONSIDER THE HEAVENS. Adapted from Psalm 8:4–5. In that psalm, the sight of the night sky inspires thoughts of humanity's smallness in relation to the Divine, but also the grandeur of being made in the divine image. This contemporary prayer, adapted from the Reform prayer book of Rabbi David Einhorn (1809–1879), also evokes the double nature of humanity: bound by earthly desires yet yearning for transcendent goodness. "You hold out Your hand" expresses the increasing sense of God's nearness in the hour of *N'ilah*.

Whatever your hands have the power to do, do with all your might.
For action and thought, skill and wisdom are yours in this world alone
— nowhere else. (Ecclesiastes 9:10)

In Praise of Hands

That they are slaves.
That each tendon's a rope
and the knuckles are pulleys.
That their white bones
line up like pieces of broken chalk.

They are bound by flesh
as leather around a Bible.
That they dance and write
in air the story
of what is lost, what is gained.

That they are soldiers
cut and bleeding, a link
to the heart's kingdom.
That they are so beautiful
a moon has landed on each finger.

That they are trained
for harps and hired for murder.
That the cuticles are shaped
like soft horseshoes.
They contain rivers.

That the ring finger's shyness
suffers when gripped by the powerful.
That the palm yields to blisters
and wears the calloused rags
of repetition.

That they are mythical
with their lifeline's hieroglyphics.
That they struggle
because of their great strength.
They are able to heal themselves.

That they know what it means
to draw the water
and work without pay.
That they will hide our eyes
and pray for our sins.

That they may lift the hammer
and lead our bodies to grace.
That they will make a print
like no other
until they wave goodbye.

IN PRAISE OF HANDS. By Jeanne Bryner (b. 1951).

פֶּתַח דָּבָר
Peitach Davar
אֵל נוֹרָא עֲלִילָה
El Nora Alilah
בִּתְהִלָּה
Bit·hilah
חֲצִי קַדִּישׁ
Chatzi Kaddish

יִתְגַּדַּל וְיִתְקַדַּשׁ שְׁמֵהּ רַבָּא,
בְּעָלְמָא דִּי בְרָא כִרְעוּתֵהּ.
וְיַמְלִיךְ מַלְכוּתֵהּ בְּחַיֵּיכוֹן
וּבְיוֹמֵיכוֹן,
וּבְחַיֵּי דְכָל בֵּית יִשְׂרָאֵל,
בַּעֲגָלָא וּבִזְמַן קָרִיב.
וְאִמְרוּ: אָמֵן.
יְהֵא שְׁמֵהּ רַבָּא מְבָרַךְ
לְעָלַם וּלְעָלְמֵי עָלְמַיָּא.
יִתְבָּרַךְ וְיִשְׁתַּבַּח וְיִתְפָּאַר
וְיִתְרוֹמַם וְיִתְנַשֵּׂא וְיִתְהַדָּר
וְיִתְעַלֶּה וְיִתְהַלָּל שְׁמֵהּ
דְּקֻדְשָׁא, בְּרִיךְ הוּא,
לְעֵלָּא **וּלְעֵלָּא מִכָּל** בִּרְכָתָא וְשִׁירָתָא,
תֻּשְׁבְּחָתָא וְנֶחֱמָתָא
דַּאֲמִירָן בְּעָלְמָא. וְאִמְרוּ: אָמֵן.

Yitgadal v'yitkadash sh'meih raba,
b'alma di v'ra chiruteih.
V'yamlich malchuteih b'chayeichon
uvyomeichon,
uvchayei d'chol beit Yisrael —
baagala uvizman kariv;
v'imru: Amen.
Y'hei sh'meih raba m'varach
l'alam ul·almei almaya.
Yitbarach v'yishtabach v'yitpaar
v'yitromam v'yitnasei v'yit·hadar
v'yitaleh v'yit·halal sh'meih
d'kudsha — b'rich hu —
l'eila ***ul·eila mikol*** *birchata v'shirata,*
tushb'chata v'nechemata
daamiran b'alma; v'imru: Amen.

May God's great name come to be magnified and sanctified in the world God brought into being. May God's majestic reign prevail soon in your lives, in your days, and in the life of the whole House of Israel; and let us say: *Amen.*

May God's great name be blessed to the end of time.

May God's holy name come to be blessed, acclaimed, and glorified; revered, raised, and beautified; honored and praised. Blessed is the One who is **entirely** beyond all the blessings and hymns, all the praises and words of comfort that we speak in the world; and let us say: *Amen.*

MAY GOD'S GREAT NAME COME TO BE MAGNIFIED יִתְגַּדַּל . . . שְׁמֵהּ רַבָּא. The *Chatzi* (half or partial) *Kaddish* has been called "a kind of liturgical punctuation mark"; and, in fact, it serves as a deep breath between major rubrics of prayer. But it is more than that. The *Chatzi Kaddish* tells us that God is the Ineffable, "entirely beyond" all the words that we speak. Why then is our worship defined by a book of words? Rabbi Henry Slonimsky (1884–1970) said this of the prayer book: "The Jewish soul is mirrored there as nowhere else, mirrored or rather embodied there." *We* are the true character and content of the book from which we pray.

Yearning

Just a moment—
a shaft of sunlight
in the fog,
a shift of mind and heart,
a breath of peace.
Just a moment—
that's all I ask:
to feel You there,
to know Your touch,
to see the truth
behind these words we speak.
At the end of this long day—
one last chance to stand before You.
Exhausted as I am,
I still have hope.
Just a moment—
let me pray.

Reverie before Prayer

Taking small steps into the New Year
I have come upon a blue lake in my heart—
the stillest of waters
in this dense word-forest of prayer—
and, like a stand of old growth,
the towers of the last *Amidah*
rise toward the Unnamable.

הַתְּפִלָּה
HaT'filah · Standing before God

כַּוָּנָה
Kavanah

אָבוֹת וְאִמָּהוֹת
Avot v'Imahot

גְּבוּרוֹת
G'vurot

קְדֻשַּׁת הַשֵּׁם
K'dushat HaShem

קְדֻשַּׁת הַיּוֹם
K'dushat HaYom

זָכְרֵנוּ
Zochreinu

הַבְּרָכוֹת
הָאַחֲרוֹנוֹת
*HaB'rachot
HaAcharonot*

כִּי־קָדוֹשׁ הַיּוֹם לַאֲדֹנֵינוּ,
וְאַל־תֵּעָצֵבוּ,
כִּי־חֶדְוַת יְיָ הִיא מָעֻזְּכֶם.

Ki-kadosh hayom laAdoneinu;
v'al-tei·atzeivu —
ki chedvat Adonai hi ma·uz'chem.

This day is holy to our God. Do not be sad,
for your rejoicing in the Holy One is the
source of your strength.

אֲדֹנָי, שְׂפָתַי תִּפְתָּח,
וּפִי יַגִּיד תְּהִלָּתֶךָ.

Adonai, s'fatai tiftach —
ufi yagid t'hilatecha.

Adonai, open my lips,
that my mouth may declare Your praise.

THIS DAY IS HOLY כִּי־קָדוֹשׁ הַיּוֹם, Nehemiah 8:10. Nehemiah's words were meant to comfort and reassure the community of Jews recently returned from exile in Babylonia (5th century BCE). When he saw the people grieving over their failure to fulfill the mitzvot, he urged them to move from repentance to celebration, teaching that the proper way to honor God is through joyful, life-affirming acts.

For those who have reached the closing hour of Yom Kippur, this verse is a reminder that we do not achieve spiritual fortitude through excessive self-recrimination and despair. Rejoicing in the Holy One is the source of our strength. We enter the last *T'filah* of this sacred day encouraged to cultivate our own sense of joy.

ADONAI, OPEN MY LIPS אֲדֹנָי, שְׂפָתַי תִּפְתָּח, Psalm 51:17.

It is written: "Listen to my words, God; understand my meditation" (Psalm 5:2). The meaning of the verse is: "Holy One, when I have the strength to stand before You in prayer and express my words, listen to me. But when I do not have the strength, understand what is in my heart."

Taught Dov Baer, the *Maggid* of Mezeritch:
There were thirteen gates to the holy Temple in Jerusalem—
one for each of the twelve tribes, and one for those
who did not know the tribe to which they belonged.
So also, there are thirteen gates of prayer,
each with its own manner of entrance.
All individuals must choose their own gate
and enter into prayer in their own way.

***To the one who wanders** I open wide My doors.*

One of our Sages taught:
Prayer is like the waters of a ritual bath, but *t'shuvah* is like the sea.
As a ritual bath is sometimes open and sometimes locked,
so the gates of prayer are sometimes open and sometimes locked.
But, as the sea is always open,
so too the gates of *t'shuvah* are always open.
Another Sage taught: Also the gates of prayer are always open.

IT IS WRITTEN, *Midrash T'hilim* 5:6.

DOV BAER. Based in the village of Mezeritch in western Ukraine, Dov Baer (d. 1772) was the successor of Israel Baal Shem Tov, the founder of Chasidism. He received the title of *Maggid* ("Preacher" or "Teller") and became known for expounding the teachings of the Baal Shem Tov.

THIRTEEN GATES OF PRAYER. Dov Baer intended this teaching to explain the diversity of Jewish practice among Ashkenazim, Sephardim, and Jews of other ethnic backgrounds. We might understand his teaching as an affirmation of our dual relationship to prayer. We connect to worship in a communal way (through our "tribal" identity as Jews) and also in a private and personal way (according to our individual needs and beliefs).

T'SHUVAH. The Hebrew word means "repentance, return, response."

TO THE ONE. Based on Job 31:32.

PRAYER IS LIKE, Midrash *Lamentations Rabbah* 3.43, section 9.

ALSO THE GATES, Midrash *D'varim Rabbah* 2.

Baruch atah, Adonai,	בָּרוּךְ אַתָּה, יְיָ,	כַּוָּנָה *Kavanah*
Eloheinu v'Elohei avoteinu v'imoteinu,	אֱלֹהֵינוּ וֵאלֹהֵי אֲבוֹתֵינוּ וְאִמּוֹתֵינוּ:	**אָבוֹת וְאִמָּהוֹת** ***Avot v'Imahot***
Elohei Avraham, Elohei Yitzchak,	אֱלֹהֵי אַבְרָהָם, אֱלֹהֵי יִצְחָק,	גְּבוּרוֹת *G'vurot*
v'Elohei Yaakov;	וֵאלֹהֵי יַעֲקֹב,	קְדֻשַּׁת הַשֵּׁם *K'dushat HaShem*
Elohei Sarah, Elohei Rivkah,	אֱלֹהֵי שָׂרָה, אֱלֹהֵי רִבְקָה,	קְדֻשַּׁת הַיּוֹם *K'dushat HaYom*
Elohei Rachel, v'Elohei Leah.	אֱלֹהֵי רָחֵל, וֵאלֹהֵי לֵאָה,	זָכְרֵנוּ *Zochreinu*
HaEl hagadol hagibor v'hanora —	הָאֵל הַגָּדוֹל הַגִּבּוֹר וְהַנּוֹרָא,	הַבְּרָכוֹת הָאַחֲרוֹנוֹת *HaB'rachot HaAcharonot*
El elyon,	אֵל עֶלְיוֹן,	
gomeil chasadim tovim, v'koneih hakol;	גּוֹמֵל חֲסָדִים טוֹבִים, וְקוֹנֵה הַכֹּל –	
v'zocheir chasdei avot v'imahot,	וְזוֹכֵר חַסְדֵי אָבוֹת וְאִמָּהוֹת,	
umeivi g'ulah livnei v'neihem	וּמֵבִיא גְאֻלָּה לִבְנֵי בְנֵיהֶם,	
l'maan sh'mo b'ahavah.	לְמַעַן שְׁמוֹ בְּאַהֲבָה.	
Zochreinu l'chayim,	זָכְרֵנוּ לְחַיִּים,	
Melech chafeitz bachayim;	מֶלֶךְ חָפֵץ בַּחַיִּים.	
***v'chotmeinu** b'sefer hachayim,*	**וְחָתְמֵנוּ** בְּסֵפֶר הַחַיִּים,	
l'maancha, Elohim chayim.	לְמַעַנְךָ אֱלֹהִים חַיִּים.	
Melech ozeir umoshia umagein.	מֶלֶךְ עוֹזֵר וּמוֹשִׁיעַ וּמָגֵן –	

You are the Source of blessing, Adonai, our God
and God of our fathers and mothers:
God of Abraham, God of Isaac, and God of Jacob;
God of Sarah, God of Rebecca, God of Rachel, and God of Leah;
exalted God, dynamic in power, inspiring awe,
God sublime, Creator of all —
yet You offer us kindness,
recall the loving deeds of our fathers and mothers,
and bring redemption to their children's children,
acting in love for the sake of Your name.

Remember us for life, sovereign God who treasures life.
Seal us in the Book of Life, for Your sake, God of life.

Sovereign of salvation, Pillar of protection —

בָּרוּךְ אַתָּה, יְיָ, מָגֵן אַבְרָהָם וְעֶזְרַת שָׂרָה.

Baruch atah, Adonai, magein Avraham v'ezrat Sarah.

Blessed are You in our lives, Adonai, Shield of Abraham, Sustainer of Sarah.

JERUSALEM 1967

בְּיוֹם כִּפּוּר בִּשְׁנַת תַּשְׁכַּ״ח לָבַשְׁתִּי
בִּגְדֵי־חַג כֵּהִים וְהָלַכְתִּי לָעִיר הָעַתִּיקָה בִּירוּשָׁלַיִם.
עָמַדְתִּי זְמַן רַב לִפְנֵי כּוּךְ חֲנוּתוֹ שֶׁל עֲרָבִי,
לֹא רָחוֹק מִשַּׁעַר שְׁכֶם, חֲנוּת
כַּפְתּוֹרִים וְרִכְסָנִים וּסְלִילֵי חוּטִים
בְּכָל צֶבַע וְלַחְצָנִיּוֹת וְאַבְזָמִים.
אוֹר יָקָר וּצְבָעִים רַבִּים, כְּמוֹ אֲרוֹן־קֹדֶשׁ פָּתוּחַ.

אָמַרְתִּי לוֹ בְּלִבִּי שֶׁגַּם לְאָבִי
הָיְתָה חֲנוּת כְּזֹאת שֶׁל חוּטִים וְכַפְתּוֹרִים.
הִסְבַּרְתִּי לוֹ בְּלִבִּי עַל כָּל עַשְׂרוֹת הַשָּׁנִים
וְהַגּוֹרְמִים וְהַמִּקְרִים, שֶׁאֲנִי עַכְשָׁו פֹּה
וַחֲנוּת אָבִי שְׂרוּפָה שָׁם וְהוּא קָבוּר פֹּה.

כְּשֶׁסִּיַּמְתִּי הָיְתָה שְׁעַת נְעִילָה.
גַּם הוּא הוֹרִיד אֶת הַתְּרִיס וְנָעַל אֶת הַשַּׁעַר
וַאֲנִי חָזַרְתִּי עִם כָּל הַמִּתְפַּלְּלִים הַבַּיְתָה.

On the Day of Atonement in the year 5728, I put on
dark holiday clothes and went to the Old City in Jerusalem.
For a long time I stood in the niche of an Arab's shop,
not far from the Nablus Gate, a store
for belts and zippers and spools of thread
in every shade and snaps and buckles.
A rare light and many colors, like a Holy Ark opened.

I said without speaking that my father
had a store like this for buttons and thread.
I told him without words about the decades,
the causes, events, that now I am here,
and my father's store was burned there and he's buried here.

When I finished it was time for the closing prayer.
He too lowered the shutter and locked the door,
and with all those who prayed, I went home.

JERUSALEM 1967. By Yehuda Amichai (1924–2000).

5728. The Jewish calendar year that began four months after the Six-Day War; its acronym (תשכ״ח) spells "you will forget."

In Hebrew, choose either hakol *or* meitim.

Atah gibor l'olam, Adonai,	אַתָּה גִּבּוֹר לְעוֹלָם, אֲדֹנָי,
m'chayeih hakol/meitim atah,	מְחַיֵּה הַכֹּל\מֵתִים אַתָּה,
rav l'hoshia.	רַב לְהוֹשִׁיעַ.
Morid hatal.	מוֹרִיד הַטָּל.
M'chalkeil chayim b'chesed,	מְכַלְכֵּל חַיִּים בְּחֶסֶד,
m'chayeih hakol/meitim	מְחַיֵּה הַכֹּל\מֵתִים
b'rachamim rabim.	בְּרַחֲמִים רַבִּים.
Someich noflim,	סוֹמֵךְ נוֹפְלִים,
v'rofei cholim umatir asurim,	וְרוֹפֵא חוֹלִים וּמַתִּיר אֲסוּרִים,
umkayeim emunato lisheinei afar.	וּמְקַיֵּם אֱמוּנָתוֹ לִישֵׁנֵי עָפָר.
Mi chamocha, baal g'vurot;	מִי כָמוֹךָ, בַּעַל גְּבוּרוֹת,
umi domeh-lach? —	וּמִי דּוֹמֶה לָּךְ,
melech meimit umchayeh	מֶלֶךְ מֵמִית וּמְחַיֶּה
umatzmiach y'shuah.	וּמַצְמִיחַ יְשׁוּעָה.
Mi chamocha, El harachamim? —	**מִי כָמוֹךָ, אֵל הָרַחֲמִים,**
zocheir y'tzurav l'chayim b'rachamim.	**זוֹכֵר יְצוּרָיו לְחַיִּים בְּרַחֲמִים.**
V'ne·eman atah l'hachayot hakol/meitim.	וְנֶאֱמָן אַתָּה לְהַחֲיוֹת הַכֹּל\מֵתִים.

Your life-giving power is forever, Adonai — with us in life and in death.
You liberate and save, cause dew to descend;
and with mercy abundant, lovingly nurture all life.
From life to death, You are the force that flows without end —
You support the falling, heal the sick, free the imprisoned and confined;
You are faithful, even to those who rest in the dust.

Power-beyond-Power, from whom salvation springs,
Sovereign over life and death — who is like You?
Merciful God, who compares with You?
With tender compassion You remember all creatures for life.
Faithful and true, worthy of our trust —
You sustain our immortal yearnings; in You we place our undying hopes.

בָּרוּךְ אַתָּה, יְיָ, מְחַיֵּה הַכֹּל\הַמֵּתִים.

Baruch atah, Adonai, m'chayeih hakol/hameitim.

Wellspring of blessing, Power eternal, You are the One who gives and renews all life.

When greeting a friend after more than a year—say:
"Praise the Power that gives life to the dead."

When the prisoner is freed and the sick one is healed—say:
"Praise the Power that gives life to the dead."

When asking forgiveness and the other forgives—say:
"Praise the Power that gives life to the dead."

When words of Torah unlock the heart and open the eyes—say:
"Praise the Power that gives life to the dead."

When evil is stopped and goodness prevails—say:
"Praise the Power that gives life to the dead."

When hope fills the spirit of one who despaired—say:
"Praise the Power that gives life to the dead."

When the hearts of the parents turn to the children
and the hearts of the children turn to the parents—say:
"Praise the Power that gives life to the dead."

בָּרוּךְ אַתָּה, יְיָ, מְחַיֵּה הַכֹּל\הַמֵּתִים.

Baruch atah, Adonai, m'chayeih hakol/hameitim.

We praise You, eternal Power—
Source of our immortal yearnings, our undying hopes.

G'vurot גְּבוּרוֹת (*facing page*). What do we believe about God's power? How do we experience it? And how can we say something meaningful about that which is ultimately beyond our grasp? The *G'vurot* prayer speaks about God's power in both physical and moral terms: God brings dew, rain, and wind; and God is a force for healing and liberation. The Reform version of the prayer presents two spiritual options: a traditional phrase (*m'chayeih meitim*), which speaks of God as the giver of life to the dead (traditionally understood as resurrection); and a modern reframing (*m'chayeih hakol*), which speaks of God as the giver of all life. Some Reform Jews understand *m'chayeih meitim* as a way of expressing a belief in the immortality of the soul; others see it as an assurance that God is "with us in death as in life." And for many it means that our dead accompany us through the power of their love, the legacy of their lessons, and the qualities we inherit from them. If we take all these words to heart, we might focus sometimes on *m'chayeih hakol* and, at other times, on *m'chayeih meitim*. The two ideas are not mutually exclusive; both help us express—directly or metaphorically—the ineffable experience of God's power in our lives.

When greeting a friend. Rabbi Joshua ben Levi said: One who sees a friend after a lapse of twelve months says: "Blessed is the One who revives the dead." (Talmud *B'rachot* 58b)

Hearts of the parents, Malachi 3:24.

שְׁמַע נָא.
סְלַח נָא הַיּוֹם,
עֲבוּר כִּי פָנָה יוֹם.
וּנְהַלֶּלְךָ נוֹרָא וְאָיֹם, קָדוֹשׁ.

Sh'ma na!
S'lach na hayom,
avur ki fanah yom.
Unhalelcha nora v'ayom, kadosh.

Hear us this day!
Forgive us, we pray — for the day begins to fade.
Your holiness awakens deepest awe.
Your praise shall be our song.

וּבְכֵן וּלְךָ תַעֲלֶה קְדֻשָּׁה,
כִּי אַתָּה אֱלֹהֵינוּ מֶלֶךְ
מוֹחֵל וְסוֹלֵחַ.

Uvchein ulcha taaleh k'dushah,
ki atah Eloheinu melech
mocheil v'solei·ach.

Our Sovereign,
God of pardon and forgiveness,
let these words of sanctity ascend to You.

פִּתְחוּ־לָנוּ שַׁעֲרֵי־צֶדֶק,
נָבֹא־בָם, נוֹדֶה יָהּ.

Pit·chu-lanu shaarei-tzedek;
navo vam, nodeh Yah.

Open the gates of righteousness for us;
open the gates that we may enter and praise the Eternal.

Open the gates for us, for all Israel, and for people everywhere:
the gates of acceptance and atonement, beauty and creativity;
the gates of dignity, empathy, and faith;
the gates of generosity and hope, insight and joy;
the gates of knowledge and love, meaning and nobility;
the gates of openness, patience, and the quest for peace;
the gates of renewal, song, and tranquility;
the gates of understanding and virtue;
the gates of wisdom and wonder; exultation, youth and old age;
the gates of Zion — reborn and rebuilt in our time.
Open the gates; open them wide — show us the way to enter.

Holy Is Your Name

Holy is your name, holy is your work, holy are the days that return to you. Holy are the years that you uncover. Holy are the hands that are raised to you, and the weeping that is wept to you. Holy is the fire between your will and ours, in which we are refined. Holy is that which is unredeemed, covered with your patience. Holy are the souls lost in your unnaming. Holy, and shining with a great light, is every living thing, established in this world and covered with time, until your name is praised forever.

Open Gate

The arc of evening
slowly turning,

the sun's blue shadows
washed away,

the gate still open
as three stars wait

to pierce the sky—
In the corridor

where night
bares its maze

you begin
to begin again.

OPEN THE GATES OF RIGHTEOUSNESS FOR US (*facing page*). This prayer is based on a traditional Sephardic *piyut* (religious poem) for *N'ilah*, whose opening verse comes from Psalm 118:19: *Open the gates of righteousness for me*. Invoking poetic license, the writer has changed "me" to "us." But the change is more than a simple adaptation of the psalm for congregational prayer: it is one of the moments in *N'ilah* that signals an emotional and spiritual turn from one sacred dimension to another. The shift here indicates a turning from the individual concerns of Yom Kippur toward a spirit of communal celebration at the end of a day devoted to self-reflection and self-judgment.

HOLY IS YOUR NAME. By Leonard Cohen (b. 1934).

OPEN GATE. By Marcia Falk (b. 1946).

וְחָתְמֵנוּ
בְּסֵפֶר הַחַיִּים
לִבְרָכָה וְלִקְדֻשָּׁה,
כִּי אַתָּה קָדוֹשׁ, וְשִׁמְךָ קָדוֹשׁ,
וּשְׁעָרֶיךָ בִּקְדֻשָּׁה נִכָּנֵס.

V'chotmeinu
b'sefer hachayim
livrachah v'likdushah —
ki atah kadosh, v'shimcha kadosh;
usharecha bikdushah nikaneis.

Seal us
for holiness and blessing in the Book of Life —
for You are holy and Your name is holy;
and we yearn to enter Your gates in holiness.

כִּי אַתָּה נוֹתֵן יָד לְפוֹשְׁעִים,
וִימִינְךָ פְּשׁוּטָה לְקַבֵּל שָׁבִים.

Ki atah notein yad l'foshim;
vimincha f'shutah l'kabeil shavim.

For You hold out Your hand to those who do wrong;
Your right hand opens wide to receive those who return.

YOU HOLD OUT YOUR HAND אַתָּה נוֹתֵן יָד. Three times in *N'ilah* the Hebrew words *atah notein yad* are spread wide across the page to proclaim this message: we have prayed, fasted, confessed, and asked forgiveness — all to the best of our ability. Now, instead of the long confession, *Al Cheit*, we say: "You hold out Your hand." That is, instead of a final litany of sin, we say: "You reach out to us."

The word *yad* can also mean "power." In that sense, *atah notein yad* ("You give us power") suggests that, in these last moments of Yom Kippur, God offers us the freedom and strength to turn our hands into instruments of blessing, to transform our myriad words of atonement into deeds of goodness.

Focusing Prayer

God of All Generations

God's Powers

The Holiness of God

The Holiness of the Day

Remember Us

Closing Words of HaT'filah

The Promise

Stay, I said
to the cut flowers.
They bowed
their heads lower.

Stay, I said to the spider,
who fled.

Stay, leaf.
It reddened,
embarrassed for me and itself.

Stay, I said to my body.
It sat as a dog does,
obedient for a moment,
soon starting to tremble.

Stay, to the earth
of riverine valley meadows,
of fossiled escarpments,
of limestone and sandstone.
It looked back
with a changing expression, in silence.

Stay, I said to my loves.
Each answered,
Always.

STAY. By Jane Hirshfield (b. 1953). Yearning for permanence, the poet says "stay" to physical parts of the natural world. But flowers and spiders cannot lie; and even her own body cannot comply with her wish. In the transitory ebb and flow of time, the promise of "always" comes only from those who love us.

A similar sense of yearning is conveyed by the prayer on the facing page. We yearn to enter God's gates in holiness—to be released from the burden of pain and guilt and be embraced by the "always" of God's love.

כּוָּנָה
Kavanah

שַׁעֲרֵי אַרְמוֹן
מְהֵרָה תִפְתַּח לְבוֹאֲרֵי אָמוֹן.
שַׁעֲרֵי גְנוּזִים
מְהֵרָה תִפְתַּח לְדָתְךָ אֲחוּזִים.
שַׁעֲרֵי הֵיכָל הַנֶּחְמָדִים
מְהֵרָה תִפְתַּח לְוֹעוּדִים.
שַׁעֲרֵי זְבוּל מַחֲנַיִם
מְהֵרָה תִפְתַּח לַחֲכְלִילֵי עֵינָיִם.
שַׁעֲרֵי טָהֳרָה
מְהֵרָה תִפְתַּח לְיָפָה וּבָרָה.
שַׁעֲרֵי כֶתֶר הַמְיֻמָּן
מְהֵרָה תִפְתַּח לְלֹא אַלְמָן.

אָבוֹת וְאִמָּהוֹת
Avot v'Imahot

גְבוּרוֹת
G'vurot

קְדֻשַּׁת הַשֵּׁם
K'dushat HaShem

קְדֻשַּׁת הַיּוֹם
K'dushat HaYom

זָכְרֵנוּ
Zochreinu

הַבְּרָכוֹת
הָאַחֲרוֹנוֹת
*HaB'rachot
HaAcharonot*

Shaarei armon —
   m'heirah tiftach l'vo·arei amon!
Shaarei g'nuzim —
   m'heirah tiftach l'dat'cha achuzim!
Shaarei heichal hanechmadim —
   m'heirah tiftach livudim!
Shaarei z'vul machanayim —
   m'heirah tiftach l'chachlili einayim!
Shaarei tohorah —
   m'heirah tiftach l'yafah uvarah!
Shaarei cheter hamyuman —
   m'heirah tiftach l'lo alman!

Gates of Heaven! Gates of Wisdom's Palace!
Open them now to the people who seek life's meaning in Torah.

Gates of Mystery! Gates of Hidden Truth!
Open them now to those who hold fast and refuse to give up.

Gates of Splendor! Gates of Beauty!
Open them now to Your faithful congregation.

Gates of Your Presence! A Vision of Glory!
Open them now to the red-eyed and weary from fasting and prayer.

Gates of Purity! Gates of Radiance!
Open them now to the people who glow with inner light.

Gates of Sovereignty! Gates of Strength!
Open them now to the people You have never abandoned.

GATES OF HEAVEN שַׁעֲרֵי אַרְמוֹן. This liturgical poem (*piyut*) by Rabbi Simeon ben Isaac Abun (ca. 925–1020) was written to introduce the *K'dushah* — a vision of the heavenly hosts joining the congregation of Israel in proclaiming God's glory. Focusing on the mutual love and loyalty that unite God and the Jewish people, the poem evokes an exhausted community yearning for a glimpse of heaven: transcendent beauty and meaning.

WISDOM'S PALACE. This translation of the words *shaarei armon* draws on the imagery in Maimonides' famous 12th-century Parable of the Palace (*Guide for the Perplexed* 3:51), which describes those who seek to draw closer to the divine Sovereign through the intellectual and spiritual quest for truth.

Alive

I aspire to
An eloquent seeing of all earth's seasons
Inspired touching of flesh, flower, and stone
True hearing of others: journey, self, and terrain,
The difficult dignity of individual thought.

An inner burning of commandment
A sometime certainty of divine presence,
Weaving of sorrow into becoming
Upwelling of seeded but surprising joy.

Into this life, courageously
Toward the unknown purpose.

Late october, and the sky is that clear blue scrim
we only see when the leaves go presto chango, garnet
and gold, and asters and chrysanthemums, the last
flowers, take their bow on center stage. The birds
are packing it up, preparing their exit, and the rest
of the garden collapses in ruin: fallen branches,
crumpled programs, dried leaves. The house light
turns everything golden, and even though we know
what's coming, the next act, we start to believe
we can stay here forever in the amber spotlight,
that night's black velvet curtain will never fall.

THE PEOPLE YOU HAVE NEVER ABANDONED לְלֹא אַלְמָן (*facing page*). This Hebrew phrase, which can also mean "the people not bereft or forsaken" (literally "not widowed"), is drawn from Jeremiah 51:5: *ki lo alman Yisrael viYhudah* (for Israel and Judah have not been forsaken by their God). The poem thus expresses both intense longing for the Divine and serene confidence in God's continuing love.

ALIVE. The majestic imagery of the 11th-century *piyut* (religious poem), on the facing page, finds expression in a contemporary poem by Rabbi Norman Hirsh (b. 1930). The modern poet, who begins with the word "I," speaks in the language of personal aspiration and desire, while the medieval poet implores God to open the gates of heaven. Yet both seek deeper vision and a more profound encounter with the holy.

LATE OCTOBER. By Barbara Crooker (b. 1945).

אַתָּה קָדוֹשׁ, וְשִׁמְךָ קָדוֹשׁ,
וּקְדוֹשִׁים בְּכָל יוֹם יְהַלְלְוּךָ סֶּלָה.

Atah kadosh, v'shimcha kadosh —
ukdoshim b'chol yom y'hal'lucha selah.

You are holy.
Your name is holy.
Seekers of holiness praise You day by day. *Selah.*

בָּרוּךְ אַתָּה, יְיָ, הַמֶּלֶךְ הַקָּדוֹשׁ.
Baruch atah, Adonai, haMelech hakadosh.
You are the Source of blessing, Eternal One —
Sovereign of the sacred.

SEEKERS OF HOLINESS PRAISE YOU DAY BY DAY וּקְדוֹשִׁים בְּכָל יוֹם יְהַלְלְוּךָ. The Talmud gives us a way of understanding what it means to be a "seeker of holiness." In *B'rachot* 17a we read: "A favorite saying of the rabbis of Yavneh was: I am God's creature and my friend is God's creature. My work is in the city and my friend's work is in the field. I rise early for my work and my friend rises early, as well. Just as my friend does not presume to do my work, so I do not presume to do my friend's work. In case you were to say, 'I study much Torah and my friend studies little' — have we not learned that, whether we do much or little, it is all one — provided we direct our hearts to heaven?" Seekers of holiness are those who devote their energies, great or small, to living in the presence of the Divine. Our tradition teaches us that the spiritual life should not be marred by competition, which leads to a "holier than thou" attitude. Rather, sincerity and intentionality define the search for holiness.

SOVEREIGN OF THE SACRED הַמֶּלֶךְ הַקָּדוֹשׁ. Throughout the High Holy Days we use the term "Sovereign" (*haMelech*) in this blessing instead of the word "God" (*haEl*). Experiencing ourselves in the presence of the Sovereign cultivates humility — a quality that is essential to asking forgiveness and confessing wrongdoing.

Help Me Listen

O Holy One,
I hear and say so many words,
yet yours is the word I need.
Speak now,
and help me listen;
and, if what I hear is silence,
  let it quiet me,
    let it disturb me,
      let it touch my need,
        let it break my pride,
          let it shrink my certainties,
            let it enlarge my wonder.

The Way It Is

There's a thread you follow. It goes among
things that change. But it doesn't change.
People wonder about what you are pursuing.
You have to explain about the thread.
But it is hard for others to see.
While you hold it you can't get lost.
Tragedies happen; people get hurt
or die; and you suffer and get old.
Nothing you do can stop time's unfolding.
You don't ever let go of the thread.

Teshuvah

Turn from evil and do good   the Psalmist says   turning
Round the turn   turn the key   clock the turn   turn in time
time to turn words into footsteps   to lead the young colt to the field
to turn from the old year   the old self   You are ready
to turn and be healed   only face   only begin

HELP ME LISTEN. By Ted Loder (b. 1930).
THE WAY IT IS. By William Stafford (1914–1993).
TESHUVAH. By Robin Becker (b. 1951); excerpted from "In the Days of Awe."

אַתָּה בְחַרְתָּנוּ מִכׇּל הָעַמִּים,
אָהַבְתָּ אוֹתָנוּ וְרָצִיתָ בָּנוּ.
וְרוֹמַמְתָּנוּ מִכׇּל הַלְּשׁוֹנוֹת,
וְקִדַּשְׁתָּנוּ בְּמִצְוֹתֶיךָ.
וְקֵרַבְתָּנוּ, מַלְכֵּנוּ, לַעֲבוֹדָתֶךָ,
וְשִׁמְךָ הַגָּדוֹל וְהַקָּדוֹשׁ עָלֵינוּ קָרָאתָ.

Atah v'chartanu mikol haamim;
ahavta otanu, v'ratzita banu.
V'romamtanu mikol hal'shonot,
v'kidashtanu b'mitzvotecha.
V'keiravtanu, Malkeinu, laavodatecha;
v'shimcha hagadol v'hakadosh aleinu karata.

You chose us, with love, to be messengers of mitzvot;
and through us You made known Your aspirations.

Among all the many peoples,
You gave us a pathway to holiness.
Among all the great nations,
You uplifted us and made Yourself our Sovereign —
and so we seek You and serve You
and celebrate our nearness to Your presence.

Your great and sacred name has become our calling.

וַתִּתֶּן־לָנוּ, יְיָ אֱלֹהֵינוּ, בְּאַהֲבָה אֶת
[יוֹם הַשַּׁבָּת הַזֶּה
לִקְדֻשָּׁה וְלִמְנוּחָה, וְאֶת]
יוֹם הַכִּפּוּרִים הַזֶּה,
לִמְחִילָה וְלִסְלִיחָה וּלְכַפָּרָה,
וְלִמְחׇל־בּוֹ אֶת כׇּל עֲוֹנוֹתֵינוּ [בְּאַהֲבָה],
מִקְרָא קֹדֶשׁ,
זֵכֶר לִיצִיאַת מִצְרָיִם.

Vatiten-lanu, Adonai Eloheinu, b'ahavah et
[Yom haShabbat hazeh
likdushah v'limnuchah, v'et]
Yom HaKippurim hazeh —
limchilah v'lislichah ulchaparah —
v'limchol-bo et kol avonoteinu [b'ahavah],
mikra-kodesh,
zeicher litziat Mitzrayim.

In Your love, Eternal our God,
You have given us this [Shabbat — for holiness and rest —
and this] Yom Kippur:
a day on which our wrongs are forgiven [with love];
a day of sacred assembly;
a day to be mindful of our people's going-out from Egypt.

How a Place Becomes Holy

Sometimes a man
will start crying in the middle of the street,
without knowing why or for whom.
It is as though someone else is standing there,
holding his briefcase, wearing his coat.

And from beneath the rust of years,
come to his tongue the words of his childhood:
"I'm sorry," and "God," and "Do not be far from me."

And just as suddenly the tears are gone,
and the man walks back into his life,
and the place where he cried becomes holy.

Psalm

redeemable, forgiven, blessed,
        by what right—only by
wanting—

        to have done
enough, to have done what is right,
        or not—

emptied out
        to make room for the unasked for,
that the soul might live—

        red poppies still bowed down
on narrowest curving stems
        after the rain has passed,

still staring
        at the darkened ground,
heedless of the light they wear—

HOW A PLACE BECOMES HOLY. By Yehoshua November (b. 1979).
PSALM. By Dan Bellm (b. 1952).

Zochreinu, Adonai Eloheinu, bo l'tovah. Amen.	זָכְרֵנוּ, יְיָ אֱלֹהֵינוּ, בּוֹ לְטוֹבָה. אָמֵן.
Ufokdeinu vo livrachah. Amen.	וּפָקְדֵנוּ בוֹ לִבְרָכָה. אָמֵן.
V'hoshi·einu vo l'chayim. Amen.	וְהוֹשִׁיעֵנוּ בוֹ לְחַיִּים. אָמֵן.

Eternal our God,
remember us, *Amen*
be mindful of us, *Amen*
and redeem us
for a life of goodness and blessing. *Amen*

Uvidvar y'shuah v'rachamim chus v'choneinu;	וּבִדְבַר יְשׁוּעָה וְרַחֲמִים חוּס וְחָנֵּנוּ,
v'racheim aleinu v'hoshi·einu —	וְרַחֵם עָלֵינוּ וְהוֹשִׁיעֵנוּ,
ki eilecha eineinu;	כִּי אֵלֶיךָ עֵינֵינוּ,
ki El melech chanun v'rachum atah.	כִּי אֵל מֶלֶךְ חַנּוּן וְרַחוּם אָתָּה.

Favor us with words of deliverance and mercy.
Show us the depth of Your care.
God, we await Your redemption,
for You reign with grace and compassion.

כַּוָּנָה *Kavanah*
אָבוֹת וְאִמָּהוֹת *Avot v'Imahot*
גְּבוּרוֹת *G'vurot*
קְדֻשַּׁת הַשֵּׁם *K'dushat HaShem*
קְדֻשַּׁת הַיּוֹם *K'dushat HaYom*
זָכְרֵנוּ *Zochreinu*
הַבְּרָכוֹת הָאַחֲרוֹנוֹת *HaB'rachot HaAcharonot*

CLOSING WORDS OF HAT'FILAH (*facing page*). This prayer brings together several essential themes of the four final blessings of *HaT'filah*. A rabbi of the 2nd–3rd centuries, Mar Shmuel of Babylonia, composed a condensed version of *HaT'filah*, known by its initial word — *Havineinu* (Give us insight) — intended for occasions when time is short. In similar manner, a sense of urgency prevails during *N'ilah*; and there is an eagerness to devote our fullest energies to the last *S'lichot* (Songs of Forgiveness) and *Vidui* (Confession) of Yom Kippur. Thus this *machzor* concludes *HaT'filah* with an abridged version of the final blessings, inspired by Mar Shmuel's *Havineinu*.

Closing Words of HaT'filah — Forgiveness, Zion, Covenant, and Peace

אֱלֹהֵינוּ וֵאלֹהֵי אֲבוֹתֵינוּ וְאִמּוֹתֵינוּ,

Eloheinu v'Elohei avoteinu v'imoteinu,

Our God and God of all generations,
on this Great Sabbath of Forgiveness,
forgive our moral failings;
on this Great Sabbath of Goodness,
teach us to be satisfied with Your goodness;
on this Great Sabbath of Atonement,
purify our hearts to serve You in truth.
Blessed are You, Adonai:
Year after year You set us on the path from guilt to holiness.

Our God and God of all generations,
let us feel Your nearness;
let us know Your love.

בָּרוּךְ אַתָּה, יְיָ, הַמַּחֲזִיר שְׁכִינָתוֹ לְצִיּוֹן.

Baruch atah, Adonai, hamachazir Sh'chinato l'Tziyon.

Let our eyes and hearts experience Your Presence in Zion.

God of goodness, mercy, and hope,
we are grateful for Your gifts of love and compassion.
Seal us today for a life of integrity, lived in covenant with You.

God of peace, grant us peace — Your most precious gift.
You have given us freedom to choose between good and evil,
life and death.
May we choose life and good,
that our children may inherit from us the blessing of peace.
May we and the whole family of Israel
be remembered and sealed in the Book of Life.

Blessed is forgiveness and blessed are goodness, mercy, and love.
Blessed is the nearness of Divine Presence and blessed is the hope for peace.

בָּרוּךְ אַתָּה, יְיָ, עוֹשֵׂה הַשָּׁלוֹם.

Baruch atah, Adonai, oseih hashalom.

You are the Blessed One, the Eternal One, Source of peace.

סְלִיחוֹת

S'lichot · Songs of Forgiveness

פְּתַח לָנוּ שַׁעַר
P'tach Lanu Shaar

אֵל עֶלְיוֹן
El Elyon

אֵל מֶלֶךְ יוֹשֵׁב
El Melech Yosheiv

סְלַח נָא
S'lach Na

סְלַח לָנוּ
S'lach Lanu

כִּי אָנוּ עַמֶּךָ
Ki Anu Amecha

Open the Gates

פְּתַח לָנוּ שַׁעַר, בְּעֵת נְעִילַת שַׁעַר,
P'tach lanu shaar, b'eit n'ilat shaar,

כִּי פָנָה יוֹם.
ki fanah yom.

הַיּוֹם יִפְנֶה, הַשֶּׁמֶשׁ יָבֹא וְיִפְנֶה.
Hayom yifneh; hashemesh yavo v'yifneh.

נָבוֹאָה שְׁעָרֶיךָ.
Navo·ah sh'arecha!

אָנָּא אֵל נָא:
Ana El na:

שָׂא נָא. סְלַח נָא.
Sa na. S'lach na.

מְחַל נָא. חֲמָל־נָא.
M'chal na. Chamol-na.

רַחֶם־נָא. כַּפֶּר־נָא.
Rachem-na. Kaper-na.

כְּבֹשׁ חֵטְא וְעָוֹן.
K'vosh cheit v'avon.

Open a gate for us when the gates are being closed,
for the day is about to fade.

The day shall end, the sun shall set.
Let us enter Your gates!

Holy One, we pray:

Please — be patient.
Please — pardon and forgive.
Please — show compassion.
Please — lead us to atonement.
And help us, please help us
to conquer injustice
and triumph over sin.

OPEN A GATE פְּתַח לָנוּ. These traditional words — likely a fragment from a lost poem — voice a yearning for a way forward, a way to connect with the Holy One, even as the gates of this holy day are closing.

THE PERSONAL SIGNIFICANCE of Yom Kippur ultimately turns on the individual's ability to believe that his or her life can be different. The main obstacle to *t'shuvah* is not whether God will forgive us but whether we can forgive ourselves — whether we can believe in our own ability to change the direction of our lives, even minimally. *T'shuvah* is grounded in the idea of an open future, in the belief that the possibilities for human change have not been exhausted, that the final chapters of our personal narratives have not been written. (Rabbi David Hartman, 1931–2013)

"Open for Me the Gates of Righteousness" — A Midrash on Psalm 118

When you are asked in the world-to-come, "What kind of work did you do?" and your answer is: "I fed the hungry," the response will be: "*This is the gate of the Eternal* (Psalm 118:20). Enter into it, you who fed the hungry."

If your answer is: "I gave drink to the thirsty," the response will be: "*This is the gate of the Eternal*. Enter into it, you who gave drink to the thirsty."

If your answer is: "I clothed the naked," the response will be: *This is the gate of the Eternal*. Enter into it, you who clothed the naked."

And the response will be the same if you answer: "I was a parent to orphans"; "I was generous to the poor"; "I performed deeds of loving-kindness."

Before

Before the gate is locked and shuttered
Before every word is said and uttered
Before I have become something different—
something other

Before the mind has lost its way
Before possessions are packed, and put away
Before the pavement hardens—
here to stay

Before the apertures of flutes are sealed
Before the laws of nature are revealed
Before the vessels break—
and can't be healed

Before decrees and edicts are imposed
Before the hand of God has closed
Before we rise to leave this place—
and go.

בְּטֶרֶם הַשַּׁעַר יִסָּגֵר,
בְּטֶרֶם כָּל הָאָמוּר יֵאָמֵר,
בְּטֶרֶם אֶהְיֶה אַחֵר.
בְּטֶרֶם יַקְרִישׁ דָּם נָבוֹן,
בְּטֶרֶם יִסָּגְרוּ הַדְּבָרִים בָּאָרוֹן,
בְּטֶרֶם יִתְקַשֶּׁה הַבֶּטוֹן.
בְּטֶרֶם יִסָּתְמוּ כָּל נִקְבֵי הַחֲלִילִים,
בְּטֶרֶם יֻסְבְּרוּ כָּל הַכְּלָלִים,
בְּטֶרֶם יִשָּׁבְרוּ אֶת הַכֵּלִים.
בְּטֶרֶם הַחֹק יִכָּנֵס לְתָקְפּוֹ
בְּטֶרֶם אֱלֹהִים יִסְגֹּר אֶת כַּפּוֹ
בְּטֶרֶם נֵלֵךְ מִפֹּה.

OPEN FOR ME THE GATES OF RIGHTEOUSNESS, *Midrash T'hilim* 118:17.
BEFORE. By Yehuda Amichai (1924–2000).

Your Promise Is Forever

God Most High, Your promise is forever.

Even when prayer is a struggle
and You seem far away
the doors open wide for the repentant.

Like the stoutness of oak trees —
so is our stubbornness.

Like thorns and thistles —
so is our malice.

And yet You say:
Return, rebellious children.
Seek My face with tears and supplication.

God Most High, Your promise is forever.

Impoverished,
we knock on Your door, seeking kindness,
lamenting our lot —

Remember us!
Recall us for a full life!
May Your ancient love come to us quickly.

And You say:
Come to Me with thanksgiving and songs.

God Most High, Your promise is forever.

פְּתַח לָנוּ שַׁעַר
P'tach Lanu Shaar

אֵל עֶלְיוֹן
El Elyon

אֵל מֶלֶךְ יוֹשֵׁב
El Melech Yosheiv

סְלַח נָא
S'lach Na

סְלַח לָנוּ
S'lach Lanu

כִּי אָנוּ עַמֶּךָ
Ki Anu Amecha

GOD MOST HIGH. Based on a *S'lichah* (liturgical poem) for Yom Kippur evening by Rashi (Rabbi Shlomo Yitzchaki, 11th century). The prayer is still found in the *Kol Nidrei* liturgy of the northern Italian cities of Asti, Fossano, and Moncalvo. The phrase "Your promise is forever" resonates with the poignant words of the *N'ilah* service: *Atah notein yad l'foshim* (You hold out Your hand to those who do wrong).

YOUR PROMISE IS FOREVER, Psalm 119:89.

THORNS AND THISTLES, Ezekiel 2:6.

RETURN, REBELLIOUS CHILDREN, Jeremiah 3:14.

SEEK MY FACE WITH TEARS AND SUPPLICATION, based on Psalm 27:8 and Jeremiah 3:21.

COME TO ME WITH THANKSGIVING AND SONGS, based on Psalm 100:2–4.

Open for Us a Gate

בְּזֶה אַחַר זֶה קוֹרִים לִי
מִקְרִים שֶׁבְּעֵת אַחֶרֶת
הָיוּ מַדְלִיקִים בִּי אֶת כָּל
פָּנָסֵי הַשִּׂמְחָה.
וְהָיִיתִי הוֹלֶכֶת יָפָה,
זְהִירָה, פֶּן יִכְבּוּ,
וְנוֹשֵׂאת בִּי הָלֹךְ וְנָשֹׂא
הַכְנָעַת הוֹדָיָה.

אֲבָל עַל הָרֶקַע הַזֶּה
הֲלֹא הֵם בִּרְקֵי־קַיִץ,
חֲזִיזִים –
וּבְהֵעָלְמָם
הֶעָבִים כֵּהִים עוֹד יוֹתֵר
וּבַמַּחֲנָק
אֵין צִפִּיָּה לְגֶשֶׁם.

הַשָּׁמַיִם עוֹמְדִים אֲטוּמִים.
פְּתַח לָנוּ שַׁעַר.

One after another things
are happening to me which
at another time would light up in me
all the lamplights of joy.
And I would walk then lovely,
careful, lest they be extinguished,
carrying back and forth
humble thanksgiving.

But in this setting
they are summer's flashes,
sparks—
and when they vanish
the clouds are even darker
and in the stifling air
there is no expectation of rain.

Heaven stands sealed.
Open for us a gate.

Day of Atonement

. . . Out of nothing I became a being,
and from a being I shall be
nothing—but until then
I rejoice, a mote in Your world,
a spark in Your seeing.

OPEN FOR US A GATE. By Lea Goldberg (1911–1970).
DAY OF ATONEMENT. By Charles Reznikoff (1894–1976).

פְּתַח לָנוּ שַׁעַר
P'tach Lanu Shaar

אֵל עֶלְיוֹן
El Elyon

אֵל מֶלֶךְ יוֹשֵׁב
El Melech Yosheiv

סְלַח נָא
S'lach Na

סְלַח לָנוּ
S'lach Lanu

כִּי אָנוּ עַמֶּךָ
Ki Anu Amecha

אֵל מֶלֶךְ יוֹשֵׁב עַל כִּסֵּא רַחֲמִים,
מִתְנַהֵג בַּחֲסִידוּת

El melech yosheiv al kisei rachamim —
mitnaheig bachasidut.

Majestic God, Your throne is mercy; love and kindness Your path.

מוֹחֵל עֲוֹנוֹת עַמּוֹ,
מַעֲבִיר רִאשׁוֹן רִאשׁוֹן,
מַרְבֶּה מְחִילָה לְחַטָּאִים,
וּסְלִיחָה לְפוֹשְׁעִים,
עוֹשֶׂה צְדָקוֹת עִם כָּל בָּשָׂר וָרוּחַ,
לֹא כְרָעָתָם תִּגְמֹל.

Mocheil avonot amo,
maavir rishon rishon,
marbeh m'chilah l'chata·im,
uslichah l'foshim —
oseh tz'dakot im kol basar varuach,
lo ch'raatam tigmol.

Though we wander and stray, Your forgiveness grows
as You pardon our wrongs, one by one —
doing what is right for every living being.
In Your mercy and love, do not treat us harshly for the harshness of our deeds.

You teach us to proclaim Your Attributes —
made known to Moses, man of humility, long ago.
This day remember, for our sake, the Covenant of Your Thirteen Ways,
as it is written:

וַיֵּרֶד יְיָ בֶּעָנָן,
וַיִּתְיַצֵּב עִמּוֹ שָׁם,
וַיִּקְרָא בְשֵׁם יְיָ.

Vayeired Adonai be·anan,
vayityatzeiv imo sham;
vayikra v'shem Adonai:

The Eternal descended in the cloud, stood with him there, and proclaimed:

יְיָ יְיָ, אֵל רַחוּם וְחַנּוּן,
אֶרֶךְ אַפַּיִם, וְרַב־חֶסֶד וֶאֱמֶת.
נֹצֵר חֶסֶד לָאֲלָפִים,
נֹשֵׂא עָוֹן וָפֶשַׁע וְחַטָּאָה, וְנַקֵּה.

"Adonai, Adonai: El rachum v'chanun;
erech apayim, v'rav-chesed ve·emet;
notzeir chesed laalafim;
nosei avon vafesha v'chataah; v'nakeih."

"Adonai, Adonai —
God, compassionate, gracious, endlessly patient, loving, and true;
showing mercy to the thousandth generation;
forgiving evil, defiance, and wrongdoing; granting pardon."

THE ETERNAL DESCENDED וַיֵּרֶד יְיָ, Exodus 34:5–7.

Open the Gates

Your Promise Is Forever

Majestic God

Forgiveness

Forgive Us

We Are Your People

Take the fruit of our lips—wholesome, true, and sweet.
Accept our offerings—our words—as we walk Your path honestly and with integrity.

Life is what You cherish and desire—not the death of human beings.
Have faith in our righteousness; diminish the voices that speak against us.

Raise us up; and let Your presence light the way. Let this day's reckoning be done.
Help us find atonement. Give us strength to stand upright in the world.

Even before we cry out, may Your forgiveness go forth.
Adonai, please receive these offerings—the sincere offerings of our lips.

So many words
They echo in my head
I'm emptied out
with no more strength to speak.
Just my life-breath
Just my heart
Just these broken shards of ancient prayer.
They say the shofar's broken
cry will reach You –
You
Rock of my heart
My portion forever.

TAKE THE FRUIT OF OUR LIPS. This poem was composed for these closing moments of Yom Kippur by a rabbi of the 10th century—Shlomo ben Yehudah the Babylonian—who "signed" his *piyut* with a Hebrew acrostic that reads: *Shlomo HaKatan* (Solomon the Small). The opening alludes to Hosea 14:3: "Take words with you and return to Adonai. . . . Instead of bulls, we will pay [the offering] of our lips." This verse was the basis for a creative revolution in Jewish belief and practice, after 70 CE, because of its assertion that prayer is equivalent to sacrifice as a way of reaching God.

EVEN BEFORE WE CRY OUT. The poet, an artist of language, nevertheless places his ultimate faith not in words but in the compassionate understanding of God, trusting that God will hear the silent language of the human heart.

SO MANY WORDS. This modern companion-piece to the above *piyut*, "Take the fruit of our lips," is based on the same hope: that the Holy One will accept our offering in all its human imperfection. "God requires the heart," says the Talmud (*Sanhedrin* 106b)—and perhaps it is through our heartfelt yearning that we connect to God, even when words and faith are lacking.

YOU . . . FOREVER, Psalm 73:26.

אל רחום

פְּתַח לָנוּ שַׁעַר
P'tach Lanu Shaar

אֵל עֶלְיוֹן
El Elyon

אֵל מֶלֶךְ יוֹשֵׁב
El Melech Yosheiv

סְלַח נָא
S'lach Na

סְלַח לָנוּ
S'lach Lanu

כִּי אָנוּ עַמֶּךְ
Ki Anu Amecha

"S'lach-na laavon haam hazeh

k'godel chasdecha,

v'chaasher nasata laam hazeh

mimitzrayim v'ad heinah."

סְלַח־נָא לַעֲוֹן הָעָם הַזֶּה
כְּגֹדֶל חַסְדֶּךָ,
וְכַאֲשֶׁר נָשָׂאתָה לָעָם הַזֶּה
מִמִּצְרַיִם וְעַד־הֵנָּה.

Moses prayed to God:

"As You have been faithful to this people ever since Egypt,

please forgive their failings now,

in keeping with Your boundless love."

"Adonai, Adonai: El rachum v'chanun;

erech apayim, v'rav-chesed ve·emet;

notzeir chesed laalafim;

nosei avon vafesha v'chataah; v'nakeih."

יְיָ יְיָ, אֵל רַחוּם וְחַנּוּן,
אֶרֶךְ אַפַּיִם, וְרַב־חֶסֶד וֶאֱמֶת.
נֹצֵר חֶסֶד לָאֲלָפִים,
נֹשֵׂא עָוֹן וָפֶשַׁע וְחַטָּאָה, וְנַקֵּה.

"Adonai, Adonai —

God, compassionate, gracious, endlessly patient, loving, and true;

showing mercy to the thousandth generation;

forgiving evil, defiance, and wrongdoing; granting pardon."

Vayomer Adonai:

"Salachti kidvarecha."

וַיֹּאמֶר יְיָ:
סָלַחְתִּי כִּדְבָרֶךָ.

And God responded:

"I forgive, as you have asked."

AS YOU HAVE BEEN FAITHFUL סְלַח־נָא, Numbers 14:19.

ADONAI, ADONAI יְיָ יְיָ, Exodus 34:6–7. Our Sages (Talmud *Rosh HaShanah* 17b) envisioned God promising that all those who recite this prayer, known as the Thirteen Divine Attributes, will receive divine compassion and forgiveness. But these words are not a magic formula intended to manipulate God for our own benefit. Rather, if we recite them with sincerity and focus, we can transform ourselves into "a chariot for God's Presence." That is, through our own actions we can make God's compassion manifest in the world. Strengthening our own sense of God's Presence within us, we become the carriers of divine love, responsible for revealing the Divine Presence to others.

AND GOD RESPONDED וַיֹּאמֶר יְיָ, Numbers 14:20.

Open the Gates
Your Promise Is Forever
Majestic God
Forgiveness
Forgive Us
We Are Your People

You Make Me Feel Safe

שַׁוְעָתִי שְׁעֵה,
וּתְפִלָּתִי תְּהֵא נְעִימָה
שְׁמַע פְּגִיעָתִי כִּפְגִיעָה תַמָּה
תְּחֹקְקֵנוּ לְחַיִּים,
וְתֵיטִיב הַחֲתִימָה
תֹּלֶה אֶרֶץ עַל־בְּלִי־מָה.

Shavati sh'eih:
utfilati t'hei n'imah;
sh'ma p'giati kifgiah tamah.
T'chok'keinu l'chayim,
v'teitiv hachatimah —
toleh eretz al-b'li-mah.

Behold my unease. Let my prayer be sweet and pleasant.
Hear it as though it were perfect, a prayer of pure innocence.
Engrave us in the Book of Life. Bring goodness to its final sealing—
for the world, and our lives with it, hover on the edge of nothingness.

יָדְךָ פְּשֹׁט,
וְקַבֵּל תְּשׁוּבָתִי בְּמַעֲמָדִי
סְלַח נָא וּמְחַל רֹעַ מַעְבָּדִי
פְּנֵה וַעֲסֹק בְּטוּבַת מְשַׁחֲרֶיךָ,
דּוֹדִי וּמְעוֹדְדִי
וְאַתָּה, יְיָ, מָגֵן בַּעֲדִי.

Yad'cha p'shot;
v'kabeil t'shuvati b'maamadi.
S'lach na umchal ro·a mabadi.
P'neih vaasok b'tovat m'shacharecha,
dodi um·od'di.
V'atah, Adonai, magein baadi.

Reach out! Extend Your hand!
I come before You: accept my return.
All the harm I have done—forgive.
The deeds I regret—please pardon.
Turn, my Beloved, to the goodness of those who seek You,
who long for You like the rays of dawn.
You, Adonai—You encourage me. You make me feel safe.

BEHOLD MY UNEASE . . . MAKE ME FEEL SAFE שַׁוְעָתִי שְׁעֵה . . . מָגֵן בַּעֲדִי. Two stanzas from the *piyut* (religious poem) known as *Adon Mo·eid K'tikach* (Our Master, It Is the Time) by Rabbi Yosef of Orleans, France (12th century). Like a musical call-and-response, the poet's cry "Reach out! Extend Your hand!" is answered with words of assurance (page 654): "You hold out Your hand to those who do wrong"—thus highlighting the connection between the Songs of Forgiveness and the Confession that follows.

FOR THE WORLD . . . NOTHINGNESS תֹּלֶה . . . בְּלִי־מָה, Job 26:7.

YOU, ADONAI . . . SAFE וְאַתָּה, יְיָ, . . . בַּעֲדִי, Psalm 3:4.

פְּתַח לָנוּ שַׁעַר
P'tach Lanu Shaar

אֵל עֶלְיוֹן
El Elyon

אֵל מֶלֶךְ יוֹשֵׁב
El Melech Yosheiv

סְלַח נָא
S'lach Na

סְלַח לָנוּ
S'lach Lanu

כִּי אָנוּ עַמֶּךָ
Ki Anu Amecha

סְלַח לָנוּ, אָבִינוּ, כִּי חָטָאנוּ,
מְחַל לָנוּ, מַלְכֵּנוּ, כִּי פָשָׁעְנוּ.
כִּי אַתָּה, אֲדֹנָי, טוֹב וְסַלָּח
וְרַב־חֶסֶד לְכָל קוֹרְאֶיךָ.

S'lach lanu, Avinu, ki chatanu;
m'chal lanu, Malkeinu, ki fashanu.
Ki atah, Adonai, tov v'salach —
v'rav-chesed l'chol korecha.

Forgive us, *Avinu*, for we have strayed;
pardon us, *Malkeinu*, for succumbing to sin—
You are generous in granting forgiveness,
all-loving to those who reach out to You.

יְיָ יְיָ, אֵל רַחוּם וְחַנּוּן,
אֶרֶךְ אַפַּיִם, וְרַב־חֶסֶד וֶאֱמֶת.
נֹצֵר חֶסֶד לָאֲלָפִים,
נֹשֵׂא עָוֹן וָפֶשַׁע וְחַטָּאָה, וְנַקֵּה.

"Adonai, Adonai: El rachum v'chanun;
erech apayim, v'rav-chesed ve·emet;
notzeir chesed laalafim;
nosei avon vafesha v'chataah; v'nakeih."

"Adonai, Adonai —
God, compassionate, gracious, endlessly patient, loving, and true;
showing mercy to the thousandth generation;
forgiving evil, defiance, and wrongdoing; granting pardon."

אֱלֹהֵינוּ וֵאלֹהֵי
אֲבוֹתֵינוּ וְאִמּוֹתֵינוּ,
סְלַח לָנוּ, מְחַל לָנוּ, כַּפֶּר־לָנוּ.

Eloheinu v'Elohei
avoteinu v'imoteinu,
s'lach lanu, m'chal lanu, kaper-lanu.

Our God and God of our fathers and our mothers —
forgive us, pardon us, lead us to atonement.

GRANTING PARDON וְנַקֵּה, Exodus 34:7. The thirteenth of the Thirteen Attributes of Mercy might be the most interesting of all. The verse in the Torah says: "God does not remit punishment" (*v'nakeih lo y'nakeh*). But the traditional liturgy omits the words *lo y'nakeh* and thereby reverses the original meaning: God does remit punishment. God does grant pardon. How can the Sages alter a verse in the Torah? The Talmud (*Yoma* 86a) answers: "God pardons those who repent — and does not pardon those who do not repent." The Sages' emendation is for us: those who are using the *machzor* to repent.

Those Who Struggle with Prayer

אֶנְקַת מְסַלְדֶיךָ,
תַּעַל לִפְנֵי כִּסֵּא כְבוֹדֶךָ.
מַלֵּא מִשְׁאֲלוֹת עַם מְיַחֲדֶךָ,
שׁוֹמֵעַ תְּפִלַּת בָּאֵי עָדֶיךָ.

Enkat m'sal'decha —
taal lifnei chisei ch'vodecha.
Malei mishalot am m'yachadecha,
Shomei·a t'filat ba·ei adecha.

May the prayers of those who struggle with prayer
reach Your presence.
May the people who say "Hear, O Israel"
come to know You as the One who hears.

Great Giver, Israel's eternal hope—
You are rich in forgiveness.
Though You dwell on high,
Your compassion is present—here and now.

Shelter us in the shade of Your presence.
When You look into our hearts, be kind; set us on the right path.
Come to us, our God. Please, be my Strength.
Hear the ache in our voices, the pain of our plea.

Most High and Hidden—we yearn to hear: "I have forgiven."
A broken people hungers for Your care and protection.
Answer us with righteousness. Inspire us with awe.
Adonai, be our Help—give us strength.

MAY THE PRAYERS. Each of these four stanzas is by a different poet: Rabbi Silano of Venosa, Italy (9th century); Rabbi Shefatya ben Amitai of Oria, Italy (9th century); Rabbi Yitzchak ben Shmuel of Dampierre, France (12th century); and Rabbi Shlomo ben Shmuel of Akko, Israel (13th century). The poem resonates with the language of Isaiah 49:2, Jeremiah 17:9, and Psalm 68:29.

BE MY STRENGTH. The individual soul, unable to hold back, bursts forth with a personal plea in the midst of this otherwise communal prayer ("Shelter us. . . . Come to us . . .").

A BROKEN PEOPLE. The Hebrew Bible tells us that God cares especially for the poor and vulnerable. The poets of this prayer present the Jewish people as spiritually impoverished and broken in spirit—an image that may also ring true for Jews living after the Shoah.

פְּתַח לָנוּ שַׁעַר
P'tach Lanu Shaar
אֵל עֶלְיוֹן
El Elyon
אֵל מֶלֶךְ יוֹשֵׁב
El Melech Yosheiv
סְלַח נָא
S'lach Na
סְלַח לָנוּ
S'lach Lanu
כִּי אָנוּ עַמֶּךָ
Ki Anu Amecha

כִּי אָנוּ עַמֶּךָ, וְאַתָּה אֱלֹהֵינוּ,
אָנוּ בָנֶיךָ, וְאַתָּה אָבִינוּ.
אָנוּ עֲבָדֶיךָ, וְאַתָּה אֲדוֹנֵנוּ,
אָנוּ קְהָלֶךָ, וְאַתָּה חֶלְקֵנוּ.
אָנוּ נַחֲלָתֶךָ, וְאַתָּה גוֹרָלֵנוּ,
אָנוּ צֹאנֶךָ, וְאַתָּה רוֹעֵנוּ.
אָנוּ כַרְמֶךָ, וְאַתָּה נוֹטְרֵנוּ,
אָנוּ פְעֻלָּתֶךָ, וְאַתָּה יוֹצְרֵנוּ.
אָנוּ רַעְיָתֶךָ, וְאַתָּה דוֹדֵנוּ,
אָנוּ סְגֻלָּתֶךָ, וְאַתָּה קְרוֹבֵנוּ.
אָנוּ עַמֶּךָ, וְאַתָּה מַלְכֵּנוּ,
אָנוּ מַאֲמִירֶךָ, וְאַתָּה מַאֲמִירֵנוּ.

Ki anu amecha, v'atah Eloheinu;
anu vanecha, v'atah avinu.
Anu avadecha, v'atah adoneinu;
anu k'halecha, v'atah chelkeinu.
Anu nachalatecha, v'atah goraleinu;
anu tzonecha, v'atah ro·einu.
Anu charmecha, v'atah notreinu;
anu f'ulatecha, v'atah yotzreinu.
Anu rayatecha, v'atah dodeinu;
anu s'gulatecha, v'atah k'roveinu.
Anu amecha, v'atah malkeinu;
anu maamirecha, v'atah maamireinu.

Our God and God of our ancestors —

We are Your people; and You are our God.
We are Your children; and You are our father, our mother.
We are the people who serve You; and You call us to serve.
We are Your community; and You are our portion.
We are Your legacy; and You are our purpose.
We are Your flock; and You are our shepherd.
We are Your vineyard; and You watch over us.
We are Your work; and You are our maker.
We are Your beloved; and You are our lover.
We are Your treasure; and You are the one we cherish.
We are Your people; and You reign over us.
We offer You our words; and You offer us Yours.

So forgive us, pardon us, lead us to atonement.

WE ARE YOUR PEOPLE כִּי אָנוּ עַמֶּךָ. With its plethora of images for God, this *piyut* (religious poem) encourages us to think beyond the narrow definition of Divinity as "Ruler of the universe." Above all, it suggests a theology that is relational, built on our capacity to respond to the Other.

In *N'ilah* we turn from the soul-searching of Yom Kippur to the world of relationships in our daily lives — encompassing love, responsibility, and commitment. This prayer may serve as a tool for exploring the multifaceted nature of those relationships.

You are our Beacon;
we are Your burden.
You are our Enigma;
we are Your frustration.
You are our Call to Conscience;
we are Your critics.
You are our Touchstone;
we are Your loyal opposition.

The future has an ancient heart
The tree still stands
Your love endures

Remind us: we are children—
still bewildered by the world;
selfish, willful;
lacking in patience, longing for praise;
in need of hugs.

Remind us: we are servants—
day-laborers, summoned every morning;
lazy, distractible;
focused on quick rewards;
ennobled by Your work.

Remind us: we are a vineyard—
watched over, yearned over;
tended these three thousand years;
scorched by fire but alive at the root;
growing slowly toward the harvest day.

The future has an ancient heart
The tree still stands
Your love endures

THE FUTURE HAS AN ANCIENT HEART. Title of a work by the painter, physician, and anti-fascist activist Carlo Levi (1902–1975): *Il Futuro ha un Cuore Antico.*
THE TREE STILL STANDS. Title of a novel by Mae Briskin (b. 1925).

וִדּוּי

Vidui · Confession

הַקְדָּמָה לַוִּדּוּי זוּטָא
Hakdamah LaVidui Zuta

וִדּוּי זוּטָא
Vidui Zuta

אַתָּה נוֹתֵן יָד
Atah Notein Yad

לֵךְ בְּשִׂמְחָה
Leich B'Simchah

How Do We Offer the N'ilah Confession?

With Honesty and Humility

אָנוּ עַזֵּי פָנִים, וְאַתָּה רַחוּם וְחַנּוּן.
אָנוּ קְשֵׁי עֹרֶף, וְאַתָּה אֶרֶךְ אַפַּיִם.
אָנוּ מְלֵאֵי עָוֹן, וְאַתָּה מָלֵא רַחֲמִים.
אָנוּ יָמֵינוּ כְּצֵל עוֹבֵר, וְאַתָּה הוּא
וּשְׁנוֹתֶיךָ לֹא יִתָּֽמּוּ.

Anu azei fanim, v'atah rachum v'chanun.
Anu k'shei oref, v'atah erech apayim.
Anu m'lei·ei avon, v'atah malei rachamim.
Anu yameinu k'tzeil oveir, v'atah hu —
ushnotecha lo yitamu.

We are insolent — but You are compassionate and gracious.
We are stubborn and stiff-necked — but You are slow to anger.
We persist in doing wrong — but You are the essence of mercy.
Our days are a shadow passing by, but You — You are existence itself,
Your years never ending.

With a Moment of Self-Reflection

אֱלֹהֵינוּ וֵאלֹהֵי אֲבוֹתֵינוּ וְאִמּוֹתֵינוּ,
תָּבֹא לְפָנֶיךָ תְּפִלָּתֵנוּ,
וְאַל תִּתְעַלַּם מִתְּחִנָּתֵנוּ.
אֲנַחְנוּ עַזֵּי פָנִים וּקְשֵׁי עֹרֶף
לוֹמַר לְפָנֶיךָ,
יְיָ אֱלֹהֵינוּ וֵאלֹהֵי אֲבוֹתֵינוּ
וְאִמּוֹתֵינוּ:
צַדִּיקִים אֲנַחְנוּ וְלֹא חָטָֽאנוּ.
אֲבָל אֲנַחְנוּ חָטָֽאנוּ.

Eloheinu v'Elohei avoteinu v'imoteinu,
tavo l'fanecha t'filateinu;
v'al titalam mit'chinateinu.
Anachnu azei fanim ukshei oref
lomar l'fanecha,
Adonai Eloheinu v'Elohei avoteinu
v'imoteinu:
Tzadikim anachnu, v'lo chatanu.
Aval anachnu chatanu.

Our God and God of all generations, may our prayers reach Your presence.
And when we turn to You, do not be indifferent.
Adonai, we are arrogant and stubborn, claiming to be blameless and free of sin.
In truth, we have stumbled and strayed.
We have done wrong.

Entering the Final Confession

The Final Confession

You Hold Out Your Hand

Go Forth In Gladness

How Do We Offer the N'ilah Confession?

With All Our Heart, with All Our Mind, with All Our Being

אָשַׁמְנוּ, בָּגַדְנוּ, גָּזַלְנוּ, דִּבַּרְנוּ דֹפִי.	*Ashamnu, bagadnu, gazalnu, dibarnu dofi.*
הֶעֱוִינוּ, וְהִרְשַׁעְנוּ, זַדְנוּ, חָמַסְנוּ,	*He·evinu, v'hirshanu, zadnu, chamasnu,*
טָפַלְנוּ שֶׁקֶר.	*tafalnu sheker.*
יָעַצְנוּ רָע, כִּזַּבְנוּ, לַצְנוּ, מָרַדְנוּ,	*Yaatznu ra, kizavnu, latznu, maradnu,*
נִאַצְנוּ, סָרַרְנוּ, עָוִינוּ, פָּשַׁעְנוּ,	*niatznu, sararnu, avinu, pashanu,*
צָרַרְנוּ, קִשִּׁינוּ עֹרֶף.	*tzararnu, kishinu oref.*
רָשַׁעְנוּ, שִׁחַתְנוּ, תִּעַבְנוּ,	*Rashanu, shichatnu, tiavnu,*
תָּעִינוּ, תִּעְתָּעְנוּ.	*ta·inu, titanu.*

Of these wrongs we are guilty:
We betray. We steal. We scorn. We act perversely.
We are cruel. We scheme. We are violent. We slander.
We devise evil. We lie. We ridicule. We disobey.
We abuse. We defy. We corrupt. We commit crimes.
We are hostile. We are stubborn. We are immoral. We kill.
We spoil. We go astray. We lead others astray.

מַה נֹּאמַר לְפָנֶיךָ, יוֹשֵׁב מָרוֹם,	*Mah nomar l'fanecha, yosheiv marom?*
וּמַה נְּסַפֵּר לְפָנֶיךָ, שׁוֹכֵן שְׁחָקִים.	*Umah n'sapeir l'fanecha, shochein sh'chakim?*
הֲלֹא כָּל הַנִּסְתָּרוֹת וְהַנִּגְלוֹת	*Halo kol hanistarot v'haniglot*
אַתָּה יוֹדֵעַ.	*atah yodei·a.*

What can we say to You whose existence is beyond time and space?
What words of ours can reach Your realm
beyond the clouds, beyond heaven itself?
Every hidden mystery, every revelation — surely, You know them all.

CONFESSION וִדּוּי (*facing page*). In all other Yom Kippur services, there are two confessions: one long (*Al Cheit*) and one short (*Ashamnu*). *N'ilah* has only the shorter confession, *Ashamnu*; and *Al Cheit* is replaced by the prayer that begins "You hold out Your hand (*Atah notein yad*)." Thus, in the closing moments of Yom Kippur, the focus shifts from our wrongs and sins to an image of God reaching out to us — encouraging our repentance with open arms, as it were. A commentary from the time of Rashi (11th century) notes that *yad* means not only "hand" but also "ability" and "freedom of action," suggesting that *Atah notein yad* can be read as a statement that God offers human beings free will, choice, and moral autonomy.

הַקְדָּמָה לְוִדּוּי זוּטָא
Hakdamah LaVidui Zuta

וִדּוּי זוּטָא
Vidui Zuta

אַתָּה נוֹתֵן יָד
Atah Notein Yad

לֵךְ בְּשִׂמְחָה
Leich B'Simchah

אתה נותן יד

You Hold Out Your Hand

אַתָּה נוֹתֵן יָד לְפוֹשְׁעִים,
וִימִינְךָ פְשׁוּטָה לְקַבֵּל שָׁבִים.
וַתְּלַמְּדֵנוּ, יְיָ אֱלֹהֵינוּ,
לְהִתְוַדּוֹת לְפָנֶיךָ עַל כָּל עֲוֹנוֹתֵינוּ,
לְמַעַן נֶחְדַּל מֵעֹשֶׁק יָדֵינוּ,
וּתְקַבְּלֵנוּ בִּתְשׁוּבָה שְׁלֵמָה לְפָנֶיךָ,
לְמַעַן דְּבָרֶיךָ אֲשֶׁר אָמָרְתָּ.

Atah notein yad l'foshim,
viminch f'shutah l'kabeil shavim.
Vat'lam'deinu, Adonai Eloheinu,
l'hitvadot l'fanecha al kol avonoteinu,
l'maan nechdal mei·oshek yadeinu,
utkab'leinu bit·shuvah sh'leimah l'fanecha,
l'maan d'varecha asher amarta.

You hold out Your hand to those who do wrong;
Your right hand opens wide to receive those who return.
You teach us the true purpose of confession:
to turn our hands into instruments of good,
to cause no harm or oppression.
Receive us, as You promised, in the fullness of our heartfelt *t'shuvah.*

וְאַתָּה יוֹדֵעַ שֶׁאַחֲרִיתֵנוּ
רִמָּה וְתוֹלֵעָה,
לְפִיכָךְ הִרְבֵּיתָ סְלִיחָתֵנוּ.
מָה אָנוּ. מֶה חַיֵּינוּ.
מֶה חַסְדֵּנוּ. מַה צִּדְקוֹתֵינוּ.
מַה יְשׁוּעָתֵנוּ. מַה כֹּחֵנוּ.
מַה גְּבוּרָתֵנוּ.

V'atah yodei·a she·achariteinu
rimah v'tolei·a;
l'fichach hirbeita s'lichateinu.
Mah anu? Meh chayeinu?
Meh chasdeinu? Mah tzidkoteinu?
Mah y'shuateinu? Mah kocheinu?
Mah g'vurateinu?

You show us many paths to forgiveness,
countless ways to make our lives count,
for You know that, in the end, we will return to the dust of the earth.
What are we? What is our life?
What is the breadth of our goodness, the depth of our righteousness,
the true measure of our achievements and success?
What use is our power? What good is our strength?

Entering the Final Confession

The Final Confession

You Hold Out Your Hand

Go Forth In Gladness

מַה נֹּאמַר לְפָנֶֽיךָ,	*Mah nomar l'fanecha,*
יְיָ אֱלֹהֵֽינוּ וֵאלֹהֵי	*Adonai Eloheinu v'Elohei*
אֲבוֹתֵֽינוּ וְאִמּוֹתֵֽינוּ,	*avoteinu v'imoteinu,*
הֲלֹא כָּל הַגִּבּוֹרִים כְּאַֽיִן לְפָנֶֽיךָ,	*halo chol hagiborim k'ayin l'fanecha,*
וְאַנְשֵׁי הַשֵּׁם כְּלֹא הָיוּ,	*v'anshei hashem k'lo hayu,*
וַחֲכָמִים כִּבְלִי מַדָּע,	*v'chachamim kivli mada,*
וּנְבוֹנִים כִּבְלִי הַשְׂכֵּל,	*unvonim kivli haskeil —*
כִּי רֹב מַעֲשֵׂיהֶם תֹּֽהוּ,	*ki rov maaseihem tohu;*
וִימֵי חַיֵּיהֶם הֶֽבֶל לְפָנֶֽיךָ.	*vimei chayeihem hevel l'fanecha.*
וּמוֹתַר הָאָדָם מִן הַבְּהֵמָה אָֽיִן,	*Umotar haadam min hab'heimah ayin —*
כִּי הַכֹּל הָֽבֶל.	*ki hakol havel.*

What can we say to You,
Eternal our God, God of all generations?
In Your presence there are no heroes
and great reputations dissolve;
the wise appear unlearned
and the discerning look foolish,
for all our deeds amount to futility
and the days of our lives — emptiness.
We human beings are no better than beasts:
all is vanity.

YOU HOLD OUT YOUR HAND אַתָּה נוֹתֵן יָד (*facing page*). The prayer focuses on God's constant presence and compassion, even in the face of sin and alienation. It recalls Psalm 73:22–23: "I was senseless and ignorant, like a brute beast before You. Yet I was always with You; You held my right hand."

In the first Hebrew prayer book ever printed — *Machzor Minhag Roma* (Prayer Book of the Roman Rite), completed on August 21, 1486 (20 Elul 5246) by Joshua Solomon Soncino in Casalmaggiore, Italy — this prayer appears in characters twice the normal size, unlike any other prayer in the book. One theory is that the printer had in mind the Conversos of 15th-century Spain (Jews forced by the Inquisition, beginning in 1391, to convert to Christianity; also known as Marranos): perhaps the enlarged letters were meant to encourage their *t'shuvah* (return to Judaism) by assuring them that God's hand remained stretched forth to them despite their forced baptisms.

YOUR RIGHT HAND OPENS WIDE וִימִינְךָ פְּשׁוּטָה (*facing page*). In the Bible, the right hand symbolizes the favored position — conveying a sense of safety, protection, and refuge. Examples include Genesis 48, when Jacob places his right hand on Ephraim's head to offer his blessing; and Psalm 16:8, "God is at my right hand; I shall never be shaken."

ALL IS VANITY, Ecclesiastes 1:2.

Atah hivdalta enosh meirosh,
vatakireihu laamod l'fanecha.

אַתָּה הִבְדַּֽלְתָּ אֱנוֹשׁ מֵרֹאשׁ,
וַתַּכִּירֵֽהוּ לַעֲמֹד לְפָנֶֽיךָ.

And yet —
from the beginning You set us apart.
We stand before You,
uplifted by Your unique awareness of humanity.

הַקְדָּמָה לַוִדּוּי זוּטָא
Hakdamah LaVidui Zuta

וִדּוּי זוּטָא
Vidui Zuta

אַתָּה נוֹתֵן יָד
Atah Notein Yad

לָךְ בְּשִׂמְחָה
Leich B'Simchah

Vatiten-lanu, Adonai Eloheinu,
b'ahavah et yom [haShabbat hazeh
v'et Yom] haKippurim hazeh —
keitz umchilah uslichah al
 kol avonoteinu,
l'maan nechdal mei·oshek yadeinu,
v'nashuv eilecha laasot chukei
 r'tzon'cha b'leivav shaleim.

וַתִּתֶּן־לָֽנוּ, יְיָ אֱלֹהֵֽינוּ,
בְּאַהֲבָה אֶת יוֹם [הַשַּׁבָּת הַזֶּה
וְאֶת יוֹם] הַכִּפֻּרִים הַזֶּה,
קֵץ וּמְחִילָה וּסְלִיחָה עַל
כָּל עֲוֹנוֹתֵֽינוּ,
לְמַֽעַן נֶחְדַּל מֵעֹֽשֶׁק יָדֵֽנוּ,
וְנָשׁוּב אֵלֶֽיךָ לַעֲשׂוֹת חֻקֵּי
רְצוֹנְךָ בְּלֵבָב שָׁלֵם.

With love You have given us this [Shabbat and this] Day of Atonement:
 to make an end of moral aimlessness, through pardon and forgiveness;
 to make an end of our abuse of power;
 to welcome our wholehearted return to the ways You desire.

V'atah b'rachamecha harabim racheim aleinu;
ki lo tachpotz b'hash·chatat olam.
Shene·emar: "Dirshu Adonai b'himatz'o;
k'ra·uhu biyoto karov."
V'ne·emar: "Yaazov rasha darko,
v'ish aven machsh'votav.
V'yashov el Adonai virachameihu —
v'el Eloheinu, ki yarbeh lislo·ach."

וְאַתָּה בְּרַחֲמֶֽיךָ הָרַבִּים רַחֵם עָלֵֽינוּ,
כִּי לֹא תַחְפֹּץ בְּהַשְׁחָתַת עוֹלָם,
שֶׁנֶּאֱמַר: דִּרְשׁוּ יְיָ בְּהִמָּצְאוֹ,
קְרָאֻֽהוּ בִּהְיוֹתוֹ קָרוֹב.
וְנֶאֱמַר: יַעֲזֹב רָשָׁע דַּרְכּוֹ,
וְאִישׁ אָֽוֶן מַחְשְׁבֹתָיו,
וְיָשֹׁב אֶל יְיָ וִירַחֲמֵֽהוּ,
וְאֶל אֱלֹהֵֽינוּ כִּי יַרְבֶּה לִסְלֽוֹחַ.

And You, in Your manifold mercy — may You be merciful to us;
 for the world's destruction is not Your desire. As it is said in the Prophets:
 "Search for Eternity while there is time; cry out when God is near.
 Let those who do evil give up their ways, and the wicked their designs.
 Let them return to God, who will show them compassion —
 to our God, whose forgiveness abounds."

SEARCH FOR ETERNITY דִּרְשׁוּ יְיָ, Isaiah 55:6–7.

You Sit, Waiting

הָהּ אֵלִי, אֵלִי,
אֲבִיר חֶלְדִּי,
חֲמָל־נָא עֲלֵי בִנְךָ נִדַּחֲךָ
אֲשֶׁר תָּעָה מִנִּי אֹרַח־אָבוֹת . . .

יָדַעְתִּי,
מָרוֹם אַתָּה מֶנִּי
וְנִשְׂגָּב מֵעֵין שִׂכְלִי
הִנְּךָ, אֵלִי.
אַךְ זֹאת גַּם זֹאת יָדַעְתִּי:
בִּמְקוֹם־מָה,
בַּמִּסְתָּרִים
תֵּשֵׁב, תְּחַכֶּה מִנִּי עוֹלָם
אֶל הָאַחֲרוֹן בַּעֲבָדֶיךָ
הַחוֹתֵר לָבוֹא שְׁעָרֶיךָ
בֶּאֱמוּנָה. . . .

My God, my God,
Mighty One of my existence,
have mercy on Your lost child
who has wandered from the ancestral path. . . .

I know
that You are far beyond me;
elevated above my ken,
are You, my God.
Yet this I know too:
Somewhere,
in the hidden places,
You sit, waiting eternally
for the last of Your servants,
who strives
to come into Your gates
in faith. . . .

YOU SIT, WAITING. From a longer poem by Hillel Bavli (1893–1961).

הַקְדָּמָה לַוִּדּוּי זוּטָא
Hakdamah LaVidui Zuta

וִדּוּי זוּטָא
Vidui Zuta

אַתָּה נוֹתֵן יָד
Atah Notein Yad

לֵךְ בְּשִׂמְחָה
Leich B'Simchah

וְאַתָּה, אֱלוֹהַּ סְלִיחוֹת,
חַנּוּן וְרַחוּם,
אֶרֶךְ אַפַּיִם, וְרַב־חֶסֶד וֶאֱמֶת.
וּמַרְבֶּה לְהֵיטִיב,
וְרוֹצֶה אַתָּה בִּתְשׁוּבַת רְשָׁעִים,
וְאֵין אַתָּה חָפֵץ בְּמִיתָתָם.
שֶׁנֶּאֱמַר: אֱמֹר אֲלֵיהֶם,
חַי אָנִי, נְאֻם אֲדֹנָי אֱלֹהִים,
אִם אֶחְפֹּץ בְּמוֹת הָרָשָׁע,
כִּי אִם בְּשׁוּב רָשָׁע מִדַּרְכּוֹ וְחָיָה.
שׁוּבוּ שׁוּבוּ מִדַּרְכֵיכֶם הָרָעִים,
וְלָמָּה תָמוּתוּ, בֵּית יִשְׂרָאֵל.

V'atah Elo·ah s'lichot,
chanum v'rachum,
erech apayim, v'rav-chesed ve·emet.
Umarbeh l'heitiv —
v'rotzeh atah bit·shuvat r'sha·im;
v'ein atah chafeitz b'mitatam.
Shene·emar: Emor aleihem,
"Chai ani, n'um Adonai Elohim,
im echpotz b'mot harasha —
ki im b'shuv rasha midarko v'chayah.
Shuvu, shuvu midarcheichem hara·im —
v'lamah tamutu, beit Yisrael?"

And You, Holy One of forgiveness —
compassionate, gracious, endlessly patient, loving, and true:
You are the wellspring of generosity —
wanting the repentance of those who do evil, not their demise.
As it is said in the Prophets:
"As I live — declares the Eternal God —
it is not My desire that the wicked shall die,
but that the wicked turn from their evil ways and live.
Turn back, turn back from all that leads you astray.
House of Israel, why choose death?"

כִּי אַתָּה סָלְחָן לְיִשְׂרָאֵל,
וּמָחֳלָן לְשִׁבְטֵי יְשֻׁרוּן
בְּכָל דּוֹר וָדוֹר,
וּמִבַּלְעָדֶיךָ אֵין לָנוּ מֶלֶךְ מוֹחֵל
וְסוֹלֵחַ אֶלָּא אָתָּה.

Ki atah solchan l'Yisrael,
umocholan l'shivtei Y'shurun
b'chol dor vador;
umibaladecha ein lanu melech mocheil
v'solei·ach ela atah.

For You are the Forgiver of Israel,
in every generation granting pardon to the tribes of Yeshurun.
We have no God of forgiveness and pardon but You, You alone.

AS I LIVE חַי אָנִי, Ezekiel 33:11.

YESHURUN. This name for the people Israel first appears in Deuteronomy 32:15. It has been understood, in folk etymology, as a reference to the Jewish people's ideal calling: to be *yashar* (straight, honorable, morally upright).

Hakarat Hatov: Recognizing the Good

אָהַבְנוּ, בָּכִינוּ, גָּמַלְנוּ, דִּבַּרְנוּ יֹפִי.
הֶאֱמַנּוּ, וְהִשְׁתַּדַּלְנוּ, זָכַרְנוּ, חִבַּקְנוּ, טָעַמְנוּ סֵפֶר.
יָצַרְנוּ, כָּמַהְנוּ, לָחַמְנוּ עֲבוּר הַצֶּדֶק, מִצִּינוּ אֶת הַטּוֹב, נִסִּינוּ,
סַרְנוּ לִרְאוֹת, עָשִׂינוּ אֲשֶׁר צִוִּיתָנוּ, פֵּרַשְׁנוּ, צָדַקְנוּ לִפְעָמִים, קָרָאנוּ בִּשְׁמֶךָ.
רָצִינוּ, שָׂמַחְנוּ, תָּמַכְנוּ.

1

We loved. And we wept. We were kind—and spoke thoughtfully.
We were faithful and trusting. We put forth effort.
We were mindful. We embraced. We took delight in the holy books.
We were creative. And we yearned.
We fought for justice—and searched out the good.
We tried our best. And we were attentive.
We did what You commanded us to do.
We found meaning in Torah. And, most of the time, we did what is right.
We proclaimed Your name. And we were accepting.
We were joyful. And we cared.

2

We have Aspired to reach higher.
We have Befriended those in need.
We have Created works of beauty.
We have Delighted in holy books.
We have Embraced our dear ones and held them close.
We have Fought for justice.
We have Given of ourselves.
We have Honored Your mitzvot.
We have Immersed ourselves in prayer.
We have Joined hands to build community.
We have Kept our word with integrity.
We have Loved faithfully and well.
We have Moved toward the light.
We have Nourished and supported.
We have Opened ourselves to hope.
We have Pursued the good.
We have Quieted our anger.
We have Remembered those who came before.
We have Sought meaning in Torah.
We have Trusted and been Trustworthy.
We have Uttered words of beauty.
We have Vigorously struggled to do right.
We have Wept over our shortcomings.
We have eXchanged blame for compassion.
We have Yearned to make life better.
We have Zestfully rejoiced.

Go Forth in Gladness

הַקְדָּמָה לַוִּדּוּי זוּטָא
Hakdamah LaVidui Zuta

וִדּוּי זוּטָא
Vidui Zuta

אַתָּה נוֹתֵן יָד
Atah Notein Yad

לֵךְ בְּשִׂמְחָה
Leich B'Simchah

Leich b'simchah, echol lachmecha,
ush'teih v'lev-tov yeinecha!

לֵךְ בְּשִׂמְחָה, אֱכֹל לַחְמֶךָ,
וּשֲׁתֵה בְלֶב־טוֹב יֵינֶךָ.

Elohim hadar bam'romecha:

Sh'ma enkat emunecha;

uvaseir et amecha:

"Salachti et z'donecha."

אֱלֹהִים הֲדַר בַּמְּרוֹמֶךָ,
שְׁמַע אֶנְקַת אֱמוּנֶיךָ,
וּבַשֵּׂר אֶת־עַמֶּךָ:
סָלַחְתִּי אֶת־זְדוֹנֶיךָ.

Leich b'simchah, echol lachmecha,
ush'teih v'lev-tov yeinecha!

לֵךְ בְּשִׂמְחָה, אֱכֹל לַחְמֶךָ,
וּשֲׁתֵה בְלֶב־טוֹב יֵינֶךָ.

Ha·eit n'ilat sh'arim,

v'eit hashemesh lavo;

v'yazeh mei kippurim al

am bachar l'chab'vo.

הָעֵת נְעִילַת שְׁעָרִים,
וְעֵת הַשֶּׁמֶשׁ לָבוֹא . . .
וְיַזֶּה מֵי כִּפֻּרִים עַל
עַם בָּחַר לְחַבְּבוֹ.

Leich b'simchah, echol lachmecha,
ush'teih v'lev-tov yeinecha!

לֵךְ בְּשִׂמְחָה, אֱכֹל לַחְמֶךָ,
וּשֲׁתֵה בְלֶב־טוֹב יֵינֶךָ.

Go forth in gladness, your heart filled with joy:
eat your bread and drink your wine!

God of glory high above, hear the cry of those who trust You;
let Your people know:
"Even the unkindest of your deeds I will forgive."

Go forth in gladness, your heart filled with joy:
eat your bread and drink your wine!

Now, as the gates are closing; now, as the sun begins to fade —
with waters of atonement bathe Your people —
the ones You embrace in love.

Go forth in gladness, your heart filled with joy:
eat your bread and drink your wine!

GO FORTH לֵךְ בְּשִׂמְחָה. By Rabbi Moses Ibn Ezra (12th century). The refrain is based on Ecclesiastes 9:7.

Our sages teach:
As soon as the fast of Yom Kippur concludes,
pound the first nail into the sukkah!

To everything there is a season—
a time for prayer and looking inward,
a time to go outside and build.

So it is written:
"One mitzvah inspires another."
May this long day of fasting and self-denial
inspire acts of creativity, generosity, and joy.
May we go from strength to strength.

As this day has been a refuge for the spirit,
may we shelter one another in the sukkah.
As we have shared worship and *t'shuvah*,
may we share hospitality and friendship in the days to come.
Mindful that our days are fleeting,
we prepare to taste the sweet fruits of this season;
to cherish life, to celebrate the light.

From this place of prayer and community,
we will soon return to our homes.
May we take with us the spirit of this day.
Melech chafeitz bachayim, Sovereign God who treasures life,
help us turn our homes into havens of Your love,
sanctuaries of Your compassion.
Let them be shelters against the storm,
dwelling-places for all that is life-giving and good.

AS SOON AS . . . INTO THE SUKKAH. From the commentary of Rabbi Moses Isserles (d. 1572) that accompanies the *Shulchan Aruch*, the authoritative code of Jewish law compiled by Rabbi Joseph Caro (1488–1575).

ISSERLES TEACHES that by starting to build the sukkah immediately after the close of Yom Kippur, we move from one sacred mitzvah to the next, thus fulfilling the words of Psalm 84:8 about the righteous: "they go from strength to strength" (*Shulchan Aruch, Orach Chayim* 624.5). The Talmud (*B'rachot* 64a) comments that the righteous are never at rest; they continue to strive for improvement throughout their lives, and even in the next world.

TO EVERYTHING THERE IS A SEASON. The opening of the third chapter of Ecclesiastes, the book traditionally read during Sukkot.

ONE MITZVAH INSPIRES ANOTHER, *Pirkei Avot* 4:2.

אָבִינוּ מַלְכֵּנוּ
Avinu Malkeinu

שְׂאוּ שְׁעָרִים
S'u Sh'arim

קַדִּישׁ שָׁלֵם
Kaddish Shaleim

הַיּוֹם מִסְתַּיֵּם
HaYom Mistayeim

תְּקִיעָה גְדוֹלָה
T'kiah G'dolah

מוּל הַשַּׁעַר

Mul HaShaar · Conclusion of the Day

Avinu Malkeinu

אָבִינוּ מַלְכֵּנוּ, קַבֵּל בְּרַחֲמִים וּבְרָצוֹן אֶת תְּפִלָּתֵנוּ.

Avinu Malkeinu, kabeil b'rachamim uvratzon et t'filateinu.

Avinu Malkeinu — Almighty and Merciful —
welcome our prayer with love; accept and embrace it.

אָבִינוּ מַלְכֵּנוּ, עֲשֵׂה לְמַעַן רַחֲמֶיךָ הָרַבִּים.

Avinu Malkeinu, aseih l'maan rachamecha harabim.

Avinu Malkeinu, act for the sake of Your boundless compassion.

אָבִינוּ מַלְכֵּנוּ, עֲשֵׂה עִמָּנוּ לְמַעַן שְׁמֶךָ.

Avinu Malkeinu, aseih imanu l'maan sh'mecha.

Avinu Malkeinu, act toward us as befits Your name.

אָבִינוּ מַלְכֵּנוּ, חָתְמֵנוּ בְּסֵפֶר פַּרְנָסָה וְכַלְכָּלָה.

Avinu Malkeinu, chotmeinu b'sefer parnasah v'chalkalah.

Avinu Malkeinu, seal us in the Book of Sustenance and Livelihood.

אָבִינוּ מַלְכֵּנוּ, חָתְמֵנוּ בְּסֵפֶר זְכֻיּוֹת.

Avinu Malkeinu, chotmeinu b'sefer z'chuyot.

Avinu Malkeinu, seal us in the Book of Worthiness and Merit.

אָבִינוּ מַלְכֵּנוּ, חָתְמֵנוּ בְּסֵפֶר סְלִיחָה וּמְחִילָה.

Avinu Malkeinu, chotmeinu b'sefer s'lichah umchilah.

Avinu Malkeinu, seal us in the Book of Forgiveness and Pardon.

SEAL US IN THE BOOK. One repeated refrain of this service — "The gates are closing" — expresses our sense of urgency and unease, perhaps fear that our time is running out. Another liturgical theme of *N'ilah* — "Open the gates" — expresses a sense of courage and hope, aspiration and faith. And when we say "seal us" — as we do five times in this last *Avinu Malkeinu* — we express our deep longing for certainty as the New Year begins. Each of us aches for some assurance that our names will be inscribed and sealed in this sacred scripture of Yom Kippur — this Torah of *T'shuvah*: the Book of Sustenance and Livelihood; the Book of Worthiness and Merit; the Book of Forgiveness and Pardon; the Book of Lives Well Lived; the Book of Redemption and Renewal. In a world of uncertainty, we want to know that our lives matter, that goodness and blessings await us in the year ahead. *Chotmeinu*, we say: "Seal us in these books. Let us know that our lives have lasting worth and meaning."

Soul-Sustainer, Source of Our Life

עֶזְרַת נַפְשֵׁנוּ, מְקוֹר חַיֵּינוּ,
Ezrat Nafsheinu, M'kor Chayeinu,
our Soul-Sustainer, Source of Our Life—
we stand as one before the One.

Each solitary soul, each fragment of the whole:
a congregation of fears, dreams, and hopes;
regret and joy, questions unanswered:

Where is justice?
When will there be peace?
Who can mend our shattered hearts?

Some are starving. Some are dying alone.
Many are suffering, in need of our love.
How far can our hands reach?

עֶזְרַת נַפְשֵׁנוּ, מְקוֹר חַיֵּינוּ,
Ezrat Nafsheinu, M'kor Chayeinu,
our Soul-Sustainer, Source of Our Life—
the gates of hope are ours to open.

Still the wind of Creation blows,
sweeping over the darkness,
building cosmos out of chaos;

evolving order and complexity;
shining light into the shadows;
wresting beauty out of brokenness and failure.

Still the wind of Creation blows:
the world is still becoming,
and we are still emerging.

עֶזְרַת נַפְשֵׁנוּ, מְקוֹר חַיֵּינוּ,
Ezrat Nafsheinu, M'kor Chayeinu,
let healing come—
let it come through deeds of *tzedakah* and *chesed*;
let it come through us—our hands, our love.

אָבִֽינוּ מַלְכֵּֽנוּ, חָתְמֵֽנוּ בְּסֵֽפֶר חַיִּים טוֹבִים.

Avinu Malkeinu, chotmeinu b'sefer chayim tovim.
Avinu Malkeinu, seal us in the Book of Lives Well Lived.

אָבִֽינוּ מַלְכֵּֽנוּ, חָתְמֵֽנוּ בְּסֵֽפֶר גְּאֻלָּה וִישׁוּעָה.

Avinu Malkeinu, chotmeinu b'sefer g'ulah vishuah.
Avinu Malkeinu, seal us in the Book of Redemption and Renewal.

אָבִֽינוּ מַלְכֵּֽנוּ, מַלֵּא יָדֵֽינוּ מִבִּרְכוֹתֶֽיךָ.

Avinu Malkeinu, malei yadeinu mibirchotecha.
Avinu Malkeinu, let our hands overflow with Your blessings.

אָבִֽינוּ מַלְכֵּֽנוּ, פְּתַח שַׁעֲרֵי שָׁמַֽיִם לִתְפִלָּתֵֽנוּ.

Avinu Malkeinu, p'tach shaarei shamayim litfilateinu.
Avinu Malkeinu, let the gates of heaven be open to our prayer.

אָבִֽינוּ מַלְכֵּֽנוּ, חַדֵּשׁ עָלֵֽינוּ שָׁנָה טוֹבָה.

Avinu Malkeinu, chadeish aleinu shanah tovah.
Avinu Malkeinu, renew us for a year of goodness.

אָבִֽינוּ מַלְכֵּֽנוּ, אֵין לָֽנוּ מֶֽלֶךְ אֶלָּא אָֽתָּה.

Avinu Malkeinu, ein lanu melech ela atah.
Avinu Malkeinu, we have no Sovereign but You.

אָבִֽינוּ מַלְכֵּֽנוּ, חָנֵּֽנוּ וַעֲנֵֽנוּ כִּי אֵין בָּֽנוּ מַעֲשִׂים,
עֲשֵׂה עִמָּֽנוּ צְדָקָה וָחֶֽסֶד וְהוֹשִׁיעֵֽנוּ.

Avinu Malkeinu, choneinu vaaneinu ki ein banu maasim.
Aseih imanu tz'dakah vachesed, v'hoshi·einu.
Avinu Malkeinu — Almighty and Merciful —
answer us with grace when our deeds are wanting.
Save us through acts of justice and love.

אָבִֽינוּ מַלְכֵּֽנוּ
Avinu Malkeinu

שְׂאוּ שְׁעָרִים
S'u Sh'arim

קַדִּישׁ שָׁלֵם
Kaddish Shaleim

הַיּוֹם מִסְתַּיֵּם
HaYom Mistayeim

תְּקִיעָה גְדוֹלָה
T'kiah G'dolah

WHEN OUR DEEDS ARE WANTING כִּי אֵין בָּֽנוּ מַעֲשִׂים. From the evening of Rosh HaShanah until the afternoon of Yom Kippur, we sing: "Answer us with grace, *for* our deeds our wanting." Now, in *N'ilah*, having engaged in the process of *t'shuvah* (return) and *cheshbon hanefesh* (accounting of the soul), we experience this final moment of *Avinu Malkeinu* in a unique way. The tiny word *ki* makes all the difference: it can mean either "for" or "when." The latter suggests that, though we are bound to miss the mark in the year ahead, we now leave behind a year's worth of guilt — serene in the knowledge that we can start fresh. Our deeds are not wanting. Truly this is a moment of joy and renewal.

As We Are Sealed — Open Us

Set me as a seal upon your heart,
as a seal upon your hand. . . .

As the Book of Life is closed and sealed—
open our hearts, open our hands.
Let those who asked forgiveness and those who gave forgiveness
depart this place in peace.
Let all God-seekers and soul-searchers of this day
depart this place inspired and renewed.
Together let us build a community of commitment.

Let all of us be sealed this day—
גְּמַר חֲתִימָה טוֹבָה . . .
g'mar chatimah tovah . . .
sealed for goodness and sealed for life
בְּסֵפֶר חַיִּים טוֹבִים . . .
b'sefer chayim tovim . . .
sealed in the Book of Life and Good,
eager to taste life's sweetness,
to enjoy the fruit of our labors,
to bring light to the darkness
and joy where sorrow dwells.

Be sealed for a year of Torah and soulful searching.
Be sealed for a year of kindness, good deeds, and love.
As the Book of Life is closed and sealed—
open our hands, open our hearts.

SET ME AS A SEAL. Song of Songs 8:6.
ENJOY THE FRUIT. Based on Psalm 128:2.

From Psalm 24

S'u sh'arim, rasheichem!	שְׂאוּ שְׁעָרִים רָאשֵׁיכֶם
Us·u pit·chei olam,	וּשְׂאוּ פִּתְחֵי עוֹלָם,
v'yavo melech hakavod.	וְיָבֹא מֶלֶךְ הַכָּבוֹד.
Mi hu zeh melech hakavod?	מִי הוּא זֶה מֶלֶךְ הַכָּבוֹד,
Adonai tz'vaot —	יְיָ צְבָאוֹת,
hu melech hakavod. Selah.	הוּא מֶלֶךְ הַכָּבוֹד סֶלָה.

Lift yourselves, gates of heaven — rise high!
Be carried aloft, everlasting portals,
that the Sovereign of Splendor may enter.

Who is the Sovereign of Splendor?
The eternal Soul of the universe, the Sublime —
this is the Sovereign of Splendor.

LIFT YOURSELVES שְׂאוּ שְׁעָרִים, Psalm 24:9–10.

GATES OF HEAVEN . . . EVERLASTING PORTALS שְׁעָרִים . . . פִּתְחֵי עוֹלָם. We might think of the gates and portals of Psalm 24 in terms suggested by Rabbi Abraham Joshua Heschel (1907–1972), who speaks of "the door to ultimate significance." For Heschel, the unlocking of that door is an experience of "wonder and awe, a sense of indebtedness . . . acts of yearning and luminous moments of insight."

WHO IS THE SOVEREIGN OF SPLENDOR מִי הוּא זֶה מֶלֶךְ הַכָּבוֹד. This question, asked twice in Psalm 24, may refer to a ritual procession that accompanied the Ark of the Covenant into the Temple of biblical times. For present-day worshipers, this question suggests that, even after the intensity of the religious experience on Yom Kippur, we do well to ask theological questions and reflect on the meaning of God in our lives.

To live life in all its fullness
is to stand, in awe, before an open gate—
to gaze into a doorway of hope,
a wondrous portal of possibilities.
Many are the gates of our lives;
many the treasures toward which they lead.
And how many close behind us—lost, forgotten, and sealed forever?
How many gates? How many years?

Standing, in awe, before the gates of a new year
we see its most precious gift:
the minutes and the hours, the days and the weeks—
the treasure house of time.
Every moment is a vessel of infinite holiness.
Every morning, noon, and night is a gateway to life's immensity.

How will we use this precious gift?

Love after Love

The time will come
when, with elation,
you will greet yourself arriving
at your own door, in your own mirror,
and each will smile at the other's welcome,

And say, sit here. Eat.
You will love again the stranger who was your self.
Give wine. Give bread. Give back your heart
to itself, to the stranger who has loved you

all your life, whom you ignored
for another, who knows you by heart.
Take down the love letters from the bookshelf,

the photographs, the desperate notes,
peel your own image from the mirror.
Sit. Feast on your life.

---

doorway of hope. In Hebrew, *petach tikvah* (Hosea 2:17).
love after love. By Derek Walcott (b. 1930).

אָבִינוּ מַלְכֵּנוּ
Avinu Malkeinu

שְׂאוּ שְׁעָרִים
S'u Sh'arim

קַדִּישׁ שָׁלֵם
Kaddish Shaleim

הַיּוֹם מִסְתַּיֵּם
HaYom Mistayeim

תְּקִיעָה גְדוֹלָה
T'kiah G'dolah

Full Kaddish

יִתְגַּדַּל וְיִתְקַדַּשׁ שְׁמֵהּ רַבָּא,
בְּעָלְמָא דִּי בְרָא כִרְעוּתֵהּ.
וְיַמְלִיךְ מַלְכוּתֵהּ בְּחַיֵּיכוֹן
וּבְיוֹמֵיכוֹן,
וּבְחַיֵּי דְכָל בֵּית יִשְׂרָאֵל,
בַּעֲגָלָא וּבִזְמַן קָרִיב.
וְאִמְרוּ: אָמֵן.

Yitgadal v'yitkadash sh'meih raba,
b'alma di v'ra chiruteih.
V'yamlich malchuteih b'chayeichon
uvyomeichon,
uvchayei d'chol beit Yisrael —
baagala uvizman kariv;
v'imru: Amen.

יְהֵא שְׁמֵהּ רַבָּא מְבָרַךְ
לְעָלַם וּלְעָלְמֵי עָלְמַיָּא.
יִתְבָּרַךְ וְיִשְׁתַּבַּח וְיִתְפָּאַר
וְיִתְרוֹמַם וְיִתְנַשֵּׂא וְיִתְהַדָּר
וְיִתְעַלֶּה וְיִתְהַלָּל שְׁמֵהּ
דְּקֻדְשָׁא, בְּרִיךְ הוּא,
לְעֵלָּא וּלְעֵלָּא מִכָּל בִּרְכָתָא וְשִׁירָתָא,
תֻּשְׁבְּחָתָא וְנֶחֱמָתָא
דַּאֲמִירָן בְּעָלְמָא.
וְאִמְרוּ: אָמֵן.

Y'hei sh'meih raba m'varach
l'alam ul·almei almaya.
Yitbarach v'yishtabach v'yitpaar
v'yitromam v'yitnasei v'yit·hadar
v'yitaleh v'yit·halal sh'meih
d'kudsha — b'rich hu —
l'eila ul·eila mikol birchata v'shirata,
tushb'chata v'nechemata
daamiran b'alma;
v'imru: Amen.

תִּתְקַבַּל צְלוֹתְהוֹן וּבָעוּתְהוֹן
דְּכָל יִשְׂרָאֵל קֳדָם אֲבוּהוֹן דִּי
בִשְׁמַיָּא.
וְאִמְרוּ: אָמֵן.

Titkabal tz'lot·hon uvaut·hon
d'chol Yisrael kodam avuhon di
vishmaya;
v'imru: Amen.

יְהֵא שְׁלָמָא רַבָּא מִן שְׁמַיָּא,
וְחַיִּים עָלֵינוּ וְעַל כָּל יִשְׂרָאֵל.
וְאִמְרוּ: אָמֵן.

Y'hei sh'lama raba min sh'maya,
v'chayim aleinu v'al kol Yisrael;
v'imru: Amen.

עֹשֶׂה שָׁלוֹם בִּמְרוֹמָיו
הוּא יַעֲשֶׂה שָׁלוֹם עָלֵינוּ
וְעַל כָּל יִשְׂרָאֵל
וְעַל כָּל יוֹשְׁבֵי תֵבֵל.
וְאִמְרוּ: אָמֵן.

Oseh shalom bimromav,
Hu yaaseh shalom aleinu,
v'al kol Yisrael
v'al kol yoshvei teiveil.
V'imru: Amen.

May God's great name come to be magnified and sanctified
in the world God brought into being.
May God's majestic reign prevail soon in your lives, in your days,
and in the life of the whole House of Israel;
and let us say: *Amen.*

May God's great name be blessed to the end of time.

May God's holy name come to be blessed, acclaimed, and glorified;
revered, raised, and beautified; honored and praised.
Blessed is the One who is entirely beyond
all the blessings and hymns,
all the praises and words of comfort
that we speak in the world;
and let us say: *Amen.*

Let the prayers and needs of all Israel be accepted
by their Creator in heaven;
and let us say: *Amen.*

Let perfect peace abound;
let there be abundant life for us and for all Israel;
and let us say: *Amen.*

May the One who makes peace in the high heavens
make peace for us, all Israel, and all who dwell on earth;
and let us say: *Amen.*

MAY GOD'S GREAT NAME COME TO BE MAGNIFIED יִתְגַּדַּל... שְׁמֵהּ רַבָּא. Ten words in praise of God distinguish the *Kaddish* from other prayers: magnified, sanctified, blessed, acclaimed, glorified, revered, raised, beautified, honored, and praised. Some have called this language excessive. But these ten words of praise are neither fulsome nor overgenerous; rather, they reflect an attempt to state the extent of our gratitude for the gift of existence — and ultimately say little about God, since God is "entirely beyond" all the praises that we can speak.

In the *Kaddish Shaleim* (Full or Complete *Kaddish*) we add the words: "Let the prayers and needs of all Israel be accepted by their Creator in heaven."

As the Day Ends

אָבִינוּ מַלְכֵּנוּ
Avinu Malkeinu

שְׂאוּ שְׁעָרִים
S'u Sh'arim

קַדִּישׁ שָׁלֵם
Kaddish Shaleim

הַיּוֹם מִסְתַּיֵּם
HaYom Mistayeim

תְּקִיעָה גְדוֹלָה
T'kiah G'dolah

We stand as one before the gates of a new year —
renewed by this Day of Atonement,
made stronger by all who are with us
and by those whose presence we feel within.

As the long day fades into dusk,
we join our voices in words of hope and dedication:

פִּתְחוּ־לָנוּ שַׁעֲרֵי־צֶדֶק, נָבֹא־בָם, נוֹדֶה יָהּ.

Pit·chu-lanu shaarei-tzedek; navo vam, nodeh Yah.

Open for us the gates of righteousness,
that we may enter and praise the Eternal Source of Life.

Open for us the gates of sacred community,
that we may enter and feel its healing power.

Open for us the gates of truth and integrity,
that we may enter and grow in faithfulness.

Open for us the gates of devotion and principle,
that we may enter and find enduring values and meaning.

Open for us the gates of repentance and return,
that we may enter and offer our best.

Open for us the gates of forgiveness,
that we may enter and offer our humanity.

Open for us the gates of kindness and compassion,
that we may enter and offer our love.

OPEN FOR US THE GATES פִּתְחוּ־לָנוּ. In the Book of Psalms (118:19) the verse reads: "Open for me the gates of righteousness" — a beautiful prayer for private devotion. But *N'ilah* is not a moment of solitude. In the last minutes of this powerful day, we express our solidarity as a congregation and our solidarity with the Jewish people. We do this by saying, "Open for us . . ."

For the Sounding of the Shofar

As the Sabbath of Sabbaths ends, we say from the heart:

Living Source — You are ours, we are Yours.

From beyond time and space,
You hold out Your hand to receive us.

Living Source — You are ours, we are Yours.

You are the Sovereign of remembrance, the Voice of holiness —
Your presence lights the way.

Living Source — You are ours, we are Yours.

Sh'ma, Yisrael — Hear the shofar —
witness to history, thunder to our souls.

Living Source — You are ours, we are Yours.

Happy are those who love the sound of the shofar —
its mystic chords of memory.

Living Source — You are ours, we are Yours.
Hear the shofar! Hear its cry of freedom, its call of courage —
cherish its promise of hope.

YOUR PRESENCE LIGHTS THE WAY, Psalm 89:16.

HAPPY ARE THOSE, Psalm 89:16, adapted.

MYSTIC CHORDS OF MEMORY. From Abraham Lincoln's first inaugural address (March 4, 1861).

SH'MA YISRAEL . . . JERUSALEM (*next two pages*). These words and sounds comprise a ritual unto itself. First, we witness the divine Unity by singing *Sh'ma Yisrael*, words recited every day when we lie down and when we rise up. Then three times (to symbolize past, present, and future) we affirm God's sovereignty, as did ancient worshipers after hearing the High Priest's three confessions on Yom Kippur. Next, the seven rungs of a "word ladder" appear on the page (for seven is the symbol of wholeness and holiness) — each rung bearing the two qualities of the righteous Judge: *Adonai*, mercy; *Elohim*, justice.

A day filled with words nears its end with a cry that echoes from deep within and far away — the ram's horn: "God ascends with the sound of *t'ruah*, Adonai with the voice of the shofar" (Psalm 47:6). Finally, "Next year in Jerusalem" — a wish, a hope, a yearning for the place where our earliest ancestors encountered the Holy, and where the Divine Presence is felt in our time.

אָבִינוּ מַלְכֵּנוּ
Avinu Malkeinu

שְׂאוּ שְׁעָרִים
S'u Sh'arim

קַדִּישׁ שָׁלֵם
Kaddish Shaleim

הַיּוֹם מִסְתַּיֵּם
HaYom Mistayeim

תְּקִיעָה גְדוֹלָה
T'kiah G'dolah

שמע ישראל יהוה

Sh'ma, Yisrael: Adonai Eloheinu, Adonai echad.
Listen, Israel: Adonai is our God, Adonai is One.

בָּרוּךְ שֵׁם כְּבוֹד מַלְכוּתוֹ לְעוֹלָם וָעֶד.
בָּרוּךְ שֵׁם כְּבוֹד מַלְכוּתוֹ לְעוֹלָם וָעֶד.
בָּרוּךְ שֵׁם כְּבוֹד מַלְכוּתוֹ לְעוֹלָם וָעֶד.

Baruch shem k'vod malchuto l'olam va·ed.
Blessed is God's glorious majesty forever and ever.

יְיָ הוּא הָאֱלֹהִים.
יְיָ הוּא הָאֱלֹהִים.
יְיָ הוּא הָאֱלֹהִים.
יְיָ הוּא הָאֱלֹהִים.
יְיָ הוּא הָאֱלֹהִים.
יְיָ הוּא הָאֱלֹהִים.
יְיָ הוּא הָאֱלֹהִים.

Adonai, hu haElohim.
Adonai is God.

Avinu Malkeinu

Psalm 24

Full Kaddish

As the Day Ends

Final Sounding of the Shofar

אלֹהינו יהוה אחד

שופר

תְּקִיעָה

שְׁבָרִים

תְּרוּעָה

תְּקִיעָה גְּדוֹלָה

T'kiah *Sh'varim* *T'ruah* *T'kiah G'dolah*

Lashanah habaah birushalayim!

Next year in Jerusalem!

הַבְדָּלָה
Havdalah

יַיִן
Yayin
בְּשָׂמִים
B'samim
נֵר
Ner
הַבְדָּלָה
Havdalah
שִׁירִים
Shirim

Wine

בָּרוּךְ אַתָּה, יְיָ,
אֱלֹהֵינוּ מֶלֶךְ הָעוֹלָם,
בּוֹרֵא פְּרִי הַגָּפֶן.

Baruch atah, Adonai,
Eloheinu melech haolam,
borei p'ri hagafen.

Adonai, our God and Sovereign, Source of blessings,
You create the fruit of the vine.

Spices

בָּרוּךְ אַתָּה, יְיָ,
אֱלֹהֵינוּ מֶלֶךְ הָעוֹלָם,
בּוֹרֵא מִינֵי בְשָׂמִים.

Baruch atah, Adonai,
Eloheinu melech haolam,
borei minei v'samim.

Adonai, our God and Sovereign, Source of blessings,
You create spices of every kind.

Lights

בָּרוּךְ אַתָּה, יְיָ,
אֱלֹהֵינוּ מֶלֶךְ הָעוֹלָם,
בּוֹרֵא מְאוֹרֵי הָאֵשׁ.

Baruch atah, Adonai,
Eloheinu melech haolam,
borei m'orei ha·eish.

Adonai, our God and Sovereign, Source of blessings,
You create the lights of fire.

YOU CREATE SPICES OF EVERY KIND. At the end of Shabbat, Havdalah, the service of separation, is recited over wine, spices, and fire (the light of a braided candle). Some derive the use of spices in Havdalah from a teaching in the Talmud (*Beitzah* 16a): "Resh Lakish said: The Holy One gives a person an additional soul (*n'shamah y'teirah*) on the eve of Shabbat; but at the end of Shabbat the additional soul is taken away." Inhaling the sweet fragrance of the spices strengthens us after the additional soul has departed.

While spices are not traditionally included in the Havdalah ceremony that concludes Yom Kippur, many Reform Jews affirm Yom Kippur as *Shabbat Shabbaton* (the Sabbath of Sabbaths; Leviticus 16:31) — and therefore include spices, even when Yom Kippur falls on a weekday.

Wine
Spices
Lights
Separation
Songs

Separation

Baruch atah, Adonai,	בָּרוּךְ אַתָּה, יְיָ,
Eloheinu melech haolam,	אֱלֹהֵינוּ מֶלֶךְ הָעוֹלָם,
hamavdil bein kodesh l'chol,	הַמַּבְדִּיל בֵּין קֹדֶשׁ לְחוֹל,
bein or l'choshech,	בֵּין אוֹר לְחֹשֶׁךְ,
bein Yisrael laamim,	בֵּין יִשְׂרָאֵל לָעַמִּים,
bein yom hash'vi·i	בֵּין יוֹם הַשְּׁבִיעִי
l'sheishet y'mei hamaaseh.	לְשֵׁשֶׁת יְמֵי הַמַּעֲשֶׂה.

Adonai, our God and Sovereign, Source of blessings—
You distinguish the holy from the everyday
and separate light from darkness.
You give each people a place in the family of nations,
and thus distinguish Israel from other peoples.
You set apart the seventh day from the six days of creation.

בָּרוּךְ אַתָּה, יְיָ, הַמַּבְדִּיל בֵּין קֹדֶשׁ לְחוֹל.
Baruch atah, Adonai, hamavdil bein kodesh l'chol.
Adonai, Source of blessings,
You distinguish the holy from the everyday.

Hamavdil bein kodesh l'chol	הַמַּבְדִּיל בֵּין קֹדֶשׁ לְחוֹל
chatoteinu hu yimchol	חַטֹּאתֵינוּ הוּא יִמְחֹל
zareinu ushlomeinu yarbeh kachol	זַרְעֵנוּ וּשְׁלוֹמֵנוּ יַרְבֶּה כַּחוֹל
v'chakochavim balailah.	וְכַכּוֹכָבִים בַּלָּיְלָה.

As You separate sacred from profane,
separate us from our wrongful ways.
Give us a future —
 our children countless as grains of sand.
Give us peace —
 majestic and beautiful as the starry night.

GIVE US PEACE וּשְׁלוֹמֵנוּ יַרְבֶּה. This 11th-century blessing exists in two versions. One asks God to increase our offspring and our prosperity (*zareinu v'chaspeinu*); the other (above) presents a vision of the future that places *sh'lomeinu* (our peace, our well-being) among our two highest values.

Songs

יַיִן
Yayin

בְּשָׂמִים
B'samim

נֵר
Ner

הַבְדָּלָה
Havdalah

שִׁירִים
Shirim

Shanah tovah, shanah tovah,

shanah tovah, shanah tovah (2x)

שָׁנָה טוֹבָה, שָׁנָה טוֹבָה,
שָׁנָה טוֹבָה, שָׁנָה טוֹבָה

A good year, a year of peace —
May gladness reign and joy increase. (2x)

Eliyahu hanavi, Eliyahu haTishbi,

Eliyahu, Eliyahu, Eliyahu HaGiladi.

Bimheirah v'yameinu yavo eileinu

im mashiach ben-David,

im mashiach ben-David.

אֵלִיָּֽהוּ הַנָּבִיא, אֵלִיָּֽהוּ הַתִּשְׁבִּי,
אֵלִיָּֽהוּ, אֵלִיָּֽהוּ, אֵלִיָּֽהוּ הַגִּלְעָדִי.
בִּמְהֵרָה בְיָמֵֽינוּ יָבֹא אֵלֵֽינוּ
עִם מָשִֽׁיחַ בֶּן־דָּוִד,
עִם מָשִֽׁיחַ בֶּן־דָּוִד.

Elijah the Prophet,
Elijah of Tishbi,
Elijah of Gilead:
may he come in our own time,
and reach us without delay.
May he yet fulfill — with love — our hope:
a world perfected and redeemed.

ELIJAH אֵלִיָּֽהוּ. II Kings 2:1–11 records Elijah's ascent to heaven, alive, in a chariot of fire. Some four centuries later, the prophet Malachi proclaimed in God's name: "I will send the prophet Elijah to you before the coming of the awesome, fearful day of Adonai. He shall reconcile parents with children and children with their parents, so that, when I come, I do not strike the whole land with destruction" (Malachi 3:23–24). Long considered a harbinger of the messianic age, Elijah is recalled particularly at the departure of Shabbat, since Shabbat is called a "sampling" (or "taste") of the world-to-come (Talmud *B'rachot* 57b).

Similarly, the prophet Miriam (*facing page*) is associated with song and healing. Her role in the story of the Israelites in Egypt (Exodus 2:7–8) makes her a redemptive figure in biblical history. Our last words on this Sabbath of Sabbaths point toward an era of *tikkun* — a world healed and at peace.

Wine
Spices
Lights
Separation
Songs

מִרְיָם הַנְּבִיאָה,
עֹז וְזִמְרָה בְּיָדָהּ,
מִרְיָם תִּרְקֹד אִתָּנוּ
לְהַגְדִּיל זִמְרַת עוֹלָם.
מִרְיָם תִּרְקֹד אִתָּנוּ
לְתַקֵּן אֶת הָעוֹלָם.
בִּמְהֵרָה בְּיָמֵינוּ הִיא תְּבִיאֵינוּ
אֶל מֵי הַיְשׁוּעָה.

Miryam han'viah —
oz v'zimrah b'yadah.
Miryam tirkod itanu
l'hagdil zimrat olam;
Miryam tirkod itanu
l'takein et haolam.
Bimheirah v'yameinu hi t'vi·einu
el mei ha-y'shuah.

Miriam the prophet —
the power of song is in her hand.
Miriam will dance among us
and the music will be heard far and wide.
Miriam will dance among us
to mend our world of suffering.
May she lead us, in our time, without delay,
to the waters of help and healing.

תִּזְכּוּ לְשָׁנִים רַבּוֹת!

Tizku l'shanim rabot!

Be worthy of your years — and may they be many!

MIRIAM THE PROPHET מִרְיָם הַנְּבִיאָה. Hebrew lyrics by Rabbi Leila Gal Berner (b. 1950).

BE WORTHY OF YOUR YEARS — AND MAY THEY BE MANY תִּזְכּוּ לְשָׁנִים רַבּוֹת. This Sephardic blessing, which appeared already near the start of the *N'ilah* service, in the poem *El Nora Alilah* (page 614), echoes a verse in *Avinu Malkeinu*: "Seal us in the Book of Worthiness and Merit." The blessing captures the purpose of Rosh HaShanah and Yom Kippur from the perspective of those who observe these holy days: to make us worthy of our lives, to instill in us the hope for an abundance of life, and, finally, to renew us as human beings who go forth in gladness.

Source and Permissions

The Central Conference of American Rabbis expresses gratitude to the publishers and writers for the permission we have received to use their material in *Mishkan HaNefesh*. Every effort has been made to ascertain the proper owners of copyrights for the selections used in this volume and to obtain permission to reprint copyrighted content where required. The Conference will be pleased, in subsequent editions, to correct any inadvertent errors or omissions that may be pointed out.

Unless otherwise noted, the translations of Hebrew prayers and other texts, original prayers in English, commentaries, and additional readings are by Rabbi Janet Marder and Rabbi Sheldon Marder.

EVENING SERVICE

3 *And why is the tallis striped*, by Yehuda Amichai, *Open Closed Open: Poems by Yehuda Amichai*, transl. Chana Bloch and Chana Kronfeld. Copyright © 2000 by Chana Bloch and Chana Kronfeld (New York: Harcourt, 2000), p. 44. Reprinted by permission of Houghton Mifflin Harcourt Publishing Company and Hana Amichai. All rights reserved.

4 *The most beautiful thing*, by Rabbi Eleazar ben Judah, *Sefer HaRokei·ach*.

4 *It is the custom*, by Rabbi Joseph Yuspa Hahn, *Yosif Ometz*.

4 *Jewish thought pays*, by Rabbi Adin Steinsaltz, *The Thirteen Petalled Rose* (New York: Basic Books, 1980), pp. 131–32.

5 *On this journey*, by Rabbi Alan Lew, *This is Real and You are Completely Unprepared: The Days of Awe as a Journey of Transformation* (New York: Little Brown and Company, 2003), pp. 8–9.

5 *Praying is more*, by Rabbi Jan Uhrbach, "Praying on the High Holy Days: An Open Letter from Rabbi Jan Uhrbach," purl.org/net/mhn15. Used by permission.

6 *The impact of erev Yom Kippur*, by Rabbi Abraham Joshua Heschel, from *Moral Grandeur and Spiritual Audacity*, ed. Susannah Heschel (New York: Farrar, Straus, and Giroux, 1996), p. 146. Copyright © 1996 Sylvia Heschel. Reprinted by permission of Farrar, Straus and Giroux, LLC.

7 *In the Bible*, by Rabbi Amy Scheinerman, "Staying in a Relationship with God: It's OK to be Angry," *Carroll County Times*. Used with permission.

7 *Yom Kippur is a Scandalous Day*, by Rabbi Michael Marmur. Used with permission.

8 *I remember*, by Pauline Wengeroff, from *Rememberings*, transl. Henny Wenkar (The Joseph and Rebecca Meyerhoff Center for Jewish Studies, University of Maryland: University Press of Maryland, 2000); adapted.

8 *Yom Kippur Sonnet*, by Jacqueline Osherow, "Yom Kippur Sonnet with a Line from Lamentations," *Dead Men's Praise* (New York: Grove Press, 1999), p. 34. Copyright © 1999 by Jacqueline Osherow. Used by permission of Grove/Atlantic, Inc. Any third party use of this material, outside of this publication, is prohibited.

11 *Of all these pleasant acts*, by Rabbi Jeffrey Cohen, *Prayer and Penitence* (Northvale, NJ: Aronson, 1994), p. 138.

15 *Rabbi Leizer survived*, by Corinna da Fonseca-Wollheim, "The Soul Breath of Kol Nidre," *Jewish World Digest* (September 20, 2006), as cited by Rabbi Nancy Wiener, purl.org/net/mhn16.

16 *that evil cannot last*, by Rabbi Samson Raphael Hirsch, *The Psalms* (New York: Feldheim, 1978), p. 186.

17 *In its emphasis*, by Rabbi David Stern, "Night Vision: A Gift of Sacred Uncertainty," in *All These Vows — Kol Nidre (Prayers of Awe)*, edited by Lawrence A. Hoffman (Woodstock, VT: Jewish Lights Publishing, 2011), p. 212. Permission granted by Jewish Lights Publishing, Woodstock, VT; jewishlights.com.

18 *Rabbeinu Tam declared*, as cited by Rabbi Hayyim Herman Kieval, *The High Holy Days, Vol. 2*, ed. David Golinkin and Monique Susskind Goldberg (Jerusalem: Schechter Institute of Jewish Studies, 2004), p. 273.

19 *The custom of reciting*, by Rabbi Hayyim Herman Kieval, "The Curious Case of Kol Nidre," *Commentary*

(October 1, 1968), purl.org/net/mhn17.

21 *Kol Nidrei*, by Nan Cohen, "*Kol Nidre*," *Rope Bridges* (Cincinnati: Cherry Grove Collections, 2005), p. 45. Copyright © 2005 WordTech Communications LLC, Cincinnati, OH.

21 *Prayer from the heart*, by Rabbi Abraham Ibn Ezra, transl. Rabbi Sheldon Marder.

22 *Chant your supplications*, as cited by Rabbi Joseph H. Hertz, *The Authorized Daily Prayer Book, Revised Edition* (New York: Bloch Publishing, 1960), p. 893; adapted.

22 *Shine praises upon God*, from *The Complete Psalms: The Book of Prayer Songs in a New Translation*, transl. Pamela Greenberg (New York: Continuum US, an imprint of Bloomsbury Publishing Inc., 2010), p. 256. © 2010 Pamela Greenberg. Used by permission of Bloomsbury Publishing Inc. Used by permission.

23 *Let us bless*, by Marcia Lee Falk, from *The Days Between: Blessings, Poems, and Directions of the Heart for the Jewish High Holiday Season*, Brandeis University Press. Copyright © 2014 by Marcia Lee Falk. Used by permission.

23 *Steal in the Prayerbook*, by Jacob Glatshteyn, "Variations on a Theme," in *American Yiddish Poetry: A Bilingual Anthology*, ed. and transl. Benjamin and Barbara Harshav (Berkeley, CA: University of California Press, 1986), p. 367. Used by permission.

25 *Day and night*, by Rabbi David Einhorn, *Olat Tamid: Book of Prayers for Jewish Congregations* (Chicago: S. Ettlinger Ptg. Co, 1896), pp. 68–69; adapted.

27 *We pause*, by Rabbi Albert Friedlander, in *Gates of Repentance* (CCAR, 1975), p. 118.

28 *You are my witnesses*, inspired by language in *Siddur Sim Shalom* (New York: The Rabbinical Assembly and the United Synagogue of Conservative Judaism), p. 285.

29 Once we affirm, by Rabbi Jeremy Kalmanofsky, "Seeking the Sacred Self," from Jewish Mysticism and the Spiritual Life: Classical Texts, Contemporary Reflections, ed. Lawrence Fine, Eitan Fishbane, and Rabbi Or N. Rose (Jewish Lights, 2010), pp. 16–17. Permission granted by Jewish Lights Publishing, Woodstock, VT; jewishlights.com.

31 *Those who reject all material possessions*, by Rabbi Abraham Isaac Kook, in *Gold from the Land of Israel*, ed. Chanan Morrison (Urim Publications, 2007), pp. 301–302; adapted from *Ein Ayah, Vol. II*, p. 328, purl.org/net/mhn18.

31 *Listen, all you who wrestle*, by Catherine Madsen, *In Medias Res: Liturgy for the Estranged* (The Davies Group Publishers: 2008). Used by permission of Catherine Madsen.

33 *At the beginning*, by Rabbi Awraham Soetendorp, "Retrieving G-d's Hidden Rays of Light: A Global Partnership Is Emerging," *Huffington Post*, purl.org/net/mhn19.

37 *Something will have gone*, by Wallace Stegner, "Coda: Wilderness Letter," in *The Sound of Mountain Water* (Penguin, 1997), pp. 145–53.

39 *Hope and trust*, as noted by Rabbi Elie Munk, *The World of Prayer* (Feldheim Publishers, 2007), p. 3.

39 *We are commanded*, by Rabbi Moses Maimonides, *Mishneh Torah, Hilchot K'riat Sh'ma* 1.3. The commentary on "all the days of your life" is in Mishnah *B'rachot* 1:5.

41 *For every exile*, by Jacqueline Kudler, "Revelation," *Sacred Precincts* (San Francisco, CA: Sixteen Rivers Press, 2003), p. 60. Used by permission

43 *When fears multiply*, by Rabbi Herschel Matt, in *Kol Haneshamah: Limot Hol* (Wyncote, PA: Reconstructionist Press, 2nd edn.), p. 287. Used by permission of The Reconstructionist Press, 1299 Church Road, Wyncote, PA 19095. Phone: 215-576-0800, email: jewishreconbooks@rrc.edu, website: jewishreconbooks.org.

43 *The Peace of Wild Things*, by Wendell Barry, *The Selected Poems of Wendell Berry* (Berkeley, CA: Counterpoint, 1998), p. 30. Copyright © 1998. Reprinted with permission of Counterpoint.

49 *From T'filah to Vidui to S'lichot*, based on a concept by Rabbi Elaine Zecher.

51 *Fall, falling, fallen*, by Edward Hirsch, "Fall," *The Living Fire: New and Selected Poems* (Knopf, reprint edn., 2011), p. 47. Copyright © 2010 by Edward Hirsch. Used by permission of Alfred A. Knopf, an imprint of the Knopf Doubleday Publishing Group, a division of Penguin Random House LLC. All rights reserved.

55 *You know how to create a heart*, by Elhanan Nir, "You Know," in *Beyond Political Messianism: The Poetry of Second-Generation Religious Zionist Settlers*, ed. David C. Jacobson (Brighton, MA: Academic Studies Press, 2011), pp. 137–39. Used by permission.

56 *the human proclivity to hatred*, by John Gray, "The Truth About Evil," *The Guardian* (October 21, 2014), purl.org/net/mhn20.

59 *Traveling to Jerusalem on a Moon Night*, by Raquel Chalfi, translated by Tsipi Keller, in *Poets on the Edge: An Anthology of Contemporary Hebrew*

Poetry (SUNY Press 2008), p. 169. Reprinted by permission of the State University of New York. Copyright © 2008 by State University of New York and by ACUM, Israel. All rights reserved.

60 *This prayer has*, by Rabbi W. Gunther Plaut, *Eight Decades: The Writing of W. Gunther Plaut* (Toronto: Dundurm Press, 2008), p. 104; adapted.

61 *Today the Jewish mission*, by Rabbi David Wolpe, *Why By Jewish* (Holt Paperbacks, 1995), p. 41.

61 *Martin Buber noted*, in "*Bechirat Yisrael*," *Darko Shel Mikra* (Jerusalem: Bialik Institute, 1964, p. 96); as cited in Nehama Leibowitz, *Studies in Vayikra*, transl. and adapted by Aryeh Newman (World Zionist Organization, Dept. for Torah Education and Culture in the Diaspora, 1980), pp. 167–68, 172; adapted.

61 *Rabbi Abraham Joshua Heschel points out*, in *The Prophets* (Harper and Row, 1962), p. 40. Copyright © by Abraham Joshua Heschel.

63 *The traditional version of this prayer*, as noted by Rabbi Jeffrey M. Cohen, *1001 Questions and Answers on Rosh Hashanah and Yom Kippur* (Jason Aronson, 1997), p. 181.

65 *They said redemption would come*, by Rivkah Miriam, *These Mountains: Selected Poems of Rivka Miriam*, transl. Linda Stern Zisquit (New Mildford, CT: The Toby Press, 2011), pp. 46–47. Used by permission.

65 *The Sages and the prophets*, by Rabbi Moses Maimonides, *Mishneh Torah, Laws of Kings* 12.4–5.

67 *The promise of Your forgiveness*, inspired by the quotation from Neuda's preface in *Hours of Devotion*, transl. M. Mayer, ed. Dinah Berland (Schocken Books, 2007).

69 *A butterfly comes and stays*, by Richard Jeffries, "The Pageant of Summer," *The Life of the Fields*, ed. Edward Thomas (London: Duckworth, 1909), pp. 270–79.

69 *Whatever is foreseen*, by Wendell Berry, *A Timbered Choir: The Sabbath Poems 1979–1999* (Berkeley, CA: Counterpoint, 1999), p. 18. Copyright © 1998 by Wendell Berry. Reprinted with permission of Counterpoint.

69 *Waking in the morning*, by Deena Metzger, reprinted from *Looking for the Faces of God* (Parallax Press, 1989) with permission of the author.

71 *On this night of Atonement*, by Rabbi Sidney Greenberg and Rabbi Jonathan D. Levine, *Mahzor Hadash* (Bridgeport, CT: The Prayer Book Press/ Media Judaica, 1978), p. 445.

73 *Every day I want*, by Marie Howe, *The Kingdom of Ordinary Time* (W.W. Norton & Company, 2009), p. 27. Copyright © 2008 by Marie Howe. Used by permission of W.W. Norton & Company.

73 *Prayer is for the soul*, based on Yehudah Halevi, *Kuzari* 3:5.

75 *It doesn't have to be*, by Mary Oliver, "Praying," *Thirst: Poems* (Boston: Beacon Press, 2006), p. 37. Copyright © 2006 by Mary Oliver. Used by permission of the Charlotte Sheedy Literary Agency, Inc.

75 *Is it not*, by Robinson Jeffers, "The Excesses of God," *The Selected Poetry of Robinson Jeffers*, ed. Tim Hunt (1938), p. 17. Copyright © 1925, 1929 and renewed 1953, 1957 by Robinson Jeffers. Used by permission of Random House, an imprint and division of Penguin Random House LLC. All rights reserved.

77 *The words I said today*, by Sivan Har-Shefi, in *Galut Halivyatan* (Hakibbutz Hameuchad, 2005), p. 78. Hebrew © Hakibbutz Hameuchad. Used by permission. Translation from "Permission," in *Beyond Political Messianism: The Poetry of Second-Generation Religious Zionist Settlers*, ed. and transl. David C. Jacobson (Academic Studies Press, 2011), pp. 133, 135–36. Used by permission.

78 *There are more expressions*, by Rabbi Sheldon Lewis, *Torah of Reconciliation* (Gefen Publishing House, 2012), pp. 2, 33.

79 *Grant us peace*, from *Gates of Prayer: The New Union Prayer Book*, ed. Chaim Stern (New York: CCAR, 1975); adapted.

79 *Eternal Source*, inspired by a prayer of Rabbi Nachman of Breslov from *Likutei T'filot*, part I, beginning of Prayer 95.

82 *Adonai, we are arrogant*; we thank Rabbi Lawrence A. Hoffman for drawing our attention to this version of the prayer, as found in *Seder Rav Amram*.

83 *Ashamnu*, by Rabbi Alan Cook. Used by permission.

83 *Rabbi Isaac Luria teaches*, as cited in *Y'sod HaT'shuvah* VI; as adduced by S.Y. Agnon and Nahum N. Glatzer, *Days of Awe*, transl. Maurice T. Galpert (New York: Schocken Books, 1965).

85 *Resh Lakish said*, by Louis E. Newman, *Repentance: The Meaning and Practice of Teshuvah* (Woodstock, VT: Jewish Lights Publishing, 2010), pp. 153–55; quoting from Pinchas H. Peli, *Soloveitchik on Repentence* (New York: Paulist Press, 1984), pp. 254–55. Permission granted by Jewish Lights Publishing, Woodstock, VT; jewishlights.com.

86 *God does not forgive us*, purl.org/net/mhn21.

87 *Force may also be used*, by Meir Tamari, *Al Chet: Sins in the Marketplace* (Jason Aronson, 1996), p. 93.

88 *Most people behave well*, Rabbi Menachem Mendel of Kotzk, as cited by Meir Tamari, *Al Chet: Sins in the Marketplace* (Jason Aronson, 1996), p. 54.

92 *God of the Covenant*, by Rabbi Ofer Sabath Beit-Halachmi, from *Barchu: A Podium for the Renewal of Prayer in Israel*, transl. Rabbi Sheldon Marder, p. 91. Used by permission.

93 *Al ha-tikkun shetikanu l'fanecha*, phrase by Rabbi Lawrence Englander.

94 *Our sins are like veils*, by Rabbi Moses Ibn Ezra, "Trembling We Seek the House of Prayer," *Documents and Texts: A Source Reader for Understanding Jewish History I*, ed. Rabbi Sol Scharfstein, transl. S. Solis-Cohen (Ktav Publishing: 1999), p. 197.

95 *Possible Answers to Prayer*, by Scott Cairns, "Possible Answers to Prayer," *Slow Pilgrim: The Collected Poems by Scott Cairns* (Paraclete Press, 2015). Reprinted with permission from the author and Paraclete Press; paracletepress.com.

99 *Will You Hear My Voice*, by Rachel Bluwstein, transl. Rabbi Ronald Aigen, *Mahzor Hadesh Yameinu*, ed. Rabbi Ronald Aigen (Montreal: Congregation Dorshei Emet), p. 430; adapted by permission. Used by permission of Rabbi Ronald Aigen.

99 *seeking spiritual connection in questions*, as posed by Celia Weisman, Gerontological Institute, Yeshiva University, 1988. For the phrase "the winter of the heart," see Martin Marty in *The Cry of Absence: Reflections for the Winter of the Heart* (Grand Rapids, MI: Eerdmans, 1997).

100 *God of forgiveness*, by Rabbi Herschel J. Matt, in *Mahzor Hadash* (Bridgeport, CT: The Prayer Book Press/Media Judaica, 1978), ed. Rabbi Sidney Greenberg and Rabbi Jonathan D. Levine, p. 453; adapted.

100 *Focusing on God's compassionate qualities*, as taught by the Geonim, as adduced by Eliyahu da Vidas, *Reishit Chochmah, Shaar Haanavah* 1; as cited at purl.org/net/mhn22; adapted.

102 *This spiritual poem from the 12th century*, by Rabbi Joel Mosbacher, based on "Of Pictures and Words: Visual and Verbal Representation of God," in *The Divine Image: Depicting God in Jewish and Israeli Art*, transl. Joel Linsider (The Israel Museum: Jerusalem, 2006).

105 *Where is God*, attributed to Rabbi Menachem Mendel of Kotzk, as cited by Rabbi Harvey J. Fields, *A Torah Commentary for Our Times*, Vol. 2: Exodus and Leviticus (New York: UAHC Press, 1991), p. 64.

106 *Rabbi Moshe Halbertal points out*, in his "Of Pictures and Words: Visual and Verbal Representation of God," in *The Divine Image: Depicting God in Jewish and Israeli Art*, transl. Joel Linsider (The Israel Museum: Jerusalem, 2006).

109 *When men were children*, by Ruth Firestone Brin, "A Woman's Meditation," *Harvest: Collected Poems and Prayers* (Duluth, MN: Holy Cow! Press, 1999), p. 4. Copyright 1986, 1999 by Ruth Firestone Brin. Reprinted by permission of The Permissions Company, Inc., on behalf of Holy Cow! Press; holycowpress.org.

109 *The Bronx, 1942*, by Linda Pastan, *An Early Afterlife: Poems* (NY: W.W. Norton & Company, 1995), p. 39. Copyright © 1995 Linda Pastan. Used by permission of W.W. Norton & Company, Inc.

112 *Avinu Malkeinu*, from a contemporary Hebrew version by Rabbi Mordechai Rotem, in *Kavvanat HaLev* (Jerusalem: IMPJ, 5749), pp. 161–62. Used by permission of the author.

118 *The Jews*, by Rabbi Jeffrey M. Cohen, *Prayer and Penitence: A Commentary on the High Holy Day Machzor* (Jason Aronson, 1994), p. 94, citing the *Iyun T'filah* commentary in the siddur *Otzar HaT'filot* (New York: Hebraica Press, 1966), p. 450; adapted.

119 *May we gain wisdom in our lives*, by Rabbi Richard Levy.

120 *How shall the heart be reconciled*, Stanley Kunitz, from "Layers," *The Collected Poems of Stanley Kunitz* (NewYork: WW Norton, 1995), p. 107. Copyright © 1978 by Stanley Kunitz. Used by permission of W.W. Norton & Company, Inc.

120 *This is the praise of the living*, based on Rabbi Harvey Fields, "In Praise of Lives Now Gone," in *Gates of Prayer*, pp. 625–26.

123 *Sow in Tears*, lyrics and music by Debbie Friedman. Used by permission.

127 *Return Again*, by Rabbi Shlomo Carlebach; BMI, used with the permission of the estate of Rabbi Shlomo Carlebach. For more information, please contact neshamacarlebach@gmail.com.

MORNING SERVICE

132 *It is written in the Book of Job*, based on Rabbi Debra Orenstein, purl.org/net/mhn23. Used by permission.

133 *Walkers with the Dawn*, by Langston Hughes, *The Collected Poems of Langston Hughes*, ed. Arnold Rampersad with David Roessel (New York: Knopf, 1994), p. 75. Copyright © 1994 by the Estate of Langston Hughes. Used by permission of Alfred A. Knopf, an imprint of the Knopf Doubleday Publishing Group, a division of Penguin Random House LLC. All rights reserved.

134 *The positive mitzvah*, by Alexander ben Mosheh of Grodno, *Yesod V'Shoresh HaAvodah*, First Gate, ch. 7 (Jerusalem, 1978), pp. 14, 15; as cited by purl.org/net/mhn24.

134 *The holiest name*, by Rabbi Lawrence Kushner, "Breathing the Name of God," *Eyes Remade for Wonder: A Lawrence Kushner Reader* (Jewish Lights, 1998), p. 144; see also Rabbi Arthur Waskow, *The Shalom Seders* (New York: New Jewish Agenda/Adama Books, 1984), p. 35. Permission granted by Jewish Lights Publishing, Woodstock, VT; jewishlights.com.

136 *May we who constantly face the temptation . . . education*, by Rabbi Allen Maller, in *Yom Kippur Readings: Inspiration, Information, Contemplation* (Jewish Lights, 2005), pp. 122–23. Permission granted by Jewish Lights Publishing, Woodstock, VT; jewishlights.com.

138 *I yearn for the I–Thou*, by Rabbi Yoel Kahn, "Mah Tovu—From Torah to Prayer," Congregation Beth El, Berkeley, CA, purl.org/net/mhn25. Used by permission of Rabbi Yoel Kahn.

139 *Deepest Good*, by Joyce Rupp, *Fragments of Your Ancient Name: 365 Glimpses of the Divine for Daily Meditation* (Sorin Books, 2011), p. 53. Copyright © 2011 by Joyce Rupp. Used by permission of Sorin Books, an imprint of Ave Maria Press, Inc., Notre Dame, IN 46556; avemariapress.com.

140 *Song of Confidence*, as per Walter Brueggemann, *The Message of Psalms* (Minneapolis: Augsburg Publishing House, 1984), p. 152.

141 *A Morning Offering*, by John O'Donohue, "Blessing: A Morning Offering," *To Bless the Space Between Us: A Book of Blessings* (Doubleday, 2008), p. 9. Copyright © 2008 by John Donohue. Used by permission of Doubleday, an imprint of the Knopf Doubleday Publishing Group, a division of Penguin Random House LLC. All rights reserved.

141 *Uses of Sorrow*, by Mary Oliver, "Uses of Sorrow," *Thirst* (Boston: Beach Press, 2007), p. 52. Used herewith by permission of the Charlotte Sheedy Literary Agency, Inc.

142 *When the mind is empty*, Rabbi Elijah ben Solomon of Vilna, as cited by Rabbi Yissachar Dov Rubin, *Talelei Oros: The Parsha Anthology — Bereishis* (Feldheim, 2002), p. 289.

143 *The Torah is like a kaleidoscope*, by Rabbi Eric Yoffie, purl.org/net/mhn26.

146 *The ancient charge against Judaism*, by Rabbi Ismar Schorsch, "Parashat Va-yetzei 5754," *Chancellor's Parashah Commentary* (Jewish Theological Seminary).

146 *put matters right*, phrasing by Rabbi Philip Blackman, *Mishnayot, Volume II* (Gateshead, England: Judaica Press, 1973), p. 312.

148 *Commentary*, by Rabbi Kenneth Chasen, in *Sh'ma: A Journal of Jewish Responsibility* (September 2010). Used by permission.

149 *When the Holy One*, from *Pirkei d'Rabbi Eliezer* 47, transl. Gerald Friedlander (New York: The Bloch Publishing Company, 1916), purl.org/net/mhn27.

149 *Commentary*, by Bryna Jocheved Levy, *Waiting for Rain: Reflections at the Turning of the Year* (Jewish Publication Society, 2008), pp. 148, 150. Used by permission.

152 *Is there any aspect*, by Rabbi Debra Orenstein, purl.org/net/mhn28. Used by permission.

153 *Free will is granted* and *Baalei t'shuvah*, by Rabbi Moses Maimonides, from *Mishneh Torah: Hilchot Teshuvah, The Laws of Repentance*, transl. Rabbi Eliyahu Touger (New York/Jerusalem: Moznaim Publishing Corporation, 1990), pp. 20–27; 114–19.

153 *The punishment of sinners*, by Rabbi Jonah of Gerona, *Gates of Repentance; Sha'arei Teshuva*, transl. Shraga Silverstein (Feldheim, 1981), pp. 4–5.

153 *Commentary*, by Erica Brown, from *Return: Daily Inspiration for the Days of Awe.*

154 *Sin, in the context of relationship*, by Rabbi Rachel Adler, *Engendering Judaism: An Inclusive Theology and Ethics* (Jewish Publication Society, 1988), p. 93. Used by permission.

154 *If even some events*, by Louis E. Newman, *Repentance: The Meaning and Practice of Teshuvah* (Jewish Lights, 2010), p. 48. Permission granted by Jewish Lights Publishing, Woodstock, VT; jewishlights.com.

155 *Yom Kippur teaches*, by Rabbi Irving Greenberg, *The Jewish Way: Living the Holidays* (Touchstone, 1993), p. 210.

155 *The Divine Voice*, by Rabbi Yoel Kahn, Congregation Beth El, Berkeley, CA, "Teshuvah and Twelve Steps" (Yom Kippur 5773 sermon), purl.org/net/mhn29. Used by permission.

156 *Who has formed the human body*, by Rabbi Sheldon Marder, "What Happens When We Use

Poetry in Our Prayer Books—And Why?" *CCAR Journal* (Summer 2013), p. 26.

157 *I can look*, by May Sarton, "Friend or Enemy," *Coming into Eighty: Poems*. Copyright © 1994 by May Sarton (New York: Norton, 1994), p. 55. Used by permission of W.W. Norton and Company, Inc.

157 *Diamonds*, inspired by Rabbi Abraham J. Twerski, *Without a Job, Who Am I? Rebuilding Your Self When You've Lost Your Job, Home, or Life Savings* (Hazeldon, 2009), p. 54.

158 *the Creator is the totality*, by Rabbi Shabtai Sheftel Horowitz, "Introduction to Shefa Tal," in *Kabbalah: Selections from Classic Kabbalistic Works From Raziel Hamalach to the Present Day*, ed. and transl. Rabbi Avraham Yaakov Finkel (Targum Press, 2003), p. 158.

159 *After a Long Insomniac Night*, by Edward Hirsch, *The Living Fire: New and Selected Poems* (Knopf, 2011), p. 235. Copyright © 2010 by Edward Hirsch. Used by permission of Alfred A. Knopf, an imprint of the Knopf Doubleday Publishing Group, a division of Penguin Random House LLC. All rights reserved.

159 *As a blade of Your grass*, by Kadya Molodowsky, "Prayers I," *Paper Bridges: Selected Poems of Kadya Molodowsky*, ed. and transl. Kathryn Hellerstein (Detroit: Wayne State University Press, 1999), p. 145. Copyright © 1999 Wayne State University Press. Used with the permission of Wayne State University Press.

161 *In uttering these blessings*, by Rabbi Micah Greenstein; adapted. Used by permission.

163 *How do I understand Akiba's response*, by Rabbi Harold M. Schulweis, "Theological Courage: Rabbinical Assembly Address, 2000," purl.org/net/mhn30. Used by permission of Valley Beth Shalom and the Harold M. Schulweis Institute.

166 *Psalm 93*, translation by Stephen Mitchell, *A Book of Psalms* (New York: HarperCollins, 1993), p. 42. Reprinted with permission of HarperCollins Publishers.

167 *I will hold you highest*, by Norman Fischer, *Opening to You: Zen-Inspired Translations of the Psalms* (Viking Compass, 2002), p. 167. Used by permission.

167 *human beings cannot truly understand animals*, Sefat Emet on Deut. 22:6, in *The Language of Truth: The Torah Commentary of the Sefat Emet*, transl. Rabbi Arthur Green (Philadelphia: Jewish Publication Society, 1998).

171 *A teaching of Rabbi Nachman*, as cited by Rabbi Yitzhak Buxbaum, *Jewish Spiritual Practices* (NY: Jason Aronson, Ltd., second edition, 1999), p. 482.

172 *Do people deserve liberation*, by Jeffrey A. Spitzer, "Did Israel Deserve Redemption," purl.org/net/mhn31. Used by permission.

174 *For often when we try*, by Rabbi Lawrence Kushner and Rabbi Nehemia Polen, in *P'sukei d'Zimra (Morning Psalms), My People's Prayer Book: Volume 3*, ed. Rabbi Lawrence Hoffman (Woodstock, VT: Jewish Lights, 1999), p. 145. Permission granted by Jewish Lights Publishing, Woodstock, VT; jewishlights.com.

175 *What Color Is Grass*, by Ruth Finer Mintz, *Traveler Through Time* (New York: Jonathan David, 1970), p. 14. Copyright © 1970 by Ruth Finer Mintz. Reprinted by permission of Jonathan David Publishers, Inc., jdbooks.com, and with permission and appreciation from Ruth's children, Rena, Aviva, and Shalom.

181 *Those who dwell*, by Rachel Carson, *The Sense of Wonder* (Harper, 1998), pp. 100–101.

181 *For at every moment God creates*, by Rabbi Levi Yitzchak of Berditchev, *K'dushat Levi*, transl. Rabbi Louis Jacobs, in *The Jewish Religion: A Companion*, ed. Rabbi Louis Jacobs (Oxford University Press, 1995), p. 317.

185 *Adonai Echad: We Proclaim You One*, inspired by Rabbi Harold M. Schulweis, "Rosh HaShanah Sermon: 'Echad,'" 1997, purl.org/net/mhn32. Used by permission of Valley Beth Shalom and the Harold M. Schulweis Institute.

187 *When Israel Baal Shem Tov*, based on Rabbi Yitzhak Buxbaum, *Jewish Spiritual Practices Second Edition* (NY: Jason Aronson: 1999), p. 18; citing *Ikkarei Emunah*, p. 11.

188 *How in the world*, by Rabbi Harold M. Schulweis, "Rosh HaShanah Sermon: 'Echad,'" 1997, purl.org/net/mhn32 (see also Talmud *Yoma* 86b). Used by permission of Valley Beth Shalom and the Harold M. Schulweis Institute.

189 *V'ahavta—When You Love*, by Rabbi Sheldon Marder, *CCAR Journal* (Spring/Summer 1996), p. 18.

189 *How do we teach children about God*, by Rabbi Harold S. Kushner, *When Children Ask about God* (New York: Schocken, 1989), p. xiv.

193 *We are impressed*, by Rabbi Abraham Joshua Heschel, "Faith," in *Moral Grandeur and Spiritual Audacity: Essays*, ed. Susannah Heschel (Farrar, Straus and Giroux, 1996), pp. 328–29. Copyright © 1996 Sylvia Heschel. Reprinted by permission of Farrar, Straus and Giroux, LLC.

195 *As long as the people allow*, by Rabbi Jill Jacobs,

"Escape from the New Mitzrayim," Jewish Funds for Justice, purl.org/net/mhn33.

197 *Who is like You . . . among the silent ones*, this line is from Rabbi Reuven Hammer, *The Classic Midrash: Tannaitic Commentaries on the Bible* (Paulist Press, 1995), p. 117.

199 *I still don't know whom*, by Kadya Molodowsky, "Tfiles," *A Question of Tradition*, transl. Kathryn Hellerstein (Stanford, CA: Stanford University, 2014), pp. 136–38. Copyright © 1999 Wayne State University Press (Detroit, MI: Wayne State University Press, 1999). Used with permission of Wayne State University Press.

200 *We see God*, by Rabbi Angela Buchdahl, "Honoring Your Parents is the Hardest Commandment (Rosh Hashanah 5775)," purl.org/net/mhn34. Used by permission.

201 *I went to my grandfather's*, by Charles Reznikoff, "Early History of a Writer," *The Poems Of Charles Reznikoff: 1918–1975*, ed. Seamus Cooney (David R. Godine, 2005), pp. 323–24. Used by permission.

201 *Without profound reverence*, by Rabbi Abraham Joshua Heschel, *The Insecurity of Freedom*, pp. 39–40. © 1966 by Abraham Joshua Heschel. Copyright renewed 1994 by Sylvia Heschel. Reprinted by permission of Farrar, Straus and Giroux, LLC.

203 *Like an Accountant*, by Abba Kovner, in *Sloan-Kettering: Poems*, translation by Eddie Levenston (New York: Schocken Books, 2002), p. 98. © 2002 by the estate of Abba Kovner. Foreword copyright © 2002 by Leon Wieseltier. Used by permission of Schocken Books, an imprint of Doubleday Publishing Group, a division of Penguin Random House LLC. All rights reserved. Hebrew used by permission of ACUM, Israel.

203 *The shattered vessel*, by Rabbi Israel Zoberman, *CCAR Journal* (Summer 1992), p. 42.

205 *Once we stop*, by Rabbi Sarah Weissman, "Yom Kippur Sermon (2014)." Used by permission.

205 *The phrase conjures up*, by Rabbi Elliot N. Dorff, in *My People's Prayer Book: Volume 2—The Amidah*, ed. Rabbi Lawrence A. Hoffman (Woodstock, VT: Jewish Lights, 1998), p. 75. Permission granted by Jewish Lights Publishing, Woodstock, VT; jewishlights.com.

206 *I sat in shul for years*, by Rabbi Edward Feinstein, in *Who By Fire, Who By Water: Unetaneh Tokef*, ed. Rabbi Lawrence A. Hoffman (Jewish Lights, 2010), pp. 145–46. Permission granted by Jewish Lights Publishing, Woodstock, VT; jewishlights.com.

207 *Judge and shepherd*, by Rabbi Margaret Moers Wenig, "Meditations on the Poetry of *Un'taneh Tokef*," in *Who By Fire, Who By Water: Un'taneh Tokef*, ed. Rabbi Lawrence A. Hoffman (Jewish Lights, 2010), p. 128. Used by permission of the author and permission granted by Jewish Lights Publishing, Woodstock, VT; jewishlights.com.

207 *Who by Fire*, lyrics by Leonard Cohen. Excerpted from *Stranger Music: Selected Poems and Songs* by Leonard Cohen. Copyright © 1993 by Leonard Cohen. Reprinted by permission of McClelland & Stewart, a division of Penguin Random House Canada Limited, a Penguin Random House Company.

211 *Untaneh Tokef, the prayer that imagines*, by Rabbi Amy Eilberg, speech presented at the National Center for Jewish Healing conference, November 10, 2003; in *Seasons for Healing: Drawing Spiritual Resources from the Jewish Holidays*. Used by permission of the author.

213 *What is at the core*, by Rabbi Alan Lew, *This Is Real and You Are Completely Unprepared: The Days of Awe as a Journey of Transformation* (Little, Brown and Co., 2003), p. 222.

214 *We who lived*, by Viktor Frankl, *Man's Search for Meaning* (Boston: Beacon Press, 2006), p. 65.

215 *And let us give ourselves over*, by Rabbi Elyse D. Frishman, in *Who By Fire, Who by Water*, edited by Rabbi Lawrence A. Hoffman (Woodstock, VT: Jewish Lights, 2010), p. 191. Permission granted by Jewish Lights Publishing, Woodstock, VT; jewishlights.com.

216 *Our mortality gains significance*, by Rabbi David Stern, in *Who By Fire, Who By Water: Un'taneh Tokef*, ed. Rabbi Lawrence A. Hoffman (Jewish Lights, 2010), p. 176. Used by permission of the author and by Jewish Lights Publishing, Woodstock, VT; jewishlights.com.

217 *The Holy Way*, inspired by Rabbi Eliezer Berkovits, *God, Man and History* (Shalem Press, 2004), pp. 119–34.

219 *Purity*, by Haim Lensky, translated by Rabbi Sheldon Marder. Written between 1927 and 1941, the poem was published in *Beyond the Waters of Lethe* (Israel, 1957).

219 *I Know Not Your Ways*, from *With Teeth in the Earth: Selected Poems of Malka Heifetz Tussman*, translated from the Yiddish by Marcia Falk, p. 134. Copyright (c) 1992 by Marcia Lee Falk. Used by permission of the translator.

220 *In I Kings 1:31*, as noted regarding Psalm 146:10 in *The Bible Psalms with the Jerusalem Commentary, Vol. 3* (Jerusalem: Mosad HaRav Kook, 2003), pp. 467–68.

221 *Letter to a Humanist*, by Ruth Brin, *Harvest: Collected Poems and Prayers* (Duluth, MN: Holy Cow! Press, 1999), p. 108. Copyright © 1986, 1999 by Ruth Firestone Brin. Reprinted with the permission of The Permissions Company, Inc., on behalf of Holy Cow! Press; holycowpress.org.

221 *God lies on his back*, by Yehuda Amichai, "And This Is Your Praise," *Shirim: 1948–1962* (Jerusalem: Schocken, 1962), p. 71 (Hebrew edition). Used by permission. Translated by Rabbi Sheldon Marder.

222 *This prayer is the first*, as noted by Rabbi Jeffrey M. Cohen, *Prayer and Penitence: A Commentary on the High Holy Day Machzor* (Jason Aronson, Inc. 1994), p. 40. Used by permission.

223 *I stand at the seashore*, by Richard P. Feynman, *The Pleasure of Finding Things Out: The Best Short Works of Richard P. Feynman*, ed. Jeffrey Robbins (Basic Books, 1999), p. 144. Used by permission.

223 *To be awake*, by Henry D. Thoreau, *Walden* (Imperia Press, 2013), pp. 65, 255.

223 *One cannot help*, by Albert Einstein, "Old Man's Advice to Youth: 'Never Lose a Holy Curiosity,'" *LIFE* (May 2, 1955), p. 64.

224 *The particular kavod*, by Rabbi Jeffrey M. Cohen, *Prayer and Penitence* (Jason Aronson, 1994), pp. 40–41. Used by permission.

227 *This rabbinic parable*, as noted by David Stern, *Parables in Midrash: Narrative and Exegesis in Rabbinic Literature* (Cambridge, MA, Harvard University Press, 1994), pp. 56–58; based on Midrash *Lamentations Rabbah* 3.21.

229 *From Mount Scopus*, by Yehuda Karni. Hebrew copyright © Yehuda Karni and ACUM. Used by permission. Translated by Rabbi Sheldon Marder.

231 *More than any event*, by Rabbi Arthur Hertzberg and Aron Hirt-Manheimer, from *Jews: The Essence and Character of a People* (HarperOne, 1999), pp. 30–31.

232 *The plural form reminds us*, by Rabbi Marc D. Angel, "Thoughts for Shabbat Teshuvah and Yom Kippur," Institute for Jewish Ideas and Ideals, purl.org/net/mhn35.

235 *It is not easy*, by Rabbi Will Berkovitz, "Forgiving God," in *We Have Sinned: Sin and Confession in Judaism — Ashamnu and Al Chet*, ed. Rabbi Lawrence Hoffman (Jewish Lights, 2012), pp. 148–49. Used by permission of the author and by Jewish Lights Publishing, Woodstock, VT; jewishlights.com.

235 *Your fellow human being*, "Thirty-Six Aphorisms of the Baal Shem Tov," purl.org/net/mhn36; adapted.

236 *The Zohar teaches*, in *Zohar Chadash, Shir HaShirim* 74d, as cited in purl.org/net/mhn37. On *Yisrael* as an acronym, see, e.g., purl.org/net/mhn38, which cites the 18th-century commentary *P'nei Y'hoshua*.

237 *Rabbi Meir Simcha of Dvinsk teaches*, in *Meshech Chochmah*.

237 *according to the Midrash*, namely, Jubilees xxxiv.15.

238 *The function of prayer*, by Leonard Fein, *Against the Dying of the Light: A Parent's Story of Love, Loss and Hope* (Jewish Lights, 2001), p. 107. Permission granted by Jewish Lights Publishing, Woodstock, VT; jewishlights.com.

239 *A blue candle is my Zion*, by William Pillin, "The Blue Candle," *To the End of Time* (Los Angeles, Papa Bach Editions, 1980), p. 154.

239 *I called God*, by Adi Assis, from *Beit T'filah Yisraeli (Singable English Translations selected from Beit Tefilah Israeli Siddur): Experimental Edition* (2013), p. 45. Hebrew copyright © Adi Assis and ACUM, Israel. Used by permission.

241 *An awe so quiet*, by Denise Levertov, *Oblique Prayers* (New York: New Directions, 1984), p. 8. Copyright © 1984 by Denise Levertov. Reprinted by permission of New Directions Publishing Corp.

241 *The Patience of Ordinary Things*, by Pat Schneider, "The Patience of Ordinary Things," *Another River: New and Selected Poems* (Amherst Writers and Artists Press, 2005). Used by permission.

242 *The Etz Yosef*, as noted by Rabbi Yissachar Dov Rubin, *Talelei Oros: The Prayer Anthology, Vol. 2* (Feldheim, 2005), p. 781.

243 *Tiny Joys*, by Rachel Bluwstein, *Found in Translation*, transl. Robert Friend (Milford, CT: Toby Press, 2006), p. 37. Used by permission.

244 *A midrash interprets*, as cited in *The Jewish Encyclopedia*, purl.org/net/mhn39.

245 *The hands of the kohanim . . . bounty on the people*, by Rabbi Levi Yitzchak of Berditchev, *K'dushat Levi*, as quoted in *The Jewish Religion: A Companion*, transl. Rabbi Louis Jacobs (Oxford University Press, 1995), p. 317.

245 *A Blessing*, Rabbi Leila Gal Berner, "A Blessing for Two Women on the Occasion of their Wedding," Ritualwell.org, purl.org/net/mhn40; adapted. Used by permission.

245 *Birkat Kohanim*, lyrics by Cantor Marsha Attie and Rabbi Judith HaLevy. Used by permission.

247 *My Child Wafts Peace*, by Yehudah Amichai, *Yehuda Amichai: A Life of Poetry, 1948–1994*, transl. Benjamin and Barbara Harshav (NY: Harper Perennial, 1995), p. 88. Used by permission.

249 *In the autumn garden*, by Pia Taavila-Borsheim, in *The Bloomsbury Anthology of Contemporary Jewish American Poetry*, ed. Deborah Ager and M.E. Silverman (New York: Bloomsbury, 2013), p. 273. Used by permission of the author.

251 *Anthem*, lyrics by Leonard Cohen, excerpted from *Stranger Music: Selected Poems and Songs* by Leonard Cohen. Copyright © 1993 by Leonard Cohen. Reprinted by permission of McClelland & Stewart, a division of Penguin Random House Canada Ltd., a Penguin Random House Company.

251 *Hope*, by Jechiel Mohar, in *The Burning Bush: Poems from Israel*, transl. Bat-Sheva Sheriff and Jon Silkin (London: W. H. Allen, 1977), p. 42. Hebrew copyright © Jechiel Mohar and ACUM, Israel.

254 *Participating in the Torah service*, by Rabbi Lawrence A. Hoffman, *My People's Prayer Book: Traditional Prayers, Modern Commentaries — Seder K'riyat Hatorah* (Jewish Lights, 2000), pp. 15–16. Permission granted by Jewish Lights Publishing, Woodstock, VT; jewishlights.com.

265 *God said to Abraham*, by Rabbi David Hartman, *A Living Covenant: The Innovative Spirit in Traditional Judaism* (Jewish Lights, 1998), pp. 147–48. Permission granted by Jewish Lights Publishing, Woodstock, VT; jewishlights.com.

265 *Rabbi Eliezer Davidovits asks*, by Rabbi Josh Zweiback, purl.org/net/mhn41, citing the Torah commentary *Eid Yaaleh* (Bne-Brak, Israel: Lipa Friedman, 1988). Used with permission. Used by permission of the author.

269 *These celestial creatures* and *Eve*, by Richard Elliott Friedman, *Commentary on the Torah* (HarperOne, 2001).

273 *Hear our Prayer*, lyrics by Cantor Lisa L. Levine. Used by permission.

273 *Mi Shebeirach*, lyrics by Debbie Friedman and Rabbi Drorah Setel, music by Debbie Friedman. Used by permission.

285 *May heaven grant*, translation and commentary by Rabbi Ronald Aigen, *Renew Our Days: A Prayer-Cycle for Days of Awe*, ed. and transl. Rabbi Ronald Aigen (Congregation Dorshei Emet, 2001), p. 242; adapted. Used by permission.

289 *I Have No Other Country*, lyrics by Ehud Manor, from "I Have No Other Country" with music by Corinne Allal. Hebrew copyright © Ehud Manor, Corinne Allal and ACUM, Israel. Used by permission. Translated by Rabbi Sheldon Marder.

290 *Your brightness lights the earth*, translation by Norman Fischer, *Opening to You* (NY: Viking Compass, 2002), p. 172. Used by permission.

291 *Richard Elliot Friedman reminds us*, in chapter 1 of his *Commentary on the Torah* (HarperCollins, 2001).

295 *Pride*, by Dahlia Ravikovitch, *Hovering at a Low Altitude: The Collected Poetry of Dahlia Ravikovitch*, transl. Chana Bloch and Chana Kronfeld (W.W. Norton and Company, 2009), pp. 131–32. Copyright © 2009 by Chana Bloch, Chana Kronfeld, and Ido Kalir; English translation copyright © 2009 by Chana Bloch and Chana Kronfeld. Used by permission of W.W. Norton and Company, Inc.

295 *Rabbi Yonah Girondi points out*, as cited in *The Pirke Avos Treasury: Ethics of the Fathers* (NY: Mesorah Publications, Ltd., 2000), p. 119.

297 *A repentant sinner*, by Rabbi Yonah Girondi, *Shaarei T'shuvah*.

297 *In a culture striving*, by Rabbi Irving Greenberg, *The Jewish Way: Living the Holidays* (Touchstone, 1993), p. 212.

299 *For the sin we committed*, by Rabbi Lionel Blue, in *Forms of Prayer for Jewish Worship, Volume 3: Prayers for the High Holydays*, ed. Assembly of Rabbis of the Reform Synagogues of Great Britain (London: Reform Synagogues of Great Britain, 1985), 304–6; adapted. Used by permission.

300 *The original Al Cheit confession*, as noted by Rabbi Jeffrey M. Cohen, *Prayer and Penitence* (Northvale, NJ: Jason Aronson, 1994), p. 159, used by permission; *Prayers for the Day of Atonement According to the Custom of the Spanish and Portuguese Jews*, ed. Rabbi David de Sola Pool (New York: Union of Sephardic Congregations, 1998), pp. 57–58.

301 *A Personal Confession*, by Rabbi Rachel Barenblat, purl.org/net/mhn42. Used by permission.

303 *On New Year's Day*, by Yehuda Amichai, from *Time*, transl. Yehuda Amichai (New York: Harper & Row, 1979), pp. 49–50; Hebrew original in *HaZ'man* (Jerusalem/Tel Aviv: Schocken, 1977), p. 45. Copyright © 1979 by Yehuda Amichai. Reprinted by permission of Harper Collins Publishers and Hana Amichai.

305 *We focused inward*, inspired by Charles H. Middleburgh, "From Staid Sins of Yesteryear to Wrongdoings of Today," in *We Have Sinned: Sin and Confession in Judaism — Ashamnu and Al Chet*, ed. Rabbi Lawrence A. Hoffman (Woodstock, VT: Jewish Lights, 2012), pp. 131–32. Permission granted by Jewish Lights Publishing, Woodstock, VT; jewishlights.com.

305 *Seven social sins*, by Mohandas Gandhi, *The*

Collected Works of Mahatma Gandhi: Volume 28 (Ahmedabad: Navajivan, 1958), p. 365.

305 *Meir Tamari relates*, in his *Al Chet: Sins in the Marketplace* (Jason Aronson, 1996), p. 163.

307 *Vidui for the Twenty-First Century*, based on a concept by Cantor Rachel Rhodes, "Environmental Tachanun" (unpublished).

310 *can only be spoken with the whole being*, by Martin Buber, *I and Thou*, transl. Ronald Gregor Smith (Edinburgh: T. & T. Clark, 1953), p. 3.

312 *Always look for the good*, from *The Empty Chair: Finding Hope and Joy: Timeless Wisdom from a Hasidic Master, Rebbe Nachman of Breslov*, adapted and ed. Moshe Mykoff and the Breslov Research Institute (Jewish Lights, 1996), pp. 33 and 99. Permission granted by Jewish Lights Publishing, Woodstock, VT; jewishlights.com.

314 *Open your heart*, based on Rabbi Rami Shapiro. Used with permission.

315 *God, God, open unto me*, by Howard Thurman, "God God," *Meditations of the Heart* (Boston: Beacon Press, 1999), pp.188–89. Copyright © 1953, 1981 by Anne Thurman. Reprinted by permission of Beacon Press, Boston.

317 *The Mystery of the Necessity to Inform You*, by Yaakov Orland, in *Israeli New Liturgy Supplement* (Tel Aviv: Beit Tefilah Israeli, 2013), p. 41; adapted. Translation by Donny Inbar. © ACUM, Israel. Used by permission.

319 *The ashes are disposed of*, by Amy Hill Shevitz, as quoted by Rabbi Steven Bayar, purl.org/net/mhn43.

AFTERNOON SERVICE

325 *Psalm* 34, the line "yearns to see goodness," by Rabbi Martin Samuel Cohen, *Our Haven and our Strength* (NY: Aviv Press, 2004); the line "do good without delay," by Rabbi Samson Raphael Hirsch, *The Psalms* (New York: Feldheim, 1978), p. 247.

326 *At this hour*, by Rabbi Chaim Stern and Rabbi Herbert Bronstein, in *Gates of Repentance* (NY: CCAR Press, 1978), pp. 394–95; adapted. For Rabbi Baeck's prayer, see "The Attorney-General of the Government of Israel v. Adolf Eichmann, Minutes of Session No. 14" (Jerusalem, 1961).

327 *Jewish thought pays*, by Rabbi Adin Steinsaltz, *The Thirteen Petalled Rose* (New York: Basic Books, 1980), pp. 131–32.

331 *Deceptions and hurts*, by Rabbi Richard Elliott Friedman, *Commentary on the Torah* (HarperSanFrancisco, 2001), p. 163.

333 *In fact, it is none other than Moses*, by Jon D. Levenson, in *The Jewish Study Bible* (Oxford University Press, 1999), p. 100. Used by permission.

335 *No station in life*, by Rabbi Samson Raphael Hirsch, *T'rumath Tzvi: The Pentateuch with a translation by Samson Raphael Hirsch and excerpts from The Hirsch Commentary*, ed. Rabbi Ephraim Oratz, transl. Gertrude Hirschler (The Judaica Press, Inc. New York, 1997), p. 451.

336 *For Reflection*, questions adapted from Synagogue 3000, purl.org/net/mhn44.

337 *On Pesach*, by Rabbi Lauren Eichler Berkun, purl.org/net/mhn45.

340 *A Prayer for Those Who Are Ill*, inspired by that of Rabbi Leila Gal Berner, from *Kol Haneshamah: Shabbat ve-Hagim* (Reconstructionist Press, 1994), p. 686.

342 *How can we pray*, by Rabbi David Wolpe, "Can You Pray What You Don't Believe?" *The Huffington Post* (March 25, 2011), purl.org/net/mhn46. Used by permission.

343 *The sailors, as representatives*, by Judy Klitsner, *Subversive Sequels in the Bible: How Biblical Stories Mine and Undermine Each Other* (Jerusalem: Maggid Books, an imprint of Koren Publishers, Ltd., 2011), pp. 21–22.

349 *Jonah inverts God's world*, by Rabbi Edward Feinstein, "A Yom Kippur Carol: Yom Kippur 5770.2009," purl.org/net/mhn47. Used by permission.

352 *Your brightness lights the earth*, by Norman Fischer, *Opening to You* (NY: Viking Compass, 2002), p. 172. Used by permission.

353 *Return Again*, by Rabbi Shlomo Carlebach, BMI; used with the permission of the estate of Rabbi Shlomo Carlebach. For more information, please contact neshamacarlebach@gmail.com.

355 *Fixing the world entails*, by Rabbi Jan Katzew, "Repairing Our World From the Inside Out," *Reform Judaism Magazine* (Winter 1999). Used by permission of Rabbi Jan Katzew.

356 *Ultimately the goal*, by Rabbi Abraham Joshua Heschel, *Man's Quest for God* (New York: Scribner, 1954), p. 17. Copyright © 1954 by Abraham Joshua Heschel.

356 *I am always*, by Louise Stirpe-Gill. Used by permission.

358 *The word chesed*, see Rabbi Nelson Glueck, *Hesed in the Bible* (Cincinnati: Hebrew Union College Press, 1967); and Rabbi Harold M. Kamsler,

"*Hesed*—Mercy or Loyalty?" *Jewish Bible Quarterly* XXVII:3 (July–September 1999).

358 *God's loving-kindness*, by Norman H. Snaith, *A Theological Word Book of the Bible*, ed. Alan Richardson (New York: Macmillan, 1951), pp. 136–37.

358 *What is chesed*, by Rabbi Jonathan Sacks, *To Heal a Fractured World: The Ethics of Responsibility* (New York: Schocken Books, 2005), pp. 45–46.

359 *Moses sought to discern*, commentary based on Rabbi Samson Raphael Hirsch.

359 *We live by the conviction*, by Rabbi Abraham Joshua Heschel, *God in Search of Man: A Philosophy of Judaism* (Farrar, Straus, and Giroux, 1955), p. 290. © 1955 by Abraham Joshua Heschel. Copyright renewed 1983 by Sylvia Heschel. Reprinted by permission of Farrar, Straus and Giroux, LLC.

361 *Why call God Magein Avraham*, based on the Sefat Emet, *Toledot* 5632.

361 *rachamanim b'nei rachamanim*, in the anonymous 13th-century work *Sefer HaChinuch* (Book of Education), number 42 (on *Parashat Mishpatim*).

362 *How should we discipline*, by Wendy Mogel, *The Blessing of a Skinned Knee: Using Jewish Teachings to Raise Self-Reliant Children* (Scribner, 2008), pp. 116–18.

362 *The quality of g'vurah*, by Rabbi Jeffrey Goldwasser, "Counting from Freedom to Covenant: Discipline," purl.org/net/mhn48; adapted. Used by permission.

363 *When kindness is misguided*, by Rabbi Abraham J. Twerski, "When Kindness is Misguided," purl.org/net/mhn49. Reprinted with permission from *Jewish Action* (Summer 1993).

365 *Parents who cannot bear*, Malbim, *Malbim on Mishley: The Book of Proverbs in Hebrew and English with the commentary of Rav Meir Leib Malbim*, abridged and adapted in English by Rabbi Charles Wengro (Feldheim, 1982), p. 140; adapted.

366 *What is the difference*, Hermann Cohen, in *Religion of Reason: Out of the Sources of Judaism*, transl. Simon Kaplan (Oxford University Press, 1995), p. 96; adapted.

366 *In the name of the daybreak*, by Diane Ackerman, "School Prayer," *I Praise My Destroyer: Poems* (New York: Vintage Books, 2000). Copyright © 1998 by Diane Ackerman. Used by permission of Random House, Inc., an imprint and division of Random House, LLC. All rights reserved.

367 *Chapters 18–20 of Leviticus*, adapted from Rabbi Bernard Bamberger, from *The Torah: A Modern Commentary*, ed. Rabbi W. Gunther Plaut, rev. ed. Rabbi David E. S. Stein (New York: URJ Press, rev. edn., 2005), pp. 808–809. Used by permission.

369 *Asked the Chofetz Chayim*, by Rabbi Yissachar Dov Rubin, *Talelei Oros: The Prayer Anthology: Volume 2*, adapted into English by Rabbi Gershon Robinson (New York: Feldheim Publishers, 2005), p. 660.

370 *The liturgy has us utter*, by Rabbi Elliot Dorff, in *P'sukei D'Zimra: Traditional Prayers, Modern Commentaries (My People's Prayerbook, vol. 3)*, ed. Rabbi Lawrence Hoffman (Jewish Lights Publishing, 1999), p. 58. Permission granted by Jewish Lights Publishing, Woodstock, VT; jewishlights.com.

371 *Be careful to visit*, Rabbi Eleazar the Great, Hebrew original in Rabbi Israel Abrahams, *Hebrew Ethical Wills*, pp. 34–50.

371 *Judaism, my child, is the struggle*, excerpt from *Wrestling with the Angel: Jewish Insights on Death and Mourning*, ed. Rabbi Jack Riemer. Copyright © 1995 by Jack Riemer. Used by permission of Schocken Books, an imprint of the Knopf Doubleday Publishing Group, a division of Penguin Random House LLC. All rights reserved.

373 *What seems to be a stone is a drama*; *Replete is the world . . . hides it all*; and *What we lack is not a will to believe but a will to wonder*; by Rabbi Abraham Joshua Heschel, *God in Search of Man: A Philosophy of Judaism* (New York: Farrar, Straus and Giroux; Reprint edition, 1976), pp. 40, 46, 85. © 1955 by Abraham Joshua Heschel. Copyright renewed 1983 by Sylvia Heschel. Reprinted by permission of Farrar, Straus and Giroux, LLC.

373 *The joy of looking*, by Albert Einstein, "What I Believe," *Forum and Century* 84 (1930) pp. 193–94. Reprinted in *Einstein on Politics*, ed. Rowe and Schulman, pp. 229–30.

373 *Study nature . . . never fail you*, by Frank Lloyd Wright, as cited by Carla Lind, *The Wright Style: Re-creating the Spirit of Frank Lloyd Wright* (New York: Simon and Schuster, 1992), p. 23.

373 *Nature is . . . garment of God*, by Johann von Goethe, as cited by Thomas Carlyle, *Sartor Resartus* (1836; reprint Nabu Press, 2010), p. 44.

373 *The poetry of earth is never dead*, by John Keats, "On the Grasshopper and Cricket," *English Romantic Writers*, ed. David Perkins (New York: Harcourt, Brace and World, Inc., 1967), p. 1127.

373 *Come to the woods*, by John Muir, *Atlantic Monthly* (January 1869).

373 *The winds will blow their own freshness*, by John Muir, in *Our National Parks* (1901), p. 56, purl.org/net/mhn50.

373 *The clearest way into the universe*, by John Muir, *John of the Mountains: The Unpublished Journals of John Muir* (1938), p. 313, purl.org/net/mhn51.

373 *Nature never hurries. . .her work*, by Ralph Waldo Emerson, "Farming," *The Portable Emerson*, ed. Carl Bode in collaboration with Malcolm Cowley (Penguin Books, 1981), p. 559.

374 *Honor is of two sorts*, by Arnold M. Eisen, "Theology and Community," in *Imagining the Jewish Future: Essays and Responses*, ed. Rabbi David A. Teutsch (State University of New York Press, 1992), p. 256; adapted.

375 *Jerusalem port city*, by Yehuda Amichai, "Jerusalem 1967," *Songs of Jerusalem and Myself*, transl. Harold Schimmel (New York: Harper & Row, 1973), pp. 58–59. Copyright © 1973 by Yehuda Amichai. Translation copyright © 1973 by Harold Schimmel. Reprinted by permission of HarperCollins Publishers and Hana Amichai.

376 *Rabbi Joseph B. Soloveitchik suggested*, as cited by Rabbi Jonathan Sacks, *To Heal a Fractured World: The Ethics of Responsibility* (Schocken Books, 2005), pp. 57–58.

376 *Another possible reading*, from *Nevarech*, transl. Philip Munishor and Michael Harumi (Jerusalem: Israel Observer Publications, 1999), p. 44.

377 *Rava taught*, based on by Ron Wolfson, *The Seven Questions You're Asked in Heaven: Reviewing and Renewing Your Life on Earth* (Jewish Lights, 2009); adapted. Permission granted by Jewish Lights Publishing, Woodstock, VT; jewishlights.com.

377 *Wallenberg*, by Danny Siegel, "Wallenberg—II," *The Garden Where Wolves and Lions Do No Harm to the Sheep and Deer* (Spring Valley, New York: The Town House Press, 1985), p. 79. Used by permission of the author.

377 *The beggar*, by Charles Reznikoff, *The Poems of Charles Reznikoff: 1918–1975* (Black Sparrow Books, 2005), p. 254. Used by permission.

379 *The Gathering*, by Jennifer Barber. © 2015 by Jennifer Barber. Used by permission.

380–81 *The most basic kind of forgiveness*, by Rabbi David R. Blumenthal, "Repentance and Forgiveness," *CrossCurrents*, purl.org/net/mhn52. Used by permission of Wiley-Blackwell.

381 *In the words*, by Rabbi Joseph Telushkin, *A Code of Jewish Ethics, Vol. 1. You Shall Be Holy* (Bell Tower, 1006), pp. 206–208.

382 *live with a sense of vocation or calling*, by Rabbi Mordecai Kaplan, as cited by Arnold M. Eisen, *The Chosen People in America: A Study in Jewish Religious Ideology* (Indiana University Press; 2nd Edition, 1983), p. 81.

383 *Even if one has a genuine grievance*, by Rabbi Ben Zion Bokser, *The Wisdom of the Talmud: A Thousand Years of Jewish Thought* (Citadel, 2001), p. 124, purl.org/net/mhn53.

384 *In the days of the Temple*, based on Cantor Macy Nulman, *The Encyclopedia of Jewish Prayer* (Northvale, NJ: Jason Aronson, 1993), pp. 361–62.

385 *Feel bad*, by Rabbi Rami Shapiro, *The Sacred Art of Lovingkindness: Preparing to Practice* (Skylight Paths, 2006) pp. 115–16. Used by permission.

386 *The Talmud associates chanun with the root chinam*, as noted by Rabbi Ezra Bick, *In His Mercy* (Maggid Books, 2010), pp. 26–28.

387 *A Prayer for Goodness and Blessing*, inspired by a Buddhist prayer, purl.org/net/mhn54.

387 *The Depth of Your Care*, by Rabbi Levi Yitzchak of Berditchev, as quoted in *Torah Gems, Bereshit, Vol. I*, compil. Aharon Yaakov Greenberg, transl. Rabbi Dr. Shmuel Himelstein (Tel Aviv: Yavneh Publishing House, Ltd; 1998), p. 328; adapted.

389 *My God*, by Lea Goldberg, "My God," *Smoke Rings* (1935); transl. Rabbi Sheldon Marder, with gratitude to Yaffa Weisman. Hebrew © by Hakibutz Hameuchad - Sifriat Poalim Publishing House, Israel. Used by permission.

390 *Each person has a Torah*, by Rabbi Lawrence Kushner, *God Was in This Place and I, I Did Not Know: Finding Self, Spirituality and Ultimate Meaning* (Woodstock, VT: Jewish Lights Publishing, 1993), p. 177. Permission granted by Jewish Lights Publishing, Woodstock, VT; jewishlights.com.

391 *the universal acceptance*, by Rabbi Reuven Kimelman, "Is Judaism Too Important to Be Left Just to Jews?" *All the World: Universalism, Particularism and the High Holy Days* (Jewish Lights Publishing, 2014), p. 105. Permission granted by Jewish Lights Publishing, Woodstock, VT; jewishlights.com.

392 *When I go to Israel*, by Rabbi Abraham Joshua Heschel, "Israel: An Echo of Eternity," *Israel: An Echo of Eternity* (Farrar, Straus and Giroux, 1987), pp. 113–14. © 1967 by Abraham Joshua Heschel. Copyright renewed 1995 by Sylvia Heschel. Reprinted by permission of Farrar, Straus and Giroux, LLC.

392 *My Heart, My Homeland*, Esther Raab, transl. Harold Schimmel, *Thistles: Selected Poems of Esther*

Raab. © 2002 by Ibis Editions. Used by permission of the publisher.

392 *A great adventure*, by Hillel Halkin, "Letters to an American Jewish Friend," *Mosaic Magazine* (November 13, 2014), purl.org/net/mhn55; excerpted there from *Letters to an American Jewish Friend: A Zionist Polemic* (Philadelphia: Jewish Publication Society of America, 1997).

393 *As a result*, by S.Y. Agnon, "Nobel Prize Acceptance Speech" (December 10, 1966).

395 *To the Father*, by Esther Raab. Translated by Rabbi Sheldon Marder. Hebrew © by Ehud Ben-Ezer. Used by permission.

395 *The Hebrew of your poets*, by Charles Reznikoff, "Jerusalem the Golden," *The Poems of Charles Reznikoff: 1918–1975* (Black Sparrow Books, 2005), p. 93. Used by permission.

395 *How difficult*, by Charles Reznikoff, "Building Boom," *The Poems of Charles Reznikoff: 1918–1975* (Black Sparrow Books, 2005), p. 58. Used by permission.

396 *The psalmist exclaims*, by Rabbi Joshua Haberman, from *Healing Psalms: The Dialogues with God That Help You Cope with Life* (Crossbook, 2010), pp. 166–67.

396–97 *My version*, by Rabbi Harold Kushner, *The Lord is My Shepherd: Healing Wisdom of the Twenty-Third Psalm* (Alfred A. Knopf, 2003), p. 155.

397 *The older we get*, by Martin Buber, quoted in *Shaarei S'lichah: A Service of Preparation for the Days of Awe*, ed. Rabbi Chaim Stern (CCAR, 1993), p. 13.

399 *Our Sages teach that miracles*, inspired by Nachmanides' introduction to his commentary on the Book of Job, as cited in *Talelei Oros: Volume 2* (op cit), p. 773. See also Rabbi Elie Munk, *The World of Prayer: Volume 1* (Feldheim Publishers, 2007), pp. 204–205.

399 *Our story tells*, by Ursula Goodenough, as cited in *The Faith of Scientists: In Their Own Words*, ed. Nancy K. Frankenberry (Princeton University Press, 2008), p. 487.

399 *Prayer is*, by Ralph Waldo Emerson, as cited in *The Faith of Scientists: In Their Own Words*, ed. Nancy K. Frankenberry (Princeton University Press, 2008), p. 487.

400 *In the end*, by Robert Emmons, as quoted by Rabbi Doug Sagal, purl.org/net/mhn56.

400 *A hundred times every day*, by Albert Einstein, *The World As I See It* (Citadel, 2000), p. 1.

401 *Ten thousand flowers*, by Wu-men Hui-k'ai, "Ten Thousand Flowers in Spring, The Moon in Autumn," in *The Enlightened Heart: An Anthology of Sacred Poetry*, transl. Stephen Mitchell (Harper Perennial, 1989), p. 47. Copyright © 1989 by Stephen Mitchell. Reprinted by permission of HarperCollins Publishers.

402 *The prosperity and success of the wicked*, by Rabbi Meir Leibush ben Yehiel Michel Weiser, as cited in *Malbim on Mishley*, abridged and adapted by Charles Wengrov, based on a draft by Avivah Gottlieb Zornberg (Jerusalem: Feldheim, 1982), p. 178.

402 *Parents and Children*, by William K. Berkson, "A Guide for the Perplexed Jewish Parent," *Reform Judaism Magazine*, purl.org/net/mhn57. Used by permission.

403 *When the Temple was destroyed*, by Rabbi Shira Milgrom, in *Living Torah: Selections from Seven Years of Torat Chayim*, ed. Rabbi Elaine Rose Glickman (URJ Press, 2005), pp. 171–72. Used by permission.

404 *Receive the light* and *Bestow favor*, comments by Rabbi Jacob Milgrom, *The JPS Torah Commentary: Numbers* (Philadelphia: Jewish Publication Society, 1989).

405 *Face*, by Sivan Har-Shefi, in *Galut Halivyatan* (Hakibbutz Hameuchad, 2005), p. 64. Hebrew © Hakibbutz Hameuchad. Used by permission. Translated by David C. Jacobson, *Beyond Political Messianism: The Poetry of Second Generation Religious Zionist Settlers* (Academic Studies Press, 2011). Used by permission.

409 *Gratitude is a function*, by Sara Yocheved Rigler, purl.org/net/mhn58. Used by permission of the author.

413 *How shall I come before You today*, by Asher Reich, in *Creator, Are You Listening? Israeli Poets on God and Prayer*, translated by David C. Jacobson (Bloomington: Indiana, 2007), p. 105. Reprinted with permission of Indiana University Press.

415 *Truly*, by Etty Hillesum, from *An Interrupted Life: The Diaries of Etty Hillesum 1941–43* (New York: Washington Square Press, 1985), pp. xv, 214–215.

418 *In biblical Hebrew*, by Rabbi Louis Jacobs, from *Returning: Exercises in Repentance*, ed. Rabbi Jonathan Magonet (New York: Bloch, 1975), p. 3; adapted.

419 *Falsehood is*, by Meir Tamari, in *Al Chet: Sins in the Marketplace* (Northvale, NJ: Jason Aronson, 1996), p. 143.

420 *Dishonesty in business*, comment based on

Rabbi Jonathan Magonet, *Returning: Exercises in Repentance* (New York: Bloch, 1978), pp. 19–21, citing *Kitzur Shulchan Aruch*.

423 *Failures of love* and *Who among us*, from *Gates of Repentance* (CCAR Press, 1978); adapted.

427 *Avinu Malkeinu*, by Rabbi Tamar Malino, Rabbi Julie Saxe-Taller, and Rabbi Joel Fleekof.

431 *Try to praise the mutilated world*, by Adam Zagajewski, "Try to Praise the Mutilated World," *Without End: New and Selected Poems*, translated by several translators (Farrar, Straus and Giroux, 2003). Copyright © 2002 by Adam Zagajewski. Translation © 2002 by Farrar, Straus, and Giroux, LLC. Reprinted by permission of Farrar, Straus and Giroux, LLC.

433 *We bend our knees and bow*, by Franz Rosenzweig, in *Returning: Exercises in Repentance*, ed. Rabbi Jonathan Magonet (New York: Bloch, 1978), pp. 102; adapted.

434 *What is the Jewish way to God*; *What is a mitzvah*, phrases from Rabbi Abraham Joshua Heschel, in *Moral Grandeur and Spiritual Audacity*, ed. Susannah Heschel (Farrar, Straus and Giroux, 1996), pp. 114, 137. Copyright © 1996 Sylvia Heschel. Reprinted by permission of Farrar, Straus and Giroux, LLC.

434 *Genuine religiosity*, phrases from Martin Buber, "Jewish Religiosity," in *The Martin Buber Reader: Essential Writings*, ed. Asher D. Biemann (Palgrave Macmillan, 2002), p. 123.

435 *We stand before God*, based on Rabbi Leo Baeck, "For all Jewish Communities in Germany," in *Documents on the Holocaust: Selected Sources on the Destruction of the Jews of Germany and Austria, Poland, and the Soviet Union*, ed. Y. Arad, Y. Gutman, and A. Margaliot (Jerusalem: Yad Vashem, 1981), pp. 87–88.

435 *Thinking of my death*, by Rabbi Norman Hirsh, *Unfolding Toward Purpose: Reflections, Commentary, and Poems 2005–2013* (self-published, 2013). Used by permission.

437 *Kadish D'rabanan,* lyrics and music by Debbie Friedman. Used by permission.

AVODAH

444 *Faith*, by Rabbi Abraham Joshua Heschel, *Moral Grandeur and Spiritual Audacity* (Farrar, Straus and Giroux, 1997), p. 339. Copyright © 1996 Sylvia Heschel. Reprinted by permission of Farrar, Straus and Giroux, LLC.

446 *We have a hunger for the spiritual*, phrase from Rabbi Eric Weiss.

449 *Life in the presence of God*, by Rabbi Arthur Green, in *Jewish Spirituality from the Bible through the Middle Ages* (New York: Crossroad, 1989), p. xiii.

449 *To say God is One*, by Rabbi Eugene B. Borowitz, in *Ehad: The Many Meanings of God is One,* ed. Rabbi Eugene B. Borowitz (Sh'ma, Inc., 1988), p. ix. Used by permission of the author.

450 *Fifteen Songs of Ascent*, based on Loren D. Crow, *The Songs of Ascent (Psalms 120–134): Their Place in Israelite History and Religion* (Scholars Press, Atlanta, GA 1996), pp. 3–27.

451 *Jerusalem*, translation by Norman Fischer, *Opening to You: Zen-Inspired Translations of the Psalms* (Viking Compass, 2002), p. 153. Used by permission.

453 *God encompasses all that exists*, inspired by Jay Michaelson, *Everything is God: The Radical Path of Nondual Judaism* (Trumpeter, 2009), pp. 1, 2.

453 *Holy*, as elaborated in Targum Jonathan, as cited by I.W. Slotki, *Isaiah*, transl. I.W. Slotki (Soncino Press, 1961), p. 29.

457 *Oneness is grounded . . . underlying unity*, by Daniel Matt, *God and the Big Bang: Discovering Harmony Between Science and Spirituality* (Jewish Lights, 1998), pp. 35–36. Permission granted by Jewish Lights Publishing, Woodstock, VT; jewishlights.com.

457 *Said the Neshkizer Rebbe*, by Rabbi Chaim Stern, *Day by Day: Reflections on the Themes of the Torah from Literature, Philosophy, and Religious Thought* (CCAR Press, 1998), p. 6.

458 *In Praise*, by Ruth Brin, *Harvest: Collected Poems and Prayers* (Holy Cow! Press, 1999). Copyright © 1986, 1999 by Ruth Firestone Brin. Reprinted with the permission of The Permissions Company, Inc., on behalf of Holy Cow! Press; holycowpress.org.

458 *Psalm 8*, translated by Stephen Mitchell, *A Book of Psalms* (HarperCollins, 1993), p. 5. Copyright © 1999 by Stephen Mitchell. Reprinted by permission of HarperCollins Publishers.

459 *Primary Wonder*, by Denise Levertov, from *Sands of the Well* (New York: New Directions, reprint edn., 1998), p. 129. Copyright © 1994, 1995, 1996 by Denise Levertov. Reprinted by permission of New Directions Publishing Corp.

460 *Island of stillness . . . attachment to the spirit*, phrases from Rabbi Abraham Joshua Heschel, *The Sabbath: Its Meaning for Modern Man* (Farrar, Straus and Giroux, 2005), p. 29. © 1951 by Abraham Joshua Heschel. Copyright renewed 1979 by Sylvia

Heschel. Reprinted by permission of Farrar, Straus and Giroux, LLC.

461 *At the time of Creation . . . hold sacred*, by Rabbi Dov Peretz Elkins, *A Shabbat Reader: Universe of Cosmic Joy* (URJ Press, 1999), p. 5; adapted. Used by permission of URJ Press.

461 *Meditation*, "For our ancestors," from *Gates of Prayer: The New Union Prayerbook* (Central Conference of American Rabbis, 1975), p. 246; adapted.

462 *Judaism teaches . . . Day of Atonement*, by Rabbi Abraham Joshua Heschel, *The Sabbath: Its Meaning for Modern Man* (Farrar, Straus and Giroux, 2005), p. 8. © 1951 by Abraham Joshua Heschel. Copyright renewed 1979 by Sylvia Heschel. Reprinted by permission of Farrar, Straus and Giroux, LLC.

462 *The festivals act . . . awakening from obliviousness*, by Rabbi Michael Strassfeld, from *The Jewish Holidays: A Guide and Commentary* (William Morrow Paperbacks, 1993), p. 1; adapted. Used by permission.

463 *When history began*, by Rabbi Abraham Joshua Heschel, *The Sabbath: Its Meaning for Modern Man* (Farrar, Straus and Giroux, 2005), p. 9. © 1951 by Abraham Joshua Heschel. Copyright renewed 1979 by Sylvia Heschel. Reprinted by permission of Farrar, Straus and Giroux, LLC.

464 *These verses reflect*, by Jeffrey H. Tigay, *The JPS Torah Commentary: Deuteronomy* (Philadelphia: Jewish Publication Society, 1996), p. 123.

468 *Dawn: The Holy Day*, from *Amitz Ko·ach*; adapted.

469 *Our Sages teach*, as cited by Angela Wood, John Logan, and Jenny Rose, *Dimensions in Religion: Teachers Resource Book* (Thomas Nelson & Sons, 1997).

470 *Within the Holy of Holies*, by Rabbi Berel Wein, "Yom Kippur and Jewish Memory," purl.org/net/mhn59.

473 *Let Israel*, translated by Pamela Greenberg, *The Complete Psalms: The Book of Prayer Songs in a New Translation* (Bloomsbury USA, 2010), p. 286. © Pamela Greenberg. Reprinted by permission of Continuum US, an imprint of Bloomsbury Publishing Inc.

474 *In the Temple*, by Yehuda Halevi, *The Selected Poems of Yehuda HaLevi*, transl. Hillel Halkin (New York: Nextbook Press, 2011), p. 20. © Nextbook Press. Used by permission.

476 *These Cry Out to Us*, from *Gates of Repentance* (CCAR, 1978, 1996), p. 403; adapted. The phrases "cry of absence" and "winter of the heart" are from Martin E. Marty, *A Cry of Absence: Reflections for the Winter of the Heart* (Eerdmans, 1997).

479 *Happy the eye*, based on the *piyut* that begins *Ashrei ayin raatah kol eileh*, in *Avonot Avoteinu*; based in turn on Ben Sira 50.

479 *My Heart Is in the East*, translation by T. Carmi, *Penguin Book of Hebrew Verse* (Middlesex, England: Penguin, 1981), p. 347.

479 *I am a memory*, by Franz Kafka, *Franz Kafka's Autobiographical Writings*, ed. Nahum Glatzer (1988).

480 *What kept the Jews going*, by Amos Oz and Fania Oz-Salzberger, *Jews and Words* (Yale University Press, 2014). Used by permission.

481 *Years since we have traveled*, by Jessica Greenbaum. Used by permission.

482 *Civilization Hangs Suspended*, by Rabbi Jacob Neusner, *Neusner on Judaism: Religion and Theology* (Ashgate Publishing, 2005), p. 426, as cited in J. Sacks *Haggadah*, p. 41.

483 *Shir HaMaalot*, translation by Pamela Greenberg, *The Complete Psalms* (Bloomsbury USA, 2010), pp. 289–90. © Pamela Greenberg. Reprinted by permission of Continuum US, an imprint of Bloomsbury Publishing Inc.

485 *To devotion*, by Ruth Brin, "They Build the Sanctuary," *Harvest: Collected Poems and Prayers* (Holy Cow! Press, 1999); adapted. Copyright © 1986, 1999 by Ruth Firestone Brin. Reprinted with the permission of The Permissions Company, Inc., on behalf of Holy Cow! Press, holycowpress.org.

486 *The Holy Book*, as cited in Rabbi Meir Zlotowitz, *Bereishis—Genesis: A New Translation* (Mesorah Publications, Ltd. 2nd edition, 1986), vol. I, p. xxxi.

486 *Do not hold yourself . . . Lev Avot*, by Moshe Lieber, *Pirke Avot: The Sages Guide to Living* (Mesorah Publications, 1995), p. 88.

487 *The Torah . . . the eyes*, from *Gates of Prayer: The New Union Prayerbook* (CCAR, 1975), pp. 698–99.

489 *When a person*, by Rabbi Eliezer Berkovits, as cited by Rabbi Jakob J. Petuchowski, *Understanding Jewish Prayer* (Ktav), as quoted in *Forms of Prayer for Jewish Worship* (Reform Synagogues of Great Britain, 1985), Vol. 3, p. 745; adapted.

490 *I say*, by Yehuda Amichai, from *Patuach sagur patuach* (Schocken, 1998), pp. 6–7. Used by permission. Translated by Rabbi Sheldon Marder.

491 *Spontaneous prayer . . . could not part with it*, as quoted in *Forms of Prayer for Jewish Worship* (Reform Synagogues of Great Britain, 1985), Vol. 3, pp. 743–45.

491 *Prayer is meaningless*, by Rabbi Abraham Joshua Heschel, "On Prayer," *Moral Grandeur and*

Spiritual Audacity: Essays by Abraham Joshua Heschel, ed. Susannah Heschel (New York: Farrar, Straus & Giroux, 1997), p. 262. Copyright © 1996 Sylvia Heschel. Reprinted by permission of Farrar, Straus and Giroux, LLC.

491 *To be able to pray*, by Rabbi Abraham Joshua Heschel, *Man's Quest for God* (New York: Scribner, 1954), p. 17. Copyright © 1954 by Abraham Joshua Heschel.

493 *Excited, my thoughts give rise*, Moses ibn Ezra, translated by Rabbi Sheldon Marder.

494 *I used to journey*, by Chaim Nachman Bialik, "Hab'reichah," in *Modern Hebrew Poetry*. Edited and translated by Ruth Finer Mintz, © 1966 by the Regents of the University of California Press. Published by the University of California Press. Used by permission. Hebrew reprinted with permission of Dvir Publishing House, Israel.

495 *God's Acrostic*, by Jacqueline Osherow, *The Hoopoe's Crown* (BOA Editions, Ltd., 2005), pp. 95–96. Copyright © 2005 by Jaqueline Osherow. Reprinted with the permission of The Permissions Company, Inc., on behalf of BOA Editions, Ltd.; boaeditions.org.

496 *The Delicate Light of My Peace*, by Zelda, in *Creator, Are You Listening? Israeli Poets on God and Prayer*, transl. David C. Jacobson (Indiana University, 2007). Hebrew copyright © Zelda Mishkovsky and ACUM. Used by permission of ACUM, Israel, and of Indiana University Press.

497 *What is the meaning*, in *Tanna de Be Eliyyahu*, ed. Meir Friedmann (Vienna, 1902), p. 116.

498–99 *A Mother's Morning Prayer*, by Hava Pinchas-Cohen, in *Creator, Are You Listening? Israeli Poets on God and Prayer*, transl. David C. Jacobson (Indiana University, 2007). Hebrew copyright © Hava Pinchas-Cohen and ACUM, Israel. Used by permission of ACUM, Israel, and of Indiana University Press.

500 *On the Day My Daughter was Born*, by Yehudah Amichai, from *A Great Tranquility: Questions and Answers* [Hebrew] (Tel Aviv: Schocken Israel, 1980), p. 44. Used by permission. Translated by Rabbi Sheldon Marder.

501 *Each of us*, based on Rabbi Samson R. Hirsch, *Psalms* (Feldheim Publishers, 1966), pp. 195–96.

503 *Rabbi Samson Raphael Hirsch*, as cited by Rabbi Joseph Telushkin, *The Book of Jewish Values: A Day-by-Day Guide to Ethical Living* (New York: Harmony, 2011), p. 96.

504 *I will not allow*, by Pamela Greenberg, *The Complete Psalms* (New York: Bloomsbury USA, 2010), p. 287–288. © Pamela Greenberg, 2010. Reprinted by permission of Continuum US, an imprint of Bloomsbury Publishing Inc. Used by permission.

505 *Whoever . . . loving-kindness*, by Rabbi Elliot N. Dorff, *The Way into Tikkun Olam: Repairing the World* (Jewish Lights, 2007), p. 15. Permission granted by Jewish Lights Publishing, Woodstock, VT; jewishlights.com.

506 *Once*, translated by Rabbi Elliot N. Dorff, *The Way into Tikkun Olam: Repairing the World* (Jewish Lights, 2007), p. 18. Permission granted by Jewish Lights Publishing, Woodstock, VT; jewishlights.com.

506 *When evil darkens our world*, based on Rabbi Chaim Stern, in *Gates of Prayer* (CCAR, 1975), p. 675.

507 *Are the hungry and the needy not the same*, phrase from Rabbi Shlomo Riskin, *A Haggadah Happening* (Efrat, Israel: Ohr Torah Stone, 2005), pp. 26–27.

508 *Truly—how splendid*, based on an original Hebrew *piyut* in *Avodah: Ancient Poems for Yom Kippur*, ed. Michael D. Swartz and Joseph Yahalom (University Park, PA: Pennsylvania State, 2005), pp. 17, 343–47.

510 *Long ago*, based on Rabbi Azrael's discourse in *The Dybbuk*, as quoted by Angela Wood, John Logan, and Jenny Rose, *Dimensions in Religion: Teachers Resource Book* (Thomas Nelson & Sons, 1997).

511 *Zion aglow with light for us and for all the world*, a phrase from Rabbi Chaim Stern, in *Gates of Repentance* (CCAR, 1978), p. 153.

511 *Faith does not spring*, by Rabbi Abraham Joshua Heschel, from *Moral Grandeur and Spiritual Audacity* (Farrar, Straus, and Giroux, 1997), p. 339. Copyright © 1996 Sylvia Heschel. Reprinted by permission of Farrar, Straus and Giroux, LLC.

EILEH EZK'RAH

517 *Therefore choose life*, lyrics by Cantor Aviva Rosenbloom and Alan Weiner (URJ Books/Music). Used by permission.

519 *Prince of Israel*, comment based on *Encyclopaedia Judaica* 12:834; 14:835.

521 *We who lived*, by Viktor E. Frankl, *Man's Search for Meaning* (New York: Simon & Schuster, 1984), p. 75.

522 *I cannot be silent*, by Shmuel Zygelboym, in *The Jew in the Modern World*, ed. Paul R. Mendes-Flohr

and Jehuda Reinharz (Oxford: Oxford University, 1980), pp. 512–13.

523 *James Chaney, Andrew Goodman, and Michael Schwerner*, based on *Bridges and Boundaries: African Americans and American Jews*, ed. Jack Salzman, Adina Back and Gretchen Sullivan Sorin (New York: The Jewish Museum, 1992), pp. 222–23.

523 *The most urgent*, by Rabbi Joachim Prinz, in *The Jewish 1960s: An American Sourcebook*, ed. Michael E. Staub (Waltham: Brandeis University Press, 2004) p. 90.

523 *I can probably do something*, as quoted in the *New York Times* (January 8 and May 24, 2007).

524 *It's tragic*, by Rita Schwerner, as quoted by Shaila Dewan, "Widow Recalls Ghosts of '64 at Rights Trial," *New York Times* (June 17, 2005).

525 *It is sometimes hard*, by Etty Hillesum, *An Interrupted Life: The Diaries of Etty Hillesum 1941–43*. (New York: Washington Square Press, 1985), pp. 140–41.

526 *Yosef Romano*, based on Giulio Meotti, *A New Shoah: The Untold Story of Israel's Victims of Terrorism*, transl. Matthew Sherry (New York: Encounter Books, 2009), pp. 13, 34, 62–63.

527 *Blessed is the match*, by Hana Senesh, in *Gates of Prayer* (CCAR), p. 590. Hebrew copyright © Hana Senesh and ACUM, Israel. Translation by Cantor Lawrence Avery. Used by permission of Transcontinental Music, URJ Books and Music.

528 *Daniel Pearl* and *Nadine Gordimer*, based on *I am Jewish: Personal Reflections Inspired by the Last Words of Daniel Pearl*, ed. Judea and Ruth Pearl (Woodstock, VT: Jewish Lights, 2004), pp. xxi, xxii, and 187. Permission granted by Jewish Lights Publishing, Woodstock, VT; jewishlights.com.

529 *God has placed*; *Her synagogue*, as quoted by Elisa Klapheck, *Fraulein Rabbiner Jonas: The Story of the First Woman Rabbi* (San Francisco, CA: Jossey-Bass, 2004), pp. 16, 56, 59, 63, 74, 86.

531 *Shir LaShalom*, Hebrew lyrics by Yaacov Rotblit and Yair Rosenblum. Hebrew copyright © Yaacov Rotblit and ACUM, Israel.

532 *Kaddish*, by Charles Reznikoff, in *The Poems of Charles Reznikoff: 1918–1975*, ed. Seamus Cooney (Jaffrey, NH: Black Sparrow Books, 2005), p. 212. Used by permission.

533 *Kadish D'rabanan*, lyrics and music by Debbie Friedman. Used by permission.

YIZKOR

540 *Like the stars*, by Rabbi Edward N. Calish, in *Union Prayerbook* (New York: CCAR, 1940), p. 75.

540 *To ask of death*, by Rabbi Jacob P. Rudin, from his collected writings.

540 *Eli, Eli*, by Hana Senesh, "Walking to Caesarea." Hebrew copyright © Hana Senesh and ACUM, Israel. Used by permission.

541 *Eternal God, we ask*, by Rabbi Chaim Stern, *Day by Day: Reflections on the Weekly Torah Portions from Literature, Philosophy and Religious Thought* (New York: CCAR, 1988), p. 173. Adapted.

542 *In reverence, suffering, and humility*, by Rabbi Abraham Joshua Heschel, *Moral Grandeur and Spiritual Audacity: Essays* (New York: Farrar, Straus, and Giroux, 1977), p. 326. Copyright © 1996 Sylvia Heschel. Reprinted by permission of Farrar, Straus and Giroux, LLC.

542 *Human beings*, by Rabbi Samuel H. Dresner, *Prayer, Humility and Compassion* (Philadelphia: Jewish Publication Society of America, 1957), p. 23; adapted. Used by permission.

543 *Where Does it End*, by Rabbi Ben Zion Bokser, in *Jewish Insights on Death and Mourning*, ed. Rabbi Jack Riemer (New York: Schocken Books, 1995). Used by permission of Rabbi Jack Riemer.

544 *Keep Me, Eternal One*, by Rabbi Chaim Stern, *Day by Day: Reflections on the Weekly Torah Portions from Literature, Philosophy and Religious Thought* (New York: CCAR, 1988), p. 172; translation adapted.

545 *A Woodpecker Taps*, by Pamela Miller Ness, excerpt from the tanka sequence "Limbs of the Ginko" (Northampton, MA: Swamp Press, 2005); reprinted in *Beyond Forgetting*, ed. Holly J. Hughes (Kent, Ohio: Kent State University Press, 2009), p. 220. Used by permission of the author.

547 *Yom Kippur without my father*, by Yehudah Amichai, "Yom Kippur," *Yehuda Amichai: A Life of Poetry, 1948–1994*, transl. Benjamin and Barbara Harshav (HarperCollins, 1995). Hebrew: *Shirei Yehuda Amichai, Volume 5* (Jerusalem: Schocken, 2004), p. 119. Used by permission.

547 *At David's Grave*, by Denise Levertov, *Poems 1968–1972* (New York: New Directions, 2002), p. 82. Copyright © 1970 by Denise Levertov. Reprinted by permission of New Directions Publishing Corp.

548 *More precious was the light*, by Edna St. Vincent Millay, "Dirge without Music," from *Collected Poems*. Copyright © 1928, 1955 by Edna St. Vincent Millary and Norman Millay Ellis. Reprinted by

the permission of The Permission Company, Inc., on behalf of Holly Peppe, Literary Executor, The Millay Society; millay.org.

549 *The death of a loved one*, by Judy Tatelbaum, *The Courage to Grieve: Creative Living, Recovery and Growth through Grief* (New York: William Morrow Paperbacks, 2009), p. 7.

550–51 *We Die*, by Diane Ackerman, *I Praise My Destroyer: Poems by Diane Ackerman* (New York: Vintage, 1998), p. 7. Copyright © 1998 by Diane Ackerman. Used by permission of Random House, an imprint and division of Penguin Random House LLC. All rights reserved.

552 *My dead*, by Rachel, in *Voices within the Ark*, ed. Howard Schwartz and Anthony Rudolf, transl. Robert Mezey (New York: Avon Books, 1980), p. 148.

552 *Together*, by Dora Kushner, "Raging Tiger" (Small Poetry Press, 1992).

553 *The Death of a Parent*, by Linda Pastan, *Carnival Evening: New and Selected Poems 1968–1998* (New York: W.W. Norton, 1998). Copyright © 1998 Linda Pastan. Used by permission of W.W. Norton & Company, Inc.

553 *Separation*, by W.S. Merwin, *The Second Four Books of Poems* (Port Townsend, Washington: Copper Canyon Press, 1993). Copyright © 1992 by W.S. Merwin. Used by permission of the Wylie Agency LLC.

557 *In the morning*, by Zelda, *Shirei Zelda*, p. 159. Hebrew copyright © Zelda Mishkovsky and ACUM, Israel (Tel Aviv: Hakibbutz Hameuchad, 1985). Used by permission. Translation by Rabbi Sheldon Marder.

557 *The Courage That My Mother Had*, by Edna St. Vincent Millay, *Collected Poems* (New York: Harper Collins Publishers, 2011), p. 459. Copyright © 1954, © 1982 by Norman Millay Ellis. Used by permission of The Permissions Company, Inc., on behalf of Holly Peppe, Literary Executor, The Millay Society; millay.org.

558 *White Apples*, by Donald Hall, "White Apples," *White Apples and the Taste of Stone: Selected Poems 1946–2006* (Houghton Mifflin Harcourt: Har/Com edition, 2006), p. 70. Copyright © 2006 by Donald Hall. Reprinted by permission of Houghton Mifflin Harcourt Publishing Company. All rights reserved.

559 *In my darkness*, by Chaim Stern, *Day by Day: Reflections on the Weekly Torah Portions from Literature, Philosophy and Religious Thought* (New York: CCAR, 1988), p. 188.

559 *Do not grieve*, by Winston Churchill, in *Winston and Clementine: The Personal Letters of the Churchills*, ed. Mary Soames (New York: Houghton Mifflin, 1999).

559 *Unnamable God*, "Psalm 16" [excerpt of 6 lines] translated by Stephen Mitchell, *A Book of Psalms* (New York: HarperCollins, 1993), p. 8; adapted. Copyright © 1993 by Stephen Mitchell. Reprinted by permission of HarperCollins Publishers.

560 *I sat down*, by Willa Cather, "I sat down," *My Antonia* (Boston: Houghton Mifflin, 1977) p. 17, 18. This interpretation is based on Dennis Sylva, *Psalms and the Transformation of Stress* (Louvain: Peeters Press, W.B. Eerdmans, 1993), p. 83.

561 *The Echo of Your Promise*, by Rabbi Harold M. Schulweis, in *Finding Each Other in Judaism: Meditations on the Rites of Passage from Birth to Immortality* (UAHC Press, 2001), p. 86. Used by permission.

562 *Han'shamah Lach*, refrain of a *pizmon* found in various *machzorim*, attributed to Rabbi Abraham ibn Ezra.

562 *My Father*, by Yehudah Amichai, in *Israeli Poetry: A Contemporary Anthology*, ed. W. Bargad and S. Chyet (Indiana University Press, 1988), p. 82. Reprinted with permission of Indiana University Press and Hana Amichai.

562 *My Mother*, by Charles Reznikoff, from "Kaddish," in *The Poems of Charles Reznikoff: 1918–1975*, ed. Seamus Cooney (Jaffrey, NH: Black Sparrow Books, 2005), p. 212. Used by permission.

563 *I Needed to Talk to My Sister*, by Grace Paley, *Fidelity: Poems* (New York: Farrar, Straus, and Giroux, 2008), p. 49. Copyright © 2000 by Grace Paley. Reprinted by permission of Farrar, Straus and Giroux, LLC.

563 *Prayer for the Dead*, by Stuart Kestenbaum, *Prayers & Run-on Sentences* (Deerbook Editions, 2007). © 2007 Stuart Kestenbaum. Used by permission.

564–65 *A Candle in a Glass*, by Marge Piercy, *The Art of Blessing the Day: Poems With a Jewish Theme* (New York: Alfred A. Knopf, 1999), pp. 48–49. Copyright © 1999 by Middlemarsh, Inc. Used by permission of Alfred A. Knopf, an imprint of the Knopf Doubleday Publishing Group, a division of Penguin Random House LLC. All rights reserved.

565 *Footprints*, by Rajzel Zychlinsky, "Footprints," *Follow My Footprints: Changing Images of Women in American Jewish Fiction*, ed. Sylvia Barack Fishman (Brandeis, 1992). Copyright © by University Press of New England, Lebanon, NH. Reprinted with permission.

565 *My Father*, by Tuvia Rubner, "My father," *Selected Poems 1957–2005* (Tel Aviv: Keshev, 2005). Copyright © Tuvia Rubner and ACUM, Israel. Used by permission.

566 *Promised Land,* by Samuel Menashe, from *The Niche Narrows: New and Selected Poems*. Copyright © 1971, 1973, 1986, 2004, 2005 by Samuel Menashe. (Jersey City, NJ: Talisman House, 2000). Reprinted by permission of the Literary Classics of the United States, Inc., New York, NY. All rights reserved.

567 *There are stars*, by Hana Senesh, *Hannah Senesh: Her Life and Diary, the First Complete Edition* (Jewish Lights), transl. Cantor Jeff Klepper and Rabbi Daniel Freedlander. Permission granted by Jewish Lights Publishing, Woodstock, VT; jewishlights.com. Hebrew copyright © Hana Senesh and ACUM, Israel. Used by permission.

572 *When we ask God*, by Rabbi Aaron Panken in *May God Remember: Memory and Memorializing in Judaism - Yizkor*, ed. Rabbi Lawrence A. Hoffman (Woodstock, VT: Jewish Lights, 2013), p. 201. Permission granted by Jewish Lights Publishing, Woodstock, VT; jewishlights.com.

573 *For an Infant or Child*, inspired by Rabbi Sandy Eisenberg Sasso, in *Rabbi's Manual* (Wyncote, PA: Reconstructionist Rabbinical Association, 1997). See also Anita Diamant, *Saying Kaddish* (Schocken, 1998), p. 194. The phrase "whose songs were left unsung" alludes to "*Acharei Moti*" by Chaim Nachman Bialik.

573 *You have to understand*, by David Grossman, as quoted in the *New York Times* (November 17, 2010).

575 *In Memory of a Parent Who Was Hurtful*, by Rabbi Robert Saks, "A Meditation in Memory of a Parent that was Hurtful." Used by permission of Rabbi Robert Saks.

576 *Psalm*, by Harvey Shapiro, "Psalm," *A Momentary Glory* (Middletown, CT: Wesleyan University Press, 2014). Copyright © 2014 by Estate of Harvey Shapiro. Used by permission of Wesleyan University Press.

576 *You are not beautiful*, by Marvin Bell, "To Dorothy," from *Nightworks: Poems 1962–2000* (Copper Canyon Press, 2003), p. 105. Copyright © 2000 by Marvin Bell. Reprinted with the permission of the Permissions Company, Inc., on behalf of Copper Canyon Press; coppercanyonpress.org.

577 *What Happens after Death*, by Rabbi David Wolpe, *Making Loss Matter* (New York: Riverhead Books, 1999), p. 203. Used by permission of the author.

578 *How shall the heart*, by Stanley Kunitz, "The Layers," *The Collected Poems* (New York: W.W. Norton, 2000), p. 217.

579 *Psalm 90*, translated by Rabbi Janet Marder.

580 *The Five Stages of Grief*, by Linda Pastan, *The Five Stages of Grief: Poems* (New York: W.W. Norton, 1978). Copyright © 1978 by Linda Pastan. Used by permission of W.W. Norton and Company, Inc.

581 *Forgiveness and the Afterlife*, by Cantor Linda Hirschhorn, sermon on Yizkor, purl.org/net/mhn61. © 2010 by Linda Hirschhorn. Used by permission.

581 *So I have spent*, by Marilynne Robinson, *The Death of Adam: Essays on Modern Thought* (New York: Houghton Mifflin, 1998), p. 216.

582 *Bright Mariner*, by Katherine Garrison Chapin, "Bright Mariner," *Bright Mariner*, woodcuts by Wharton Esherick (Duffleld & Green, 1933).

583 *Let Evening Come*, by Jane Kenyon, "Let Evening Come," *Collected Poems*. Copyright © 2005 by the Estate of Jane Kenyon. Reprinted with permission of The Permissions Company, Inc., on behalf of Graywolf Press; graywolfpress.org.

584 *God of pity and love*, from *The Union Prayerbook* (New York: CCAR, 1945); adapted.

586 *If life is a pilgrimage*, by Rabbi Abraham Joshua Heschel, from *Moral Grandeur and Spiritual Audacity: Essays*, ed. Susannah Heschel (New York: Farrar, Straus, and Giroux, 1977), pp. 377–78. Copyright © 1996 Sylvia Heschel. Reprinted by permission of Farrar, Straus and Giroux, LLC.

587 *Leisure*, by Zelda, *Shirei Zelda* (Tel Aviv: Hakibbutz Hame'uchad, 1985), p. 67. Hebrew copyright © Zelda Mishkovsky and ACUM. Used by permission. Translated by Rabbi Sheldon Marder.

587 *One leaf*, by David Ignatow, "One Leaf," in *Earth Prayers: 365 Prayers, Poems, and Invocations from Around the World*, ed. Elizabeth Roberts and Elisa Amidon (New York: HarperCollins, 1991), p. 319. Used by permission.

588 *Day Three*, by Judy Katz, "Day Three," *Cercise Press 3/7* (Cercise Press, Summer 2011). Used by permission.

589 *Father*, by Ted Kooser, *Delights & Shadows* (Port Townsend, WA: Copper Canyon Press, 2012). Copyright © 2004 by Ted Kooser. Reprinted with the permission of the Permissions Company, Inc., on behalf of Copper Canyon Press; coppercanyonpress.org.

589 *Our Ability*, by Harold Kushner, *The Lord is My Shepherd: Healing Wisdom of the Twenty-third*

Psalm (New York: Anchor, 2004), p. 155.

590 *Remember Me*, by Hal Sirowitz, *Mother Said (Poems)* (New York: Crown Publishers, 1996). Copyright © 1996 by Hal Sirowitz. Used by permission of Crown Books, an imprint of the Crown Publishing Group, a division of Penguin Random House LLC. All rights reserved.

591 *Blessed is the pilgrimage*; the phrases "great Artist" and "to hold on to life and let it go" are adapted from Rabbi Milton Steinberg's 1946 sermon "To Hold with Open Arms."

592 *One morning*, by Diane Cole, *After Great Pain, A New Life Emerges* (New York: Simon and Schuster, 1992).

593 *contains and supports us*, by Rabbi Joshua Loth Liebman, *Peace of Mind* (New York: Simon & Schuster, 1948), p. 145.

594 *A Psalm of David*, from *The Holy Scriptures* (Jewish Publication Society of America, 1917).

595 *The Shechinah*, by Phyllis Appell Bass, "Psalm 23: A Feminist Version," adapted. Used by permission.

595 *God is my shepherd*, by Rabbi Daniel Jeremy Silver, "The 23rd Psalm: A Modern Rabbinic Commentary," *Journal of Reform Judaism* (Spring 1978), pp. 45–53; adapted.

596 *My version*, by Harold Kushner, *The Lord is My Shepherd: Healing Wisdom of the Twenty-third Psalm* (New York: Anchor, 2004).

596 *Blessed is peace*; the phrases "inner serenity" and "at-homeness" are adapted from Rabbi Joshua Loth Liebman, *Peace of Mind* (New York: Simon & Schuster, 1948), p. 145.

600 *For Those Who Died for Our Country*, "Memorial Prayer for those Fallen in Battle," in *Prayer Book (abridged) for Jews in the Armed Forces of the United States* (New York: National Jewish Welfare Board, 1943), pp. 312–13; adapted. Used by permission.

601 *What is the correct way to stand at a memorial ceremony*, by Yehuda Amichai, *Open Closed Open*, transl. Chana Bloch and Chana Kronfeld (New York: Harcourt, 2000), pp. 169–70. Copyright © 2000 by Chana Bloch and Chana Kronfeld. Reprinted by permission of Houghton Mifflin Harcourt Publishing Company and Hana Amichai. All rights reserved.

601 *A Remembrance for Those Who Fell*, translated and adapted from *Kavanat HaLev*, (Jerusalem: IMPJ), p. 259. Used by permission.

602 *May God's name*, by Rabbi James Kaufman and Rabbi David Frank; adapted. Used by permission.

603 *Strange now*, this one line is by Allen Ginsberg "Kaddish" from *Kaddish and Other Poems 1958–1960* (San Francisco, CA: City Lights Publishers, 2010), p. 7.

603 *If every life*, by Rabbi Donald B. Rossoff; adapted. Used by permission.

604 *Deep contemplation*, adapted from Claude Montefiore, in the *Hertz Siddur*, pp. 298–99, and in *Gates of Prayer*, pp. 622–23; adapted.

605 *All you who mourn*, from *The Union Prayerbook* (New York: CCAR, 1945); adapted.

N'ILAH

612 *The long day*, by Charles Reznikoff, *The Poems of Charles Reznikoff: 1918–1975*, ed. Seamus Cooney (Jaffrey, NH: Black Sparrow Books, 2005), p. 224. Used by permission.

612 *Why should this prayer*, by Arthur Green, *These Are the Words: A Vocabulary of Jewish Spiritual Life* (Woodstock, VT: Jewish Lights Publishing, 2nd edn., 2012), p. 256. Permission granted by Jewish Lights Publishing, Woodstock, VT; jewishlights.com.

613 *when the gates are being closed*, a phrase from *The Penguin Book of Hebrew Verse*, ed. and transl. T. Carmi, (1981), p. 241.

613 *Again the day rolls*, by Lucille Day, "Ne'ilah," from "Yom Kippur," *Self-Portrait with Hand Microscope: Poems* (Berkeley Poets Workshop and Press, 1982). Used by permission.

616 *When we refrain*, by Rabbi Mordecai M. Kaplan, *The Meaning of God in Modern Jewish Religion* (Wayne State University Press, 1994), p. 169.

618 *When I consider the heavens*, adapted from Rabbi David Einhorn, *Olat Tamid*.

619 *In Praise of Hands*, by Jeanne Bryner, from *Tenderly Lift Me*. Copyright © 2004 by The Kent State University Press. (Kent State University Press, 2004), p. 173. Reprinted with permission.

620 *a kind of liturgical punctuation mark*, by Jeffrey M. Cohen, *Prayer and Penitence* (Northvale, New Jersey: Jason Aronson, 1994), p. 66.

620 *The Jewish soul is mirrored*, by Rabbi Henry Slonimsky, *Essays* (Cincinnati: Hebrew Union College Press; Chicago: Quadrangle Books, 1967), p. 120.

621 *Reverie before Prayer*; the phrases "blue lake in my heart" and "dense word-forest" are by Rukhl Fishman, excerpts from "My Poems Fall

Like Snow" and "What Do I Do," *I Want to Fall Like This: Selected Poems of Rukhl Fishman*, transl. Seymour Levitan (Detroit: Wayne State University, 1994), pp. 95, 181. Copyright © 1994 by Wayne State University Press. Used with the permission of the publisher. Similarly, "the stillest of waters" alludes to Psalm 23:2; "the Unnamable" is from Martin Buber, "From the Beginnings of Our Bible Translation," *Scripture and Translation*, transl. Lawrence Rosenwald with Everett Fox (Indianapolis: Indiana University, 1994), p. 183.

623 *Taught Dov Baer*, as quoted in *Maggid D'varav L'Yaakov* 141, as cited in *Chasidic Masters: History, Biography and Thought*, ed. and transl. Aryeh Kaplan (Moznaim, 1991).

625 *Jerusalem 1967*, by Yehuda Amichai, *Achshav B'Raash* (Schocken, 1975), pp. 11–12. Translation by Shirley Kauman, "On the Day of Atonement," *Celebrating the Jewish Holidays: Poems, Stories, Essays*, ed. Steven J. Rubin (Hanover & London: Brandeis University Press / University Press of New England, 2003), p. 156. Used by permission.

627 *What do we believe about God's power*, from *Gates of Prayer: The New Union Prayer Book* (New York: CCAR, 1975), p. 357.

629 *Holy Is Your Name*, by Leonard Cohen, "Psalm 43," excerpted from *Stranger Music: Selected Poems and Songs* by Leonard Cohen. Copyright © 1993 Leonard Cohen. Reprinted by permission of McClelland & Stewart, a division of Penguin Random House Canada Limited, a Penguin Random House Company.

629 *Open Gate*, by Marcia Lee Falk, from *The Book of Blessings: New Jewish Prayers for Daily Life, the Sabbath, and the New Moon Festival*. Copyright © 1996 by Marcia Lee Falk. Used by permission of the author.

631 *The Promise*, by Jane Hirshfield, "The Promise," *Come, Thief: Poems* (New York: Knopf, 2011), p. 22. Copyright © 2011 by Jane Hirshfield. Used by permission of Alfred A. Knopf, an imprint of the Knopf Doubleday Publishing Group, a division of Penguin Random House LLC. All rights reserved. Used by permission.

633 *Alive*, by Rabbi Norman Hirsh, *God Loves Becoming* (self-published, 2005). Used by permission.

633 *Late October*, by Barbara Crooker, "Vaudeville," *Gold* (Cascade Books, 2013), p. 4. Used by permission of Wipf and Stock Publishers; wipfandstock.com.

635 *Help Me Listen*, by Ted Loder, *Guerillas of Grace: Prayers for the Battle* (Minneapolis, MN: Augsburg Books, 1984, 2005), p. 31. Used by permission.

635 *The Way It Is*, by William Stafford, "The Way It Is," *Ask Me: 100 Essential Poems* (Minneapolis, MN: Graywolf Press, 1999, 2014). Copyright © 1998, 2014 by The Estate of William Stafford. Reprinted with permission of The Permissions Company, Inc., on behalf of Graywolf Press; graywolfpress.org.

635 *Turn from evil and do good*, by Robin Becker, "In the Days of Awe," *The Horse Fair: Poems* (University of Pittsburgh Press, 2000), p. 44. Used by permission.

637 *How a Place Becomes Holy*, by Yehoshua November, *God's Optimism* (Charlotte, NC: Main Street Rag Publishers, 2010). Used by permission of the author.

637 *Psalm*, by Dan Bellm, *Practice: A Book of Midrash* (San Francisco: Sixteen Rivers Press, 2008). Used by permission.

640 *The personal significance of Yom Kippur*, by Rabbi David Hartman, "Reflections on Rosh Hashanah and Yom Kippur," *Jerusalem Post* (October 7, 2008).

640 *when the gates are being closed*, a phrase from *The Penguin Book of Hebrew Verse*, ed. and transl. T. Carmi, (1981), p. 241.

641 *Before*, by Yehuda Amichai, Yehuda Amichai, *Shirim: 1948–1962* (Jerusalem/Tel Aviv: Schocken, 1962), page 167. Used by permission. Translated by Rabbi Sheldon Marder.

642 *Your promise is forever*, an interpretive translation by Rabbi Sheldon Marder of "God of Hosts," in *Rashi's Commentary on Psalms*. Comment based on Rabbi Jonathan Sacks, *The Koren Yom Kippur Machzor* (Jerusalem: Koren, 2012), pp. 1166–67.

643 *Open for Us a Gate*, by Lea Goldberg, in *Selected Poetry and Drama*, transl. Rachel Tzvia Back (New Milford, CT: The Toby Press, 2005), p. 200. Used by permission.

643 *Day of Atonement*, by Charles Reznikoff, from "Day of Atonement," *The Poems of Charles Reznikoff: 1918–1975*, ed. Seamus Cooney (Boston: Black Sparrow, 2005), p. 224. Used by permission.

649 *Great Giver*; the phrase "great Giver" is from Charles Reznikoff's poem "Day of Atonement" (see just above).

653 *In all other Yom Kippur services*, anonymous, in *Otzar Ha-tefillot* (New York: Hebraica Press, 1966),

p. 582; as cited by Jeffrey M. Cohen, *Prayer and Penitence* (Northvale, NJ: Jason Aronson, 1994), p. 285.

655 *In the first Hebrew prayer book ever printed,* based on Abraham J. Karp, *From the Ends of the Earth: Judaic Treasures of the Library of Congress* (New York: Rizzoli/Library of Congress, 1991), pp. 182–84.

657 *You Sit, Waiting*, by Hillel Bavli, "T'filah," from *Sanctuary in the Wilderness: A Critical Introduction to American Hebrew Poetry*, ed. and transl. Alan Mintz (Stanford University Press, 2012), pp. 180–81. Reprinted with permission of Dr. Samuel Bavli.

659 *We have aspired*, Hebrew text by Binyamin Holtzman, inspired by Rabbi Abraham Isaac Kook (1865–1935), *Ein Ayah* (his commentary on *Ein Yaakov*), who commended the confession of successes as well as failures.

666 *the door to ultimate significance*, Rabbi Abraham Joshua Heschel, "Depth Theology," in *The Insecurity of Freedom* (New York: Farrar, Straus & Giroux, 1967), p. 124. © 1966 by Abraham Joshua Heschel. Copyright renewed 1994 by Sylvia Heschel. Reprinted by permission of Farrar, Straus and Giroux, LLC.

667 *To live life*, inspired by Rabbi Milton Steinberg.

667 *Love After Love*, by Derek Walcott, "Love After Love," *Collected Poems: 1948–1984*, selected by Glyn Maxwell (Farrar, Straus and Giroux, 1987), p. 328. Copyright © 2014 by Derek Walcott. Reprinted by permission of Farrar, Straus and Giroux, LLC.

677 *Miriam the Prophet*, Hebrew lyrics by Rabbi Leila Gal Berner. Hebrew used by permission of Rabbi Leila Gal Berner. Translation by Rabbi Sheldon Marder.